NHM (CHO)

[Community Health Officer Competition Guide]

By Experienced Teachers

AF809302

Jain Publications

780, Banwalon Ka Darwaza, Chaura Rasta, Jaipur-03

NHM (CHO)

PUBLISHER
CHINMAY JAIN
JAIN PUBLICATIONS
780, Banwalon Ka Darwaza,
Chaura Rasta, Jaipur-302003
PH. : 0141-4012716, 9602011100
E-Mail : jainpublicationjp@gmail.com

Distributor
RAJ PUSTAK MANDIR
241, CHAURA RASTA, JAIPUR
PH. : 0141- 2578098, 9414020100
E-Mail : rajpustakmandir1@gmail.com

₹ 450/-

Typesetting By
S. V. Computers, Jaipur

Printers
Sheetal Printers

Contents

❑❑❑

UP CHO Exam. Paper 2021 (Memory Based)
Test Date : 09/09/2021

Section : Midwifery and Obstetrical Nursing

1. **A nurse midwife has to develop .... based knowledge and practice of midwifery and take part in research activities.**
(a) Social evidence (b) Political evidence
(c) Scientific evidence (d) Economical evidence **(c)**

2. **The period of life when the body undergoes changes leading to reproductive maturity is called:**
(a) Adulthood (b) Childhood
(c) Infancy (d) Adolescence **(d)**

3. **The first menstrual flow begins at puberty and is termed:**
(a) Chromosome (b) Menopause
(c) Sex chromosome (d) Menarche **(d)**

4. **The emryo continues to develop in which part of the female body?**
(a) Oviduct (b) Testis
(c) Uterus (d) Ovary **(c)**

5. **The female pelvisc exists exactly in which part of the body?**
(a) The upper part of the abdomen
(b) It is located between the upper and lower part of the abdomen
(c) The lower part of the hipbones
(d) The lower part of the abdomen, it is located between the hip bones **(d)**

6. **Which of the following is male reproductive system?**
(a) Vagina (b) Testis
(c) Uterus (d) Ovary **(b)**

7. **Babies born through IVF or in vitro fertilisation technique are called:**
(a) Test babies (b) Tube babies
(c) Test-tube babies (d) Artificial babies **(c)**

8. **The ovary produces female gametes called:**
(a) sperm duct (b) ova (eggs)
(c) zygote (d) sperms **(b)**

Section : Community Health Nursing

1. **सामुदायिक स्वास्थ्य नर्सिंग, शरीर संबंधी ज्ञान को सार्वजनिक स्वास्थ्य विज्ञान और............से संश्लेषित करती है।**
(a) सामुदायिक नर्सिंग सिद्धांत
(b) सार्वजनिक नर्सिंग सिद्धांत
(c) वृत्तिपरक (पेशेवर) नर्सिंग सिद्धांत
(d) व्यक्तिगत नर्सिंग सिद्धांत **(c)**

2. **In India, a community health nurse should hold a registration certificate as a nurse and as a midwife from which organisation?**
(a) Indian Council of Medical Research
(b) Ministry of Health and Family Welfare
(c) Medical Council of India
(d) State Registration Nursing Council **(d)**

3. **In which year was India declared a polio free nation?**
(a) 2019 (b) 2014
(c) 2010 (d) 2011 **(b)**

4. **The Epidemic Diseases Act was passed in which year in India?**
(a) 1958 (b) 1858
(c) 1897 (d) 1997 **(c)**

5. **निम्नलिखित में से कौन सी, सामुदायिक स्वास्थ्य नर्सिंग की एक विशेषता है?**
(a) औद्योगीकरण और नगरीकरण
(b) समुदाय में सामाजिक प्रदूषण को समझन
(c) सार्वजनिक व्यवहार
(d) इसमें अंतर्वेषयिक सहयोग शामिल होता है। **(d)**

6. **In which city is the headquarters of the World Health Organization situated?**
(a) Geneva (b) New York
(c) Vienna (d) London **(a)**

7. **The Arabic system of medicine practised in India is known as:**
(a) the homeopathy system
(b) the siddha system
(c) the unani system
(d) the ayurveda system **(c)**

8. **संयुक्त राष्ट्र के सतत विकास लक्ष्यों (SDG) का तीसरा लक्ष्य कौन सा है?**
(a) स्वच्छ जल और स्वच्छता।
(b) अच्छा स्वास्थ्य और कल्याण
(c) किफायती और स्वस्थ ऊर्जा
(d) लिंगानुपात में सुधार **(b)**

Section : Child Health Nursing

1. बैसिलस कालमेट गुएरिन (बी.सी.जी.) (Bacillus Calmette-Guein (BCG) का टीका, बच्चों को निम्नलिखि में से किस रोग से सुरक्षित रखने के लिए उपयोग किया जाता हैं?

(a) डिप्थीरिया (b) पोलियो
(c) तपेदिक (टी.बी.) (d) टिटनेस **(c)**

2. Live birth is defined as complete expulsion or extractoni from the mother of a product of conception, and which after separaton shows signs of life for at least..........

(a) 24 hours (b) 2 days
(c) 1 hour (d) 10 days **(c)**

3. पोलियो (poliomyelitis) मुख्यतः .... से कम आयु के बच्चों को प्रभावित करता है।

(a) 2 वर्ष (b) 4 वर्ष
(c) 5 वर्ष (d) 6 वर्ष **(c)**

4. पांच से कम मृत्यु दर (USMR) क्या हैं?

(a) जन्म से पांचवें सप्ताह से पूर्व मृत्यु होने की प्रायिकता
(b) जन्म के पांचवें माह से पूर्व मृत्यु होने की प्रायिकता
(c) पांचवी वर्षगांठ से पूर्व मृत्यु होने की प्रायिकता
(d) जन्म के पांचवें दिन से पूर्व मृत्यु होने की प्रायिकता **(c)**

5. विश्व स्वास्थ्य संगठन (WHO) के अनुसार, जन्म के समय शिशु का वजन......... या इससे कम होना, जन्म के समय कम वजन (low birth weight) कहलाता है, उसकी गर्भाधान की अवधि चाहे जो भी रही हो।

(a) 2.5 kg (b) 3 kg
(c) 6 kg (d) 4 kg **(a)**

6. Which of the following is a disorder of the white blood cells?

(a) Purpura-ITP (b) Leukaemia
(c) Haemophillia (d) Anaemia **(b)**

7. The integrated Child Development Service (ICDS) Scheme was launched in which year?

(a) 1980 (b) 1975
(c) 1999 (d) 1988 **(b)**

8. Immediately at birth, irrespective of the condtion of the baby which of the following should be the first step?

(a) Positioning (b) Warmath
(c) Tactile stimulation (d) Suctioning **(b)**

Section : Medical Surgical Nursing

1. निलय (ventricvles) .... द्वारा एक-दूसरे से पृथक होते हैं।

(a) अंतरा अलिंद पट (interatrial septum)
(b) अंतरानिलय पट (interventricular septum)
(c) शिरानाल (sinus)
(d) अलिन्द (auricle) **(b)**

2. मानव हृदय एक शंकु की आकृति वाला...........पेशीय पम्प होता है।

(a) छह प्रकोष्ठ वाला (b) चार प्रकोष्ठ वाला
(c) दो प्रकोष्ठ वाला (d) तीन प्रकोष्ठ वाला **(b)**

3. 'चिकित्सकीय-सर्जिकल नर्सिंग' के अनुसार, संक्रमणों का प्रसार रोकने और नियंत्रित करने के लिए सर्वाधिक महत्वपूर्ण तथा सर्वाधिक आधारभूत तकनीक कौन सी है?

(a) जीवाणुनाशन (b) हाथ धोना
(c) विसंक्रमण (d) मुंह की सफाई **(b)**

4. 'घावों की देखभाल और मरहम-पट्टी' सिद्धांत के अनुसार, एक खरोंच वाले घाव की देखभाल की प्रक्रिया का प्रथम चरण कौन सा हैं?

(a) पीड़ित या स्वयंसेवी को बैठाना या लिटाना
(b) किसी भी कंकड़ या अन्य विजातीय पदार्थ को हटाना
(c) हाथों को धोना
(d) घाव के प्रकार पर ध्यान देना और खरोचों को चिन्हित करना **(c)**

5. What is asepsis?

(a) The removal of all foreign material such as soild or organic material
(b) The presence of pathogens like bacteria, vfirus and other microbes
(c) The act of soiling or contamnation.
(d) The absence of pathogens like bactera, virus and other microbes. **(d)**

6. The fluid part of the blood is known as:

(a) Plasma (b) Platelets
(c) Haemoglobin (d) White blood calls **(a)**

7. पूयन (sepsis) क्या हैं?

(a) यह एक संक्रमित व्यक्ति से अन्य तक रोगजनकों का प्रसार है।
(b) यह शरीर के किसी भाग में, जहां सूक्ष्मजीव संक्रमण उत्पन्न कर सकते हो, उनके प्रवेश को रोकने के लिए किए जाने वाले प्रयासों का संयोजन है।
(c) यह मवाद बनाने वाले जीवाणुओं द्वारा या शरीर में जीवाणु और उनके विषों की उपस्थिति, (प्रायः घाव के संक्रमण के पश्चात्) जो मवाद उत्पन्न करता है, के कारण शरीर का संक्रमण है।
(d) इसका अभिप्राय मानव शरीर के बाहर सभी रोगजनकों को किसी रसायन या अभिकर्मक के प्रत्यक्ष संपर्क द्वारा नष्ट किए जाने से है। **(c)**

8. A nosocomial infecton is also known as:

(a) A respiratory tract infection
(b) An interfection with which a patient may have come to the hospital
(c) A hospital acquired infection
(d) A urinary tract infection **(c)**

Section : Health Education and Communication Skills & Enviropnmental Hygiene

1. The World Health Organization has defined 'Health' as-

(a) Physical, mental and social well-being
(b) Mental and physical well-being only
(c) Social well-being only
(d) Physical well-being only **(a)**

2. Which of the following is NOT a vector borne disease?

(a) Malaria (b) Encephalitis
(c) Typhoid (d) Yellow fever **(c)**

3. Which of the following nutrients are also known as 'energy giving foods'?

(a) Proteins
(b) Minerals
(c) Carbohydrates and fats
(d) Vitamins **(c)**

4. The atmosphere of asbestos mines contains asbestos dust. Which of the following diseases can be caused by long-term exposure to this?

(a) Asbestosis (b) Asbestosis silica
(c) Silicosis (d) Silica asbestosis **(a)**

5. जल, भोजन इत्यादि के माध्यम से रोगजनक सूक्ष्मजीवों के प्रसार की प्रक्रिया क्या कहलाती हैं?

(a) वाहन प्रसार
(b) संपर्क प्रसार
(c) केवल भौतिक संपर्क प्रसार
(d) रोगाणुवाहक प्रसार **(a)**

6. किस/किन खाद्य (घों) को छोटे बच्चों के लिए सर्वोत्तम और संपूर्ण भोजन माना जाता हैं?

(a) दूध (b) फल
(c) अंडे और मांस (d) दालें **(a)**

7. Which of the following schemes has been launched by the Government of India to make India as 'Open Defection Free (ODF) nation?

(a) Swachh Bharat Mission
(b) Bharat ki Swachhata Bharat Ki Sundarta Yojana
(c) Safe Disposal of Human Excreta Mission
(d) Open Defecation Free Mission **(a)**

8. Which of the following schemes has been launched by the Government of India to ensure safe drinking water to every rural household through 'Functional Household Tap Connection (FHTC)'?

(a) Jal Jeevan Mission
(b) Swachh Gramin Peyjal Yojana
(c) Jal Jeevan Hariyali Mission
(d) Swachh Jal Khushi Ke Do Pal **(a)**

Section: Mental Health Nursing

1. जिस प्रकार हम स्वयं को देखते हैं और अपनी सक्षमताओं तथा गुणों के संबंध में हम जो विचार रखते हैं, उसे........भी कहा जाता है।

(a) आत्म सम्मान
(b) आत्म–अवधारणा
(c) तार्किक स्वत्व (relational self)
(d) आत्म–नियमन (self-regulation) **(b)**

2. .... को प्रायः भय और अवबोध की विसरित, अस्पष्ट, अत्यन्त अरूचिकर अनुभूति के रूप में पारिभाषित किया जाता है।

(a) सामाजिक फोबिया (b) एगोराफोबिया (Agoraphobia)
(c) आसक्त व्यवहार (d) व्यग्रता (Anxiety) **(d)**

3. Raymond Cattell had applied a statistical technique for mental health called:

(a) Source traits (b) Source analysis
(c) Factor analysis (d) Surface traits **(c)**

4. सकारात्मक लक्षणों और नकारात्मक लक्षणों के साथ स्किजोफ्रेनिया (schizophrenia) के लक्षणों की तीसरी श्रेणी निम्नलिखित में से कौन सी है?

(a) मनः प्रेरक लक्षण (Psychomotor symptoms)
(b) श्रवणात्मक लक्षप (Psychomotor symptoms)
(c) उदासीन लक्षण (Psychomotor symptoms)
(d) विभ्रम लक्षण (Delusional symptoms) **(a)**

5. Leucocytes are also known as:

(a) Red blood cells (RBCs)
(b) White blood cells (WBCs)
(c) Plasma
(d) Haemoglobin **(b)**

6. 'Preoccupation with delusions or auditory hallucinations; no disorganised speech or behaviour or inappropriate affect' is a sub type of........

(a) Undifferentiated type (b) Paranoid type
(c) Disorganised type (d) Catatonic type **(b)**

7. A biologically based characteristic way of reaching is known as:

(a) Habit (b) Trait
(c) Disposition (d) Temperament **(d)**

8. निम्नलिखित में से कौन सा विकल्प, व्यक्ति के उन गुणों से संबंधित है, जो उसे अन्य से भिन्न बनाते हैं?

(a) सामाजिक पहचान (b) सामाजिक स्वत्व
(c) आत्म सम्मान (d) व्यक्तिगत पहचान **(d)**

Section : Nutrition

1. Which human organ secretes mucous, hydrochloric

acid and digestive juices?

(a) Mouth (b) Liver

(c) Pancreas (d) Stomach **(d)**

2. **Which of the following eating disorders often begins in late adolescence or early adulthood after a series or various unsuccessful oweight reduction diets?**

(a) Anorexia (b) Bulimia

(c) Anorexia bulimia (d) Anorexia nervosa **(b)**

3. **Which of the largest gland in the human body?**

(a) Gall bladder (b) Liver

(c) Large intestine (d) Small intestine **(b)**

4. **आहार नाल मुख्यतः एक लंबी नलिका होती है जो मुंह से लेकर. ....तक विस्तृत होती है।**

(a) बड़ी आंत (b) गुदा

(c) यकृत (d) पेट **(b)**

5. **Which of the following statements describes 'healthy eating habits'?**

(a) Eat 5 balanced meals of average size each day, plus 4 nutritious snacks. One can skip one meal.

(b) Eat 2 normal meals of average size each day, can skip nutritious snacks.

(c) Eat 1 balanced meals of average size each day, plus two nutritious snacks. One must try not to skip meals.

(d) Eat 3 balanced meals of average size each day, plus two nutritious snacks. One must try not to skip meals. **(d)**

6. **'वसा' के संबंध में निम्नलिखित में से कौन सा कथन सही हैं?**

(a) एक ग्राम वसा, 15 kcal ऊर्जा मुक्त करती है।

(b) एक ग्राम वसा, 11 kcal ऊर्जा मुक्त करती है।

(c) एक ग्राम वसा, 16 kcal ऊर्जा मुक्त करती है।

(d) एक ग्राम वसा, 9 kcal ऊर्जा मुक्त करती है। **(d)**

7. **मुख्यतः किस पोषक तत्व की कमी के कारण रक्ताल्पता (Anaemia) रोग होता है?**

(a) वसा (b) विटामिन ए

(c) आयरन (d) प्रोटीन **(c)**

8. **किस पोषक तत्व की कमी के कारण घेंघा रोग होता हैं?**

(a) विटामिन B-12 (b) विटामिन A

(c) विटामिन K (d) आयोडीन **(d)**

Section : First Aid

1. **आग से घायल होने की स्थिति में, ... में त्वचा की अधिचर्म कहलाने वाली केवल बाहरी परत जली होती है।**

(a) आंशिक मोटाई तक जलना (partial thickness burns)

(b) सतही जलना (superficial burns)

(c) पूर्ण मोटाई तक जलना (full thickness burns)

(d) अतिशय जलना (hyper burns) **(b)**

2. **A new born baby has how many bones at the time of birth?**

(a) 310 (b) 300

(c) 295 (d) 206 **(b)**

3. **निम्नलिखित में से कौन सा किसी बीमारी या चोट के लिए आरंभिक देखभाल का प्रावधान है?**

(a) सैनिटाइजर का उपयोग (b) परिरक्षित चिकित्सा

(c) बीमारी का अवलोकन (d) प्राथमिक चिकित्सा **(d)**

4. **Which of the following drugs is used very commonly in the treatment of allergies?**

(a) Saridon tablet (b) Cetirizine tablet

(c) Aspirin tablet (d) Paracetamol tablet **(b)**

5. **'अस्थि के दीर्घ अक्ष के समकोण पर टूटना'...........को वर्णित करता है।**

(a) एक आघात अस्थिभंग (b) एक कुंडलित अस्थिभंग

(c) एक तिर्यक अस्थिभंग (d) एक अनुप्रस्थ अस्थिभंग **(d)**

6. **What is the initial first aid technique in a food-borne illness?**

(a) The patient needs immediate hospitallisation

(b) Remove excess clothing and keep the person in a cool place

(c) Oral Rehydration Salts (ORS) should be given with luckewarm water

(d) Massage the front part of the belly **(c)**

7. **........ खतरे, रेडियोधर्मी पदार्थो के संपर्क में आने से संबंधित होते हैं।**

(a) मनोसामाजिक (b) विकिरण

(c) श्रम–दक्षता (d) जैविक और रासायनिक **(b)**

8. **निम्नलिखित में से कौन सा, चिकित्सकीय आपातस्थिति में 3Cs का एक भाग नहीं हैं?**

(a) जांच (b) सहयोग

(c) देखभाल (d) कॉल **(b)**

Section : Basic Anatomy and Physiology

1. **विज्ञान की निम्नलिखित में से कौन सी शाखा, शरीर के विविध ा अंगों की सामान्य संरचना, आकृति, अकार और अवस्थिति के अध्ययन से संबंधित हैं?**

(a) आंकोलॉजी (b) फिजियोलॉजी

(c) ओटोलैरिगोलॉजी (d) एनाटॉमी **(d)**

2. **The abnormal frequency of bowl movement and increased liquidity of faecal discharge is known as:**

(a) Jaundice (b) Diarrhoea

(c) Indigestion (d) Constipation **(b)**

3. **मेरूरज्जू, किस तंत्रिका तंत्र का भाग होता हैं?**

(a) केंद्रीय तंत्रिका तंत्र (b) अंतरांगी तंत्रिका तंत्र

(c) परानुकंपी तंत्रिका तंत्र (d) परिधीय तंत्रिका तंत्र **(a)**

4. **The neural system of all animals is composed of highly**

specialised cells called:

(a) Dendrites (b) Neurons

(c) Axon (d) Neurotransmitters **(b)**

5. **The oesophagus and the trachea (wind pipe) open into the ....**

(a) Pharynx (b) Larynx

(c) Cartilaginous flap (d) Cardiac portion **(a)**

6. **The pons is connected with the medulla on one side and with the .... on the other side.**

(a) Forebrain (b) Midbrain

(c) Hindbrain (d) Spinal cord **(b)**

7. **Each cell is equipped with different machineries known as:**

(a) Cell walls (b) Cell membrances

(c) Cytoplasm (d) Organelles **(d)**

8. **आंत्रीय श्लेष्मल उपकला में........होते हैं, जो श्लेष्मा का स्त्राव करते हैं।**

(a) काइम (chyme)

(b) कलश कोशिकाऐं (goblet cells)

(c) बोलस (bolus)

(d) निगलन (deglutition) **(b)**

Section: Administration and Ward Management

1. **भारत में स्वास्थ्य देखभाल को भारतीय संविधान की सातवीं अनुसूची के अंतर्गत......... में शामिल किया गया है।**

(a) केंद्रीय सूची (b) समवर्ती सूची

(c) राज्य सूची (d) अवशिष्ट सूची **(c)**

2. **निम्नलिखित में से कौन सी, सामूहिक सौदेबाजी की एक विशेषता नहीं हैं?**

(a) लोचशीलता (b) संबंध विकास

(c) सामूहिक गतिविधि (d) कर्नचारी मूल्यांकन **(d)**

3. **Which of the following includes inpatient services, involving medical, surgical and other specialities, and specific diagnostic procedures?**

(a) Diagnostic activity (b) Rehabilitative activity

(c) Curative activity (d) Preventive activity **(a)**

4. **Which hospital care deals with highly specialised medical facilties?**

(a) Tertiary care

(b) Secondary care

(c) Primary care

(d) Super speciality hospital care **(a)**

5. **In the healthcare system, an activity or service that is organised by an individual or company is known as:**

(a) A co-operative medical facility

(b) Private health care

(c) Medical tourism

(d) Public health care **(b)**

6. **In which method of nursing are nurses assigned specific functions such as administering medications, taking and recording vitals or providing general nursing care to a group of patients?**

(a) Individual method (b) Team method

(c) Patient method (d) Functional method **(d)**

7. **Which of the following organisations is a national regulatory body for nurses and nurse education in India?**

(a) National Nursing Council

(b) Nursing Council of India

(c) Indian Nursing Council

(d) Provincial Nursing Council **(c)**

8. **बचाव के कार्यों में किस प्रकार का स्ट्रेचर उपयोग किया जाता हैं?**

(a) नील राबर्टसन स्ट्रेचर (b) फर्ले स्ट्रेचर

(c) पैरागार्ड स्ट्रेचर (d) यूटाइल स्ट्रेचर **(a)**

Section: General Aptitude and Reasoning General Awareness and Basic Computer Knowledge

1. **ग्रीन-ब्लू इंफ्रास्ट्रक्चर नीति ('Green-Blue' infrastructure policy) किस राज्य/केंद्रशासित प्रदेश द्वारा प्रस्तावित की गई हैं?**

(a) तमिलनाडु (b) उत्तरप्रदेश

(c) दिल्ली (d) कर्नाटक **(c)**

2. **'Blue Screen of Death' indicates a major error in..... .**

(a) Free Fire (b) Wireless routers

(c) Microsoft Windows (d) Facebook **(c)**

3. **दिए गए विकल्पों में से उस संख्या का चयन करें, जो निम्नलिखित श्रेणी में प्रश्नवाचक चिह् (?) के स्थान पर आ सकती हैं?**

12, 6, 6, 9, 18, ?

(a) 36 (b) 48

(c) 40 (d) 45 **(d)**

4. **यदि एक 250- मीटर-लंबी रेलगाड़ी को रेल्वे लाइन के किनारे स्थित एक खंभे को पार करने में 45 सेकंड का समय लगता है, तो रेलगाड़ी की चाल कितनी होगी?**

(a) 15 km/h (b) 25 km/h

(c) 18 km/h (d) 20 km/h **(d)**

5. **दो मंदिरों T1 और T2 के बीच की दूरी 120 km है। एक जीप, 20 km/h की औसत चाल से T1 से T2 की ओर चलना प्रारंभ करती है। एक अन्य जीप, पहली जीप से 10 मिनट पहले 30 km/h की औसत चाल से T2 से T1 की ओर चलना प्रारंभ करती है। दोनों जीपें, क्रमशः T1 और T2 से कितनी दूरी पर मिलेंगी?**

(a) 51.78 km और 98.22 km
(b) 54.60 km और 95.470 km
(c) 41.81 km और 78.19 km
(d) 45.16 km और 74.84 km **(c)**

6. निम्नलिखित में से कौन सा कथन असत्य हैं?
(a) प्रयुक्त जल या अपशिष्ट जल को साफ करने के बाद पुनः प्रयोग नहीं किया जा सकता।
(b) जल स्वच्छ करने की प्रक्रिया में प्रदूषकों और हानिकारक पदार्थो को हटाया जाता है।
(c) अपशिष्ट जल में मानव मल–मूत्र भी मिला हो सकता है।
(d) स्वच्छ जल हमारे जीवन की मूलभूत आवश्यकता है। **(a)**

7. P1 और P2 को अपनी कारों से पूणे से मुंबई तक यात्रा करनी है। P1, 80 km/h की चाल से चल रहा है; जबकि P2, 60 km/h की चाल से चल रहा है। यदि P1 को इस यात्रा में 9 घंटे का समय लगता है, तो P2 को इस यात्रा में कितना समय लगेगा?
(a) 20 घंटे (b) 12 घंटे
(c) 14 घंटे (d) 16 घंटे **(b)**

8. A bullet train is travelling at a speed of 131 km/h. How many seconds will it take to cover a distance of 9/8 km?
(a) 75 s (b) 90 s
(c) 120 s (d) 105 s **(b)**

9. निम्नलिखित में से कौन सी अंतरिक्ष एजेंसी सुपरबिट (Super Bit) नामक दूरदर्शी का निर्माण कर रही हैं?
(a) ई.एस.ए. (ESA)
(b) नासा (NASA)
(c) रोस्कॉस्मॉस (Roscosmos)
(d) इसरो (ISRO) **(d)**

10. .... is a mobile application developed by the Government of India to connect essential health services with people in the fight against COVID-19.
(a) MedWatch (b) Aarogya Setu
(c) Aam Aadmi (d) Doctor Desk **(b)**

11. Operating systems and other programs typically access a hardware device through a ...., which provides a software interface to the device.
(a) Macro assembler (b) Device driver
(c) Dynamic linker (d) Compiler **(b)**

12. चार अक्षर समूह दिए गए हैं, जिनमें से तीन संगत है और एक असंगत है। असंगत का चयन कीजिए।
(a) HLOP (b) SVXY
(c) KNPQ (d) RUWX **(a)**

13. 19 हाथियों की आयु का औसत 31 है। बाद में, यह पाया गया कि 14, 24 और 31 की आयु वाले हाथियों की आयु त्रुटिवश 41, 42 और 43 अंकित कर ली गई थी। सही औसत ज्ञात कीजिए।
(a) 27 (b) 30
(c) 29 (d) 28 **(d)**

14. 'A # B' means 'A is the son of B'
'A & B' means 'A is the wife of B'
'A @ B' means 'A is the brother of B'
'A $ B' means 'A is the husband of B'
If M @ K # J & O @ L, then how is K related to L?
(a) Nephew (b) Son
(c) Niece (d) Cousin **(a)**

15. Which of the following is the first particle discovered which is believed to be elementary, that is, not made up of further constituents?
(a) Glucon (b) Photon
(c) Electron (d) Proton **(c)**

16. In operating system, a pipe is used for ....
(a) Inter-process communication
(b) Network data transmission
(c) Connecting two chips
(d) Process synchronisation **(a)**

17. चार अक्षर समूह दिए गए हैं, जिनमें से तीन संगत हैं और एक असंगत है। असंगत का चयन कीजिए।
(a) GKIM (b) FJHL
(c) PTRV (d) CHEJ **(d)**

18. एलेक जेफरी..........से संबद्ध हैं।
(a) आर.एन.एफ. फिंगर प्रिंटि
(b) डी.एन.डी. अनुक्रमण
(c) डी.एन.डी. फिंगर प्रिंटिंग
(d) साइट–डाइरेक्टेड म्यूटाजेनेसिस **(c)**

19. ...... used in a computer has a switching regulator to convert electrical power efficiently.
(a) HDD (b) ROM
(c) USB (d) SMPS **(d)**

20. यदि 'A # B' का अर्थ है- 'A, B का भाई है', 'A ^ B' का अर्थ है- 'A, B की पुत्री है', 'A * B' का अर्थ है- 'A, B का पति है', 'A & B का अर्थ है- 'A, B' की बहन है और 'A % B' का अर्थ है- 'A, B की माता है तो निम्नलिखित व्यंजक में 'K' का 'O' से क्या संबंध हैं?

J * K % L & M # N % O

(a) नानी (b) दादी
(c) मामी/मौसी (d) माता **(a)**

Rajasthan CHO Exam

10 November 2020

1. निम्नलिखित में से कौनसा Macronutrient नहीं हैं।
(a) Proteins (b) Fats
(c) Vitamins (d) Carbohydrates

2. निम्नलिखित में से कौनसा water soluble vitamin है?
(a) Vitamin A (b) Vitamin C
(c) Vitamin D (d) Vitamin E

3. निम्नलिखित में से कौन-से खाद्य पदार्थ से विटामिन ई की सबसे अधिक मात्रा मिलती है?
(a) Meat (b) Sunflower oil
(c) Vetetable (d) Fruits

4. Vitamin C की कमी से कौनसी बीमारी होती है?
(a) Night blindness (b) Scurvy
(c) Rickets (d) Beri Beri

5. बच्चे को पूरक आहार (Complementary Feeding) कब से शुरू कर देना चाहिए?
(a) पैदा होते ही (b) छः माह की उम्र पर
(c) एक वर्ष की उम्र पर (d) दो वर्ष की उम्र पर

6. निम्नलिखित में से कौनसा पोषक तत्व tissue repair के लिए आवश्यक है?
(a) Vitamin (b) Carbohydrate
(c) Fat (d) Protein

7. निम्नलिखित में से कौनसा लक्षण डेंगू बीमारी का नहीं है?
(a) तेज बुखार (b) हल्का बुखार
(c) आँखों में दर्द (d) जोड़ों में दर्द

8. VVM का full form क्या है?
(a) Vaccine Viability Monitor
(b) Vaccine Vial Monitor
(c) Vaccine Verification Monitor
(d) Viral Viability Monitor

9. 9 माह पर Vitamin A की dose कितनी होती है?
(a) 50000 IU (b) 100000 IU
(c) 200000 IU (d) 300000 IU

10. किसी वस्तु/सतह को coronavirus से संक्रमणमुक्त (decontamination) किस रासायनिक पदार्थ से किया जा सकता है?
(a) फोरमलडिहाइड (b) मेथेनोल
(c) ग्लूटरिल्डिहाइड (d) सोडियम हाइपोक्लोराइट

11. Multi-drug Resistant Tuberculosis के इलाज की अवधि । कितनी होती है?
(a) कम से कम 6-8 माह (b) कम से कम 12 माह
(c) कम से कम 20-24 माह (d) कम से कम 24-27 माह

12. गर्भवती महिला को टिटनेस टोक्सोइड (tetaus toxoid) के दो टीके लगाने के बीच कम से कम कितना अन्तराल रखना चाहिए?
(a) कम से कम एक सप्ताह (b) कम से कम दो सप्ताह
(c) कम से कम चार सप्ताह (d) कम से कम बारह सप्ताह

13. निम्नलिखित में से कौन-कौन सी vaccine जन्म के समय दी जाती है?
(a) BCG, OPV, Hepatitis B
(b) BCG, OPV, Hepatitis C
(c) BCG
(d) BCG, OPV, Pentavalent (पेंटावलेंट)

14. कोविड-19 बीमारी का कारक क्या है?
(a) Bectria (b) Virus
(c) Fungus (d) Protozoa

15. मानव शरीर में कितनी हड्डियाँ होती है?
(a) 202 (b) 204
(c) 206 (d) 208

16. टी.बी. की जाँच के लिए किये जाने वाले Tuberculin Test को क्या कहते हैं?
(a) Schick test (b) Mantoux Test
(c) VDRL Test (d) ELISA Test

17. मानव शरीर में सबसे बड़ी ग्रन्थि (largest gland) कौन-सी है?
(a) Pancreas (b) Liver
(c) Splen (d) Gallbladder

18. Testes द्वारा बनाये जाने वाला हार्मोन कौन-सा है?
(a) Testosterone (b) TSH
(c) Cortisol (d) Insulin

19. Liver में Carbohydrate किस रूप में संग्रहित (store) होता है?
(a) Glucose (b) Sucrose
(c) Galactose (d) Glycogen

20. किसी आबादी/समुदाय मे कोई संक्रमित रोग के पहले रोगी (first case) को क्या कहते है?
(a) Index case (b) Primary case
(c) Secondary case (d) Carrier

21. विश्व स्वास्थ्य दिवस कब मनाया जाता है?
(a) 10 मई (b) 01 दिसम्बर
(c) 11 मार्च (d) 07 अप्रैल

22. भारत के वर्तमान राष्ट्रपति कौन है?
(a) श्री वैंकैया नायडू (b) श्री प्रणब मुखर्जी
(c) श्री रामनाथ कोविन्द (d) श्री लालकृष्ण आडवाणी

23. MTP act भारतीय संसद द्वारा कब लागू किया गया?
(a) 1962 (b) 1971
(c) 1965 (d) 1984

24. निम्नलिखित बीमारियो में से कौनसी बीमारी का भारत से उन्मूलन किया जा चुका है?
(a) क्षय रोग (b) मलेरिया
(c) पोलियो (d) एड्स

25. हरित क्रान्ति (Green revolution) का आवाहन किसने किया था?
(a) वरगीज कुरियन (b) त्रिभुवनदास पटेल
(c) एम.एस. स्वामीनाथन (d) एम.एस. दलाया

26. भारत में स्वच्छ भारत अभियान का शुभारम्भ कब किया गया था?
(a) 2 सितम्बर 2014 (b) 2 अक्टूबर 2014
(c) 15 अगस्त 2014 (d) 2 अक्टूबर 2013

27. निम्नलिखित में से कौनसी प्रक्रिया को (Global warming) का जिम्मेदार ठहराया गया है?
(a) ग्रीनहाऊस इफेक्ट (b) कोयला खदानों में आग
(c) सूखी खेती (d) मानसून

28. निम्नलिखित नें से कौनसा रोग फीको-ओरल (Feeo-oral) माध्यम से नहीं फैलता?
(a) खसरा (b) टायफाइड
(c) कोलेरा/हैजा (d) हेपेटाइटिस ए

29. दस्त रोग में मृत्यु का मुख्य कारण कौन-सा है?
(a) उल्टी (b) पेट में दर्द
(c) निर्जलीकरण (d) सुस्ती

30. निम्नलिखित में से 5 वर्ष से छोटे बच्चों की मृत्यु का मुख्य कारण क्या है?
(a) दस्त रोग (b) निमोनिया
(c) खसरा (d) छोटी माता

31. बच्चों में सामान्य कैपिलरी रीफिल समय (Normal Capillary Time) कितना होता है?
(a) एक सैकेण्ड से कम (b) तीन सैकेण्ड से कम
(c) पाँच सैकेण्ड (d) सात सैकेण्ड

32. आप एक छः माह के बच्चे के विकास का आकलन कर रहे हैं। सामान्यतः निम्नलिखित में से आप क्या उम्मीद कर सकते है?
(a) बच्चा छोटे वाक्य बोल सकता है।
(b) बच्चा चम्मच से स्वयं खाना खा सकता है।
(c) बच्चा स्वयं बैठ सकता है।
(d) बच्चा स्वयं उठ कर खड़ा हो सकता है?

33. भारत में जन्म के समय नवजात का वजन सामान्यतः कितना होता है?
(a) 1.5 से 2.5 किलो (b) 2.0 से 3.0 किलो
(c) 2.5 से 3.5 किलो (d) 3.0 से 4.0 किलो

34. जब कंगारू मदर केयर (KMC) प्रदान की जाती है, वह कम से कम कितने समय के लिए प्रदान की जानी चाहिए?
(a) कम से कम 15 मिनट (b) कम से कम 1 घण्टा
(c) कम से कम 3 घण्टे (d) कम से कम छः घण्टे

35. लेबर रूम का तापमान (°C में) कितना होना चाहिए?
(a) 20 - 24 (b) 26 - 28
(c) 28 - 30 (d) 34 - 37

36. निम्नलिखित में से कौन सा Immunoglobulin मानव के दूध (human milk) में पाया जाता है?
(a) IgG (b) IgM
(c) IgA (d) IgA

37. BCG वैक्सीन का इंजेक्शन किस प्रकार लगाया जाता है?
(a) Intradermal (b) Subcutaneous
(c) Intramiscular (d) Intravenous

38. Koplik's spots किस बीमारी में देखने को मिलते हैं?
(a) छोटी माता (chickenpox) (b) Mumps
(c) खसरा (Measles) (d) पोलिया

39. समेकित बाल विकास सेवायें योजना (ICDS Scheme) के लाभार्थी कौन हैं?
(a) छः वर्ष से छोटे बच्चे
(b) गर्भवती तथा स्तनपान कराने वाली महिलायें
(c) बुजुर्ग व्यक्ति
(d) (a) तथा (b) दोनों

40. निम्नलिखित में से कैल्शियम (Calcium) का सबसे बढ़िया स्त्रोत क्या है?
(a) माँस (b) फल (c) दूध (d) सब्जी

41. प्रसवोत्तर रक्तस्त्राव (postpartum hemorrhage) में कौन-सी दवा काम में नहीं ली जाती है?
(a) Oxytocin (b) Methergin
(c) Mifepristone (d) Misoprostol

42. प्रसव की सम्भावित तिथि (Expected date of delivery) पता लगाने के लिए पिछली माहवारी के पहले दिवस से कितने दिन जोडने चाहिये?
(a) 9 माह (b) 9 माह 2 दिन
(c) 9 माह 7 दिन (d) 9 माह 14 दिन

43. गर्भवती महिला में सामान्य श्वसन दर (Normal respiratory rate) कितनी होती है?
(a) 12-16 प्रति मिनट (b) 18-20 प्रति मिनट
(c) 18-24 प्रति मिनट (d) 20-24 प्रति मिनट

44. Fetoscope से Fetal heart sound गर्भ धारण की कितनी अवधि के बाद सुनी जा सकती है?
(a) 12 सप्ताह (b) 20 सप्ताह
(c) 24 सप्ताह (d) 32 सप्ताह

45. रक्त में हीमोग्लोबिन (Hb) की मात्रा कितने से कम होने पर गर्भवती महिला को एनिमिक कहा जाता है?
(a) 13 g% (b) 12g% (c) 11g% (d) 10g%

46. IUCD का क्या तात्पर्य है?
(a) Intrauterine control device
(b) Intrauterine copper device
(c) Intrauterine contraceptive device
(d) Intrauterine continuous device

47. सामान्यतः Fetal Heart Rate कितनी होती है?
(a) 60-80 प्रति मिनट (b) 100-120 प्रति मिनट
(c) 120-160 प्रति मिनट (d) 160-180 प्रति मिनट

48. प्रत्येक प्रसव पूर्व जाँच में निम्नलिखित जाँचे की जानी चाहिये?
(a) Hemoglobin, Urine sugar, HCG
(b) Hemoglobin, Urine sugar, Urine Albumin
(c) Hemoglobin, Blood sugar, Urine sugar
(d) Hemoglobin, Urine sugar, HPL

49. एक गर्भवती महिला को चार माह के गर्भ पर Tetanus Toxoid (TT) का पहला टीका लगा था। अब वह आंठवे माह में जाँच हेतु आई है आप TT के टीके के बारे में क्या निर्णय लेंगे?
(a) TT का टीका नहीं लगायेंगे
(b) TT का दूसरा टीका लगायेंगे
(c) TT का 0.5 ml की जगह 1.0 ml का टीका लगायेंगे।
(d) आज TT का टीका लगायेंगे और महिला को 15 दिन बाद TT के एक और टीके के लिए बुलायेंगे

50. Hemoglobin की मात्रा को जाँचने के लिए क्या इस्तेमाल किया जाता है?
(a) NaCl (b) N/10 HCl (c) NaOCl (d) NaOH

51. गर्भवती महिला को कौन-कौन से संक्रमणों के लिए जाँचना चाहिए?
(a) HIV, Hepatitis A, Syphilis
(b) HIV, Hepatisis B, Hyphilis
(c) HIV, Hepatitis C, Syphilis
(d) HIV, Hepatitis E, Syphilis

52. Partograph में Alert line और Action line में कितने घण्टों का अन्तराल होता है?
(a) 2 घण्टे (b) 3 घण्टे
(c) 4 घण्टे (d) 6 घण्टे

53. जन्म के कितने समय बाद नवजात शिशु को स्तनपान शुरू करवा देना चाहिए?
(a) एक घण्टे की भीतर (b) दो घण्टे बाद
(c) चिकित्सक के कहने पर ही (d) छः घण्टे के बाद

54. सामान्य प्रसव में औसतन कितना खून बह जाता है?
(a) 100 ml (b) 300 ml
(c) 500 ml (d) 700 ml

55. Bio medical waste rules के अनुसार नाल (Placenta) को कौन-सी थैली में डाला जाता है?
(a) पीली थैली (b) लाल थैली
(c) काली थैली (d) नीली थैली

56. भारत में मातृ मृत्यु का सबसे प्रमुख कारण क्या है?
(a) संक्रमण (Sepsis)
(b) Toxemia
(c) असुरक्षित गर्भपात (unsafe abortion)
(d) रक्तस्राव

57. असुरक्षित यौन सम्बन्ध (Unprotected coitus) के बाद कितने 'समय के भीतर' आपातकालीन गर्भनिरोधक गोली लेने से गर्भ ठहरने की संभावना कम होती है?
(a) 24 घण्टे (b) 48 घण्टे
(c) 72 घण्टे (d) 120 घण्टे

58. प्रसवोत्तर बन्ध्याकरण (postpartum sterilization) प्रसव के कितने समय के बाद किया जाना चाहिए?
(a) 12 घण्टे से 7 दिन (b) 24 घण्टे से 7 दिन
(c) 48 घण्टे से 7 दिन (d) 72 घण्टे से 7 दिन

59. Vasectomy के बाद कितने समय तक किसी को परिवार योजना का अन्य तरीका इस्तेमाल करना चाहिए?
(a) एक माह तक (b) तीन माह तक
(c) दो माह तक (d) पाँच माह तक

60. Levonorgestel (LNG) IUCD को कितने समय में बदल देना चाहिये?
(a) पाँच वर्ष (b) दस वर्ष
(c) पन्द्रह वर्ष (d) बीस वर्ष

61. राजस्थान की शिशु मृत्यु दर कितनी है?
(a) 14/1,000 (b) 28/1,000
(c) 37/1,000 (d) 56/1,000

62. BMW से क्या तात्पर्य है?
(a) Basic medical waste (b) Bio medical waste
(c) Blood medical waste (d) Bio manpower waste

63. रक्तचाप (BP) को मापते समय instrument की नलियों (tubes) को हाथ के किस ओर रखना चाहिए?
(a) बाहर की ओर (lateral)
(b) अन्दर की ओर (medial)
(c) पीछे की ओर (posterior)
(d) पीछे की बाह की ओर (Postero-lateral)

64. वर्तमान में भारत की कुल प्रजनन दर (Total Fertility Rate) कितनी है?
(a) 1.8 (b) 2.2 (c) 2.5 (d) 2.6

65. टायफाइड (Typhoid) बीमारी का पता लगाने के लिए कौनसा टेस्ट किया जाता है?
(a) Widal test (b) Millard's test
(c) Kahn test (d) Mantoux test

66. विश्व स्वास्थ्य संगठन (WHO) का मुख्यालय कहाँ है?
(a) New york (b) Genva
(c) Paris (d) London

67. जल के शुद्धिकरण के लिये कौन-सा रासायनिक पदार्थ इस्तेमाल किया जाता है?
(a) Lime (b) Bleaching Powder
(c) Potassium Permanganate (d) Formaldehyde

68. एक प्राथमिक स्वास्थ्य केन्द्र औसतन कितनी आबादी के लिए स्थापित किया जाता है?
(a) 5,000 (b) 10,000 (c) 30,000 (d) 50,000

69. वर्तमान में राजस्थान की मातृ मृत्यु दर (MMR) कितनी है?
(a) लगभग 100/1,00,000 (b) लगभग 150/1,00,000
(c) लगभग 200/1,00,000 (d) लगभग 250/1,00,000

70. देश में पिछली जनगणना कब की गयी थी?
(a) 2005-06 (b) 2011
(c) 2012-14 (d) 2019

71. विश्व की कितनी जनसंख्या भारत में रहती है?
(a) लगभग 7 प्रतिशत (b) लगभग 12 प्रतिशत
(c) लगभग 17 प्रतिशत (d) लगभग 22 प्रतिशत

72. पीने के पानी में free residual chlorine की मात्रा कितनी होनी चाहिए?
(a) 0.25 mg per liter (b) 0.5 mg per litre
(c) 1.0 mg per litre (d) 2.0 mg per litre

73. भारत में राष्ट्रीय जनसंख्या नीति (National Pupulation policy) कब लागू की गयी?
(a) 1952 (b) 1965 (c) 1985 (d) 2000

74. राष्ट्रीय ग्रामीण स्वास्थ्य मिशन का शुभारम्भ किस वर्ष में किया गया?
(a) 2000 (b) 2002 (c) 2005 (d) 2007

75. आशा (ASHA)/आशा सहयोगिनी सामान्यत: कितनी आबादी के लिए सेवायें प्रदान करती है?
(a) 500 (b) 1000 (c) 2500 (d) 5000

76. निम्नलिखित में से कौनसी बीमारी का भारत से उन्मूलन कर दिया गया है?
(a) मलेरिया (b) नारु रोग
(c) एस.आई.वी (d) घेंघा

77. जन्म तथ मृत्यु पंजीकरण अधिनियम (Birth and deaths Registration Act) के अनुसार जन्म का पंजीकरण कितनी अवधि में करवा लेना चाहिए।
(a) 7 दिवस (b) 10 दिवस (c) 14 दिवस (d) 21 दिवस

78. खसरा (Measles) वैक्सीन का Route of administration क्या है?
(a) Intradermal (b) Subeutaneous
(c) Intramuscular (d) Intravenous

79. एक व्यस्क आदमी का Body mass Index कितना होना चाहिए?
(a) 15-19 (b) 20-25 (c) 26-30 (d) 31-35

80. बच्चों में दस्त रोग के इलाज के लिये ORS के साथ निम्नलिखित में से क्या दिया जाता है?
(a) Calcium (b) Iron
(c) Vitamin (d) Zinc

81. सामान्य व्यक्ति में HbA1C की मात्रा कितनी होती है?
(a) 6.0% से कम (b) 6.5% से 7.0%
(c) 7.0% से 8.0% (d) 3.0% से कम

82. किसी व्यस्क में Random Blood Sugar की कितनी मात्रा से मधुमेह (Diabetes Mellitus) का संदेह होना चहिए?
(a) 20 mg/dl से 100 mg/dl
(b) 100 mg/dl से 140 mg/dl
(c) 140 mg/dl से ज्यादा
(d) 200 mg/dl से ज्यादा

83. मधुमेह (Diabetes Mellitus) की सबसे ज्यादा पाई जाने वाली जटिलता (Complication) क्या है?
(a) Galactosemia (b) Hyperglycemia
(c) Hypoglycemia (d) Stroke

84. मानव शरीर में कैंसर किस प्रकार फैलता है?
(a) त्वचा के माध्यम से
(b) Lymphatic system के माध्यम से
(c) रक्त के माध्यम से
(d) (b) तथा (c) दोनों

85. निम्नलिखित सभी कारण स्तन कैंसर का जोखिम बढाते हैं सिवाय एक के-
(a) Late Menopause
(b) अत्यधिक वजन
(c) कई व्यक्तियों के साथ यौन सम्बन्ध
(d) शारीरिक व्यायाम न करना

86. स्तन की स्वयं जाँच करने पर (Breast Self-examination) का सबसे उपयुक्त समय कब होता है?
(a) माहवारी के दौरान
(b) माहवारी के प्रथम दिन के 7-10 दिन बाद
(c) माहवारी शुरू होने के 10 दिन पहले
(d) यदि महिला हार्मोन ले रही हो तो रक्तस्त्राव (withdrawal bleeding) शुरू होने के अगले दिन

87. गर्भावस्था के दौरान तम्बाकू सेवन से क्या हो सकता है?
(a) समय से पहले प्रसव (Premature Labour)
(b) बढ़े वजन वाला नवजात शिशु (Overweight Baby)
(c) कम वजन वाला बच्चा (Low birth weight baby)
(d) नपुंसकता (Impotence)

88. Insulin इंजेक्शन सामान्यत: किस के लिए दिये जाते है?
(a) Type I diabetes Mellitus
(b) Type II diabetes Mellitus
(c) Type III diabetetes Mellitus
(d) Both type I and Type III diabetes Mellitus

89. सामान्य मानव विकास के लिये प्रतिदिन आयोडीन की कितनी मात्रा की आवश्यकता होती है?
(a) 50-100 माइक्रोग्राम (b) 50-100 मिलीग्राम
(c) 100-150 माइक्रोग्राम (d) 100-150 मिलीग्राम

90. Cervical Cancer से बचाव के लिए कौन-सी वैक्सीन इस्तेमाल ली जा सकती है?
(a) IPV वैक्सीन (b) Hepatitis वैक्सीन
(c) DPT वैक्सीन (d) HPV वैक्सीन

91. NETEN (Norethirdrone enanthate) गर्भधारण से कितने समय के लिए बचाता है?
(a) एक माह (b) दो माह
(c) तीन माह (d) चार माह

92. IUCD का सबसे अधिक पाया जाने वाला प्रतिकूल प्रभाव (side effect) क्या है?
(a) Ectopic Prégnancy
(b) Excessive Menstrual Flow
(c) Rupture of Uterus
(d) Expulsion of IUCD

93. HIV संक्रमण का पता लगाने के लिए कौन-सी तकनीक अपनायी जाती है?
(a) Northern Blot तथा ELISA
(b) Immunoblot तथा ELISA
(c) Southern Blot तथा ELISA
(d) Western Blot तथा ELISA

94. किशोरावस्था में सबसे ज्यादा पायी जाने वाली पोषण संबंधी कमी कौन सी है?
(a) Iron Deficiency Anemia
(b) Hypothyroidism
(c) Calcium Deficiency
(d) Zomc Deficiency

95. विश्व में किशोरावस्था में मृत्यु का सबसे बड़ा कारण क्या है?
(a) आत्महत्या (b) दस्त रोग
(c) सड़क दुर्घटना (d) एनीमिया

96. Testosterone एक हार्मोन है जो पाया जाता है?
(a) केवल पुरूषों में
(b) केवल महिलाओं में
(c) केवल पुरूषों में यौवन के समय
(d) पुरूष तथा महिलाओं दोनों में

97. किशोर बालक-बालिकाओं में de-worming के लिए Albendazole की dose कितनी है?
(a) 100 mg BD (b) 200 mg OD,HS
(c) 400 mg OD, HS (d) 800 mg, BD

98. गैर-संक्रामक रोग (Non-Communicable Diseases) –
(a) एक व्यक्ति से दूसरे व्यक्ति का फैल सकते है
(b) एक व्यक्ति से दूसरे व्यक्ति को सम्पर्क द्वारा नहीं फैलते
(c) Vectors द्वारा फैलते हैं
(d) उपरोक्त में से कोई नहीं

99. किसी वयस्क व्यक्ति का सामान्य रक्तचाप (Normal Blood pressure) कितना होता है।
(a) 120/80 mm Hg (b) 130-139/80-89 mm Hg
(c) 140-159/90-99 mm Hg (d) उपरोक्त में से कोई नहीं

100. मधुमेह (Diabetes Mellitus) के रोगी के प्रमुख लक्षण क्या होते है?
(a) Polyuria (अत्यधिक पेशाब आना)
(b) Polydypsia (अत्यधिक प्यास लगना)
(c) Polyphagia (अत्यधिक भूख लगना)
(d) उपरोक्त सभी सही हैं

ANSWERS

1.[c]	2.[b]	3.[b]	4.[b]	5.[b]	6.[d]	7.[b]	8.[b]	9.[b]	10.[d]
11.[d]	12.[c]	13.[a]	14.[b]	15.[c]	16.[b]	17.[b]	18.[a]	19.[d]	20.[b]
21.[d]	22.[c]	23.[b]	24.[c]	25.[c]	26.[b]	27.[a]	28.[a]	29.[c]	30.[b]
31.[b]	32.[c]	33.[b]	34.[d]	35.[b]	36.[d]	37.[a]	38.[c]	39.[d]	40.[c]
41.[c]	42.[c]	43.[c]	44.[b]	45.[c]	46.[c]	47.[c]	48.[b]	49.[b]	50.[c]
51.[b]	52.[c]	53.[a]	54.[c]	55.[a]	56.[d]	57.[c]	58.[c]	59.[b]	60.[a]
61.[c]	62.[b]	63.[b]	64.[b]	65.[a]	66.[b]	67.[b]	68.[c]	69.[b]	70.[b]
71.[c]	72.[b]	73.[d]	74.[c]	75.[b]	76.[b]	77.[d]	78.[b]	79.[b]	80.[d]
81.[a]	82.[c]	83.[c]	84.[d]	85.[c]	86.[b]	87.[c]	88.[a]	89.[c]	90.[d]
91.[b]	92.[b]	93.[d]	94.[a]	95.[a]	96.[a]	97.[c]	98.[b]	99.[a]	100.[d]

◆◆◆

MP CHO Paper 2020 (Memory Based)

1. The data required for analysing the health situation and defining the health problem of a community includes all except?

(a) Socio economic factors
(b) Cultural factors
(c) Spiritual factors
(d) Demographic factors

2. The roles and responsibilities of ASHA includes all except?

(a) Provide primary medical care for minor illnesses like diarrhoea
(b) Provide medical care using IMNCI guidelines
(c) Provide DOTS treatment
(d) Create awareness about nutrition and basic sanitation

3. The concept of primary health care was recommended by?

(a) Bhore committee
(b) Mudaliar committee
(c) Mukheijee committee
(d) Kartar singh committee

4. The gross motor development of a 6 - 8 months old infant is?

(a) Holds head erect
(b) Sits without support
(c) Crawling
(d) Stands with support

5. Flattening or falling of the childs weight curve is an earliest indication of?

(a) Vitamin deficiency
(b) Micronutrient deficiency
(c) Protein energy malnutrition
(d) Worm infestation

6. ICDS means?

(a) International Child Development Scheme
(b) Indian Child Development Scheme
(c) Integrated Child Development Scheme
(d) Initiated Child Development

7. A 3 to 6 years old child belongs to the developmental stage?

(a) Infant (b) Toddler
(c) Pre-schooler (d) School age

8. Playing alone with toys different from those used by other children, in an area enjoying the presence of other children and making no effort to speak with them is called?

(a) Onlooker play (b) Solitary play
(c) Parallel play (d) Associative

9. The recommended dietary intake of protein for an Indian adult is?

(a) 1 gm per kg body weight
(b) 2 gm per kg body weight
(c) 3 gm per kg body weight
(d) 4 gmper kg body weight

10. Vitamin D deficiency results in?

(a) Club foot (b) Osteomalacia
(c) Osteomyelitis (d) Osteoporosis

11. The production or release of certain coagulation factors is stimulated by which Vitamin?

(a) Vitamin B_{12} (b) Vitamin A
(c) Vitamin E (d) Vitamin K

12. The assigning of various roles to be performed by nurses working in the ward is called?

(a) Planning (b) Staffing
(c) Controlling (d) Organising

13. The objectives of nursing personnel management includes all except:

(a) To upgrade and promote existing staff wherever possible
(b) To maintain discipline
(c) To take all steps to have excessive hours of work
(d) To maintain standards of remuneration

14. Assigning a group of patients to a group of staff members under the leadership of a professional nurse is called?

(a) Functional method (b) Team method
(c) Primary nursing (d) None of these

15. The employees state insurance act covers employees drawing wages not exceeding?
(a) Rs. 19,000 per month (b) Rs. 20,000 per month
(c) Rs. 21,000 permonth (d) Rs. 22,000 permonth

16. During an accident severe blood loss results in?
(a) Hypo glycemia (b) Shock
(c) Anaphylaxis (d) Sepsis

17. The parameters assessed using Glasgow coma scale
(a) Eye opening response, best verbal response, best motor response
(b) Eye response, best verbal response, best stimuli response
(c) Eye response, best response, best motor response
(d) None ofthese

18. Heimlich maneuver's is performed to?
(a) To treat insufficient breathing
(b) To improve circulation
(c) To remove blockage from victim's airway
(d) To provide effective ventilation

19. In adult anuria refers to urine output less than?
(a) 50 ml per day (b) 100 ml per day
(c) 150 ml per day (d) 200 ml per day

20. The hormones secreted by isletsofLangerhans are?
(a) Insulin,Glucagon
(b) Insulin,Glucagon, Somatostatin
(c) Insulin,Glucagon,ACTH
(d) Insulin,ACTH, Somatostatin

21. The primary role of aldosterone is?
(a) Conserve sodium, promote potassium excretion
(b) Conserve potassium, promote sodium excretion
(c) Conserve sodium and potassium
(d) Promote excretion of Sodium and Potassium

22. The sub Centre isrenamed as?
(a) Health & sciences Centre
(b) Health Centre
(c) Health and wellness Centre
(d) Health Science, treatment and palliative Centre

23. The procedure by which amniotic fluid is obtained for testing is?
(a) Chorionic villus sampling
(b) Amniocentesis
(c) Fetal blood sampling
(d) None of these

24. Before birth, the alveoli in a baby's lungs are expanded and filled by?
(a) Air (b) Fluid
(c) Blood (d) Meconium

25. The diagnostic tests of malaria includes all, except?
(a) Rapid diagnostic test (b) Serological test
(c) Microscope (d) Hemoglobin test

26. The mode of transmission of Hepatitis C is?
(a) Feco oral route (b) Droplet nuclei
(c) Contaminated blood (d) None of these

27. What is the dose of Vitamin A for an infant at 9 months of age?
(a) l lakh IlJ (b) 2 lakh IU
(c) 3 lakh lU (d) 4 lakh lU

28. The first line of drugs for treatment of tuberculosis are?
(a) Isoniazid, Rifampicin, Pyrazinamide, Ethambutol and streptomycin
(b) Rifampicin, NH, streptomycin, PAS andAmikacin
(c) Rifampicin, NH, streptomycin, Kanamycin and Ethambutol
(d) NH, Streptomycin, Kanamycin and PAS

29. The various drugs used for lactation suppression are all except?
(a) Tab Cabergoline (b) Tab pyridoxine
(c) Injection mixogen (d) Injection Methergin

30. The essential characters of a good nursing service department includes all except?
(a) Evaluating nursing services periodically
(b) Formulation of written statement of purpose and objectives of nursing service
(c) Availability of written procedures for nurses
(d) Running the hospital with minimal staffing

31. Recommended disinfectant specific to killing t Corona Virus is?
(a) Carbolic acid (b) Lyzol
(c) Phenyl (d) Sodium Hypochiorite

32. Which of the following is a DNA virus?
(a) Hepatitis A (b) Hepatitis B
(c) Hepatitis C (d) Hepatitis D

33. Rubella is also known as?
(a) Tetanus (b) Whooping cough
(c) Measles (d) German Measles

34. SARS stands for?
(a) Standard Acute Respiratory Syndrome
(b) Severe Acute Respiratory Syndrome
(c) Sub-Acute Respiratory Syndrome
(d) Showing All Respiratory Symptoms

35. The mode of transmission of Leprosy is?
(a) Droplet infection (b) Fecal oral route
(c) Sexual contact (d) None ofthese

36. Botulism is caused by?
(a) Staphylococci (b) Salmonellosis
(c) Clostridiumtetani (d) Clostridium botulinum

37. Which animal is amplifier of Japanese encephalitis?
(a) Cow (b) Monkey
(c) Pig (d) Cat

38. In which communicable diseases the Acid Fast Bacilli Test is positive?
(a) Tetanus and Leprosy
(b) Diphtheria and Tetanus
(c) Poliomyelitis and Tetanus
(d) Tuberculosis and Leprosy

39. Which behavioral risk factors contribute to a person developing a Non Communicable Disease?
(a) Physical inactivity
(b) Harmful Alcohol consumption
(c) Tobacco use
(d) All of these

40. Contributing factors for causation of cardiovascular disease are?
(a) Genetic, Tobacco, Alcohol and Physical inactivity
(b) Genetic, Alcohol, Air pollution
(c) Diabetes, Water pollution, Obesity
(d) Diabetes, Genetic, Obesity, Congenital heart problem

41. Approach for cancer prevention policy are?
(a) Early detection & treatment
(b) Screening
(c) Palliative care
(d) All of these

42. The infection by which organism can cause cervix cancer?
(a) Hepatitis B (b) HIV
(c) HPV (d) H. Pylori

43. What is Palliative Care?
(a) It is an approach to improve quality of life of patients and their family who are facing life threatening illness
(b) It is an approach to improve quality of life of patients with terminal cancer
(c) It is an approach to reduce cost of treatment
(d) It is an approach to reduce mortality and morbidity of the country

44. Brachytherapy refers to?
(a) Giving anti cancerous drugs through intravenous route
(b) Procedure of placing radioactive material inside the body
(c) Passing radioactive rays in the body
(d) None of these

45. When was National Family Health and welfare program started in India?
(a) 1947 (b) 1952
(c) 1953 (d) 1980

46. Tuberculosis accelerates the progression of which disease?
(a) Asthma (b) HIV
(c) Leprosy (d) Rubeola

47. Which of the following diseases eradicated from India?
(a) Leprosy, Tuberculosis, Small Pox
(b) Measles, Polio, Small Pox
(c) Small Pox, Guinea worm, Polio and Yaws
(d) SARS, Polio, Small Pox

48. When was India declared Polio free?
(a) 27th March 2014 (b) 27th March 2019
(c) Not yet declared (d) 27th March 2020

49. Notifiable diseases as per (WHO) under IHR are?
(a) Cholera, Plague, Yellow Fever
(b) Polio, Tetanus, Typhoid, Hepatitis
(c) Plague, Yaws, Influenza
(d) Cholera, Polio, Influenza

50. INAP stands for?
(a) India Nurses And Pediatrician
(b) India New Association with Public
(c) India Nurses and Public Initial
(d) India Newborn Action Plan

51. Mission Indradhanush was launched in which year?
(a) December 2014 (b) December 2004
(c) March 2014 (d) December 2019

52. National Non Communicable Disease Prevention & Control Program includes?
(a) Cancer, Hypertension, Cardiovascular & diabetes
(b) Cancer, Diabetes, Cardiovascular& stroke
(c) Cancer, Leprosy, Diabetes & tuberculosis
(d) Cancer, Diabetes, Leprosy & Tuberculosis

53. Immediate first aid treatment for dog bite is?
(a) Cover with dressing
(b) Apply antiseptic lotion

(c) Wash with soap and water
(d) Suture the big wound

54. The first aid treatment for choking is?
(a) Try to remove the object with your fingers
(b) Give five sharp back blows between shoulder blades
(c) Call for ambulance
(d) Give something to drink

55. The ratio of cardiac compression and artificial breathing is?
(a) 15:2 (b) 60:6
(c) 12:3 (d) 30:2

56. What immediate nursing intervention will you take in case of blood reaction?
(a) Inform the physician
(b) Inform blood bank
(c) Monitor vital signs
(d) Stop the transfusion immediately and monitor vital signs

57. The order to perform CPR as per American Heart Association is?
(a) Airway breathing compression
(b) Breathing airway compression
(c) Compression airway breathing
(d) None of these

58. Which of these is a permanent method of contraception?
(a) Tubal ligation
(b) Vasectomy
(c) MTP
(d) Tubal ligation and vasectomy

59. Which one is a natural method of family planning?
(a) BBT
(b) Tracing changes in cervical mucous
(c) MTP and Tracing changes in cervical mucous
(d) Both (a) and (b)

60. The copper used in Copper T has the following action?
(a) Blastocidal (b) Bacteriostatic
(c) Bacteriocidal (d) Spermicidal

61. Which of contraceptive method prevents the ovulation?
(a) Barrier (b) Surgical
(c) Natural (d) Hormonal

62. The age and sex of a country can be described by?
(a) Pie Chart (b) Density of Population
(c) Population Pyramid (d) All ofthese

63. The NRR means?
(a) Net Reproduction Rate
(b) National Reproductive Rate
(c) National Respiratory Rate
(d) All ofthese

64. How many NFHS has been successfully completed in India till now?
(a) 2 (b) 3
(c) 4 (d) 5

65. The Adolescent people are in which age group as per WHO?
(a) 9-19 years (b) 12-19 years
(c) 10-19 years (d) More than 19 years

66. The characteristics of adolescents are?
(a) Rapid physical, psychological cognitive growth
(b) Behavior change and development
(c) Academic excellence
(d) Rapid physical, psychological cognitive growth and Behavior change and development

67. National AIDS control program includes?
(a) IEC activities
(b) AIDS education
(c) University talk AIDS program
(d) All of these

68. Kishori Shakti Yojana is catering to the need of girls in the age group?
(a) 10-19 yrs (b) 11-18 yrs
(c) 12-19 yrs (d) 13-19 yrs

69. The meaning of ARSH under RMNCH+A Program is?
(a) Adolescent Reproductive and Sexual Health
(b) Adolescent Reproductive and Social Health
(c) Adolescent Regulation and Sexual Health
(d) Adolescent Reward and Sexual Health

70. Benefits of investing in adolescent health are except?
(a) Economic, Social and Political
(b) Economic, Health and Social
(c) Economic, Health and Human right
(d) Economic, Political and Social

71. Weekly Iron and Folic Acid Supplementation (WIFS) Programme is meant for?
(a) Adolescent girls & lactating mothers
(b) Adolescent boys, pregnant mother & lactating mothers
(c) Pregnant women

(d) Adolescent boys and girls

72. As per National population policy of India the minimum age of girls for marriage is?

(a) 15 years (b) 18 years
(c) 21 years (d) 19 years

73. The normal chromosome complement in males is?

(a) 45XY (b) 46XX
(c) 44XY (d) 46YY

74. The hormones involved in the functioning of male reproductive system are?

(a) Follicle stimulating Hormcne, Oxytocin, Leutenizing hormone
(b) Follicle stimulating hormone, Testosterone, Leutenizing hormone
(c) Follicle stimulating hormone, Oxytocin, Testosterone
(d) Follicle stimulating hormone, Prolactin, Testosterone

75. The hormones that do not cross the placenta are?

(a) Thyroxine and Steroids
(b) Insulin and Thyroxine
(c) Insulin and Steroids
(d) Parathormone and Calcitonin

76. Softening of cervix to facilitate its dilatation during labour is called?

(a) Hegar's sign (b) Goodell's sign
(c) Braxton Hicks sign (d) Chadwick's sign

77. Estimated date of delivery is calculated using?

(a) McDonald's (b) Naegele's rule
(c) Rule of nine (d) Dawn's formula

78. The earliest symptom of pregnancy is?

(a) Morning sickness (b) Amenorrhea
(c) Quickening (d) Constipation

79. The exercise that helps to maintain the tone of pelvic floor muscles is called?

(a) Breathing exercise (b) Kegel exercise
(c) Pelvic exercise (d) Abdominal exercise

80. A graphical representation of the progress of labor in which cervical dilatation and descent of fetal head is plotted against time is called?

(a) Partogram (b) Parturition
(c) Road to health chart (d) Cardiotocography

81. After delivery of the newborn baby umbilical cord should be clamped and cut within?

(a) 1 to 3 secs (b) 1 to 3 minutes
(c) 5 to 10 minutes (d) 30-35 minutes

82. The most important and effective action in neonatal resuscitation is?

(a) Stimulation (b) Ventilation
(c) Chest compression (d) Administering drugs

83. The preferred route of administration of epinephrine hydrochloride is?

(a) Oral (b) Intramuscular
(c) Intravenous (d) Endotracheal

84. The aim of mission INDRADHANUSH is related to?

(a) Mid day meal (b) Water sanitation
(c) Covid prevention (d) Immunization

85. The hormone primarily responsible for the milk ejection?

(a) Oestrogen (b) Progesterone
(c) Oxytocin (d) Prolactin

86. Nosocomial Pneumonia is pneumonia that is acquired from?

(a) The community (b) Home
(c) Hospital envircmnent (d) Animals

87. Breast feeding week is celebrated in?

(a) 1st week of July (b) 1st week of August
(c) 1st week of September (d) 1st week of November

88. The type of cell division that occurs in reproductive cells is?

(a) Mitosis (b) Meiosis
(c) Mutation (d) All of these

89. The mode of transmission of NIPAH virus is?

(a) Bats (b) Pigs
(c) Humans (d) All of these

90. The etiological agent of chicken pox is?

(a) Herpes zoster (b) Varicella zoster
(c) HIV (d) Rhabdo virus

91. Indian Air Force Day is celebrated on ....?

(a) October 8 (b) October 30
(c) November 15 (d) September 15

92. Who is the governor of Maharashtra?

(a) Anandiben Patel
(b) Jayant Patil
(c) Nitin Raut
(d) Bhagat Singh Koshyari

93. Which of the following is the capital of Meghalaya?

(a) Gangtok (b) Imphal
(c) Shillong (d) Agartala

94. World Mental Health Day is observed globally on every year?

(a) 10th October (b) 15th November
(c) 20th September (d) 20th August

95. Who won the French open men's singles title in 2020?
(a) Novak Djokovic (b) Rafael Nadal
(c) Roger Federer (d) Stefanos Tsitsipas

96. Kuchipudi is the Classical Dance of ....State.
(a) Andhra Pradesh (b) Tamil Nadu
(c) Karnataka (d) Kerala

97. Who is the author of the book 'Grandparents' Bag of Stories?
(a) ParoAnand (b) Ruskin Bond
(c) Anushka Ravishankar (d) SudhaMurty

98. International Nurses Day is observed around the world on?
(a) 12th August (b) 12th September
(c) 12th May (d) 12th November

99. Who is the Chairman of Board of Control for Cricket in India (BCCI)?
(a) Rahul John (b) Anil Kumble
(c) Sourav Ganguly (d) Shashank Manohar

100. Vishal Anand, who passed away recently was associated with which fleld?
(a) Sports (b) Writing
(c) Journalism (d) Acting

Answers

1. (c)	2. (b)	3. (a)	4. (b)	5. (c)	6. (c)	7. (c)	8. (b)	9. (a)	10. (d)
11. (d)	12. (b)	13. (c)	14. (b)	15. (c)	16. (b)	17. (a)	18. (c)	19. (b)	20. (b)
21. (a)	22. (c)	23. (b)	24. (b)	25. (d)	26. (c)	27. (a)	28. (a)	29. (d)	30. (d)
31. (d)	32. (b)	33. (d)	34. (b)	35. (a)	36. (d)	37. (c)	38. (d)	39. (d)	40. (a)
41. (d)	42. (c)	43. (a)	44. (b)	45. (b)	46. (b)	47. (c)	48. (a)	49. (d)	50. (d)
51. (a)	52. (a)	53. (c)	54. (b)	55. (d)	56. (d)	57. (c)	58. (d)	59. (d)	60. (d)
61. (d)	62. (c)	63. (a)	64. (c)	65. (c)	66. (d)	67. (d)	68. (b)	69. (a)	70. (c)
71. (d)	72. (b)	73. (c)	74. (b)	75. (d)	76. (b)	77. (b)	78. (b)	79. (b)	80. (a)
81. (b)	82. (b)	83. (d)	84. (d)	85. (c)	86. (c)	87. (b)	88. (b)	89. (d)	90. (b)
91. (a)	92. (d)	93. (c)	94. (a)	95. (b)	96. (a)	97. (d)	98. (c)	99. (c)	100. (d)

Madhya Pradesh. CHO Paper-2019 Set-I

1. **Which part of pancreas produce and secrete insulin?**
   a. Glomerulus b. Bowman's capsule
   c. Islets of Langerhans d. Loop of Henle
2. **In High grade fever, the body temperature is–**
   a. 99 F – 100 F b. > 100 F – 102 F
   c. 103 F – 107 F d. More than 107 F
3. **Which of the following is NOT an endocrine gland?**
   a. Pituitary b. Parathyroid
   c. Pancreas d. Hypothalamus
4. **When pulse rate is less than 60 beats per minute, it is called–**
   a. Bradycardia b. Bradypnea
   c. Tachycardia d. Tachypnea
5. **Decreased amount of oxygen in blood is known as–**
   a. Hypoxia b. Hypocapnea
   c. Hypoxemia d. Hypercapnea
6. **Which of the following comprised of seven bones?**
   a. Cervical vertebrae b. Carpals
   c. Cranial bones d. Lumbar vertebrae
7. **How many lobes liver have–**
   a. 1 b. 2
   c. 3 d. 4
8. **Collar bone is known as–**
   a. Clavilce b. Scapula
   c. Humerus d. Radius
9. **Which type of blood cells are associated with clotting–**
   a. WBC b. RBC
   c. Platelets d. Lymphocytes
10. **Central Nervous System is made up of–**
    a. Spinal cord
    b. Cerebrum
    c. Brainstem and cerebellum
    d. All of the these
11. **When was India declared polio free?**
    a. 2011 b. 2012
    c. 2013 d. 2014
12. **What is the sex ratio in Madhya Pradesh–**
    a. 923 b. 931
    c. 947 d. 963
13. **What is life expectancy at birth in India–**
    a. 64 b. 69
    c. 72 d. 75
14. **Infant Mortality Rate in India is–**
    a. 55 b. 47
    c. 41 d. 33
15. **What will be the approximate number of pregnant woman in a year in a Sub Health Centre area with a population of 4800 and birth rate of 25–**
    a. 90–100 b. 100–110
    c. 120–130 d. 140–150
16. **Which statement is not true–**
    a. Rubella is not a bacterial disease
    b. Filariasis is a parasitic disease
    c. Malaria is transmitted by Aedes aegypti mosquito
    d. Typhoid spread through contaminated food and water
17. **Incubation period is the period between–**
    a. Calling ambulance and reaching hospital
    b. Giving vaccine and developing immunity
    c. Taking medicine and getting its response
    d. Entry of organism and development of symptoms
18. **What is virulence–**
    a. A disease of intestine
    b. Fungus infection of nails
    c. Disease causing capacity of organisms
    d. Liver
19. **Ability of a pathogen to establish an infection is called–**
    a. Inflammation b. Infectivity
    c. Allergy d. None of the above
20. **Agent, host and................make it a epidemiological triad.**
    a. Immunity b. Susceptibility
    c. Environment d. Medicines
21. **Secondary prevention means–**
    a. Health Promotion b. Specific Protection
    c. Rehabilitation d. None of them
22. **Bronchial asthma is relates to–**
    a. A non communicable disease
    b. Wheezing sound
    c. Occurs in all age groups
    d. All of them

23. Restriction on the movement of people to prevent the spread of disease is called–
a. Quarantine b. Isolation
c. Detention d. Seperation

24. Hydrophobia is a disease in which the patient……
a. Shows normal behaviour
b. Feels Drowy and sleepy
c. Is scared of the water
d. Drinks lot of water

25. All are water borne disease except–
a. Hepatitis–A b. Typhoid fever
c. Dysentry d. Tuberculosis

26. How many ANC check–up are minimum necessary–
a. 1 b. 2
c. 3 d. 4

27. All are signs of High Risk Pregnancy except–
a. Eclamsia b. Previous still birth
c. Previous C–Section d. None of them

28. What is not true about severe anemia in pregnancy–
a. ANC Check–up by MO
b. Iron Sucrose Injection
c. Advise rest
d. 1 IFA Tab daily

29. Eclamsia means–
a. Pre–eclampsia + convulsions
b. Hypertension + Diabetes
c. Hypertension + Severe anemia
d. Hypertension + Oedema

30. What is true about Gestational diabetes–
a. A diabetic lady coceives
b. Increase in Blood sugar only in 3rd trimester of pregnancy
c. No medication is required
d. High blood sugar develops during pregnancy

31. Menarche usually occurs at the age of–
a. 8 – 10 years b. 11 – 13 years
c. 14 – 16 years d. 15 – 16 years

32. First day of a lady's menstrual period was July 12, 2019. What is the estimated date of delivery?
a. May 7, 2020 b. April 22, 2020
c. March 6, 2020 d. April 19, 2020

33. Maternal Death means death of a pregnant women–
a. From conception till 28 days of delivery
b. From conception till 30 days of delivery
c. From conception till 42 days of delivery
d. Death only during delivery

34. The period of about six weeks after childbirth is known as–
a. Convalescence b. Recovery
c. Recuperation d. None of these

35. What is labelled as severe anemia in a pregnant women?
a. 9 – 11 gm/dl b. 7 – 9 gm/dl
c. Less than 7 gm/dl d. 12 – 14 gm/dl

36. A child is SAM if MUC is–
a. < 12.5 cm
b. < 11.5 cm
c. < 13.5 cm
d. Between 12.5 cm–13.5 cm

37. What is the ideal age for starting complementary feeding?
a. 4–6 months b. 6 month
c. 8 month d. 10 month

38. Scurvy is caused by deficiency of–
a. Vitamin D b. Vitamin A
c. Vitamin B d. Vitamin C

39. What is neonatal period–
a. 0–7 days b. 0–14 days
c. 0–21 days d. 0–28 days

40. Which disease is transmitted mainly by faeco oral route–
a. Hepatitis–B b. Diphtheria
c. Polio d. Tetatus

41. A 5 yrs old having loose motion, has adequate urine output and is playful. What should you do?
a. Give ORS to drink b. Start IV fluids
c. Stop feeding d. All of these

42. Diarroea means loose stools………in one day.
a. 2 or more times b. 3 or more times
c. 4 or more times d. 5 or more times

43. Who can provide Kangaroo Mother Care (KMC)?
a. Mother b. Father
c. Grand mother d. All of these

44. All are true for dysentry, except–
a. Presence of blood in stools
b. Increased frequency of motion
c. Tenesmus
d. Presence of worms in stools

45. What is not true about severe pneumonia in a child aged 11 months–
a. Respiratory rate is > 50 per minute
b. Only X ray can confirm
c. Child is drowsy
d. Refusal to drink or feed

46. PCV vaccine is given to protect against–
a. Typhoid b. Diarroea
c. Pneumonia d. Meningitis

47. Measles should not be used if has been more than.......hours after reconstitution.
a. 1 hr b. 2 hrs
c. 3 hrs d. 4 hrs

48. Dose of vitamin A, given along with measles vaccine is for a child of 16 months is–
a. 0.5 lac IU b. 1 lac IU
c. 2 lac IU d. 2.5 lac IU

49. Which vaccine prevents congenital rubella syndrome–
a. Measles b. DPT
c. MR d. TT

50. All of the following are given intramuscularly, except–
a. DPT Vaccine
b. Hepatitis B Vaccine
c. Pentavalent
d. MR

51. The minimum legal age limit for employment of children is–
a. 10 years b. 12 years
c. 14 years d. 16 years

52. First sign of puberty in girls is–
a. Breast bud development
b. Pubic hair
c. Height spurt
d. Axillary hair

53. ICTC stands for–
a. Integrated Centre for Testing of Chronic diseases
b. Integrated Counseling and Training Centre
c. Integrated Counseling and Testing Centre for HIV/AIDS
d. Integrated Child Training Centre

54. The counseling tips for adolescents include all of the following, except–
a. Maintain menstrual hygiene
b. Avoid unprotected sexual behavior
c. Keep classmates informed
d. Have a positive outlook

55. Adolescent mothers are at a high risk of–
a. Low birth weight babies
b. Miscarriage
c. Still birth
d. All of these

56. What is different amongst the choices given–
a. Copper T b. Chhaya
c. Insulin d. Condom

57. What is true about male sterilization–
a. Not a permanent method
b. Failure rate is very high
c. Can not be done after the age of 60
d. Known as Vasectomy

58. What is 'Antara'?
a. An injectable contraceptive
b. Progestin–only pill
c. Combination oral contraceptive
d. None of these

59. Women of reproductive age refers to all women aged–
a. 18–45 years b. 15–49 years
c. 21–45 years d. 18–40 years

60. What is not true about male contraception–
a. Vasectomy is effective permanent method
b. Condoms prevent STD
c. Absteinence is not the method of contraception
d. None of these

61. Syphilis is a complex systemic sexually transmitted infection caused by–
a. A helminth b. A fungus
c. A virus d. A spirochaete

62. What is the total duration of treatment of Multi–drug–resistant tuberculosis–
a. Atleast 24–27 months
b. Atleast 20–24 months
c. Atleast 6–8 months
d. Atleast 12 months

63. A combination of drugs is used in the treatment of tuberculosis in order to–
a. Reduce resistance of the pathogen to treatment
b. Check sensitivity of drugs
c. Check reactivity of drugs
d. Check hypersensitivity of drugs

64. **DOTS in reference to tuberculosis means–**
a. Duration of tuberculosis treatment schedule
b. Directly observed treatment, short course
c. The spots that appear on the skin during treatment
d. Drugs of tuberculosis, short course

65. **Dengue is caused by the bite of–**
a. Culex mosquito
b. Aedes aegypti mosquito
c. Female Anopheles mosquito
d. Mites

66. **All among the following are complications of hookworm infestation, except–**
a. Iron deficiency anemia
b. Nutritional deficiencies
c. Ascites
d. Meningitis

67. **Which among the following virus is responsible for most incidence of common cold?**
a. Rhino virus b. T4 virus
c. MSZ virus d. Simian virus 40

68. **Fever followed by Maculo popular Rashes and Any of the cough/coryza/conjunctivitis–**
a. Small pox b. Measles
c. Tetanus d. Chicken pox

69. **What is not true about Rabies–**
a. Caused by Rabies Virus
b. Transmitted by bite of rabid animals
c. Nothing can be done post exposure
d. All of them

70. **Symptoms of typhoid include all, except–**
a. Abdominal pain b. Headache
c. Loss of appetite d. Seizures

71. **What is meant by COPD–**
a. Chronic obstructive pleural disease
b. Chronic obstructive pelvic disease
c. Chronic obstructive pulmonary disease
d. None of these

72. **Stroke is caused by–**
a. Lack of blood supply to cerebral blood vessels
b. Lack of blood supply to carotid artery
c. Lack of blood supply to coronary artery
d. None of these

73. **Full form of NPCDCS–**
a. National Programme for Prevention and Control of Cancer, Diabetes Cardiovascular Diseases and Stroke
b. National Programme for Chronic Obstructive Pulmonary Diseases, Diabetes Cardiovascular Diseases and Stroke
c. National Programme for Prevention and Control of Cancer, Dengue Hemorrhagic fever, Cardiovascular Diseases and Stroke
d. National Programme for Chronic Obstructive Pulmonary Diseases, Diabetes Cardiovascular Diseases and Sickle Cell Anemia

74. **What is the formula used to calculate BMI?**
a. Weight in kgs / height in centimeter2
b. Weight in kgs / (height in meter)2
c. Weight in kg / height in feet2
d. None of these

75. **Stroke is defined as–**
a. Brain damage due to roadside accident
b. Interruption of blood supply to brain leading to damage of brain tissue
c. Brain tissue damage due to high bilirubin
d. None of these

76. **Which of these is not a non–modifiable risk factor–**
a. Age b. Family history
c. Overweight d. All of these

77. **Beta Blocker and ACE Inhibitors are prescribed for the management of–**
a. Hypertension b. Diabetes
c. COPD d. None of these

78. **Iodine deficiency disorder form a spectrum of abnormalities, EXCEPT–**
a. Goitre b. Mental retardation
c. Deaf mutism d. Neck rigidity

79. **The daily requirement of Iodine for normal human growth and development is–**
a. 50–100 micrograms
b. 100–150 micrograms
c. 150–200 micrograms
d. 200–250 micrograms

80. **Benefits of weight reduction include–**
a. Lowering risk of cardiovascular diseases
b. Reduction of harmful blood fats/hyperlipidemia
c. Correction of sleeping disorder
d. All of these

81. National Leprosy Eradication Programme was launched in–
a. 1983 b. 1988
c. 1993 d. 2002

82. Pradhan Mantri Surakshit Matritva Abhiyan (PMSMA) was launched in–
a. 2015 b. 2016
c. 2017 d. None of these

83. Full form of MAA program is–
a. Maternal Absolute Affection
b. Mother Assited Attention
c. Mother's Absolute Affection
d. Mother's and Father's Absolute Attention

84. First National AIDS Control Programme–I launched in–
a. 1992 b. 1994
c. 1996 d. 1997

85. India aims to eliminate TB with zero deaths–
a. 2021 b. 2022
c. 2030 d. 2025

86. Target Population covered under Rashtriya Kishore Swasthya Karyakram (RKSK) –
a. 10–19 years age male and female of rural areas
b. 10–19 years age male and female of urban areas
c. Both a and b
d. Only a

87. The objective of National Deworming Day is to deworm all preschool and school–age children (enrolled and non–enrolled) between the ages of–
a. 1 – 19 years b. 2 – 20 years
c. 3 – 18 years d. 4 – 16 years

88. National Tobacco Control Program launched by Government of India in?
a. 2013–14 b. 2008–09
c. 2010–11 d. 2007–08

89. National Programme for Healthcare of Elderly (NPHCE) covers beneficiaries above the age of–
a. Above 59 years b. Above 60 years
c. Above 61 years d. Above 65 years

90. The three main components of National Mental Health Programme (NMHP) are–
A. Treatment of Mentally ill
B. Rehabilitation
C. Prevention and promotion of positive mental health
a. Only C b. Only A and B
c. Only A and C d. All of these

91. Statue of unity is situated in which state–
a. West Bengal b. Gujarat
c. Delhi d. Madhya Pradesh

92. When is the International Yoga Day celebrated?
a. 21–Jun b. 21–Mar
c. 22–Apr d. 31–May

93. Laddakh is part of which state–
a. Jammu and Kashmir
b. Himachal Pradesh
c. Haryana
d. None of these

94. The first Indian State to go wholley organic is–
a. Meghalaya b. Sikkim
c. Madhya Pradesh d. Kerala

95. Which district of Madhya Pradesh has highest female–male ratio as per Census 2011–
a. Jhabua b. Dindori
c. Mandla d. Balaghat

96. Madhya Pradesh State was constituted on–
a. 1st November, 1959
b. 1st November, 1958
c. 1st November, 1957
d. 1st November, 1956

97. ISRO HQ is situated in
a. Dehradun b. Sriharikota
c. Hyderabad d. Bangalore

98. National Rural Health Mission has been launched in the country in–
a. 2003 b. 2004
c. 2005 d. 2009

99. All India Institute of Ayurveda will work with which country for integrating Ayurveda principles with modern medicine?
a. Russia b. Japan
c. Israel d. Australia

100. India's first private train–
a. Tejas b. Shatabdi
c. Duronto d. Garib Rath

Answer Sheet

1. C.	2. C.	3.D.	4 .A.	5. C.	6.A.	7.D.	8.A.	9.C.	10.A.
11.D.	12.B.	13.B.	14.D.	15.C.	16.C.	17.D.	18.C.	19.B.	20.C.
21.D.	22.D.	23.A.	24.C.	25.D.	26.D.	27.D.	28.D.	29.A.	30.D.
31.B.	32.D.	33.C.	34.D.	35.C.	36.B.	37.B.	38.D.	39.D.	40.C.
41.A.	42.B.	43.D.	44.D.	45.B.	46.C.	47.D.	48.C.	49.C.	50.D.
51.C.	52.A.	53.C.	54.C.	55.D.	56.C.	57.D.	58.A.	59.B.	60.C.
61.D.	62.A.	63.A.	64.B.	65.B.	66.D.	67.A.	68.B.	69.C.	70.D.
71.C.	72.A.	73.A.	74.B.	75.B.	76.C.	77.A.	78.D.	79.B.	80.D.
81.A.	82.B.	83.C.	84.A.	85.D.	86.B.	87.A.	88.D.	89.B.	90.D.
91.B.	92.A.	93.D.	94.B.	95.D.	96.D.	97.B.	98.C.	99.D.	100.A.

Madhya Pradesh CHO Paper-2019 Set – II

1. **Who is the Governor of Madhya Pradesh–**
a. Anandiben Patel
b. Kalraj Mishra
c. Bhagat Singh Koshiyari
d. Lalji Tandon

2. **Who is PV Sindhu–**
a. Cricket Player
b. Badminton Player
c. Hockey Player
d. Shooting Champion

3. **Who is Union Health Minister–**
a. Tulsiram Silawat b. Rajnath Singh
c. JP Nadda d. Harsh Vardhan

4. **When is World Health Day celebrated–**
a. 5–Jan b. 10–Feb
c. 7–Apr d. 1–May

5. **What is not true–**
a. Cricket is not the national game of India
b. Saina Nehwal is not the present world badminton champion
c. India has never won a gold medal in Olympic hockey
d. PT Usha has won a Gold medal in 100 meter race in Olympics

6. **Which statement is true–**
a. Dengue is a mosquito–borne viral infection
b. Malaria is a non–infectious disease
c. HIN1 is not directly associated with Swine Flu
d. Typhoid doesn't spread through contaminated food and drinking water

7. **Which is the largest state in India–**
a. Madhya Pradesh b. Rajasthan
c. Maharashtra d. Uttar Pradesh

8. **Which is the largest internal organ in human body–**
a. Brain b. Heart
c. Kidney d. Liver

9. **What is Rafale–**
a. Fighter aircarft b. Nuclear submarine
c. Assault Rifle d. Anti Tank missile

10. **Where is Gurdwara Darbar Sahib Kartarpur located–**
a. Jammu and Kashmir
b. Himachal Pradesh
c. Haryana
d. Pakistan

11. **What is normal body temperature in fahrenheit–**
a. 98.2 b. 98.6
c. 99.2 d. 99.6

12. **Which gland or organ doesn't work right in type 1 diabetes?**
a. Pituitary gland b. Pancreas
c. Adrenal glands d. Kidneys

13. **Poor output of urine is known as?**
a. Oliguroia b. Pyruria
c. Enuresis d. Diuresis

14. **Which cell secretes antibody?**
a. Monocytes b. Lymphocytes
c. Neutrophils d. Eosinphils

15. **Long standing high blood pressure may result in–**
a. Cardiomegaly b. Cardiac failure
c. Heart attack d. All of these

16. **The respiratory system is made up of trachea, the lungs and the–**
a. Diaphragm b. Pancreas
c. Esophagus d. Liver

17. **The opening of right atrium into right ventricle is guarded by–**
a. Mitral valve
b. Tricuspid valve
c. Bicuspid valve
d. Aortic semilunar valve

18. **A band of tough, flexible connective tissue which connects two bones or cartilages or hold together a joint is called–**
a. Joint b. Cartilage
c. Tendon d. Ligament

19. **What is true about small intestine–**
a. Duodenum is not part of small intestine
b. Digestion is completed
c. Ileum is middle part of small intestine
d. All of the these

20. **Moving arm towards the body's midline–**
a. Abduction b. Flexion
c. Adduction d. Extension

21. **Which of the following is used to take cervical smear–**
a. Colposcope b. Vaginoscepe
c. Ayre's Spatula d. Laparoscope

22. All are included in hypertensive disorder of pregnancy except–
a. Pre eclampsia
b. Chronic hypertension with superimposed pre eclampsia
c. Gestational Hypertension
d. None of these

23. How many weeks does a typical pregnancy last–
a. 40 b. 38
c. 42 d. 44

24. Worldwide most common problem during pregnancy is–
a. Diabetes
b. Pre eclampsia
c. UTI
d. Iron deficiency Anaemia

25. Fetal tachycardia is defined as foetal heart rate greater than–
a. 120 – 140 beats/min
b. 140 – 160 beats/min
c. 150 – 170 beats/min
d. 160 – 180 beats/min

26. The nurse is caring for a client who had a spontaneous abortion. The nurse's priority should be assessing the client for–
a. Heamorrhage b. Dehydration
c. Hypertension d. Sub–involution

27. Woman who has a hemoglobin level below.........g/dl at any time during the pregnancy is considered to be suffering from severe anaemia–
a. 9 – 11 gm/dl b. 7 – 9 gm/dl
c. Less than 7 gm/dl d. 12 – 14 gm/dl

28. The following should be tested at every ANC visit–
a. Haemoglobin, Urine sugar and HCG
b. Haemoglobin, blood and urine sugar
c. Haemoglobin, Urine sugar and protein
d. Haemoglobin, Urine sugar and HPL

29. Eclampsia is–
a. Pre–eclampsia + convulsions (Hypertension + Proteinuria and convulsions)
b. Hypertension + convulsions
c. Hypertension + Proteinuria
d. Pre–eclampsia + Hypertension

30. The most frequent cause of maternal death during child birth is–
a. Sepsis b. Toxemia
c. Asphyxia d. Hemorrhage

31. PPIUCD stands for–
a. Postpartum intrauterine contraceptive device
b. Post–Puerperium intrauterine contraceptive device
c. Post Pregnancy intrauterine contraceptive device
d. Post Parturition intrauterine contraceptive device

32. Which of the following is not an example of a barrier contraceptive–
a. Condon
b. Diaphragm
c. Oral Contraceptive Pills
d. Cervical cap

33. Oral Contraceptive Pills can have–
a. Oestrogen and Progestin
b. Progestin only
c. Both of these
d. None of the above

34. What do male condoms offer that other forms of birth control do not?
a. Least chance of failure
b. Best protection against STDs
c. Cheapest to use
d. All of these

35. World population day falls on–
a. 11–Jul b. 11–May
c. 11–Aug d. 11–Sep

36. Full form of SAM is–
a. Serious Anemic Malnutrition
b. Severely Anemic Mother
c. Severe Acute Malaria
d. Severe Acute Malnutrition

37. A baby is called an infant upto what age?
a. 1 month b. 28 days
c. 6 months d. 1 year

38. Rickets is caused by deficiency of–
a. Vitamin D b. Vitamin A
c. Vitamin B d. Vitamin C

39. What is sign of severe Pneumonia–
a. Restlessness
b. Not taking feeds
c. In drawing of chest wall
d. All of these

40. Which disease is not transmitted mainly by faeco oral route–
a. Measles b. Cholera
c. Hepatitis A d. Enteric fever

41. Vitamin A solution protects children against–
a. Myopia b. Hypermetropia
c. Xeropthalmia d. Cretinism

42. The most common cause of death due to Dirrhoea is–
a. Vomiting b. Abdominal pain
c. Lethargy d. Dehydration

43. Koplicks spots are seen in which disease–
a. Measles b. Mumps
c. Rubella d. Polio

44. What is LBW?
a. Birth weight < 2.5 kg
b. Birth weight < 3 kg
c. Birth weight < 1.5 kg
d. Birth weight < 1 kg

45. Which is not the viral infection–
a. Hepatitis–B b. Measles
c. Hib Disease d. Chicken Pox

46. Vaccines should be stored at what temperature–
a. 0–4 Deg Celsius b. 2–6 Deg Celsius
c. 2–8 Deg Celsius d. 0–8 Deg Celsius

47. All are minor reactions of DPT vaccine except–
a. Mild Fever
b. Pain at the injection site
c. Rashes
d. Excessive crying

48. Route of administration and dose of BCG vaccine for a 3 month old baby is–
a. Intra Dermal, 0.1 ml
b. Sub Cutaneous, 0.1 ml
c. Intra Muscular, 0.5 ml
d. Sub Cutaneous, 0.5 ml

49. Dose and Route of administration of rotavirus vaccine is–
a. 2 drops, oral b. 5 drops, oral
c. 10 drops, oral d. 1 ml, Intramuscular

50. After which age BCG vaccine should not be given–
a. 6 Months b. 1 year
c. 2 year d. 5 years

51. When was national Health Mission Launched–
a. 2001 b. 2005
c. 2009 d. 2012

52. Pulse polio immunization covers–
a. 0–5 Years Children
b. 0–1 Years Children
c. 1–5 Years Children
d. 0–2 Years Children

53. The process, which destroys all microbial life including spores is known as–
a. Disinfection b. Antisepsis
c. Deodorization d. Sterilization

54. JSY is an acronym for–
a. Janani Suraksha Yojana
b. Jeevan Suraksha Yojana
c. Jeevan Shakthi Yojana
d. Jan Suraksha Yojana

55. Goitre is caused by deficiency of which hormone–
a. Insulin b. Estrogen
c. Serotonin d. Thyroid

56. What is a Sex ratio–
a. Number of Males and Females in 1000 population
b. Number of females per 1000 males
c. Number of males per 1000 females
d. Number of female birth per 1000 male birth

57. Infant Mortality Rate is–
a. The infant deaths per thousand live births
b. The infant deaths per thousand deliveries
c. The infant deaths per 1 lakh live births
d. Number of infant deaths in 1000 poulation every year

58. What is the % Fully Immunized Children for Madhya Pradesh as per NFHS–4–
a. 47.5 b. 53.6
c. 61.5 d. 64.2

59. PMJAY is an acronym for–
a. Pradhan Mantri Jan Arogya Yojana
b. Pradhan Mantri Janani Arogya Yojana
c. Pradhan Mantri Jan–swasthya Arogya Yojana
d. None of these

60. Sudden increase in occurrences of a disease in a particular time and place is known as–
a. Outbreak b. Inbreak
c. Disease crisis d. All of these

61. All are levels of prevention except–
a. Health Promotion b. Early diagnosis
c. Rehabilitation d. None of these

62. What is the population of Madhya Pradesh as per Census 2011–

a. 7.2 Cr b. 7.5 Cr
c. 8.2 Cr d. 8.6 Cr

63. What is the insurance cover under the Ayushman Bharat Scheme–

a. Rs 4 Lakh b. Rs 5 Lakh
c. Rs 10 Lakh d. Rs 3 Lakh

64. Number of children who would be born per woman if she passes through the childbearing years bearing children according to a current schedule of age–specific fertility rates is known as–

a. Age–specific fertility rate
b. Crude birth rate
c. Total Fertility rate
d. Total birth rate

65. As per SRS 2015–17, Maternal Mortality Ratio (MMR) of MP is–

a. 229 b. 188
c. 165 d. 173

66. Under the Ayushman Bharat, government has announced two major initiatives, namely National Health Protection Scheme and............

a. Health Centre
b. Health and Yoga Centre
c. Health and Welliness Centre
d. Wellness centre

67. Mission Indradhanush is related with?

a. Children Safety b. E–Commerce
c. Child Vaccination d. None of these

68. The National AIDS Control Programme (NACP) was launched in–

a. 1990 b. 1989
c. 1979 d. 1992

69. True about Mission Parivar Vikas is–

a. Launched on World Population Day
b. A new family planning initiative
c. Focus on 146 high fertility districts in 7 states with high TFR
d. All of these

70. ASHA stands for–

a. Accredited Social Health Activist
b. Additional Social Help Available
c. Active Society Help Agent
d. All of these

71. RNTCP stands for–

a. Review of National Tuberculosis Control Programme
b. Renewed National Tuberculosis Control Programme
c. Revised National Tuberculosis Control Programme
d. None of these

72. The National Leprosy Control Programme was launched by the Govt. of India in–

a. 1955 b. 1965
c. 1975 d. 1985

73. To address the huge burden of mental disorders Government of India has launched which program–

a. National Psychiatric Program
b. National Program for Mentally Handicapeed
c. National Mental Health Program
d. National Program for Spirituality

74. Which program was launched in 1976–

a. National Tuberculosis Control Program
b. National Malaria control Program
c. National Program for control of Blindness
d. None of these

75. National Vector Borne Disease Control Programme was launched to–

a. To control Typhoid b. To control Cholera
c. To control Malaria d. All of these

76. WHO defines "Adolescents" as individuals in the age group of–

a. Less than 10 years b. 11–15 years
c. 10–19 years d. 20–29 years

77. Which among the following is the top cause of mortality among adolescents in the world–

a. Suicide
b. Communicable Diseases
c. Road Traffic Accidents
d. Iron Deficiency Anemia

78. RKSK stands for–

a. Rashtriya Kishor Swasthya Karyakram
b. Rajasthan Kishor Swasthya Karyakram
c. Rural Kalyan Swasthya Karyakram
d. Railway Kalyan Swasthya Karyakram

79. What is the dose of Weekly Iron and Folic Acid Supplementation Scheme (WIFS)?

a. 100 mg elemental iron and 500 mcg folic acid
b. 50 mg elemental iron and 100 mcg folic acid

c. 150 mg elemental iron and 50 mcg folic acid
d. 100 mg elemental iron and 150 mcg folic acid

80. The focus of adolescent health according to RMNCHA + is all except–
a. Strengthen ARSH clinic
b. Address teenage pregnancy
c. Menstrual hygiene
d. Cancer counseling

81. Which of the following is a communicable disease–
a. Diabetes b. Pertussis
c. Hypertension d. Kwashiorkor

82. The objects/articles contaminated by HIV can be decontaminated using–
a. Formaldehyde
b. Methanol
c. Glutaraldehyde
d. Sodium hypochlorite

83. Which of the following statements is incorrect?
a. Tuberculosis is caused by Mycobacterium tuberculosis
b. People who are exposed to TB may or may not develop the disease
c. Persons with latent TB infection are not infectious and cannot spread infection to others
d. Every individual who is exposed to TB develops the disease

84. Symptoms of Dengue include all, except–
a. High Fever b. Low grade Fever
c. Eye pain d. Joint pain

85. Painful and profoundly swollen limb/limbs are a long term physical consequence of–
a. Lymphatic Filariasis
b. Dengue
c. Malaria
d. Yellow Fever

86. Which among the following is a sign of dehydration?
a. Decrease thirst
b. Dry Mouth
c. Increased urine output
d. Fever

87. The following diseases spread through respiratory route, except–
a. Influenza b. Mumps
c. Measles d. Typhoid

88. Which of the following pair of diseases is caused by viruses?
a. Rabies, Mumps b. AIDS, Syphilis
c. Typhoid, Tetanus d. Cholera, Tuberculosis

89. Typhoid fever is caused by–
a. Salmonella typhi
b. Human papilloma virus
c. Fungi
d. Plasmodium vivax

90. Koplik spots can be seen in–
a. Measles b. Chicken pox
c. Typhoid d. Mumps

91. What is not true about Diabetes–
a. Develops only after the age of 30 yrs
b. Polyuria, polydipsia and polyphagia are common symptoms
c. Normal fasting blood sugar level should be less than 120
d. All of these

92. VIA is used to–
a. Diagnose oral cancers
b. Treat lung cancer
c. Radiation therapy for intestinal cancer
d. Screening for cervical cancer

93. CBAC stands for–
a. Communication based assessment checklist
b. Community based assessment checklist
c. Compliance based assessment checklist
d. Calculation based assessment checklist

94. Symptoms of stroke are–
a. Confusion and Difficulty in speech
b. Severe headache and dizziness
c. Difficulty in swallowing and Face drooping
d. All of these

95. Complications of diabetes are all except–
a. Diabetic Ketoacidosis
b. Arthritis
c. Neuropathy
d. Retinopathy

96. What is not true about Hypertension–
a. Occurs in urban population
b. Normally affects people above 30 yrs of age
c. Cannot be cured permanently by antihypertensive drugs
d. 90–150 is not the correct range for systolic BP

97. All are risk factors for Hypertension except–
a. Obesity
b. Family History
c. Contaminated water
d. Smoking

98. Osteomalacia in adults and Rickets in children is caused by deficiency of–
a. Vitamin C b. Vitamin D
c. Vitamin A d. Vitamin E

99. The common signs of breast cancer are–
a. Lump or thickening in the breast
b. A change in size of breast
c. Discharge from nipples
d. All these

100. Diagnosis of obesity can be done by calculating BMI, which stands for–
a. Body mind index
b. Body metabolic index
c. Basal metabolic index
d. Body mass index

Answer Sheet

1. D.	2. B.	3. D.	4 . C.	5. C.	6.A.	7.B.	8.D.	9.A.	10.D.
11.B.	12.B.	13.A.	14.B.	15.C.	16.A.	17.B.	18.D.	19.B.	20.C.
21.C.	22.D.	23.A.	24.D.	25.D.	26.A.	27.C.	28.C.	29.A.	30.D.
31.A.	32.C.	33.C.	34.B.	35.A.	36.D.	37.D.	38.A.	39.D.	40.A.
41.C.	42.D.	43.A.	44.A.	45.C.	46.C.	47.C.	48.A.	49.B.	50.B.
51.B.	52.A.	53.D.	54.A.	55.D.	56.B.	57.A.	58.B.	59.A.	60.A.
61.D.	62.A.	63.B.	64.C.	65.B.	66.C.	67.C.	68.D.	69.D.	70.A.
71.C.	72.A.	73.C.	74.C.	75.C.	76.C.	77.C.	78.A.	79.A.	80.D.
81.B.	82.D.	83.D.	84.B.	85.A.	86.B.	87.D.	88.A.	89.A.	90.A.
91. A.	92. D.	93. B.	94. D.	95. B.	96.A.	97. C.	98. B.	99. D.	100. D.

❑❑❑

Madhya Pradesh CHO Papers – 2019 Set–III

1. Which of the following is a communicable disease?

a. Diabetes b. Diphtheria
c. Hypertension d. Kwashiorkor

2. Which among the following is not a common symptom of tuberculosis?

a. Cough for three weeks or more
b. Fever, especially at night
c. Weight gain
d. Loss of appetite

3. What is the full form of VVM?

a. Vaccine verification monitor
b. Vaccine viability monitor
c. Vaccine vial monitor
d. None of these

4. What is the preferred site for administering DPT vaccine in infants?

a. Dorso gluteal Muscle
b. Gluteus Maximus
c. Vastus Lateralis
d. Gluteus Medius

5. All among the following "Home Available Fluids (HAF)" can be given to a diarrhea patient, except–

a. Lemon water b. Butter milk
c. Sugarcane juice d. Coconut water

6. The suggested dose of vitamin–A given at 9 months of age is–

a. 2 lakh IU b. 3 lakh IU
c. 1 lakh IU d. 50,000 IU

7. Fever, abdominal tenderness, slow pulse, delirium and rose colored rash indicative the disease–

a. Small pox b. Measles
c. Tetanus d. Chicken pox

8. Leprosy is caused by–

a. Mycobacterium leprae
b. Mycobacterium tuberculous
c. Rota virus
d. Mosquito

9. Which first line anti TB drug is contraindicated for a pregnant women?

a. Streptomycin b. Isoniazid
c. Ethambutol d. Pyrazinamide

10. Symptoms of stroke are–

a. Confusion and Difficulty in speech
b. Severe headache and dizziness
c. Difficulty in swallowing and Face drooping
d. All of these

11. Gestational diabetes occurs in–

a. Lactating mothers b. Adolescents
c. Elderly population d. Pregnant women

12. How does cancer spread in the human body?

a. Through lymphatic system
b. Through blood stream
c. Skin
d. Both lymphatic system and Through blood stream

13. The common method of screening for Cervical Cancer in the community is–

a. Ultra sound
b. Blood smear
c. Visual inspection with acetic acid
d. CT scan

14. How many steps are involved in doing breast self examination–

a. Four b. Five
c. Two d. Three

15. Asthma can be prevented by–

a. Preventing exposure to allergens
b. Take vaccine against asthma
c. Taking medicines regularly
d. None of the above

16. Beta Blocker and ACE Inhibitors are prescribed for the management of–

a. Hypertension b. Diabetes
c. COPD d. None of these

17. The following are fat soluble vitamins except–

a. Vitamin A b. Vitamin D
c. Vitamin E d. Vitamin C

18. Vitamin needed for blood clotting–

a. Vitamin A b. Vitamin B
c. Vitamin E d. Vitamin K

19. Oral Rehydration Therapy is recommended for patient suffering with–

a. Cholera b. Tetanus
c. Typhoid d. Tuberculosis

20. Which procedure will help in the management of atonic PPH?
a. Uterine muscle dilators
b. Bimanual compression of uterus
c. Suturing of cervical and vaginal tears
d. Intra vaginal packing

21. In eclampsia, the initial loading dose of intramuscular Inj MgSo4 is–
a. 5 grams in each buttock
b. 10 grams in each buttock
c. 10 grams in single buttock
d. 5 grams in single buttock

22. In shock one should preferably not use–
a. Normal saline
b. Dextrose Normal saline
c. Dextrose 5%
d. Ringer lactate

23. In a crying baby, when should the cord be clamped normally?
a. 10 mins of delivery
b. Immediately after delivery
c. Once the cord pulsation stops
d. Delivery of placenta

24. The FIRST step in thermal protection for the newborn includes–
a. Drying the baby thoroughly immediately after birth
b. Drying the baby thoroughly after the cord has been cut
c. Covering the baby with a clean, dry cloth immediately after birth
d. Covering the baby with warmed blanket

25. Counseling of IUCD insertion should be done–
a. Starting from Antenatal visits
b. Only when she is delivering
c. Only after delivery
d. Can be done after 2 days of delivery

26. A mother should be assessed for the following within one hour of the delivery–
a. Excessive bleeding b. Temperature
c. Uterine contraction d. All of these

27. What should be the room temperature in the labour room?
a. 23 – 25 Degree Celsius
b. 26 – 28 Degree Celsius
c. 30 – 35 Degree Celsius
d. 20 – 25 Degree Celsius

28. What is the depth of chest compression for an adult?
a. 2–3 cm b. 3–4 cm
c. 4–5 cm d. 6–7 cm

29. The sign of increased ICP in a child, 18 month old is–
a. Increased irritability
b. Narrowing pulse pressure
c. Pinpoint pupils
d. Tachycardia

30. Quality assurance refers to–
a. Standard practice b. Measurement scale
c. Evaluation scale d. Rating scale

31. Islets of Langerhans are present in–
a. Brain b. Stomach
c. Ovary d. Pancreas

32. Mrs. Leela has placenta previa. The most likely symptom she will present is a–
a. Painless bleeding
b. A board like abdomen
c. Intermittent pain with spotting
d. A dull pain in the lower abdomen

33. Which of the following test result is useful to assess the liver function?
a. Glucose tolerance test
b. Creatine clearance test
c. Serum transaminase d.
d. Serum electrolytes

34. The Panchayat Raj Institution at block level–
a. Gram panchayat b. Zilla Parishad
c. Grama Sabha d. Panchayati Samiti

35. In adult during ear irrigation to straighten the ear canal hold the pinna–
a. Upward
b. Downward backward
c. Straight backward
d. Upward and backward

36. Heat regulation centre is–
a. Thalamus b. Hypothalamus
c. Basal nuclei d. Central cortex

37. Increased pulsation felt in lateral fornices of vagina in pregnancy is termed as a–
a. Chadwick's sign b. Osiander's sign
c. Goodell's sign d. Hegar's sign

38. Priority attention required for an unconscious patient is–
a. Nutrition b. Elimination
c. Airway patency d. Exercise

39. The most appropriate nursing action in the first 48 hours of hospitalization of a patient with full thickness burns over 30% of the body is directed towards preventing–
a. Pneumonia b. Shock
c. Contractures d. Hypertension

40. Dysphasia is a defect that cause difficulty in–
a. Walk b. Speech
c. Swallowing d. Vision

41. The largest gland in the human body–
a. Pancreas b. Liver
c. Spleen d. Gallbladder

42. Enlargement of the thyroid gland due to lack of iodine–
a. Cretinism b. Goitre
c. Hyperthyroidism d. Graves disease

43. Inanimate objects that can transmit the disease are termed as–
a. Droplet b. Dust
c. Fomites d. Reservoir

44. Person or animal or object from which the infectious agent is transmitted–
a. Agent b. Host
c. Source d. Reservoir

45. Infection occurring in a patient while in a hospital or health care agency–
a. Opportunistic infection
b. Nosocomial infection
c. Iatrogenic infectio
d. Indirect infection

46. A widespread occurrence of an infectious disease in a community at a given period of time is called–
a. Endemic b. Epidemic
c. Pandemic d. Sporadic

47. Proponent of germ theory of disease–
a. Louis Pasteur b. Robert Hook
c. Charles Darwin d. Robert Brown

48. What does BMW stand for?
a. Bio Medical Waste
b. Basic Medical Waste
c. Blood Medical Waste
d. Bio Manpower Waste

49. Vaccines produce–
a. Natural immunity b. Active immunity
c. Passive immunity d. Acquired immunity

50. The time interval between the entry of the disease agent into the body and the appearance of first sign or symptom of the disease is–
a. Incubation period b. Transmission
c. Infection d. Epidemic

51. Under ICDS programme, there is an anganwadi worker for every–
a. 3,000 population b. 1,000 population
c. 10,000 population d. 5,000 population

52. Full form of DOTS is–
a. Directly Observed Treatment Short–Course
b. Distantly Observed Treatment Short course
c. Distinctly Overviewed Tele Short–Course
d. Differently Overviewed Tuberculosis Strategy

53. According to Central Birth and Registration Act, 1969, an event of death is required to be registered in–
a. 21 days b. 7 days
c. 10 days d. 14 days

54. Most common site to administer BCG vaccine is–
a. Left Thigh b. Right thigh
c. Left deltoid d. Right deltoid

55. Carrier of Dengue disease is–
a. Aedes mosquito
b. Culex mosquito
c. House fly
d. Anopheles mosquito

56. Difficulty in getting off to sleep or in maintaining sleep is called a–
a. Amnesia b. Narcolepsy
c. Insomnia d. Hypersomnia

57. What is the amount of solution placed in a nebulization chamber while providing nebulization?
a. 3 ml b. 6 ml
c. 2 ml d. 10 ml

58. The most critical factor in the care of an infant after repair of a cleft lip is–
a. Prevent vomiting
b. Maintaining a patent airway
c. Maintaining parenteral fluid infusions
d. Administering medications that reduce oral secretions

59. Which of the following disease is transmitted mainly by faeco–oral route?
a. Polio b. HIV
c. Measles d. Syphilis

60. The characteristic features of Measles (Rubeola) that differentiate it from German measles (Rubella) are–

a. A high fever and koplik spots
b. A rash on the trunk with pruritus
c. Nausea, vomiting and abdominal cramps
d. Signs that are similar to those of a cold, followed by a rash

61. What is the major cause of death in children under 5 years of age among the following diseases?

a. Pneumonia b. Measles
c. Chicken pox d. Hepatitis

62. The reflex that causes the baby's toes to spread when the sole of the foot is stroked is–

a. Babinski reflex b. Rooting reflex
c. Moro reflex d. Sucking reflex

63. What is the normal capillary refill time in children?

a. Less than 3 secs b. More than 3 secs
c. ess than 1 sec d. 5 secs

64. What is the age group of a neonate?

a. 0 to 7 days
b. 0–28 days
c. 1 month to one year
d. 0 to 1 year

65. The site for needle prick in a neonate for blood glucose monitoring is–

a. Heel b. Palm
c. Forearm d. Leg

66. The nurse is aware that a neonate of a mother with diabetes is at risk for what complication?

a. Hypoglycemia b. Anemia
c. Dehydration d. Acidos

67. If an HIV–positive mother chooses to breastfeed, she should–

a. Alternate breastfeed with infant formula feedings
b. Breastfeed exclusively along with anti retroviral therapy until weaning by 6 months
c. Feed the baby the freshly expressed milk using katori and spoon
d. Breast feed only during night or when the baby is sick

68. The birth weight of the baby doubles at the age of–

a. 3 months b. 6 months
c. 9 months d. 12 month

69. Ophthalmic neonatorum is caused by–

a. Neisseria gonorrhoea
b. Cytomegalovirus
c. Herpes virus
d. Human papilloma virus

70. Expected time of closure of anterior frontalle is–

a. 4–6 weeks b. 6–8 weeks
c. 9–12 weeks d. 16–18 weeks

71. Yellow, thick secretion from the breasts in the first three days of the delivery–

a. Colostrum b. Transitional milk
c. Mature milk d. Fatty milk

72. Clinical sign seen in tetanus–

a. Koplik's spot b. Pseudomembrane
c. Opisthotonus d. Hydrophobia

73. Which among the following is the top cause of mortality among adolescents in the world–

a. Suicide
b. Communicable diseases
c. Road Traffic Accidents
d. Iron Deficiency

74. ICTC stands for–

a. Integrated Centre for Testing of Chronic diseases
b. Integrated Counseling and Training Centre
c. Integrated Counseling and Testing Centre for HIV/AIDS
d. Integrated Child Training Centre

75. Adolescence is a transitional phase between–

a. Teenage and Adulthood
b. Childhood and teenage
c. Childhood and adulthood
d. Childhood and old age

76. In pregnancy kit test women is said to be pregnant if–

a. Single line appears
b. Two lines appear
c. Two lines where one is not clear appears
d. No band appears

77. A client tells the nurse that the first day of her last menstrual period was July 22, 2008. What is the estimated date of delivery?

a. May 7, 2009 b. April 29, 2009
c. April 22, 2009 d. March 6, 2009

78. **The presence what levels of urine albumin together with high blood pressure is sufficient to categorize her as having pre–eclampsia?**
a. +3 b. +4
c. +5 d. +2

79. **Sucking breasts during breastfeeding helps predominantly in the release of which hormone–**
a. HCG b. Prostaglandin
c. Estrogen d. Oxytocin

80. **At 24 weeks of gestation, the fundus of the uterus is–**
a. At the level of umbilicus
b. At the level of xiphi sternum
c. At the level of symphysis pubis
d. Above the umbilicus

81. **A bloody, sticky discharge from the vagina is known as–**
a. Show b. Goodells sign
c. Osianders sign d. Hegars sign

82. **The following should be tested at every ANC visit–**
a. Haemoglobin, Urine sugar and HCG
b. Haemoglobin, blood and urine sugar
c. Haemoglobin, Urine sugar and protein
d. Haemoglobin, Urine sugar and HPL

83. **If a soft irregular foetal pole is felt in pelvic grip, then it may be–**
a. Vertex presentation
b. Breech presentation
c. Transverse lie
d. Occipito posterior positio

84. **Exclusive breastfeeding for young infants means–**
a. Feeding the infant with extra milk
b. The infant receives only breast milk and nothing else
c. Feeding the infant with breast milk and water only
d. Exclude breast milk from young infants' feeds

85. **The most frequent cause of maternal death during child birth is–**
a. Sepsis b. Toxemia
c. Asphyxia d. Hemorrhage

86. **The dose of Vitamin K for a newborn weighing less than 1000 g is?**
a. 0.5 mg b. 1 mg
c. 1.5 mg d. 2 mg

87. **Within how many minutes should the placenta be delivered before referring to the higher facility?**
a. 15 mins b. 30 min
c. 45 mins d. 1 hour

88. **Episiotomy should be done when–**
a. Head is crowning the vulva and recedes back into the vagina when the contractions pass off
b. Head is crowning the vulva and does not recede back into the vagina when the contractions pass off
c. Head has not crowned and recedes back into the vagina
d. Head has not crowned and does not recede back into the vagina

89. **Active Management of third stage of labour should be practiced–**
a. Only for women who have a history of postpartum hemorrhage
b. Only for the primipara
c. Only for the multipara
d. For all women

90. **Which of the following fetal positions is the most favorable for birth?**
a. Vertex presentation
b. Transverse lie
c. Frank breech presentation
d. Posterior position of the fetal head

91. **Which of the following are the signs of true labour pain?**
a. Pain increases in frequency, intensity and duration of contraction and does not subside even after rest
b. Pain remains the same throughou
c. Pain increases only in frequency and intensity
d. Pain increases in frequency, intensity and duration of contraction but it subside after rest

92. **Pinkish linear marks found in abdominal wall, thighs and breasts during pregnancy–**
a. Linea nigra b. Linea albicans
c. Striae gravidarum d. Striae albicans

93. A positive sign of pregnancy–

a. Hegar's sign b. Osiander's sign
c. Fetal heart sound's d. Morning sickness

94. The pituitary hormone that stimulates the secretion of milk from the mammary glands–

a. Oxytocin b. Progesterone
c. Estrogen d. Prolactin

95. The common complaints of a woman with IUCD is–

a. Vaginal bleeding b. Pelvic infection
c. Uterine perforation d. Abdominal pain

96. Sperm count less than 20 million/mL–

a. Aspermia b. Oligospermia
c. Azoospermia d. Asthenospermia

97. Emergency contraceptives are effective if administered within following period after unprotected coitus?

a. 24 hrs b. 48 hrs
c. 72 hrs d. 120 hrs

98. What is male sterilization called?

a. Tubectomy b. Vasectomy
c. Salphingectomy d. None of these

99. Injectables contraceptives inhibit ovulation by–

a. Preventing the LH surge and lowering FSH and LH
b. By thickening the cervical mucous and rendering the endometrium less suitable foı implantation
c. By hindering the rate of ovum transport
d. All of these

100. A safe, simple, temporary and reliable form of male contraception is–

a. Use of condom b. Vasectomy
c. Abstinence d. All of these

Answer Sheet

1.B.	2. C.	3. C.	4 . C.	5. C.	6.C.	7.B.	8.A.	9.A.	10.D.
11.D.	12.D.	13.C.	14.B.	15.A.	16.A.	17.D.	18.D.	19.A.	20.B.
21.A.	22.C.	23.C.	24.A.	25.A.	26.D.	27.B.	28.C.	29.A.	30.A.
31.D.	32.A.	33.A.	34.D.	35.D.	36.B.	37.B.	38.C.	39.B.	40.B.
41.B.	42.B.	43.C.	44.C.	45.B.	46.B.	47.A.	48.A.	49.D.	50.A.
51.B.	52.A.	53.A.	54.D.	55.A.	56.C.	57.A.	58.B.	59.A.	60.A.
61.A.	62.A.	63.A.	64.B.	65.A.	66.A.	67.B.	68.B.	69.A.	70.D.
71.A.	72.C.	73.C.	74.C.	75.C.	76.B.	77.B.	78.D.	79.D.	80.A.
81.A.	82.C.	83.B.	84.B.	85.D.	86.A.	87.B.	88.B.	89.D.	90.A.
91.A.	92.C.	93.C.	94.D.	95.A.	96.B.	97.C.	98.B.	99.D.	100.A.

□□□

Madhya Pradesh CHO Papers – 2019 Set–IV

1. What is true about Oedema–
a. It is fluid retention in body
b. Affected tissues become swollen
c. It is reversible
d. All of these

2. What is main function of liver–
a. Produes Insulin
b. Bile production and excretion
c. Secretion of Gastric Juice
d. All of them

3. What is true about Gallblader–
a. Helps in gaining weight
b. Produces insulin
c. Stores bile
d. None of them

4. Semen contains what?
a. Prostatic fluid b. Sperms
c. Seminal Fluid d. All of them

5. Normal respiratory rate per minute for an adult at rest–
a. 12 to 20 breaths b. 10 to 14 breaths
c. 10 to 20 breaths d. 15 to 25 breaths

6. Which muscle is most typically used to give injection in arm–
a. Biceps b. Triceps
c. Deltoid d. Brachialis

7. Tube connecting kidney to urinary bladder is–
a. Trachea b. Urethra
c. Ureter d. Fallopian tube

8. Part of eye where image is formed–
a. Lens b. Cornea
c. Sclera d. Retina

9. Which statement is incorrect–
a. Ossicles are 2 bones
b. Tympanic membrane is also known as eardrum
c. Cochlea is the part of inner ear
d. Pinna is part of external ear

10. What is true about lungs–
a. Right lung has two lobes
b. They have Brochi and Bronchioles
c. They are covered by pericardium
d. Situated just below diaphragm

11. Births in India must be registered within–
a. 7 days b. 14 days
c. 21 days d. 1 month

12. What is the population of MP as per census 2011–
a. 7.26 Cr b. 7.56 Cr
c. 8.1 Cr d. 8.34 Cr

13. As per SRS–2017, Infant mortality rate of MP is–
a. 33 b. 30
c. 29 d. 47

14. As per SRS–2017, under–five mortality rate (U5MR) of MP is–
a. 37 b. 47
c. 55 d. 49

15. Census is conducted in every............years in India–
a. 25 b. 15
c. 10 d. 20

16. Crude birth rate is a simplest measure of fertility because it includes–
a. Total population
b. Mid year population
c. Live births only
d. Pre–term births

17. In the demographic cycle, India is in the–
a. High stationary stage
b. Early expanding stage
c. Late expanding stage
d. Low stationary stage

18. 'Demographic Processes' does not include–
a. Fertility b. Morbidity
c. Mortality d. Social mobility

19. Incidence is determined by–
a. Prospective study
b. Case Control study
c. Cross sectional study
d. Retrospective study

20. Definition of health given by WHO includes which of the following dimensions–
a. Social b. Physical
c. Mental d. All of these

21. Which of the following is a mortality indicator?
a. Life Expectancy b. Notification Rate
c. DALY d. Bed turn–over ratio

22. Primary prevention of dental caries includes–

a. Chlorination
b. Dental health education
c. Mass screening
d. Dental fitting, teeth extraction

23. School health check up come under............level of prevention–

a. Premordial b. Primary
c. Secondary d. Tertiary

24. Maternal Mortality Ratio (MMR) is–

a. The proportion of maternal deaths per 1,00,000 live births
b. The proportion of maternal deaths per 10000 live births
c. The proportion of maternal deaths per 1000 live births
d. The proportion of maternal deaths per 1,00,000 deliveries

25. National Vector Borne Disease Control Programme is related with–

a. Tuberculosis b. Malaria
c. AIDS d. Leprosy

26. The first day of a lady's last menstrual period was 15 Sep 2019. What is the estimated date of delivery?

a. Jun–08, 2020 b. Jun–15, 2020
c. Jun–22, 2020 d. Jun–29, 2020

27. What is not a High risk pregnancy with–

a. Hb 11 g/dl
b. Pre–eclampsia
c. Previos Caessarian section
d. Diabetes

28. Some common complications of pregnancy include all except–

a. High Blood Pressure
b. Gestational Diabetes
c. Eclampsia
d. Malaria

29. Common cause of maternal death is–

a. Twin pregnancy b. Eclamsia
c. Hemorrhage d. None of these

30. In ectopic pregnancies fertile egg usually implants in–

a. An Ovary b. A fallopian tube
c. The Cervix d. The uterine wall

31. What is excessive bleeding during menstruation called–

a. Menorrhagia b. Metrorrhagia
c. Oligomenorrhoea d. Polymenorrhoea

32. The fertilization of an egg in a medium and subsequent transfer to mother's Uterus is known as–

a. Zygote intrafallopian transfer
b. In vitro fertilization
c. Intra cytoplasmic injection
d. Gamete intrafallopian transfer

33. Most common cause of infertility in women is–

a. Endometriosis
b. PCOS
c. Cancinoma Cervix
d. Sexually Transmitted disease

34. During antenatal examination the information regarding fetal presenting part engagement is obtained by–

a. Fundal grip b. Right lateral grip
c. Left lateral grip d. Pelvic grip

35. For typing the B.P. Apparatus cuff while measuring blood pressure, it should be placed–

a. 1 cm above the elbow
b. 3 cm above the elbow with tubing placed at posterior
c. 3 cm above the elbow with tubing placed medially
d. 2 cm above the elbow

36. All is true for Exclusive breast feeding except–

a. Medication can be given
b. Only branded Ghutti can be given
c. Only breast feeding
d. Upto Six months

37. Early Neonate is a baby upto what age?

a. 0–3 days b. 0–7 days
c. 0–14 days d. 0–21 days

38. A child with SAM having Hypothermia should be–

a. Kept under warmer
b. Given feeds
c. Screened for infections
d. All of the above

39. Which babies are eligible for Kangaroo Mother Care (KMC) –

a. Less than 1.5 Kg Wt
b. Less than 2 Kg Wt
c. Less than 2.5 Kg Wt
d. Less than 3 Kg Wt

40. An infant might start walking at what age?
a. 6–9 Months b. 9–12 Months
c. 13–15 Months d. None of these

41. What should be applied over umblical cord–
a. Spirit b. Betadine
c. Antibiotic ointment d. Nothing

42. What causes pneumonia in infants–
a. Virus
b. Bacteria
c. Fungi and parasites
d. All of the above

43. A newborn requires initial steps of resuscitation if he is–
a. Not crying b. Full Term
c. Good muscle tone d. Crying

44. What should be done to prevent hypothermia?
a. KMC b. Breast feeding
c. Covering head d. All of the above

45. Albendazole is given to treat–
a. Diarrhoea b. Pnumonia
c. Worm infestation d. Amoebiasis

46. Which of the following is not given at birth?
a. OPV
b. Hepatitis B Vaccine
c. BCG
d. Pentavalent

47. Which of the following is included in open vial policy–
a. Measles b. Pentavalent
c. Rotavirus vaccine d. BCG

48. A 14 months old child with mild cold and cough is brought for vaccination. What should be done?
a. Ask parents to bring child later
b. Vaccinate the child
c. Tell them to get the child vaccinated in district hospital
d. Give half dose of vaccine

49. BCG vaccine can be given after birth, if not, can be given upto–
a. 1 month b. 6 months
c. 9 months d. 12 months

50. A child is Fully Immunized Child if received these vaccines before completing 1 year of age–
a. BCG, DPT3 and OPV3
b. Hepatitis–B, OPV and Measles
c. Pentavalent3, OPV3 and MR1
d. None of the above

51. Counseling for problems related to sexual health is done at which level of service provision?
a. District hospital
b. Primary health centre
c. Community health centred.
d. All of the above

52. What is the full form of BMI?
a. Body Metabolic Index
b. Basic Metabolic Index
c. Body Mass Index
d. Basic Mass Index

53. Overweight refers to a BMI of?
a. Less than 18.5 kg/m2
b. More than 25.0 kg/m2
c. Less than 25.0 kg/m2
d. More than 18.5 kg/m2

54. ICTC stands for–
a. Integrated Centre for Testing of Chronic diseases
b. Integrated Counseling and Training Centre
c. Integrated Counseling and Testing Centre for HIV/AIDS
d. Integrated Child Training Centre

55. Adolescence is a transitional phase between–
a. Teenage and Adulthood
b. Childhood and teenage
c. Childhood and adulthood
d. Childhood and old age

56. Choose side effect of Oral contraceptive Pills–
a. Pain in abdomen
b. Increased appetite
c. Loose Motions
d. Intermittent spotting

57. Which method of contraception has highest failure rates–
a. Coitus interruptus
b. Condoms
c. Oral Contraceptive Pills
d. Tubal ligation

58. What is 'Chhaya'–
a. A contraceptive Pill
b. An injectable contraceptive
c. Brand name of a female condom
d. None of the above

59. How can healthy BIRTH SPACING be accomplished?
a. Rhythm Method
b. Barrier Method
c. Hormonal Method
d. All of the above

60. What is true about Mission Pariwar Vikas–
a. New name for Family Planning program
b. Relates to Contraceptives and family planning services
c. Giving all health services under Ayushman Bharat
d. Family Health Insurance Scheme

61. Which of the following is not a Sexually Transmitted Disease–
a. Syphilis b. Gonorrhoea
c. Fibroid uterus d. HIV

62. Chikungunya is caused by a–
a. Bacterium b. Virus
c. Parasite d. Protozoan

63. Cholera is a–
a. Water borne disease b. Air borne disease
c. Genetic disorder d. None of the above

64. Who is considered a new case of Tuberculosis–
a. TB patient who has never had any treatment for TB or has taken any anti TB drugs
b. TB patient who has taken treatment for TB for less than one month
c. Both of these
d. None of these

65. All of the following are water borne diseases, except–
a. Cholera b. Mumps
c. Hepatitis A d. Typhoid

66. Measles can be eliminated by–
a. Proper treatment b. Vaccination
c. Both of these d. None of these

67. Artemisinin–based combination therapies (ACTs) are used for treatment of–
a. Dengue b. Chicken guinea
c. Tuberculosis d. Malaria

68. HIV infection is caused by–
a. Virus b. Bacteria
c. Fungi and parasites d. None of these

69. What is true about Hepatitis A–
a. Communicale disease
b. Transmitted through contaminated food and water
c. Caused by hepatitis A virus
d. All of these

70. What is true about Typhoid–
a. It is caused by a virus
b. Spreads by droplet infection
c. Affects Intestine
d. Affects kidneys

71. What is the name of the vaccine against Cervical Cancer–
a. IPV vaccine b. Hepatitis
c. HPV vaccine d. Anti viral vaccine

72. Asthma can be prevented by–
a. Preventing exposure to allergens
b. Take vaccine against asthma
c. Taking medicines regularly
d. None of the above

73. Which of these is not a reason for hypoglycaemia–
a. Skipping a meal
b. Less physical activity
c. Taking more than recommended dose of insulin
d. Side effect of anti–diabetic drugs

74. Cardiovascular disease may damage–
a. Heart b. Brain
c. Kidney and eyes d. Any one of these

75. Full form of IDD is–
a. Idiopathic dilation disorder
b. Impetigo deficiency disorder
c. Iodine deficiency disorder
d. Infantile digital disorder

76. In Atherosclerosis, the blood vessels become–
a. Thick and stiff b. Fragile
c. Elastic d. None of the above

77. Which ingredient has high content of Fluoride–
a. Black rock salt b. Iodine salt
c. Sugar d. All the above

78. The types of screening test available for cervical cancer are?
a. Pap Smear Test
b. Visual Inspection with Acetic Acid
c. Testing for Human Papilloma Virus for high risk HPV types
d. All the above

79. The common risk factors for cancer are, except–
a. Tobacco and family history
b. Alcohol and smoking
c. Pollution and radiation
d. Exposure and contact with cancer patient

80. Osteoporosis is due to deficiency of which mineral–
a. Potassium b Iron
c. Calcium d. Zinc

81. In order to achieve the vision of Universal Health Coverage (UHC), Government of India initiated–
a. Aarogya Bharat Yojana
b. Pradhan Mantri Jan Aaarogya Yojana
c. Ayushman Bharat Yojana
d. Ujjwala Yojana

82. Mission Parivar Vikas is initiated under?
a. Maternal Health b. Nutrition
c. Family Planning d. Adolescent Health

83. "Mera Aaspatal" Mobile based application and web portal is initiated for?
a. Map of District Hospital
b. Patient Feedback
c. Online Registration
d. Online Consultation

84. National Family Welfare Program was launched in–
a. 1950 b. 1951
c. 1952 d. 1953

85. Pulse Polio Examination was launched in–
a. 2005 b. 1995
c. 1996 d. 1998

86. Which of the following is not a national health programme?
A. National Programme for Control of Blindness and Visual Impairment
B. National Tobacco Control Programme (NTCP)
C. National Oral Health Programme
D. National Programme for Prevention and Control of Deafness (NPPCD)
a. Only A and B b. Only A, B and C
c. Only A and C d. None of these

87. DASTAK Abhiyan is related to–
a. Nutrition b. Maternal Health
c. Elderly Health d. Blindness

88. UIP program was launched in–
a. 1975 b. 1980
c. 1985 d. 1990

89. DOTS therapy is was started under–
a. RNTCP
b. Malaria Control Programme
c. Leprosy Control Programme
d. HIV AIDS Control Programme

90. The National Viral Hepatitis Control Program has been launched–
a. 2015 b. 2016
c. 2017 d. 2018

91. Who is present ISRO Chief–
a. Dr. PKK Ayyangar b. Dr. R. Valiathan
c. A. S. Kiran Kumar d. K. Sivan

92. W. Harvey discovered–
a. Laws of heredity
b. Dynamite
c. Circulation of blood
d. Crystal dynamics

93. Which state has its own separate state constitution–
a. Nagaland
b. Jammu and Kashmir
c. Arunachal Pradesh
d. None of these

94. Who is chief of the army staff–
a. General V. K. Singh
b. General Bipin Rawat
c. General Bipin Chandra Joshi
d. General Deepak Kapoor

95. Mary Kom is famous for–
a. Singing b. Dancing
c. Boxing d. Wrestling

96. Who is chief justice of India–
a. Justice Ranjan Gogoi
b. Justice Sharad Arvind Bobde
c. Justice Dipak Mishra
d. Justice T. S. Thakur

97. Who is vice–president of India–
a. Sri Venkaiah Naidu
b. Sri Ram Nath Kovind
c. Sri Lal Krishna Advani
d. Sri J. P. Nadda

98. Red Cross was founded by–
a. A. Cursetji
b. Badel Powell
c. J. H. Durant
d. Trygve Lie

99. Stethoscope was invented by–
a. Dunlop b. Lainnec
c. Bessemer d. Auenbrugg

100. Which gas caused the Bhopal gas tragedy incident–
a. Isoamyl acetate b. Propionic acid
c. Methyl trichloride d. Methyl isocyanate

Answer Sheet

1.C.	2. B.	3. C.	4 . D.	5. A.	6.C.	7.C.	8.D.	9.A.	10.B.
11.C.	12.A.	13.D.	14.C.	15.C.	16.B.	17.C.	18.B.	19.A.	20.D.
21.A.	22.B.	23.C.	24.A.	25.B.	26.C.	27.A.	28.D.	29.C.	30.B.
31.A.	32.B.	33.D.	34.D.	35.C.	36.B.	37.B.	38.D.	39.B.	40.B.
41.D.	42.D.	43.A.	44.D.	45.C.	46.D.	47.B.	48.B.	49.D.	50.D.
51.D.	52.C.	53.B.	54.C.	55.C.	56.D.	57.A.	58.A.	59.D.	60.B.
61.C.	62.B.	63.A.	64.C.	65.B.	66.B.	67.D.	68.A.	69.D.	70.C.
71.C.	72.A.	73.B.	74.D.	75.C.	76.A.	77.A.	78.D.	79.D.	80.C.
81.C.	82.C.	83.B.	84.B.	85.B.	86.D.	87.A.	88.C.	89.A.	90.D.
91. D.	92. C.	93. D.	94. B.	95. C.	96. B.	97. A.	98. C.	99. B.	100. D.

□□□

1. Fundamental of Nursing (MCQ)

1. **Pathogenic organisms are**
   A. Used in the pasteurization process
   B. More plentiful than any other type of organism
   C. Important to industry
   D. Harmful to humans

2. **For giving CPCR, after ascertaining unresponsiveness one should:**
   A. Call for help
   B. Establish an airway
   C. Check the carotid pulse
   D. Give chest compression

3. **Local cold application transfer heat from the body by:**
   A. Radiation B. Evaporation
   C. Convection D. Conduction

4. **Autoclaving a means of sterilization will destroy**
   A. All microorganisms
   B. Pathogenic microorganisms
   C. Non pathogenic microorganisms
   D. Just yeasts and molds

5. **Position in which the patient is to be cared after lower extremity amputation is:**
   A. Left lateral
   B. Supine with head turned to one side
   C. Side lying with amputated side up
   D. Prone

6. **When giving a patient intramuscular preoperative medications, the practical nurse must remember to inject into site no more than ?**
   A. 1ml B. 2ml
   C. 3ml D. 4ml

7. **The safest position for a lady with cord prolapse in labor is:**
   A. Fowler's position B. Prone
   C. Supine D. Trendelenburg

8. **The percentage of water in human body is:**
   A. 60% B. 80%
   C. 35% D. None of these

9. **Daily care of patient's room would consist of**
   A. Disinfecting and sterilizing items in his immediate area
   B. Providing fresh water for his flowers
   C. Scrubbing and waxing the floor
   D. Damp dusting and straightening

10. **The most important electrolyte of intracellular fluid is:**
    A. Potassium B. Calcium
    C. Sodium D. Chloride

11. **During the bath observation of skin include ?**
    A. Temperature integrity and condition
    B. Colour, warmth and bruising
    C. Markings made by wrinkles in the sheet or crumbs
    D. Distribution and colour of hair

12. **Patient recovering from general anaesthesia should be positioned in:**
    A. Supine position
    B. Fowler's position
    C. Trendelenburg position
    D. Side lying position

13. **Included as a part of charting is the recording of observations and assessment of the patient. Basic skills used by the nurse in assessment are**
    A. Subjective and objective observation
    B. Communications of the patient
    C. Laboratory data and patient's response to tests
    D. Recording of all data in a legal manner

14. **Lugol's solution contains:**
    A. Potassium iodide
    B. Sodium bromide
    C. Ammonium chloride
    D. Calcium chloride

15. **Which of the following feature is not related to Gushing's triad?**
    A Systolic BP
    B. Hypothermia
    C. Bradycardia
    D. Widening pulse pressure

16. **Signs of a local infection include**
    A. Redness,.pain, swelling and decreased temperature
    B. Increase and decreased blood pressure
    C. Redness, pain and swelling of the area
    D. Increased temperature, pain, redness and decreased urine output

17. **The mount of bleaching powder for disinfection of 1000 gallons of water is:**
    A. oz B. loz
    C. 50 gm D. 10 gm

18. The physician writes the following order, "Obtain a sterile urine specimen for C & S".Which of the following is true concerning a sterile urine specimen?

A. May be obtained from the catheter bag if the patient has a Foley catheter

B. May be obtained using the "clean catch" or "mid stream" method as long as you use a sterile container

C. Must be obtained either by catheterizing the patient or from the catheter itself if the patient has a Foley catheter

D. May be obtained only by clamping off a Foley catheter for 15 minutes and then taking the specimen from the catheter tubing

19. Best method of oxygen administration to a 2 month old baby is:

A. Oxyhood B. Nasal cannula

C. Face mask D. Oxygen tent

20. Best method of oxygen administration to a Burn patient is:

A. Oxyhood B. Nasal cannula

C. Face mask D. Oxygen tent

21. Nursing observation that should be reported to physician immediately include ?

A. Pulse, hypotention and decreased urinary output

B. Obstruction of the intravenous tubing and inflammation at the puncture site

C. Removal of the signs of local infection

D. Three hundred fifty millimetre of yellow green drainage from nasogastric tube during the 8 hour shift.

22. Best mask of oxygen administration to a facial Burn patient used as:

A. Aerosol mask

B. Venturi mask

C. Face mask

D. Non Rebreather mask

23. To check the placement of nasogastric tube the nurse can ?

A. Order a chest xray examination after injecting 5cc of air into the stomach

B. Ask the patient if the tube feels as if it is in the stomach

C. Ask the patient to take tree deep breaths while pinching the nasogastric tube

D. Inject 5cc of air into the nasogastric tube while listening with a stethoscope for air entering the stomach

24. Best mask of oxygen administration are used in clinical practice when patient need higher humidify oxygen :

A. Aerosol mask

B. Venturi mask

C. Face mask

D. Non rebreather mask

25. Amount of blood used for exchange transfusion in a neonate is:

A. 50 ml/kg body weight

B. 65 ml/kg body weight

C. 80 ml/kg body weight

D. 100 ml/kg body weight

26. In case of accident what would you first examine

A. Patent airway

B. Hemorrhage

C. Fractures

D. Possible head injury

27. For eye examination the instrument used is:

A. Percussion hammer

B. Otoscope

C. Stethoscope

D. Opthalmoscope

28. The important nursing intervention prior to administration of preanesthetic medication is:

A. Ask patient to empty the bladder

B. Do deep breathing and coughing exercises

C. Shave the skin

D. Regulate IV accurately

29. All these are sterilized by chemicals except:

A. Endoscopes B. Gauze

C. Scissors D. Cables

30. You would use the following methods of artificial respiration

A. Mouthto mouth

B. Pronepressure

C. Back pressure

D. Mouthtonose

31. The important nursing intervention prior to surgery is:

A. Ask patient to empty the bladder

B. Do deep breathing and coughing exercises

C. Shave the skin

D. Regulate IV accurately

32. In order to stop oozing bleeding you would first try ?

A. Pressure points

B. Direct pressure to the wound

C. Tourniquet

D. Ice packs

33. Who invented thermometer:

A. Celsius

B. Galileo Galilee

C. Lord Kelvin

D. Thomas J. Manning

34. Characteristic sign of heat exhaustion are ?
A. Profuse perspiration, normal body temperature, fainting
B. Unconsciousness, incontinence and bradycardia
C. Elevated body temperature, hot dry skin and tachycardia
D. Flushed face, rigidity of body muscles and excessive salivation

35. A clinical thermometer indicates temperatures in degree fahrenhait from:
A. 95 to 110 B. 94 to 110
C. 98 to 110 D. 96 to 112

36. The normal breath rate of human beings is:
A. 12-15 per minute
B. 22-25 per minute
C. 15-18 per minute
D. 20-24 per minute

37. If a patient asks you to pray with him you should ?
A. Summon the hospital chaplain or minister of the patient faith
B. Ask him about his faith because you may not agree with his religious belief
C. Comply with his request, asking him if he has any special prayer he would like to say
D. Ignore his request, realizing that illness after causes a patient concern about spiritual welfare

38. If would eviscerations occurs, the immediate nursing action is:
A. Cover the would with sterile dry gauze
B. Leave the wound uncovered and pull the skin edges together
C. Cover the wound with sterile gauze moistened with sterile NS
D. Cover the wound with water-soaked gauze

39. How frequent should the nurse monitor the Vital Sign of the patient in the recovery room?
A. Every 15 minutes B. Every 60 min
C. Every 30 min D. Every 45 min

40. A common blood test is that is used in a urologic workup is the blood urea nitrogen BUN) test. The normal level for this test is
A. 10 to 20 mg/100ml of whole blood
B. 25 to 40 mg/100ml of whole blood
C. 50 to 80 mg/100ml of whole blood
D. 70 to 120 mg/100ml of whole blood

41. The most important factor in the prevention of postoperative infection is:
A. Frequent change of wound dressings
B. Proper administration of antibiotics
C. Fluid intake of 2-3 L/day
D. Practice of strict aseptic techniques

42. Mr. X is to have a suprapubic prostatectomy. In this procedure the gland is approached through the
A. Bladder B. Perineum
C. Urethra D. Ureter

43. Which of the following nursing actions should be given highest priority when admitting the patient into the operating room?
A. Level of consciousness
B. Patient identification and correct operative consent
C. Positioning and skin preperation
D. Vital signs

44. After a cast has been applied, the nurse should suspect circulatory impairment if the patient of?
A. Stiffness of the digits
B. Itching of the part
C. Numbness or tingling or both of the digits
D. Excessive sweating under the cast

45. ALT exceeds AST in:
A. Viral hepatitis B. Cholestatic hepatitis
C. Toxic hepatitis D. All the above

46. Information necessary for complete pain assessment would include ?
A. Precipitating event description and location
B. Medication preference and location
C. Emotional state of the patient and nutritional need
D. Time since last injection and physician order

47. Test for hypersensitivity is called:
A. Patch test B. None of the above
C. Patrick's test D. Post-coital test

48. Humidified oxygen is administered via tracheostomy after a laryngectomy because
A. Humidified oxygen contains more water
B. The upper airway is no longer connected to the lower airway
C. The lower airway heals more quickly if humidity is utilized
D. Humidified oxygen administration facilitates suctioning

49. Choosing the appropriate catheter depends on:
A. Knowledge of any allergies to latex or plastic
B. The expected duration of catheterization
C. The size of the patient's urethral canal
D. All the above

50. The purpose of steam inhalation is to
A. Produce thicker secretions,which may be expectrated more easily
B. Increase the oxygen content coming in contact with the mucous membranes

C. Prevent drying of the trachea or tracheitis
D. All of the Above

51. Curved or coude catheters have:
A. A rounded curved tip
B. A single lumen with a small 11/24 cm opening
C. A single lumen with a small 11*A* cm opening
D. An inflatable balloon that encircles the tip near the lumen or opening

52. The patient with bleeding esophagus varices can be treated with a SengstakenBlakemore Tube. In caring for the patient with this type of tube; the nurse should be most alert for
A. Loss of balloon pressure
B. Irritation of nares
C. Airway obstruction
D. Atelectasis

53. The skin is shaved prior to surgery in order to:
A. Facilitate skin incision
B. To prevent wound infection
C. Reduce post operation scarring
D. Indicate the site to be draped

54. When interpreting the results of the tes Tape on urine, orange indicate
A. 1+ sugar B. 2+sugar
C. 3+ sugar D. 5+ sugar

55. Quantity of sodium chloride required to make 1 litre of normal saline is:
A. 900 grams B. 0.9 grams
C. 9 grams D. 90 grams

56. A patient is to be started on an eternal feeding. What important steps should nurse take before the patient in started on eternal feeding
A. Evaluate the familiar perception of eternal feeding
B. Assess the understanding of eternal feeding
C. Assess patient allergy to lactogen
D. Make sure patient had nothing by mouth while eternal feeding is started

57. White doing CPR the compression ventilation ratio in an adult should be:
A. 25:2 B. 30:2
C. 15:2 D. 20:2

58. A 4year old client was brought to the health centre with chief complaint of severe diarrhea and the passage of "rice water". The client is most probably suffering from which condition?
A. Giardiasis B. Cholera
C. Amebiasi D. Dysentery

59. You are irrigating a draining wound with sterile saline solution. Which of the following would be the most appropriate procedure to follow:
A. Prepare sterile field, put on sterile gloves and remove soiled dressing, wash hands
B. Wash hands, wear clean gloves, remove soiled dressing, remove gloves, wash hands, wear sterile gloves, prepare sterile field
C. Remove solid dressing, flush wound and wash hands, prepare sterile field
D. Pour solution, wash hands and remove soiled dressing, prepare sterile field

60. To diagnosis meningitis which type of sample is collected:
A. Urine B. CSF
C. Bone-marrow D. Stool

61. A patient who decides to leave the hospital against medical advice (LAMA) must sign a form. What is the purpose of this form?
A. To release the physician and hospital from legal responsibility for the patient's health status
B. To ethically illustrate that the patient has control of his or her won care and treatment
C. To use in the event of readmission
D. To indicate the patient's wishes

62. Which of the following is not a parameter for "Glasgow coma scale"
A. Eye opening B. Pupillary response
C. Verbal response D. Motor response

63. Tracheostomy is usually performed between the tracheal rings of cartilage of:
A. Fourth and fifth B. All of the above
C. Second and third D. Third and fourth

64. "Rice Water Stool" is a typical finding in cases of :
A. Cholera B. Typhoid
C. Ulcerative colitis D. Amoebiasis

65. Patient has intravenous fluids infusing in the right arm when taking a blood pressure on thi patient, the nurse would:
A. Take the blood pressure in the left arm
B. Take the blood pressure in the right arm
C. Use the smallest possible cuff
D. Report inability to take the blood pressure

66. Full form of CPR is :
A. Cardio Pulmonary Resuscitation
B. Cardio-Pulmonary Relapse
C. Cardio Pulmonary Restriction
D. Chronic Pulmonary Replace

67. Infectious non sharp waste is collected in:
A. Black bag B. White bin
C. Yellow bag D. Red bag

68. What concentration of NaCl in intravenous fluid is termed "Isotonic":
A. 0.25% B. 0.45%
C. 0.75% D. 0.90%

69. What is the other name of thumb forceps?
A. Needle holder B. Mosquito forceps
C. Kelly's forceps D. Mouse's teeth

70. Surgical needles are:
A. 5/8 circle B. Straight
C. 1/4 circle D. All of the above

71. A nursing intervention in thrombophlebitis would be contraindicated:
A. Maintaining strict bed rest
B. Turning the patient from side to side
C. Applying warm packs to the affected leg
D. Massaging the affected leg

72. The most effective position for a women in labor with cord prolapsed is:
A. Lithotomy B. Trendelenburg
C. Sims D. Knee chest

73. A patient with acute pancreatitis has NG tube for low intermittent suction to prevent:
A. Chronic distortion
B. Gastric reflux
C. Pancreatic stimulation
D. Peristalsis

74. Intraocular pressure is measured with a instrument called:
A. Tonometer B. Manometer
C. Oculometer D. Perimeter

75. With aging blood pressure is often higher due to:
A. Decreased peripheral resistance
B. Decreased elasticity in arterial walls
C. Loss of muscle mass
D. Changes in exercise and diet

76. Eye padding is applied on unconscious patients to prevent:
A. Dryness of eye B. Blinking of eyes
C. Corneal ulcer D. Eye movement

77. AED stands for:
A. Arrhythmia eliminating device
B. Advanced emergency defibrillator
C. Authorised emergency defibrillator
D. Automated external defibrillator

78. Top priority treatment of ventricular fibrillation includes:
A. ECG monitoring B. Proper positioning
C. CPR D. Catherization

79. Carotid pulse should be checked for:
A. 15-20 seconds
B. Less than 5 seconds
C. 5-10 seconds
D. 10-15 seconds

80. In following which disease occur due to deficiency of thiamine:
A. Beri-Beri B. Pellagra
C. Anaemia D. Scurvy

81. Heimlich Maneuver involves the following:
A. Abdominal thrusts
B. Blind finger sweep in throat
C. Chest compressions
D. Jaw thrust

82. To prevent legal implications,. What should be done by a nurse during pre-operative period:
A. Provide psychological support
B. Obtain written consent
C. Provide comprehensive nursing care
D. Explain the patient and his relatives about post-operative complications

83. Recommended disinfectant used for handling spills is:
A. 10% sodium hypochlorite
B. 5% bleach solution
C. 1% sodium hypochlorite
D. 2% bleach solution

84. Chest compression in an unresponsive victim will be started:
A. After giving two breaths to victim
B. After making an emergency call to ambulance service
C. After checking carotid pulse of the victim and find the pulse is absent
D. As soon as you find an unresponsive victim

85. Clinical menifestations of anaemia include except:
A. Low Hb level B. Fatigue
C. Hyperactivity D. Lassitude

86. Universal precautions in hospital involve:
A. Gloving B. Mask, gowning
C. Hand washing D. All of the above

87. A patient in ventricular fibrillation is about to be defibrillated. A nurse knows that to convert this rhythm effectively, the machine should be set at which of the following energy levels for the best delivery?
A. 200 Joules B. 360 Joules
C. 50 Joules D. 100 Joules

88. Priority basis management of a unconscious patient include:
A. I.V. therapy
B. I.V. mannitol
C. Clearance of airway
D. Pain at Mc burny point

89. Cesol, and chloroxylenol are:
A. Acids B. Aldehydes
C. Halogens D. Phenols

90. In oliguria volume of urine is:
A. Less than 100 ml B. Less than 400 ml
C. Less than 800 ml D. Absence of urine

91. A comprehensive health assessment of an older person includes:
A. Functional assessment
B. Clinical assessment
C. Psychosocial assessment
D. All of the above

92. Management of cardiac arrest include except:
A. Massive I.V. infusion
B. O2 Therapy
C. Clearance of airway
D. Cardiac compression

93. Which of the following chemical is most powerful disinfectant?
A. Dettol B. Lysol
C. Phenol D. KMnO4.

94. During head injury what is the cause of increase in body temperature:
A. Pons injury
B. Hypothalamus injury
C. Cerebellum injury
D. Medulla injury

95. Temporary hardness of water is also called as
A. Chloride hardness B. Sodium hardness
C. Carbonate hardness D. None

96. In a patient of fever, "Fastigium" is term given to which of the following period?
A. Onset of fever
B. When body temperature has reached its maximum and remains constant
C. When the body temperature is gradually returning to normal
D. When body temperature is suddenly returning to normal

97. Anemometer is used to measure:
A. Air temperature B. Air velocity
C. Humidity D. Air pollution

98. Florence Nightingale was born in which country:
A. England B. Germany
C. Italy D. France

99. What is the colour coding of bag in hospitals to dispose off human anatomical wastes such as body parts?
A. Black B. Yellow
C. Blue D. Red

100. Criteria of a profession include except:
A. A profession should be intellectual
B. It should be self governing
C. In a profession there is no place for higher education
D. A profession should be service-oriented

101. Fresh bleaching power contains:
A. 0.033% chlorine B. 33% chlorine
C. 0.33% chlorine D. 3.3% chlorine

102. Qualities of a nurse include except:
A. Caring attitude B. Honesty
C. Talkative D. Well balanced life

103. The most effective method of well disinfection is done by:
A. Chlorine tablets B. KMnO4
C. Per chlorine D. CaOCl 2

104. Use of code of ethics in nursing profession includes:
A. It guides professional behaviour
B. It prevent a nurse from practicing below the standard set by the code
C. It can be used to protect a nurse who is falsely accused of doing something wrong
D. All of the above

105. The size of respirable dust is:
A. 10-15 jam B. 1-5 jam
C. 5-10 Am D. 15-20 urn

106. A failure in professional duty, practice or skill that leads to injury or harm to the patient, is termed as:
A. Malpractice B. Negligence
C. Crime D. Misunderstanding

107. The reagent used for testing urine sugar is:
A. Bendict's regent B. Sahli's agent
C. Rothera's agent D. None

108. What is the full term of TNAI?
A. Training in Nursing at All India Level
B. Trained Nurses of All India
C. Trained Nurses Association of India
D. Training in Nurses at International Level

109. A patient request that an I.V. not be initiated in his hand, which site is the next best of choice:
A. Antecubital fossa B. Forearm
C. Lower extremity D. Upper arm

110. Which one of the following is correct with regard to meaning of the term "Hyperkalemia"?
A. Increased Blood sugar level
B. Increased blood cholesterol level
C. Increased blood potassium level
D. Increased urine sodium level

111. Soap is valuable in cleansing the skin, because it is:
A. Lathers freely
B. Alkaline
C. Acidic
D. Lowers surface tension

112. The nurse is obtaining a sample from wound for culture. The patient asks what a culture is. Which of the following is the best response by the nurse to explain what a culture is?
A. A culture identifies presence of pathogens
B. It is for measuring antibiotic levels
C. It identifies an antibiotic's effect on pathogen
D. It determines the appropriate medication dosage

113. After a laryngectomy, which of the following assessment takes priority:
A. Nutritional status
B. Lung sounds
C. Airway patency and respiratory function
D. Fluid balance

114. Following is needed by all the pathogens to multiply?
A. Moisture B. Light
C. A Host D. Oxygen

115. When the body temperature raised to 105°F or above it is called:
A. Hyperpyrexia B. Hyperthermia
C. Rigor D. High pyrexia

116. The exit of client from hospital is :
A. Admission B. Discharge
C. Absconded D. AMA

117. Appropriate position for a client with severe ascites:
A. Sidelying B. Fowler's
C. Sim's D. Dorsal

118. Nursing and clients goal are set in which phase of nursing process?
A. Assessment B. Planning
C. Implementation D. Nursing diagnosis

119. In a Blood pressure recording, it is 110/80 mm of Hg, the pulse pressure in this value is:
A. 30 B. 110 C. 80 D. 190

120. A systematic rational method of planning and providing nursing care for individual, family and community is called as nursing process
A. Comprehensive nursing
B. Primary Nursing
C. Nursing process
D. Therapeutic nursing

121. The normal number of cardiac cycles per minute range from:
A. 90-100 B. 60-100
C. 60-80 D. 50-60

122. Biographic data of history taking exclude which of the following?
A. Age B. Gender
C. Diagnosis D Family history

123. Which one of the following is not necessary in the mangement of pulmonary oedema?
A. Mechanical ventilation
B. Diuretics
C. O_2 at high flow rate
D. Thoracentesis

124. Inflammation of the tissue surrounding nail is known as :
A. Paronychia B. Cellulitis
C. Keratosis D. Callosis

125. Which one of the following is not a sign of fluid overload:
A. Eleaved C.V.P. reading
B. Dyspnea
C. Bounding pulse
D. Abdominal distension

126. Bending of head towards chest is an example of which movement?
A. Abduction B. Adduction
C. Flexion D. Extension

127. A wound with uneven edges in known as:
A. Bruised B. Incised
C. Punctured D. Lacerated

128. 18 G Intra Venous canula is used for :
A. Blood Transfusion
B. Medication
C. New born baby
D. Sub cutaneous injection

129. Code of ethics for nurses is:
A. Guide for professional behaviour
B. Set of rules
C. Set of right behaviour
D. Set of wrong behaviour

130. Which of the following term denote reduced urine out put?
A. Dysurea B. Poly urea
C. Pyurea D. Oligurea

131. The greatest advantage of CAT scan is:
A. Non invastive procedure with no risks to client
B. The accuracy of diagnosis is nearly 100%
C. Shows the actual anatomical relationship of all structures
D. Image all tissues in three dimensions

132. Sharp instruments should not be sterilized by:
A. Autoclaving B. Boiling
C. Hot air oven D. Antiseptic solution

133. Mercury is a liquid metal used in thermometer because:
A. It reflects the temperature reading
B. It fluctuates and falls easily after reading
C. Expansion is uniform and is easily visible
D. Expansion is quick and easy to read

134. Appropriate needle size for insulin injection is :
A. 18G, 11/2" long B. 22G, 1" long
C. 22G, 11/2" long D. 25G, 5/8" long

135. The caloric test provides information about
A. Functions of vestibular portion of 8th cranial nerve
B. Functions of external auditory canal
C. Functions of the middle ear
D. None of the above

136. A drug has been prescribed to administer " PRN". The nurse understands that, PRN means,
A. As needed B. At night
C. Early Morning D. Stat

137. Which pulse is palpated to see the effectiveness of CPR ?
A. Radial B. Temporal
C. Carotid D. Femoral

138. The normal PH of blood is :
A. 6.3- 6.8 B. 6.55-7.55
C. 7.35-7.45 D. 7.55-7.65

139. Which one of the following solution is not indicated for bladder irrigation?
A. Sodium Bicarbonate
B. Potassium permanganate
C. Sodium nitrate
D. Boric acid

140. Which of the following intravenous solutions is hypotonic?
A. Normal Saline
B. 0.45% saline
C. Ringer's lactate
D. 5% Dextrose in normal saline

141. Nosocomial infection is the infection;
A. Acquired from the hospital
B. Acquired from outside the hospital
C. Acquired from the diseased person
D. Acquired from the relatives

142. Decreased level of potassium in blood is known as:
A. Hyperkalemia B. Hypokalemia
C. Hypernatrmia D. Hpocalcemia

143. Which one of the following is not a manual mobilization technique used while performing chest physiotherapy?
A. Coughing B. Clapping
C. Percussion D. Vibration

144. Which of the following size of the rectal tube is indicated for bowel wash for an adult patient?
A. 22-30 Fr B. 12-18 Fr
C. 20-24 Fr D. 18-24 Fr

145. Which one of the following route is not indicated for administering analgesic medicine
A. Intra venous B. Intra muscular
C. Epidural D. Intra abdominal

146. A patient has orders to receive 1 L (one litter) of 5% dextrose to be infused over 8 hours. How many ml to be infused per hour?
A. 80 ml B. 100 ml
C. 125 ml D. 150 ml

147. A patient has order to receive 50 ml of an antibiotic to be infused over 1 (one) hour. The tubing drip factor of 60. How many drops/minute should be set?
A. 66 B. 17 C. 50 D. 100

148. Which of the following is an indication of mild shock?
A. Blood Pressure : 88/50 mm Hg
B. Pulse: 110/minute
C. Lethargy
D. Urine output 18 ml/hr

149. The nurse is admitting a trauma patient to the emergency department. Which of the following should be her priority intervention?
A Circulation
B. Breathing
C. Maintaining open airway
D. Disability

150. While providing care, the nurse understands that, the last sense to leave in a terminally ill patient is ?
A. Taste B. Smell
C. Touch D. Hearing

151. Which of the following positions is recommended for a patient with a nasal bleeding?
A. Lying down with feet elevated
B. Sitting up with neck extended
C. Lying down with a small pillow under the head
D. Sitting up with head slightly leaning forward

152. Which the following type of bandaging is used for supporting and immobilizing elbow, ankle and knee
A. Circular B. Figure of eight
C. Spiral reverse D. Spiral

153. A strip of material used mainly to support and immobilize a part of the body is called as
A. Bandage B. Sling
C. Restrain D. Plaster

154. Which of the following is used as antiseptic:
A. Baking soda B. Aspirin
C. Dettol D. Rentidine

155. Which of the following type of fluid is considered as non-purulent
A. Cerebro-spinal fluid CSF)
B. Pericardial fluid
C. Ascites fluid
D. All of the above

156. Temperature regulating centre of the body is situated in the following part of the brain
A. Cerebellum
B. Medulla Oblongata
C. Hypothalamus
D. Thalamus

157. Which is the angle of insertion for intramuscular injection
A. 45 Degree B. 90 Degree
C. 75 Degree D. 95 Degree

158. To facilitate breathing of the patient following position may be given
A. Fowler's position
B. Recumbent position
C. Raising foot end
D. Supine Position

159. To measure rectal temperature in children the thermometer is inserted in anus up tocPpks
A. 1 to 1.5 Inch B. 1.5 to 2.0 inch
C. 2.0 to 2.5 inch D. 0.5 to 1.0 inch

160. An individual whose blood group is "B" can donate blood to a person whose blood group is
A. 'A' and 'B' B. 'A' and 'AB'
C. 'B' and 'AB' D. 'A' and 'O'

161. If a child develops cyanosis early during a tonic clonic seizures, it is most appropriate for the nurse to
A. Insert an airway
B. Administration of oxygen
C. Use a Padded tongue blade
D. Observe without intervening

162. Restraints are used as
A. Injury devices
B. Holistic devices
C. Relaxation devices
D. Protective devices

163. MRI stands for an imaging equipment
A. Magnetic Red Imaging
B. Modern Radio Imaging
C. Manual Routine Imaging
D. Magnetic Resonance Imaging

164. As soon as the patient enters the post anesthesia care unit, first priority assessment by the nurse
A. Urinary output
B. ECG Monitoring
C. Level of consciousness
D. Airway Patency and respiratory status

165. Intramuscular injections can be injected in all of the following muscles, except
A. Triceps B. Deltoid
C. Vastus lateralis D. Gluteal

166. Tidal Volume in a normal adult is about
A. 50 ml B. 500 ml
C. 1500 ml D. 2500 ml

167. Observation is the method of
A. Data collection B. Evaluation
C. Planning D. Assessment

168. Which among the following is not one of the major methods of data collection
A. Observation B. Questionnaires
C. Interviews D. Checklists

169. Patient centered nurse will use
A. Empathy B. Desensitization
C. Ego State D. Racket System

170. Drugs that cause expulsion of gas from the intestinal track
A. Astringent B. Carminatives
C. Cathartics D. Emetics

171. Post-operative position following cleft palate repair is:
A. Supine B. Prone
C. In an infant seat D. On the side

172. The one difference between a leader and a manager is that the manager does not have
A. Formal authority B. Subordinates
C. Followers D. Responsibility

173. A team member who does not want to contribute for fear of making a mistake is a
A. Pleaser B. Criticiser
C. Passive members D. Controller

174. To avoid pulling the urinary catheter nurse should tape the catheter on patient's
A. Upper thigh B. Lower thigh
C. Hind leg D. Foot

175. Cross infection occurs usually in
A. Community B. Home
C. Hospital D. Schools

176. Platelets are stored at
A. 40 to 50° C B. 30° C
C. 4° C D. 22-24° C

177. Fresh frozen plasma contains
A. Plasma proteins and clotting factor
B. RBCs
C. Platelets
D. None of the above

178. The amount of blood that is ejected from the heart in one contraction is called the
A. Cardiac output B. Stroke volume
C. Preload D. After load

179. For a patient who is on contact precaution instructions, to give a bed bath, what would nurse instruct to use to a nursing assistant
A. Gown and goggles
B. Gown and gloves
C. Gloves and shoe protectors
D. Gloves and goggles

180. Which of the following positions, the patient is placed for giving epidural regional block
A. Lithotomy B. Supine
C. Prone D. Lateral

181. The patient with CHF is placed in a high Fowler's position .What is the rationale for placing the patient in this position?
A. To increase the volume of blood returning to heart
B. To increase cardiac output and stroke volume
C. To reduce the volume of blood returning to heart
D. To reduce ankle edema and prevent dysrhythmias

182. Which nursing intervention is appropriate for a client with skeletal traction?
A. Prone positioning
B. Intermittent weights
C. Pin care
D. 5 pound weight

183. An individual whose blood type is B may in emergency donate blood to a person whose blood type is?
A. B or A B. AB or A
C. A or O D. AB or B

184. Which of the following medication is useful for reducing raised intracranial pressure?
A. I V mannitol B. I V phenytoin
C. I V diazepam D. I V nitroglycerine

185. An important aspect of nurse-patient relationship is:
A. Therapeutic B. Personal
C. Social D. Casual

186. Following are the strategies to promote effective human relations, except
A. Individualized goals
B. Common organizational goals
C. Group cohesiveness
D. Sense of oneness

187. Self understanding is facilitated by the study of:
A. Newman's window B. Kothari window
C. Johari window D. Bohari window

188. A ward in charge starts establishing ' Best Nurse' award on a monthly basis. She is appreciating the phenomenon of :
A. Motivation B. Persuasion
C. Communication D. Information

189. Why nurse should keep unit ready for admission:
A. Nurse will be ready to receive the patient
B. Patient feel expected and welcome
C. Patient feel at home and ease
D. Nurse will be ready for treatment

190. Why humidification is important when patient is on oxygen therapy:
A. To prevent drying of nasal mucosa
B. To prevent drying of mouth
C. To help patient to breath
D. To help patient to be at ease

191. Objective to maintain body mechanics by a nurses is to:
A. Maintain posture
B. Have good muscle strength
C. Avoid strain and fatigue
D. Make less mistakes

192. If patient is on IV it is important for the nurse to check the tubing for knots and clots so that:
A. There is no swelling
B. No pain at site
C. Patient is not uncomfortable
D. Fluid flow at proper rate

193. Saline water is used to inflate the catheter balloon because:
A. Saline crystallizes and result in incomplete deflation of balloon
B. Saline crystallizes and result in deflation of balloon
C. If leakage occur it does not irritate the skin
D. If helps in optimal drainage

194. When patient is given fowlers position the head of the bed is elevated to:
A. 20 to 30 degree B. 30 to 40 degree
C. 45 to 60 degree D. 65 to 90 degree

195. In which of the following stage of pressure ulcer nurse will observe there is partial thickness loss of dermis with open ulcer with wound without slough:

A. First B. Second
C. Third D. Fourth

196. Which description best suits serous drainage from a wound:

A. Free bleeding
B. Thick and yellow
C. Brown and foul smelling
D. Clear watery plasma

197. Nosotracheal suctioning is contraindicated in case patient is having:

A. Laryngeal oedema and spasm
B. Hypoxia
C. Dysrthmias
D. Increase ICP

198. Patient with appendicitis complains of pain, nurse can reduce pain by:

A. Giving analgesics
B. Applying ice bag
C. Giving rest and medicine
D. Giving position and comfort

199. To avoid the infection during I/V infusion the nurse should:

A. Change I/V site and assessment
B. Cover the needle site and check vitals
C. Check and cover needle site and change I/V bottle 24 hourly
D. Assessment of site and check vitals

200. In case child have I/V canula, nurse should give heparin lock as it will help in:

A. Intermittent administration of I/V medication
B. Continuous flow of I/V fluids
C. To keep the site under restrain to use for medication
D. To assess the site before giving I/V

201. Features of ' Kussmaul ' respiration are

A. Respirations ceases for more than 20 seconds
B. Regular but abnormally slow respiration
C. Laboured respiration with increased rate
D. Abnormally deep, regular with increased respiration

202. Delayed transfusion related complication is

A. Circulatory overload B. Septicemia
C. Iron overload D. Hypocalcemia

203. Material required for applying pressure at the I/V site is

A. Alcohol swab B. Betadine swab
C. Sterile swab D. Adhesive bandage

204. Donation of patient's own blood prior to his scheduled surgery is

A. Autologous B. Homologous
C. Monologous D. Hetrologous

205. Effect of platelet transfusion is checked by

A. Increased hematocrit level
B. Increased hemoglobin level
C. Reduced oozing of blood from puncture site
D. Reduced body temperature

206. Maneuver used to relieve the upper airway obstruction is

A. Valsalva B. Heimlich
C. Leopord D. Military

207. The signs of pulmonary embolism are all EXCEPT

A. Dyspnoea
B. Rise in blood pressure
C. Cynosis
D. Tachycardia

208. Principles related to body mechanics are-

A. Bernoulli B. Archimedes
C. Ergonomics D. Newton

209. Position used to promote emptying of gut is

A. Side line
B. Prone
C. Lithotomy
D. Reverse Trendelenburg

210. Head end of a hemorrhagic stroke patient is kept

A. Straight B. Lowered to 30º
C. Elevated to 30º D. Lateral

211. Chest tube drainage helps in relieving the symptoms of patient with pneumothorax by maintaining

A. Negative pressure in pleural cavity
B. Positive pressure in pleural cavity
C. Zero pressure in pleural cavity
D. Square positive pressure in pleural cavity

212. Which of the postoperative instruction following tonsillectomy is incorrect

A. Monitor for bleeding
B. Suction every 2 hourly
C. Give clear fluid when patient is awake
D. Give no milk products

213. A client drank 217 oz of orange juice, 6 oz of tea and 8 oz of milk. The calculated intake will be:

A. 515 ml. B. 585 ml.
C. 625 ml. D. 645 ml.

214. The endotracheal tube is put into the:

A. Oesophagus B. Stomach
C. Trachea D. Nasal cavity

215. To avoid an error while measuring blood pressure, the nurse should:
A. Use a narrow cuff
B. Stand close to the manometer
C. Elevate the client's
D. Read at eye level

216. In case of ventricular fibrillation, a nurse must prepare for the first step of treatment:
A. Intravenous infusion
B. Continuous cardiac monitoring
C. Oxygen administration
D. Cardiopulmonary resuscitation and defibrillation

217. When it is discovered that the patient has no carotid pulse or respirations, the nurse:
A. Clears the airway
B. Gives four full lung inflations
C. Compresses lower sternum 15 times
D. Checks for radial pulse

218. Neonates exposed to oxygen for a longer period may suffer from:
A. Glaucoma
B. Retrolental fibroplasias
C. Eye infection
D. None of the above

219. What is the nurse's responsibility in an unusual situation when she administers wrong medicine orally:
A. Keep it secret
B. Inform the sister in charge next day
C. Ask the patient to vomit it out immediately and inform the doctor
D. Write it in the report book

220. Sign and symptoms of cardiogenic shock:
A. Oliguria
B. Bradycardia
C. Elevated blood pressure
D. Fever

221. A nurse assess the patients respiratory status. Which of the following symptoms be an early indicator of hypoxia in an unconscious patient:
A. Cyanosis
B. Decreased respiration
C. Restlessness
D. Hypotension

222. The nurse evaluates the adequacy of the neonates oxygen by monitoring:
A. Cyanosis of hands and feet
B. Pulse rate continuously
C. Arterial blood gas levels
D. The percentage of oxygen received

223. Catgut is made from intestine of:
A. Domestic cat B. Wild cat
C. Sheep D. Horse

224. Fumigation with formalin vapor is commonly used to sterilize and disinfect:
A. Operation room B. Scrubbing room
C. Nursing room D. Sterilization room

225. An autoclave is used for:
A. Dry heat sterilization
B. Moist heat sterilization
C. Chemical sterilization
D. Gaseous sterilization

226. Which of following suture materials can be autoclaved for sterilization:
A. Silk & Linen
B. Catgut & Polyglactin
C. PDS & Polyster
D. Polyglycolic acid & Collagen

227. For an operation OT nurse should prepare:
A. Dressing trolley B. Emergency trolley
C. Mayo trolley D. Washing trolley

228. Lateral position of extension is used for operations of:
A. Kidney B. Gall bladder
C. Appendix D. Ovary

229. Lithotomy position is used for operations on:
A. Vagina B. Perineum
C. Anal canal D. All of these

230. Knee elbow position is used for:
A. Lumbar laminectomy
B. Hamerroidectomy
C. Hysterectomy
D. Cholecystectomy

231. Proctoscope is used to see:
A. Anal canal B. Sigmoid colon
C. Vagina D. Oral cavity

232. Lead rubber aprons are used in OT when following equipment is used:
A. Electric Cautery B. Ventilator
C. Image intensifier D. Pulse oxymeter

233. Which forceps are non traumatic
A. Allis' forceps
B. Kocher's forceps
C. Tooth thumb forceps
D. Babcock's forceps

234. Endotracheal intubation is used in:
A. General anesthesia B. Spinal anesthesia
C. Regional anesthesia D. Local anesthesia

235. Tuohy's needle is used for:
A. Spinal anesthesia
B. Epidural anesthesia
C. Local anesthesia
D. Nerve block

276. Who developed the first theory of nursing
A. Hammurabi B. Alexander
C. Fabiola D. Nightingale

277. A nurse administers an intravenous solution of 0.45 sodium chloride .With respect to human blood cells, to which category of fluids does this solution belong
A. Isotonic B. Isomeric
C. Hypotonic D. Hypertonic

278. Clay colored stools indicate
A. Upper GI bleeding
B. Impending constipation
C. An effect of medication
D. Bile obstruction AND Jaundice

279. Which of the following is the principal mode of heat exchange in an infant incubator
A. Radiation B. Evaporation
C. Convection D. Conduction

280. The blood group that contains no antibodies
A. A B. B C. O D. AB

281. Who decreased the mortality by improving sanitation in the battlefields, resulting in a decrease in illness and disease
A. Florence Nightingale
B. Clara Barton
C. Dorthea Dix
D. Lillian Wald

282. How will you position a patient prior to abdominal examination
A. Supine with knees flexed
B. Prone
C. Lying on back
D. Sim's

283. Disposal of expired and cytotoxic drugs is by
A. Separate landfill disposal
B. Municipal waste
C. Autoclaving
D. Chemical treatment

284. Which of the following burns the waste at very high temperatures and thus reduces its volume
A. Incinerator B. Autoclave
C. Hot air oven D. All of the above

285. Dose that can be given by IM route
A. 2 ml B. 3 ml
C. 4 ml D. 6 ml

286. During Adult CPR, Chest should be compressed in a minute
A. 30 times B. 60 times
C. 72 times D. 100 times

287. The most reliable method of taking pulse is
A. Radial B. Apical
C. Cephalic D. Femoral

288. The action phase of nursing process is
A. Assessment B. Diagnosis
C Implementing D. Evaluating

289. Complete Name of CSSD
A. Central Supper Sterile Department
B. Central Storage Supply Department
C. Central Sterile Supply Department
D. Central Supply Storage Department

290. The choice of IV fluid in burn patient is
A. N.S. B. R.L.
C. D.N.S. D. Mannitol

291. Which is not an Isotonic Solution
A. 0.9 % NS
B. Ringer Lactate
C. Dextrose 5%
D. DNS (5% dextrose with 0.9% NS)

292. Which of these is not a investigation for Dysphagia
A. Barium Swallow B. Endoscopy
C. Manometry D. Colonoscopy

293. Asepsis means Asepsis
A. Freedom from infection
B. Freedom from sterility
C. Freedom form environmental pollution
D. Freedom from anxiety

294. The lumber puncture is contraindicated in Lumber Puncture
A. Increased ICP
B. Mental Retardation
C. Cerebral Palsy
D. Bacteremia

295. A two-year-child with tetralogy of fallot suddenly falls on floor. The best Nursing actions is:
A. Put the child in the bed immediately
B. Allow the child on the sitting position
C. Place the child on the chair
D. Call physician immediately

296. A 3-year-old child had Cardiac Catherization. The Nurse should include the following in care Plan:
A. Monitoring for responses to general anaes-thesia
B. Bed rest for 24 hours
C. NPO for 12 hours
D. Observe for severe pain and medicate as needed

297. A patient had chemical burn, the best initial action is:
A. Roll the patient in the blanket
B. Flush the area with copious amount of water or normal saline
C. If chemical is an acid neutralize with a base
D. Move the patient away from the chemical

298. When administering blood to a patient, it is important to:
A. Administer each unit within a 6-hour period
B. Use a volume control infusion pump to ad-minister the blood
C. Run the blood at a slower rate during the first 5 to 10 minutes
D. Draw blood samples from the patient immediately after each unit is transfused

299. The colour of the urine of a patient with suspected choecystitis will most likely be:
A. Pale-yellow B. Greenish brown
C. Red D. Yellow-orange

300. The first aid measure at the scene of an accident, to minimize the immediate life-threatening systemic complication of injury to the long bones of the injured person is by:
A. Handling and transporting gently
B. Elevating the affected limb
C. Maintaining functional aligment
D. Encouraging deep breathing and coughing

301. A patient is to receive an intravenous infusion containing potassium chloride. When starting this I.V. infusion, the nurse should select:
A. The anticubital space in the client's arm
B. A vein in the back of the client's dominant arm
C. The largest possible vein in the client's arm
D. A vein in the back of the client's non-domi-nant arm

302. A patient has been in coma for 2 months. The nurse understands that to prevent the effects of shearing force, the head of the bed should be at an angle of:
A. 30° B. 45° C. 60° D. 90°

303. Reverse cold chain is used for:
A. Carrying stool samples of polio patients from Primary Health Centre(PHC)to the laboratory
B. Transporting outdated vaccine from the PHC to the district hospital
C. Transporting the vaccine to the laboratory to check its potency
D. Transporting the vaccine from camps to sub-centres

304. HIV contaminated waste products can be decontaminated by the following agents except:
A. Sodium hypochlorite
B. Formaldehyde
C. Glutaraldehyde
D. Methanol

305. The results of which diagnostic test that confirm the diagnosis of tuberculosis:
A. Bronchoscopy B. Sputum culture
C. Tuberculin test D. Saline test

306. If temperature of an object is 140 degree Fahrenheit, then its temperature in centigrade is:
A. 105 degree centigrade
B. 32 degree centigrade
C. 140 degree centigrade
D. 60 degree centigrade

307. ....is the method of transfer of heat by circulating air or liquid
A. Evaporation B. Radiation
C. Conduction D. Convection

308. The apex heart beat can be best heard at
A. 3rd intercostals space
B. 7th intercostals space
C. 5th intercostals space
D. Centre of the sternum

309. All of the following all components of Glasgow coma scale except
A. Eye opening B. Verbal response
C. Motor response D. pain status

310. It is an increase in depth of respiration
A. Apnoea B. Hyperpnoea
C. Dyspnoea D. Orthopnoea

311. Infection which occur as a result of diagnostic procedure or treatment is called
A. Iatrogenic infection
B. Cross infection
C. Contagious disease
D. Communicable disease

312. .... Is the separation and description of previously joined wound edges.
A. Evisceration B. Contracture
C. Dehiscence D. Scarring

313. What is the primary reason for the gradual change of position of the patient after surgery?
A. To prevent muscle injury
B. To prevent sudden drop of BP
C. To prevent respiratory distress
D. None of the above

314. To correctly palpate the patient's skin for temperature determination, a nurse will use the:
A. Fingertips of hands
B. Dorsal surface of hands
C. Palmer surface of hands
D. Base of hands

315. The correct position to palpate the apical pulse is at the:
A. Left midclavicular line at the level of second intercostals space
B. Line axillary line at the level of fifth intercostals space
C. Left midclavicular line at the level of fifth intercostals space
D. Left midclavicular line at the level of seventh intercostals space

316. Rapid administration of blood containing citrate causes:
A. Hypocalcaemia B. Hypercelcemia
C. Hypokalaemia D. Hyperkalemia

317. Increased respiratory rate is called:
A. Tachycardia C. Tachypnea
B. Bradycardia D. Bradypnea

318. Oxygen saturation is measured by:
A. Manometer B. Pulse transducer
C. Pulse oximeter D. Thermometer

319. The position used to assess the extension of hip joint is:
A. Prone B. Supine
C. Sitting D. Dorsal recumbent

320. Difference between diastolic and systolic pressure is:
A. Pulse pressure B. Cardiac output
C. Blood pressure D. Pulse deficit

321. Ethical dilemmas can be best solved by:
A. Homecare nurse
B. Code of ethics for nurses
C. Relationship
D. Ethical principle

322. The immediate nursing action where patient has cardiac arrest:
A. Begin mouth-to-mouth respiration
B. Put him on ventilation
C. O_2 not to be given
D. Begin O_2 therapy

323. Increased sweating leads to:
A. Hypervolaemia B. Oedema
C. Hyponatramia D. Hypernatremia

324. When providing a patients hydration status, a nurse would initiate:
A. Provide ice clips
B. Provision of variety of fluids
C. Maintain inflow and outflow chart
D. Give fluid on patients demand

325. Which of the instructions are most appropriate to be provided by the nurse to a patient undergone cataract surgery:
A. Elevate the head of the bed while sleeping
B. Take a stool softener daily at right
C. Keep the room environment cool and dry
D. Avoid climbing stairs

326. The nurse evaluates the adequacy of the neonates oxygen by monitoring:
A. Pulse rate continuously
B. Arterial blood gas levels
C. Cyanosis of hands and feet
D. The percentage of oxygen received

327. The patient anxiety during the preoperative period would decrease by which of the following nursing actions:
A. Reassuring the patient that the surgical staff are competent professional
B. Encouraging sleep
C. Explaining all procedures thoroughly
D. Spending time listening to the patient and answering questions

328. The drip that is running satisfactorily may stop because:
A. Blood dotted in the Cannula
B. The vein is obstructed by too tight a bandage
C. The head of pressure is too low
D. None of the above

329. A jerky pulse with full expansion and sudden collapse is:
A. Corrigan's pulse B. Collapsing pulse
C. Bounding pulse D. Running pulse

330. Application of cool clothes to the skin decreases the body temperature through:
A. Evaporation B. Radiation
C. Conduction D. Convection

331. A positive Benedict's test is not given by:
A. Maltose B. Sucrose
C. Lactose D. Glucose

332. The following are absorbable sutures, except:
A. Nylon B. Monocryl
C. Catgut D. Vicryl

333. Cessation of breathing for a short period is:
A. Apnoea B. Bradypnea
C. Orthopnoea D. Dyspnea

334. Blood pressure is measured by:
A. Sphygmomanometer B. Nanometre
C. Barometer D. Calorimeter

335. To assess the patients posterior tibial pulse a nurse would palpitate:
A. Below the medial malleolus
B. Below the lateral malleolus
C. Behind the knee
D. Over the medial malleolus

336. The nurse is assessing the colostomy of a patient who has had an abdominal perineal resection for a bowel tumour. Which of the following assessment indicate that the colostomy is beginning to function?
A. Absent bowel sounds
B. The passage of flatus
C. The patient ability to tolerate foods
D. Bloody drainage from the colostomy

337. Cyanosis is caused in case of:
A. Lack of water B. Lack of oxygen
C. Lack of glucose D. Lack of blood

338. To maintain normal breathing pattern, which position is beneficial:
A. Sim's position
B. Knee-chest position
C. Fowler's position
D. Dorsal position

339. Intraosseous injection is given in:
A. Vein B. Bone marrow
C. Spinal cavity D. Muscles

340. Stages of malaria fever includes all except:
A. Cold stage B. Hot stage
C. Fever state D. Sweating stage

341. What is the meaning of Census Report in the hospital?
A. Number of population around hospital
B. Number of employees
C. Number of babies born in hospital
D. Number of patients at midnight in the hospital

342. The importance of research in nursing is to provide:
A. Quality nursing care
B. Comprehensive nursing care
C. Evidence based nursing care
D. Individualized nursing care

343. A nursing intervention in thrombophlebitis would be contraindicated:
A. Maintaining strick bedrest
B. Turning the patient from side to side
C. Applying warm packs to the affected leg
D. Massaging the affected leg

344. The most common accurate way to determine the need for oxygen in a patient with CoPD is by:
A. Observing the skin colour
B. Noting changes in the vital signs
C. Asking how the patient feels
D. Arterial Blood gas analysis

345. A patient with acute pancreatitis has NG tube for low intermittent suction to prevent:
A. Chronic distortion
B. Gastric reflux
C. Pancreatic stimulation
D. Peristalsis

346. Cystitis is the inflammation of:
A. Gallbladder B. Urinary bladder
C. Cyst D. Liver

347. An informed consent is obtained from a preoperative patient to prevent:
A. Complications B. Infection
C. Any fall D. Legal implications

348. A patient with cardiovascular disorder had a diminished gag reflex, the nurse will:
A. Instill artificial tears
B. Maintain side lying position
C. Offer small sips of dear fluids
D. Test cranial nerves III, IV, VI

349. The nurse practitioner's role may be categorized in all of the following except:
A. Traditional B. Extended
C. Expanded D. Evaluative

350. Which protective items a nurse require to provide colostomy care to the patient with nosocomial infection?
A. Gloves and goggles
B. Gloves and a gown
C. Gloves, gown and shoes protector
D. Gloves, gown and goggles

351. Infusion of 1000 ml of normal saline over 12 hours requires how many drops per minute when the drop factor is 15 drops/minute?
A. 15 drops/minute B. 17 drops/minute
C. 21 drops/minute D. 23 drops/minute

352. 7.5 mg of morphine sulphate I/M start from an ampule of 10 mg is to be administered. How many ml of this drug is to be administered in correct dose?
A. 0.5ml B. 0.75ml
C. 0.85ml D. 1.5ml

353. Eye padding is applied on unconscious patients to prevent:
A. Dryness of eyes B. Blinking of eyes
C. Corneal ulcer D. Eye movement

354. While pouring the liquid medicine from a bottle into an ounce, glass, the lablel of the bottle is held:
A. Against the hand 1 B. Right side
C. Leftside D. Any side

355. Insulin is injected into:
A. Intradermal B. Subcutaneous
C. Intrathecal D. Intramuscular

356. Before administering the medicine to a patient nurse checks the prescription:
A. Two times B. Three times
C. One time D. Four times

357. Nursing intervention designed to decrease the risk of infection in a patient with an indwelling catheter include:
A. Cleanse area around meatus
B. Empty catheter drainage bag at least daily
C. Change catheleter tubing and bag every 48 hours
D. Maintain fluid intake of 1200-1500 ml everyday

358. While lifting a patient, a nurse bends on her
A. Hips and back \ B. Hips and knees
C. Back and knees D. Back only

359. To give Fowler's position to a patient, the head end of the bed is raised to:
A. 35° angle B. 15° angle
C. 60° angle D. 45° angle

360. Wound dressing is done by using:
A. Septic technique
B. Medical asepsis
C. Surgical asepsis
D. Medical and surgical asepsis

361. Urine sample for culture is collected from:
A. First urine B. Last urine
C. Midstream urine D. First and last urine

362. Tonicity of Ringer Lactate solution is:
A. Isotonic B. Normotonic
C. Hypotonic D. Hypertonic

363. A nursing diagnosis represents the:
A. Assessment of client data
B. Proposed plan of care
C. Client's health problems
D. Actual nursing intervention

364. To instill ear drops to a small child, pull the pinna:
A. Straight back B. Down and back
C. Forward D. Up and back

365. Nurse-patient relationship is
A. Human to human relation
B. Subordinate superior relation
C. Employer employee relation
D. Superior subordinate relation

366. Administration of a medicine just below the skin is called:
A. Intravenous B. Subcutaneous
C. Intramuscular D. Intradermal

367. A patient is to have an enema. The rectal tube show be inserted:
A. 2 inches B. 6 inches
C. 8 inches D. 4 inches

368. The simplest method of prevent cross infection is:
A. Disinfection B. Sterilization
C. Fumigation D. Handwashing

369. Pap smear examination is done to diagnose:
A. Ca breast B. Ca bladder
C. Ca cervix D. Ca rectum

370. A patient has an IV infusion. If the IV infusion infiltrates, the nurse should first:
A. Discontinue the infusion
B. Elevate the IV site
C. Flush the tube
D. Apply warm, moist soaks

371. Which of the following is a waterborne disease?
A. Filariasis B. Influenza
C. Poliomyelitis D. Dengue fever

372. The best position to give enema is:
A. Prone B. Supine
C. Left lateral D. Right lateral

373. The best position to give enema is:
A. Prone B. Sims lateral
C. Left lateral D. Right lateral

374. The most preferred intramuscular injection site for children is:
A. Deltoid B. Dorsogluteal
C. Vastus lateralis D. Ventrogluteal

375. Which of the following is related to vision testing?
A. Litmus paper B. Tuning fork
C. Snellen's chart D. Acetic acid

376. A 5% dedtrose salien 1000 mL is ordered for a patient to run in 8 hours. A drip set with a drop factor of 15 per mL is used. What is the flow rate to be set?
A. 21 drops/min B. 31 drops/min
C. 11 drops/min D. 41 drops/min

377. The position recommended for a patient with epistaxis is:
A. Supine
B. Prone
C. Sitting with head turning backward
D. Sitting with head turning forward

378. While receiving blood transfusion, the patient develops chills and headache. The nurse's first action is to:
A. Slow the blood flow
B. Lightly cover the patient
C. Notify the physician
D. Stop the transfusion immediately

379. The safest position for a woman in labor with prolapsed cord is:
A. Lithotomy B. Trendelenburg
C. Supine D. Fowler's

380. Nasogastric tube feeding is to be given slowly to reduce the hazard of:
A. Distention B. Indigestion
C. Flatulence D. Regurgitation

381. Which of the following is an isotonic solution?
A. 10% dextrose B. 5% dextrose
C. Normal saline D. 5% dextrose

382. Infection from urinary catheters can be best prevented by:
A. Cleansing around the meatus periodically
B. Encouraging adequate fluid intake
C. Changing position frequently
D. Irrigating the catheter daily

383. An agent that inhibit the growth of bacteria is:
A. Carrier B. Vaccine
C. Bacteriostat D. Bactericide

384. Total score of Glasgow coma scale is:
A. 5 B. 15
C. 10 D. 20

385. The most important aspect of hand washing is
A. Time B. Water
C. Friction D. Soap

386. The most appropriate time to collect sputum specimen from a patient is:
A. On awakening B. Before meals
C. After meals D. After activity

387. When a person is unconscious, the person is unable to:
A. Control elimination
B. Move spontaneously
C. React to painful stimuli
D. None of them

388. Position to be given to a patient recovering from general anesthesia is:
A. Side lying position
B. Supine position
C. Fowler's position
D. Trendelenburg position

389. The position of an unconscious patient should be changed at least every
A. 2 hours B. 4 hours
C. 6 hours D. 8 hours

390. Site of BCG vaccination is:
A. Outer aspect of upper Left thigh
B. Left deltoid or Left outer aspect of upper arm
C. Outer aspect of upper Right thigh
D. Right deltoid or Right outer aspect of upper arm

391. Airborne precautions for a patient with pulmonary tuberculosis has to be taken until:
A. Tuberculin test is negative
B. No tubercle bacilli in the sputum
C. The patient no longer has the disease
D. Patient's temperature has returned to normal

392. Route of a administration of measles vaccine is:
A. Intramuscular B. Oral
C. Intradermal D. Subcutaneous

393. Before doing paracentesis for a patient with ascites, instruct the patient to:
A. Eat food low in fat
B. Remain NPO for 24 hours
C. Empty the bladder
D. Assume supine position

394. The percentage of fluid in the infant's body is:
A. 20% B. 40% C. 60% D. 80%

395. The most important electrolyte of intracellular fluid is:
A. Sodium B. Potassium
C. Chloride D. Calcium

396. The position in which a patient with dyspnea should be placed is:
A. Sims B. Orthopneic
C. Supine D. Prone

397. The temperature of water for a tepid sponge bath should be approximately:
A. 92°to94°F B. 95°to97°F
C. 98° to 100°F D. 101° to 103°F

398. A person's body temperature of 98.6 F is converted is
A. 36.5°C B. 37.0°C
C. 37.7°C D. 38.2°C

399. Which of the following is an independent nursing function?
A. Administration of oral medicine
B. Administration of injection
C. Giving blood transfusion
D. Health education

400. Which of the following destroys HIV?
A. Dettol
B. Savlon
C. Sodium hypochlorite
D. Lysol

401. The most commonly used site of bone morrow-aspiration in child is:
A. Lateral aspect of the wrist
B. Middle of the chest
C. Distal end of the thigh
D. Posterior iliac crest

402. The best and safest method of sterilization is:
A. Immersion in chemical germicide
B. Boiling for 30 minutes
C. Flaming
D. Autoclaving

403. A patient with COPD should have oxygen administered by nasal canula at the rate of:
A. 10 L/minute B. 1-2 L/minute
C. 5 L/minute D. 7.5L/minute

404. Temperature of solution used for simple evacuant enema for adult is:
A. 95-100 °F B. 105-100 °F
C. 90-95 °F D. 85-90 °F

405. An increase in rate and depth of respiration alternating with a period of apnea is:
A. Stridor
B. Polypnea
C. Cheyne-Stoke's respiration
D. Wheezing

406. AN Agent inhibits growth of microorganism?
A. Antiseptic B. Bacteristatic
C. Bactericide D. Disinfectant

407. In hyperpyrexia the temperature will be:
A. Above 105 °F
B. Between 103-105 °F
C. Between 101-103°F
D. Above 100 up to 101 °F

408. The instrument used for measuring intraocular pressure is:
A. Ophthalmoscope B. Gonipscope
C. Tonometer D. Keratometer

409. Painful micturition is referred to as:
A. Dysuria B. Enaresis
C. Encopresis D. Dyspepsia

410. When assessing for signs of blood transfusion reaction the nurse has to assess for which of the following:
A. Warm skin B. Diaphoresis
C. Polyuria D. Hypertension

411. Common cause of bedsore is:
A. Immobility
B. Nasogastric tube feeding
C. Fracture forearm
D. Vomiting

412. The most important person in a hospital:
A. Physician
B. Nursing superintendent
C. Patient
D. PRO

413. Maintaining continuous bladder drainage in the dependent position prevent:
A. Urinary reflux
B. Urinary retention
C. Urinary incontinence
D. Urinary retention with over

414. Stiffening of the body after death is:
A. Keloid B. Contracture
C. Postmortem D. Rigor mortis

415. Stat dose of medication is administered:
A. Once a day B. At bedtime
C. At once D. If needed

416. Most effective method of destroying microorganism is:
A. Dry heat B. Boiling
C. Cold sterilization D. Autoclave

417. International Nurse's day celebrated is on:
A. 5th September B. 7th April
C. 1st December D. 12th May

418. Which vein should be used first when initiating IV therapy:
A. Jugular vein
B. Basilic vein
C. Brachiocephalic vein
D. Auxiliary vein

419. Which the of pain maybe accompanied changes in vital signs?
A. Acute pain B. Chronic pain
C. Referred pain D. Cancer pain

420. A small quantity of a qualifies the whole is?
A. Blood B. Specimen
C. Substance D. Food

421. Mackintosh should never be folded, because:
A. Difficult to store
B. Chance of wet surface
C. Tearing occurs
D. Becomes rough

422. Respiration is increased soon after exercises because:
A. BMR increases
B. Oxygen consumption decrease
C. BMR decrease
D. Weakness increases

423. Immediately after fracture, the body part should be:
A. Raised from the body level
B. Moved towards the unaffected areas
C. Immobilized till medical aid is available
D. Lowered from the body level

424. Pulse should not be counted with thumb because:
A. It will cause pain
B. It will not be comfortable to the patient
C. It causes feeling of self pulse
D. It impedes pulse

425. Handwashing is essential before doing any procedure:
A. To avoid dust contamination
B. To prevent self-infection
C. To prevent cross infection
D. To observe economy of materials

426. Dental root abscess is the result of:
A. A neglected mouth B. Glossitis
C. Stomatitis D. Chrysalis

427. The use of documentation is:
A. To diagnose the condition
B. To communicate
C. To educate
D. All of the above

428. Decubitus ulcer is prevented by:
A. Lowered mobility
B. Improved circulation
C. Low residue food
D. Impaired circulation

429. **Domestic method of purification of water:**
A. Boiling
B. Filter control
C. Water purification plant
D. None of the above

430. **Reaction of normal urine is:**
A. Acidic B. Slightly acidic
C. Neutral D. Alkaline

431. **Match it.**

Wound drainage	Color and Consistency
A. Serous	1. Red with blood, thin
B. Sanguinous thin	2. Clear, light yellow,
C. Sero Sanguinous	3. Creamy, yellow, green,White
D. Purulent	4. Pink to light red

A.B.C.D
A. 2 1 4 3 B. 1 2 3 4
C. 4 3 2 1 D. 1 3 2 4

432. **What is level of raise during ovulation?**
A. 1°F B. 5°C
C. 3°F D. 2°C

433. **The reasons for using the parenteral route to administer Medications include**
A. Parenteral Medication lasts longer than an oral medication
B. It is the least expensive method
C. It is easier to measure an accurate dose
D. The parenteral route allows more rapid, absorption than the oral route

434. **Match the following:**

I	II
A. Facal Incontinence	1. Cramping and Hyperactive Bowel sounds
B. Fecal Impaction	2. Involuntary elimination of feces
C. Flatulence	3. Large, hard, stool in folds of rectum
D. Diarrhea	4. Accumulation of gas in CI tract

A. B. C. D.
A. 4 3 2 1 B. 3 2 4 1
C. 1 2 3 4 D. 2 3 4 1

435. **While instilling eye drops, instruct your patient to**
A. Look down and away
B. Look up and away
C. Look straight a head
D. Look up and directly at the dropper

436. **Which gait should you teach a patient who can bear weight on both legs?**
A. Three point B. Four point
C. Two point D. Five point

437. **The term 'Nurture' refers to the effect of one of the following on human development**
A. Heredity B. Environment
C. Food and Safety D. Rewards

438. **The person who harbours the pathogen without suffering from any ill effect of that is called**
A. Source B. Latent infection
C. Host D. Healthy carrier

439. **What are the responsibilities of a circulatory nurse?**
I. Verify consent
II. Ensure proper temperative, humidity, lighting and safe functioning of equipment
III. Monitory acceptic practices
IV. Responsible for ensuring the second verifica-tion of surgical procedure and site
A. I, II and III B. II, III and IV
C. I, III and IV D. All of the above

440. **The following are the complications of oxygen administration**
I. It supports combustion
II. Causes CO_2 Narcosis
III. Oxygen Toxicity
IV. Absorption Atelectasis
A. I, II and III B. II, III and IV
C. I, II and IV D. I, II, III and IV

441. **Urge incontinence, incomplete bladder emptying - Bladder/Sphincter incoordination are the features of which dys functions.**
A. Atonic Bladder
B. Hypertonic Bladder
C. Flaccid Bladder
D. Cortical Lesion

442. **Match List I with List II and select the correct answer using the codes given below the lists:**

I	II
A. Rhonchi	1. High pitched squeaking or musical sounds
B. Wheezes	2. Discontinuous, high- pitched sounds
C. Stridor	3. Snoring or ratling sounds from obstruction of larg air-ways
D. Crackles	4. Musical or crowing sound from partial obstruction Of Larynx or Trachea

	A.	B.	C.	D.
A.	3	1	4	2
B.	1	2	4	3
C.	2	4	3	1
D.	4	2	3	1

443. Arrange the stages of team growth
A. Performing, Norming, Storming and Forming
B. Forming,Storming, Norming and Performing
C. Storming,Norming, Forming and Performing
D. Norming,Forming, Performing and Storming

444. OSCE means
A. Objective Structured Clinical Examination
B. Observation Structured Clinical Examination
C. Objective Subjective Clinical Examination
D. Observation Subject Course Examination

445. Amount of solution administered for evacuant enema for adults:
A. 250-500 ml B. 500-1000 ml
C. 1000-1500 ml D. 1500-2000 ml

446. One pint is equal to:
A. 250ml` B. 500ml
C. 750ml D. 1000ml

447. What is the standard method of removal impacted cerumen from the external canal?
A. Irrigation
B. Suction
C. Instrumentation
D. Instillation of oil drops

448. The partial or total separation of wound layers is termed as
A. Evisceration B. Dehiscence
C. Pressure sore D. Infection

449. Infectious hospital waste is disposed by the process of
A. Autoclaving B. Deepburial
C. Incineration D. Shredding

450. Size of needle for intramuscular injection:
A. 18-20 gauge B. 21-23 gauge
C. 24-25 gauge D. 26-27 gauge

451. Rate of oxygen administration through nasal catheter:
A. 0.5-1 liter B. 1.0-2 liter
C. 2-4 liter D. 4-6 liter

452. The assessment of wound indicates healing is occurring when
A. The centre tissue is white
B. Bleeding has stopped
C. There is no further drainage from wound
D. Pink granulation tissue is visible

453. Massage promotes increased circulation and softening of connective tissues. It also has which effect?
A. Narrows blood wessels
B. Eases muscle spasms
C. Causes hyper ventilation
D. Widens blood vessels

454. Which of the following is the appropriate route of administration for insulin?
A. Intramuscular B. Intradermal
C. Subcutaneous D. Intravenous

455. The most suitable laxative for a patient with spastic constipation is
A. Dietary fibre B. Bisacodyl
C. Castor oil D. Phenolphthalein

456. Thrombocytopenia means
A. Decreased number of platelets
B. Increased number of platelets
C. Decreased number of leukocytes
D. Increased number of leukocytes

457. The binocular instrument providing a magnification to map the abnormal areas on the cervix is:
A. Colposcope B. Cystoscope
C. Colonoscope D. Proctoscope

458. Painful Micturition:
A. Eneuresis B. Dysuria
C. Rentention of urine D. Diarrhoea

459. Amount of solution used for evacuant enema hi adults:
A. 100-250 ml B. 250-350 ml
C. 500-1000 ml D. 1000-1500 ml

460. Drugs used to relieve pain:
A. Anti inflammatory B. Antipyretics
C. Antibiotics D. Analgesics

461. One teaspoon contains .... ml
A. 2ml B. 5ml
C. 10ml D. 15ml

462. One ml contains......... drops
A. 5 drops B. 10 drops
C. 15 drops D. 20 drops

463. How much salt must be added to one litre of water to make a solution of normal saline?
A. 2 grams B. 5 grams
C. 6 grams D. 9 grams

464. The blood group contains no antibodies:
A. A B. B
C. O D. AB

465. A healthy person can donate blood .... times a year.
A. Six or seven B. Five or six
C. Three or four D. Two or three

466. To relieve from dyspnoea position to be used is:
A. Prone position B. Supine position
C. Side lying position D. Fowler's position

467. Normal blood urea level is:
A. 40-60 mg%   B. 20-40 mg%
C. 10-20 mg%   D. 80-120 mg%

468. A method of making the victim to breath passively
A. Artificial respiration
B. Spontaneous respiration
C. Deep breathing
D. Kusmal breathing

469. Information given by the sufferer about his illness:
A. Sign   B. Symptom
C. Observation   D. Diagnosis

470. Normal respiratory rate in adults is:
A. 20 breathes per/min
B. 40 breathes per/min
C. 16 breathes per/min
D. 10 breathes per/min

471. The normal body temperature is .... °C.
A. 35 °C   B. 37°C
C. 40 °C   D. 42 °C

472. Characteristic of the blood flow due to arterial bleeding is the following except:
A. Bright red in colour
B. Spunts at each cartrachian of the heart
C. Flow is pulsatile
D. Dark red in colour

473. An agent that has power to kill Micro-organism:
A. Bacteriostat   B. Bacteriocide
C. Antiseptic   D. Bacteriostasis

474. Strength of savlon for cleaning of wounds:
A. 1:10   B. 1:100
C. 1:1000   D. 1:10000

475. Which complication of IV infusion can cause pulmonary edema or heart failure?
A. Infiltration
B. Circulatory overload
C. Infection
D. Pyrogenic reactions

476. All of the following can be used to determine a chromosome analysis of the fetus except:
A. Chrionic vilus sampling
B. Percutaneous umbilical blood sampling (PUBS)
C. Aminocentesis
D. Fetal umbilical Doppler velocimetry

477. All of the following are precautions in the care of a patient with high fever except:
A. Never leave a patient with high fever alone
B. Tepid cold sponging is not useful in patient not responding to antipyretics
C. Rigors and convulsions may occur at any time
D. Administer antipyretic drugs

478. All of the following precautions are true while recording oral temperature of a patient except-
A. Measurement of temperature should be done on a fixed time of the day
B. It is measured at least 3 min. after keeping the thermometer sublingually with lips closed
C. Not to record in a patient who have recently smoked
D. In patients on oxygen inhalation, stop the oxygenation before recording oral temperature

479. Inflammation of the tongue:
A. Glossitis   B. Gingivitis
C. Stomatitis   D. Parotitis

480. Inoculating loop is sterilized by:
A. Hot air oven   B. Flaming
C. Radiation   D. Autoclave

481. Blood drawn for complete blood count CBC.is collected in
A. EDTA vial   B. Chloride vial
C. Plain vial   D. Citrate vial

482. In case of delay in transportation of cerebrospinal fluid (CSF) sample, it should be:
A. Keptat-20°C
B. Kept in ice bucket
C. Kept at room temperature
D. Refrigerated at 4°C

483. Normally cerebrospinal fluid (CSF) sample is used:
A. At 20°C
B. Kept in ice bucket
C. At room temperature
D. At 4°C

484. In Benedict's test which is the end colour indicates absence of sugar in urine?
A. Yellow   B. Orange
C. Blue   D. Green

485. The difference between systolic and diastolic blood pressure is known as:
A. Pulse difference   B. Cardiac pressure
C. Systolic pressure   D. Pulse pressure

486. The micelles Associated colloids) are formed only above a particular temperature called:
A. Curie temperature
B. Critical temperature
C. Kraft temperature
D. Boyle temperature

487. The appropriate needle size for insulin is
A. 22G, Wz" long   B. 22G, 1" long
C. 18G, IVz" long   D. 25G, 5/8" long

488. All of the following nursing interventions are correct when using the Z-track method of injection except
A. Aspirate for blood before injection
B. Rub the site vigorously after the injection
C. Prepare the injection site with alcohol
D. Use a needle that's a least 1" long

489. Bradenscale is used for assessing the risk of
A. Decubitus ulcer
B. Urinary tract infection
C. Hypertension
D. Diabetes mellitus

490. The percentage and the flow of oxygen in a green colour venture mask is
A. 31% and 6 lit/minute
B. 60% and 15 lit/minute
C. 35% and 8 lit/minute
D. 60% and 15 lit/minute

491. Which of the following intervention can best present bed sore?
A. Use special water mattress
B. Change the position every 1 hour
C. Keep skin clean and dry
D. Massage reddened areas with lotion or oils

492. Pre-operative preparation for appendectomy include all of the following except
A. Remove the jewelries
B. Skin preparation
C. Enema Stat
D. Consent

493. Which of the following, position is given to a patient with severe breathing difficulty?
A. Supine B. Trendlenberg
C. Dorsal recumbent D. Fowlers

494. Which of the following medication order is immediately and once only administration?
A. Single order B. Prn order
C. Stat order D. Standing order

495. Which type of solution causes water to shift from cells to plasma?
A. Alkaline B. Isotonic.
C. Hypotonic D. Hypertonic

496. How much oxygen a nurse should give to a patient with chronic respiratory failure?
A. 1 liter/mt with nasal probe
B. 2 liters/mt with nasal mask
C. 10 liters/mt with nasal mask
D. 12 liters/mt with nasal probe

497. What is the usual site of intramuscular injection a nurse will choose in an adult for Z-track technique?
A. Deltoid B. Rectus Femoris
C. Ventrogluteal D. Vastus lateralis

498. Which of the following method of oxygen inhalation are used in emergency?
A. Nasal catheter B. Nasal mask
C. Nasal Cannula D. Tracheostomy

499. Thirty year old patient has an ulcer over lateral malleolus. Nurse caring for this patient understands the pain of the patient is due to
A. Edema B. Exudate
C. Infection D. Ischemia

500. Nurse has to apply erythromycin ointment to a newborn child. Which area of eye she is supposed place it?
A. On the cornea
B. Under the eyelid
C. Lower conjunctiva
D. Upper conjunc-tiva

501. Fluid overload in a patient may cause
A. Anglo edema B. Peripheral edema
C. Pulmonary edema D. Cerebral edema

502. To do percussion and postural drainage of lungs in bronchiectasis. What body position of the patient, a nurse should use?
A. Supine position
B. Prone position
C. Decubitus position
D. Semi Fowlers position

503. How a nurse will have to collect urine sample for culture from urinary collecting system?
A. With needle aspiration
B. Empty urine from bag
C. Collect from catheter
D. Disconnect bag and collect

504. Which of the following method of oxygen inhalation will be provide accurate oxygen concentration in emergency?
A. Nasal catheter B. Nasal mask
C. Nasal Cannula D. Venturi Mask

505. How much oxygen a nurse should give to a patient with COPD patient?
A. 4 liter/mt with nasal probe
B. 2 liters/mt with nasal canulla
C. 10 liters/mt with nasal mask
D. 12 liters/mt with nasal probe

506. The most appropriate time for the nurse to obtain a sputum specimen for culture is
A. Early in the morning
B. After chest physiotherapy
C. After aerosol therapy
D. After the patient eats a light breakfast

507. Nurse working in an ICU must be aware of the ratio of chest compression to ventilation in CPR procedure is
A. 12:1 B. 12:2 C. 15:1 D. 15:2

508. How long should a nurse wait after taking cold milk for recording oral temperature?
A. 5 to 10 mts B. 10 to 20 mts
C. 20 to 30 mts D. 30 to 40 mts

509. Apical pulse is assessed by placing the diaphragm of the stethoscope at the area of
A. Pulmonic area B. Aortic area
C. Tricuspid area D. Mitral area

510. Ineffectual straining at stool is known as
A. Constipation B. Tenesmus
C. Borborygnii D. Steatorrhoea

511. Which of the following is used to assess the function of brain stem?
A. Braden scale
B. Glosgow coma scale
C. Cold caloric test
D. Intracranial pressure

512. While performing tracheostomy suctioning, suction time should not be more than
A. 30 seconds B. 10 seconds
C. 20 seconds D. 45 seconds

513. Color coding for nitrous oxide cylinder is
A. Light blue
B. Black
C. Gray
D. Black with white shoulders

514. Sensitivity and reaction is tested by administering the drug
A. Subcutaneously B. Intramuscularly
C. Intradermally D. Intravenously

515. Lateral curvature of the spine is called as
A. Lordosis
B. Kyphosis
C. Scoliosis
D. Pectus excavatum

516. Which of the following is used for assessing the pain children?
A. Brief pain inventory
B. Wong-Baker faces pain rating scale
C. Visual analogue scale
D. Numerical rating scale

517. The equipment used in the examination of ear is
A. Laryngoscope B. Otoscope
C. Proctoscope D. Ophthalmoscope

518. Which of the following procedure always requires surgical asepsis?
A. Nasogastric tube insertion
B. Vaginal irrigation
C. Colostomy irrigation
D. Urinary catheterization

519. Which of the following is used to assess the level of consciousness?
A. Braden scale B. Snellen's chart
C. Glasgow coma scale D. Apgar score

520. While giving NG tube feeding, which of the following nursing actions prevents complications?
A. Plug the air vent during feeding
B. Flush with 20 mL of air
C. Advance rube 2 cm
D. Provide high Fowler's position

521. Normal serum potassium level in meq/L is
A. 5.5 to 6.5 B. 6.5 to 7.5
C. 2.5 to 3.5 D. 3.5 to 5

522. The method used for refining semiconductors known as:
A. Mond process B. Van arkel method
C. Electrolytic refining D. Zone refining

523. Which of the following is known as 'syngas'?
A. CO + C12 B. $CO + O_2$
C. $CO + H_2$ D. $CO + N_2$

524. Ortolani's test is diagnostic in:
A. Congential hip dislocation
B. Induction of labour
C. Respiratory distress
D. Congential anomalies

525. The size of the intravenous cannula used for neonates is
A. 18 B. 22 C. 24 D. 20

526. Bleeding from the nose is known as
A. Hematuria B. Epistaxis
C. Hematemesis D. Hemoptysis

527. Mode of spread of polio infection is:
A. Through vectors B. Droplet infection
C. Faeco-oral route D. Through blood

528. Vastus lateralis is a site lot
A. Intravenous injection
B. Intramuscular injection
C. Intradermal injection
D. Subcutaneous injection

529. Which of the following need to be performed before radial arterial cannulation to evaluate radial and ulnar arterial patency?
A. Capillary refill test B. Alien's test
C. Anglography D. Buerger's test

530. Acute pancreatitis is manifested by an elevated
A. Serum creatinine
B. Serum amylase
C. Serum bilirubin
D. Serum alkaline phosphatase

531. Dorsalis pedis is the pulse felt over:
A. Lower limb B. Trunk
C. Upper limb D. Neck

532. The solution used to disinfect the bed linen of HIV positive patient is
A. Savlon
B. Sodium hypochlorite
C. Dettol
D. Lysol

533. Which of the following procedure always requires surgical asepsis?
A. Colostomy irrigation
B. Vaginal irrigation
C. Urinary catheterization
D. Nasagastric tube insertion

534. The characteristic fever found in typhoid is:
A. Relapsing fever
B. Step ladder fever
C. Intermittent fever
D. Continuous fever

535. The amount of moisture in the air is recorded with:
A. Anemometer B. Hygrometer
C. Barometer D. Six's thermometer

536. The waves used in telecommunication is:
A. Microwaves B. Cosmic rays
C. Infra red D. Ultra violet

537. A phylum with pseudocoelom
A. Arthropoda B. Platyhelminthes
C. Annelida D. Asheliminthes

538. Photo electric effect can be explained on the basis of:
A. Quantum theory
B. Electromagnetic theory
C. Corpuscular theory
D. Wave theory

539. The linear product obtained by the condensation polymerization of phenol and formaldehyde is:
A. Novolac B. Melamine
C. Nylon 6,6 D. Bakelite

540. Classic barrel shaped chest is seen in patients with:
A. Congestive cardiac failure
B. COPD
C. Bronchiectasis
D. Pulmonary effusion

541. Sudden fall of temperature is called:
A. Crisis B. Lysis
C. Relapse D. Quotidian

542. Which of the following solution is isotonic?
A. 0.9% saline B. Dextran
C. 0.45% saline D. Dextrose saline

543. Instrument to detect the colour of a solution is:
A. Flame photometer
B. Calorimeter
C. Clorimeter
D. Chromatography

544. The maximum height at which the enema can should be held while giving enema is:-
A. 66 cm B. 45 cm C. 37cm D. 30cm

545. Best method to prevent foot drop in client on bed rest is to use:
A. Splints B. Blocks
C. Cradles D. Sandbags

546. Florence Nightingale was born on:
A. May 12th 1820 B. May 12th 1832
C. April 7th 1820 D. June 7th 1842

547. Temporary hardness of water is removed by:
A. Addition of chlorine B. Filtration
C. SODS method D. Boiling

548. All of the following instruction are given to a patient before computed tomography CT) scan except:
A. Wear comfortable, loose-fitting clothing
B. Remove all metallic objects such as hairpin, dentures, jewellery etc
C. It will not effect the outcome of pregnancy in case of female patient
D. Nil orally several hours before the scan

549. Out of the following, which medicines are used for intestinal evacuation ?
A. Cathartics B. Carminatives
C. Astringents D. Antimycotics

550. Prior to feeding an infant by gastrostomy tube, the nurse should:
A. Aspirate the tube
B. Slowly instill 5 ml of water
C. Provide the baby with a pacifier
D. Place the baby in semi-fowler's position

551. The nursing care of a patient with dongue fever include all of the following except:
A. Low grade dengue fever can be treated at home.
B. Provide cold compression
C. Provide proper hydration and electrolyte balance
D. Symptomatic treatment is given irrespective of the grade of the disease

552. Following are predisposing cause for bedsore except:
A. Impaired circulation B. Lowered vitality
C. Emaciation D. Anorexia

553. Inability to sleep is termed as:
A. Dyspepsia B. Dyspnaea
C. Anorexia D. Insomnia

554. What should be the temperature of water used for cold sponging ?
A. 98°F B. 105°F C. 70° F D. 0°F

555. Which of the following is not found in urine?
A. Only glucose B. Only protein
C. Only Red blood cells D. All of the above

556. Instrument used to examine the rectum:
A. Autoscope B. Proctoscope
C. Endoscope D. Ophthalmoscope

557. Florence Nightingale was born on:
A. January 12 B. April 12
C. May 5 D. May 12

558. Acetic acid is used for testing urine for:
A. Sugar B. Acetate
C. Albumin D. Bile salts

559. Enema given to destry or expel the worms from the intestine:
A. Astringent enema
B. Anthelmintic enema
C. Purgative enema
D. Carminative enema

560. Examination with the help of stethoscope is called:
A. Percussion B. Palpation
C. Auscultation D. Inspection

561. When pulse rate is less than 60 per minute it is called:
A. Bradycardia B. Bradypnea
C. Tachycardia D. Tachypnea

562. The most important point in nursing care of a patient after tracheostomy is:
A. Administration of antibiotics
B. Maintenance of intake output
C. Oxygen administration
D. Suctioning

563. In a patient of fever, "fastigium" is term given to which of the following period?
A. Onset of fever
B. When body temperature has reached its max-imum and remains constant
C. When the body temperature is gradually re-turning to normal
D. When the body temperature is suddenly re-turning to normal

564. In which of the following positions, patient is not lying down?
A. Trendelenburg B. Sim's
C. Fowler's D. Rose

565. When a drug is to be given at bed time, which of the following coded instructions is used?
A. Ac B. Hs C. Pc C. Prn

566. The process of assessing patients who come to emergency department and determining the management priorities is called:
A. Gavages B. Triage
C. Lavage D. Mirage

567. Method of administering friction over skin is called:
A. Instillation C. Inunction
B. Insufflation D. Insertion

568. While measuring blood pressure in upper arm, the chest piece of stethoscope is placed over which of the following arteries?
A. Axillary B. Radial
C. Ulnar D. Brachial

569. How much blood is drawn from a donor when one unit of blood is donated?
A. 400ml B. 300ml
C. 200ml D. 100ml

570. Blankets can be sterilized by
A. Dry heat method
B. Ethylene oxide treatment
C. Autoclaving
D. Ionizing radiation

571. Gloves are sterilized by
A. Ethylene oxide
B. Hot air over method
C. Dry heat
D. Radiant heat

572. Diseases transferred through contact are called
A. Communicable Disease
B. Infectious Disease
C. Contagious Disease
D. Epidemic Disease

573. The position commonly used for pelvic surgeries is:
A. Supine B. Trendelenburg
C. Sims's position D. Prone

574. The apex beat is felt at which intercostals space?
A. 6th B. 3rd
C. 4th D. 5th

575. Tablespoon is equal to
A. 5 ml B. 10 ml
C. 15 ml D. 30 ml

576. Bleeding from the nose is termed:
A. Epistaxis B. Hyper emesis
C. Hemoptysis D. Haematemesis

577. The colour of bag in which the infectious solid wastes are disposed is:
A. Yellow B. Red
C. Black D. Blue

578. The compression to ventilation ratio in CPR in case of single rescuer is:
A. 30:2 B. 5:2
C. 15:2 D. 3:1

579. The position to be maintained for a patient with increased ICP is:
A. Semi Fowler's position
B. Trendelenburg position
C. Sidelying
D. Prone position

580. In triage yellow colour indicates:
A. Dead B. Emergent
C. Urgent D. No urgent

581. An intentional touching of the patient's body without consent is termed:
A. Malpractice B. Negligence
C. Assault D. Battery

582. The style of leadership that dominates and commands the group is:
A. Laiseez-faire B. Autocratic
C. Democratic D. Situational

583. The injury of which nerve leads to Wrist Drop'?
A. Ulnar nerve B. Axillary nerve
C. Median nerve D. Radial nerve

584. for disposable items, the best method for sterilization is:
A. Boiling heat B. Dry heat
C. Incineration D. Gamma radiation

585. Vertical transmission is by:
A. Placenta B. Mosquito
C. water contact D. Droplet

586. Which is most difficult to block spreading of?
A. Waterborne B. Iatrogenic
C. Airborne D. Vector

587. The period after entry of the organism to produce maximum infection is known as:
A. Lead time
B. Incubation period
C. Generation time
D. Serial interval period

588. in lumbar puncture, the needle is inserted between:
A. L4-L5 B. L1-L2
C. L3-L4 D. L2-L3

589. The pressure set in autoclave for sterilization is:
A. 20 Ib B. 25lb
C. 15 Ib D. 30 Ib

590. The transmission of infection from the mother to the fetus through placenta is termed:
A. Iatrogenic Transmission
B. Vertical born transmission
C. Nosocomial infection
D. Horizontal transmission

591. Zinc-oxide bandage is
A. Adhesive bandage
B. Impregnated bandage
C. Elastic bandage
D. Non elastic bandage

592. Which of the following is used in colposcopy?
A. Povidone icdine B. Acetic acid
C. Methylene blue D. Gentian violet

593. The blood pressure of a normal healthy person is:
A. 120/70 mm Hg B. 120/80 mm Hg
C. 100/60 mm Hg D. 140/70 mm Hg

594. Bradycardia refers to heart rate below:
A. 60 beats/min B. 70 beats/min
C. 100 beats/min D. 60 beats/min

595. Bluish discoloration of the skin is referred as:
A. Hypoxia B. Dyspnea
C. Apnoea D. Cyanosis

596. Prolonged bedridden patients have the risk of developing:
A. Decubitus ulcer B. Cellulites
C. Scabies D. Psoriasis

597. The most preferred site for giving IM injection of an average adult is:
A. Deltoid B. Umbilicus
C. Gluteus region D. Forearm

598. Sharp instruments may be sterilized with:
A. Radiation B. Hot air
C. Lysol D. All of the above

599. Which of the following is powerful disinfectant?
A. Dettol B. Lysol
C. Phenol D. Xylocaine

600. Act of soiling or making impure by contact
A. Sepsis B. Contamination
C. Colonization D. Culture

601. Immediately after cholecystectomy, the nursing action that should assume the highest priority is
A. Encouraging the client to take adequate deep breaths by mouth
B. Encouraging the client to change the position frequency
C. Changing the dressing at least BID
D. Irrigate the T-tube frequency

602. Dehydration in child with diarrhea, thirst present, tears absent is
A. Mild B. Moderate
C. Severe D. None

603. What is the position for thoracentesis
A. Orthopneic
B. Knee-chest
C. Low-fowlers
D. Side-lying position on the affected side

604. Vaccination is not contraindicated in
A. High Fever
B. Infection
C. Immunosuppressive disease
D. Diabetes

605. Diabetic coma results from excessive accumulation of
A. Nitrogen
B. Ketones
C. Glucose
D. Sodium bicarbonate

606. A child is getting 5% Dextrose 1000 ml IV in 24 hours, the mini dropper delivers 60 drops/ml. the rate of flow will be
A. 10 drops per minute
B. 32 drops per minute
C. 38 drops per minute
D. 42 drops per minute

607. A nurse measures a patient's Temperature at 102° F, what is equivalent centigrade temperature
A. 40.1°C B. 38.9° C
C. 48°C D. 38°C

608. Tuberculin test denotes
A. Previous or present sensitivity to tubercle proteins
B. Patient is resistant to tuberculosis
C. Patient is susceptible to tuberculosis
D. Protective immune status of individual against tuberculosis

609. The most appropriate time for the nurse to obtain a sputum specimen for culture is
A. Early in the morning
B. After the patient eat light breakfast
C. After aerosol therapy
D. After chest physiotherapy

610. A disease characterized by precipitation of uric acid crystals in articular tissue
A. Rheumatoid arthritis
B. Gout
C. Osteoarthritis
D. Rheumatic fever

611. The most common feature in tracheoesophageal fistula without atresia is
A. Excessive secretions at birth
B. Abdominal distention
C. Recurrent aspiration pneumonia
D. Regurgitation of food

612. A patient has been admitted with a diagnosis of acute lymphoblastic leukemia. When he is receiving chemotherapy, nurse should assess for the development of lifethreatening thrombocytopenia by monitoring the patient for?
A. Fever B. Diarrhea
C. Headache D. Hematuria

613. Most common type of surgery of BPH
A. Suprapubic prostatectomy
B. Perinal prostatectomy
C. Transurethral resection
D. Retropublic prostatectomy

614. Which plasmodium causes Malignant Malaria
A. P. Ovale B. P. Malariae
C. P. Falciparum D. P. Vivax

615. All of the following statement are true about donning sterile gloves except
A. The first glove should be picked up grasping the inside of the cuff
B. The second glove should be picked up by inserting the gloved fingers under the cuff outside the glove
C. The glove should be adjusted by sliding the gloved fingers under the sterile cuff and pulling the glove over the wrist
D. The inside of the glove is considered sterile

616. Deep palpation is used to assess of the following?
A. Skin turgor B. Hydration
C. Organs D. Temperature

617. In which step of the nursing process would the nurse ask a patient if the medication she administered relieved his pain
A. Assessment B. Analysis
C. Planning D. Evaluation

618. Which of the following is a sign symptom of a hemolytic reaction to blood transfusion
A. Hemoglobinuria& Urticaria
B. Chest Pain
C. Muscle cramp
D. Distended neck veins

619. Nurse is caring for a patient with active upper GI bleeding. What is the appropriate diet for this client during the first 24 hour after admission?
A. Regular diet B. Skim milk
C. Nothing by mouth D. Clear liquids

620. Discharge teaching for a patient with post operative inguinal hernia includes
A. Telling him to avoid heavy lifting for 4 to 6 weeks
B. Instructing him to have a soft bland diet for two weeks
C. Telling him to resume his previous daily activities without limitations
D. Recommending him to drink eight glasses of water daily

621. Palpating the mid clavicular line is the correct technique for assessing
A. Base line vital sign
B. Systolic blood pressure
C. Respiratory rate
D. Apical pulse

622. Which of the following drug is to be infused fast
A. Aminophylline B. Mannitol
C. Dopamine D. Potassium chloride

623. The nurse explain to a patient that a cough
A. Is a protective response to clear the respiratory tract irritants
B. Is primarily a voluntary action
C. Is induced by the administration of an antitussive drug
D. Can be inhibited by splinting the abdomen

624. The position given to the patient for abdominal paracentesis is:
A. Supine position
B. Lithotomy position
C. Fowler's position
D. Knee chest position

625. Leukoplakia is the earliest sign of
A. Liver cirrhosis B. Leukemia
C. Lymphoma D. Oral Cancer

626. Floating tip of Iceberg indicates
A. Subclinical cases B. Clinical cases
C. Fatal cases D. Unidentified cases

627. For 10 months old child, IM injection can be given in
A. Deltoid
B. Antero lateral Thigh
C. Buttock
D. Abdomen

628. Flame photometer is used for estimation of
A. Blood Electrolytes
B. Blood Urea
C. Bile Pigments
D. Hemoglobinopathies

629. Anticoagulants used for prothrombin time is
A. Sodium citrate B. Heparin
C. EDTA D. Any of these

630. Acid used in process of decalcification is
A. HBr B. H2SO4
C. HCl D. HCN

631. Icterus index is measure of the degree of yellowish-green color in plasma or serum in
A. Jaundice B. Meningitis
C. Glomerulonephritis D. Conjunctivitis

632. Normal value of blood urea is
A. 2 to 5 mg/dl B. 10 to 50 mg/dl
C. 10 to 50 μ/l D. 2 to 5 μ/l

633. Normal value of serum chloride is
A. 95 to 115 mEq/L B. 25 to 50 mEq/L
C. 150 to 200 mEq/L D. 120 to 160 mEq/L

634. Reagent used for detection of Urobilinogen is
A. HCl B. NaCl
C. Benedict's reagent D. Ehrlich's reagent

635. Which of the following is not a protozoa found in stool
A. E. Coli B. E.Histolytica
C. Giardia D. Balantiduim Coli

636. Measurement of creatinine is used as a test of
A. Liver function B. Stomach
C. Kidney D. Pancreas

637. Auramin O is a
A. Colorless dye B. Florescent dye
C. Natural dye D. Ordinary dye

638. Full form of EDTA is
A. Ethenoldiamine Tetra Acetic Acid
B. Ethylenediamine Tetra Acetic Acid
C. Ethylenediamine Tri Acetic Acid
D. Ethenoldiamine Tri Acetic Acid

639. Which of the following is preferred for obtaining blood sample
A. Vein
B. Artery
C. Capillary (Skin puncture)
D. All of the above

640. Capillary blood is not taken from the following in infants
A. Ball of the thumb B. Great Toe
C. Heel D. Lobe of ear

641. Casoni's test is performed to diagnose
A. Leishmaniasis B. Hydatid cyst
C. Grannuloma D. Syphillis

642. Fouchet's Test is done for
A. Bile pigments B. Urobilinogen
C. Ketones D. LDH

643. Sodium nitroprusside is used in test for
A. Occult blood
B. Urobilinogen
C. Bence Jones Proteins
D. Acetone or Ketone

644. VDRL test is for screening of syphilis
A. True B. False
C. May be false D. Don't know

645. Basophilia is seen in
A. Megaloblastic Anemia
B. Jaundice
C. Chronic Myeloid Leukemia
D. Rheumatoid Arthritis

646. CSF examination helps in diagnosis of
A. Otosclerosis
B. Urinary tract infection
C. Thyroid dysfunction
D. Meningitis

647. 1 ml of ACD solution is sufficient to prevent coagulation of
A. 4 ml of blood B. 5 ml of blood
C. 6 ml of blood D. 8 ml of blood

648. Thyroid function tests are
A. TSH and T4
B. T3, T4, TSH
C. Creatinine, urea, BUN
D. BUN and TSH

649. Best method of diagnosing enterobius infection is
A. Rectal Biopsy
B. Perianal Swab
C. Stool Examination
D. None of these

650. Toluenesulfonic acid test is used to detect presence in Urine of
A. Sugar
B. Bence Jones Protein
C. Casts
D. Mucin

651. Minimum level of hemoglobin required for donating blood
A. 10.0 gm/dl B. 12.0 gm/dl
C. 12.5 gm/dl D. 11.0 gm/dl

652. Rheumatoid factors are not exclusively found in rheumatoid arthritis but also in
A. Syphilis
B. SLE
C. Hypergammaglobulinaemia
D. All of these

653. The sample of urine should be fresh and should be examined immediately and not kept at room temperature for long because
A. Its reaction might change
B. Casts might disintegrate
C. bacterial growth may take place
D. All of these

654. Urea and Creatinine tests are used to assess
A. Liver function
B. Gastric Function
C. Glomerular filtration
D. Cardiac Function

655. Minimum interval between two whole blood donations should be
A. 6 months B. 12 months
C. 3 months D. 2 weeks

656. Osmotic fragility test is done for the diagnosis of
A. Sickle cell anemia
B. Iron deficiency anemia
C. Hereditary spherocytosis
D. Megaloblastic anemia

657. Benedict's test is done to estimate
A. Cholesterol B. Sodium
C. Creatinine D. Sugar

658. In a pregnant women anemia is hemoglobin level less than :
A. 12 gm/dl B. 10.0 gm/dl
C. 12.5 gm /dl D. 11.0 gm/dl

659. Normal Renal Threshold for glucose is
A. 140 mg/dl B. 180 mg/dl
C. 120mg/dl D. 110mg/dl

660. Direct Coomb's test may be positive in pregnant ladies
A. True B. False
C. May be true D. Don't know

661. Which of the following is true for hypothyroid
A. High T3, Low TSH
B. Normal T3, Low TSH
C. Raised T3, Normal TSH
D. Low T3, Raised TSH

662. Wintrobe method is used in
A. ESR estimation B. Hb Estimation
C. Centrifugal D. None of the above

663. To assess blood gas saturation, which is the most preferred site to take a sample from
A. Capillary B. Artery
C. Vein D. Venous shunt

664. Which of the test of urine is positive in myeloma
A. Bence Jones Protein B. Heller's Test
C. Foam Test D. Benedict's test

665. 'qs' in prescription means
A. Every hour B. Sufficient quantity
C. Every time D. Every day

666. Example for osmotic purgative
A. Magnesium sulphate B. Liquid paraffin
C. Phenophthalein D. Castor oil

667. What is rectified sprit?
A. 75 % ethanol B. 100% ethanol
C. 90% ethanol D. 50% ethanol

668. Preservative useful in eye drops
A. Mercuric chloride
B. Chlorine water
C. Bromine water
D. Phenyl mercuric nitrate

669. Drug obtained by recombinant DNA technology
A. Tetanus toxoid B. Penicillin
C. Human insulin D. Zidovudine

670. The Antibiotics are manufactured in large scale by
A. Surface culture in liquid medium
B. Surface culture in solid medium
C. Submerged culture in liquid medium
D. Submerged culture in solid medium

671. Antibodies are
A. Immunogens B. Haptens
C. Immunoglobulins D. Allergens

672. In what disease Heart fails to pump?
A. Angina pectoris
B. Hepatic coma
C. Congestive cardiac failure
D. Nephrotic syndrome

673. Drug obtained from plant source
A. Reserpine B. Penicillin
C. Ethanol D. Sulfamethoxazole

674. One teaspoonful is equal to
A. 30 ml B. 15 ml
C. 10 ml D. 5 ml

675. Opioid derivative used in cough syrup
A. Pentazocine B. Diphenoxylate
C. Noscapine D. Buprenorphine

676. The term 'bd' in prescription means?
A. Twice daily B. Thrice daily
C. Once a day D. Four times a day

677. Example for physical incompatibility
A. Alkali + Acid
B. Alkakoid + Acid
C. Magnesium hydroxide + acid
D. Castor oil + water

678. In a prescription –D5W means
A. Distilled water 5 ml
B. Daily 5 times
C. 5 drops of water
D. Dextrose 5% in water

679. Uses of isotonic saline do not include
A. I.V. injection
B. Intra-cutaneous injection
C. Sub-cutaneous injection
D. Injection into varicose veins

680. Sterilizing the eye drops are done by following methods except
A. Heating in an autoclave
B. Filtration
C. Adding an antiseptic
D. Maintaining at 98° C for 30 minutes

681. 'Rx' in a prescription means
A. Repeat B. Rectify
C. Take D. Supply

682. Morphine is contraindicated for patients with head injury because it produces
A. BVG
B. Hyperactive spinal refluxes
C. Respiratory depression
D. Analgesia

683. Chicken pox is Spread by :
A. Droplet infection B. Body fluids
C. Contaminated foods D. Fomites

684. One ounce by volume is equal to
A. 30 ml B. 60 ml
C. 90 ml D. 15 ml

685. In a prescription "QID' means
A. One fourth B. One quart
C. Once in four days D. Four times a day

686. What is the meaning of 'ou' in a prescription?
A. One unit B. Once a day
C. Orally D. Both eyes

687. One kilogram is equal to
A. 2.2 pounds B. 3.0 pounds
C. 3.3 pounds D. 4 pounds

688. Cardiac glycoside
A. Enalapril
B. Hydralazine
C. Digitalis
D. Hydrochlorothiazide

689. What advise will you give to the patient while giving tetracycline?
A. To take with milk
B. Not to take with milk
C. To take with fatty diet
D. To take in evening

690. Increased frequency of Defecation and water content in stools is called
A. Constipation B. Diarrhea
C. Steatorrhea D. Malaena

691. Method of sterilizing metal instruments
A. Adding antiseptic solution
B. Steam under pressure
C. Hot air oven
D. Radioactive isotopes

692. Vehicle in ophthalmic drops include all except
A. Ethanol B. Isotonic phosphate
C. Special boric acid D. Boric acid

693. What is a liniment?
A. Liquid medicament applied with friction on the affected area
B. Liquid medicament applied as a paint
C. Liquid medicament given as enema
D. Liquid medicament given orally

694. Catgut is sterilized by
A. Dry heat method B. Autoclaving
C. Ionizing radiation D. Chemical method

695. Enzyme responsible for conversion of glucose to glucose-6-PO4
A. Glycogen synthase B. G-6 phosphatase
C. Glucokinase D. Phosphorylase

696. What is 'sos' in a prescription order?
A. If needed B. Subcutaneous
C. Without D. At once

697. Elbow crutches are indicated for the persons with
A. Strong upper extremities and strong trunk
B. Strong upper extremities and weak trunk
C. Weak upper extremities and strong trunk
D. Weak upper extremities and weak trunk

698. Push up is an example of
A. Close kinetic chain exercise
B. Active free weight bearing exercise
C. Both of these
D. None of these

699. Cock up splint is used in the management of:
A. Ulnar nerve palsy
B. Brachial plexus palsy
C. Radial nerve palsy
D. Combined Ulnar and Median nerve

700. Which of the following would be most representative of a normal oxygen saturation rate?
A. 45% B. 60% C. 80% D. 95%

701. Low resistance high repetition exercise is used to improve muscle
A. Strength B. Endurance
C. Volume D. Co-ordination

702. Which muscle is known as Kicking muscle which is a two joint muscle that is active during both hip flexion and knee extension
A. Iliopsoas B. Rectus femoris
C. Sartorius D. Pectineus

703. What is the first functional task that should be taught to a patient with a T2 spinal cord injury?
A. Rolling
B. Self range of motion
C. Ambulation which long leg braces
D. Bed to wheelchair transfer

704. Hemarthrosis develops within ....of injury
A. Minutes to hours B. Hours to days
C. Days to weeks D. Weeks to months

705. In poliomyelitis destruction occurs in
A. Muscle
B. Peripheral nerve
C. Anterior horn cells
D. Posterior horn cells

706. Stiff knee gait is characterized by
A. Lurching B. Hand to knee
C. Hip hiking D. Steppage gait

707. Stress fracture is treated by:
A. Rest B. Immobilization
C. Internal fixation D. Closed reduction

708. What is geriatrics?
A. Study of old age people
B. Study of human behavior
C. Study of human population
D. Physical and psychological function

709. Which of the following techniques does not require radiation?
A. Computerized tomography
B. Conventional radiography
C. Magnetic resonance imaging
D. None of the above

710. Hopping, skipping, jumping are form of..........
A. Eccentric exercise
B. Plyometrics
C. Concentric followed by eccentric
D. None of the above

711. Wrist drop is seen in palsy of:
A. Ulnar nerve B. Radial nerve
C. Median nerve D. A and B

712. For the traction to be effective, the force must exceed the frictional resistance encountered by the body part. For lumbar traction the force should be-------------------
A. More than 1/10 of body weight
B. More than 1/3 of body weight
C. More than 1/2 of body weight
D. More than 1/5 of body weight

713. Serum uric acid level is higher in.......................
A. SLE B. Stills disease
C. Gout D. None of the above

714. The confirmatory test for Paralytic poliomyelitis
A. Stool Examination
B. CSF Examination
C. Blood Examination
D. Nerve Examination

715. Inanimate objects that can transmit the disease
A. Droplet B. Dust
C. Fomites D. Reservoir

716. The best and useful method of household waste disposal in rural area is
A. Dumping B. Composting
C. Incineration D. Controlled tipping

717. Cause of temporary hardness of water
A. Carbonates B. Sulphates
C. Chlorides D. Calcium

18. In a patient with perforated duodenal ulcer, which of the following you would expect to observe as the primary initial symptoms
A. Fever B. Pain
C. Dizziness D. Vomiting

19. Trichomonal infection is caused by
A. Protozoa B. Fungus
C. Yeast D. Bacteria

20. Kussmaul's breathing is
A. Shallow breaths interrupted by apnea
B. Prolonged gasping inspiration followed by a very short, usually inefficient aspiration
C. Marked rhythmic waxing and waning of respirations from very deep to very shallow breathing and temporary apnea
D. Increased rate and depth of respiration

21. What is the best method used to assess the temperature of an alert patient admitted to the hospital with dehydration secondary to vomiting and diarrhea
A. Oral B. Axillary
C. Radial D. Heat sensitive tape

2. Histology is the study of
A. Cells and membranes
B. Skin
C. Organs and organ system
D. Tissues

3. Paul-Bunnell test is used to diagnose
A. Cytomegalo virus infection
B. Infectious mononucleosis
C. Herpes simplex infection
D. Cacervix

4. According to Maslow's theory of hierarchy of needs, the most basic or first-level needs include
A. Esteem and self esteem
B. Self actualization
C. Love and belonging
D. Air, water and food

5. Safe disposal of mercury
A. Bury under earth
B. Collect carefully and reuse
C. Combustion
D. Treat with chemical

. After 1 week of hospitalization, patient develops hypokalemia. Which of the following is the most significant symptom of his disorder
A. Lethargy
B. Increased pulse rate and blood pressure
C. Muscle weakness
D. Muscle irritability

727. Oral thrush is caused by
A. Bacteria B. Fungus
C. Virus D. Protozoa

728. Which substance increases the amount of urine produced
A. Caffeine containing drinks, such as coffee and cola
B. Beets
C. Urinary analgesics
D. Kaolin with pectin (Kaopectate)

729. The nurse is admitting a patient with a suspected fluid imbalance. The most sensitive indicator of body fluid is
A. Daily weight
B. Serum sodium levels
C. Measured intake and output
D. Blood pressure

730. Milk sugar is
A. Lactose B. Glucose
C. Sucrose D. Cellulose

731. The maximum transfusion time for a unit of packed red blood cells (RBCs) is
A. 6 hours B. 4 hours
C. 3 hours D. 2 hours

732. Brauns splint is used for
A. Fracture of the arms
B. Fracture of pelvis
C. Fracture of the lower limbs
D. Fracture of collar bone

733. The goal of mammography is
A. Early detection of breast cancer
B. Early detection of mouth cancer
C. Early detection of chest cancer
D. Early detection of cervical cancer

734. The method of applying medication to the skin
A. Inhalation B. Ingestion
C. Injection D. Inunction

735. The antibodies are
A. Proteins B. Carbohydrates
C. Lipids D. Germs

736. For occult blood test, what specimen will you collect
A. Blood B. Urine
C. Stool D. Gastric Juice

737. Gout is generally associated with
A. Smoking
B. Low-protein diet
C. Increased xanthine oxidase activity
D. Increased urate deposition in joints

738. Pigeon chest seen in
A. Osteoporosis B. Ricketts
C. Osteosarcoma D. Costochondritis

739. Which of the following is administered by subcutaneous (S/C).route

A. BCG
B. Insulin
C. Mantoux test
D. Drug sensitivity test

740. Hepatic disease leads to major elevation of

A. Biliverdin B. Total bilirubin
C. Albumin D. Haem

741. An increased myoglobin level suggests which of the following in a patient with chest pain

A. Liver disease
B. Myocardial damage
C. Hypertension
D. Cancer

742. Acromegaly is most frequently diagnosed in

A. Middle aged adults
B. Newborns
C. Children ages 2 to 5
D. Person aged 65 and older

743. T-tube drainage is used after

A. Lobectomy B. Appendectomy
C. Cholecystectomy D. Ileostomy

744. To clear secretions after performing postural drainage techniques, what position would allow the patient to produce the most forceful cough

A. Prone B. Sidelying
C. Supine D. Upright sitting

745. Milwaukee brace is used in

A. Scoliosis B. Fracture skull
C. Fracture tibia D. CTEV

746. Language disorder is.........................

A. Alexia B. Aphasia
C. Dyslexia D. Broca's aphasia

747. The mode of heat transfer by hot pack, whirl pool bath, paraffin wax bath is.................:

A. Conduction and radiation
B. Conduction and convection
C. Radiation and convection
D. Conduction, radiation and convection

748. Terminal disinfection is carried out

A. On admission of a patient
B. When Patient is in ward
C. After patient goes home
D. After patient dies in ward

749. Euthenesia is called

A. Painless death B. Good death
C. Both 1 & 2 D. None of the above

750. Hyperthermia is the complication of

A. Hot application B. Cold application
C. Both 1 & 2 D. None of the above

751. Steam inhalation is

A. Dry heat B. Moist heat
C. Both 1 & 2 D. None of the above

752. Which assessment indicates to the nurse th development of cardiogenic shock in M.I patient at I.C.U.

A. Bradycardia
B. Increase B.P.
C. Oliguria
D. Warm & Flushed skin

753. Role of nurse in physical examination

A. Preparation of environment & equipment
B. Preparation of the patient
C. Provide assistance
D. All of the above

754. What type of diet is restricted in renal failure

A. Protein B. Carbohydrates
C. Vitamins D. Iron supplements

755. Cardinal signs of inflammation are all except

A. Pain B. Redness
C. Swelling D. Hypothermia

756. Keton bodies in urine is detected by which test

A. Benedict's B. Hay's
C. Rothera's D. Gemelin

757. Position provided to the patient of acute M.I.

A. Fowler's position
B. Recumbent position
C. Sit upright position
D. Dorsal position

758. The Sitz-bath helps in

A. Circulation
B. Defecation
C. Healing of wound& Decrease pain
D. Vaginal Discharge

759. A puncture proof bucket is used for the dispos of

A. I.V. Set
B. Wrappers of Syringe
C. Body parts of patient
D. Needles & broken ampoules

760. Which of the following is a cause of constipatio

A. Lack of fibre in food
B. Less intake of liquid in food
C. Irregular habit of defecation
D. All of the above

761. Wound dressing is done by using

A. Septic technique
B. Medical asepsis
C. Surgical asepsis
D. Medical and surgical asepsis

762. The Nurses take the following Pledge

A. The Nightingale Pledge
B. The Christian Pledge
C. The Catholic Pledege
D. The Hippocrates Pledge

63. Which of these is not incinerated
A. Waste sharps B. Human organs
C. Bandage D. Solid waste

64. Information given by the sufferer about his illness is called
A. Sign B. Symptoms
C. Observation D. Diagnosis

65. What are the indications of Hemodialysis
A. Uremia
B. Hepatic Coma
C. Chronic Renal Failure
D. All of the above

66. In Biomedical waste management which colour coded bin is used to dispose plastic waste
A. Green B. Red
C. Yellow D. Black

67. Placenta should be disposed in which Color Bucket
A. Black B. Yellow
C. Green D. Red

68. "Black Death" is related with
A. Cholera B. Plaque
C. Malaria D. Dengue

69. Blood is stored at what temperature
A. At 2° to 8 ° C
B. - 2 ° to 6 ° C
C. At 20 °C to 22 ° C
D. At room temperature

70. During ABG following analysis is done
A. HCO_3, PO_2
B. HCO_3, PCO_2
C. PO_2, PCO_2, PH
D. HCO_3, PO_2, PCO_2, PH

71. Body temperature below 950F is called
A. Hyperthermia B. Lysis
C. Hypothermia D. Pyrexia

72. Sharp waste to be dumped in:
A. Red Bag B. Blue Bag
C. Yellow Bag D. Black Bag

73. Ratio of Dettol Solution to disinfect thermometer:
A. 1: 20 B. 1 : 40
C. 1: 30 D. 1: 10

74. Formula to Convert Fahrenheit to Celsius.
A. ° C = (F-32) 9/5 B. °C = (F-32) 5/9
C. °C = (32-5) 9/5 D. °C = (32.5) 5/9

75. Chemical Formula of Plaster of Paris
A. $MgSO_4$, $7H_2O$ B. $CaSO_4$, $7H_2O$
C. Al(PO4)3 D. Anhydrous CaSO4

76. Intraosseous injection given in
A. Vein B. Muscles
C. Bone D. Skin

777. Colour coding of most hazardous pesticides
A. Red B. Green
C. Yellow D. Black

778. Boiling water helps in killing all organism except
A. Fungi B. Protozoa
C. Bacteria D. Spores

779. What is the method of disposal of waste of yellow coloured bin
A. Incineration B. Microwaving
C. Shredding D. Autoclaving

780. Who is the Founder of nursing?
A. Neetu Sharma
B. Deergha Sharma
C. Sister Nancy
D. Florence nightingale

781. Where is the Florence night angles born?
A. England B. USA
C. Italy D. London

782. When was the Florence nightingales born?
A. 25 may 1811 B. 12 may 1820
C. 13 august 1910 D. 13 may 1820

783. When was the Florence nightingale's death?
A. 13 may 1810 B. 13 august 1910
C. 13 august 1920 D. 12 may 1820

784. What do you mean by Nutrition?
A. All of above
B. To nourish
C. To cherish
D. To protect support & sustain

785. How does the Florence nightingales provide services?
A. To provide money B. To give Medicine
C. Provide Hygiene D. To provide shelter

786. International nurse day celebrate on:
A. 12 august B. 12 June
C. 13 august D. 12 may

787. Who is the Founder of modern nursing?
A. Verginia handerson
B. Pratibhia patil
C. Sr. nancy
D. Florence nightingales

788. What do you mean by Core of nursing means?
A. Promotion & prevention of health
B. All of the above
C. alleviation from suffering
D. Restoration of health

789. What do you mean by Comprehensive nursing?
A. Meeting of family need
B. Meeting of old its need
C. Meeting of whole patent need
D. Meeting of society

790. **Which are the essentials in nursing?**
A. The science B. All of the above
C. The spirit D. The art

791. **Which is the extent of nursing?**
A. The individual B. The family
C. All of the above D. The society

792. **What are the main principal of Nursing procedure?**
A. All of the above B. Use of resource
C. Individuality D. Safety & comfort

793. **Who explain the "nursing is novel profession"?**
A. W.H.O B. A.N.A
C. I.C.N. D. I.N.C.

794. **Who is the Lady with lamp?**
A. Florence Night angles
B. Henderson
C. Deergha Sharma
D. Florida

795. **Who is the Professional nurse?**
A. Who registered in District nursing council
B. Who registered in State nursing council
C. Diploma nurse
D. G.N.M, B.Sc, M.sc. nursing competed nurse

796. **Who is the head of Health team?**
A. Nurse B. Dietician
C. Physician D. Physiotherapist

797. **Health is the**
A. The absence of illness
B. The apposite of disease
C. A sate of complete physical mental & social wellbeing
D. A condition B/W disease and good health

798. **From where was the word name come hospital?**
A. Greek word B. Latin word
C. French word D. Chine word

799. **What is the function of hospital?**
A. Care of sick & injured patient
B. Diagnosis & treatment of disease
C. Promotion of health
D. All of the Above

800. **What do you mean by word "hospes"?**
A. Hostel
B. Care of terminal ill patient
C. Hotel
D. All of the above

801. **A hospital which have Bed capacity less than 100 is known as:**
A. Medium hospital B. Small hospital
C. Large hospital D. Teaching hospital

802. **Teaching hospital bed capacity is?**
A. More than 300 B. More than 100
C. More than 500 D. Less than 400

803. **A hospital which have Bed capacity more tha 300 is known as:**
A. Teaching hospital B. Large hospital
C. Small hospital D. Medium hospital

804. **What do you mean by asepsis?**
A. Present of microorganism
B. Contamination
C. Inhibits of bacteria
D. Absence of microorganism

805. **What do you mean by Bacteriostate?**
A. A agent which inhibits growth of bacteria
B. A agent inhibits of microorganism
C. A agent which kills the bacteria
D. A agent which kills of the microorganism

806. **Which is the disinfection done after Patie discharge from the ward?**
A. Concurrent disinfection
B. Terminal disinfection
C. Droplet disinfection
D. Isolation

807. **What do you mean Bactericide agent?**
A. To kill the Bacteria.
B. To stop Bacteria growth.
C. All
D. To kill the Microorganism.

808. **What do mean by droplet infection?**
A. By sneezing and coughing
B. Bed-sheet, furniture infection.
C. Vessels and cloths
D. By garbage

809. **Which type of the immunity provided b immunization ?**
A. Imitate B. Natural
C. Artificial D. None

810. **What is the Quarantine?**
A. Prevention B. Treatment
C. Diagnosis D. Isolation

811. **What is Sterization?**
A. Destroyed of pathogenic & non pathogen microorganism with their spores
B. Destroyed of pathogenic & non pathogen microorganism
C. Growth of pathogenic & non pathogen microorganism
D. Destroyed pathogenic microorganism

812. **What do you mean by cross infection?**
A. To stop the infection
B. Free from infection
C. None of them
D. To transmit the infection to one person another

813. HIV transfer from mother to her newborn child it is known as:
A. Iatrogenic mode of transmission
B. Horizontal mode of transmission
C. Vector mode of transmission
D. Vertical mode of transmission

814. Which place is related to nosocomial infection?
A. Hospital B. House
C. Community D. All

815. Infection transfer during fault procedure (eg.catheterization, blood transfusion) it is known as:
A. Vertical mode of transmission
B. Horizontal mode of transmission
C. Vector mode of transmission
D. Iatrogenic mode of transmission

816. When is the nosocomial infection occur after admission?
A. 48 hrs to 28 days after discharge
B. 48 hrs to 15 days after discharge
C. After discharge
D. Before admission

817. How do you prevent the Cross infection in hospital?
A. Proper cleanliness
B. Safe disposal of excreta urine stool & sputum
C. Well ventilated & safe water & food supply
D. All of the above

818. What is primary precaution used by nurse to prevent the Cross infection in hospital?
A. Safe disposal of excreta urine stool & sputum
B. Use of mask
C. None of them
D. Proper hand washing

819. A nurse is teaching a. client how to use the call bell system. Which level of Maslow's Hierarchy of Needs does this nursing action address?
a. Physiologic b. Self – Esteem
c. Interpersonal d. Safety

820. Nurses are held responsible for the commission of a tort. The nurse understands that a tort is:
A. The application of force to the body of another by a reasonable individual.
B. An illegality committed by one person against the property or person of another.
C. An illegality committed against the public and punishable by the law through the courts.
D. Doing something that a reasonable person under ordinary circumstances would not do.

821. A graduate nurse is preparing to apply to the State Board of Nursing for licensure to practice as a registered professional Nurse. What group primarily is protected under the regulations of the practice of nursing?
A. The public
B. Practicing nurses
C. The emplcying agency
D. People with health problems.

822. When being interviewed for a position as a registered professional nurse, the applicant is asked to identify an example of an intentional tort. What is the appropriate response?
A. Breach of duty B. Malpractice
C. False imprisonment D. Negligence

823. During a newborn assessment the nurse identifies that the temperature, pulse, respirations, and other physical characteristics are within the expected range. The nurse records these findings on the clinical record. Legally, how should the nurse's action be interpreted?
A. This is a medical diagnosis and the nurse overstepped the legal boundary.
B. The nurse met the requirements set forth in the Nurse Practice Act.
C. Nursing assessments are not equivalent to a health care provider's assessments.
D. The initial assessment of the infant's physical status is the responsibility of the client's health care provider

824. A nurse is evaluating a client's knowledge of ambulating with crutches. The nurse identifies the need for further teaching when the client status, "I must practice:
A. Sitting down and standing up."
B. Doing active exercises on a regular schedule."
C. Ambulating several hours a day."
D. Standing and maintaining balance."

825. What is the priority nursing action in nursing process.
A. Identify goals for care.
B. Develop a plan of care.
C. Obtain client's nursing history.
D. State client's nursing needs.

826. Based on the client's reported pain level, the nurse administers 8 mg of the prescribed morphine. The medication is available in a 10 mg syringe. Wasting of the remaining 2 mg of morphine should be done by the nurse and a witness. Who should be the witness?
A. Nursing supervisor
B. Licensed Practical nurse
C. Designated nursing assistant
D. Client's health care provider

827. How can a nurse best evaluate the effectiveness of communication with a client?

A. Medical assessments
B. Health care team conferences
C. Client's physiologic responses
D. Client feedback

828. A physically ill client is being verbally aggressive to the nursing staff. What is the most appropriate initial nursing response?

A. Explore the situation with the client.
B. Accept the client's behaviour.
C. Withdraw from contact with the client.
D. Tell the client the reason for the staff's actions.

829. What principle must a nurse consider when caring for a client with a closed wound drainage system?

A. Gravity causes fluids to flow down a pressure gradient.
B. Fluid flow rate is determined by the diameter of the lumen.
C. Siphoning causes fluids to flow from one level to a lower level.
D. Fluids flow from an area of higher pressure to one of lower pressure.

830. A client had extensive, prolonged surgery. Which electrolyte level should the nurse monitor most closely?

A. Calcium B. Chloride
C. Potassium D. Sodium

831. A nurse administers an intravenous solution of 0.45% sodium chloride. In what category of fluids does this solution belong?

A. Isomeric B. Hypotonic
C. Isotonic D. Hypertonic

832. A nurse is caring for a client with diarrhea. In which clinical indicator does the nurse anticipate a disease?

A. Pulse rate B. Tissue turgor
C. Specific gravity D. Body temperature

833. A client reports vomiting and diarrhea for 3 days. What clinical finding will most accurately indicate that the client has a fluid deficit?

A. Loss of body weight.
B. Decrease in blood pressure.
C. Presence of dry skin.
D. Altered general appearance.

834. A client is admitted with metabolic acidosis. The nurse considers that two body systems interact with the bicarbonate buffer system to preserve healthy body fluid pH. What two body systems should the nurse assess for compensatory changes?

A. Circulatory and urinary
B. Respiratory and urinary
C. Muscular and endocrine.
D. Skeletal and nervous

835. A nurse assesses a client's serum electrolyte levels in the laboratory report. What electrolyte in intracellular fluid should the nurse consider most important?

A. Sodium B. Calcium
C. Potassium D. Chloride

836. A client is in a state of uncompensated acidosis. What approximate arterial blood pH does the nurse expect the client to have?

A. 7.35 B. 7.45
C. 7.48 D. 7.20

837. In what position should the nurse place a client recovering from general anesthesia?

A. Side- lying B. Supine
C. High- Fowler D. Trendelenburg

838. The nurse is teaching a client about adequate hand hygiene. What component of hand washing should the nurse include that is most important for removing microorganisms?

A. Soap B. Friction
C. Water D. Time

839. A nurse in the surgical intensive care unit is caring for a client with a large surgical incision. What medication does the nurse anticipate will be prescribes for this client?

A. Cyanocobalamin (Cobex)
B. Phytonadione(Mephyton)
C. Ascorbic acid (Ascorbicap)
D. Vitamin A (Aquasol A)

840. A nurse applies an ice pack to a client's leg for 20 minutes. What client indicator helps the nurse determine the effectiveness of the treatment?

A. Peripheral vasodilatation
B. Local anesthesia
C. Depression of vital signs.
D. Decreased viscosity of blood.

841. Most reliable method of measuring body temperature is :-

A. Oral B. Axillary
C. Elbow D. Rectal

842. In following which statement regarding intravenous infusion is incorrect :-

A. A running I.V. should be checked every 30 minutes for adults and every 15 minutes for children.

B. 'Speed up' an I.V. in order to compensate for being behind schedule on the amount to infuse.

C. No solution or product other than normal saline should be added to blood or blood product.

D. Don't select an I.V. site on a paralyzed arm and don't take blood pressure on the arm that has an infusing I.V

843. Which of the following sentence is correct about plaster cast :-

A. The casted extremity should be elevated continuously for first 24-48 hours to minimize swelling and promote venous drainage.

B. Pulmonary embolism, infection and a vascular necrosis are the complication of plaster cast

C. All of the above sentences are correct.

D. Turn the casted extremity every 1-2 hour to allow air circulation and promote drying

844. Mannitol is a :-

A. Hypertonic solution and osmotic diuretic

B. Isotonic solution and osmotic diuretic

C. Hypotonic solution and osmotic diuretic

D. Hypertonic solution and thiazide diuretic

845. When performing tracheostomy suctioning the nurse should withdraw the catheter after applying intermittent suction for maximum:-

A. 20 Seconds B. 10 Seconds

C. 1-2 Minute D. 3-4 Minute

846. Collapsing pulse is also known as

A. Water-hammer pulse

B. Bounding pulse

C. Pulse-alterans

D. Bigeminal pulse

847. Which of the following type of bandage is used for head injury

A. Circular B. Capline

C. Spiral D. Spica

848. Which of the following table is used by the patient for the purpose of reading, writing and taking meal

A. Over bed table B. Bed-side table

C. None of the above D. Bed-table

849. Rectal tube should not be kept in place for not more than

A. 20 Minute B. 10 Minute

C. 30 seconds D. 5 Minute

850. Which of the following position is preferred for a patient after mastectomy

A. Fowler's position with affected arm elevated above the level of heart

B. Side-lying position with the affected arm

C. Prone position

D. High-fowler's position with affected arm elevated above the level of heart

851. What is the correct order of 5 stages of dying person

A. Denial – anger – bargaining – depression – acceptance

B. Anger – depression – bargaining – denial – acceptance

C. Denial – depression – bargaining – anger – acceptance

D. Depression – denial – anger – bargaining – acceptance

852. In the following which is the most important part of nursing process

A. Planning and determining the goal

B. Nursing intervention

C. Evaluation

D. Assessment of the problems or needs of the patient

853. In the following which bone is generally preferred for bone marrow aspiration

A. Humerus B. Sternum

C. Tibia-fibula D. Iliac crest

854. Oedema, pain and coolness at the I.V. site indicates which of the following complication of intravenous therapy

A. Infilteration

B. Infection

C. Circulatory overload

D. Air embolism

855. Drugs used to cause intestinal evacuation is

A. Carminatives B. Astringents

C. Cathartics D. Antimycotics

856. Which of the following position should be provided to the patient during sigmoidoscopy –

A. Sim's lateral B. Genu pectoral

C. Lithotomy D. Supine

857. Drugs which increase the action of sweat glands

A. Diuretics B. Digestants

C. Diaphoretics D. Ecbolics

858. Application of the drug to the skin is known as

A. Inhalation B. Insertion

C. Inunction D. Instillation

859. **SLE (Systemic lupus erythematous) :-**
A. An autoimmune disease
B. An endocrine disorder
C. A cardiac disorder
D. An allergic reaction

860. **Beneficial effects of exercise are except – .**
A. Maintains the muscles tone
B. Stimulates the blood circulation
C. Stimulates venous stasis
D. Increases oxygen consumption and metabolic rate

861. **When a drug is to be given at bed time, which of the following coded instruction is used?**
A. Ac B. Od C. Sos D. Hs

862. **During giving enema the distance to which the tube is inserted in an adult is**
A. 3-4 meter B. 3-4 inch
C. 1-1½ meter D. 1-2 cm

863. **Therapeutic uses of local hot application are except**
A. Heat controls haemorrhage
B. Heat promotes healing
C. Heat provide warmth
D. Heat reduces pain

864. **While giving hot application temperature of water in hot water bottle should be –**
A. 90° to 100°f B. 120° to 149°f
C. 200° to 210°f D. 100° to 110° f

865. **Examples of dry heat application are except –**
A. Hot water bottle B. Heating lamps
C. Hot fomentations D. UV rays

866. **Example of dry cold application are except –**
A. Ice pack B. Cold compress
C. Ice bag D. Ice cradle

867. **Suffix 'ostomy' means –**
A. Cutting into or incision of body part
B. Repair or suture of body part
C. Creation of opening into body part
D. Excision or removal of body part

868. **Laboratory findings during respiratory alkalosis are**
A. pH>7.45, $PaCO_2$ < 35 mmHg, PaO_2 < 80 mmHg
B. pH<7.35, $PaCO_2$ > 45 mmHg, PaO_2 < 80 mmHg
C. pH<7.45, $PaCO_2$ < 35 mmHg, PaO_2 < 80 normal
D. pH<7.35, $PaCO_2$ = 40 mmHg, PaO_2 < 80 mmHg

869. **In hospital the method most commonly used for administering oxygen to the patients is**
A. Nasal catheter B. Nasal cannula
C. By mask D. Oxygen tent

870. **Solution used for eye irrigation is –**
A. 2% boric acid B. 1% silver nitrate
C. All D. Normal saline

871. **Prolonged suctioning of the tracheostomy may cause –**
A. Anorexia
B. Hypoxia & cardiac arrest
C. Nausea & vomiting
D. Myocarditis & endocarditis

872. **What is the normal arterial PCo2 level-**
A. 30 to 40 mm of Hg B. 35 to 45 mm of Hg
C. 25 to 35 mm of Hg D. 40 to 50 mm of Hg

873. **Penicillin V (Veetids), 250 mg. PO every 8 hours is prescribe for a child with a respiratory infection. The child's weight is 44 Ib. The safe pediatric dosage is 25 to 50 mg per kg. per day. This dose is-**
A. High B. Low C. None D. Safe

874. **ESR increases in**
A. Allergic Reaction B. None of the above
C. Sickle Cell anemia D. Dehydration

875. **Increase level of Enzyme suggest skeletal muscle damage –**
A. CK-BB B. CK-MM
C. CK-MB D. None

876. **Level of LDH begins to rise about hrs. after MI.**
A. 48-72 hrs B. 4-6 hrs.
C. 24 hrs. D. 12 hrs.

877. **In Myocardial infarction (MI) :**
A. $LDH_2 > LDH_1$ B. $LDH_1 > LDH_2$
C. $LDH_3 > LDH_3$ D. $LDH_1 > LDH_3$

878. **A pt diagnosed with chronic pancreatitis. Which of the laboratory value is in fovour of chronic pancreatitis.**
A. Serum amylase level 45 Units/L
B. Serum amylase level 100 Units/L
C. Serum amylase level 500 Units/L
D. Serum amylase level 300 Units/L

879. **A pt having Mild degree of Renal insufficiency if witch of the following serum creatinine level is found :**
A. 0.5 mg/dl B. 1.9 mg/dl
C. 0.2 mg/dl D. 3.5 mg/dl

880. **Therapeutic level of serum pheyntoin is :**
A. 10-20 ug/dl B. 20-40ug/dl
C. 10-30 ug/ dl D. 5-12 ug/ml

881. **Which of the following is abnormal serum electrotype value :**
A. Na= 148 mEq/L
B. Potassium – 3.8mEq/L
C. Chloride -101 mEq/L
D. HCO_3= 26 mEq/L

882. A client is been admitted to the hospital for UTI & Dehydration & nurse evaluate that the client has received adequate volume replacement if the blood urea nitrogen level drops to :
A. 35 mg/dl B. 15 mg/dl
C. 29 mg/dl D. 3 mg/dl

883. Hospice is the treatment concept for –
A. Cardiac Pt B. Psychiatric Pt
C. Terminally ill Pt D. All

884. The process of assessing Pt who come to emergency department & determining the management priorities is called :
A. mirage B. Collage
C. Triage D. Strage

885. Site for recording Apical pulse :
A. 5 left intercostals space
B. 5& 6 left intercostals space
C. 3& 4 left intercostals space
D. All

886. Which of the following solution can be given with the blood transfusion.
A. R/L
B. 5% dextrose in ½ NS
C. 0.9 % Nacl
D. None

887. Antidote for potassium overload is –
A. Protamine Sulphate B. Desferoxamine
C. Keyaxalate D. N-accetyl cystein

888. A physician order 2000 ml of 5 % Dextrose & ½ NS to infuse over 24 hours. The drop factor is 15 drops/1 ml. A nurse set the flow rate at how many drops/minute?
A. 17 B. 21 C. 15 D. 28

889. Following liver biopsy the nurse plan to place the client in which of the followings position:
A. Left Sims Position
B. Right Sims Position
C. On the right side of the body.
D. On the side of the body.

890. Other name for Gas sterilization :
A. Fumigation
B. Autoclaving
C. Disinfection
D. Hot air sterilization

891. Complication of blood transfusion is :
A. Hypercalcemia B. Hypokalemia
C. Hyperkalemia D. Hypenatremia

892. Leg elevated position is providing in :
A. DVT B. Varicose Vein
C. Amputation D. All

893. Grains of paper like appearance of urine indicate presence of _______ in.
A. Stone B. Pus
C. Urea D. Uric acid

894. Size of endotracheal tube for neonate is
A. 8 mm B. 6 mm
C. 4.5 mm D. 3.5 mm

895. Gallow's traction is also known as –
A. Bryant's traction B. .Buck's Extension
C. Russell's traction D. skeletal traction

896. Chloride level in CSF is
A. 20-40 mg/dl B. 40-60 meq/L
C. 720-750 mg/dl D. 720-750 meq/L

897. Vital capacity of lungs is
A. 3500 ml B. 4500ml
C. 5000 ml D. 3000 ml

898. CAT Scan is
A. Computerized Axial Tomography scan
B. Computerized Automatic Tomography scan
C. Computerized Arial Tomography scan
D. Computerized Active Tomography scan

899. Most commonly used ventilator is 900. Site for giving Adrenaline injection directly into the heart-
A. 5th intercostals space
B. 6th intercostals space
C. 4th intercostals space
D. 7th intercostals space

900. When patient is in terminal stage of life, he wants the self decided death to pain relief called as:
A. Murder B. Euphonise
C. Entire D. Euthanasia

901. The client in a sitting position respiration is best for
A. Asthma
B. COPD pt
C. Cardiac patient
D. Nervous system problem

902. Which of the following Disinfectant solution is used for disinfection of endoscope?
A. Eusol
B. Cidex(2%-glutereldyhyde)
C. Mercurochrome
D. Both A & C

903. Painting of body cavity infected with fungus infection is done by –
A. Mercurochrome B. Lysol
C. Gentian Violet D. Eusol

904. Warm bed is also known as –
A. Stump Bed B. Recovery Bed
C. Fracture Bed D. Renal Bed

905. Rigar mortis first involve muscle of –
A. Jaw B. Neck C. Arm D. Legs

906. Which of the following ointment is used for treatment of Decubitus ulcer
A. ZnO B. Gentian Violet
C. Powder D. Both B & C

907. Calories requirement of a infant is –
A. 150 calories/kg bd wt/day
B. 130 calories/kg bd wt/day
C. 165 calories/kg bd wt/day
D. 110 calories/kg bd wt/day

908. Wound dressing is done by using-
A. Medical Asepssis B. Surgical Asepsis
C. Septic technique D. Both A & B

909. Which of the following solution reading available on the nursing unit should the nurse hang until another TPN solution is mixed & delivered to the nursing unit.
A. 5% dextrose in water
B. 5% dextrose in 0.9% Nacl
C. 5% dextrose in R/L
D. 10% dextrose in water.

910. A nurse is performing CPR on an adult client, when performing chest compression, the nurse understand that correct hand placement is located over the-
A. Lower 3rd of the sternum
B. Lower half of Ster
C. Upper half of Sternum
D. Upper 3rd of the sternum

911. Which of the following is most appropriate location to assess the pulse of an infant while giving BLS.
A. Carotid B. Popliteal
C. Radial D. Brachial

912. A nurse is performing CPR on an adult client. The nurse understand that when performing chest compression one should depress the sternum
A. 2 to 2.5 inch B. 1/2 to 3/4 inch
C. 3/4 to 1 inch D. 2.5 to 3 inch

913. Immediate disinfection of all contaminated articles during the course of disease-
A. Terminal disinfection
B. Concurrent disinfection
C. Sterilization d. Autoclaving
D. All of above

914. The fall of temperature in a Zigzag manner to normal is:
A. Crisis B. Decline
C. Stadium D. Lysis

915. In subnormal temp.the body temp. is:
A. 98-100^{0}F B. 95-97^{0}F
C. 35-36^{0}F D. 92-95^{0}F

916. X-ray is discovered by
A. Roentgen (1975) B. Roentgen (1885)
C. Roentgen (1895) D. Rovsing(1985)

917. T-Wave represents -
A. Repolarization of Ventricle
B. Repolarization of atrium
C. Depolarization of atrium
D. Depolarization of Ventricle

918. A client admitted with symptoms of systolic BP.70 mm of hg.,pulse 130/m,r.r rate 24,set priority action by nurse.
A. Start iv infusion B. Call physician
C. Lower head of bed D. Call cpr team

919. nurse caring client of 70 year old with hypovolamia who is receiving blood transfusion assessment finding crackle on chest auscultation and distend neck vein ,coughing what is nurse initial action ?
A. No need of any action
B. Slow the transfusion
C. Assess the client's pupil
D. Stop transfusion and push normal saline

920. A client with malnutrition place on total parentral nutrition nurse noted entering air in central line which initial action most appropriate?
A. Elevated head of bed
B. Place pt.leftlateral decubitus position
C. Notify physician
D. Stop TPN and infuse dextrose 5%

921 A client with crohns disease required TPN nurse find TPN bag empty what fluid nurse to select hang until another bag to prepared in pharmacy?
A. Normal saline B. Ringer lactate
C. D10W D. D5W

922. A pt under go for bone marrow aspiration from sternum what position nurse would assist in procedure?
A. Supine position
B. Dorsal recumbent
C. Lithotomy
D. Foetal attitude position

923. A client with COPD in respiratory failure which result is most sensitive indicator that the pt. require mechanical ventilator?
A. PH 7.22 B. SaO_2-90
C. PCO_2-58 D. HCO3-27

924. When nurse preparing client for MRI nurse should implement following?
A. Remove jewellery and inquiry about metal implant
B. Scrub inj.site till 15 minute
C. Obtain inform conscent and administer.4mg atropine
D. None

925. A pneumonectomy is performed on a client with lung cancer which of following would probable plan for client care?
A. Deep breathing exercise
B. Pain control measure
C. Suppliment oxygen
D. Close chest drain

926. Which assessment finding first in COPD pt. indicate to nurse about respiratory problem is chronic?
A. Clubbing of fingers B. Coughing
C. Cyanosis D. Wheezing

927. When providing care for a client with pancreatitis nurse would anticipated which of following order?
A. Fluid intake 3000ml/day
B. Place client in reverse trendlenburg position
C. NBM to pt.
D. Insert n .g.tube connect with low intermittent suction

928. Nurse assisting the physician with removing chest tube to remove instruct to client.
A. Hold breath 2 minute and exhale slow
B. Contineous breath in and out during remove
C. Take a deep breath ,exhale and bearing down
D. None

929. Nurse when performing pulmonic auscultation correctly when stethoscope is placed .
A. Between apex and sternum
B. 5th inter costal space in midclavicular line
C. At manibrium
D. 2nd intercostals space between left of sternum

930. Which clinical manifestation most indicative of carbon mono oxide poisoning.
A. Pulse oximeter reading 80%
B. Stridor respiration
C. Presence of carbon particle in mucus
D. Cherry red colour to mucus membrane

931. A client with chest tube noted with tube disconnected what is most appropriate action.
A. Clamp the tube immediately
B. Reconnect the tube at system again
C. Place him on left side
D. Put the end of tube in sterile cup of normal saline

932. A client with Hepatitis-c who has cirrhosis changes has just returned after liver biopsy nurse place the client in .
A. Rt.side lying B. Trendlenburg
C. Supine D. Left sims

933. The chest tube drainage system has continuous bubbling in the water seal chamber when the nurse clamp different area of tube to find out to find out where bub bling stop she is checking for.
A. The suction being too high
B. Tension pneumothotax
C. The suction being too low
D. An air leak

934. When percussing the lungs of a patient with emphysema, the nurse would probably hear which of the following sounds?
A. Hyperresonance B. Resonance
C. Tympany D. Dullness

935. When percussing a normal lung, which of the following sounds should be heard?
A. Tympany B. Dullness
C. Hyperresonance D. Resonance

936. In performing a bacterial wound swab, why is it necessary to cover the wound with appropriate dressing?
A. Facilitates wound healing, absorbs exudate, and reduces risk of bacterial colonization.
B. Promotes patient's comfort.
C. It reduces the transmission of microorganisms.
D. It decreases trauma to the tissue.

937. Which of the following types of burn injury is more frequent?
A. Chemical burns
B. Electrical burns
C. Thermal burns
D. Radiation related burns

938. What kind of technique used for assessing the extent of burn that gives reproducible accuracy especially age-related cases?
A. Wallace's "rule of nines" tool
B. Fitzpatrick's Scale
C. Both A and B
D. Lund and Browder chart

939. A nurse is inserting a nasogastric tube in an adult male client. During the procedure, the client begins to cough and has difficulty breathing. Which of the following is the appropriate nursing action?

A. Quickly insert the tube
B. Notify the physician immediately
C. Pull back on the tube and wait until the respiratory distress subsides
D. Remove the tube and reinsert when the respiratory distress subsides

940. Nurse Ryan is assessing for correct placement of a nosogartric tube. The nurse aspirates the stomach contents and check the contents for pH. The nurse verifies correct tube placement if which pH value is noted?

A. 7.0 B. 7.35 C. 7.5 D. 3.5

941. Nurse Joy is preparing to administer medication through a nasogastric tube that is connected to suction. To administer the medication, the nurse would:

A. Position the client supine to assist in medication absorption
B. Clamp the nasogastric tube for 30 minutes following administration of the medication
C. Aspirate the nasogastric tube after medication administration to maintain patency
D. Change the suction setting to low intermittent suction for 30 minutes after medication administration

942. The nurse is performing a colostomy irrigation on a male client. During the irrigation, the client begins to complain of abdominal cramps. What is the appropriate nursing action?

A. Notify the physician
B. Increase the height of the irrigation
C. Medicate for pain and resume the irrigation
D. Stop the irrigation temporarily

943. The nurse is teaching a female client how to perform a colostomy irrigation. To enhance the effectiveness of the irrigation and fecal returns, what measure should the nurse instruct the client to do?

A. Place heat on the abdomen
B. Perform the irrigation in the evening
C. Reduce the amount of irrigation solution
D. Increase fluid intake

944. "The client with O+ blood is in need of an emergency transfusion but the lab does not have any O+ blood available. Which potential unit of blood could be given to the client?

A. A+ unit B. B+ unit
C. Any Rh+ unit. D. 0- unit

945. "The physician orders 2 units of packed RBCs to be administered to the client. At 6pm.the night shift nurse initiates the first unit's transfusion before going off shift. At 10am. the day shift nurse notes the IV line has clotted off and the transfusion has not been completed. The nursing assessment revealed the transfusion was only approximately 75% complete. Which of the actions by the nurse is most appropriate?

A. Discontinue the transfusion.
B. Advise the blood bank about the delay for the next unit.
C. Restart another peripheral line with 0.9% NS and restart The blood transfusion with the remaining blood unit.
D. Document the amount infused thus far and continues the transfusion.

946. The nurse has obtained a unit of blood from the blood bank and has checked the blood bag properly with another nurse. Just before the beginning transfusion, the nurse assesses which of the following items?

A. Skin Colour
B. Urine output
C. Vital signs
D. Latest Hematocrit level.

947. "Before starting a transfusion of packed red blood cells for an anaemic patient, the nurse would arrange for a peer to monitor his or her other assigned patients for how many minutes when the nurse begins the transfusion?

A. 5 minutes B. 60 minutes
C. 30 minutes D. 15 minutes

948. "The nurse is caring for a patient who is to receive a transfusion of two units of packed red blood cells. After obtaining the first unit from the blood bank, the nurse would ask which of the following health team members in the nurses" station to assist in checking the unit before administration.

A. Unit Secretary
B. A Phlebotomist
C. Another Registered Nurse
D. A Physician's Assistant

949. The nurse who is about to give a blood transfusion knows that blood cells start to deteriorate after a certain period of time. Which of the following items is important to check regarding the age of blood cells before the transfusion is begun?

A. Presence of clots
B. Blood group
C. Blood identification number
D. Expiration date

950. The nurse is caring for a 70-year-old client with hypovolamia who is receiving a blood transfusion. Assessment findings reveal crackles on chest auscultation and distended neck veins. What is the nurse's initial action?
A. Assess the client's pupils.
B. Document the finding as the only action.
C. Stop the blood transfusion and turn normal saline.
D. Slow the transfusion.

951. The nurse is aware that the following solutions is routinely used to Flush an IV device before and after the administration of blood to a Patient is:
A. 5 percent dextrose in water solution
B. Sterile water
C. Heparin sodium
D. 0.9 percent sodium chloride

952. "Following surgery, the client requires a blood transfusion. The main reason the nurse wants to complete the unit transfusion within a four-hour period that blood:
A. Hanging for a longer four hours creates an increased risk of sepsis
B. May clot in the bag
C. May evaporate
D. May not clot in the recipient after this time period

953. "The nurse determines that a client is having a transfusion reaction. After the nurse stops the transfusion, which action should immediately be taken next?
A. Runs normal saline at a keep-vein-open rate
B. Removes the intravenous line
C. Runs a solution of 5% dextrose in water
D. Obtain a culture of the tip of the catheter device removed from the client

954. Besides high blood pressure values, what other signs and symptoms may the nurse observe if hypertension is present?
A. Unexplained pain and hyperactivity
B. Dizziness, mental confusion, and mottled extremities
C. Restlessness and dusky or cyanotic skin that is cool to the touch
D. Headache, flushing of the face, and nosebleed

955. The client, who has been on bed rest for 2 days, asks to get out of bed to go to the bathroom. He has new orders for "up ad lib." What action should the nurse take?
A. Give him some slippers and tell him where the bathroom is located.
B. Obtain orthostatic blood pressure measurements
C. Ask the nursing assistant to assist him to the bathroom.
D. Tell him it is not a good id

956. Using an oral electronic thermometer, the nurse checks the early morning temperature of a client. The client's temperature is 36.1° C (97° F). The client's remaining vital signs are in the normally acceptable range. What should the nurse do next?
A. Document the results; temperature is normal.
B. Recheck the temperature every 15 minutes until it is normal.
C. Get another thermometer; the temperature is obviously an error
D. Check the client's temperature history.

957. The client has an oral temperature of 39.2° C (102.6° F). What are the most appropriate nursing interventions?
A. Reduce external coverings and keep clothing and bed linens dry; administer antipyretics as ordered
B. Provide an alcohol sponge bath and monitor laboratory results.
C. Remove excess clothing, provide a tepid sponge bath, and administer an analgesic.
D. Provide fluids and nutrition, keep the client's room warm, and administer an analgesic.

958. The hypothalamus controls body temperature. The anterior hypothalamus controls heat loss, and the posterior hypothalamus controls heat production. What heat conservation mechanisms will the posterior hypothalamus initiate when it senses that the client's body temperature is lower than comfortable?
A. Vasodilatation and redistribution of blood to surface vessels
B. Sweating, vasodilatation, and redistribution of blood to surface vessels
C. Vasoconstriction, reduction of blood flow to extremities, and shivering
D. Vasoconstriction, sweating, and reduction of blood flow to extremities

959. The nurse's documentation indicates that a client has a pulse deficit of 14 beats. The pulse deficit is measured by:
A. Subtracting 60 (bradycardiafrom) the client's pulse rate and reporting the difference
B. Subtracting the client's pulse rate from 100 (tachycardiaand) reporting the difference

C. Assessing the apical pulse and 30 minutes later assessing the carotid pulse and subtracting the difference
D. Assessing the apical pulse and the radial pulse for the same minute and subtracting the difference

960. During the enema the client begins to complain of pain. The nurse notes blood in the return fluid and rectal bleeding. The nurse's next action is to:
A. Slow down the rate of instillation
B. Stop the instillation and measure vital signs
C. Stop the instillation.
D. Tell the client to breathe

961. The nurse is instructing the client about the use of opioids for pain relief. Included in the teaching is the fact that opioids may cause:
A. Headaches. B. Hypertension
C. Constipation D. Muscle weakness

962. A female client reports that she is experiencing burning on urination, frequency, and urgency. The nurse notes that a clean-voided specimen is marked cloudy. The probable cause of these symptoms and findings is:
A. Renal stone B. Haemorrhage
C. Cystitis D. Incontinence

963. Hospital-aquired urinary tract infections (UTIs) are often related to poor hand washing and:
A. Poor perineal hygiene
B. Use of urinary drainage bags
C. Improper catheter care
D. Poor urinary output

964. The nurse recognizes that the organism that most frequently causes urinary tract infections (UTIs) in women is:
A. Streptococcus
B. Escherichia coli
C. Aspergillus
D. Staphylococcus aureus

965. A female client is having difficulty voiding after childbirth. The nurse implements which of the following interventions to promote voiding?
A. Ambulating the client to the bathroom
B. Trickling warm water over the mons pubis
C. Turning the water tap on
D. All the above.

966. Most common site for blood transfusion in neonate are.
A. Femoral vein B. Sephanous vein
C. Basilic vein D. Umblical vein

967. The blood is stored on.
A. 2 to 8 degree centigrade
B. 8 degree centigrade
C. 1 degree centigrade
D. 4 degree centigrade

968. The drug which are used for the dilation of the eye?
A. Myotics B. Galactagogue
C. Mydriatics D. Expectorant

969. Which solution is given in nutrient enema except?
A. N.S. B. Glycerine
C. Glucose saline D. Peptonized milk

970. Normal height of the retention eneme is .
A. 45 cm. B. 20 cm. C. 8 cm. D. 18 cm.

971. stimulant enema is used in .
A. To reduce the inflammation
B. Elimination of the gases
C. To destroy the parasites
D. Shock

972. Transfer of heat directly through a substances from hot part to the cold part is known as.
A. Convection B. Radiation
C. Conduction D. Evaporation

973. Thermometer should be wipe after taking the temperature.
A. From bulb to stem B. From stem to bulb
C. Both A and B D. None of them

974. The high pitch musical whistling sound that occur with partial obstruction of bronchi is known as.
A. Wheezing B. Sign
C. Stridor D. Rale

975. If the B.P.cuff is too narrow the reading will be.
A. Low B. High
C. Normal D. None of them

976. Powder or gel form of drug encased in a hard or soft outercasing that dissolve in the stomach.
A. Caplet B. Elixir
C. Suppository D. Capsule

977. The small air sacs at the end of the terminal bronchioles that are the sites of gas exchange are known as which of the following?
A. Lobules. B. Pleurae
C. Alveoli D. Bronchioles

978. A patient who has difficulty breathing, increased respiratory and pulse rates, and pale skin with regions of cyanosis may be suffering from which of the following?
A. Hyperventilation B. Atelectasis
C. Perfusion D. Hypoxia

979. When inspecting a patient's chest to assess respiratory status, the nurse should be aware of which of the following normal findings?

A. The contour of the intercostal spaces should be rounded.
B. The chest should be slightly convex with no sternal depression.
C. The anteroposterior diameter should be greater than the transverse diameter.
D. The skin at the thorax should be cool and moist.

980. When percussing a normal lung, which of the following sounds should be heard?

A. Tympany B. Hyperresonance
C. Dullness D. Resonance

981. Which of the following normal breath sounds should be heard over the trachea?

A. Bronchial B. Bronchovesicular
C. Vesicular D. Tympanic

982. A patient who develops air in the pleural space is experiencing which of the following conditions?

A. Pneumothorax B. Hemothorax
C. Pleural effusion D. Pleura thorax

983. A patient who complains of difficulty breathing should be placed in which of the following positions?

A. Fowler's position B. Lateral position
C. Supine position D. Prone position

984. To drain the apical sections of the upper lobes of the lungs, the nurse should place the patient in which of the following positions?

A. Left side with a pillow under the chest wall
B. High Fowler's position
C. Side-lying position
D. Trendelenburg position

985. Which of the following inhalers is used to liquefy or loosen thick secretions?

A. Mucolytic agents
B. Bronchodilators
C. Corticosteroids
D. Metered-dose inhalers

986. The brain is sensitive to hypoxia and will sustain irreversible brain damage after how many minutes?

A. 4 to 6 minutes. B. 2 to 4 minutes
C. 6 to 8 minutes D. 8 to 10 minutes

987. Mr. Parks has chronic obstructive pulmonary disease. His nurse has taught him pursed-lip breathing, which helps him in which of the following ways?

A. Increases carbon dioxide, which stimulates breathing
B. Decreases the amount of air trapping and resistance
C. Helps liquefy his secretions
D. Teaches him to prolong inspiration and shorten expiration

988. A nurse suctioning a patient through a tracheostomy tube should be careful not to occlude the Y-port when inserting the suction catheter because it would cause which of the following to occur?

A. Loss of sterile field
B. Prevention of suctioning
C. Trauma to the tracheal mucosa
D. Suctioning of carbon dioxide

989. When caring for a patient with a tracheotomy, the nurse should be aware of which of the following?

A. The wound around the tube and inner cannula, if one is present, should be cleaned atleast every 24 hours.
B. Suctioning of the tracheostomy tube must be done using sterile technique.
C. A newly inserted tracheostomy tube requires no immediate attention.
D. The patient has no impairment of speaking function.

990. When percussing the lungs of a patient with emphysema, the nurse would probably hear which of the following sounds?

A. Resonance B. Dullness
C. Tympany D. Hyperresonance

991. Which of the following is a function of the upper airway?

A. Conduction of air
B. Purification of inspired
C. Production of pulmonary surfactant
D. Mucociliary clearance air

992. Which of the following accurately reflect the role of water in the human body?

A. Water acts as a solvent for electrolytes and nonelectrolytes.
B. Water facilitates cellular metabolism and proper chemical functioning.
C. Water helps maintain normal body temperature.
D. All of the above

993. Which of the following are proper actions for preparing an IV solution and tubing when starting an IV infusion?

A. Clamp tubing, uncap spike, and insert into entry site on bag as manufacturer directs.
B. Maintain aseptic technique when opening sterile packages and IV solution.
C. Remove cap at end of tubing, release clamp, and allow fluid to move through tubing
D. All of the above.

994. Following preparation of the IV solution and tubing, which of the following actions would be performed by the nurse when selecting a site and palpating a vein to start an IV infusion?

A. Select an appropriate site and palpate accessible veins.
B. Direct the ends of the tourniquet away from the site and check that the radial pulse is still present
C. Both A and B
D. None of them

995. Which of the following are signs of complications and their probable causes that may occur when administering an IV solution to a patient?

A. Local or systemic manifestations may indicate an infection is present at the site.
B. Redness, swelling, heat, and pain at the site may indicate phlebitis.
C. Swelling, pain, coolness, or pallor at the insertion site may indicate infiltration of the IV.
D. All of the above

996. Which of the following statements accurately describe the function or regulation of sodium in the human body?

A. Sodium participates in the generation and transmission of nerve impulses.
B. Sodium is the primary regulator of ECF volume.
C. Both A and B
D. None of them

997. Which of the following statements accurately describe the function or regulation of potassium in the body?

A. The kidneys conserve potassium when cellular potassium is decreased.
B. Potassium is the chief regulator of cellular enzyme activity and cellular water content.
C. Potassium is the major cation of ICF and works reciprocally with sodium.
D. All of the above

998. Which of the following statements accurately describe fluid and electrolyte movement?

A. A hypertonic solution has a greater concentration of particles in solution, causing water to move out of the cells and into the intravascular compartment in which the fluid is hypertonic, causing the cells to shrink.
B. Through the process of osmosis, the solvent water passes from an area of lesser solute concentration to an area of greater solute concentration until equilibrium is established.
C. In the process of diffusion, the solute moves from an area of higher concentration to an area of lower concentration until equilibrium is established.
D. All of the above.

999. Which of the following is the liquid constituent of blood?

A. Intracellular fluid B. Intravascular fluid
C. Interstitial fluid D. Extracellular fluid

1000. Which of the following food items is a leading source of potassium?

A. Canned vegetables
B. Bananas
C. Bread
D. Cheese

1001. Which of the following is the most abundant electrolyte in the body?

A. Sodium B. Potassium
C. Calcium D. Magnesium

1002. "Pumping uphill" would describe which of the following means of transporting materials to and from intracellular compartments?

A. Osmosis B. Diffusion
C. Filtration D. Active transport

1003. When determining a site for an IV infusion, the nurse should consider which of the following guidelines?

A. Antecubital veins should be used for long-term infusions.
B. Veins in the leg should be used to keep the arms free for the patient's use.
C. Veins in surgical areas should be used to increase the potency of medication.
D. Scalp veins should be selected for infants because of their accessibility.

1004. Individuals with which of the following blood types are often called universal donors?

A. Type A B. Type B
C. Type AB D. Type O

1005. A nurse who has diagnosed a patient as having "fluid volume excess" related to

compromised regulatory mechanism (kidneys) may have been alerted by which of the following symptoms?
A. Muscle twitching
B. Fingerprinting over sternum
C. Distended neck veins
D. Nausea and vomiting

1006. Which of the following short- or long-term venous access devices is usually introduced into the subclavian or internal jugular veins and passed to the superior vena cava just above the right atrium?
A. Electronic infusion device
B. Implanted port
C. Central venous catheter
D. Peripherally inserted central catheter

1007. When teaching a patient about foods that affect his fluid balance, the nurse will keep in mind that the electrolyte that primarily controls water distribution throughout the body is which of the following?
A. K_ B. Ca_
C. Na__ D. Mg__

1008. Which of the following nursing diagnoses would you expect to be based on the effects of fluid and electrolyte imbalance on human functioning?
A. Constipation related to immobility
B. Pain related to surgical incision
C. Health Risk for Infection related to inadequate personal hygiene
D. Altered Thought Processes related to cerebral edema, including mental confusion

1009. A woman who notices an involuntary loss of urine following a coughing episode is most likely experiencing which of the following types of incontinence?
A. Urge incontinence
B. Overflow incontinence
C. Stress incontinence
D. Functional incontinence

1010. Measurement of residual urine by catheterization after voiding verifies which of the following conditions?
A. Urinary tract infection
B. Urinary retention
C. Urinary incontinence
D. Urinary suppression

1011. Which of the following catheters should be used to drain a patient's bladder for short periods (5 to 10 minutes)?
A. Straight catheter
B. Suprapubic catheter
C. Indwelling urethral catheter
D. Foley catheter

1012. Which of the following facts about the lower urinary tract system should be kept in mind when considering catheterization?
A. A normal bladder is as susceptible to infection as an injured one.
B. The external opening to the urethra should always be sterilized.
C. Pathogens introduced into the bladder remain in the bladder.
D. The bladder normally is a sterile cavity.

1013. Which of the following collection devices is a nurse's best option when collecting urine from a nonambulatory male patient?
A. Specimen hat
B. Large urine collection bag
C. Bedpan
D. Urinal

1014. Pt. is being transferred to the hospital from a nursing home with a diagnosis of dehydration and urinary bladder infection. His skin is also excoriated from urinary incontinence. Which of the following is the most appropriate nursing diagnosis for pt.?
A. Impaired Skin Integrity related to urinary tract infection and dehydration.
B. Urinary Incontinence related to urinary tract infection
C. Impaired Skin Integrity related to functional incontinence
D. Risk for Urinary Tract Infection related to dehydration

1015. Which of the following nursing interventions would be least effective when trying to maintain safety for the patient with an indwelling catheter?
A. Maintain a closed drainage system.
B. Apply a topical antibiotic to urinary meatus.
C. Restrict fluid intake.
D. Report signs of infection immediately.

1016. A nurse determines that her patient has costovertebral tenderness. Which of the following conditions is indicated by this physical finding?
A. An inflamed kidney
B. A Bladder obstruction
C. A bladder infection
D. The presence of a kidney stone

1017. The doctor has ordered the collection of a fresh urine sample for a particular examination. Which urine sample would the nurse discard?

A. The sample collected immediately after lunch
B. The first voiding of the day
C. The voiding collected at 4 p.m.
D. The bedtime voiding.

1018. Which of the following statements accurately describe the function and composition of the urinary bladder?

A. The urinary bladder muscle is innervated by the autonomic nervous system.
B. The urinary bladder serves as a reservoir for urine.
C. Both A and B
D. None of them

1019. Tympany, the normal sound percussed over the abdomen, is caused by which of the following?

A. Hollow organs B. Excess flatus
C. Intestinal fluid D. Fecal contents

1020. Which of the following drugs acts by increasing intestinal bulk to enhance mechanical stimulation of the intestine?

A. Magnesium sulphate
B. Bisacodyl
C. Cascara.
D. Phenolphthalein

1021. Which of the following measures are appropriate when a nurse collects a stool specimen?

A. Handwashing is performed before and after glove use when handling a stool specimen.
B. Medical aseptic techniques are always followed.
C. The patient should be instructed not to place toilet tissue in the bedpan or specimen container.
D. All of the above

1022. Which of the following assessment measures is used to assess the location, shape, size, and density of tissues?

A. Observation B. Percussion
C. Palpation D. Auscultation

1023. When percussing the stomach, which of the following sounds would most likely be heard?

A. Flatness B. Hyperresonance
C. Dullness D. Tympany

1024. A patient who presents with a dusky, bluish skin color is experiencing which of the following conditions?

A. Cyanosis B. Jaundice
C. Flushing D. Pallor

1025. Which of the following are soft, low-pitched sounds heard best over the base of the lungs during inspiration?

A. Bronchial sounds
B. Adventitious breath sounds
C. Bronchovesicular sounds
D. Vesicular breath sounds

1026. A soft, high-pitched, flat sound that is usually percussed over muscle tissue is which of the following?

A. Resonance B. Flatness
C. Hyperresonance D. Dullness

1027. Mr. Rogers has a large tumor in his left lung. Which assessment technique would be used to determine the size of this tumor?

A. Percussion B. Palpation
C. Auscultation D. Inspection

1028. A rubbing, grating sound that is loudest on the lower lateral anterior surface of the thorax and is auscultated during inspiration is known as which of the following?

A. Wheeze B. Rhonchi
C. Friction rub D. Crackles

1029. Which of the following assessment techniques would a nurse use to assess the thyroid gland?

A. Percussion B. Inspection
C. Palpation D. Auscultation

1030. Which of the following is an accurate description of vesicular breath sounds?

A. They are soft, low-pitched sounds heard best over the base of the lungs during respiration. Inspiration is longer than expiration.
B. They are noisy, strenuous respirations.
C. They are high-pitched sounds heard on inspiration when there is a narrowing of the upper airway.
D. They are high-pitched, harsh sounds, with expiration being longer than inspiration.

1031. A weak, thready pulse found after the nurse palpates peripheral pulses may indicate which of the following conditions?

A. Decreased cardiac output.
B. Hypertension and circulatory overload
C. Impaired circulation
D. Inflammation of a vein

1032. Which of the following statements describe the tone that may be per-cussed at specific body locations.

A. Loud tympany may be heard over a gastric air bubble.

B. A dull sound is generally heard over the liver.

C. A flat tone may be heard over the thigh.

D. All of the above

1033. Which of the following is the primary source of heat in the human body?

A. Hypothalamus

B. Hormones

C. Sympathetic neurotransmitters

D. Metabolism

1034. What would be the cardiac output of an adult with a stroke volume of 75 mL and a pulse of 78 beats/minute?

A. 5,000 mL B. 5,550 mL

C. 6,000 mL D. 5,850 mL

1035. Which of the following conditions occurs when an adult has a pulse rate of 100 beats/minute?

A. Bradycardia B. Tachycardia

C. Pulse amplitude D. Arrhythmia

1036. Which of the following statements concerning respiratory rates is accurate?

A. An increase in intracranial pressures stimulates the respiratory center and increases the respiration rate.

B. Healthy adults breathe about 12 to 20 times per minute.

C. The respiratory rate decreases in response to the increased metabolic rate during pyrexia.

D. Infants and young children have a lower respiratory rate than adults.

1037. Which of the following statistics regarding blood pressure is accurate?

A. Men usually have a lower blood pressure than women of the same age..

B. Blood pressure tends to be lower in a prone or supine position than in a seated or standing position.

C. Blood pressure decreases after eating.

D. Blood pressure is usually highest on arising in the morning.

1038. The average normal temperature in degrees Fahrenheit for adults in the rectal site in which of the following?

A. 99.0 B. 97.6

C. 98.6 D. 594.0

1039. Which of the following clearly describes a stage 3 pressure injury?

A. It includes a full thickness skin loss; subcutaneous fat may be visible.

B. It includes a partial thickness loss of dermis and shallow open ulcers.

C. It includes a full thickness tissue loss with exposed bone, tendon, and muscle.

D. It is present on areas of persistent, non-blanchable redness when compared with the surrounding skin.

1040. Which of the following is considered as a major factor in determining pressure injuries to patients?

A. Pain B. Abscess

C. Edema D. Redness

1041. Which of the following strategy is not essential in preventing pressure injuries?

A. Prevent shear and friction.

B. Monitor patient's nutrition and hydration.

C. Maintain good skin hygiene.

D. Promote rubbing and massaging the bony prominences.

1042. Which of the following step in the nursing process where a nurse will continue, modify, or terminate the client's plan based on the outcomes gathered?

A. Diagnosing B. Implementing

C. Assessing D. Evaluating

1043. There are various types of assessment use by a nurse which depends on the situation. Which of the following is performed during any physiologic or psychological crisis of the patient?

A. Emergency Assessment

B. Initial Assessment

C. Problem-Focused Assessment

D. Time-Lapsed Reassessment

1044. Obtaining data is a very crucial part in planning patient's care. Which of the following types of data is also referred as the overt data?

A. Subjective data B. Objective data.

C. Constant data D. Inherent data

1045. There are different types of nursing diagnosis that a nurse can choose from. Which of the following types is considered as a client problem which is present at the time of assessing the patient?

A. Syndrome diagnosis.

B. Wellness diagnosis

C. Risk nursing diagnosis

D. Actual diagnosis

1046. Which of the following is not a characteristic of Maslow's hierarchy of needs?

A. It is self-centered rather than problem centered.

B. Has superior perception, is more decisive.

C. It is realistic, sees life clearly, and is subjective about his or her observations.

D. It is highly effective, flexible, spontaneous, courageous, willing to make mistakes.

1047. Which of the following describes a secondary level of prevention?

A. Family planning services

B. Referring a client to a support group

C. Denver Developmental Screening Test.

D. Hepatitis B Immunization

1048. Which of the following models of health and wellness describes that a person is considered healthy as long as they can perform their roles in the society?

A. Adaptive Model

B. Role Performance model

C. Role Status Model

D. Role Consistency Model

1049. Andragogy is defined as the art and science use in teaching adults. Which of the following concepts can be used as a guide for client teaching?

A. An adult's readiness to learn is often not related to a developmental task or social role.

B. As people mature, they move from independence to dependence.

C. An adult's previous experiences can be used as a resource for learning.

D. An adult is more oriented in learning when material is use sometime in the future.

1050. A leader is someone who can influence others to accomplish a specific goal. Which of the following leadership styles that has a minimal leader activity level?

A. Authoritarian Leadership Style

B. Laissez-Faire Leadership Style

C. Democratic Leadership Style

D. A and C

1051. Which of the following interventions that a nurse should not perform in patients suffering from hypothermia?

A. Cover the client's scalp with a cap

B. Keep limbs far from the body.

C. Provide a warm environment.

D. Apply warm blankets.

1052. The nurse assesses a client with an ileostomy for possible development of which of the following acid-base imbalances?

A. Respiratory acidosis

B. Metabolic alkalosis

C. Metabolic acidosis

D. Respiratory alkalosis

1053. The nurse anticipates which of the following responses in a client who develops metabolic acidosis

A. Respiratory rate of 30 cpm

B. Urinary output of 15 ml

C. Heart rate of 105 bpm

D. Temperature of 39 degree Celsius

1054. A client has a phosphorus level of 5.0mg/dL. The nurse closely monitors the client for?

A. Hypoglycemia

B. Elevated blood glucose

C. Cardiac dysrhythmias

D. Signs of tetany

1055. A nurse is caring for a child with pyloric stenosis. The nurse would watch out for symptoms of?

A. Vomiting large amounts

B. Projectile vomiting

C. Watery stool

D. Dark-colored stool

1056. Which of the following has mostly likely occurred when there is continuous bubbling in the water seal chamber of the closed chest drainage system?

A. Air leak in the system.

B. The connection has been taped too tightly

C. Lung expansion

D. The connection tubes are kinked.

1057. The nurse plans to frequently assess a post-thyroidectomy patient for?

A. Polyuria

B. Laryngospasm

C. Hypertension

D. Hypoactive deep tendon reflex .

1058. A nurse is preparing to give an IM injection of Iron Dextran that is irritating to the subcutaneous tissue. To prevent irritation to the tissue, what is the best action to be taken?

A. Use the z-track technique

B. Administer drug at a 45 degree angle

C. Use a 24-gauge-needle

D. Apply ice over the injection site

1059. What should a nurse do prior to taking the patient's history?
A. Offer the patient a glass of water
B. Ask information for insurance purposes.
C. Ask the patient to put on gown
D. Establish rapport

1060. A nurse is going to administer ear drops to a 4-year-old child. What is the correct way of instilling the medicine after tilting the patient's head sidewards?
A. Pull the pinna up then backwards.
B. Pull the pinna back then upwards
C. Pull the pinna back then downwards
D. Pull the pinna down then backwards

1061. Exchange of gases between the blood andbody cell is known is
A. Diffusion B. Oxygenation
C. Transportation D. None of the Above

1062. During a basic life support class, the instructor said that blind finger sweeping is not advisable for infants. Which among the following could be the reason?
A. The mouth is still too small
B. The infant might bite
C. Sharp fingernails might injure the victim
D. The object may be pushed deeper into the throat

1063. A nurse enters a room and finds a patient lying on the floor. Which of the following actions should the nurse perform first?
A. Call for help
B. Assess vital signs
C. Ask the patient what happened
D. Establish responsiveness of patient

1064. A patient with complaints of chest pain was rushed to the emergency department. Which priority action should the nurse do first?
A. Administer morphine sulfate intravenously
B. Administer oxygen via nasal cannula
C. Initiate venous access by performing venipunture
D. Complete physical assessment and patient history

1065. Several patients from a reported condominium fire incident were rushed to the emergency room. Which should the nurse attend to first?
A. A 40-year-old woman with complaints of severe pain on the left thigh
B. A 28-year-old man with burns on all extremities
C. A 4-year-old child who is crying inconsolably and reports severe headache
D. A 15-year-old girl, with burns on the face and chest, reports hoarseness of the voice

1066. The doctor ordered 1 pack of red blood cells (PRBC) to be transfused to a patient. The nurse prepares the proper IV tubing. The IV tubing appropriate for blood transfusion comes with?
A. Air vent
B. In-line filter
C. Microdrip chamber
D. Soluset

1067. The expected yet negative (harmful) result for post hemodialysis is a decrease in?
A. Creatinine
B. Red blood cell count
C. Phosphorus
D. BUN

1068. A patient was brought to the emergency room after she fell down the stairs. Which of the following is the best indicator for increased intracranial pressure in head and spinal injury?
A. Inability to move extremities
B. Decrease level of consciousness
C. Increase in pulse and blood pressure
D. Decreased respiratory rate

1069. A new nurse is administering an enema to a patient. The senior nurse should intervene if the new nurse?
A. Positions the client on the right side
B. Hangs the enema bag 18 inches above the anus
C. Advances the catheter 4 inches into the anal canal
D. Lubricates 4 inches of the catheter tip

1070. The medication nurse is going to give a patient his morning medications. What is the primary action a nurse should do before administering the medications?
A. Check client's identification bracelet
B. Raise head of the bed
C. Give distilled water
D. Provide privacy

1071. A cardiac patient came in to the hospital for his daily cardiac rehabilitation. This type of activity is included in the following:
A. Tertiary Disease Prevention
B. Secondary Disease Prevention
C. Primary Disease Prevention
D. All of the above

1072. When will be the best time to work with termination phase in a community immersion?

A. Orientation Phase
B. Pre-Interview Phase
C. Working Phase
D. Termination Phase

1073. Which of the following conditions tends to lower blood pressure?

A. High viscosity of the blood
B. Strong pumping action of blood
C. Decreased elasticity of walls of arterioles
D. Low blood volume into arteries

1074. Which of the following are normal variations in vital signs that occur at various ages?

A. The normal blood pressure for a newborn is 73/55.
B. Normal oral temperature for an adult is 37_C.
C. Both A & B
D. None of them

1075. Which of the following statements regarding blood pressure are accurate?

A. The highest pressure is the systolic pressure; the lowest pressure is the diastolic pressure
B. Blood pressure rises as the ventricle contracts and falls as the heart relaxes.
C. When the radial pulse is irregular, counting at the apex of the heart and at the radial artery simultaneously may assess the apical radial pulse rate.
D. All of the above

1076. Which of the following guidelines would be implemented when properly assessing a patient's blood pressure?

A. Have the patient assume a comfortable lying or sitting position.
B. Inflate the cuff while continuing to palpate the artery. Pump the pressure 30 mm Hg above the point at which the systolic pressure was palpated and estimated.
C. Center the bladder of the cuff over the brachial artery, about midway on the arm,so that the lower edge of the cuff is about 2.5 to 5 cm above the inner aspect of theelbow.
D. All of the above

1077. In examining a patient with asthma in exacerbation, what lung sound is predominant?

A. Crackles B. Pleural rub
C. Wheezes D. Gurgles.

1078. What is the proper order in the physical assessment when it comes to examination of the abdomen?

A. Auscultation, Inspection, Percussion, Palpation
B. Inspection, Percussion, Palpation, Auscultation
C. Palpation, Percussion, Inspection, Auscultation
D. Inspection, Auscultation, Percussion, Palpation

1079. A client is diagnosed to have Congestive Heart Failure. Upon auscultating the client's lungs the nurse hears crackling sounds bilaterally at the bases. What term should you use in documenting this finding?

A. Rhonchi B. Rales
C. Wheezing D. Atelectasis

1080. In a burn patient, in order to promote adequate fluid within 24 hours, what intravenous fluid is appropriate?

A. D5 Water
B. D5NS
C. 0.9% NaCl Solution
D. Lactated Ringer's Solution

1081. You were assigned to a patient with a nasogastric tube attached for almost three days. It is time to irrigate it, what is the protocol that you will follow?

A. A 30 mL sterile saline must be forcefully instilled and provide a basin to catch the return flow.
B. A 20 mL sterile saline must be gently instilled and provide a basin to catch the return flow.
C. Gently instill 30 mL normal saline and then withdraw solution.
D. Instill 30 mL sterile water and then withdraw solution.

1082. You were assigned to a patient. Upon assessment, the patient elicited Homan's sign. What is the nursing priority using this assessment?

A. Encourage fluid and electrolyte balance
B. Encourage good venous circulation
C. Secure patent airway
D. Promote skin care

1083. A 28-month-old child with severe diarrhea is admitted. Upon assessment the child is feverish, has dry lips and irritable. What is your first nursing priority upon admission?

A. Weigh the child
B. Assess the skin turgor
C. Asses the hydration status
D. Obtain the apical-radial cardiac rate.

1084. The nurse is to administer digoxin elixir to a 6-month-old with a congenital heart defect. The nurse auscultates an apical pulse rate of 100. The nurse should:

A. Record the heart rate and call the physician
B. Hold the medication and recheck the heart rate in 30 minutes
C. Administer the medication and recheck the heart rate in 15 minutes
D. Record the heart rate and administer the medication 269. A mother of a 3-year-old hospitalized

1085. With lead poisoning asks the nurse to explain the treatment for her daughter. The nurse's explanation is based on the knowledge that lead poisoning is treated with:

A. Chelating agents B. Gastric lavage
C. Antiemetics D. Activated charcoal

1086. An 18-month-old is scheduled for a cleft palate repair. The usual type of restraints for the child with a cleft palate repair are:

A. Wrist restraints
B. Full arm restraints
C. Elbow restraints
D. Mummy restraints

1087. The nurse should instruct the client to do which of the following just before the nurse remove the NG tube.?

A. Take and hold a deep breath.
B. Inhale and exhale quickly
C. Exhale
D. Perform a valsalva maneuver

1088. To determine the accurate measurement of the length of the naso-gastric tube to be inserted ,the nurse should:

A. Mark the tubeat10inch
B. Place the tube at the tip of the nose and measure by extending the tube to the ear lobe and then down to the lower part of sternum
C. Mark the tube at 32 inch
D. Place the tube at the tip of the nose and measure by extending the tube to the ear lobe and then down to the top part of sternum.

1089. Which of the following solution can be given with the blood transfusion.

A. R/L
B. 5% dextrose in ½ NS
C. 0.9 % Nacl
D. None

1090. When performing tracheostomy suctioning the nurse should withdraw the catheter after applying intermittent suction for maximum:-

A. 10 Seconds B. 30 Seconds
C. 1-2 Minute D. 3-5 Minute

1091. Collapsing pulse is also known as

A. Bounding pulse
B. Bigeminal pulse
C. Pulse-alterans
D. Water-hammer pulse

1092. A nurse is inserting a nasogastric tube in an adult male client. During the procedure, the client begins to cough and has difficulty breathing. Which of the following is the appropriate nursing action?

A. Quickly insert the tube
B. Notify the physician immediately
C. Pull back on the tube and wait until the respiratory distress subsides
D. Remove the tube and reinsert when the respiratory distress subsides .

1093. Nurse Joy is preparing to administer medication through a nasogastric tube that is connected to suction. To administer the medication, the nurse would:

A. Clamp the nasogastric tube for 30 minutes following administration of the medication
B. Aspirate the nasogastric tube after medication administration to maintain patency
C. Position the client supine to assist in medication absorption.
D. Change the suction setting to low intermittent suction for 30 minutes after medication administration

1094. The nurse is teaching a female client how to perform a colostomy irrigation. To enhance the effectiveness of the irrigation and fecal returns, what measure should the nurse instruct the client to do?

A. Place heat on the abdomen
B. Increase fluid intake
C. Perform the irrigation in the evening
D. Reduce the amount of irrigation solution

1095. "The client with O+ blood is in need of an emergency transfusion but the lab does not have any O+ blood available. Which potential unit of blood could be given to the client?

A. B+ unit B. A+ unit
C. 0- unit D. Any Rh+ unit.

1096. "The physician orders 2 units of packed RBCs to be administered to the client. At 10pm. the night shift nurse initiates the first unit's transfusion before going off shift. At 10am. the day shift nurse notes the IV line has clotted off and the transfusion has not been completed Which of the actions by the nurse is most appropriate?

A. Advise the blood bank about the delay for the next unit.
B. Restart another peripheral line with 0.9% NS and restart the blood transfusion with the remaining blood unit.
C. Document the amount infused thus far and continue the transfusion.
D. Discontinue the transfusion.

1097. The nurse has obtained a unit of blood from the blood bank and has checked the blood bag properly with another nurse. Just before the beginning transfusion, the nurse assessess which of the following items?

A. Urine ouput.
B. Skin Color
C. Vital signs
D. Latest hematocrit level.

1098. "Following surgery, the client requires a blood transfusion. The main reason the nurse wants to complete the unit transfusion within a four-hour period that blood:

A. May evaporate
B. May clot in the bag
C. Hanging for a longer four hours creates an increased risk of sepsis
D. May not clot in the recipient after this time period

1099. "The nurse determines that a client is having a transfusion reaction. After the nurse stops the transfusion, which action should immediately be taken next?

A. Remove the intravenous line
B. Run normal saline at a keep-vein-open rate
C. Run a solution of 5% dextrose in water.
D. Obtain a culture of the tip of the catheter device removed from the client

1100. A female client is having difficulty voiding after childbirth. The nurse implements which of the following interventions to promote voiding?

A. Turning the water tap on
B. Trickling warm water over the mons pubis
C. Ambulating the client to the bathroom
D. All of the above.

1101. Maximum temperature of femalc

A. During menstruation
B. Just before menstrual period.
C. After ovulation
D. None of the Above

1102. Formula which is used by nurse to convert Celsius in to Fahrenheit.

A. (F – 32) * 5/9 B. 5/9 C. +3
C. 9/5 C. +23 D. 9/5 C. +32

1103. Period when the body temp has reached its maximum & remains fairly constant at a high level

A. Remittent B. Continuous
C. Fastigium D. Inter mitten

1104. Oxygen consumption increases for each °C rise in temperature

A. 7% B. 7% C. 1.3% D. 13%

1105. Which are the stages of fever Except?

A. Shivering B. Fever stage
C. Cold D. Hot stage

1106. Nurse when caring of a client who diagnosed as hyperthermia , she start the sponge bath as priority action on side except?

A. Legs B. Chest
C. Head D. Hand

1107. Carotid artery at the palpate at side

A. Behind the knee.
B. Posterior border of sterno cleido mastoid muscles
C. Horizontals border of sterno cleido mastoid muscles
D. Anterior border of sterno cleido mastoid muscles

1108. Drug digoxine should be avoided in condition of

A. Pulse below 60/m
B. Pulse above 120/m
C. Pulse 80/m
D. Pulse 100/m

1109. Pulse rate is rapid during inspiration & slow during expiration which are otherwise known as normal arrhythmia ?

A. Bradycardia B. Sinus arrhythmia
C. Arrhythmia D. Dicrotic pulse

1110. nurse who is caring with restrain patient for
A. 30 minute B. 5 minute
C. 10 minute D. 45 second

1111. Suture are more sensitive
A. Plain catgut B. Nylon
C. Chromic catgut D. Silk

1112. Catgut are received from
A. Larva of cocoon
B. Brain of sheep
C. Intestine of sheep
D. Intestine of cat

1113. Suture which should cut from abdomen with in
A. 7-10 days B. 2-5 days
C. 10-14 days D. 10-40 days

1114. Normal length of suture is
A. 15 cm. B. 10 inch
C. 15 inch D. 10 cm.

1115. Uncuffed tracheostomy tubes
A. Provide aspiration protection.
B. Are used mostly for children.
C. Facilitate positive-pressure ventilation.
D. Don't allow for airway clearance.

1116. A patient may need a tracheostomy due to
A. Nasal polyps.
B. Long-term mechanical.
C. Esophageal fissures.
D. Bronchodilation. ventilation.

1117. Current guidelines recommend a tracheostomy instead of an ET tube
A. To lower the risk of complications.
B. For patients needing an artificial airway for more than 21 days.
C. For patients needing any type of mechanical ventilation.
D. For patients needing an artificial airway for 10 days or less.

1118. An adult has been diagnosed as having pulmonary tuberculosis. Which test would the nurse expect to be ordered?
A. Blood test B. Monteux test
C. Sputum D. Chest X-ray

1119. An adult patient has been bile obstruction . Which test would the nurse expect
A. White colour stool
B. Clay colour stool
C. Blood in stool
D. Soup like stool

1120. An Patient 65 year old age has been diagnosed as having pulmonary oedema. Which test would the nurse expect to be ?
A. Manipulation B. Percussion
C. Palpation D. Auscultation

1121. An Patient 35 year old age has been examine by Nurse Rina for bowl sound. Sound would the nurse expect to be ?
A. High pitch B. Gurglish
C. Low pitch D. Resonance

1122. An patient has been bile presence in urine . colour of urine expected by nurse
A. Pink B. White
C. Brown green D. Blue

1123. The nurse is positioning an adult who has just returned to the surgical nursing care unit following a pneumonectomy. What is the most appropriate position in which to place the client?
A. Semi-Fowler's on his back.
B. Semi-Fowler's on the affected side.
C. Sims position on the unaffected side.
D. Semi-Fowler's on the unaffected side.

1124. An order is written for oxygen by nasal cannula at 2 liters per minute. In assessing the adequacy of the oxygen therapy, which of the following is most effective?
A. Measurement of arterial blood gasses.
B. Checking the color of mucous membranes.
C. Measurement of pulmonary functions.
D. Checking the respiratory rate.

1125. The nurse is performing tracheal suctioning. Which action is essential to prevent hypoxemia during suctioning?
A. Administer 100% oxygen before suctioning.
B. Encouraging the client to deep breathe and cough.
C. Removal of oral and nasal secretions.
D. Auscultate the lungs.

1126. Client complaint to nurse after removal of Et tube about stridor or horseness sound respiration, instruction should given by nurse to pt.
A. Abnormal after removal of tube and client should more talking
B. Normal after removal of tube and client should limit talking
C. Infection are very severe take antibiotic
D. I do not know contact to doctor

1127. Nurse rosy caring pt. with tracheotomy tube sudden dislodgment the tube set the priority nursing action.
A. Inform the physician
B. Grasp the retention suture to spread the opening
C. Use the tracheal dilator to hold the stoma open,
D. Extend the neck and open air way

1128. An Patient 65 year old age has been diagnosed as having pulmonary oedema. Which best position provide to pt.

A. Semi fowler B. High fowler
C. Prone D. Low fowler

1129. Best position provided by nurse in pt. who is suffering from GERD

A. Semi fowler
B. Reverse Trendelenburg
C. Fowlers
D. High fowler

1130. Nurse working in ICU , during examination doctor told patient have Increase ICP,Best position provided by nurse to pt. :-

A. Semi fowler
B. Reverse Trendelenburg
C. Fowlers
D. High fowler

1131. Nurse caring 2-year age child with minor fracture of femur which is most initial treatment of this pt.?

A. Apply the Bryant traction
B. Placing the child in skeletal traction
C. Immediate setting and casting the fracture
D. Setting the fracture with pin during surgery.

1132. A client 15 months had a spica cast applied,which is nursing action as priority:-

A. Avoid give him medication they cause constipation
B. Assess sensation ,circulation ,and motion of feet and toe
C. Limited fluid give so urination can wet cast
D. Instruct parents carry child in car.

1133. Nurse is prepare in 2 year age child as injection in left side leg identify the area where nurse give the inj.

A. Intra muscular B. Vastus lateral
C. Deltoid muscle D. Ventro glutial

1134. Prolonged suctioning of the tracheostomy may cause:

A. Hypoxia & Cardiac
B. Nausea & Vomiting
C. Anorexia
D. Myocarditis & Endocarditis

1135. A client has Buck's extension traction applied to the right leg. The nurse plans which of the following interventions to prevent complications from the device?

A. Aprovide pin care once a shift
B. Inspect the skin on the right leg at least once every 8 hours
C. Massage the skin of the right leg with lotion every 8 hours
D. Release the weights on the right leg for range of motion exercises daily

1136. A client has head halter traction applied to the head. The nurse plans which of the following interventions to prevent complications from the device?

A. Massage the skin of the right leg with lotion every 8 hours
B. Aprovide pin care once a shift
C. Inspect the skin on the right leg at least once every 8 hours
D. Release the weights on the right leg for range of motion exercises daily

1137. A nurse obtained a client's pulse and found the rate to be above normal. The nurse document this findings as:

A. Tachypnea B. Tachycardia
C. Arrythmia D. Hyper pyrexia

1138. Which of the following actions should the nurse take to use a wide base support when assisting a client to get up in a chair?

A. Face the client, bend knees and place hands on client's forearm and lift
B. Bend at the waist and place arms under the client's arms and lift
C. Spread his or her feet apart
D. Tighten his or her pelvic muscles

1139. Which intervention is an example of primary prevention?

A. Administer immunization to an infant
B. Administering digoxin to a patient with heart failure
C. Obtaining a smear to screen for cervical cancer
D. Using occupational therapy to help a patient cope with arthritis

1140. A client who is unconscious needs frequent mouth care. When performing a mouth care, the best position of a client is:

A. Fowler's position
B. Side lying
C. Supine
D. Trendelenburg

1141. A client enters into the clinic with a chief complaint of abdominal pain and diarrhea. What phrase of nursing process is being implemented here by the nurse?

A. Implementation B. Diagnosis
C. Planning D. Assessment

1142. It is best describe as a systematic, rational method of planning and providing nursing care for individual, families, group and community
A. Nursing Process B. Assessment
C. Diagnosis D. Implementation

1143. Which of the following symptoms should be watched for in a patient increase stroke volume?
A. Restlessness and agitation
B. Weak irregular pulse
C. Increased blood pressure
D. Bounding pulse

1144. The most appropriate technique to assess skin for temperature and moisture is.
A. Auscultation. B. Palpation
C. Thermometer D. Percussion

1145. While examining a client's leg, the nurse notes an open ulceration with visible tissue in the wound. which type of dressings is most appropriate for the nurse in charge to apply?
A. Moist, sterile saline gauze
B. Sterile petroleum gauze
C. Dry sterile dressing
D. Povidone-iodine-soaked gauze

1146.Platelet count decreases in:
A. Malaria B. Filaria
C. Dengue D. Typhoid

1147. If a blood pressure cuff is wide for a client, blood pressure readings taken with such a cuff may do which of the following?
A. Fail to show changes in blood pressure
B. Produce a false-low measurement
C. Cause sciatic nerve damage
D. Produce a false-high measurement

1148. A client who has glaucoma is to have miotic eyedrops instilled in both eyes. The nurse knows that the purpose of the medication is to:
A. Anesthetize the cornea
B. Constrict the pupils
C. Dilate the pupils
D. Paralyze the muscles of accommodation

1149. Resonance is best describe as:
A. Short, high pitch and thudding.
B. Sounds created by air filled lungs
C. Moderately loud with musical quality
D. Drum-like

1150. How much potassium is normally present in the intra cellular fluid?.
A. 135-145 MEq/L B. 9-11 mg/dl.
C. 140meq/lit D. 3.5 -5.1 meq/l

1151. Which of the following is an hypotonic solution except?
A. Mannitol
B. Half –Normal Saline
C. One-third Normal Saline
D. 1/4 normal saline

1152. The separation and disruption of previously joined wound edges is termed as?
A. eviscerstion. B. Dehiscence
C. extravesation D. hernia

1153. A client is admitted with complaints of chest pain shortness of breath. The nurse's assessment crackel sound. The nurse knows that when a client has crackel sound due to:
A. A neck tumor
B. Fluid overload
C. Dehydration
D. An electrolyte imbalance

1154. Transfer of heat directly through air from .
A. Conduction. B. Radiation
C. Evaporation D. Convection

1155. How many micro drops in one millilitres?
A. 60 B. 15 C. 30 D. 40

1156. The snoring sound respiration in alcoholism are
A. Rale B. Sign
C. Stretrous D. Stridor

1157. most common site for iv infusion in neonate are.
A. Scalp vein B. Umblical vein
C. Sephanous vein D. Basilic vein

1158. Which oxygen delivery system would the nurse apply that would provide the highest concentrations of oxygen to the client?
A. Venturi mask
B. Non-rebreather mask
C. Partial rebreather mask
D. Simple face mask

1159. nurseperforming CP Ronanadultclient, when performing chestcom pression, thenurse understand dtht correct hand placement is located over the-
A. Lower 3rd of the Sternum
B. Lower half of Sternum
C. Upper 3rd of the Sternum
D. Upper half of Sternum

1160 BLS:
A. Brachial B. Radial
C. Popliteal D. Carotid

1161. A nurse is inserting a Nasogastric tube in During the procedure, the client begins to cough and has difficulty breathing. Which of the following is the appropriate nursing action?

A. Pull back on the tube and wait until the respiratory distress subsides
B. Notify the physician immediately
C. Remove the tube and reinsert when the respiratory distress subsides
D. Quickly insert the tube .

1162. The nurse is caring for a 70-year-old client with hypovolemia who is receiving a IV infusion Assessment findings reveal crackles on chest auscultation and distended neck veins. What is the nurse's initial action except?

A. Slow the transfusion.
B. Assess the client's pupils.
C. Start oxygen inhalation .
D. High fowler position of pt.

1163. What heat conservation mechanisms will the anterior hypothalamus initiate when it senses that the client's body temperature is higher than comfortable?

A. Sweating, vasodilation, and redistribution of blood to surface vessels
B. Vasodilation and redistribution of blood to surface vessels.
C. Vasoconstriction, sweating, and reduction of blood flow to extremities
D. Vasoconstriction, reduction of blood flow to extremities, and shivering

1164. If the nurse sees vigorous and continuous bubbling in the second bottle, she should:

A. Momentarily clamp the tube to note for air leak
B. Administer oxygen to the patient
C. Attempt to change a new bottle
D. Pull the chest tube out to remove the air leak

1165. A client is discharged following hospitalization for congestive heart failure. The nurse teaching the family suggests they encourage the client to rest frequently in which of the following positions?

A. Supine. B. High Fowler's
C. Left lateral D. Low Fowler's

1166. Which of the following conditions correlate with the following information: High pH, neutral HCO_3 High PO_2 , low pCO_2

A. Metabolic alkalosis
B. Respiratory acidosis
C. Metabolic acidosis
D. Respiratory alkalosis

1167. If the nurse sees fluid moving up and down during inspiration and expiration on the water seal bottle, she should:

A. Call the physician immediately and damp the chest tube.
B. Immediately check the bottle for leaks
C. Do nothing as this is expected
D. Cover the wound with wet sterile gauze and send someone to calf the physician

1168. How many macro drops in one millilitres?

A. 40 B. 60 C. 30 D. 15

1169. when a patient fall from roof and comes in emergency , method is used to by nurse to provide support for maintain airway of patient.

A. Jaw thrush method
B. Heimlich maneuver
C. Head tilt chin lift method
D. None of the Above

1170. Initial support is given to patient by Defibrillation.

A. 300 jule B. 350 jule
C. 200 jule D. 100 jule

1171. A nurse find the client unresponsive .the client is not breathing and does not have pulse,and the nurse immediately calls out for the help.the next nursing actionis which of the following ?

A. Open the airway
B. Start chest compression
C. Give the oxygen
D. Ventilate with a mouth to mask device

1172. The a PTT most commonly is used to monitor & screen for coagulation disorder.

A. Warfarin therapy
B. Heparin therapy
C. Anemia D calcium therapy
D. All of the above

1173. The test for is performed to detect myocardial damage

A. CK-BB B. CK-MB
C. CK-MM D. None of the Above

1174. In acute pancreatitis the level is greatly Increased.

A. Ammonia B. Lipase
C. Bilirubin D. Amylase

1175. Normal value of total billirubin is

A. 0.2 to 0.7 mg/dl B. 0.1 to 0.3 mg/dl
C. 0.2 to 1.2 mg/dl D. None of the Above

1176. A physician order 1000 ml of normal Saline to infuse over 12 hours. A nurse prepare to set the flow rate at how many drops / minute

A. 15 drop/minute B. 17 drop/minute

C. 23 drop/ minute D. 21 drop/ minute

1177. Made for a client with amputation to keep comfort to pt.

A. Blancket Bed B. Cardiac bed

C. Admission bed D. Divided bed

1178. dressing apply on forehead is

A. Spical B. Forehead dressing

C. Capline D. Figure of 8

1179. Test is performing to assess the normal functioning for 8th cranial nerve.

A. Cranial test B. Caloric test

C. Vital test D. Functional test

1180. When collecting data on a client with cellulitis of the right leg, which of the following would the nurse expect to find?

A. Painful skin that is swollen and pale in color

B. Cold, red skin

C. Red, swollen skin with inflammation spreading to surrounding tissues

D. Small, localized blackened area of skin

1181. An elderly patient was hydrated with lactated Ringer's solution last hour. During the most recent evaluation of the patient by the nurse, a finding of a rapid bounding pulse and shortness of breath were noted. the nurse suspects that the patient now shows signs of:

A. Hypovolemia, and needs more fluids

B. Needing no adjustment in fluid administration

C. An acid-base disturbance

D. Hypervolemia, and needs the fluids adjusted

1182. A client suffering from a narcotic overdose whenVital signs of noted are T 102.6, HR 128, R 24, and BP 130/86. A blood gas analysis sample was drawn on room air, and the results are as follows: pH 7.33, Paco2 53, Pao2 72, HCO3 24. This client is at risk for

A. Respiratory alkalosis

B. Respiratory acidosis

C. Metabolic acidosis

D. Metabolic alkalosis

1183. A client with cancer is admitted to the oncology unit. Stat lab values reveal Hgb 12.6, WBC 6500, K+ 1.9, uric acid 7.0, Na+ 136, The nurse evaluates that the client is experiencingwhich of the following?

A. Hypokalemia

B. Hypernatremia

C. Myelosuppression

D. Leukocytosis

1184. The nurse is working in the emergency room when a client arrives with severe burns of the left arm, hands, face, and neck. Which action should receive priority?

A. Applying oxygen

B. Starting an IV

C. Obtaining blood gases

D. Medicating the client for pain

1185. A client has rectal cancer and is scheduled for an abdominal perineal resection. What should be the priority nursing care during the post-op period?

A. Teaching how to irrigate the illeostomy

B. Facilitating perineal wound drainage

C. Encouraging a high-fiber diet

D. Stopping electrolyte loss in the incisional area

1186. A removal of the left lower lobe of the lung is performed on a client with lung cancer. Which post-operative measure would usuallybe included in the plan?

A. A mediastenal tube

B. A tracheostomy

C. Closed chest drainage

D. Percussion vibration and drainage

1187. A client arrives in the emergency room with a possible fractured femur. The nurse should anticipate an order for:

A. Buck's traction

B. Ice to the entire extremity

C. Trendelenburg position.

D. An abduction pillow

1188. The nurse is preparing a client for surgery. Which item is most important to remove before sending the client to surgery?

A. Hearing aid B. Wedding ring

C. Contact lenses D. Artificial eye

1189. Which of the following nursing action is considered a malpractice

A. If nurse fails to read the label written on the medicine

B. If nurse administer wrong medicine

C. If nurse forget to give medicine

D. All of the above condition

1190. The nurse recognizes that which of the following would be mostappropriate to wear when providing direct care to a client with a cough?

A. Gown. B. Mask

C. Gloves D. Shoe covers

1191. The physician has ordered that the client's medication be administered intrathecally. The nurse is aware that medications will be administered by which method?
A. Into the cerebrospinal fluid.
B. Rectally
C. Intramuscularly
D. Intravenously

1192. The client is receiving total parenteral nutrition. Which labtest should be evaluated while the client is receiving TPN?
A. Blood glucose
B. Creatinine
C. Hemoglobin
D. White blood cell count

1193. Which laboratory test would be the least effective in making thediagnosis of a myocardial infarction?
A. Troponin B. AST
C. CK-MB D. Myoglobin

1194. A 25-year-old male is brought to the emergency room with a pieceof metal in his eye. Which action by the nurse is correct?
A. Cover both eyes with paper cups.
B. Rinse the eye thoroughly with saline.
C. Use a magnet to remove the object.
D. Patch the affected eye only.

1195. The nurse is taking the blood pressure of an obese client. If theblood pressure cuff is too small, the results will be:
A. A blood pressure reading that is correct.
B. A false low reading
C. A false elevation
D. A subnormal finding

1196. A 20-year-old is admitted to the rehabilitation unit following accident. Which would be the appropriate method for measuring the client for crutches?
A. Measuring the client with the elbows flexed 10°
B. Measuring five finger breaths under the axilla
C. Measuring 3 inches under the axilla
D. Measuring the client with the crutches 20 inches from the side of the foot

1197. The nurse is caring for a client with peripheral vascular disease.To correctly assess the oxygen saturation level, the monitor maybe placed on the:
A. Abdomen B. Earlobe
C. Ankle D. Chin

1198. A client who has experienced prolonged exposure to the cold is admitted to the hospital. Which method of taking a temperature would be most appropriate for this client?
A. Rectal with an electronic thermometer
B. Oral with a glass thermometer
C. Axillary with an electronic thermometer.
D. Tympanic with an infrared thermometer

1199. While teaching a health promotion group of adults, the nurse notices one person who is clutching his throat with both hands. What should the nurse do first?
A. Ask, "Are you choking?"
B. Encourage the person to cough vigorously.
C. Call Emergency
D. Give five back blows.

1200. The nurse notes a lesion that appears to be caused by tissue compression on the right hip of a patient who suffered a stroke 5 days ago. How should the nurse document this finding?
A. Maceration B. Abrasion
C. Pressure ulcer D. Excoriation

1201. For a morbidly obese patient, which intervention should the nurse choose to counteract the pressure created by the skin folds?
A. Cover the mattress with a sheepskin.
B. Apply petrolatum barrier creams.
C. Separate the skin folds with towels.
D. Keep the linens wrinkle free.

1202. What is the rationale for hand washing? Hand washing is expected to remove:
A. All microorganisms from the skin.
B. Resident flora from the skin.
C. Transient flora from the skin.
D. Media for bacterial growth.

1203. The charge nurse on the medical surgical floor assigns vital signs to the nursing assistive personnel and medication administration to the licensed vocational nurse. Which nursing model of care is this floor following?
A. Functional nursing
B. Case method nursing
C. Team nursing
D. Primary nursing

1204. Which of the following is the primary mechanism or site of heat loss?
A. Skin surface
B. Warming and humidifying of inspired air
C. Contraction of pilomotor muscles of the skin.
D. Urine and feces

1205. A patient is admitted with shortness of breath, so the nurse immediately listens to his breath sounds. Which type of assessment is the nurse performing?

A. Focused physical assessment.
B. Comprehensive assessment
C. Ongoing assessment
D. Psychosocial assessment

1206. The nurse is assessing vital signs for a patient just admitted to the hospital. Ideally, and if there are no contraindications, how should the nurse position the patient for this portion of the admission assessment?

A. Lying flat on the back with knees flexed
B. Sitting upright
C. Lying flat on the back with arms and legs fully extended
D. Side-lying with the knees flexed

1207. What is the preferred order for the nurse to perform the following examination techniques?

A. Auscultation B. Palpation
C. Inspection D. Percussion

A. D, A, B, C B. C, B, D, A
C. A, C, D, B D. A, B, C, D

1208. An adult is about to have a tracheostomy performed. Which action is of highest priority for the nurse before the procedure is done?

A. Doing a surgical prep of the neck and upper chest wall
B. Drawing blood for serum electrolytes and blood gases.
C. Inserting an indwelling catheter and attaching it to dependent drainage.
D. Establishing means of postoperative communication.

1209. The nurse is performing tracheal suctioning. Which action is essential to prevent hypoxemia during suctioning?

A. Administer 100% oxygen before suctioning
B. Encouraging the client to deep breathe and cough.
C. Removal of oral and nasal secretions.
D. Auscultate the lungs

1210. An order is written for oxygen by nasal cannula at 2 liters per minute. In assessing the adequacy of the oxygen therapy, which of the following is most effective?

A. Measurement of pulmonary functions.
B. Checking the color of mucous membranes.
C. Checking the respiratory rate.
D. Measurement of arterial blood gasses

1211. During the review of systems in a nursing history, a nurse learns that the patient has been coughing mucus. Which of the following nursing assessments would be best for the nurse to use to confirm a lung problem?

A. Chest examination
B. Family report
C. Physical examination with auscultation of the lungs
D. Blood investigation

1212. Your ungloved hands come in contact with the drainage from your patient's wound. What is the correct method to clean your hands?

A. Use an alcohol-based hand cleaner.
B. Wash them with soap and water
C. Rinse them and use the alcohol-based cleaner
D. Wipe them with a paper towel

1213. The nurse is assessing a postoperative adult patient. Which of the following should the nurse document as subjective data?

A. Laboratory test result.
B. Vital signs
C. Patient's description of pain
D. Electrocardiographic (ECG) waveforms

1214. A male patient has a soft wrist-safety device. Which assessment finding should the nurse consider abnormal?

A. A palpable radial pulse
B. A palpable ulnar pulse
C. Pink nail beds
D. Cool, pale fingers

1215. What is the best method to sterilize a straight urinary catheter and suction tube in the home setting?

A. Use boiling water.
B. Use an autoclave
C. Use ethylene oxide gas
D. Use chemicals for disinfection

1216. When a nurse is performing surgical hand asepsis, the nurse must keep hands:

A. Above elbows.
B. Below elbows
C. At a 45-degree angle
D. In a comfortable position

1217. The nurse in charge is transferring a patient from the bed to a chair. Which action does the nurse take during this patient transfer?

A. Helps the patient dangle the legs.
B. Position the head of the bed flat
C. Stands behind the patient
D. Places the chair facing away from the bed

1218. Before administering the evening dose of a prescribed medication, the nurse on the evening shift finds an unlabeled, filled syringe in the patient's medication drawer. What should the nurse in charge do?

A. Obtain a label for the syringe from the pharmacy
B. Discard the syringe to avoid a medication error
C. Use the syringe because it looks like it contains the same medication the nurse was prepared to give
D. Call the day nurse to verify the contents of the syringe

1219. Put the following steps for removal of protective barriers after leaving an isolation room in order:

1. Perform hand hygiene
2. Remove gown, rolling it onto itself without touching the contaminated side
3. Remove gloves
4. Remove eyewear or goggles
5. Untie top, then bottom mask strings and remove from face

A. 3, 1, 2, 4, 5 B. 5, 4, 3, 2, 1
C. 3, 2, 5, 1, 4 D. 5, 3, 1, 4, 2

1220. A female patient is being discharged after cataract surgery. After providing medication teaching, the nurse asks the patient to repeat the instructions. The nurse is performing which professional role?

A. Educator B. Manager
C. Caregiver D. Patient advocate

1221. The nurse has redressed a patient's wound and now plans to administer a medication to the patient. Which is the correct infection control procedure?

A. Leave the gloves on to administer the medication
B. Remove gloves and perform hand hygiene before administering the medication
C. Remove gloves and administer the medication
D. Leave the medication on the bedside table to avoid having to remove gloves before leaving the patient's room

1222. A scrub nurse in the operating room has which responsibility?

A. Positioning the patient
B. Assisting with gowning and gloving
C. Handling surgical instruments to the surgeon
D. Applying surgical drapes

1223. The physician orders heparin, 7,500 units, to be administered subcutaneously every 6 hours. The vial reads 10,000 units per milliliter. The nurse should anticipate giving how much heparin for each dose?

A. ¾ ml B. ½ ml
C. ¼ ml D. 1 ¼ ml

1224. The nurse in charge measures a patient's temperature at 102 degrees F. what is the equivalent Centigrade temperature?

A. 39 degrees C B. 38.9 degrees C
C. 47 degrees C D. 40.1 degrees C

1225. To evaluate a patient for hypoxia, the physician is most likely to order which laboratory test?

A. (ABG) analysis
B. Sputum culture
C. Total haemoglobin
D. Red blood cell count

1226. The nurse uses a stethoscope to auscultate a male patient's chest. Which statement about a stethoscope with a bell and diaphragm is true?

A. The bell detects high-pitched sounds best
B. The diaphragm detects low-pitched sounds best
C. The bell detects thrills best
D. The diaphragm detects high-pitched sounds best

1227. Which of the following is the most effective way to break the chain of infection?

A. Placing patients in isolation.
B. Wearing gloves
C. Hand hygiene
D. Providing private rooms for patients

1228. The nurse wears a gown when:

A. The patient's hygiene is poor
B. Blood or body fluids may get onto the nurse's clothing
C. The patient has AIDS or hepatitis
D. The nurse is assisting with medication administration

1229. An employer establishes a physical exercise area in the workplace and encourages all employees to use it. This is an example of which level of health promotion?

A. Tertiary prevention
B. Secondary prevention
C. Primary prevention
D. Passive prevention

1230. What does the nurse in charge do when making a surgical bed?

A. Rolls the patient to the far side of the bed.
B. Places the pillow at the head of the bed
C. Leaves the bed in the high position when finished
D. Tucks the top sheet and blanket under the bottom of the bed

1231. The physician prescribes 250 mg of a drug. The drug vial reads 500 mg/ml. how much of the drug should the nurse give?

A. 2 ml B. ½ ml
C. 1 ml D. ¼ m

1232. A nurse is administering eardrops to an 22 year age patient with an ear infection. How does the nurse puli the patient's ear when administering the medication?

A. Outward
B. Back
C. Upward and outward
D. Upward and back

1233. Which nursing action is essential when providing continuous enteral feeding?

A. Warming the formula before administering it
B. Positioning the patient on the left side
C. Elevating the head of the bed
D. Hanging a full day's worth of formula at one time

1234. When teaching a female patient how to take a sublingual tablet, the nurse should instruct the patient to place the table on the:

A. Floor of the mouth
B. Roof of the mouth
C. Top of the tongue
D. Inside of the cheek

1235. Which action by the nurse in charge is essential when cleaning the area around a Jackson-Pratt wound drain?

A. Wearing sterile gloves and a mask
B. Removing the drain before cleaning the skin
C. Cleaning briskly around the site with alcohol
D. Cleaning from the center outward in a circular motion

1236. The doctor orders dextrose 5% in water, 1,000 ml to be infused over 8 hours. The I.V. tubing delivers 15 drops per milliliter. The nurse in charge should run the I.V. infusion at a rate of:

A. 32 drop per minute
B. 21 drop per minute
C. 15 drop per minute
D. 125 drops per minute

1237. A male patient undergoes a total abdominal hysterectomy. When assessing the patient 10 hours later, the nurse identifies which finding as an early sign of shock?

A. Heart rate of 110 beats/minute.
B. Pale, warm, dry skin
C. Restlessness
D. Urine output of 30 ml/hour

1238. Which pulse should the nurse palpate during rapid assessment of an unconscious male adult?

A. Carotid B. Brachial
C. Femoral D. Radial

1239. A position in which a patient is in a side-lying position on either side, with the top leg flexed up toward the abdomen; used to assess the rectum

A. Fowlers position
B. Lateral sign
C. Sim's Position
D. Lithotomy position

1240. In the patient's chart on a Chronological Record of Medical Care , local forms, flow sheets, or electronic documentation.

A. Fever B. Pulse
C. Blood pressure D. Vital signs

1241. Which route for taking temperature is safer and less disturbing to infants and children?

A. Rectal B. Axillary
C. Oral D. None of the Above

1242. The nurse is performing nasotracheal suctioning. After suctioning the client's trachea for fifteen seconds, large amounts of thick yellow secretions return. What action should the nurse implement next?

A. Encourage the client to cough to help loosen secretions.
B. Re-oxygenate the client before attempting to suction again.
C. Rotate the suction catheter to obtain any remaining secretions.
D. Advise the client to increase the intake of oral fluids.

1243. A client is receiving a cephalosporin antibiotic IV and complains of pain and irritation at the infusion site. The nurse observes erythema, swelling, and a red streak along the vessel above the IV access site. Which action should the nurse take at this time?

A. Initiate an alternate site for the IV infusion of the medication.

B. Administer the medication more rapidly using the same IV site.

C. Notify the healthcare provider before administering the next dose.

D. Give the client a PRN dose of aspirin while the medication infuses.

1244. Three days following surgery, a male client observes his colostomy for the first time. He becomes quite upset and tells the nurse that it is much bigger than he expected. What is the best response by the nurse?

A. Reassure the client that he will become accustomed to the stoma appearance in time.

B. Offer to contact a member of the local ostomy support group to help him with his concerns.

C. Instruct the client that the stoma will become smaller when the initial swelling diminishes.

D. Encourage the client to handle the stoma equipment to gain confidence with the procedure.

1245. An elderly male client who suffered a cerebral vascular accident is receiving tube feedings via a gastrostomy tube. The nurse knows that the best position for this client during administration of the feedings is

A. Prone B. Sims'

C. Fowler's D. Supine

1246. When assisting an 45-year-old client to ambulate, it is important for the nurse to realize that the center of gravity for an person is the

A. Arms. B. Head.

C. Hips. D. Feet.

1247. Which assessment data would provide the most accurate determination of proper placement of a nasogastric tube?

A. Examining a chest x-ray obtained after the tubing was inserted.

B. Hearing air pass in the stomach after injecting air into the tubing.

C. Aspirating gastric contents to assure a pH value of 4 or less.

D. Checking the remaining length of tubing to ensure that the correct length was inserted.

1248. The nurse is caring for a client who is receiving 24-hour total parenteral nutrition (TPN) via a central line at 54 ml/hr. When initially assessing the client, the nurse notes that the TPN solution has run out and the next TPN solution is not available. What immediate action should the nurse take?

A. Infuse 10 percent dextrose and water at 54 ml/hr.

B. Discontinue the IV and flush the port with heparin.

C. Infuse normal saline at a keep vein open rate.

D. Obtain a stat blood glucose level and notify the healthcare provider.

1249. Which intervention is most important for the nurse to implement for a male client who is experiencing urinary retention?

A. Apply a skin protectant.

B. Apply a condom catheter.

C. Encourage increased fluid intake.

D. Assess for bladder distention.

1250. When assessing a client with wrist restraints, the nurse observes that the fingers on the right hand are blue. What action should the nurse implement first?

A. Palpate the right radial pulse.

B. Apply a pulse oximeter to the right hand.

C. Compare hand color bilaterally.

D. Loosen the right wrist restraint.

1251. The nurse is administering medications through a nasogastric tube (NGT) which is connected to suction. After ensuring correct tube placement, what action should the nurse take next?

A. Flush the tube with water.

B. Clamp the tube for 20 minutes.

C Administer the medications as prescribed.

D. Crush the tablets and dissolve in sterile water.

1252. An elderly client with a fractured left hip is on strict bedrest. Which nursing measure is essential to the client's nursing care?

A. Massage any reddened areas for at least five minutes.

B. Encourage active range of motion exercises on extremities.

C. Position the client laterally, prone, and dorsally in sequence.

D. Gently lift the client when moving into a desired position.

1253. The nurse must examine a patient who is weak and unable to sit unaided or to get out of bed. How should she position the patient to begin and perform most of the physical examination?

A. Semi-Fowler's B. Dorsal recumbent
C. Lithotomy D. Sims'

1254. A patient is admitted with shortness of breath, so the nurse immediately listens to his breath sounds. Which type of assessment is the nurse performing?

A. Focused physical assessment
B. Comprehensive physical assessment
C. Ongoing assessment
D. Psychosocial assessment

1255. The nurse notes a lesion that appears to be caused by tissue compression on the right hip of a patient who suffered a stroke 5 days ago. How should the nurse document this finding?

A. Maceration B. Pressure ulcer
C. Excoriation D. Abrasion

1256. While teaching a health promotion group of adults, the nurse notices one person who is clutching his throat with both hands. What should the nurse do first?

A. Call emergency
B. Encourage the person to cough vigorously.
C. Give five back blows.
D. Ask, "Are you choking?"

1257. If a patient who is receiving IV fluids develops tenderness, warmth, erythema, and pain at the site, the nurse suspects:

A. Sepsis B. Infiltration
C. Phlebitis D. Fluid overload

1258. An elderly patient was hydrated with lactated Ringer's solution last hour. During the most recent evaluation of the patient by the nurse, a finding of a rapid bounding pulse and shortness of breath were noted. the nursing action are

A. Inform to doctor
B. Stop the transfusion
C. Administer oxygen
D. Provide high fowler position

259. The nurse should use the diaphragm of the stethoscope to auscultate which of the following?

A. Bowel sounds
B. Jugular venous hums
C. Heart murmurs
D. Carotid bruits

1260. The nurse is assessing a patient admitted to the hospital with rectal bleeding. The patient had a hip replacement 2 weeks ago. Which position should the nurse avoid when examining this patient's rectal area?

A. Semi-Fowler's
B. Supine
C. Dorsal recumbent
D. Sims'

1261. Which of the following actions should the nurse take to use a wide base support when assisting a client to get up in a chair?

A. Bend at the waist and place arms under the client's arms and lift
B. Spread his or her feet apart
C. Face the client, bend knees and place hands on client's forearm and lift
D. Tighten his or her pelvic muscles

1262. A client had oral surgery following a motor vehicle accident. The nurse assessing the client finds the skin flushed and warm. Which of the following would be the best method to take the client's body temperature?

A. Axillary B. Oral
C. Arterial line D. Rectal

1263. A client who is unconscious needs frequent mouth care. When performing a mouth care, the best position of a client is:

A. Side lying B. Fowler's position
C. Supine D. Trendelenburg

1264. A client is hospitalized for the first time, which of the following actions ensure the safety of the client?

A. Keep side rails up at all time
B. Keep the lights on at all time
C. Keep unnecessary furniture out of the way
D. Keep all equipment out of view

1265. The ability of the body to defend itself against scientific invading agent such as baceria, toxin, viruses and foreign body

A. Hormones B. Immunity
C. Secretion D. Glands

1266. It is a transparent membrane that focuses the light that enters the eyes to the retina.

A. Lens B. Cornea
C. Sclera D. Pupils

1267. Which of the following cluster of data belong to Maslow's hierarchy of needs

A. Physiologic needs
B. Love and belonging
C. Self actualization
D. All of the above

1268. This is characterized by severe symptoms relatively of short duration.
A. Acute Illness B. Chronic Illness
C. Pain D. Syndrome

1269. Which of the following is the nurse's role in the health promotion
A. Teach client to be effective health consumer
B. Health risk appraisal
C. Worksite wellness
D. None of the Above

1270. Which of the following is the abbreviation of drops?
A. Gtts B. Gtt
C. Dp D. Dr

1271. The abbreviation for micro drop is...
A. Gtt B. μgtt
C. Mdr D. Mgts

1272. Which of the following is the meaning of PRN?
A. When advice B. When necessary
C. Immediately D. Now

1273. Which of the following is the appropriate meaning of CBR?
A. Cardiac Board Room
B. Complete Bed Rest
C. Complete Bathroom
D. Complete Board Room

1274. One (1) tsp is equals to how many drops?
A. 15 B. 10 C. 60 D. 30

1275. The nurse prepares to administer buccal medication. The medicine should be placed...
A. On the client's skin
B. On the client's conjunctiva
C. Under the client's tongue
D. Between the client's cheeks and gums

1276. Which of the following is the most important purpose of handwashing
A. To prevent the transfer of microorganism
B. To promote hand circulation
C. To avoid touching the client with a dirty hand
D. To provide comfort

1277. The first techniques used examining the abdomen of a client is:
A. Palpation B. Auscultation
C. Inspection D. Percussion

1278. A technique in physical examination that is use to assess the movement of air through the tracheobronchial tree:
A. Palpation B. Inspection
C. Auscultation D. Percussion

1279. The best position for examining the rectum is:
A. Prone B. Knee-chest
C. Sim's D. Lithotomy

1280. It refers to the manner of walking
A. Range of motion
B. Gait
C. Flexion and extension
D. Hopping

1281. The nurse asked the client to read the Snellen chart. Which of the following is tested:
A. Olfactory B. Optic
C. Oculomotor D. Troclear

1282. The nurse is preparing to suction the client with a tracheotomy. The nurse notes a previously used bottle of normal saline on the client's bedside table. There is no label to indicate the date or time of initial use. The nurse should:
A. Obtain a new bottle and label it with the date and time of first use.
B. Lip the bottle and use a pack of sterile 4×4 for the dressing.
C. Ask the ward secretary when the solution was requested.
D. Label the existing bottle with the current date and time.

1283. A technique in physical examination of tapping the body with the fingertips to evaluate the size, borders, and consistency of some internal organs, and to discover the presence of and evaluate the amount of fluid in a cavity of the body
A. Palpation. B. Percussion
C. Auscultation D. Olfaction

1284. A client with pancreatic cancer has an infusion of TPN (Total Parenteral Nutrition). The doctor has ordered for sliding-scale insulin. The most likely explanation for this order is:
A. Total Parenteral Nutrition leads to negative nitrogen balance and elevated glucose levels.
B. Total Parenteral Nutrition is a high-glucose solution that often elevates the blood glucose levels.
C. Total Parenteral Nutrition cannot be managed with oral hypoglycemics.
D. Total Parenteral Nutrition leads to further pancreatic disease.

1285. The physician has ordered an MRI for a client with an orthopedic ailment. An MRI should not be done if the client has:
A. A permanent pacemaker
B. A history of claustrophobia
C. The need for oxygen therapy
D. Sensory deafness

1286. A 30-year-old male from Haiti is brought to the emergency department in sickle cell crisis. What is the best position for this client?
A. Side-lying with knees flexed
B. Semi-Fowler's with legs extended on the bed
C. High Fowler's with knees flexed
D. Knee-chest

1287. The client arrives in the emergency department after a motor vehicle accident. Nursing assessment findings include BP 80/34, pulse rate 120, and respirations 20. Which is the client's most appropriate priority nursing diagnosis?
A. Fluid volume deficit
B. Alteration in cerebral tissue perfusion
C. Ineffective airway clearance
D. Alteration in sensory perception

1288. The nurse is caring for the client following a laryngectomy when suddenly the client becomes nonresponsive and pale, with a BP of 90/40. The initial nurse's action should be to:
A. Increase the infusion of normal saline
B. Place the client in Trendelenburg position.
C. Administer atropine intravenously.
D. Move the emergency cart to the bedside.

1289. The client admitted two days earlier with a lung resection accidentally pulls out the chest tube. Which action by the nurse indicates understanding of the management of chest tubes?
A. Cover the insertion site with Vaseline gauze.
B. Reinsert the tube.
C. Order a chest x-ray.
D. Call the doctor.

1290. The best size for administration of a blood transfusion to a 19-year-old is:
A. 20 gauge B. 19 gauge
C. 22 gauge D. 18 gauge

1291. A client is admitted to the unit two hours after an explosion causes burns to the face. The nurse would be most concerned with the client developing which of the following?
A. Hypovolemia
B. Hyperkalemia
C. Hypernatremia
D. Laryngeal edema

1292. The client is admitted following cast application for a fractured ulna. Which finding should be reported to the doctor?
A. Pain at the site
B. Paresthesia of the fingers
C. Pulses rapid
D. Warm fingers

1293. Before administering eardrops to a toddler, the nurse should recognize that it is essential to consider which of the following?
A. The IQ of the child
B. The child's weight
C. The developmental level of the child
D. The age of the child

1294. The first action that the nurse should take if she finds the client has an O2 saturation of 68% is:
A. Apply oxygen by mask.
B. Recheck the O2 saturation in 30 minutes.
C. Elevate the head.
D. Assess the heart rate.

1295. The obstetric client's fetal heart rate is 80–90 during the contractions. The first action the nurse should take is:
A. Ask the client to ambulate.
B. Turn the client to her left side.
C. Reposition the monitor.
D. Prepare the client for delivery.

1296. A two-year-old is admitted for repair of a fractured femur and is placed in Bryant's traction. Which finding by the nurse indicates that the traction is working properly?
A. The infant no longer complains of pain.
B. The pins are secured within the pulley.
C. The legs are suspended in the traction.
D. The buttocks are 15° off the bed.

1297. What is the colour of Oxygen cylinder?
A. Black on top and base is white.
B. Yellow colour.
C. Blue colour.
D. White on top and base in black.

1298. What is the height of enema can in the retained enema?
A. 12 inch B. 22 inch
C. 8 inch D. 18 inch

1299. What is the normal temperature of feeding of infant?
A. 100° F B. 110°F
C. 99° F D. 98.8°F

1300. For the absorption in the body the large amount fluid is slowly gives that called as
A. Proctoclysis B. Colonic irrigation
C. Suppository D. Suppression

1301. What is the amount of solution in the adult enema?
A. Less than 250 ml
B. 250-500 ml
C. 500-1000 ml
D. 500-600 ml

1302. Which of the examination is done by stethoscope?
A. Inspection B. Percussion
C. Palpation D. Auscultation

1303. What is the use of the Bed side commode?
A. To provide support
B. Sputum collection.
C. To pass the urine and stool
D. All of the above

1304. The Paraffin bath use for:
A. Rheumatoid arthritis
B. Appendicitis
C. In Burn
D. Pelvic problem

1305. Which of the component is not essential in the communication?
A. Message B. Receiver
C. Sender D. Sound

1306. What is distance between two beds in ideal setup?
A. 6 feet B. 12 feet
C. 3 feet D. 9 feet

1307. When was the S.N.A established?
A. 1922 B. 1920 C. 1929 D. 1950

1308. When was the T.N.A.I established?
A. 1929 B. 1947 C. 1922 D. 1950

1309. When was the I.N.C established?
A. 1946 B. 1949 C. 1948 D. 1947

1310. Dysuria means.
A. Painful micturation
B. Painful pus formation
C. Painful Defecation
D. Painful sweating

1311. Pyuria mean presence in urine?
A. Blood B. Protein
C. Sugar D. Pus

1312. Enuresis mean involuntary passing of urine due to.
A. Non pathological
B. Path physiological causes
C. Defects in urethra
D. Renal stone

1313. Nocturia is passing of urine.
A. Afternoon B. Morning
C. At night D. All of the Above

1314. Oligouria mean formation & execration of urine less than.
A. 400 ml B. 100 ml
C. 3000 ml D. 2000 ml

1315. Polyuria mean urine output more than ?
A. 2000 ml/24 hrs B. 2500 ml/24 hrs
C. 100 ml/24 hrs D. 400 ml/24 hrs

1316. Presence of blood in urine is called.
A. Glycosuria B. Albuminemia
C. Hematuria D. None of them

1317. Glucose present in urine.
A. Glycaemia B. Glycosuria
C. Glycolipidemia D. None of the Above

1318. Which of the following is the cause of acute Diarrhoea?
A. E.coli B. Nervous tension
C. Vibrio cholera D. All of the above

1319. Which of the following is called as the increase amount of urine?
A. Pyuria B. Hematuria
C. Polyuria D. All of the above

1320. Which of the complication can occur in lithotomy position?
A. Bed sore B. None
C. Thrombosis D. Foot drop

1321. Which of the following condition shown bounding pulse?
A. Dehydration
B. Increase stroke volume
C. Decrease stroke volume
D. Shock

1322. Which is the bandage use for head?
A. Spical B. Capeline
C. Circular D. Spiral

1323. Difficulty in sollowing is called as:
A. Dysphagia B. Nausea
C. Dyspepsia D. Alopecia

1324. Which of the solution is not used for mouth wash?
A. NaCl B. Glucose
C. $KMnO_4$ D. H_2O_2

1325. Which of the surgery sitz's bath use postoperatively?
A. breast cancer and Mastoidectory
B. Rectal surgery and haemorr- hoidectomy
C. Myopia and cataract
D. Liver biopsy and Appendicitis

1326. Which of the following condition enema is contraindicated?
A. Mega colon
B. Peptic ulcer
C. Respiration disease
D. Acute appendicitis

1327. What is the haemoptysis?
A. Blood in sputum.
B. Blood in urine.
C. Blood is from nose
D. Blood in stool.

1328. Which of the substance has maximum energy?
A. Fat B. Water
C. Protein D. Conbodydrate

1329. Urine output less than 100 ml. in a day is called as:
A. Anuria B. Polyuria
C. Oligouria D. Suppression

1330. Which of the following condition respiration stop during sleeping time?
A. Dyspnea B. Apnoea
C. Sleep apnoea D. Sleep Bradypnea

1331. What is the water temperature during Sitz bath?
A. 100-115 F B. 115-115 F
C. 120 F D. 120-125 F

1332. What is the scale in Glasgow coma scale?
A. 3-15 B. 2-15
C. 0-15 D. All of the Above

1333. Which is not an element of communication?
A. Storage B. Receiver
C. Sender D. Message

1334. What is normal concentration of CO_2 in blood ?
A. 22-27meq/lit B. 135-145meq/lit
C. 35-45mmog hg D. 3.5-5.1 mEq/lit

1335. CO_2 level increase in blood is called:
A. Dyspnea B. Hypercapnia
C. Hypocapnea D. Apnoea

1336. What is the normal venous pressure?
A. 40 to 110 mm of hg
B. 40 to 110 mm of water
C. 140 to 90 mm of water.
D. 120 to 180 mm of hg

1337. What is the normal venous pressure?
A. 14 to 29 mm of water
B. 3 to 8 mm of hg
C. 4 to 11 mm of water
D. 12 to 18 mm of hg

1338. Bad odour from mouth is called as:
A. Stomatitis B. Halitosis
C. Cheilosis D. Gingivitis

1339. Which of the bacteria coating on the teeth?
A. Gonocacas B. Stephylococas
C. Neumococas D. Streptococas.

1340. What is the Stomach wash?
A. Instillation B. Gavage
C. Irrigation D. Lavage

1341. Which of the examination is done by palm of hands of the internal organs?
A. Palpation B. Auscultation
C. Inspection D. Percussion

1342. Which of the examination is done by taping on the finger of the internal organs?
A. Inspection B. Percussion
C. Palpation D. Auscultation

❑❑❑

Answer Sheet

1.D.	2.A.	3.D.	4.A.	5.C.	6.C.	7.D.	8.A.	9.A.	10.A.
11.A.	12.D.	13.A.	14.A.	15.B.	16.C.	17.D.	18.A.	19.A.	20.D.
21.A.	22.A.	23.D.	24.A.	25.A.	26.A.	27.D.	28.A.	29.B.	30.A.
31.C.	32.B.	33.B.	34.A.	35.A.	36.C.	37.C.	38.C.	39.A.	40.A.
41.D.	42.A.	43.B.	44.C.	45.D.	46.A.	47.A.	48.B.	49.D.	50.D.
51.A.	52.C.	53.B.	54.C.	55.C.	56.B.	57.B.	58.B.	59.B.	60.B.
61.A.	62.B.	63.D.	64.A.	65.A.	66.A.	67.D.	68.D.	69.D.	70.D.
71.D.	72.B.	73.C.	74.A.	75.B.	76.C.	77.D.	78.C.	79.C.	80.A.
81.A.	82.B.	83.B.	84.C.	85.C.	86.D.	87.A.	88.C.	89.D.	90.B.
91.D.	92.A.	93.C.	94.B.	95.C.	96.B.	97.B.	98.C.	99.B.	100.C.
101.B.	102.C.	103.D.	104.D.	105.B.	106.A.	107.A.	108.C.	109.B.	110.C.
111.D.	112.A.	113.C.	114.A.	115.A.	116.B.	117.B.	118.D.	119.A.	120.C.
121.C.	122.C.	123.D.	124.A.	125.D.	126.C.	127.D.	128.A.	129.A.	130.D.
131.B.	132.B.	133.C.	134.D.	135.A.	136.A.	137.C.	138.C.	139.A.	140.B.
141.A.	142.B.	143.B.	144.A.	145.D.	146.C.	147.C.	148.B.	149.C.	150.D.
151.D.	152.B.	153.A.	154.C.	155.A.	156.C.	157.B.	158.A.	159.D.	160.C.
161.B.	162.D.	163.D.	164.C.	165.A.	166.B.	167.D.	168.D.	169.A.	170.B.
171.B.	172.C.	173.C.	174.A.	175.C.	176.D.	177.A.	178.B.	179.B.	180.D.
181.C.	182.C.	183.D.	184.A.	185.A.	186.A.	187.C.	188.A.	189.B.	190.A.
191.C.	192.D.	193.A.	194.C.	195.B.	196.D.	197.A.	198.B.	199.C.	200.A.
201.D.	202.C.	203.C.	204.A.	205.C.	206.B.	207.B.	208.C.	209.D.	210.B.
211.A.	212.B.	213.D.	214.C.	215.D.	216.D.	217.C.	218.B.	219.C.	220.A.
221.A.	222.C.	223.C.	224.A.	225.B.	226.A.	227.C.	228.A.	229.D.	230.A.
231.A.	232.C.	233.D.	234.A.	235.B.	236.A.	237.A.	238.A.	239.D.	240.D.
241.D.	242.B.	243.C.	244.B.	245.C.	246.B.	247.B.	248.B.	249.D.	250.D.
251.D.	252.B.	253.B.	254.D.	255.C.	256.A.	257.B.	258.C.	259.C.	260.D.
261.D.	262.D.	263.A.	264.A.	265.D.	266.A.	267.A.	268.C.	269.D.	270.D.
271.C.	272.A.	273.A.	274.B.	275.C.	276.D.	277.C.	278.D.	279.C.	280.D.
281.A.	282.A.	283.A.	284.A.	285.B.	286.D.	287.B.	288.C.	289.C.	290.B.
291.D.	292.D.	293.A.	294.A.	295.B.	296.D.	297.D.	298.C.	299.B.	300.A.
301.C.	302.A.	303.A.	304.D.	305.B.	306.D.	307.D.	308.C.	309.D.	310.B.
311.A.	312.C.	313.B.	314.B.	315.C.	316.A.	317.C.	318.C.	319.A.	320.A.
321.B.	322.A.	323.C.	324.C.	325.B.	326.B.	327.D.	328.A.	329.A.	330.C.
331.B.	332.A.	333.A.	334.A.	335.A.	336.B.	337.B.	338.C.	339.B.	340.C.
341.D.	342.C.	343.D.	344.D.	345.C.	346.B.	347.D.	348.B.	349.B.	350.C.
351.C.	352.B.	353.C.	354.A.	355.B.	356.B.	357.A.	358.B.	359.D.	360.C.
361.C.	362.A.	363.C.	364.B.	365.A.	366.D.	367.D.	368.D.	369.C.	370.A.
371.C.	372.C.	373.B.	374.C.	375.C.	376.B.	377.D.	378.D.	379.B.	380.D.
381.C.	382.A.	383.C.	384.B.	385.C.	386.A.	387.A.	388.A.	389.A.	390.B.
391.B.	392.D.	393.C.	394.C.	395.B.	396.B.	397.C.	398.B.	399.D.	400.C.
401.D.	402.D.	403.B.	404.B.	405.C.	406.B.	407.A.	408.C.	409.A.	410.B.
411.A.	412.C.	413.A.	414.D.	415.C.	416.A.	417.D.	418.B.	419.A.	420.B.
421.C.	422.A.	423.C.	424.C.	425.C.	426.A.	427.D.	428.B.	429.A.	430.B.
431.A.	432.A.	433.D.	434.D.	435.B.	436.B.	437.B.	438.D.	439.D.	440.D.
441.B.	442.A.	443.D.	444.A.	445.B.	446.B.	447.A.	448.B.	449.C.	450.B.
451.C.	452.D.	453.B.	454.C.	455.A.	456.A.	457.A.	458.B.	459.C.	460.D.
461.B.	462.C.	463.D.	464.D.	465.C.	466.D.	467.B.	468.A.	469.B.	470.C.

471.B.	472.D.	473.B.	474.A.	475.B.	476.D.	477.B.	478.D.	479.A.	480.B.
481.A.	482.D.	483.C.	484.C.	485.D.	486.C.	487.D.	488.B.	489.A.	490.D.
491.B.	492.C.	493.D.	494.C.	495.D.	496.B.	497.C.	498.B.	499.D.	500.C.
501.C.	502.B.	503.A.	504.D.	505.B.	506.A.	507.D.	508.B.	509.D.	510.B.
511.C.	512.B.	513.A.	514.C.	515.C.	516.B.	517.B.	518.D.	519.C.	520.D.
521.D.	522.D.	523.C.	524.A.	525.C.	526.B.	527.C.	528.B.	529.B.	530.B.
531.A.	532.B.	533.C.	534.B.	535.B.	536.A.	537.D.	538.A.	539.D.	540.B.
541.A.	542.A.	543.D.	544.B.	545.D.	546.A.	547.D.	548.C.	549.A.	550.D.
551.B.	552.D.	553.D.	554.C.	555.D.	556.B.	557.D.	558.C.	559.B.	560.C.
561.A.	562.D.	563.B.	564.C.	565.B.	566.B.	567.C.	568.D.	569.A.	570.B.
571.A.	572.C.	573.B.	574.D.	575.C.	576.A.	577.B.	578.A.	579.A.	580.B.
581.D.	582.B.	583.D.	584.D.	585.A.	586.C.	587.C.	588.A.	589.C.	590.B.
591.B.	592.B.	593.B.	594.A.	595.D.	596.A.	597.C.	598.D.	599.C.	600.B.
601.A.	602.B.	603.A.	604.D.	605.B.	606.D.	607.B.	608.A.	609.A.	610.B.
611.C.	612.D.	613.C.	614.C.	615.A.	616.C.	617.D.	618.A.	619.C.	620.A.
621.D.	622.B.	623.A.	624.C.	625.D.	626.B.	627.B.	628.A.	629.A.	630.C.
631.A.	632.B.	633.A.	634.D.	635.A.	636.C.	637.B.	638.B.	639.A.	640.D.
641.B.	642.B.	643.D.	644.A.	645.C.	646.D.	647.A.	648.B.	649.B.	650.B.
651.C.	652.D.	653.D.	654.C.	655.C.	656.C.	657.D.	658.D.	659.B.	660.B.
661.D.	662.A.	663.B.	664.A.	665.B.	666.A.	667.C.	668.D.	669.C.	670.D.
671.C.	672.C.	673.A.	674.D.	675.C.	676.A.	677.D.	678.D.	679.B.	680.C.
681.C.	682.C.	683.A.	684.A.	685.D.	686.D.	687.A.	688.C.	689.B.	690.B.
691.B.	692.A.	693.A.	694.D.	695.C.	696.A.	697.A.	698.C.	699.C.	700.D.
701.B.	702.B.	703.A.	704.A.	705.C.	706.C.	707.A.	708.A.	709.C.	710.B.
711.B.	712.B.	713.C.	714.A.	715.C.	716.B.	717.A.	718.B.	719.A.	720.D.
721.B.	722.D.	723.B.	724.D.	725.B.	726.C.	727.B.	728.A.	729.C.	730.A.
731.B.	732.C.	733.A.	734.D.	735.A.	736.C.	737.D.	738.B.	739.B.	740.B.
741.B.	742.A.	743.C.	744.D.	745.A.	746.B.	747.B.	748.D.	749.C.	750.A.
751.B.	752.C.	753.D.	754.A.	755.D.	756.C.	757.A.	758.C.	759.D.	760.D.
761.C.	762.A.	763.A.	764.B.	765.D.	766.B.	767.B.	768.B.	769.A.	770.D.
771.C.	772.B.	773.B.	774.B.	775.D.	776.C.	777.A.	778.D.	779.A.	780.D.
781.C.	782.B.	783.B.	784.D.	785.A.	786.D.	787.D.	788.B.	789.C.	790.B.
791.C.	792.A.	793.C.	794.A.	795.B.	796.C.	797.C.	798.B.	799.D.	800.C.
801.B.	802.B.	803.B.	804.D.	805.A.	806.B.	807.A.	808.A.	809.C.	810.D.
811.A.	812.D.	813.D.	814.A.	815.D.	816.A.	817.D.	818.D.	819.D.	820.D.
821.A.	822.C.	823.B.	824.B.	825.C.	826.B.	827.D.	828.B.	829.D.	830.C.
831.B.	832.B.	833.C.	834.B.	835.C.	836.D.	837.A.	838.B.	839.C.	840.B.
841.D.	842.B.	843.C.	844.A.	845.B.	846.A.	847.B.	848.A.	849.A.	850.A.
851.A.	852.D.	853.D.	854.A.	855.C.	856.B.	857.C.	858.C.	859.A.	860.C.
861.D.	862.B.	863.A.	864.B.	865.C.	866.B.	867.C.	868.A.	869.A.	870.C.
871.B.	872.B.	873.D.	874.B.	875.B.	876.A.	877.B.	878.D.	879.B.	880.A.
881.A.	882.C.	883.C.	884.C.	885.A.	886.C.	887.C.	888.B.	889.C.	890.A.
891.C.	892.D.	893.D.	894.D.	895.A.	896.C.	897.B.	898.A.	899.C.	900.D.
901.B.	902.B.	903.C.	904.D.	905.A.	906.A.	907.D.	908.B.	909.D.	910.B.
911.D.	912.A.	913.B.	914.D.	915.B.	916.C.	917.A.	918.C.	919.B.	920.B.
921.C.	922.B.	923.A.	924.A.	925.D.	926.A.	927.D.	928.C.	929.D.	930.D.
931.D.	932.A.	933.D.	934.A.	935.D.	936.A.	937.C.	938.D.	939.C.	940.D.
941.B.	942.D.	943.D.	944.D.	945.A.	946.C.	947.D.	948.C.	949.D.	950.D.
951.D.	952.A.	953.A.	954.D.	955.B.	956.D.	957.A.	958.C.	959.D.	960.B.

961.C.	962.C.	963.C.	964.B.	965.D.	966.D.	967.A.	968.C.	969.B.	970.B.
971.D.	972.C.	973.B.	974.A.	975.B.	976.D.	977.C.	978.D.	979.B.	980.D.
981.A.	982.A.	983.A.	984.B.	985.A.	986.A.	987.B.	988.C.	989.B.	990.D.
991.B.	992.D.	993.D.	994.C.	995.D.	996.C.	997.D.	998.D.	999.B.	1000.B.
1001.C.	1002.D.	1003.D.	1004.D.	1005.C.	1006.C.	1007.C.	1008.D.	1009.C.	1010.B.
1011.A.	1012.D.	1013.D.	1014.C.	1015.C.	1016.A.	1017.B.	1018.C.	1019.A.	1020.A.
1021.D.	1022.C.	1023.D.	1024.A.	1025.D.	1026.B.	1027.A.	1028.C.	1029.C.	1030.A.
1031.A.	1032.D.	1033.D.	1034.D.	1035.B.	1036.B.	1037.B.	1038.A.	1039.A.	1040.A.
1041.D.	1042.D.	1043.A.	1044.B.	1045.D.	1046.A.	1047.C.	1048.B.	1049.C.	1050.B.
1051.B.	1052.C.	1053.A.	1054.D.	1055.B.	1056.A.	1057.B.	1058.A.	1059.D.	1060.A.
1061.A.	1062.D.	1063.D.	1064.B.	1065.D.	1066.B.	1067.B.	1068.B.	1069.A.	1070.A.
1071.A.	1072.A.	1073.D.	1074.C.	1075.D.	1076.D.	1077.C.	1078.D.	1079.B.	1080.D.
1081.C.	1082.B.	1083.C.	1084.D.	1085.A.	1086.C.	1087.A.	1088.B.	1089.C.	1090.A.
1091.D.	1092.C.	1093.A.	1094.B.	1095.C.	1096.D.	1097.C.	1098.C.	1099.B.	1100.D.
1101.B.	1102.D.	1103.C.	1104.D.	1105.B.	1106.B.	1107.D.	1108.A.	1109.B.	1110.A.
1111.C.	1112.C.	1113.A.	1114.C.	1115.B.	1116.B.	1117.B.	1118.C.	1119.B.	1120.D.
1121.B.	1122.C.	1123.A.	1124.A.	1125.A.	1126.B.	1127.D.	1128.B.	1129.B.	1130.A.
1131.A.	1132.B.	1133.B.	1134.A.	1135.B.	1136.B.	1137.B.	1138.A.	1139.A.	1140.B.
1141.D.	1142.A.	1143.D.	1144.B.	1145.A.	1146.C.	1147.B.	1148.B.	1149.B.	1150.C.
1151.A.	1152.B.	1153.B.	1154.D.	1155.A.	1156.C.	1157.A.	1158.B.	1159.B.	1160.D.
1161.A.	1162.B.	1163.A.	1164.A.	1165.B.	1166.D.	1167.C.	1168.D.	1169.C.	1170.C.
1171.B.	1172.B.	1173.B.	1174.D.	1175.C.	1176.C.	1177.D.	1178.C.	1179.B.	1180.C.
1181.D.	1182.B.	1183.A.	1184.A.	1185.B.	1186.C.	1187.A.	1188.C.	1189.D.	1190.B.
1191.A.	1192.A.	1193.B.	1194.A.	1195.C.	1196.C.	1197.B.	1198.A.	1199.A.	1200.C.
1201.D.	1202.C.	1203.A.	1204.A.	1205.A.	1206.B.	1207.B.	1208.D.	1209.A.	1210.D.
1211.C.	1212.B.	1213.C.	1214.D.	1215.A.	1216.A.	1217.A.	1218.B.	1219.A.	1220.A.
1221.B.	1222.C.	1223.A.	1224.B.	1225.A.	1226.D.	1227.C.	1228.B.	1229.C.	1230.C.
1231.B.	1232.D.	1233.C.	1234.A.	1235.D.	1236.A.	1237.C.	1238.A.	1239.C.	1240.D.
1241.B.	1242.B.	1243.A.	1244.C.	1245.C.	1246.C.	1247.A.	1248.A.	1249.D.	1250.D.
1251.A.	1252.D.	1253.A.	1254.A.	1255.B.	1256.D.	1257.C.	1258.B.	1259.A.	1260.D.
1261.C.	1262.A.	1263.A.	1264.A.	1265.B.	1266.B.	1267.D.	1268.A.	1269.D.	1270.A.
1271.B.	1272.B.	1273.B.	1274.C.	1275.D.	1276.A.	1277.C.	1278.C.	1279.B.	1280.B.
1281.B.	1282.A.	1283.B.	1284.B.	1285.A.	1286.B.	1287.A.	1288.A.	1289.A.	1290.D.
1291.D.	1292.B.	1293.D.	1294.A.	1295.B.	1296.D.	1297.D.	1298.C.	1299.A.	1300.A.
1301.C.	1302.D.	1303.C.	1304.A.	1305.D.	1306.A.	1307.B.	1308.C.	1309.D.	1310.A.
1311.D.	1312.B.	1313.C.	1314.A.	1315.B.	1316.C.	1317.B.	1318.A.	1319.C.	1320.C.
1321.B.	1322.B.	1323.A.	1324.B.	1325.B.	1326.D.	1327.A.	1328.A.	1329.A.	1330.C.
1331.B.	1332.A.	1333.A.	1334.C.	1335.B.	1336.B.	1337.B.	1338.B.	1339.D.	1340.D.
1341.A.	1342.B.								

❑❑❑

2. Anatomy & Physiology with Microbiology (MCQ)

1. **The radius is located**
   A. In the upper part of the arm
   B. On the thumb side of the lower arm
   C. On the little finger side of the lower arm
   D. At the shoulder arm
2. **Antibodies are produced by:**
   A. Plasma cells B. Lymphocytes
   C. Erythrocytes D. Basophills
3. **Normally respiratory centre is stimulated by:**
   A. Oxygen B. Blood PH
   C. Carbon dioxide D. Lactic acid
4. **The type of muscle found in the visceral organs and blood vessels is called**
   A. Voluntary B. Cardiac
   C. Myocardium D. Involuntary
5. **In human body unoxygenated blood is purified by:**
   A. Heart B. Lungs
   C. Lever D. Kidney
6. **All microorganisms ....?**
   A. Form spores
   B. Have a waxy coating
   C. Are protoplasm consisting of protein
   D. Adapt to adverse environment
7. **Which of the following bone is the largest bone in human body:**
   A. Tibia B. Radius
   C. Femur D. Humerus
8. **Factors influencing inhibition of growth and destruction of microorganisms include?**
   A. Temperature and contact
   B. Absence of organic material
   C. Time
   D. Spore formation
   A. B, C and D B. A, B and D
   C. A, C and D D. A, B and C
9. **Which part of body is affected in typhoid:**
   A. Lungs B. Intestines
   C. Liver D. Pancreas
10. **Vitamin essential for coagulation of biood is:**
    A. A B. B
    C. K D. D
11. **In the complex sense of vision the image of an object focused on the retina and is transmitted to the brain**
    A. Cornea B. Optic nerve
    C. Lens D. Iris
12. **Volume remaining in the lungs and airways following a maximum expiratory effort is known as:**
    A. Residual volume B. Total lung capacity
    C. Vital capacity D. Tidal capacity
13. **If pericardial fluid exceed above 50 ml. This is known as -**
    A. Pericardial oedema
    B. Pericardial transudate
    C. Cardiac tamponade
    D. Cardiac asthma
14. **Thyroid gland is present in:**
    A. Chest B. Back
    C. Abdomen D. Neck
15. **Many children with tonsillitis develop ear infection this is because the ear and throat are connected by the**
    A. Larynx B. Eustachian Tube
    C. Epiglottis D. Esophagus
16. **Smooth muscle tissue is located in:**
    A. The stomach B. Urinary bladder
    C. Intestines D. All of the Above
17. **The respiratory centre is located in the part of brain**
    A. Medulla B. Thalamus
    C. Midbrain D. Cerebellum
18. **Powerhouse of the cell is:**
    A. Mitochondria B. Nucleus
    C. Golgi bodies D. Cell wall
19. **Water is mostly absorbed from the digestive tract in the**
    A. Esophagus B. Stomach
    C. Small Intestine D. Large Intestine
20. **The breakdown products of hemoglobin is:**
    A. Phosphclipids B. Bile pigments
    C. Fibrin D. Prothrombin
21. **Thyroid is effective only in the presence of ?**
    A. Calcium B. Iodine
    C. Potassium D. Sodium chloride
22. **Largest internal organ of human body is:**
    A. Liver B. Lungs
    C. Kidney D. Heart
23. **The normal pH for body fluids is**
    A. 9.1 to 9.6 B. 7.35 to 7.45
    C. 4. 4. To 5.4 D. 7 to 7.1
24. **Prothrombin is produced by:**
    A. Blood B. Liver
    C. Ovary D. Spleen
25. **Number of pairs of spinal nerves that exit from the spinal cord are:**
    A. 31 B. 33
    C. 24 D. 30
26. **Total no. Of bones in the body?**
    A. 206 bones B. 256 bones
    C. 215 bones D. 201 bones

27. **A compound within a cell nucleus that consists of a protein bound to a nucleic acid is called:**
A. Nucleoprotein B. Albumin
C. Glycoprotein D. All of the Above

28. **The fibrous tissue connecting bone to bone is called?**
A. Cartilage B. Tendon
C. Muscle D. Ligament

29. **The bonds that hold the antigen to the antibody combining site are?**
A. Covalent bond
B. Co-ordinate covalent bond
C. Hydrophilic bond
D. None of the Above

30. **Heat regulating centre is located in?**
A. Thalamus
B. Hypothalamus
C. Medulla oblongata
D. Cerebrum

31. **Meningitis is an?**
A. Inflammation of the membranes that surround the liver
B. Inflammation of the membranes that surround the brain and the spinal cord
C. Inflammation of the membranes that surround the heart
D. Inflammation of the membranes that surround the kidney

32. **Corticosteroid is naturally produced by?**
A. Thalamus B. Ovary
C. Thyroid gland D. Adrenal glands

33. **Aspartate aminotransferase enzyme?**
A. Plays a role in processing proteins
B. Plays a role in metabolism, the process that converts food into energy
C. Both A and B
D. None of the Above

34. **Gall bladder is located in?**
A. Upper right part of abdomen
B. On right side of liver
C. On the left side of liver
D. Below the liver

35. **The smallest bone of human body is?**
A. Stapes B. Phallanges
C. Metacarpals D. Xiphisternum

36. **Measure of the overall strength of binding of an antigen with many antigenic determinants and multivalent antibodies is called?**
A. Avidity B. Affinity
C. Activity D. None of the Above

37. **The function of fallopian tube is?**
A. Secretion of oestrogen and progesterone
B. Passage way for foetus
C. Occurrence of fertilization
D. Developing foetus

38. **The autonomic nervous system regulates visceral activities such as?**
A. Respiration
B. Contraction of smooth muscles
C. Gastroinstestinal motility
D. All the Above

39. **Normal respiration of healthy person is?**
A. 5-10/min B. 10-15/min
C. 15-20/min D. 20-30/min

40. **The widal test is positive if TO antigen titer is more than?**
A. 1: 70 in an active infection
B. 1:160 in an infection
C. 1: 80 in an active infection
D. 1:90 in an active infection

41. **Kidney is situated?**
A. In abdominal cavity
B. In pelvic cavity
C. In thoracic cavity
D. In dorsal cavity

42. **In normal person the percentage of glycosylated haemoglobin is?**
A. 6 B. 14.5 C. 15.5 D. 17.9

43. **Total number of chambers in human heart is?**
A. 4 B. 1 C. 2 D. 3

44. **Which part of the brain controls and integrates activities of the autonomic nervous system?**
A. Hypothalamus B. Epithalamus
C. Midbrain D. Thalamus

45. **The only artery which supplies deoxygenated blood:**
A. Pulmonary artery B. Hepatic artery
C. Gastric artery D. Renal artery

46. **The difference between the apical and radial pulse rates is called the:**
A. Rhythm deficit B. Heart amplitude
C. Pulse deficit D. Pulse amplitude

47. **Fault in male that may cause infertility includes:**
A. Mumps orchitis
B. Raised scrotal temperature
C. Undescended testes
D. All of the Above

48. **Inability of the liver to metabolize and remove bilirubin from the biliary system is:**
A. Haemolytic jaundice
B. Obstructive jaundice

C. Hereditary hyperbilirubinemia
D. Hepatocellular jaundice

49. The structural and functional unit of kidney is called as
A. Neuron B. Glomeruli
C. Axone D. Nephrone

50. The bone that protect the brain is called as
A. Sternum B. Cranium
C. Clavicle D. Pelvis

51. Excetory unit of kidney is:
A. Nephron
B. Henle's loop
C. Bowman's capsule
D. Glomerulus

52. The pancreas produces which two hormone:
A. Insulin and glucagon
B. Epinephrine and insulin
C. Melatonin and glucagon
D. Glucagon and epinephrine

53. Which of muscle is Rectus Femoris?
A. Fusiform B. Elongated
C. Triangular D. Pinnate

54. Heart sounds are the result of:
A. Movement of blood into the heart form the aorta
B. Blood flow through the heart
C. Closure of the heart valves
D. Contraction of the cadiac muscle

55. Which of the following hormone stimulate contraction of the uterus at the end of the pregnancy and stimulate milk from the mammary gland
A. Oxytocin
B. Adrenocortico Tropic Hormone (acTH)
C. Vasopressin
D. Estrogen

56. As a part of the assessment of the cranial nerves, the nurse asks the patient to arise the eyebrows, smile and show the teeth, these actions provide information about which cranial nerve?
A. Facial B. Vagus
C. Olfactory D. Optic

57. The Growth hormone or Somatotropin is secreted by which of the following gland
A. Adrenal gland
B. Testis
C. Hypothalamus
D. Pituitary gland

58. Which of the following represents the correct pathway for conduction of an action potential through the heart?
A. AV node, AV bundle, SA node, Purkinje fibers, bundle branches
B. Sa node, bundle of his, bundle ranches, AV node, purkinje fibers
C. SA node, Av node bundle of his, bundle branches, purkinje fibers
D. AV node, bundle branches, bundle of His, SA node, purkinje fibers

59. Which part of the brain is concerned with hearing, short term memory and sense of smell?
A. Temporal lobe B. Parietal lobe
C. Cerebellum D. Hypothalamus

60. The last product in the process of blood coagulation is:
A. Thromboplastin B. Prothrombin
C. Fibrin D. Thrombin

61. What is the name of the membrane that covers lungs?
A. Meninges B. Pleura
C. Peritoneum D. Periosteum

62. A person with one of the following blood groups of considered a universal recipient:
A. A B. AB C. O D. B

63. Which Muscle is located on the anterior part of the thigh?
A. Vastus lateralis B. Rectus femoris
C. Vastus medialis D. Sartorius

64. The part of brain, which is responsible for the co-ordination of movement is:
A. Brain stem B. Thalamus
C. Cerebellum D. Hypothalamus

65. Which of the following structures carries bile and pancreatic juice to the duodenum?
A. Pancreatic duct B. Cystic duct
C. Hepatic duct D. Common bile duct

66. The hereditary determinants of humans are received from:
A. Allele B. Genes
C. Nucleus D. Cytopalsm

67. Which of the following is not a cranial nerve?
A. Accessory B. Abducent
C. Trochlear D. Coccygeal

68. Corpus luteum is found in:
A. Foetus B. Placenta
C. Uterus D. Ovary

69. Mechanical digestion in the stomach is accomplished by which of the following structures?
A. Mucosa
B. Smooth muscle layer
C. Striated muscle layer
D. Gastric glands

70. Heart burn refers to an uneasy burning sensation in the:
A. Jejunum B. Duodenum
C. Oesophagus D. Stomach

71. Which of the following mineral is necessary for blood clotting ?
A. Iron B. Sodium
C. Potassium D. Calcium

72. Total number of facial bone:
A. 12 B. 10 C. 14 D. 16

73. Each normal heart beat is initiated by which of the following ?
A. Sino atrial Node
B. Bundle of His
C. Cardiac center of Medulla
D. Sympathetic nerves

74. The process by which ova are discharge from ovary is called:
A. Menstruation B. Oogenesis
C. Ovulation D. Fertilization

75. When blood pressure falls, which of the following is secreted by kidney to raise it ?
A. Renin B. Epinephrine
C. Aldosterone D. Erythropoetin

76. The heart of the activated sludge process is:
A. Sludge digester
B. Primary sedimentation tank
C. Aeration tank
D. Final setting tank

77. Permanent pacemaker is indicated in which of the following dysrhythmias ?
A. Ventricular fibrillation
B. Asymptomatic bradycardia
C. Atrial fibrillation
D. Third degree heart block

78. The type of memberane that lines the knee joint:
A. Mucous B. Epithelial
C. Serous D. Synovial

79. Which of the following structure covers the larynx during swallowing?
A. Hydroid cartilage B. Vocal cords
C. Soft palate D. Epiglottis

80. Which of the following is the heriditary meaterial of cells?
A. D.N.A in the chromosomes
B. Protein in the ribosomes
C. R.N.A in the nucleus
D. Ribosomes in the cytoplasm

81. Which one of the following is considered as a part of the endomembrane system?
A. Vacuole B. Ribosome
C. Mitochondria D. Peroxisome

82. Which results from too much cortisol secretion in the body?
A. Addison's disease
B. Cushing's syndrome
C. Hypothyroidism
D. None of the Above

83. Which of the following is the function of companion cells?
A. It provides water to xylem
B. Loading of sucrose into sieve elements
C. It provides energy to sieve elements for passive transport
D. Loading of sucrose into sieve elements by active transport

84. A primary central organ of the lymphatic system, plays vital in immunity:
A. Liver B. Spleen
C. Thymus D. Tonsills

85. In Kranz anatomy, which of the following do the bundle sheath cells have?
A. Thick walls, no intercellular spaces and several chloroplasts
B. Thin walls, many intercellular spaces and few chloroplasts
C. Thin walls, few intercellular spaces and no chloroplasts
D. Thick walls, no intercellular spaces and large number of chloroplasts

86. The largest cavity in the human body:
A. Thoracic cavity B. Abdominal cavity
C. Pelvic cavity D. Cranial cavity

87. For the birth of a normal female child of human which of the following conditions of the zygotic cell is a must?
A. Two Y chromosome
B. One X and two Y chromosome
C. Two X chromosome
D. One Y and two X chromosome

88. The primary function fo the prostate glands:
A. To produce a secretion that aids the nourishment and passage of sperm
B. To store under developed sperm before ejaculation
C. To regulate proper sperm development
D. To stimulate the production and maturation of sperms

89. Which of the following immunoglobulin is involved in allergic reaction?
A. Ig A B. Ig D
C. Ig G D. Ig E

90. Smallest unit of culture is:
A. Trait B. Complex
C. Moral D. Subculture

91. Four pairs of microbe and its industrial product are given below: Which one of the following is a wrong matching?
A. Clostridium butylicum lactic acid
B. Saccharomyces ethanol
C. Trichoderma polysporum cyclosporuma
D. Penicillium notsatum penicillin

92. The strongest joint in the body is:
A. Shoulder joint B. Knee joint
C. Sacroiliac joint D. Hip joint

93. The PcR is a technique that
A. Is used for in vivo replication of DNA
B. Is used for in vivo synthesis of MRNA
C. Is used for in vitro synthesis of MRNA
D. Is used for in vitro replication of specific DNA sequence using thermostable DNA polymerase.

94. Which of the following bacteria is not a source of restriction endonuclease
A. Haemophilus infleunza
B. Escherichia coli
C. Agrobacterium tumefaciens
D. Bacillus amyloli

95. A saprophyte which can act as a parasite is
A. Facultative saprophyte
B. Obligate saprophyte
C. Facultative parasite
D. Obligate parasite

96. Okazaki is known for his contribution to the understanding of
A. Transcription B. Translation
C. DNA replication D. Mutation

97. The basis of DNA fingerprinting is
A. The double helix
B. Errors in base sequence
C. Polymorphism in sequence
D. DNA replication

98. Turner syndrome is
A. XO B. XXY
C. XXX D. XYY

99. Which of the following structure is not related with inner ear
A. Cochlea B. Vestibule
C. Organ of corti D. Malleus

100. Natural pacemaker of the heart is
A. Sa node B. aV node
C. Purkinjie fibre D. bundle of His

101. Oxytocine Hormone is secreted by
A. Anterior Pituitary Gland
B. Posterior Pituitary Gland
C. Thyroid Gland
D. Adrenal cortex

102. All of the following are acid-fast except
A. Mycobacterium tuberculosis
B. Nocardia
C. Isospora belli
D. Staphylococcus

103. An example of holocrine gland is
A. A sweat gland
B. A salivary gland
C. A pancreatic gland
D. A sebaceous gland

104. Hypoglossal nerve is
A. 6th cranial nerve B. 7th cranial nerve
C. 12th cranial nerve D. 9th cranial nerve

105. Which of these structure holds the small intestine in its position?
A. Mesentery B. Mesocolon
C. Lesser omentum D. Greater omentum

106. Which one of the following organs breaks fat to produce cholesterol?
A. Intestine B. Liver
C. Lungs D. Kidneys

107. Which of the following is secreted through lacrymal gland?
A. Sebum B. Mucous
C. Tears D. Sweat

108. The thickest human skin is ?
A. Palm B. Sole
C. Neck D. Head

109. Which of the following is an example of tissue ?
A. Brain B. Blood
C. Liver D. Stomach

110. Through which of the following organs maximum nutritional elements in the blood are absorbed
A. Mouth B. Large intestine
C. Small intestine D. Abdomen

111. Which one of the following enzymes is found in the Saliva ?
A. Renin B. Ptyalin
C. Tenin D. Resin

112. The total number of bones in human body are ?
A. 212 B. 206 C. 202 D. 102

113. The longest bone of the human body is?
A. Stepis B. Fibula
C. Tibia D. Femur

114. In which of the following structure the human body vermiform appendix is included ?
A. Large Intestine B. Small Intestine
C. Gall bladder D. Stomach

115. Example of ball and socket joint is?
A. Elbow
B. Hip joint
C. Thumb and fingers
D. Between wrist bones

116. During clotting, the prothombin is changed to thrombin in the presence of?
A. Calcium ions and fibrogen
B. Thromboplastin and Vitamin K
C. Calcium ion and Vitamin K
D. Calcium ion and Thromboplastin

117. A failure in lymphatic system to return body fluids adequately results in?
A. Swelling of hands and legs
B. Swelling of face and hands
C. Oedema in spleen
D. Swelling of tissues as oedema

118. The trachea or wind pipe is made up of cartilage rings; shape of the rings is?
A. C shaped B. S shaped
C. Cone shaped D. Straight

119. Acid base balance is regulated by kidney by excreting hydrogen ion and electrolytes to maintain the?
A. Electrolyte balance in body
B. Specific gravity of urine
C. Filter the protein from urine
D. Normal PH of blood plasma

120. Which of the following is a master gland which influences the endocrine glands:
A. Thyroid B. Parathyroid
C. Hypothalamus D. Pituitary

121. One of the functions of cerebellum is to:
A. Serve as a passage between spinal cord and brain
B. Maintain balance, coordination and muscular control
C. Conduct nerve impulse
D. Maintain area of reason, thought, memory and sensation

122. Most of the infections spread to the ear from throat through?
A. Eustachian tube
B. Cochlea
C. Ear canal
D. Tympanic membrane

123. Germ cell theory was proposed by?
A. Robert Koch B. Ronald Ross
C. Louis Pasteur D. Walter Reed

124. Most microbial structures and enzymes in human beings are composed of?
A. Lipids B. Proteins
C. Carbohydrates D. Minerals

125. Mycology is the study of
A. Fungi B. Virus
C. bacteria D. Nucleic acid

126. Most commonly used bacterium for genetic engineering is
A. E. coli B. Klebsiella
C. Proteius D. Serratia

127. Adenine in DNA structure pairs with?
A. Thymines B. Cytosine
C. Guanines D. Pyrimidine

128. The process of copying the DNA sequence of a gene into messenger RNA (MRNA). is called
A. Transference B. Transcription
C. Translocation D. Translation

129. Which mode of information transfer usually does not occur?
A. DNA to DNA
B. DNA to RNA
C. DNA to protein
D. All occur in a working cell

130. A medical disorder resulting from mutation in the DNA repair system is
A. Bloom syndrome
B. Nephrotic syndrome
C. Poly syndrome
D. Pierrerobin syndrome

131. Functional unit of bronchial tree ?
A. Respiratory bronchiole
B. Alveolar duct
C. Alveoli
D. Acinus

132. All of Hyaline cartilage of larynx EXCEPT -
A. Cricoid B. Corniculate
C. Areytenoid D. Thyroid

133.' Voice box' is the term for
A. True – vocal cord B. False vocal cord
C. Larynx D. Laryngopharynx

134 After forcefull inspiration the maximum volume of air exhaled out of the lung is known as
A. ERV B. FRC
C. Vc D. IRV

135 All one cause of portal hypertension EXCEPT -
A. Thrombophlebitis B. DVT
C. Cirrhoris D, Jaundice

136. All are seen in portal hypertension except -
A. Ascitis
B. Caput medusae
C. Haemorrhoid
D. Urinary bladder obstruction

137. **Anterior 2/3 of the tongue carries taste sensation with the help of**
A. Glossopharyngeal B. Vagus
C. Hypoglossal D. Facial

138. **Muscle of tongue is mainly supplied -**
A. IX C.N. B. X CN.
C. XI C.N. D. XII CN.

139. **The neurotransmitter serotonin is derived from which precursor amino acid?**
A. Dopamine B. Tyrosine
C. Tryptophan D. Glutamine

140. **Glucagon hormone is secreted by the**
A. Thyroid gland B. Adrenal gland
C. Pancreas D. Pituitary gland

141. **The concentration of sodium chloride in our blood per 100 ml is**
A. 0.9% B. 0.8%
C. 0.5% D. 0.1%

142. **Simple squamous epithelium is a term for ?**
A. Tissue B. Cell
C. Organ D. Pathology

143. **Which of the following is not one of the 3 external coverings of the kidney?**
A. Renal capsule B. Adipose capsule
C. Renal adventitia D. Renal Fascia

144. **A system is defined as a group of......... that function together?**
A. Cells B. Tissues
C. Molecules D. Organs

145. **The junction at which an impulse travels from one neuron to another is called ?**
A. Synapse B. Stimulus
C. Nerve message D. Axon

46. **The following are sinus areas except which one?**
A. Frontal B. Maxillary
C. Ethmoid D. Cranial

47. **Which is the biggest cell in the body?**
A. Nerve cells B. Cardiac cells
C. Renal cells D. Ovum

48. **Find out the odd one**
A. Trachea B. Bronchi
C. Esophagus D. Larynx

49. **Anatomy is a term, which means the study of ?**
A. Physiology B. Morphology
C. Cell Function D. Human Function

50. **A major function of the large intestine is to ?**
A. Secrete digestive enzymes
B. Remove waste material
C. Regulate the release of bile
D. Secrete water in order to regulate blood volume

151. **The total volume of CSF is ?**
A. 50 ml B. 100 ml
C. 150 ml D. 275 ml

152. **All are motor nerve except?**
A. Accessory B. Abducent
C. Trochlear D. Trigeminal

153. **Length of female urethra is?**
A. 18 cm B. 4 cm
C. 10 cm D. 18 inches

154. **Which of the following would not be lined by pericardium?**
A. Heart B. Stomach
C. Intestine D. Liver

155. **The terminal portion of the large intestine is?**
A. Duodenum B. Ileum
C. Rectum D. Colon

156. **B-cells of pancreas secrete which hormone?**
A. Insulin B. LH
C. FSH D. TRH

157. **Iron absorption c̲ part of intestine?**
A. Duedonum B. Large Intestine
C. Stomach D. Colon

158. **The largest gland in the human body?**
A. Pancreas B. Liver
C. Spleen D. Gall bladder

159. **Chemical signals released by an organism that influence the behavior of other individuals of the same species are called?**
A. Pheromone B. Insulin
C. Androgen D. Steroid

160. **The functional unit of kidney is called?**
A. Bowman's capsule
B. Malphigian corpuscles
C. Pyramid
D. Nephron

161. **Mobile bone of skull?**
A. Maxilla B. Mandible
C. Ethmoid D. Sphenoid

162. **The natural pacemaker of the heart is?**
A. Bundle of His B. Av Node
C. Sa Node D. Purkinje Fiber

163. **Mitral valve is also referred as?**
A. Bicuspid valve B. Tricuspid valve
C. Pulmonary valve D. Aortic valve

164. **The gland that is located below Hypo-physeal Fossa of Sphenoid bone is?**
A. Thyroid gland B. Pineal gland
C. Pituitary gland D. Adrenal gland

165. **Antibodies are produced by?**
A. Leucocytes B. Monocytes
C. Lymphocytes D. Spleen

166. **Carbonic anhydrase occurs in?**
A. Lymphocytes B. Blood plasma
C. Rbc D. Leucocytes

167. **A moth sex attraction would be due to ?**
A. Hormone B. Neurotransmitter
C. Pheromone D. Steroid

168. **The central nervous system consist of?**
A. The brain and spinal cord
B. Spinal nerves only
C. The brain stem and cerebellum
D. The cerebellum and the spinal column

169. **The left ureter is slightly longer than the right ureter because the?**
A. Left ureter has a three layered wall
B. Left kidney is higher than the right
C. Right kidney is higher than the left
D. Left kidney performs more functions

170. **The primary muscles of inspiration?**
A. Abdominals and external intercoastal
B. Diaphragm and external intercoastal
C. Abdominals and internal intercoastal
D. Diaphragm and internal intercoastal

171. **Clotting can be prevented by using ?**
A. Antiemitics B. Antibiotics
C. Anticoagulants D. Analgesics

172. **Which arrangement of gastro intestinal layer is correct from inside out?**
A. Serous, mucosa, submucosa and muscular layer
B. Mucosa, submucosa, serous and muscular layer
C. Mucosa, submucosa, muscular and serous
D. Muscular, serous, submucosa and mucosa

173. **Match the following?**
A. Pleural cavity filled with blood — 1. Pneumo-thorax
B. Pleural cavity filled with pus — 2. Pleural ef-fusion
C. Pleural cavity filled with air — 3. Heamo -thorax
D. Pleural cavity filled with fluid — 4. Pyothorax

	A.	B.	C.	D
A.	4	2	3	1
B.	3	4	1	2
C.	2	3	4	1
D.	4	1	2	3

174. **Duration of one cardiac cycle in a normal person at rest is?**
A. 0.3 sec B. 0.5 sec
C. 0.8 sec D. 0.10 sec

175. **Hormone secreted by the testes?**
A. Oestrogen B. Pitocin
C. Androgens D. Progesterone

176. **........ is the immunity get by the body after the first attack of disease.**
A. Natural immunity
B. Passive immunity
C. Artificial immunity
D. Acquired immunity

177. **The cells that are responsible for the production of antibodies are ?**
A. Red blood cells B. Platelets
C. Plasma D. White blood cells

178. **The following organs are situated in the abdominal cavity except?**
A. Stomach B. Oesophagus
C. Liver D. Spleen

179. **The system of body which helps for the removal of waste matter from body?**
A. Digestive system
B. Endocrine system
C. Respiratory system
D. Excretory system

180. **The condition where bacteria circulate and multiply in the blood is called?**
A. Fibrinolysins B. Bacteremia
C. Pyemia D. Septicemia

181. **A condition characterized by moving of bones out joint:**
A. Fracture B. Sprain
C. Strain D. Dislocation

182. **A tube of muscular tissue carrying ingested food from the mouth to stomach?**
A. Oesophagus B. Duodenum
C. Trachea D. Pharynx

183. **A red pigment in the blood cells which combines with oxygen and carbon dioxide for carrying them?**
A. Red blood cells B. Haemoglobin
C. Platelet D. Plasma

184. **Hormones are transported to all parts of the body through ?**
A. Nerves B. Blood
C. Lymph D. Muscles

185. **Deficiency of ...... in food causes simple goiter.**
A. Sodium B. Iron
C. Iodine D. Calcium

186. **The "basic unit of life" is**
A. The atom
B. Water
C. The cell
D. The chemical level of organization

187. **The outer layer of the eye ball is**
A. Sclera B. Choroids
C. Retina D. Pars Plana

188. The primary function of the ascending loop of Henle in the kidney is?
A. The active re-absorption of sodium
B. The active re-absorption of chloride ions
C. The passive re-absorption of potassium
D. The passive re-absorption of urea

189. The middle layer of the urinary bladder is identified as ?
A. Mucous Coat B. Sub mucous Coat
C. Muscular Coat D. Sphincter Coat

190. Short sightedness can be corrected by using spectacles with ..... lens.
A. Concave B. Convex
C. Cylindrical D. Opaque

191. Which artery supplies oxygenated blood to the stomach ?
A. Carotid artery B. Gastric artery
C. Celiac artery D. Cephalic artery

192. The organs of the excretory system consist of the following except
A. Blood vessels B. Skin
C. Liver D. Kidneys

193. The 10th cranial nerve is:
A. Hypoglossal B. Abdu cent
C. Vagus D. Facial

194. The middle layer of meninges is:
A. Choroid Plexus B. Dura mater
C. Piamater D. Arachnoids mater

195. The anterior transparent part of the eye is:
A. Sclera B. Pupil
C. Conjunctiva D. Cornea

196. Hormones from anterior pituitary
A. Growth hormone
B. acTH
C. TSH
D. Somatostatin

197. Which of the following match with the definition: a poor output of urine?
A. Oligouria B. Pyruia
C. Enuresis D. Diuresis

198. Which valve prevents backward flow of blood into the left atrium ?
A. Aortic valve B. Pulmonary valve
C. Tricuspid valve D. Mitral valve

199. The ______ membranes surround the lungs?
A. Pericardial B. Mediastinal
C. Pleural. D. Peritoneal

200. Which division of the nervous system initiates a response known as fight and flight?
A. The parasympathetic nervous system
B. The sympathetic nervous system
C. The somatic nervous system
D. None of these

201. Most commonly fractured carpal bone
A. Hamate B. Lunate
C. Scaphoid D. Capitate

202. Identify the hip bone from the following:
A. Sacrum B. Femur
C. Humerus D. In nominate

203. The pH of arterial blood is:
A. 5.40 B. 7.65
C. 7.80 D 7.40

204. Life span of Rbc's is:
A. 12 days B. 40 days
C. 120 days D. 50 days

205. The lobe of the brain that can decode and interpret visual information:
A. Temporal B. Frontal
C. Parietal D. Occipital

206. After ovulation corpus luteum formed in the ovary releases:
A. Testosterone B. Aldosterone
C. Progesterone D. Estrogen

207. The main function of kidney is to:
A. Eliminate oxygen
B. Regulate fluid balance and removing waste products
C. Metabolise vitamins
D. Eliminate carbon dioxide

208. Which one of the following brain area that regulates body temperature?
A. Cerebellum B. Cerebrum
C. Hypothalamus D. Hippocampus

209. Which one of the following sugar concentration is highest in body?
A. Maltose B. Lactose
C. Glucose D. Fructose

210. The micturation reflex center is located in the
A. Pons B. Midbrain
C. Lumbar plexus D. Sacral plexus

211. Biopesticides are produced by:
A. Bacillus thuringiensis
B. Agrobacterium tumfeciens
C. Pseudomonas sp
D. Bacillus anthracis

212. Hyper functioning of anterior pituitary in pre-pubertal children causes
A. Gigantism
B. Acromegaly
C. Addison's disease
D. Cushing's disease

213. **Which one of the following gymnosperm is said to have double fertilizations?**
A. Ephedra B. Cycas
C. Pinus D. Ginko

214. **Where is cardiac sphincture located?**
A. Lungs B. Liver
C. Stomach D. Heart

215. **Tunica adventitia is a layer of:**
A. Bloodvessels B. Uterus
C. Testis D. Lungs

216. **Islets of Langerhans are concentrated in which portion of Pancreas?**
A. Head B. Body
C. Tail D. Uncinate process

217. **Which of the following hormones owes its discovery to tissue culture technique?**
A. Auxin B. Cytokinins
C. Gibberellin D. Abscisicacid

218. **Light year is the unit of:**
A. Speed B. Mass
C. Time D. Distance

219. **Pollen grains in the angiosperm represent:**
A. Male gamete
B. Microsporophyll
C. Male gametophyte
D. Microsporangium

220. **Germ theory of disease was founded by:**
A. Hippocrates B. Louis pasteur
C. William harvey D. Alexander fleming

221. **Robert Koch discovered the etiologic agent of**
A. Typhoid B. Tuberculosis
C. Smallpox D. Polio

222. **What is the best method to dispose hospital waste?**
A. Composting B. Chemical treatment
C. Incineration D. Dumping

223. **The optimum temperature for the growth of most pathogenic bacteria is:**
A. 30°c B. 25°c
C. 37°c D. 42°c

224. **In majority of the cases the causative organism for sore throat is:**
A. Gonococci B. Streptococci
C. Meningococci D. Staphylococci

225. **Mitosis is a condition of:**
A. Cell division with half chromosomes
B. Cell division without reduction
C. Cell breakdown
D. Cell death

226. **Which one of the disease is not caused by an acid fast bacilli aFB.?**
A. Leprosy B. Nocardiasis
C. Tuberculosis D. Typhoid

227 **Which of the following conditions is caused by long-term exposure to high levels of cortisol**
A. Addison's disease
B. Crohn's disease
C. Adrenal insufficiency
D. Cushing syndrome

228. **All are parts of the light microscope except:**
A. Condenser
B. Slide with cover slip
C. Objective lens
D. Eye-piece

229. **An agent which kills pathogenic bacteria is called:**
A. Asepsis B. Disinfectant
C. Fomite D. Bacteriostat

230. **In which organ does the maximum absorption of Iron take place ?**
A. Stomach B. Small Intestine
C. Colon D. Liver

231. **The 'p' wave on the electrocardiogram corresponds to**
A. Atrial depolarization
B. Atrial repolarization
C. Ventrical depolarization
D. Ventrical repolarization

232. **Which colour of light has the longest wavelength:**
A. Violet B. Blue
C. Red D. Green

233. **Bowman's glands are found in**
A. Jux tamedullary Nephrons
B. Olfactory Epithelium
C. External auditory canal
D. Cortical Nephrons Only

234. **The effect of antidiuretic Hormone (ADH) is**
A. Decreased urine output
B. Oligouria
C. Anuria
D. Increased urine output

235. **The collapse of the alveoli is prevented by:**
A. Pleural Fluid B. Cilia
C. Mucus D. Surfactant

236. **The Nissl's granules of nerves cell are made up of?**
A. DNA B. RNA
C. Ribosome D. Protein

237. **Payer's patches are found in**
A. Esophagus B. Duodenum
C. Small Intestine D. Large Intestine

238. **Part of brain that helps in maintaining posture and equilibrium is:**
A. Medulla B. Cerebellum
C. Cerebrum D. Thalamus

239. **Neurons that release acetylcholine are refer to as:**
A. Adrenergic B. Cholinergic
C. Dopaminergic D. None of the Above

240. **Total pairs of cranial nerves are:**
A. 122 B. 20
C. 12 D. 14

241. **The average tidal volume is**
A. 600 ml B. 400 ml
C. 700 ml D. 500 ml

242. **Differentiate the essential amino acid in the following:**
A. Valine B. Proline
C. Tyrosine D. Glycine

243. **Synthesis of glucose from no carbohydrate source is referred as:**
A. Glycogenesis B. Glycolysis
C. Gluconeogenesis D. Glycogenolysis

244. **A largest organ in abdominal cavity that filters blood is?**
A. Lymph nodes B. Palatine Tonsils
C. Spleen D. None of the Above

245. **A hormone that controls closure of stomata in response to water stress is?**
A. Auxins B. Cytokinins
C. Gibberellins D. Abscisicacid

246. **An animal that warms itself mainly by the heat of cellular respiration is?**
A. A poikilotherm B. A hoineotherm
C. Anectotherm D. Anendotherm

247. **Abnormal lateral deviation of vertebral column is?**
A. Osteoporosis B. Lordosis
C. Kyphosis D. Scoliosis

248. **The abnormal dilatation of the wall of an artery is referred as?**
A. Phlebitis B. Aneurysm
C. Hemisphere D. Atherosclerosis

249. **The paralysis of both upper and lower extremities is known as?**
A. Quadriplegia B. Hemiplegic
C. Paraplegia D. Monoplegia

250. **Rice or bread taste sweet on prolonged chewing because of the breakdown of starch in them. The enzyme in the saliva which takes part in this reaction is:**
A. Pepsin C. Amylase
B. Renin D. Invertase

251. **Bell's Palsy is due to the injury of which cranial nerve?**
A. Hypoglossal B. Trigeminal
C. Facial D. Trochlear

252. **The urethra which opens on the dorsal surface of the penis is termed?**
A. Anorchidism B. Epispadiasis
C. Hypospadiasis D. Cryptorchidism

253. **The number of chromosomes in pollen grains of Pinus is 6. The chromosome number in its endosperm after fertilization will be:**
A. 6 B. 12
C. 24 D. 36

254. **The hyper secretion of growth hormone leads to:**
A. Grave's diseases B. Cretinism
C. Myxoedema D. Acromegaly

255. **The aV node is located in the:**
A. Right atrium
B. Atrio ventricular septum
C. Pericardium
D. Myocardium

256. **Proteins that are to be used outside the cell are synthesized:**
A. In the mitochondria
B. On the rough endoplasmic reticulum
C. On the smooth endoplasmic reticulum
D. On free ribosome

257. **The human eye forms the image of an object at its:**
A. Cornea B. Iris
C. Pupil D. Retina

258. **Root of the hair is:**
A. Multi cellular B. Uni cellular
C. Both A & B D. None of them

259. **The normal value of Hb in female is**
A. 8-10 gm% B. 12-14 gm%
C. 10-12 gm% D. 16-18 gm%

260. **Mitral valve is situated between**
A. Aorta and left ventricle
B. Right atrium and right ventricle
C. Left atrium and left ventricle
D. Pulmonary artery and right ventricle

261. **7th cranial nerve is?**
A. Facial B. Occulomotor
C. Glossophayngal D. Abducens

262. **The causative organism for tetanus is?**
A. Salmonella typhi
B. Treponema palladium
C. Clostridium welchie
D. Clostridium tetani

263. Angiotensin IInd is a
A. Vasoconstrictor B. Muscle relaxant
C. Vasodilator D. Bronchodilator

264. Acetabulam is the part of?
A. Humerus B. Radius
C. Scapula D. Femur

265. Circle of Willis is related with circulation of
A. Heart B. Brain
C. Kidney D. Liver

266. Erythropoietin is secreted by?
A. Liver B. Adrenals
C. Kidney D. Pancreas

267. The heat regulatory centre is located in the:
A. Thalamus B. Hypothalamus
C. Medulla D. Limbic system

268. Longest bone human body is:
A. Femur B. Humerus
C. Tibia D. Fibula

269. Skull consists of:
A. 14 bones B. 22 bones
C. 12 bones D. 14 bones

270. Chyme is called to?
A. Food in the mouth
B. Food in the stomach
C. Food reached in the stomach
D. Food reached in the nectum

271. Insulin is secreted by?
A. Alpha cells B. Beta cells
C. Gamma cells D. Delta cells

272. The artery which supply blood to head and neck is
A. Coronary artery B. Carotid artery
C. Mesenteric artery D. Infracostal artery

273. A nerve which helps in the process of smelling is:
A. Optic nerve B. Occulomotor nerve
C. Olfactory nerve D. Facial nerve

274. A normal respiration of healthy person is:
A. 5-10/minute B. 10-15/minute
C. 16-20/minute D. 20-30/minute

275. Enzyme which helps in digestion of fat:
A. Amylase B. Lipase
C. Enterokinase D. Tripsin

276. Which of the following sphincter does not prevent reflux of material?
A. Lower oesophageal sphincter
B. Gastroducodenal sphincter
C. Ileocolonic sphincter
D. Internal anal sphincter

277. A gland which can be classified as an endocrine except?
A. Thyroid B. Thymus
C. Pancreas D. Pituitary

278. Active transport of substance from blood into the nephrone is called:
A. Filteration
B. Tubular secretion
C. Tubular reabsorption
D. Osmosis

279. Taste buds for sensing bitterness are located on which part of the tongue?
A. Anterior part of the tongue
B. Posterior part of the tongues
C. Lateral part of the tongue
D. Under surface of the tongue

280. A junction between two or more bones or cartilage:
A. Synovial joint B. Sutures
C. Joint D. Fontenelle

281 The outermost covering of the bone is:
A. Pericardium B. Periosteum
C. Peritoneum D. Perimetrium

282. Head of the femur articulates with the:
A. Obturator foramen
B. Foramen magnum
C. Acetabulum
D. Cerebellum

283. How many chromosomes are found in a cell of human being?
A. 23 B. 28 C. 46 D. 48

284. Which part of the heart is responsible for circulating blood through the lungs?
A. Left ventricle B. Right ventricle
C. Left atrium D. Right atrium

285. "Powerhouse" of the human cells is:
A. Nucleus B. Golgi bodies
C. Mitochnodria D. Ribosome

286. Transformation of one type of cell into another type is called:
A. Hyperplasia B. Metaplasia
C. Dysplasia D. Anaplasia

287. "Sino atrial node" is located in which part of the heart?
A. Right atrium B. Right ventricle
C. Left atrium D. Left ventricle

288. The number of thoracic vertebrae in human being is:
A. 5 B. 7 C. 9 D. 12

289. Blood groups were first discovered by:
A. Robert Koch
B. Karl Landsteiner
C. Paul Ehrlich
D. An ton von Lueowenhock

290. **Which of the following extraocular muscles is not supplied by third cranial nerve?**
A. Superior oblique B. Inferior oblique
C. Superior rectus D. Inferior rectus

291. **The regulation of blood glucose is maintained by the hormone:**
A. Insulin B. Prolactin
C. Oxytocin D. Testosterone

292. **The color of the Rbc's is given by:**
A. Actin B. Globin
C. Chyme D. Heme

293. **Out of the following which hormone is secreted by the posterior pituitary gland?**
A. Growth hormone B. Prolactin
C. ACTH D. ADH

294. **The junction through which neurons communicate with one another is:**
A. Dendrite B. Axon
C. Synapse D. Node of Ranvier

295. **Which is found in the highest concentration in the urine?**
A. Uric acid B. Urea
C. Glucose D. Creatinine

296. **Enzyme responsible for conversion of glucose to glucose-6-PO_4**
A. Glycogen synthase
B. G-6 phosphatase
C. Glucokinase
D. Phosphorylase

297. **The blood groups referred as "Universal donor' is:**
A. O -ve B. B
C. AB D. A

298. **Normal values for HCO3 are considered:**
A. 15-30 mEq/L B. 20-35 mEq/L
C. 22-27 mEq/L D. 24-29 mEq/L

299. **Total number of chromosomes in our body is:**
A. 44 B. 47 C. 46 D. 48

300. **The normal hemoglobin level is:**
A. 19-23 g/dl B. 14-16 g/dl
C. 8-10 g/dl D. 11-14 g/dl

301. **The normal blood glucose level of an average adult is:**
A. 70-110mg/dl B. 50-100 mg/dl
C. 180-210 mg/dl D. 140-180 mg/dl

302. **The outer covering of the heart is:**
A. Peritoneum B. Pleura
C. Pericardium D. Myocardium

303. **The volume of blood pumped from the left ventricle is termed:**
A. Circulatory volume
B. Stroke volume
C. Cardiac output
D. Cardiac response

304. **Speech centre is:**
A. Broca's area B. Premotor area
C. Frontal area D. Postcentral area

305. **The pituitary hormone that stimulate secretion of milk is:**
A. Prolactin B. Oxytotin
C. Estrogen D. Progesterone

306. **The ear bones that transmit the vibrations to cochlea are situated in:**
A. Middle ear B. Inner ear
C. Outer ear D. Eustachian rube

307 **All of the following can cause tachycardia except**
A. Fever
B. Exercise
C. Sympathetic nervous system stimulation
D. Parasympathetic nervous system stimulation

308. **Downward displacement of enlarged spleen is prevented by**
A. Lienorenal ligament
B. Phrenicocolic ligament
C. Sigmoid colon
D. Upper pole of rt. Kidney

309. **Which of the following sphincters is under voluntary control**
A. Pyloric B. Cardiac
C. Internal anal D. External anal

310. **The ELISa test is used to**
A. Screen blood donors for antibodies to human immunodeficiency virus (HIV)
B. Test blood to be used for transfusion for HIV antibodies
C. Aid in diagnosing a patient with AIDS
D. All of the Above

311. **The major cause of transfusion viral hepatitis is**
A. Hepatitis A B. Hepatitis B
C. Hepatitis C D. Hepatitis D

312. **Hemophillia occurs due to deficiency of clotting factor**
A. VI B. VII
C. VIII D. IX

313. **The most important parameter of aPGaR score is**
A. Heart rate B. Respiratory rate
C. Grimace D. Reflex

314. **The leading cause of MMR is**
A. Diabetes B. Infections
C. Toxaemia D. Hemorrhage

315. **Structure that pass from thorax to abdomen behind the diaphragm are all except**
A. Azygos vein
B. Aorta
C. Thoracic duct
D. Greater splanchnic nerve

316. Prothrombin time is increased in
A. Heparin therapy
B. Obstructive Jaundice
C. Haemorrhagic disease of newborn
D. All of the Above

317. Find out the odd one
A. Head B. Arm
C. Neck D. Trunk

318. Mullerian inhibiting substance is produced by
A. Stroma B. Sartoli cells
C. Leyding cells D. All of the Above

319. All increase the chances of deep vein thrombosis except
A. Oral contraceptive pills
B. Hypertension
C. Superficial thrombophlebitis
D. Myocardial Infarction

320. Wrist drop is caused by all except
A. Lead poisoning
B. Radial nerve palsy
C. Ulnar nerve palsy
D. Both A and B

321. The hormone known to participate in metabolism of calcium and phosphorous is
A. Mineralocorticoids
B. Calcitonin
C. Glucagon
D. Glucocorticoids

322. Neurotransmitters
A. Are electrical impulse
B. Are found only in neuron with myelin shea the
C. Are signal molecules released at synapses
D. Are produced by muscles

323. Lymphatics are found in
A. Brain B. Choroid
C. Vertebrae D. Dermis of skin

324. Deficiency of clotting factor IX leads to
A. Christmas disease
B. Thrombocytopenia
C. Hemophilia
D. Thalassemia

325. Concentration of the urine is controlled by
A. MSH B. ADH
C. Oxytocin D. ACTH

326. The gas most commonly used in cryosurgery is
A. O_2 B. CO_2
C. N_2 D. H_2

327. ECG changes in Myocardial infarction is:
A. ST segment elevation
B. Wide QRS complex
C. Presence of U wave
D. Prolonged PR interval

328. The structure called .... are intracellular areas with specific function?
A. Inclusions B. Organs
C. Organelles D. Macromolecules

329. The following structure pass through the greater sciatic foramen except?
A. Superior gluteal artery
B. Sciatic nerve
C. Obturator internus tendon
D. Pudenal nerve

330. Which of the following is not a type of immunoglobulin?
A. IgE B. IgA
C. IgG D. IgC

331. Normal level of HDL cholesterol is?
A. 20-35 mg/dl B. 50-80 mg/dl
C. 40-65 mg/dl D. 75-100mg/dl

332. Bilirubin is a breakdown product of which of the following
A. Wbc B. Rbc
C. Enzymes D. Platelets

333. Precursor cells of Rbc are
A. Reticulocyte B. Band Forms
C. Myelocytes D. Melanomyelocytes

334. PcR stands for
A. Polymerase reaction
B. Polymerase circular reaction
C. Polymerase chain reagent
D. Polymerase chain reaction

335. Vitamin D regulates the level of
A. Calcium and Phosphorus
B. Phosphorus and Magnesium
C. Calcium and Magnesium
D. All of the Above

336. Which of the following is an example of delayed hypersensitivity reaction?
A. Tuberculin reaction
B. Type II hypersensitivity
C. Immune complex mediated hypersensitivity
D. Anaphylaxis

337. Optimum temperature required for wax during embedding?
A. 100°c B. 65° c
C. 45° c D. 85° c

338. Low Prothrombin levels in absence of jaundice indicates?
A. Serious damage to liver
B. Serious damage to Kidney
C. Portal Hypertension
D. IHD

339. Hemolyzed serum should not be used for the estimation of enzymes?
A. True B. False
C. May be false D. Don't know

340. Facilitated diffusion of glucose takes place in all sites except?
A. Skeletal muscle
B. Adipose tissue
C. Insulin dependant tissues
D. Renal tubules

341. Hypothalamic functions include all except?
A. Regulation of posterior pituitary
B. Regulation of anterior pituitary
C. Control of reproduction
D. Control of respiration

342. What is the normal cardiac output?
A. 1 litres/minute B. 2 litres/minute
C. 4 litres/minute D. 5 litres/minute

343. Rod shaped bacteria are called?
A. Cocci B. Bacilli
C. Spirochetes D. Vibrio

344. Reflex are functions at the level of
A. Cerebellum
B. Cerebral hemispheres
C. Medulla
D. Spinal cord

345. Blood pressure is regulated by all except
A. Vasomotor centre
B. Aortic baro receptors
C. Juxtaglomerular cells
D. Loop of Henle

346. Site of action for anti emetics
A. Basal ganglia
B. Spinal chord
C. Chemoreceptor trigger zone
D. Cerebral hemispheres

347. A physical therapist performs a manual muscles test on the primary hip abductor. The therapist should perform the test while palpating the:
A. Rectus femoris B. Gluteus medius
C. Sartorius D. Gluteus minimus

348. All are dilators of pupil except
A. Adrenalin B. Pilocarpine
C. Atropine D. Phenylephrine

349. Erb's palsy effects
A. Lumbar plexus B. Sacral plexus
C. Brachial plexus D. Cranial nerves

350. What is the initial reaction of cryotherapy?
A. Vasodilatation
B. Vasoconstriction
C. Increased blood flow
D. Reduced metabolic rate

351. A patient with a C3 spinal cord injury is positioned in supine. Which area is most susceptible to pressure in this position?
A. Greater trochanter
B. Anterior iliac crest
C. Medical malleolus
D. Sacrum

352. What should be the progression of exercise protocol following musculoskeletal injury?
A. Isometric- eccentric – concentric
B. Isometric – concentric – concentric and eccentric
C. Concentric-eccentric- concentric and eccentric
D. Isometric-concentric- eccentric

353. Locking is a feature of ....injury?
A. Collateral ligament
B. Meniscus
C. Cruciates
D. All of the Above

354. All are the features of spinal tuberculosis except:
A. Kyphosis B. Scoliosis
C. Paraplegia D. Abscess

355. The systemic effects of cryotherapy is?
A. Increased blood pressure
B. Decreased blood pressure
C. Decreased cardiac output
D. None of the Above

356. Which of the following bones is considered a sesamoid bone?
A. Sternum B. Ethmoid
C. Phalanx D. Patella

357. There are ....long bones in hand
A. 15 B. 17 C. 19 D. 22

358. Best to visualize corneal endothelium
A. Fundoscopy
B. Specular microscopy
C. Slit lamp
D. Gonioscopy

359. Vagus is which cranial nerve?
A. X B. IX C. VII D. V

360. The interferons are?
A. Antigen proteins
B. Antiviral proteins
C. Antibiotic proteins
D. All of these

361. A natural body defense that plays an active role in preventing infections is?
A. Yawning
B. Body hair
C. Hiccupping
D. Rapid eye movements

362. **Repair of tympanic membrane is**
A. Tympanoplasty B. Myringoplasty
C. Myringotomy D. Septoplasty

363. **Signs of pseudophakia?**
A. Surgical Scar
B. Shining reflex in papillary area
C. Deep ac
D. All of the Above

364. **Pus in the pleural cavity**
A. Pleural effusion B. Empyema
C. Emphysema D. Pyorrhea

365. **The part of the digestive system where no digestion takes place is**
A. Mouth B. Oesophagus
C. Ileum D. Stomach

366. **Which of the following is a mydriatic**
A. Atropine B. Adrenaline
C. Novocaine D. Silver nitrate

367. **Protein synthesis occurs in**
A. Ribosomes B. Golgi apparatus
C. Lysosomes D. Endosomes

368. **The most serious complication of fracture is**
A. Infection B. Fat embolism
C. Hemorrhage D. Air embolism

369. **Tubular vision is caused by**
A. Retinitis pigmentosa
B. Glaucoma
C. Cataract
D. Papilloedema

370. **The ciliary body**
A. Consists of the pars plicata and pars plana
B. Produces aqueous humor
C. Is responsible for accommodation
D. All of the Above

371. **The growth and multiplication of microorganisms is known as**
A. Staining B. Culture
C. Isolation D. Autoclaving

372. **Malaria is a**
A. Zoonotic disease B. Viral disease
C. Bacterial disease D. Protozoal disease

373. **Latent squint also known as**
A. Hypertropia B. Exotropia
C. Esotropia D. Heterophoria

374. **An instrument that can sterilize surgical implements through use of pressurized steam is known as**
A. Autoclave B. Keratome
C. Tonometer D. Curette

375. **Uveal tissue consist of all except?**
A. Choroid B. Iris
C. Ciliary body D. Vitreous

376. **Topical NSAIDS for ophthalmic use is?**
A. Ibuprofen B. Nepafenac
C. Aspirin D. Vancomycin

377. **The site of production of cholecystokinin and secretin is the?**
A. Stomach B. Pancreas
C. Small intestine D. Large intestine

378. **The most common injury among elderly persons is**
A. Atheroscleotic changes in the blood vessels
B. Increased incidents of gallbladder disease
C. Urinary tract infection
D. Hip fracture

379. **Hypermetropia is a condition in which all are found except?**
A. Axial length of eyeball is small
B. Correction with convex lens
C. Image formed in front of the retina
D. Refractive error can be diagnosed by retinoscopy

380. **Advantages of indirect ophthalmoscopy are all except?**
A. Peripheral retina can be visualized
B. Wider retinal field
C. More bright image
D. Opacity in the media visualized

381. **Forward displacement of eyeball is?**
A. Proptosis B. Enopthalmos
C. Ptosis D. None

382 **The endocrine system is quicker than the nervous system**
A. True B. False
C. May be true D. Don't know

383. **Colour of the retina is due to?**
A. Anterior border layer
B. Stroma
C. Anterior epithelium layer
D. Posterior pigmented layer

384. **Most common primary intraocular tumour in adults**
A. Choroidal melanoma
B. Retinoblastoma
C. Melanocytoma
D. Astrocytoma

385. **In anterior uveitis the pupil is generally**
A. Of normal size B. Constricted
C. Dilated D. None

386. **Dysphasia is a defect that causes difficulty in**
A. Walk B. Speech
C. Swallowing D. Vision

387. Which stain is also known as acid fast stain
A. Albert stain
B. Ziehl Neelsen stain
C. Pasteur's stain
D. Lister stain

388. Black Tarry stool is evidence of
A. Gastric hemorrhage
B. Hemorrhoids
C. Anal fissure
D. Intestinal obstruction

389. DDT is
A. Contact poison B. CNS poison
C. Stomach poison D. None of these

390. Treatment of aphakia is
A. Spectacles B. Intraocular lens
C. Contact lens D. All of the Above

391. Which of the following is a carbonicanhydrase inhibitor
A. Mannitol B. Acetazolamide
C. Pilocarpine D. Latanoprost

392. Types of corneal opacity are
A. Macular B. Nebular
C. Leucoma D. All of the Above

393. Shape of the orbit is
A. Spherical
B. Quadrangular truncated Pyramidal Shape
C. Triangular
D. None

394. Hyaluronic acid is present in
A. Aqueous humor B. Vitreous humor
C. Cornea D. Lens

395. Sensory pigmented layer of eye is
A. Cornea B. Retina
C. Sclerotic D. Iris

396. RNA is present in
A. Cytoplasm B. Nucleus
C. Ribosome D. All of the Above

397. Normal values for pCO_2 are considered:
A. 20-40 mm Hg B. 25-30 mm Hg
C. 30-40 mm Hg D. 35-45 mm Hg

398. Colour of fluorescein staining in corneal ulcer is
A. Yellow B. Blue
C. Green D. Red

399. Red-green glasses are used for
A. Diplopia charting B. Worth's 4 dot test
C. Friend test D. All of the Above

400. Surgical procedure to treat glaucoma is
A. Sics B. Phacoemulsification
C. Becca D. Trabeculectomy

401. Which is the most important muscle to produce upwards rotation of the scapula?
A. Serratus anterior B. Trapezius
C. Levator Scapulae D. Deltoid

402. At what distance, distant direct ophthalmoscopy is performed
A. 20-25 cm B. 30-33 cm
C. 35-40 cm D. 40-44 cm

403. Pilocarpine causes all except
A. Salivation B. Meiosis
C. Sweating D. Cycloplegia

404. All actions done by superior oblique except
A. Elevation B. Depression
C. Intorsion D. Abduction

405. Staphylomas are
A. Localized bulging of wall of eyeball
B. Localized bulging of wall of orbit
C. Condition related to eye lid
D. Condition related to optic nerve

406. Plica semilunaris is also known as
A. First eyelid B. Second eyelid
C. Third eyelid D. Ptosis

407. Locking position of shoulder joint is
A. Flexion, abduction and internal rotation
B. External rotation, abduction and internal rotation
C. Extension, abduction, external rotation
D. Flexion, abduction, external rotation

408. The commonest deformity at hip in post polio residual paralysis is:
A. Flexion deformity
B. Extension deformity
C. Flexion adduction deformity
D. Flexion abduction deformity

409. Best site where Intra Occular Lens (IOL) is fitted
A. Capsular ligaments
B. Endosulcus
C. Ciliary supported
D. Capsular bag

410. Dendritic ulcer can be treated with
A. Topical acyclovir
B. Topical natamycin
C. Topical steroids
D. Laser

411. The crystalline lens derives its nourishment from
A. Blood vessels
B. Aqueous humor and vitreous humor
C. Connective tissue
D. Zonules

412. Aqueous humour is produced by?
A. Ciliary body B. Retina
C. Vitreous D. Cornea

413. Adduction of eye is?
A. Upward movement of eye
B. Downward movement of eye
C. Nasal movement of eye
D. Temporal movement of eye

414. Dysdiadokokinesia is feature of?
A. Cerebellar lesion
B. Basal ganglia lesion
C. Cortical lesion
D. None of the Above

415. Arterial supply of uveal tract
A. Anterior ciliary arteries
B. Long posterior ciliary arteries
C. Short posterior arteries
D. All of the Above

416. Choroid is composed of all except
A. Haller's layer B. Sattler's layer
C. Henley's layer D. Choriocapillaris

417. Causes of coloured halos in eyes?
A. Acute congestive Glaucoma
B. Early stages of cataract
C. Mucopurulent conjunctivitis
D. All of the Above

418. Newborn eye is?
A. Myopic B. Hypermetropic
C. Emmetropic D. All of the Above

419. Cobb's angle is used to quantify the magnitude of deformity of
A. Hip B. Spinal column
C. Elbow D. Knee

420. In fracture neck of femur the blood supply to the head of the femur is retained by?
A. Circumflex artery
B. Nutrient artery
C. Artery to ligament of the head of femur
D. Femoral artery

421. The end feel of loose body inside the joint is
A. Elastic B. Hard
C. Leathery D. Springy rebound

422. Lateral rectus supplied by
A. Trochlear nerve
B. Abducent nerve
C. Occulomotor nerve
D. Trigeminal nerve

423. Proper sterilization of all surgical instruments is part of what strategy
A. Scrubbing
B. Septic technique
C. Aseptic technique
D. Universal precaution

424. All are seen in 3rd nerve palsy except
A. Ptosis
B. Diplopia
C. Miosis
D. Outwards eye deviation

425. Schirmer test is used in diagnosis of?
A. Keratitis B. Dry eye
C. Uveitis D. None

426. All of the following are signs of herpes zoster ophthalmicus except?
A. Keratitis B. Episcleritis
C. Uveitis D. Retinitis

427. All occur in process of accommodation of eye except?
A. Contraction of sphincter pupillae
B. Dilatation of pupil
C. Change in lens curvature
D. Contraction of ciliary muscle

428. Spirometry does not determine the?
A. Tidal volume
B. Inspiratory reserve volume
C. Vital capacity
D. Residual volume

429. The number of spinal nerves that emerge from spinal cord is?
A. 33 pairs B. 32 pairs
C. 31 pairs D. None of the Above

430. Deep tendon reflex is exaggerated in lesion ?
A. Upper motor neuron
B. Lower motor neuron
C. Peripheral nerve injury
D. None of the Above

431. Drop of QRS complex is found in?
A. 1st degree heart block
B. 2nd degree heart block
C. 3rd degree heart block
D. Both A & B

432. Charcoat joints are?
A. Ankylosed joint
B. Progressively degenerating joints
C. Infective joint
D. Painless arthritis joint

433. Meralgia parasthetica occurs in .... nerve.
A. Sciatic
B. Superficial peroneal
C. Lateral femoral cutaneous
D. Sural

434. In parkinsonism, the lesion is due to
A. Lateral thalamus
B. Substantia nigra
C. Caudate nucleus
D. Subthalamic nucleus

435. Corneal sensation are diminished in
A. Herpes simplex keratitis
B. Conjunctivitis
C. Fungal keratitis
D. Marginal keratitis

436. All are the common causes of childhood blindness except
A. Malnutrition
B. Glaucoma
C. Ophthalmia neonatorum
D. Congenital dacryocystitis

437. Normal eye is
A. Monochromatic B. Dichromatic
C. Trichromatic D. Polychromatic

438. Commonest type of retinal detachment is?
A. Rhegmatogenous B. Exudative
C. Tractional D. None

439. Optic disc diameter is
A. 1 mm B. 1.5 mm
C. 2 mm D. 3 mm

440. Treatment of acute anterior uveitis includes
A. Topical steroids B. Cycloplegics
C. Both D None

441 Most common nerve damage in shoulder dislocation
A. Radial nerve B. Axillary nerve
C. Flexion D. Extension

442. Damage to Nerve of bell results in
A. CTEV
B. Winging of the scapula
C. Claw hand
D. Policeman's tip hand

443. Tenodesis grip is important for............... Level ScI patient.
A. C5 B. C6 C. C8 D. T1

444. Polymyositis is,?
A. Infective myopathy
B. Muscle degenerating disease
C. Not myopathy
D. Inflammatory myopathy

445. Inward misdirection of cilia is known as?
A. Trichiasis B. Entropion
C. Ectropion D. None

446. Treatment of choice for congenital glaucoma?
A. Goniotomy B. Trabeculotomy
C. Iridotomy D. None

447. Peripheral iridectomy is must in which of the following?
A. POAG
B. Closed angle glaucoma
C. Cataract
D. All of the Above

448. Laser seen in LASIK
A. Excimer laser B. Argon
C. Nd-YaG D. Holmium

449. Nasociliary nerve supplies
A. Lacrimal sac B. Cornea
C. Dilator papillae D. Ethmoidal sinus

450. KF ring seen in
A. Wilson disease B. Blunt trauma
C. Chemical injury D. Thermal injury

451. All are the features of Vitamin A deficiency except
A. Bitot's spots B. Tranta's spot
C. Keratomalacia D. Conjunctival xerosis

452. Which is not an effect of strengthening of cVS
A. Increased heart rate
B. Decreased systolic BP
C. Increased Diastolic BP
D. Decreased cholesterol

453. Motor supply of diaphragm is
A. Thoraco dorsal B. Intercostal nerves
C. Phrenic nerve D. Symphathetic

454. Tardy ulnar nerve palsy is due to:
A. Cubitus valgus
B. Fixation of nerve in the groove by osteoarthritis
C. Excision of elbow joint
D. Fracture of internal condyle

455. Burst fracture is seen in ?
A. Talus fracture
B. Vertebral fracture
C. Femoral head fracture
D. Scaphoid

456. Timolol is?
A. Carbonic anhydrase inhibitor
B. Antibiotic
C. B-blocker
D. Alpha agonist

457. Gonioscopy is done to visualize?
A. Angle of cornea
B. Angle of anterior chamber
C. Angle of posterior chamber
D. Angle of retina

458. Term Myopia is used for
A. Far Sightedness B. Near-Sightedness
C. Abnormal vision D. Normal vision

459. Foreign body sensation can be produced by all except
A. Allergic conjunctivitis
B. Contact lens wear
C. Cataract
D. Trichiasis

460. Which of the following is not a proper method of solid waste disposal
A. Dumping B. Controlled tipping
C. Manure pits D. Composting

461. Pus in anterior chamber is known as
A. Hypopyon B. Hyphaema
C. Exudates D. Flare

462. Horner's syndrome is characterized by all except
A. Miosis B. Sweating
C. Proptosis D. Ptosis

463. All of the following eye diseases are included in vision 2020 except?
A. Cataract B. Childhood blindness
C. Trachoma D. Glaucoma

464. In indirect ophthalmoscopy the image is?
A. Real and inverted
B. Virtual and inverted
C. Real and erect
D. Virtual and erect

465. Bitot's spots are seen in?
A. Vitamin A deficiency
B. Vitamin B Deficiency
C. Vitamin C Deficiency
D. All of the Above

466. All of the following are near vision chart except?
A. Jager's chart
B. Roman test type
C. Snellen's
D. Pelli – Robson chart

467. Which of the following visual problem need immediate attention
A. Photo sensitivity B. Flashes of light
C. Redness of eye D. Tearing

468. Which is the master gland of the body?
A. Adrenalin B. Thyroid
C. Hypothalamus D. Ovary

469. All are the tests for tear film adequacy except?
A. Schirmer test
B. Tear film break-up time
C. Vital staining by flurescein
D. Flurescien dye disappearance test

470. Observation system of slit lamp include?
A. Eyepiece B. Objective Lens
C. Prisms D. All of the Above

471. More then one pupil is known as?
A. Polycoria B. Correctopia
C. Heterochromia D. Aniridia

472. Which bone is also known as 'collar bone'
A. Clavicle B. Scapula
C. Radius D. Humerus

473. Perimetry is used for
A. Visual fields charting
B. Central corneal Thickness
C. IOP monitoring
D. None

474. Ophthalmia Neonatorum within first 48 hours of birth is caused by
A. Adenovirus
B. Neisseria gonorrhoeae
C. Candia albicans
D. Chlamydia trachomatis

475. Stye is inflammation of
A. Glands of moll B. Glands of zeis
C. Meibomian gland D. Glands of Krause

476. Place where Rbcs are produced is
A. Liver B. Blood
C. Testes D. Red bone marrow

477. Ectropion is
A. Outward turning of eyelid
B. Inward turning of eyelid
C. Drooping of eyelid
D. Misdirection of cilia

478. What types of anesthetic is used for minor procedure?
A. Systemic B. Local
C. None D. Both A and B

479. concave spherical lenses are used in?
A. Myopia B. Hypermetropia
C. Astigmatism D. All of these

480. What is the power of the convex lens most commonly used in indirect ophthalmoscopy?
A. 90 d B. 78 d C. 20 d D. 60 d

481. Largest salivary gland is?
A. Parotid B. Submandibular
C. Sublingual D. Pancreas

482. Most common cause of viral conjunctivitis is
A. Pox Virus B. Adeno Virus
C. Herpes D. Cmv

483. Meibomian glands are
A. Sebaceous glands B. Sweat glands
C. Mixed D. None

484. Site of aqueous production is
A. Ciliary body B. Trabeculum
C. Iris D. Scschlemm's cannal

485. Recovery in cataract surgery is fastest with which of the following
A. IccE B. EccE
C. Sics D. Phacoemulsification

486. The space between arachnoid & pia matter is called
A. Epidural B. Subdural
C. Subarachnoid D. Extradural

36. The famous Hawthorne experiments were conducted by
A. Elton Mayo B. Max Weber
C. Henry Ford D. F.W Taylor

37. Bhore Committee is also known as
A. Health Survey and Development Committee
B. Health Survey and Planning Committee
C. Hospital review committee
D. Mudaliar Committee

38. Which definition of quality of care represents the entire continuum from structure to process and to outcome?
A. Deming's B. WHO.
C. Donabedian D. Kurt Schneider

39. Following are the principle of management .EXCEPT?
A. Unity of command B. Order
C. Scalar Chain D. Indiscipline

40. Quality Council of India sponsored accreditation system for hospitals and health care providers:
A. NABH
B. Joint Commission International
C. BIS
D. NABET

41. Which of the following principle of administration describes about "union is strength and extension of unity of command for establishing team work"?
A. Remuneration of personnel
B. Unity of command
C. Division of work
D. Espirit de crops

42. Theory of bureaucracy in management was proposed by
A. Henry Gantt B. Max Weber
C. Henry Fayol D. Peter Ducker

43. All statements are true about administration. EXCEPT?
A. Administration is the organization of human and physical mean to get an object.
B. Administration is concerned with "what and how" of government.
C. Administration can be explained for these group activities which are prescribed in co-operative form to achieve an aim.
D. Administration is not common to all organizations.

44. Plan-Do-Check -Act cycle is related to:
A. Donabedian B. Deming
C. Henry Gantt D. B.F. Skinner

45. Which of following principle of management describe as "Communication up and down each position in line of authority"
A. Authority B. Espirit de corps
C. Scalar Chain D. Unity of command

46. An administration is ....
A. Ongoing B. Goal oriented
C. Social and human D. All of the Above

47. A broad statement by which the organization specifies how it will achieve its goals is
A. Vision Statement
B. Mission Statement
C. Policy statement
D. Protocol

48. Which of following system of management is a demanding and rewarding style of managing a business?
A. Management by exception
B. Management by motivation
C. Management by results
D. Management by objectives

49. Which of the following is present in every experimental study?
A. Manipulation of the independent variable
B. A Control group
C. Random assignment of subjects to groups
D. Random selection of subjects from the population.

50. Which of the following characteristics is related to Laissez-faire leadership?
A. Very little guidance from leaders & Group members are expected to solve problems on their own
B. Complete freedom for followers to make decisions
C. Leaders provide the tools and resources needed
D. All of the Above

51 Which of following system of material management is based on cost criteria in analysis of store items?
A. ABC analysis
B. VED analysis
C. Cost benefit analysis
D. Data analysis

52. The code of ethics in nursing received by india?
A. 1963 B. 2004 C. 1953 D. 1973

53. The code of ethics in nursing given by:
A. ICN B. WHO
C. INC D. Govt of India

54. Code of ethics in nursing profession includes:
A. What is right and what is wrong
B. SET of principles
C. Responsibilities of a nurse
D. All of the Above

55. Scientific Management Theory was developed by
A. Max Weber B. Frederick Taylor
C. Adam Smith D. Rensis Likert

56. Which of the following is a core of a nursing?
A. To alleviate suffering
B. To promote health
C. To prevent illness
D. All of the Above

57. A failure in professional duty or practice that leads to harm to the patient, is termed as :
A. Negligence B. Crime
C. Malpractice D. Battery

58. Components of a nursing diagnosis include all, EXCEPT
A. Problem Statement (diagnostic label)
B. Etiology (related factor)
C. Defining Characteristic
D. Outcome statement

59. Indian Red Cross society was established in :
A. 1922 B. 1920 C. 1918 D. 1908

60. What is the meaning of trends in nursing?
A. Code of ethics in nursing profession
B. Movement in a particular direction in nursing field
C. Job description of a profession nurse
D. Professional qualification required for a nurse

61. Where is the headquarter of international council of nurses?
A. Rome B. Newyork
C. Geneva D. New Delhi

62. The Indian Nursing Council act was passed in:
A. 1947 B. 1950 C. 1948 D. 1949

63. Network analysis in management of health services include,
A. Cost accounting
B. Cost benefit analysis
C. Cost effective analysis
D. PERT

64. Which of the following Activities of INC?
A. Maintain uniform standards in nursing education in all over India
B. Registration of nursing students after completion of course for abroad
C. To decide rules and regulations for establishing new college of nursing
D. All of the Above

65. The target "health for all by 2000 A.D." was declared by
A. WHO B. TNAI
C. INC D. UNICEF

66. The organization which is responsible for registration of nursing personnel
A. International council of nurse's
B. INC
C. State nurse's council
D. SNA

67. Who is associated with the concept of Total Quality Management?
A. Rensis Likert
B. Kurt Lewin
C. Max Weber
D. W. Edwards Deming

68. In India, in which year LHV course was started:
A. 1967 B. 1948 C. 1918 D. 1945

69. What is Activity of IRCS ?
A. Provision of blood banks and first aid services
B. Provide fund for development
C. Maternal and child welfare services
D. Relief during disaster

70. Father of management by objectives (MBO)
A. Peter Drucker B. Frederick Taylor
C. Henri Fayol D. Max Weber

71. WHO was established on:
A. 7th April - 1945 B. 7th April- 1948
C. 1 April 1948 D. 7th April - 1899

72. Where is the Head quarter of WHO ?
A. London B. Geneva
C. New Delhi D. Newyork

73. Where is the South-East region Head quarter of WHO?
A. London B. Geneva
C. New Delhi D. Newyork

74. The food and agriculture organisation was established in
A. 1945 B. 1965 C. 1947 D. 1948

75. Where is the Head quarter of food and agriculture organisation?
A. Rome B. Geneva
C. New Delhi D. Newyork

76. Which of the following health agency mainly assisting the national TB control programme in India?
A. ILO
B. USAID
C. WHO
D. The Colombo plans

77. Which of the following is the most important characteristic of administration?
A. It is creative
B. It is an going process
C. It is universal
D. All of the Above

78. What are the Principle of a good administration?
A. Scalar of chain
B. Unity of command
C. Authority, responsibility ,accountability and Division of work
D. All of the Above

79. Fourteen Principle of an administration given by:
A. Luther Gullick B. Bulls
C. Watson D. Henri Fayol

80. What is nurse-patient ratio for each shift should be In ICU?
A. 1 : 3 B. 1 : 9 C. 1 : 1 D. 4 : 1

81. What is nurse patient ratio for each shift should In general ward ?
A. 1 : 9 B. 1 : 1 C. 1 : 10 D. 1 : 3

82. Who is the administrative head of school of nursing?
A. Tutor B. Principal
C. Chairman D. Vice-principal

83. What is the administrative level in college of nursing?
A. Chairman - Vice-principal- Principal-associate professor- lecturer
B. Principal - Vice-principal-associate professor- lecturer-clinical instructor
C. Chairman - Vice-principal-associate professor- lecturer-clinical instructor
D. Chairman - Vice-principal- lecturer-clinical instructor

84. The government of India anoounced the first National Health Policy in the year:
A. 1951 B. 1982 C. 1977 D. 1991

85. Qualities and abilities that are required for a particular work or task, is known as :
A. Negligence B. Competence
C. Administraticn D. Capacity

86. What is the nurse patient ratio should be In ICU?
A. 1 : 3 for 24 hours B. 1 : 9 for 24 hours
C. 1 : 1 for each shift D. 1 : 1 for 24 hours

87. Which management theory states " when managers make a decision, they must take into account all aspects of the current situation and act on those aspects that are key to the situation at hand"?
A. Systems theory
B. Chaos Theory
C. Contingency Theory
D. Bureaucratic Management Theory

88. Which of the following nursing personnel is considered as first level professional nurse who provides direct patient care?
A. Nursing superintendent
B. DNS
C. Head nurse
D. Staff nurse

89. An anganwari worker is expected to cover the population of:
A. 3000 B. 5000 C. 2000 D. 1000

90. Which of the following is important for an effective administration?
A. Lack of communication
B. Organisation should be decentralised
C. Organisation should be centralised
D. Both A & C

91. "A clinical judgment about an individual, a family or a community's responses to actual and potential health problems/life processes" - refers to
A. Nursing Diagnosis
B. Outcome Identification
C. Quality assurance
D. System analysis

92. Which of the following type of services is provided by a hospital?
A. Curative& Preventive
B. Research and Rehabilitative

C. Training and education
D. All of the Above

93. What is the dictionary meaning of word supervision?

A. Overseeing B. Evaluation
C. Guidance D. Caring

94. Which of the following are the most important tools of supervision?

A. Teaching B. Anecdotal records
C. Check-list D. Staff meeting

95. A list which is filled by supervisor in form of yes or no is known as:

A. Rating scale
B. Performance record
C. Check list
D. Anecdotal records

96. Nursing may be defined as "the diagnosis and treatment of human responses to health and illness". This definition of of nursing was given by

A. Nightingale
B. American Nurses Association (ANA, 1995)
C. Henderson
D. World Health Organization (WHO)

97. Who gives the 'POSDCORB' elements of administration?

A. Luther Gullick B. Bulls
C. Watson D. Henri Fayol

98. Periodic formal evaluation of the nursing employee about his duties and performance during a specified time period is known as:

A. Supervision
B. Rating scale
C. Check list
D. Performance-appraisal

99. A Total Quality Management (TQM) strategy developed by Motorola Company in 1986:

A. Plan-Do-Check –Act
B. MBO
C. Six Sigma
D. PERT

100. Which of the following is a feature of budget?

A. It should have the support by top management
B. It should be flexible
C. It should be planned
D. All of the Above

101. What is The minimum age of admission in nursing training programme ?

A. 21 years B. 18 years
C. 17 years D. 15 years

102. The type of nursing diagnosis which is a judgment on client's response to a present health problem

A. Actual Diagnosis
B. High Risk Nursing Diagnosis
C. Possible Nursing Diagnosis
D. Wellness Diagnosis

103. A quality of a person where he has ability to influence others it is known as:

A. Administration B. Counselling
C. Leadership D. Direction

104. The organization where top level has most of the decision making capacity is known as:

A. Authentic B. Decentralise
C. Centralised D. Organization

105. Time taken for any project is estimated by

A. Work sampling
B. Input-output analysis
C. Network analysis
D. System analysis

106. The technique of counselling in which emotional aspects are more significant than the intellectual aspects is known as:

A. Purposive counselling
B. Counsellor centered counselling
C. Element centered counselling
D. Client centered counselling

107. Finding the most cost-effective way doing a project:

A. Network analysis B. System analysis
C. Cost analysis D. Field analysis

108. Which of the following is sentence related to good ward management?

A. Delegation of responsibilities
B. Maintenance of suitable environment
C. Proper record keeping and reporting
D. All of the Above

109. The word administration is derived from?

A. Greek word B. French word
C. English word D. Latin word

110. As per the North Atlantic Treaty Organization (NATO) triage system, green colour code refers to

A. Injuries are life-threatening but survivable with minimal intervention.
B. Injuries are significant and require medical care, but can wait hours without threat to life or limb.
C. Injuries are minor and treatment can be delayed hours to days.
D. Injuries are extensive and chances of survival are unlikely even with definitive care.

111. What is meaning of 'S' in elements of administration in the word POSDCORB?

A. Staffing B. Shy
C. Systematic D. Supervision

112. W. Edward Deming is known for his contribution in modern management for introducing

A. Application of psychology in advertisement and marketing
B. Time and motion studies
C. Quality control
D. PERT Technique

113. What is meaning of 'P' in elements of administration in the word POSDCORB?

A. Programme B. Presentation
C. Planning D. Power

114. Who give the elements of administration Word POSDCORB?

A. Professor Luther Gullick
B. WHO
C. Sigmund Freud
D. Blooms

115. Who is the head of The union ministry of health & family welfare ?

A. Health director
B. Health Minister of state
C. Cabinet minister
D. Health secretary

116. What is teacher student ratio according to INC for GNM?

A. 1: 50 B. 1: 1 C. 1: 15 D. 1: 10

117. Who is the president present of INC?

A. Mr. Jogendra Sharma
B. Mr. Amadudding Ahmed
C. Mr. Mahesh Sharma
D. Mr. T. Dileep Kumar

118. PHCs under public health care system in India was introduced as result of recoomendatinos by:

A. Bhore committee
B. Kartar Singh Committe
C. Mudaliyar Committee
D. Planning Commission

119. What is the size of the hospital for affiliation for GNM School ?

A. 100 beds B. 300 beds
C. 50 beds D. 150 beds

120. Which of the following should be nurse patient ratio in OPD of a hospital?

A. 1 : 125 B. 1 : 10
C. 1 : 25 D. 1 : 100

121. In material management, the period in days that elapses between placing an order and receiving the stores is termed as

A. Lead time
B. Economic Order Quantity
C. Quantity survey
D. Reorder time

122. Which of the following is the component of administration except?

A. Direct patent care
B. Evaluation of report
C. Budget
D. Organizat on

123. What are the Job responsibilities of nursing superintendent in the hospital?

A. Nursing rounds or supervision
B. Planning and implementation of policies
C. Preparaticn of organisation chart
D. All of the Above

124. The extent of resemblance between the purpose of healthcare and the truly granted care is referred to

A. Standard B. Audit
C. Quality D. Outcome

125. Which of the following are the components of the in-service education programme?

A. Planning
B. Leadership development
C. Skill trairing
D. All of the Above

126. Which of the following is the patient clinical record?
A. Staff development and performance record
B. Duty chart maintain by staff nurse
C. Intake & output and vital charting
D. All of the Above

127. WHO constitution was made in
A. 1947 B. 1950 C. 1952 D. 1956

128. What is the census report in the hospital?
A. Number of patients at midnight in the hospital
B. Number of staff in hospital at night
C. Number of patients born in hospital
D. Number of death of patient in hospital

129. Which of the following is the responsibility of state nursing council?
A. Transferor of nursing staff
B. Preparation the job for nursing staff
C. Formulation of objectives of nursing care
D. Registration of nurses & Implementation the standard for patient care prepared by INC

130. Which of the following inventory control method is based on the criteria of rate of consumption of the items?
A. ABC Analysis (Always Better Control)
B. VED Analysis (Vital, Essential, Desirable)
C. HML Analysis (High, Medium, Low)
D. FSN Analysis (Fast, Slow moving and Non-moving)

131. The NS of hospital is considered as:
A. Training level manager
B. First level manager
C. Middle level manager
D. Operating level manager

132. A group of trained persons who have same objectives and goal is known as :
A. Organization B. Management
C. Administration D. Hospital

133. Standard Operating Procedure (SOP) refers to:
A. An optimal balance between possibilities realized and a framework of norms and values.
B. Doing the right thing right, right away, the first time
C. Detailed, written instructions to achieve uniformity of the performance of a specific function.
D. A process of meeting the needs and expectations of the customers, both internal and external.

134. When authority flows directly from superior to a subordinate, it is known as:
A. Staff authority
B. Functional authority
C. Line authority
D. All of the Above

135. Which of the following education term related to Planned educational activities provided in a job setting?
A. Job analysis
B. In-service education
C. Continuing education
D. None of them

136. Part of a quality system covering the manufacture and testing of pharmaceutical dosage forms or drugs and active pharmaceutical ingredients, diagnostics, foods, pharmaceutical products, and medical devices:
A. Good manufacturing practice (GMP)
B. Good regulatory practice (GRP)
C. Good Clinical Practice (GCP)
D. Good laboratory practice (GLP)

137. Which of the following regulatory body is associated with registration of nurses in the state?
A. Indian Medical Association
B. Indian Nursing Council
C. State Nursing Council
D. ICN

138. What leadership style A utilized to maintain a strong control in the department?
A. Laissez- faire B. Democratic
C. Collegial D. Autocratic

139. This is a common trait of a leader which is defined as his ability to possess honesty, responsibility and maturity in the working area.
A. Integrity B. Personality
C. Intelligence D. Flexibility

140. You are the head nurse in the pediatric department. Your roles in the planning process in the hospital include the following, except one:
A. Act as link between higher- level managers and non managers

B. Directly responsible for the actual production of nursing services

C. Represent the organization

D. Both B & C

141. What is true about patient classification system or PCS?

A. It is a method of grouping patients according to length or duration of nursing care

B. It is a measuring tool used to describe the progress of patient's status

C. It depends on the complexity of nursing care requirements of the patient

D. All of the Above

142. It is a managerial function that indicates leading the staff in the most effective method.

A. Planning B. Directing

C. Organizing D. Controlling

143. Which describes an informal leader?

A. Anju who is appointed because of her competencies and continuing education

B. Mina who becomes the leader of the team because of her years of experience in the department

C. Abdul who is considered the leader of the team since he was given the legitimate authority to act as one.

D. Helan who is chosen by the administration because of her age and knowledge in the area of work.

144. Why is good communication important in managing personnel?

A. It motivates personnel to do their jobs well

B. It promotes independence and collaboration

C. It fosters influence and power

D. All of the Above

145. Downward communication is described below. Which one is correct?

A. The communication is between two supervisors

B. The flow of communication is from the head nurse to supervisor

C. The flow of communication is from the chief nurse to the head nurse

D. The flow of communication is from the staff nurse to the chief nurse

146. During controlling and evaluating phase, the following are quality improvement methods utilized by institutions. Which one refers to a review process used by healthcare organization to assure that the hospital may provide care to clients?

A. Credentialing and licensing

B. Standards of care

C. Clinical pathways

D. Benchmarking

147. Which type of conflict management technique is described as cooperating and that one side gives in to the other?

A. Avoiding B. Accommodating

C. Competing D. Compromising

148. Supervision and delegation fall to what phase of the management process?

A. Organizing B. Directing

C. Controlling D. Planning

149. What kind of staffing is considered the most common pattern and the oldest type?

A. Cyclical staffing

B. Full time equivalent staffing

C. Conventional staffing

D. Decentralized staffing

150. SNA established in:

A. 1929 B. 1920 C. 1945 D. 1950

151. ANA established in:

A. 1950 B. 1929 C. 1922 D. 1908

152. TNAI (Trained Nurses Association of India) Established in:

A. 1905 B. 1908 C. 1922 D. 1929

❑❑❑

Answer Sheet

1.B.	2. D.	3. A.	4. D.	5. A.	6. A.	7. A.	8. A.	9. A.	10. B.
11. C.	12. D.	13. C.	14. D.	15. D.	16. D.	17. D.	18. C.	19. D.	20. B.
21. D.	22. A.	23. D.	24. C.	25. B.	26. D.	27. B.	28. C.	29. A.	30. A.
31. D.	32. B.	33. B.	34. D.	35. C.	36. A.	37. B.	38. C.	39. D.	40. A.
41. D.	42. B.	43. D.	44. B.	45. C.	46. D.	47. B.	48. B.	49. A.	50. D.
51. A.	52. D.	53. A.	54. D.	55. A.	56. D.	57. C.	58. D.	59. B.	60. B.
61. C.	62. A.	63. D.	64. D.	65. A.	66. C.	67. D.	68. B.	69. D.	70. A.
71. B.	72. B.	73. C.	74. A.	75. A.	76. D.	77. D.	78. D.	79. D.	80. A.
81. A.	82. B.	83. B.	84. B.	85. B.	86. D.	87. C.	88. D.	89. D.	90. D.
91. A.	92. D.	93. A.	94. C.	95. C.	96. B.	97. A.	98. D.	99. C.	100. D.
101. C.	102. A.	103. C.	104. C.	105. C.	106. D.	107. C.	108. D.	109. D.	110. C.
111. A.	112. C.	113. C.	114. A.	115. C.	116. D.	117. D.	118. A.	119. C.	120. A.
121. A.	122. A.	123. D.	124. C.	125.D.	126. C.	127. A.	128. A.	129. D.	130. D.
131. C.	132. A.	133. C.	134. C.	135. B.	136. A.	137. C.	138. D.	139. B.	140. A.
141. D.	142. B.	143. B.	144. D.	145. C.	146. B.	147. B.	148. B.	149. D.	150. A.
151. A.	152. C.								

487. Corneal thickness is measured by
A. Pachymetry B. Tonometry
C. Keratometry D. Asthesiometry

488. Fluoroscein stain is used in detecting
A. Corneal Ulcer B. Dry Eyes
C. Both A & B D. None of the Above

489. Most common organism infecting contact lens
A. Staphylococcus B. Streptococcus
C. Acanthamoeba D. Chalmydia

490. Calculation of IOL power is called?
A. Pachymetry B. Tonometry
C. Keratometry D. Biometry

491. Ecchymosis is
A. Conjuctival oedema
B. Conjuctival inflammation
C. Sub conjuctival haemorrhage
D. Conjuctival dryness

492. Acuity of Near Vision is Tested by
A. Snellen's chart B. Jaeger's chart
C. Logmar chart D. Ishihara chart

493. The magnification obtained with a direct ophthalmoscope is
A. 5 times B. 10 times
C. 15 times D. 20 times

494. All of the following are antifungal except
A. Amphotericin B B. Natamycin
C. Clotrimazole D. Acyclovir

495. Visual acuity with pinhole is decreased in all conditions except
A. Posterior polar cataract
B. Central corneal opacity
C. Early Nuclear sclerosis
D. Macular scar

496. Keratometry is?
A. Measurement of curvature of anterior surface of cornea
B. Measurement of curvature of anterior surface of lens
C. Measurement of curvature of posterior surface of cornea
D. Measurement of curvature of posterior surface of lens

497. Human natural lens is?
A. Biconcave structure
B. Biconvex structure
C. Plano concave structure
D. Plano convex structure

498. Physiological insufficiency of accommodation is?
A. Myopia B. Hypermetropia
C. Presbyopia D. None of the Above

499. The most common cause of reduced vision in the world is
A. Trachoma B. Diabetic retinopathy
C. Refractive error D. Glaucoma

500. Reflexes Move in Opposite direction in Retinoscopy in
A. Myopia of Less than 1 D
B. Myopia of More than 1 D
C. Myopia of 1 D
D. None of the Above

501. Intraocular lens is made up of
A. PMMa B. Hydrophilic acrylate
C. Silicone D. All of the Above

502. Drooping of upper lid is known as
A. Ptosis B. Entropion
C. Ectropion D. Chalazion

503. Sjogren syndrome is due to deficiency of which layer of tear film
A. Aqueous deficiency B. Lipid deficiency
C. Mucous deficiency D. All of the Above

504. Wing shaped fold of conjunctiva encroaching on cornea is
A. Pterygium B. Pinguecula
C. Concretion D. Chalazion

505. Following are the conjuctival Glands except
A. Glands of Zeis B. Glands of Wolfring
C. Glands of Manz D. Glands of Krause

506. Light passes through the following structures in which order?
A. Vitreous Humor, Lens, aqueous Humor, cornea
B. Cornea, aqueous Humor, Lens, Vitreous Humor
C. Cornea, Vitreous Humor, Lens, aquous Humor
D. Aquous Humor, cornea, Lens, Vitreous Humor

507. Rhodopsin is present in
A. Rods B. Cones
C. Both D. None of the Above

508. Treatment of corneal ulcer include
A. Antibiotic
B. Cycloplegic
C. Corneal Scrapping
D. All of the Above

509. Chalazion is a chronic inflammatory granuloma of
A. Meibomian gland B. Zeiss gland
C. Sweat gland D. Wolfring gland

510. Use of convex lens, except
A. For correction of Hypermetropia
B. For correction of aphakia
C. For correction of Presbyopia
D. For correction of Myopia

511. Schirmer's test is used for
A. Dry Eyes B. Corneal Ulcer
C. Both D. None of the Above

512. Commonest cause of cataract is
A. Trauma B. Biabetes
C. Old age D. TORCH infections

513. Definition of blindness according to WHO is
A. V/a of <3/60 or its equivalent
B. V/a of <4/60 or its equivalent
C. V/a of <5/60 or its equivalent
D. V/a of <2/60 or its equivalent

514. Arcus senilis refer to an annular lipid infiltration of
A. Cornea B. Limbus
C. Conjunctiva D. Sclera

515. Age related opacification of lens is known as
A. Senile cataract
B. Complicated cataract
C. Traumatic cataract
D. Congenital cataract

516. Uses of prisms in ophthalmology are
A. Measurement of angle of deviation
B. Slit lamp biomicroscopy
C. Applanation tonometry
D. All of the Above

517. Which of the following structures can be examined with a slit lamp without any additional aid except
A. Conjunctiva B. Cornea
C. Iris D. Retina

518. All are the gland of eyelid except
A. Meibomian gland
B. Glands of Manz
C. Glands of zeis
D. Glands of Moll

519. Refractive index of human lens is
A. 1.39 B. 1.79 C. 1.99 D. None

520. Which type of lenses are used for correction of myopia?
A. Convex B. Concave
C. Plano D. Planoconcave

521. Atropine is contraindicated in
A. Narrow angle glaucoma
B. Open angle glaucoma
C. Congenital glaucoma
D. Steroid induced glaucoma

522. Safe strategy is used for
A. Onchocerciasis B. Trachoma
C. Trichiasis D. None of the Above

523. Renin is secreted from:
A. Collecting ducts
B. Juxtaglomerular apparatus
C. PcT
D. dcT

524 Which organ does Jaundice affect
A. Lungs B. Heart
C. Liver D. Stomach

525. Which part of the eye is affected in cataract
A. Pupil B. Lens
C. Iris D. Retina

526. Which body part separates abdominal and thoracic cavity
A. Liver B. Diaphragm
C. Spleen D. Ribs

527. Microorganisms which need oxygen to survive and multiply
A. Anaerobic B. Spores
C. Aerobic D. Zoonosis

528. Stapes is smallest bone it is situated in
A. In wrist joint B. In ear
C. In nose D. In ankle joint

529. Development of Mature Ovum is called as
A. Oogenesis B. Ovulation
C. Fertilization D. All of the Above

530. Fight and Flight response made by the body in emergency situation is associated with increased activity of
A. Adrenal Gland B. Pituitary Gland
C. Thyroid Gland D. Pancreas

531. Bile is stored in human body in
A. Liver B. Pancreas
C. Intestine D. Gall-bladder

532. Bile is secreted in human body by
A. Liver B. Pancreas
C. Intestine D. Gall-bladder

533. Taste buds for sensing bitterness are located on which part of the tongue
A. Anterior part of tongue
B. Posterior part of tongue
C. Lateral part of tongue
D. Under surface of tongue

534. Largest gland of body
A. Pancreas B. Salivary gland
C. Liver D. Pyloric gland

535. The lens found in human eye is
A. Biconcave B. Biconvex
C. Uniconcave D. Uniconvex

536. In following which is the inner most layer of the eye
A. Sclera B. Cornea
C. Retina D. Iris

537. Thermophillic bacteria can survive at............ temperature
A. Extremely high B. Extremely low
C. Moderate D. Any

538. Anatomical Snuff box is present in
A. Hand B. Leg
C. Neck D. Ear

539. Vasopressin hormone is also known as
A. Thyroxin hormone
B. Parathyroid haromone
C. Anti-diuretic hormone
D. Prolactin hormone

540. The relay center of brain is
A. Medulla B. Pons
C. Brain stem D. Thalamus

541 A bone embedded within a tendon or a muscle is called?
A. Sesamoid B. Ethmoid
C. Platypoid D. None of the Above

542. A gland which is both endocrine and exocrine?
A. Thyroid gland B. Thymus gland
C. Pancreas D. Pituitary gland

543. The breast is a modification of?
A. Sebaceous Gland B. Sweat Gland
C. Thyroid Gland D. Pituitary gland

544. Lower part of pharynx is attached to?
A. Stomach B. Larynx
C. Trachea D. None of the Above

545. What cell type secrets surfactant?
A. Plasma cell
B. Type I alveolar cell
C. Type II alveolar cell or Pneumocytes cell
D. Type III alveolar cell

546. In Human body rods and cones are related with
A. Vision B. Hearing
C. Touch D. Smell

547. Cholelithiasis is?
A. Inflammation of gall bladder
B. Stone in Kidney
C. Stone in gall bladder
D. Infection in Kidney

548. Type of the c-Shaped cartilage in Trachea
A. Costal cartilage B. Hyaline cartilage
C. Fibro cartilage D. Elastic cartilage

549. The Organ which establishes connection between mother and fetus is called
A. Amniotic Fluid B. Umbilical cord
C. Placenta D. Deciduas

550. Neurotransmitter involved in pain relief is:
A. Acetycholine B. Norepinephrine
C. Serotonin D. Endorphins

551. Which of the following is the main function of ovaries
A. Ovulation
B. Nourishment of embryo
C. Implantation
D. Delivery of foetus

552. Hormone not secreted by placenta is?
A. Estrogen B. Progesterone
C. HcG D. Testosterone

553. Which of the following is power house of the cells
A. Cytoplasma B. Cell Membrane
C. Nucleus D. Mitochondria

554. Goiter is related to?
A. Thyroid gland
B. Deficiency of Iodine
C. Swelling in thyroid
D. All of the Above

555. Which of the following tube is ligated during vasectomy?
A. Ejaculatory duct B. Seminal Vesicles
C. Seminal Tubules D. Vas deferens

556. Disease causing bacteria which appears to be comma shaped after staining under the microscope is
A. Bacilli B. Cocci
C. Vibrio D. Spirall

557. Hormone which is responsible for production and secretion of milk in breast
A. Oestrogen
B. Progesterone
C. Luteinising Hormone
D. Prolactin

558. Who is the carrier of Haemophilia
A. Female
B. Male
C. Both Male and Female
D. None of the Above

559. Benign tumor of fatty tissue is?
A. Lipoma B. Sarcoma
C. Mixoma D. Neuroma

560. Leukopenia is?
A. Reduced number of WBC
B. Increased number of WBC
C. Reduced number of RBC
D. Increased number of RBC

561. Standard temperature and pressure of autoclave is
A. 200°C, 20 lbs/inch 2 for 30 m
B. 121°F, 151 lbs/inch 2 for 30 m
C. 121°C, 15 Kg/Cm 2 for 30 m
D. 121°C, 15 lbs/inch 2 for 30 m

562. Sense organ responsible for balance in body
A. Eye B. Ear
C. Nose D. Skin

563. Growth hormone is secreted from?
A. Pituitary Gland
B. Adrenal Gland

C. Thymus Gland
D. Hypothalamus Gland

564. Placenta and Fetal membrane is formed by which
A. Inner cell mass B. Trophoblast
C. Mesoderm D. Endoderm

565. The immunity that is developed as a result of infection or by specific immunization is called
A. Herd Immunity B. Passive immunity
C. Active immunity D. None of the Above

566. Which of the following is the correct order for the passing of food through the digestive system?
A. Oesophagus, large intestine, stomach, small intestine
B. Mouth, oesophagus, stomach, large intestine
C. Oesophagus, small intestine, stomach, anus
D. Mouth, Oesophagus, stomach, small intestine, large intestine

567. Light rays entering the eye is controlled by?
A. Pupil B. Iris
C. Cornea D. Lens

568. Which of the following is not a muscle identified in the rotator cuff?
A. Teres Major B. Teres Minor
C. Infraspinatus D. Supraspinatus

569. Which of the following is not included in the femoral triangle?
A. Femoral artery B. Femoral Nerve
C. Femoral Vein D. Femoral Ligament

570. Which of the following is not a component of the carotid sheath?
A. Cranial nerve X
B. Common carotid artery
C. Internal jugular vein
D. Cranial nerve IX

571. Which of the following spinal dermatome level corresponds with the landmark of the inguinal ligament?
A. T10 B. L1
C. L3 D. L5

572. Which of the following nerves innervates the deltoid?
A. Radial B. Cranial nerve XI
C. Subscapular D. Axillary

573. Wrist extensors are primarily controlled by what nerve?
A. Radial B. Ulnar
C. Median D. Tibial

574. Adductor pollicis in the hand is controlled by which nerve?
A. Radial B. Ulnar
C. Median D. Tibial

575. Which of the following arteries is the most frequent site of coronary artery stenosis?
A. LCA B. RCA
C. LADA D. Pd

576. Which of the following nerves is not directly linked to the L2-L3 spinal level?
A. Tibial B. Obturator
C. Femoral D. None of the Above

577. Which of the following passageways contain the maxillary nerve and blood vessels?
A. Stylomastoid foramin
B. Inferior orbital fissure
C. Foramen ovale
D. Carotid canal

578. Which of the following passageways contain the facial nerve and blood vessels?
A. Stylomastoid foramin
B. Inferior orbital fissure
C. Foramen ovale
D. Carotid canal

579. Which of the following passageways contain the internal carotid artery?
A. Foramen rotundum
B. Condylar canal
C. Foramen ovale
D. Carotid canal

580. Which of the following is the most common site of disc herniation?
A. C_6-C_7
B. T_{12}-L_1
C. L_4-L_5
D. L_5-S_1

581. Which of the following ligaments is not found in the knee?
A. Patellar ligament
B. Oblique popliteal ligament
C. Arcuate popliteal ligament
D. Deltoid ligament

582. Which of the following nerves innervates the teres minor muscle?
A. Subscapular nerve
B. Suprascapular nerve
C. Axillary nerve
D. Pectoral nerve

583. Which of the following nerves innervates the pronator teres muscle?
A. Radial
B. Median
C. Musculocutaneous
D. Ulnar

584. Which of the following supplies the muscles of the perineum?
A. Pudendal nerve
B. Sciatic nerve
C. Femoral nerve
D. Tibial nerve

585. Which of the following eye muscles rotates the eye downward and away from midline?
A. Inferior oblique
B. Superior oblique
C. Inferior rectus
D. Superior rectus

586. Which of the following eye muscles rotates the eye upward and toward midline?
A. Inferior oblique B. Superior oblique
C. Inferior rectus D. Superior rectus

587. In following which is a vector borne disease?
A. Measles B. Diptheria
C. Dengue D. Tetanus

588. Father of antiseptic surgery-
A. Robert Koch B. Robert hook
C. Louise pasture D. Lord lister

589. Antibody involve in allergic asthma-
A. IgG B. IgM
C. IgE D. IgA

590. Which of the following is the father of microbiology?
A. Landsteiner
B. Louis Pasteur
C. Robert Koch
D. Antonie van Leeuwenhoek

591. The most common inhibitory neurotransmitter in the human brain is:
A. Acetycholine B. Serotonin
C. GABA D. Dopamine

592. Streptomycin antibiotic was discovered by:
A. Alexander Fleming
B. Louis Pasteur
C. Robert Koch
D. Waksman

593. Who discovered the penicillin?
A. Edward Jenner
B. Alexander Fleming
C. Louis Pasteur
D. Robert Koch

594. Who developed modern microscope?
A. Edward Jenner
B. Deergha Sharma
C. Antonievan Leeuwenhoek
D. Mr. Pagoda

595. Bacteria those are unable to synthesize their own food known as?
A. Autotrophs. B. Carnivorous
C. Heterotrophs D. Saprotrophs

596. The techniques of sterilization were introduced by?
A. Robert Koch. B. Deergha Sharma
C. Louis Pasteur D. John dew

597. Which of the following bacteria can grow in alkaline pH?
A. Shigella
B. Lactobacilli Acidophilus
C. Vibrio cholera
D. Salmonella typhi

598. Antibody passes though placenta-
A.. IgG B. IgM
C. IgE D. IgA

599. Hib is a———— vaccine-
A. Live viral B. Killed viral
C. Live bacterial D. Killed bacterial

600. Which of the following bacteria dies just after drying?
A. Treponema palladium
B. Mycobacterium tuberculosis
C. Staphylococcus
D. Pseudomonas

601. TY_{21a} is a———— vaccine-
A. Live viral B. Killed viral
C. Live bacterial D. Killed bacterial

602. The motor cortex is situated:
A. Frontal lobe B. Parietal lobe
C. Temporal lobe D. Occipital lobe

603. Chicken pox is a?
A. Respiratory infection
B. Enteric infection
C. Skin infection
D. None of the Above

604. Who proposed the germ theory?
A. Louis Pasteur. B. Robert Koch
C. Lord Lister D. Alexander Fleming

605. Polio is a ?
A. Respiratory infection
B. Enteric infection
C. Skin infection
D. C.N.S. infection

606. Who introduced the method of vaccination to prevent smallpox?
A. Robert Koch B. Edward Jenner
C. Louis Pasteur D. John Hunter

607. Which is triple antigen vaccine-
A. DPT B. BCG
C. Hep.B D. Hib

608. Who made first successful immunization against smallpox?
A. Waksman B. Robert Koch
C. Louis Pasteur D. Edward Jenner

609. Serum sterilize through-
A. Filtration B. Hot air oven
C. Autoclave D. Radiation

610 Mycobacterium tubercle Bacillus discovered by:
A. Robert Koch. B. Loeffler
C. Hansen D. Deergha Sharma

611. Schick test use to diagnose-
A. Diphtheria B. Scarlet fever
C. Thyphoid D. Cholera

612. Toxoids are-
A. Modified bacterial exotoxin
B. Modified bacterial endotoxin
C. Both A & B
D. None of the Above

613. Bacteria possess?
A. Only D.N.A. B. Only R.N.A.
C. Both A & B D. None of the Above

614. Fluminating infection means?
A. Pus forming infection
B. Long term infection
C. Local area infection
D. Infection occurring suddenly with intensity

615. Which of the following is not a gram-negative bacteria?
A. Clostridium perfringens
B. Vibrio cholerae
C. Escherichia coli
D. Bordetella pertussis

616. The term vaccine was introduced by:
A. Loeffler B. Deergha Sharma
C. Edward Jenner D. Louis Pasteur

617. Which of the following is not true related to endotoxins?
A. Endotoxins are liberated from bacterial cells.
B. Produced mainly by gram positive microorganisms
C. Produced mainly by gram negative microorganisms
D. Can cause fever

618. Which of the following diseases and bacteria are matched up incorrectly?
A. Typhoid – Salmonella typhi
B. Syphilis – Trepenoma pallidum
C. Gastritis – Heliobacter pylori
D. Tuberculosis– Yersinia pestis

619. Which of the following diseases and bacteria are matched up incorrectly?
A. Treponema pallidum – Syphilis
B. Clostridium botulinum- Botulism
C. Borrelia burgdorferi – Lyme disease
D. Yersinia enterocolitica – Diphtheria

620. Which of the following is not true concerning Staphylococcus aureus?
A. S. aureus is related to cocci Gram poitive.
B. S. aureus can cause pneumonia
C. S. aureus can lead to acute bacterial endocarditis
D. S. aureus is related to cocci Gram negative

621. Which of the following signs and symptoms is not linked to Haemophilus influenzae?
A. Otitis media B. Pneumonia
C. Gastroenteritis D. Epiglottis

622. The Tsetse fly is a transmission factor for which of the following organisms?
A. Trepenoma pallidum
B. Trypanosoma gambiense
C. Entamoeba histolytica
D. Toxoplasma

623. Which of the following is not fungal related?
A. Cryptococcus neoformans
B. Candida albicans
C. Tinea nigra
D. Chlamydiae

624. Which of the following is not a DNA virus?
A. Adenovirus B. Hepatitis-A virus
C. Papovirus D. Poxvirus

625. Which of the following test is done for scarlet fever?
A. Schick test.
B. Widal test
C. ZEIL NELSON test
D. Dick test

626. Which of the following is not a RNA virus?
A. Reovirus B. Heptitis-B virus
C. Deltavirus D. Herpesvirus

627. The parietal lobe hosts:
A. Primary visual cortex
B. Primary auditory cortex
C. Somatosensory cortex
D. Motor cortex

628. Which of the following viruses is not a double strand DNA virus?
A. Poxvirus B. Parvo virus
C. Adenovirus D. Herpesvirus

629. Which of the following viruses is not a single strand RNA virus?
A. Togavirus B. Retrovirus
C. Poxvirus D. Picornavirus

630. Which of the following microorganisms is not concern to UTI's?
A. E. coli B. Pseudomonas
C. Klebsiella D. Haemophilus

631. Disease that affects many people at different countries is termed as
A. Sporadic B. Pandemic
C. Epidemic D. Fluminent

632. Which of the following is not a gram-positive bacteria?
A. Streptococci B. Pseudomonas
C. Mycobacteria D. None of these

633. Gram-positive bacteria, responsible for food poisoning-
A. E. Coli
B. Pseudomonas aerogenosa
C. Clostridia
D. All of these

634. Which of the following gram-positive bacteria causes otitis media?
A. Neisseria B. Streptococcus
C. Staphylococcus D. Shigella

635. Which of the following gram-positive bacteria is not aerobic?
A. Pseudomonas B. Salmonella
C. Clostridium D. None of these

636. Gram-negative bacteria, that are responsible for food poisoning?
A. Salmonella B. Shigella
C. E.coli D. All of these

637. Which of the following is a gram-negative bacteria?
A. Shigella B. Clostridia
C. Staphylococci D. None of these

638. Which of the following is a gram-positive bacteria?
A. Lactobacillus B. Staphylococci
C. Corny bacterium D. All of these

639. Tuberculosis is a
A. Water borne disease
B. Air borne disease
C. Food borne disease
D. Arthropod borne disease

640. Life cycle of malarial parasite was first described by:
A. Banting and Best B. Ronald Ross
C. Robert Koch D. Louis Pasteur

641. Primary mediators involve in anaphylaxis
A. Histamine B. Serotonin
C. Heparin D. All of these

642. Cold like symptoms are caused by which bacteria
A. Pseudomonas
B. Shigella
C. Haemophilus influenza
D. Haemophilus streptococcus

643. Which of the following is not a species of plasmodium parasite?
A. Plasmodium vivax
B. Plasmodium ovale
C. Plasmodium maxicana
D. Plasmodium malariae

644. The viruses that live as parasites on bacteria are called
A. Saprophyte B. Commensels
C. Bacteriophages D. None of these

645. Diphtheria is caused by
A. Corynebacterium
B. Staphylococcus
C. Diplococcus
D. Mycobacterium

646. Koplic spots observed in the mucous membrane is seen in
A. Diphtheria B. Measles
C. Mumps D. Influenza

647. The most infectious food borne disease is
A. Tetanus B. Dysentery
C. Typhoid D. Botulism

648. "Klebs loeffler bacillus" is the name of which of the following bacteria?
A. Lactobacillus.
B. Clostridium tetani
C. Hemophilus influenza
D. Corynebacterium diphtheriae

649. An example for common air borne epidemic disease?
A. Influenza B. Typhoid
C. Encephalitis D. Jaundice

650. Amoebic dysentery in humans is caused by?
A. Plasmodium
B. Paramecium
C. Shigella
D. Entamoeba histolytica

651. The test used for detection of typhoid fever?
A. WIDAL test B. ELISA
C. Montaux test D. Western blotting

652. Which is an example of spirochete ?
A. Pneumococci
B. Staphylococci
C. Treponema pallidum
D. Streptococci

653. Interferons are effective against-
A. Bacteria B. Virus
C. Fungi D. All of these

654. **For effective sterilization, steam in an autoclave should be at a pressure of 15 pounds per square inch for 30 minutes and at a temperature of:**
A. 131°C B. 100°C
C. 110°C D. 121°C

655. **A facultative anaerobic is**
A. Only grow in presence of CO_2
B. Only grow in the presence of O_2
C. Ordinarily an anaerobe but can grow with O_2
D. Ordinarily an aerobe but can grow in absence of O_2

656. **Rod shaped bacteria are known as**
A. Cocci B. Mycoplasma
C. Bacilli D. Riketsia

657. **All the groups of bacteria have cell wall except**
A. Mycobacteria B. Mycoplasmas
C. Clostridia D. Rickettsia

658. **Benedict's test in a urine sample is done for the detection of:**
A. Bile pigment B. Acetone
C. Glucose D. Bile salt

659. **Gram positive bacteria appear as?**
A. Pink B. Violet
C. Green D. None of these

660. **Gram negative bacteria appear as?**
A. Pink B. Violet
C. Yellow D. None of these

661. **The primary visual cortex is situated in the:**
A. Frontal lobe B. Parietal lobe
C. Temporal lobe D. Occipital lobe

662. **The Largest virus is**
A. Parvo virus B Pox virus
C. Rhabdo virus D. Adeno virus

663. **The smallest virus is?**
A. Parvo virus B. Rhabdo virus
C. Pox virus D. Adeno virus

664. **Asepsis means?**
A. Freedom from infection
B. Freedom from pain.
C. Freedom from noise
D. Freedom from anxiety

665. **Infection that results in pus formation are called?**
A. Pyrogenic infection
B. Acute infection
C. Pyogenic infection
D. Focal infection

666. **Cholera vaccine provides protection for**
A. 1 – 3 months B. 3 – 6 months
C. 6 – 12 months D. 12-18 months

667. **Widal test is performed:**
A. To identify the cause of dysentery
B. To identify the typhoid fever
C. To identify the AIDS
D. To identify the cause of diarrhoea

668. **Acid fast bacteria are**
A. Neisseria B. Staphylococci
C. Mycobacteria D. Streptococci

669. **Mycobacteria are stained with**
A. Gram's staining
B. Simple staining
C. Albert staining
D. Ziehl – Neelsen's staining

670. **Trichomonal infection is caused by:**
A. Bacteria B. Protozoa
C. Fungus D. Yeast

671. **Streptococcus forms cause which type of infections?**
A. Fever B. Zoonotic
C. Pyogenic D. All of these

672. **HIV is belonging to**
A. Retro Viridae B. Rhabdo Viridae
C. Toga Viridae D. Orthomyxo Viridae

673. **Immunity means?**
A. Acquired immunity by immunization.
B. Antibodies and antigen reactions
C. Transfer of maternal antibodies across the placenta
D. Level of resistance of a person to a particular disease

674. **The interval period between HIV infection and appearance of antibodies in serum is called?**
A. Intrinsic period B. Incubation period
C. Window period D. Latent period

675. **Screening test for AIDS is**
A. Western blot test B. ELISA test
C. Both A and B D. VDRL test

676. **Urine sample for culture is collected from?**
A. First and last urine
B. First urine
C. Last urine
D. Midstream urine

677. **Confirmatory test for AIDS is?**
A. Western blot test
B. ELISA test
C. Shick test
D. Seliwanoff's test

678. **The causative organism of tuberculosis is:**
A. Meningococci
B. Micrococci
C. Mycobacterium tubercle bacilli
D. Steptococci bacilli

679. The first antibody to contact invading microorganisms?
A. IgG B. IgM
C. IgA D. IgE

680. The following factors influence microbial growth, except:
A. Disinfection B. Temperature
C. Moisture D. Darkness

681. During AIDS, HIV infects?
A. CD_3 lymphocytes
B. CD_4 lymphocytes
C. CD_2 lymphocytes
D. Blastocytes

682. The most often cells from blood infected by IV is:
A. Polymorph
B. CD_4 (Helper) T.Lymphocyte
C. B-Lymphocyte
D. CD_3 (Suppressor) T. Lymphocyte

683. Which of the following process is known as sporicidal?
A. Sterilization. B. Cold sponging
C. Antiseptic D. Disinfection

684. A process of destruction of microorganisms is known as:
A. Detergent B. Sterilization
C. Sterility D. Disinfectant ion

685. Which infecting serotype of dengue virus is most dangerous?
A. Type-4 B. Type-1
C. Type-2 D. Type-3

686. A chemical used for destruction of microorganisms is known as:
A. Detergent B. Sterilization
C. Sterility D. Disinfectant

687. Lysol is a?
A. Antibiotic B. Disinfectant
C. Antiseptic D. Antifungal agent

688. HIV virus belongs to which of the following groups?
A. Hepadnavirus B. Flavivirus
C. RNA-Retrovirus D. Rhabdovirus.

689. Temperature required for pasteurization is?
A. Above 150°C B. Below 100° C
C. 110°C D. None of these

690. Milk pasteurization by high-temperature-short time (HTST)method employs:
A. 13.8°C for 10sec
B. 82.8°C for 30 min.
C. 71.7°C for l5sec.
D. 61.7°C for 15 sec.

691. Separation of a single bacterial colony is called
A. Isolation B. Separation
C. Pure culturing D. Smear

692. Which of the following is ionizing radiation?
A. U.V. rays B. IR
C. Y-rays D. Sun light

693. Pathogen means:
A. Organism which are found in plants.
B. Micro-organism which causes disease
C. Organism which are found in animals
D. Organism which are beneficial for us

694.. Viruses can be cultivated in?
A. Agar media B. Broth
C. Living cells D. None of these

695. Sterilization of endoscope is done:
A. By 2% gluteraldehyde
B. By Autoclaving
C. By U.V.rays
D. By 2% phenol

696. Temperature used for hot air oven is?
A. 100°C for 1 hour
B. 120°C for 1 hour
C. 160°C for 1 hour
D. 80°C for 1 hour

697. Thermophilic bacteria grow at following minimum temperature:
A. 85°C B. 20°C C. 35°C D. 55°C

698. Infrared radiation is a method of sterilization by
A. Dry heat B. Moist hea
C. Barrier method D. Mechanical method

699. Which of the following stage not takes place in the mouth?
A. Food is fashioned into a bolus
B. Carbohydrate digestion begins
C. Food becomes partially liquefied
D. Absorption of food

700. Which of the following known as protein factory?
A. Ribosome. B. Mitochondria
C. Lysosome D. Ovary

701. The chemical digestion begins in the stomach through the action of the enzyme?.
A. Fat; lipase
B. Fat; bile
C. Carbohydrate; salivary amylase
D. Protein; pepsin

702. In following which is not sterilized by antiseptic solution?
A. NG tube B. Suction catheter
C. Rectal tube D. Scissor.

703. Digestion of proteins:
A. Consumes water (hydrolysis) and amino acids
B. Consumes water (hydrolysis) and releases amino acids
C. Releases water (dehydration) and amino acids
D. Releases water (dehydration) and consumes amino acids

704. Which of The following epithelial tissue is found in uterine tubes ?
A. Squamoush B. Simple
C. Columnar D. Ciliated

705. The small intestine is the main site of absorption of:
A. Carbohydrates absorbed as monosacchorides
B. Carbohydrates absorbed as amino acids by active transport
C. Fats absorbed into lacteals of the lymphatic system
D. Both A and C

706. Which of the function of Golgi apparatus cell organelle is helpful in?
A. Pinocytosis B. Exocytosis
C. Endocytosis D. None of them

707. General functions of the stomach include the:
A. Metabolism of consumed foods and vitamins
B. Absorption of many of the digested nutrients
C. Mixing of the gastric contents to form chyme
D. Secretion of alkaline enzymes

708. Which of The epithelial tissue lines the urinary bladder?
A. Connective B. Columnar
C. Stratified D. Transitional

709. Digestion involves:
A. Transport of nutrient molecules from the intestine to cells
B. Intracellular change of nutrient molecules into essential intracellular nutrients
C. Splitting polymers into absorbable monomers in the GI tract
D. Secretion of insulin and glucagon

710. Spiral organ of Corti is related with:
A. Vision. B. Respiration
C. Speech D. Hearing

711. Secretin produced by the mucosa of the duodenum is stimulated by:
A. Distention of the stomach
B. Large quantities of bile
C. A fatty Chyme
D. Acidity of the Chyme

712. Thick band of neurons that connects the right and left cerebral hemispheres is:
A. Corpus callosum B. Hippocampus
C. Fornix D. Amygdala

713. Amino acids, monosaccharide's, glycerol and fatty acids are:
A. Transported in the lymph to all the lymph nodes in the body
B. All hormones
C. Products of carbohydrate metabolism
D. End products of digestion

714. Liver is found in:
A. Cranial cavity B. Pelvic cavity
C. Abdominal cavity D. Thoracic cavity

715. Which of these is false about "gastric juice?"
A. Is highly acidic because of its HCL content
B. Contains the intrinsic factor for absorption of vitamin B_{12}
C. Is controlled in part by a hormone called Gastrin
D. None of the Above

716. What is normal Length of pharynx in an adult?
A. 6-10 cm B. 40-50 cm
C. 20-30 cm D. 12-14 cm

717. Which of the following conditions lead to release of bile into the duodenum?
A. Presence of fat into the duodenum
B. Release of CCK into blood
C. Contraction of gallbladder
D. Both B and C

718. Which of the following structure is known as voice box?
A. Pharynx B. Nasopharynx
C. Trachea D. Larynx

719. What is small intestine?
A. Measures about one inch in diameter and 22 feet in length
B. Completes the digestion of foods
C. Secretes hormones which aid digestion
D. All of the Above

720. Which of The following organ help in production of sound?
A. Trachea B. Tongue
C. Pharynx D. Larynx

721. The bile salts are:
A. Enzymes for digesting food in the small intestines
B. Detergents for breaking up large fat globules to small ones
C. Stimulants to pancreatic secretion of enzymes
D. The major ingredients of gallstones

722. Which organ is Inferior associated with the Larynx?
A. Larynx B. Pharynx
C. Trachea D. Bronchi

723. The sodium bicarbonate in pancreatic juice helps to raise the pH of chyme. What substance originally lowered the pH of chyme?
A. Chyle B. H_2CO_3
C. HCl D. Alkali

724. Which of the following organ prevents the food from passing into the lower respiratory tract?
A. Pharynx B. Larynx
C. Epiglottis D. Large intestine

725. Which of the following is not a function of the pancreas?
A. Secretes insulin as well as glucagon into pancreatic duct
B. Secretes alkaline juice which neutralizes chyme while chyme is stored in the stomach
C. Secretes both endocrine and exocrine substances
D. Secretes lipase which acts on bile-emulsified fats to convert them to fatty acids and glycerol

726. Length of trachea is about:
A. 10-12 cm B. 18-20 cm
C. 20-25 cm D. 25-30 cm

727. Only one type of digestive juice contains carbohydrate, protein and fat-digesting enzymes. Which one is it?
A. Pancreatic Juice B. Saliva
C. Bile D. Intestinal Juice

728. What is the shape of cartilage rings found in trachea?
A. I-shaped B. J-shaped
C. T-shaped D. C-shaped

729. What action does pancreatic juice have on carbohydrate digestion?
A. Converts maltose to glucose
B. Converts sucrose to glucose and fructose
C. Converts polysaccharides and starches to maltose
D. All of the Above

730. Number of rings found in trachea ?
A. 12-14 B. 20-25
C. 16-20 D. 10-12

731. Retinoscopy is used for?
A. Testing visual acuity
B. To visualize angle structures
C. For fundus examination
D. To determine degree of refraction

732. Which part of ear is also known as labyrinth?
A. Outer ear B. Middle ear
C. Inner ear D. None of them

733. The major function of the watery bicarbonate secretion of the exocrine portion of the pancreas is:
A. To complete the digestion initiated in the stomach
B. To add water to the rather dry chyme entering the duodenum from the stomach
C. To facilitate the digestion of lipids
D. To neutralize the acid chyme from the stomach

734. Which of the following auditory ossicle is hammer shaped?
A. Incus B. Maleous
C. Stapes D. None of the Above

735. The major stimulus for the release of CCK is the presence of:
A. Bile in the intestine
B. Pancreatic juice in the intestine
C. Fatty acids and amino acids in the stomach or duodenum
D. Acidic chyme in the intestine

736. Semicircular canals are found in:
A. Outer ear B. Lateral ear
C. Inner ear D. Middle ear

737. Gastrin, which is secreted by stomach cells, functions to:
A. Inhibit the production of hydrochloric acid
B. Increase the secretions of the gastric glands
C. Change pepsin into pepsinogen
D. Initiate the cephalic phase of digestion

738. Which of the following structure separates the outer ear from the middle ear?
A. Vestibule membrane
B. Ear canal
C. Cochlear nerve
D. Tympanic membrane

739. Which of the following is not a characteristic of the large intestine?
A. A absorbs much of the water remaining in the waste material of undigested food
B. It is divided into ascending, transverse, and descending portions
C. Contains bacteria which synthesize certain vitamins
D. Serves as the main absorptive surface for digested foods

740. Which of The following artery supplies blood to the eye ?
A. Internal carotid artery
B. Left arch
C. Right Subclavian
D. External carotid

741. The most important function of the large intestine is:
A. Absorption of water and electrolytes
B. Secretion of enzymes
C. Digestion of incompletely digested foods
D. Removal of toxic substances

742. Macula lutea is found in:
A. Cornea B. Lens of eye
C. Iris of eye D. Retina of eye

743. Which of the following is a true statement?
A. Villi increase the absorptive surface of an organ
B. Digestion does not occur in the large intestine
C. Mass peristalsis occurs in the Large Intestine (LI) during defecation
D. All of the Above

744. Which of the following structure also known as blind spot?
A. Macula lutea. B. Rod and Cons
C. Optic disc D. Fovea centralis

745. Formation has occurred any excess glucose in the blood is:
A. Converted to lipid and stored as fat
B. Excreted by the kidney
C. Converted to urea
D. Is used in protein synthesis

746. Which of The following fluid found in Posterior segment of the eye is known as:
A. Vitreous body B. Cerumen
C. Aqueous fluid D. None of them

747. Blood glucose is actually:
A. Absorbed from GI tract
B. Released by the muscles into the blood when it isn't needed as energy source for contraction
C. Glycogen from the liver
D. The kinetic energy of the blood

748. What is the normal Intra ocular pressure ?
A. 30-40 mm Hg. B. 5-10 mm Hg
C. 25-30 mm Hg D. 10-20 mm Hg

749. Production of bile is one of several important functions of the
A. Gallbladder B. Liver
C. Pancreas D. Small intestine

750. Outer layer of skin is known as?
A. Dermis. B. Subcutaneous
C. Epidermis D. None of them

751. Bile is stored and concentrated in the
A. Gall bladder B. Liver
C. Biliary apparatus D. Duodenum

752. Which of The following maintain colour of skin?
A. Melanin B. Bile pigment
C. Hb D. None of them

753. After the hepatic treshhold for glycogen formation has occurred, any excess glucose in the blood is
A. Converted to lipid and stored as fat
B. Excreted by the kidneys
C. Converted to urea
D. B and C are correct

754. Which of the following coloured light has the longest wavelength?
A. Blue B. Yellow
C. Red D. Green

755. If an incision has to be made in the Small intestine (SI) to remove an obstruction, the first layer of tissue to be cut into is the
A. Muscularis B. Mucosa
C. Submucosa D. Serosa

756. Taste buds of sweet and salty tastes are found on:
A. Tip of tongue B. Sides of tongue
C. Back of tongue D. All of the Above

757. The fat-covered membrane protecting the SI and LI anteriorly is
A. Meninges B. Pleura
C. Peritoneum D. Mesentery

758. Which of The following part of eye generate impulses and help to see in dim light?
A. Rods B. Lens
C. Conjunctiva D. Cones

759. Gluconeogenesis?
A. Is concerned with synthesis of glycogen
B. Refers to the conversion of glycogen into glucose
C. Refers to the ability of the liver to form precursors for glucose using fats and proteins
D. Is a process resulting from deamination of amino acids

760. The Taste buds of bitter taste are found on?
A. Tip of tongue B. Sides of tongue
C. Back of tongue D. None of them

761. The end product of sugar metabolism is/are?
A. Maltose, lactose and sucrose
B. Carbon dioxide, water and heat and energy
C. Urea
D. Glucose and other simple sugars

762. Blood vessels are present in:
A. Epidermis layer B. Adipose tissue
C. Dermis layer D. None of them

763. The production of glucose-breakdown products from protein is called
A. Glycolysis B. Gluconeogenesis
C. Glycogenesis D. Glycogenolysis

764. Zygote is a:
A. Meeting of penis and vagina
B. Meeting of ovum and penis
C. Meeting of penis and uterus
D. Meeting of ovum and spermatozoa

765. Sternum is a:
A. Flat bone B. Sesamoid
C. Irregular bone D. Long bone

766. Example of irregular bone is:
A. Vertebrae B. Patella bones
C. Ribs D. Sternum

767. Bone destroying cells are:
A. Osteocytes B. Osteoblasts
C. Osteoclasts D. All of the Above.

768. Number of cervical vertebra are:
A. 5 B. 12 C. 3 D. 7

769. Number of thoracic vertebra are:
A. 4 B. 5 C. 12 D. 7

770. Number of lumbar vertebra are:
A. 5. B. 8 C. 7 D. 6

771. Total number of ribs are:
A. 12 pairs B. 10 pairs
C. 6 pairs D. 11 pairs

772. Hip bones are, except:
A. Ileum B. Pubis
C. Femur D. Ischium

773. Shoulder and hip joints are the examples of:
A. Ball and socket joint
B. Gliding joint
C. Pivot joint
D. Hinge joint

774. Synovial fluid is found in:
A. Ball and socket joint
B. Synovial joint
C. Pivot joint
D. All of the Above.

775. The joint found between humerus and radius ulna is:
A. Ball and socket joint
B. Hinge joint
C. Fixed joint
D. Pivot joint

776. Which vitamin is required for calcium and phosphate absorption from the intestinal tract:
A. Vitamin A B. Vitamin K
C. Vitamin D D. Vitamin B

777. Total number of muscles in the body are:
A. 200 B. 639
C. 402 D. 432

778 Which is the neurotransmitter believed to be decreased in cognitive disorders, such as Alzheimer's disease?
A. Acetylchcline B. Dopamine
C. Serotonin D. GABA

779. Which are the largest vertebra?
A. Cervical. B. Sacrum
C. Lumbar D. Thoracic

780. Total number of floating ribs are:
A. 5 pairs B. 1 pair.
C. 3 pairs D. 2 pairs

781. Only movable bone of skull is:
A. Nasal bones B. Mandible
C. Ethmoid D. Maxilla

782. Bones of cranium are except:
A. Frontal bone B. Ear ossicles
C. Temporal bone D. Sphenoid bone.

783. Number of parietal bones in cranium are:
A. 1. B. 4
C. 6 D. 2

784. The suture that joins the parietal bone with occipital bone is:
A. Coronal B. Frontal
C. Lambdoidal D. Sagittal

785. First bone of the vertebral column is:
A. Frontal B. Cervical
C. Stapes D. Atlas

786. Examples of long bones are, except:
A. Femur B. Fibula
C. Sternum D. Tibia

787. The bacteria which normally present in vagina?
A. Streptococci.
B. Corynebacterium
C. Lactobacillus acidophilus
D. E.coli

788. What is the benefit of acidity of vagina?
A. It makes sexual act easy.
B. It keeps vagina moist
C. It prevents the growth of microbes
D. It maintains normal temperature

789. Length of male urethra is approximately:
A. 18-20 cm B. 10-15 cm
C. 30-40 cm D. 10-12 cm

790. Weight of non-pregnant uterus is:
A. 1000 gms B. 150 gm
C. 50 gm D. 100 gms

791. The size of non-pregnant uterus in an adult is about (length, width and thick-ness):
A. 7.5 x 5 x 2.5 cm. B. 7.5 x 2.5 x 1.5cm
C. 5 x 2 x 1 cm D. 12.5 x 10 x 2.5 cm

792. Testosterone is secreted by:
A. Prostate gland
B. Testes
C. Interstitial cells of Leydig
D. Spermatic cord

793. Sperm are stored in:
A. Testes. B. Spermatic cord
C. Epididymis D. Prostate gland

794. The part of sperm which contains its DNA?
A. Head B. Legs
C. Tailed Body D. All of the Above

795. Which of the following is NOT true for the large intestine?
A. Secretes no enzymes
B. Absorbs large quantities of water
C. Secretes large quantities of mucus
D. Houses bacteria that synthesize Vit K

796. Maximum heat loss from the body occurs through the:
A. Lungs B. Liver
C. Skin D. Kidney

797. The first step in fat digestion is:
A. Formation of micelles
B. Breakdown of fatty acids by lipases
C. Formation of monoglycerides
D. Emulsification

798. Pancreatic secretions are stimulated by
A. Secretin
B. CCK
C. Impulses from the vagus nerve
D. All of the Above

799. Which of the following site take place for Fertilization?
A. Ampulla B. Fallopian tube
C. Uterus D. Isthmus

800. Which of the following is true of vitamins?
A. They function as coenzymes
B. They are not energy sources
C. They cannot generally be synthesized by the body
D. All of the Above

801. What is normal Length of fallopian tube?
A. 10 cm B. 5.5 cm
C. 1.5 cm D. 20 cm

802. Which of the following groups contain only water soluble vitamins?
A. A , B B. B , C
C. C , D D. D , E

803. Heat regulating centre is present in :
A. Pons
B. Cerebellum
C. Medulla oblongata
D. Hypothalamus

804. Glycogenolysis refers to
A. The formation of glycogen
B. The formation of urea
C. Conversion of fat and/ or protein to glucose
D. Conversion of glycogen to glucose

805. Which of the following site take place for Fertilization?
A. Vagina B. Fallopian tube
C. Uterus D. Ovarian duct

806. Glycogenolysis is promoted by
A. Glucagon
B. Growth hormone
C. Insulin
D. Both A and D are correct

807. Which of the following hormone is responsible for maturation of the follicles?
A. FSH.
B. ADH
C. Progesterone and Oxytocin
D. LH

808. The regulation of normal blood sugar level is accomplished by
A. Insulin, glucagons and adrenalin
B. Cell tissue absorption of glucose from the blood
C. The breakdown of glycogen by the liver
D. All of the Above

809. What is important Function of HCG?
A. Secretion of FSH
B. Help in fertilization
C. Secretion of LH
D. It stimulates the corpus luteum to continue secrete progesterone

810. Which aspect of swallowing is voluntary?
A. Movement of food into the pharynx
B. Movement of food through the pharynx
C. Movement of food into the esophagus
D. Movement of food through esophagus

811. Which of the following Thickest layer of uterine wall?
A. Perimetrium B. Myometrium
C. Endometrium D. None of them

812. Mixing of chime with digestive juices in the SI is achieved by
A. Mastication B. Segmentation
C. Peristalsis D. Churning

813. What is the normal Period of proliferative phase during Menstrual Cycle?
A. 28 days. B. 3 days
C. 10 days D. 7 days

814. **Stimulation of the parasympathetic nerve supply to the stomach**
A. Would increase peristalsis
B. Would decrease peristalsis
C. Would have no effect on peristalsis
D. All of the Above

815. **What is the normal interval of menstrual cycle?**
A. 7 days. B. 28 days
C. 14 days D. 10 days

816. **Which of the following is NOT correct?**
A. Final digestion of disaccharides is done by enzymes from pancreas
B. Sugars are absorbed as monosaccharides
C. Glucose is absorbed by active transport
D. Fructose is absorbed by facilitated diffusion

817. **What is the normal Period of secretory phase during Menstrual Cycle?**
A. 28 days. B. 3 days
C. 7 days D. 14 days

818. **Which of the following is NOT true of salivary amylase?**
A. It is an enzyme
B. It has a stable range of pH , from pH 4 to pH 9
C. It function best at pH 6.9 – 7.0
D. It splits starch into polysaccharides

819. **Sperms produced by:**
A. FSH a.ovary
B. Seminiferous tubules
C. Epididymis
D. None of the Above

820. **Which of the following is not part of the circulatory system.**
A. Heart B. Lungs
C. Blood D. Blood vessels

821. **Which is not a pulse in the body**
A. Carotid B. Radial
C. Femoral D. Temprial

822. **Progesterone is secreated by:**
A. FSH B. Oxytocin
C. LH D. Corpus luteum

823. **What is the thickness of Capillaries**
A. 1 cell thick B. 10 Cells Thick
C. 100 Cells Thick D. 100,000 Cells thick

824. **What is Menopause?**
A. Ovulation start
B. Join sperm and ovum
C. Cessation of Menstrual Cycle
D. Onset of Menstrual Cycle

825. **Which of the following Correct spelling ?**
A. Hemoglobin B. Haemoglobin
C. Hemoglowbin D. Heamowglobin

826. **What are the name of the Walls of uterus?**
A. Perimetrium B. Myometrium
C. Endometrium D. All of the Above

827. **What is normal Age of puberty in females?**
A. 8-10 years B. 18-20 years
C. 14-16 years D. 11-13 years

828. **What is normal Position of uterus?**
A.. Anteverted and retroflexed
B. Anteverted and ante flexed
C. Retrovertec and retroflexed
D. Extrovertec and ante flexed

829. **What is normal Blood pressure ?**
A. 140/80 B. 140/100
C. 120/80 D. 120/100

830. **What is the normal pH of vagina?**
A. 3.5-5. B. 6.5-7.5
C. 8-10 D. 1-3

831. **What is carried mainly in plasma**
A. White blood cells
B. Glucose
C. Carbon Dioxide
D. Oxygen

832. **Which of the following maintain ph of vagina?**
A. Bartholin's glands
B. Adrenal gland
C. Hypothalamus
D. None of the Above

833. **Vasodilatation is**
A. Vessels under the skin expand
B. Muscles expand
C. Vessels under the skin shrink
D. Muscles shrink

834. **Bartholin's glands are found in:**
A. Vagina B. Ureter
C. Uterus D. None of the Above

835. **Too cold is term known as:**
A. Hyperthermia B. Hypothermia
C. Lowthermic D. Hythermic

836. **What is an average Heart rate of a adult at rest?**
A. 40 B. 72
C. 85 D. 120

837. **The area of the brain which is involved in the understanding of meaning is:**
A. Broca's area
B. Association areas
C. Wernicke's area
D. Motor speech area

838. **During exercise**
A. Cell respiration increases
B. Cell respiration decreases
C. Oxygen production increases
D. CO_2 production decreases

839. How many red blood cells are there in a drop of blood
A. 15 million B. 50,000
C. ½ Million D. 5 million

840. What gives red blood cells their colour
A. Muscle B. Oxygen
C. Haemoglobin D. Plasma

841. Which of the following produce Cell mediated immunity?
A. Platelets B. RBCs
C. T-Lymphocytes D. B-lymphocytes

842. Which has no nucleus
A. White blood cells
B. Red blood cells
C. Heart cells
D. Lung cells

843. Which of the following is not Effect of histamine?
A. Vasodilatation.
B. Bronchoconstriction
C. Vasoconstriction
D. Increased vascular permeability

844. Which contains Oxygenated blood
A. Pulmonary artery
B Right ventricle
C. Left Ventricle
D. Venules

845. What is the normal pH of saliva?
A. <7 B. 10
C. >7 D. None of the Above

846. The neurons of motor pathway control:
A. Stress reaction
B. Organs and glands
C. Involuntary muscles
D. Voluntary muscles

847. Fetal blood cell formation takes place in:
A. Spleen B. Bone marrow
C. Liver D. All of the Above

848. In the circulatory system, which is correct
A. Right ventricle, Semi-lunar valve, Pulmonary artery, Lungs
B. Left ventricle, Semi-lunar valve, Pulmonary artery, Lungs
C. Right ventricle, Semi-lunar valve, Pulmonary Vein, Lungs
D. Left ventricle, Semi-lunar valve, Pulmonary Vein, Lungs

849. Which of the following is the final product of blood clotting process?
A. Prothrombine B. Fibrin
C. Fibrinogen D. Thrombopastin

850. What is the correct name for red blood cells
A. Erythrocytes B. Leucocytes
C. Phagocytes D. Megabytes

851. What is responsible for blood clotting
A. Plasma B. Platelets
C. Corpuscules D. Protein

852. Spleen lies in:
A. Left hypochondriac region
B. Hypochondriac region
C. Pelvic cavity
D. Right hypochondriac region

853. How much % of water is in blood
A. 60 B. 70
C. 80 D. 90

854. A substance which produces vasoconstriction and released by platelets is called:
A. Prothrombine B. Prostaglandins
C. GABA D. Serotonin

855. What is not a function of blood
A. Carries waste products away
B. Controls temperature
C. Controls balance of chemicals in body
D. Produces acid

856. Which of the following electrolyte is helpful in blood clotting?
A. Na^+ B. Ca^{+2}
C. Iron D. K^+

857. The life span of platelets are?
A. 5-7 days B. 28-35 days
C. 120 days D. 8-11 days

858. Phagocytes do what ?
A. Eat germs
B. Produce bacteria
C. Stop smokers smoking
D. Make red blood cells

859. What is normal number of WBC in an healthy adult ?
A. 2.5-4.5 million/mm^3 blood
B. 1.5-4.5 lack
C. 4000-11000/mm^3 blood
D. 8-12 million/mm^3 blood

860. Smallest blood vessels are
A. Arteries B. Arterioles
C. Venules D. Capillaries

861. What is the normal platelet count in human blood ?
A. 4000-11000/mm^3 blood.
B. 10000-110000/mm^3 blood
C. 150000-450000/mm^3 blood
D. 50,000-150000/mm^3 blood

862. How much blood is in the body
A. 5 litres B. 5 pints
C. 15 litre D. 15 pints

863. The blood cells help in phagocytises and produce immunity in a client?
A. WBCs B. RBCs
C. Platelets D. None of the Above

864. Where does oxygenated blood giver up its oxygen
A. Lungs B. Muscles
C. Right ventricle D. Left ventricle

865. Largest blood cell is:
A. Erythrocyte. B. Platelets
C. Thrombocytes D. Leucocytes

866. Which is the only artery to carry de-oxygenated blood
A. Carotid B. Femoral
C. Bracial D. Pulmonary

867. The main site for destruction of RBC is?
A.. Liver B. Spleen
C. Bone marrow D. Kidney

868. Another name for the bicuspid valve is the?
A. Mitral B. Pitral
C. Vitral D. Bitral

869. The condition which primarily increases erythropoiesis, is:
A. Hypoxia B. Low temperature
C. Low pH D. High pH

870. Heart muscle is
A. Voluntary muscle
B. Muscle
C. Carotid muscle
D. Involuntary Cardiac muscle

871. What is normal number of RBC count in an adult ?
A. 1-3 million/mm^3 blood.
B. 1000-1200/mm^3 blood
C. 8-10 million
D. 4.5-6.5 million/mm^3 blood

872. Formula for cardiac output is ?
A. SV/HR B. HR/SV
C. HR + SV D. HR x SV

873. Colour of blood is bright red due to presence of?
A. Hb and iron
B. Carboxyhaemoglobin
C. Oxyhaemoglobin
D. RBC and platelets

874. If individual has Heart rate of 60, Stroke rate of 150ml Cardiac output is ?
A. 900 ml B. 9000 ml
C. 2.5 ml D. 25 ml

875. RBC is produced in?
A. Liver
B. Heart
C. Red bone marrow
D. Blood brain barrier

876. Wall down the middle of the heart is called the ?
A. Hexum B. Pentum
C. Octum D. Septum

877. Which of the following is not associated with the role of the kidneys?
A. Release of erythropoietin (hormone)
B. Release of renin (enzyme)
C. Release of Vitamin E
D. Activate Vitamin D

878. The highest blood pressure is found in the ?
A. Venules B. Aorta
C. Arteries D. Veins

879. The diameter of RBC is about?
A. 5 u B. 10 u
C. 12 u D. 7.2 u

880. Walls are thickest in the?
A. Right atrium B. Right ventricle
C. Left atrium D. Left ventricle

881. Which brain structure is most responsible for our balance, posture and muscle tone?
A. Medulla oblongata
B. Cerebellum
C. Reticular system
D. Pons

882. Where would you find valves
A. Arterioles B. Capillaries
C. Veins D. Lungs

883. Formation of large molecule from smaller molecules is called as:
A. Anabolism B. Metabolism
C. Digestion D. Catabolism

884. What circulation carries oxygenated blood to the body
A. Systemic B. Bodily
C. Muscular D. Pulmonary

885. The process of breakdown of large molecule into smaller molecules is known as:
A. Anabolism B. Metabolism
C. Digestion D. Catabolism

886. What colour is oxygenated blood
A. Red B. Blue
C. Purple D. White

887. What is normal Shape of gallbladder ?
A. Pear B. Round
C. O shape D. Bean

888. S.A node is the pacemaker of heart because of
A. Location in the right atrium
B. Neural control
C. Natural leakiness to Na+
D. Natural leakiness to K+

889. Kuffer cells are found in:
A. Brain B. Small Intestine
C. Liver D. Stomach

890. Absolute refractory period in the heart
A. Corresponds to the duration of relaxation
B. Lasts till half of cardiac contraction
C. Shorter than refractory period in skeletal muscle
D. Lasts till cardiac contraction

891. Normal Brown colour of stool is due to presence of:
A. Urobillinogen B. Intake of food
C. Stercobilin D. Bile

892. First heart sound occurs during the period of
A. Isometric relaxation
B. Isotonic relaxation
C. Isovolumetric contraction
D. Isovolumetric relaxation

893. What is normal Length of large intestine?
A. 1 meter. B. 2.0 meter
C. 2.5 meter D. 1.5 meter

894. Which of these vessels does not have sympathetic control
A. Cerebral B. Splanchnic
C. Cardiac D. Cutaneous

895. What is function of Bile?
A. Digestion of fat
B. Emulsification of glucose
C. Digestion of protein
D. Emulsification of fat

896. Blood brain barrier is made up of
A. Astrocytes B. Oligodendrocytes
C. Oligodendroglia D. Microglia

897. Amount of bile secreted daily is:
A. 300-500 ml. B. 1800-2000 ml
C. 1200-1500 ml D. 500-1000 ml

898. Positive bathmotropic effect on heart is produced by
A. Stimulation of vagus nerve
B. Stimulation of sympathetic nerves
C. Atropin
D. Sectioning of vagus

899. What is the name of end product after digestion of protein?
A. Glucose B. Amino acid
C. Lactic acid D. Fatty acid

900. Mary's law denotes relationship between heart and
A. Contractility and conductivity
B. Rate and contraction
C. Rate and BP
D. Contraction and BP

901. What is the name of largest part of small intestine ?
A. Jejunum B. Duodenum
C. Ileum D. None of them

902. Which of the following conducting systems has the slowest conducting velocity
A. SA Node B. Atrial muscle
C. Purkinje fibres D. AV Node

903. Most important component of oral contraceptive agents is
A. Thyroxine B. LH
C. Progesterone D. GH

904. In heart, within physiological limits the force of contraction is directly proportional to the
A. Pacemaker activity
B. AV nodal delay
C. Initial length of the cardiac muscle
D. Respiratory rate

905. What is normal Length of duodenum?
A. 25 cm. B. 10 cm
C. 30 cm D. 15 cm

906. The diacrotic notch on aortic pressure curve is caused by
A. Closure of mitral valve
B. Closure of tricuspid valve
C. Closure of atrial valve
D. Closure of pulmonary valve

907. Which of the following organ absorbed maximum part of food?
A. Small intestine B. Intrinsic factor
C. Large intestine D. Abdomen

908. The PR interval of ECG corresponds to
A. Ventricular repolarization
B. Ventricular repolarization
C. Atrial repolarization and conduction through AV node
D. Repolarization of AV node and bundle of His

909. Which of the following is not a Function of stomach?
A. Temporary storage of food.
B. Production of intrinsic factor
C. Absorption of food
D. Digestion of food

910. Increased vagal tone causes
A. Hypertension
B. Tachycardia
C. Bradycardia
D. Increase in cardiac output

911. Which of the following is not increased during exercise
A. Stroke volume
B. Total peripheral resistance
C. Systolic BP
D. Heart rate

912. ADH has which of the following effects on the distal convoluted tubule?
A. Decrease water re-absorption
B. Increase water re-absorption
C. Decrease the concentration of urine
D. Increase the urine volume

913. Which of the following takes longest time to return to normal after 1L of blood is removed from a normal individual
A. Number of RBC's in peripheral blood
B. Plasma volume
C. Renin secretion
D. Blood pressure

914. What is the main Function of intrinsic factor ?
A. Digestion of food.
B. Digestion of food
C. Absorption of glucose and amino acid
D. Absorption of Vitamin B_{12}

915. When a pheochromocytoma suddenly discharges a large amount of epinephrine into the circulation the patients heart rate would be expected to
A. Increase because epinephrine has a direct chronotropic effect on the heart
B. Increase because of increased parasympathetic discharge to the heart
C. Decrease because the increase in blood pressure stimulates the carotid and aortic baroreceptors
D. Decrease because of increased tonic parasympathetic discharge to heart

916. Which of the following Enzyme present in gastric juice?
A. Tripsin B. Gastrin
C. Pepsin D. Ptyalin

917. In a patient with mitral stenosis one would expect to hear
A. Continuous murmur
B. A systolic murmur loudest over the base of heart
C. A diastolic murmur loudest over the apex of heart
D. A diastolic murmur loudest over the base of heart

918. Intrinsic factor found in gastric juice which is secreted by:
A. Mammary gland B. Goblet cells
C. Parietal cells D. Salivary glands

919. The 's' wave in ECG is below isoelectric line because of
A. Repolarization of ventricles
B. Change in direction of the impulse when the base of the ventricles are getting depolarised
C. Depolarisation of apex of heart
D. Repolarisation of apex of heart

920. Which of the following is not present in Gastric juice?
A. Pepsin B. Intrinsic factor
C. Amylase D. HC1

921. Which of the following is least likely to cause hypertension
A. Chronically increased secretion of adrenal medulla
B. Treatment with OCP
C. Chronically increased secretion of thyroid gland
D. Chronically increased secretion by zona glomerulosa of adrenal cortex

922. What is The normal amount of gastric juice secreted in a day?
A. 2 litter B. 0.5 litter
C. 1.0 litter D. 1.5 litter

923. Lymph flow from the foot is?
A. Increased when an individual rises from the supine to standing position
B. Increased by massaging the foot
C. Increased when capillary permeability is decreased
D. Decreased by exercise

924. Stomach is continuous with duodenum at?
A. Cardiac sphincter B. Oddi's sphincter
C. Pyloric sphincter D. None of them

925. The pressure in the radial artery is determined by?
A. The degree of constriction of brachial vein
B. The rate of discharge in sympathetic nerve fibres to the arm
C. Pressure in the hepatic portal vein
D. Pressure in the brachial vein

926. Largest salivary gland is?
A. Parotid gland B. Pancreas gland
C. Sublingual gland D. None of them

927. **The 'T' wave in ECG is above the isoelectric line because of**
A. Depolarisation of ventricles
B. Depolarisation of bundle of His
C. Change in the direction of repolarisation from the wave of depolarization of the ventricles
D. Repolarisation of purkinje fibres

928. **What is the normal Length of oesophagus ?**
A. 25cm B. 20 cm
C. 10 cm D. 15 cm

929. **Which is LEAST LIKELY to cause high-output heart failure?**
A. Anemia
B. High fever
C. Hypertrophic cardiomyopathy
D. Hyperthyroidism

930. **Which of the following artery supply Blood to intestine ?**
A. Coeliac artery
B. Superior mesenteric artery
C. Inferior mesenteric artery
D. All of the Above.

931. **"Fibrolipomatosis", a newly-discovered cause of sudden death in athletic young people, is usually found by the pathologist in the**
A. Aortic valve cusps
B. Right atrium
C. Right ventricle
D. Left atrium

932. **The enzyme present in saliva is:**
A. Pepsin B. Insulin
C. Amylase D. Tripsin

933. **At autopsy of a "victim" of cocaine abuse, which of these would be most helpful to the pathologist in confirming that cocaine actually caused the death?**
A. Amyloid deposition
B. Contraction band necrosis
C. Endocardial fibrosis
D. Mycotic aneurysm(s)

934. **Which of the following are cutting teeth?**
A. Premolar
B. Molar
C. Incisor and Canine
D. None of them

935. **What did the brewers in Quebec add to their beer, causing the epidemic cardiomyopathy?**
A. Adriamycin B. Cobalt
C. Dioxin D. Homocysteine

936. **What are the Number of temporary teeth ?**
A. 18 B. 24 C. 28 D. 32

937. **Which of these bacteria is most likely to set up acute bacterial endocarditis on a previously-normal valve?**
A. Clostridia
B. Staphylococcus
C. Streptococcus pyogenes
D. Streptococcus viridiens

938. **What are the Functions of tongue ?**
A. Speech B. Deglutition
C. Mastication D. All of the Above.

939. **Cardiomyopathy of pregnancy is most closely related epidemiologically to**
A. Alcohol abuse
B. Folic acid deficiency
C. High salt intake
D. Poverty

940. **Temporary teeth starts to erupt in children by?**
A. 6 months. B. 4 months
C. 8 months D. 1 year

941. **Which systemic disease often features sterile vegetations located on the surfaces of valve leaflets, and not just their lines of closure?**
A. Amyloidosis B B. Hemophilia
C. Lupus D. Rheumatoid arthritis

942. **Which bone attached base of Tongue?**
A. Stapes bone B. Scapoid bone
C. Hyoid bone D. Palatine bones .

943. **What accumulates in the heart in Pompe's disease?**
A. Cholesterol B. Glycogen
C. Lipofuscin D. Mitochondria

944. **Largest taste buds is called:**
A. Celiac B. Vallate
C. Filiform D. Fungi form

945. **Which is most likely to produce tricuspid valve stenosis?**
A. Carcinoid heart disease
B. Ebstein's anomaly
C. Endocarditis from IV drug use
D. Severe atherosclerosis

946. **Bile is stored in?**
A. Gallbladder B. Lungs
C. Pancreas D. Liver

947. **In Kawasaki's disease, you will probably NOT see**
A. Enlarged lymph nodes containing granulomas
B. Erythema of the palms
C. Fever
D. Reddening of the oral mucosa

948. **What's the major risk factor for Buerger's thromboangiitis obliterans?**
A. Alcohol abuse B. Cocaine use
C. Old age D. Smoking

949. Mesenteric/Auerbach's plexus is found in:
A. Muscle layer
B. Hair
C. Gastric Mucosa layer
D. Sub mucosa layer

950. In Osler-Weber-Rendu, you'll first notice the little vascular malformations on the
A. Conjunctiva B. Digits
C. Lips D. Retina

951. Unable to make HDL
A. Common familial hypercholesterolemia
B. Milroy's disease
C. Noonan's syndrome
D. Tangier's disease

952. Outer layer of blood vessels tract is known as:
A. Perimetrium B. Endometrial
C. Adventitia D. Sub mucosa

953. Which is most typical in Down's syndrome?
A. Atrial septal defect just above crux of heart
B. Coarctation of the aorta
C. Sinus venosus defect
D. Very low-placed tricuspid valve

954. Which of the following is the largest serous membranes of the body?
A. Pericardium B. Peritoneum
C. Myometrium D. None of them

955. Sudden death during sleep in a 30 year old Laotian man with no known coronary risk factors suggests
A. Brugada's
B. Cardiac syndrome X
C. Lipoprotein LpS2
D. Lpa

956. Which fact about a group of vegetations would be most helpful in letting you know that it's Libman-Sacks (as in lupus anticoagulant syndrome) rather than marantic endocarditis (as in cancer of the pancreas)?
A. Contain numerous plasma cells
B. Cause damage to the underlying valve
C. Contain hematoxylin bodies
D. Not confined to lines of closure

957. Sperms produce an enzymatic substance for dissolving egg coverings. It is called
A. Hyaluronic acid B. Hyaluronidase
C. Androgamone D. Diastase

958. What's the eponym for angina caused by coronary spasm?
A. Buerger's B. Ebstein's
C. Heberden's D. Prinzmetal's

959. A healthy, sedentary adult's heart usually weighs no more than
A. 150 gm B. 250 gm
C. 350 gm D. 450 gm

960. Which of the following organ acts as a temporary reservoir of urine?
A. Kidney B. Urinary bladder
C. Ureter D. Henal of loop

961. Wavy fibers in the absence of other myocardial pathology suggest what to the autopsy pathologist?
A. Amyloidosis
B. Cobalt cardiomyopathy
C. Hypertrophic cardiomyopathy
D. Sudden coronary death

962. Most "unstable angina" is probably due to
A. A thrombus forming and lysing
B. Extreme hypercholesterolemia and rapid atherogenesis
C. Multiple emboli to the coronaries
D. Serial hemorrhages within a plaque

963. What is normal weight of adult kidney?
A. 30 gm. B. 50 gm
C. 100 gm D. 150 gm

964. Which is most likely to produce dextrocardia, i.e., a heart on the right side instead of the left?
A. Down's syndrome
B. Fetal alcohol syndrome
C. Immotile cilia syndrome
D. Rubella in the unborn child

965. Which of The following hormone increases water reabsorption ?
A. ADH.
B. Parathyroid hormone
C. Calcitonin
D. Thyroxin

966. Which structure is most likely to rupture as a result of Barlow's syndrome?
A. Mitral chorda
B. Papillary muscle body
C. Posterior leaflet, longitudinally
D. Posterior leaflet, transversely

967. Erythropoietin hormone produces and secretes by:
A. Liver B. Heart
C. Kidney D. Lung

968. Which is LEAST LIKELY to give you a dilated cardiomyopathy?
A. Amyloid cardiomyopathy
B. Autoimmune cardiomyopathy
C. Chagas's cardiomyopathy
D. Duchenne's cardiomyopathy

969. Listen carefully to your ankylosing spondylitis patients because they are much more likely than other folks to develop
A. Aortic insufficiency
B. Aortic stenosis
C. Carotid bruits
D. Mitral insufficiency

970. The normal pH of urine is:
A. 7.35 B. 8.4
C. 7.4 D. 6.8

971. Finding a Weibel-Palade body on electron microscopy establishes that the cell is
A. Endothelium B. Myocardium
C. Myointima D. Neoplastic

972. Glucose is completely reabsorbed by is:
A. Convoluted tubules
B. Urethra
C. Kidney
D. Uric acid

973. A folic-acid deficient diet probably places a person at risk for coronary disease by raising plasma
A. Homocysteine B. Homogentisic acid
C. Oxidized LDL D. Lipoprotein A

974. What is normal GFR in adult?
A. 20 ml/min. B. 300 ml/min
C. 125 ml/min D. 100 ml/min

975. You are LEAST LIKELY to see hyper plastic arteriolar sclerosis as a result of
A. Hemolytic-uremic syndrome from E. coli
B. Malignant hypertension
C. Scleroderma
D. Severe diabetes

976. Bowman's capsule is found in:
A. Kidney B. Brain
C. Lung D. Stomach

977. The myocardial hypertrophy seen in patients with aortic stenosis, which is often extreme but which usually allows the heart to empty adequately, is considered an example of:
A. Concentric hypertrophy
B. Eccentric hypertrophy
C. Egocentric hypertrophy
D. Hypertrophic cardiomyopathy

978. Which of The following artery supplies blood to kidney ?
A. Hepatic artery B. Common iliac artery
C. Renal artery D. Common artery

979. Which of the following techniques uses a sugar to look at the functioning of the brain?
A. EEG B. CT scan
C. MRI scan D. PET scan

980. Which of The following gland is situated on superior part of kidney ?
A. Thymus gland B. Parathyroid gland
C. Adrenal gland D. Pituitary gland

981. In "sudden cardiac death" without an acute coronary artery lesion, the pathologist usually finds at least what percent stenosis of all three coronary arteries?
A. 50-55% B. 60-65%
C. 70-75% D. 80-85%

982. Kidneys are situated in:
A. Thoracic cavity B. Oral cavity
C. Pelvic cavity D. Abdominal cavity

983. In long QT syndrome caused by a potassium channel mutation, sudden death commonly occurs during participation in what sport?
A. Basketball
B. Being struck in the chest by a baseball
C. Skiing (cold exposure)
D. Swimming

984. Renin hormone is produced and secreated by:
A. Lungs B. Liver
C. Kidney D. Brain

985. In classic tertiary syphilis, the valve lesion was
A. Aortic insufficiency
B. Aortic stenosis
C. Mitral stenosis
D. Papillary fibroelastoma

986. Which of The following blood vessels link the artery and vein ?
A. Coronary artery B. Aorta
C. Capillaries D. Arterioles

987. Which portion of the mitral valve is most likely to calcify as a result of old age?
A. Annulus B. Anterior leaflet
C. Chordae D. Papillary muscle

988. What's the common cardiac malformation in fetal alcohol syndrome?
A. Chiari meshwork
B. Ebstein's anomaly
C. Patent ductus arteriosus
D. Ventricular septal defect

989. Sebaceous glands are not found on:
A. Axilla B. Palms of the hands
C. Soles of feet D. Both B and C

990. A very widely patent foramen ovale, causing an atrial septal defect, is described as
A. Lutembacher's syndrome
B. Ostium primum defect
C. Ostium secundum defect
D. Roger's disease

991. Which of the following is the longest vein in the body?
A. Femoral vein.
B. Superior vena cava
C. Inferior vena cava
D. Great sephaneous vein

992. Uncomplicated hypertension and diabetes are most likely to produce what change at the level of the arterioles?
A. Amyloidosis
B. Atherosclerosis
C. Hyaline sclerosis
D. Intimal onionskinning

993. A newborn infant presents with cyanotic heart disease and fails to thrive. On examination of the heart, it was revealed that the aorta arose from the right ventricle and the pulmonary trunk arose from the left ventricle. What is the name given to this type of cardiac malformation?
A. Transposition of the great vessels
B. Ventricular septal defect (VSD)
C. Atrial-septal defect (ASD)
D. Tetralogy of Fallot

994. Which of the following is the largest vein in the body?
A. Superior vena cava B. Sephaneous vein
C. Inferior vena cava D. Femoral vein

995. Which of the choices below is not a functional process performed by the respiratory system?
A. Pulmonary ventilation
B. Transport of respiratory gases
C. External respiration
D. Pulmonary respiration

996. Melanin is secreted in:
A. Cornium layer. B. Germinative layer
C. Granulosum layer D. Dermis layer

997. Complete the following statement using the choices below. Air moves out of the lungs when the pressure inside the lungs is
A. Less than the pressure in the atmosphere.
B. Greater than the pressure in the atmosphere.
C. Equal to the pressure in the atmosphere.
D. Greater than the intra-alveolar pressure.

998. Unlike inspiration, expiration is a passive act because no muscular contractions are involved Expiration, however, depends on two factors. Which of the choices below lists those two factors?
A. The recoil of elastic fibers that were stretched during inspiration and the inward pull of surface tension due to the film of alveolar fluid
B. The expansion of respiratory muscles that were contracted during inspiration and the lack of surface tension on the alveolar wall
C. The negative feedback of expansion fibers used during inspiration and the outward pull of surface tension due to surfactant
D. Combined amount of CO_2 in the blood and air in the alveoli

999. Which of the following artery supplies the pancreas?
A. Coronary B. Abdominal
C. Hepatic D. Splenic artery

1000. Which of the following is NOT a function of the lungs?
A. Metabolism
B. Serves as a reservoir of blood for the left ventricle.
C. It is a filter to protect the systemic vasculature
D. All of the Above

1001. Part of sperm involved in penetrating egg membrane is
A. Tail B. Acrosome
C. Allosome D. Autosome

1002. Which of the following is NOT an effector of respiration?
A. Heart B. Diaphragm
C. Intercostals D. Trapezius.

1003. Which of the following is the first branching of the bronchial tree that has gas exchanging capabilities?
A. Terminal bronchioles.
B. Respiratory bronchioles.
C. Alveoli
D. Segmental bronchi

1004. Which of the following could NOT be part of an acinus?
A. Alveolar sacs
B. Alveolar ducts
C. Terminal bronchioles
D. Respiratory bronchiole

1005. The heart sound lub is heard due to:
A. Closure of the atrioventricular valves
B. Opening of the aortic and pulmonary valves
C. Closure of the aortic and pulmonary valves
D. Opening of the atrioventricular valves

1006. If you increased the left atrial pressure from 5 mmHg to 15 mmHg, what effect would that have on pulmonary circulation?
A. It would force blood the opposite direction.

B. It would increase the speed at which blood moves through the pulmonary circulation.
C. No change.
D. Blood flow would almost or completely stop.

1007. Which of the following Taste buds found at the sides of the tongue?
A. Sweet taste buds B. Bitter taste buds
C. Salty taste buds D. Sour taste buds

1008. Which of the following concerning average lung volumes and capacities of a person at rest is TRUE?
A. TLC>VC>TV>FRC
B. TLC>FRC>VC>TV
C. TLC>VC>FRC>TV
D. TLC>FRC>TV>VC

1009. The heart sound 'dub' is heard due to:
A. Closure of the atrioventricular valves.
B. Opening of the aortic and pulmonary valves
C. Closure of the aortic and pulmonary valves
D. Opening of the atrioventricular valves

1010. Which of the following is NOT a normal occurance with increasing age?
A. Vital capacity of the lung decreases.
B. Residual volume increases.
C. Functional residual capacity increases.
D. Expiratory reserve volume increases.

1011. Which of the following spirometry measurements has the greatest sensitivity for detecting early air flow obstruction?
A. FVC B. FEV1
C. FFE D. FEF25-75

1012. Which of the following known as pulse regulation center ?
A. SANode B. Bundle of His
C. Purkinje fibers D. AV Node

1013. Which of the following does NOT happen during inspiration?
A. The ribs move upward.
B. The diaphragm lifts up.
C. The antero-posterior dimensions of the chest are increased.
D. The tranverse dimensions of the thorax are increased.

1014. Which of The following vein carries oxygenated blood?
A. Hepatic B. Pulmonary
C. Gastric D. All of the Above

1015. During inspiration, how does alveolar pressure compare to atmospheric pressure?
A. Alveolar pressure is greater than atmospheric.
B. Alveolar pressure is less than atmospheric.
C. Alveolar pressure is the same as atmospheric.
D. Alveolar pressure is one of the few pressures where the reference pressure is not atmospheric.

1016. Failure of testis to descend into the scrotum is called
A. Paedogenesis B. Castration
C. Cryptorchidism D. Impotency

1017. Which of the following represents the pressure difference that acts to distend the lungs?
A. Alveolar pressure
B. Airway opening pressure
C. Transthoracic pressure
D. Transpulmonary pressure

1018. Which of the following is not considered a component of kidney stones?
A. Calcium phosphate B. Uric Acid
C. Calcium oxalate D. HCO_3

1019. According to the Law of Laplace, air should flow from the smaller alveoli to the larger, collapsing them. In the lungs, several factors counter that tendency, and stabilize the alveolar structures. Which of the following is NOT one of them?
A. Surfactant lowers surface tension to a greater degree when it is on a smaller surface area, allowing the smaller alveoli to stay open.
B. Mechanical stability is given by surrounding alveoli.
C. Transpulmonary pressure is lower for smaller alveoli, allowing them to stabilize in comparison to the bigger ones.
D. Surface tension at the gas-liquid interface increases as alveolar surface area increases.

1020. Which of the following is FALSE concerning the production and role of lung surfactant?
A. It is part of a lipoprotein called dipalmitoyl phosphatidyl-choline.
B. It is synthesized by alveolar type II cells.
C. As the alveolar surface area decreases during the compression curve, the surfactant decreases the surface tension at a constant rate.
D. When surfactant density is decreased during expansion, surface tension initially rises rapidly, then slows down until it reaches the starting point.

1021. What is the function of vasopressin?
A. Vasoconstriction
B. Reduction in urine output
C. Increase in systemic BP
D. All of the Above

1022. Which of the following is NOT true concerning respiratory distress syndrome in premature infants?
A. Their ability to synthesize DPPC is limiteD.
B. Higher pressures are required to ventilate the lungs.
C. Lung compliance is low
D. Alveoli tend to over expand and sometimes burst at the end of inspiration.

1023. A patient have vasopressin deficiency ,what is expectation by nurse?
A. Reduction in urine output
B. Increase in systemic BP
C. Increase in urine output
D. None of them

1024. Which of the following is NOT true at FRC?
A. It is about 75% TLC.
B. The elastic recoil of the chest wall is outward.
C. The elastic recoil of the lung is inward.
D. The relaxation pressure of the lung and chest wall combined is at atmospheric pressure.

1025. If the lung were punctured, which of the following would happen?
A. The lung would collapse on the side of the puncture.
B. Both the lung and the chest wall would collapse on the side of the puncture.
C. The relaxation pressure of the chest wall would increase until it surpassed the atmospheric.
D. The relaxation pressure of the chest wall would increase, but stop before it reached atmospheric pressure.

1026. Which of the following hormone is responsible and essential for milk production in female?
A. Prolactine B. FSH
C. ADH D. Oxytocin

1027. Which of the following is FALSE concerning the airflow in the lungs?
A. During inspiration and expiration, the flow in the trachea and larger bronchi is turbulent.
B. Towards the middle of the bronchial tree, the flow is turbulent at the branches and laminar in between.
C. Near the end of the bronchial tree, the flow is laminar.
D. The acini have very small radii which significantly increases the total air flow resistance of the bronchial tree.

1028. Which of the following is FALSE concerning airway resistance?
A. Up to 50% is in the nose.
B. The maximum resistance in the bronchial tree occurs at the fourth generation.
C. In the later generations, the radii are smaller, increasing the total resistance at each successive generation.
D. Airway resistance can be increased by loss of tissue elasticity and contraction of bronchial smooth muscles.

1029. Which of the following hormone is also known as vasopressin?
A. ADH B. TSH
C. Oxytocin D. ACTH

1030. Which of the following is FALSE concerning the effect of effort on airflow and volume during inspiration and expiration?
A. During inspiration, greater effort always results in greater flow.
B. Peak expiratory flow occurs at the beginning of expiration.
C. At low and moderate lung volumes, the greater the effort above threshold, the greater the airflow in expiration.
D. Portions of the expiration curve are effort independent.

1031. Which of the following hormone plays an important role in milk ejection?
A. Prolaction B. FSH
C. TSH D. Oxytocin.

1032. If the equal pressure point during expiration is in the lobar bronchi, which of the following is TRUE?
A. Expiratory flow would be effort dependent.
B. Expiratory flow would be effort independent.
C. The bronchi beyond the equal pressure point would compress.
D. This situation would only occur during medium and low lung volumes.

1033. Which of the following does NOT apply to the alveoli at the base of the lungs?
A. They are less elastic than the alveoli at the apex.
B. The pleural pressure is lower.
C. At FRC they are less inflated than the alveoli at the apex.
D. They are closed at RV.

1034. Which of the following is FALSE concerning the closing volume for the lung?
A. Comes between Phase 3 and Phase 4 on the single breath N2 washout curve.
B. Marks the point where the alveoli at the apex close.
C. Marks a sudden increase in nitrogen concentration in the expelled breath.
D. Marks when the overinflated, poorly ventilated alveoli at the apex expel their air with high N2 concentrations.

1035. Oxytocin is secreted by:
A. Thymus gland B. Adrenal cortex
C. Anterior pituitary D. Posterior pituitary

1036. Which of the following is TRUE if a patient breathes slower than normal with increased tidal volumes?
A. More resistive work is done.
B. The total work done decreases.
C. More elastic work is done.
D. Compliance is decreased.

1037. Which of the following is INCORRECT concerning the efficiency of breathing and the oxygen consumption of the respiratory muscles?
A. Efficiency is defined as the ratio of mechanical work done to move air to the amount of metabolic energy used by the respiratory muscles.
B. The respiratory system uses less than 3% of the body's total oxygen consumption at rest.
C. Respiratory muscles are more efficient than large muscle groups.
D. Emphysema increases the oxygen requirement for respiratory muscles.&

1038. An area of neurons running through the middle of the medulla and pons, and is responsible for keeping people alert and aroused as well selective attention to certain information:
A. Cerebellum B. Hypothalamus
C. Limbic system D. Reticular system

1039. In what situation would the gas exchange ratio be decreased compared to the respiratory quotient?
A. During slowed breathing.
B. Holding your breath.
C. During hyperventilation.
D. Impossible. The two are always equivalent.

1040. Which of the following endocrine gland secretes FSH and LH?
A. Posterior pituitary B. Anterior pituitary
C. Adrenal gland D. Thymus gland

1041. A 140 lb woman would have approximately how much dead space in her lungs?
A. 140 ml. B. 70 ml.
C. 280 ml. D. 35 ml.

1042. How do you calculate how much inspired air actually ventilates the alveoli during one minute?
A. Subtract the volume of dead space from the tidal volume.
B. Subtract both the dead space volume that was already in the lungs plus the dead space of the inspired air that won't reach the alveoli from the tidal volume.
C. Subtract the volume of dead space from the tidal volume and multiply it by the number of breaths per minute.
D. It is equal to the tidal volume times the frequency of breathing.

1043. Which of the following is NOT a function of dead space?
A. Warms expired air to body temperature.
B. Saturates inspired air with water vapor.
C. Removes bacteria and other particulate matter.
D. Conducts the warmed air to the respiratory membranes.

1044. The pituitary gland lies in the:
A. Fossa of ethmoid bone
B. Fossa of occipital bone
C. Fossa of sphenoid bone
D. None of them

1045. To which of the following is alveolar PCO2 directly proportional?
A. Rate of CO_2 production and alveolar ventilation.
B. Rate of CO_2 production and rate of O_2 consumption.
C. Alveolar ventilation and rate of O_2 consumption.
D. Alveolar ventilation, rate of O_2 consumption, and rate of CO_2 production.

1046. Which of the following gland secretes tears?
A. Sweat gland B. Adrenal
C. Lacrimal D. Sebaceous

1047. If a patient's blood carries 10 grams of Hb per deciliter, what is the O2 carrying capacity of his blood?
A. 18 milliliters per deciliter.
B. 20 milliliters per deciliter.
C. 10 milliliters per deciliter.
D. 13 millliliters per deciliter.

1048. Loss of sense of smell is known as:
A. Agnosia B. Aphasia
C. Apraxia D. Anosmia .

1049. Which of the following definitions is FALSE?

A. O_2 content of blood is the actual amount of O_2 in one deciliter of blood.

B. O_2 saturation of blood is the ratio of O_2 content to its O_2 capacity.

C. The O_2 uptake curve of blood is the functional relationship between O_2 content and PO_2.

D. The O_2 content of blood depends completely on the amount of Hb in the blood.

1050. Which of the following statements about Hb is FALSE?

A. A higher P50 than normal means that the O_2 binds less tightly to HB.

B. An increase in 2,3-DPG shifts the O_2 uptake curve to the left.

C. An increase in PCO_2 causes a right shift of the O_2 uptake curve.

D. An decrease in pH increases P50.

1051. Which of the following is a specific investigation to detect seizures?

A. CT scan B. MRI scan

C. EEG D. BEAP

1052. Which of the following in FALSE concerning CO_2 uptake?

A. If PO_2 = PCO2, then there will be more total CO_2 in the blood.

B. Oxygenation moves the CO_2 uptake curve downward.

C. The CO_2 uptake curve is generated by comparing the total CO_2 per unit volume of blood, and the PCO2.

D. Deoxygenated blood carries less CO_2 than oxygenated

1053. Water in percentage of water in adult human body ?

A. 45% B. 80%

C. 20% D. 60%

1054. Which of the following is INCORRECT concerning the O_2 / CO_2 movement and processing through the lungs and tissues?

A. Binding of O_2 to Hb changes its configuration so that CO_2 and H+ ions are more likely to dissociate.

B. When CO_2 diffused into the alveoli, the $PaCO_2$ is lowered.

C. Carbonic acid is an intermediate in the reaction combining H+ with HCO_3- to form H_2O and CO_2.

D. Arterial blood flows to the tissues where H+ ions combine with HCO_3- to form H_2O and CO_2.

1055. Which of the following can cause stagnant hypoxia?

A. COPD

B. Shock or heart failure.

C. Cyanide poisoning.

D. Carbon monoxide poisoning.

1056. If you blocked the blood supply to an alveolus, which of the following would NOT occur as a result?

A. The ventilation perfusion ratio would be 0.

B. The PAO_2 would be greater than normal.

C. The $PACO_2$ would be 0.

D. All of the Above are true.

1057. Which of the following is FALSE concerning the ventilation and perfusion of different regions of the lung?

A. Alveoli at the top of the lung have a smaller dynamic compliance.

B. The Hb moving through the base of the lung is less saturated than that at the apex of the lung.

C. PAO_2 at the apex of the lung is higher than that at the base of the lung.

D. Regional variation in ventilation-perfusion is more efficient for oxygenating blood than is uniform ventilation-perfusion.

1058. Which of the following pairs is INCORRECT concerning central nervous systems and a factor they respond to by affecting respiration?

A. Cerebellum: Mechanoreceptor input

B. Limbic system: emotional states

C. Cerebral cortex: voluntary control

D. Cerebral motor cortex: exercise

1059. Which of the following will NOT increase the minute ventilation?

A. An increase in arterial pH.

B. An increase in arterial partial pressure of carbon dioxide.

C. Increase in alveolar pressure of carbon dioxide.

D. Exercise

1060. Which of the following is the primary regulating variable of the central chemoreceptors?
A. PaO_2.
B. $PaCO_2$
C. Arterial Ph
D. Input from stretch receptors.

1061. In which situation would the response to hypoxia be limited?
A. In a patient with obstructed airways.
B. When hypoxia is accompanied by hypercapnea.
C. In the hypoxia induced by high altitude.
D. During hypoventilation.

1062. Which of the following is FALSE concerning chemoreceptor input to the respiratory centers?
A. CSF is a poor buffer and a drop in PCO_2 produces a large change in pH initiating a change in respiration.
B. The body can adjust to chronic hypercapnea by using an active HCO3- transport process in the choroid plexus.
C. The carotid and aortic bodies detect increases in $PaCO_2$ and pH, and decreases in PaO_2 .
D. 75% of ventilatory response is regulated by chemoreceptors in the CSF and 25% by the carotid and aortic bodies.

1063. Which of the following pairs is NOT a pulmonary mechanoreceptor paired to a possible stimulus?
A. Stretch receptor: inflation
B. Irritant receptor: inhaled dust
C. Juxtacapillary receptors: decreases interstitial fluid volume in alveolar walls.
D. Bronchial C receptors: large inflations.

1064. Intrapulmonary pressure is ?
A. Pressure within the pleural cavity
B. Pressure within the alveoli of the lungs
C. Negative pressure in the intrapleural space
D. Difference between atmospheric pressure and respiratory pressure

1065. Surfactant helps to prevent the alveoli from collapsing by ?
A. Umidifying the air before it enters
B. Warming the air before it enters
C. Interfering with the cohesiveness of water molecules, thereby reducing the surface tension of alveolar fluid
D. Protecting the surface of alveoli from dehydration and other environmental variations

1066. Which of the following statements is incorrect?
A. During fetal life, lungs are filled with fluid.
B. Respiratory rate is lowest in newborn infants.
C. Descent of the diaphragm results in abdominal breathing.
D. The chest wall becomes more rigid with age.

1067. Tidal volume is air ________.
A. Remaining in the lungs after forced expiration
B. Exchanged during normal breathing
C. Inhaled after normal inspiration
D. Forcibly expelled after normal expiration

1068. Possible causes of hypoxia include ________.
A. Too little oxygen in the atmosphere
B. Obstruction of the esophagus
C. Taking several rapid deep breaths
D. Getting very cold

1069. Because the lungs are filled with fluid during fetal life, which of the following statements is true regarding respiratory exchange?
A. Respiratory exchanges are made through the ductus arteriosus.
B. Respiratory exchanges are not necessary.
C. Respiratory exchanges are made through the placenta.
D. Because the lungs develop later in gestation, fetuses do not need a mechanism for respiratory exchange.

1070. Which of the following is not a stimulus for breathing?
A. Rising carbon dioxide levels
B. Rising blood pressure
C. Arterial PO_2 below 60 mm Hg
D. Arterial pH resulting from CO_2 retention

1071. Respiratory control centers are located in the ________?
A. Midbrain and medulla
B. Medulla and pons
C. Pons and midbrain
D. Upper spinal cord and medulla

1072. The amount of air that can be inspired above the tidal volume is called ________?
A. Reserve air
B. Epiratory reserve
C. Inspiratory reserve
D. Vital capacity

1073. Oxygen and carbon dioxide are exchanged in the lungs and through all cell membranes by ?
A. Osmosis B. Diffusion
C. Filtration D. Active transport

1074. Select the correct statement about the pharynx.?
A. The pharyngeal tonsil is located in the laryngopharynx.
B. The auditory tube drains into the nasopharynx.
C. The laryngopharynx blends posteriorly into the nasopharynx.
D. The palatine tonsils are embedded in the lateral walls of the nasopharynx.

1075. Which of the following is not found on the right lobe of the lung?
A. Middle lobe B. Cardiac notch
C. Horizontal fissure D. Oblique fissure

1076. Which of the choices below is not a role of the pleura?
A. Allows the lungs to inflate and deflate without friction
B. Helps divide the thoracic cavity into three chambers
C. Helps limit the spread of local infections
D. Aids in blood flow to and from the heart because the heart sits between the lungs

1077. Which of the following provide the greatest surface area for gas exchange?
A. Alveolar sacs
B. Alveoli
C. Respiratory bronchioles
D. Alveolar ducts

1078. Gas emboli may occur because a ________.
A. Person holds his breath too long
B. Diver holds his breath upon ascent
C. Pilot holds her breath upon descent
D. Person breathes pure oxygen in a pressurized chamber

1079. Inspiratory capacity is ________.
A. The total amount of air that can be inspired after a tidal expiration
B. The total amount of exchangeable air
C. Functional residual capacity
D. Air inspired after a tidal inhalation

1080. The nose serves all the following functions except ________.
A. As a passageway for air movement
B. As the initiator of the cough reflex
C. Warming and humidifying the air
D. Cleansing the air

1081. A premature baby usually has difficulty breathing. However, the respiratory system is developed enough for survival by ________.
A. 17 weeks B. 24 weeks
C. 28 weeks D. 36 weeks

1082. Which of the following statements is true regarding the respiratory rate of a newborn?
A. The respiratory rate of a newborn is slow.
B. The respiratory rate of a newborn varies between male and female infants.
C. The respiratory rate of a newborn is approximately 30 respirations per minute.
D. The respiratory rate of a newborn is, at its highest rate, approximately 40-80 respirations per minute.

1083. Most inspired particles such as dust fail to reach the lungs because of the ________.
A. Ciliated mucous lining in the nose
B. Abundant blood supply to nasal mucosa
C. Porous structure of turbinate bones
D. Action of the epiglottis

1084. Which of the disorders below is characterized by destruction of the walls of the alveoli producing abnormally large air spaces that remain filled with air during exhalation?
A. Pneumonia B. Tuberculosis
C. Emphysema D. Coryza

1085. Another term for the swallowing of food is–
A. Digestion B. Ingestion
C. Deglutition D. Peristalsis

1086. The serous membrane that passes from the lesser curvature of the stomach and the upper duodenum to the inferior surface of the liver is the–
A. Visceral peritoneum B. Mesentery
C. Greater omentum D. Lesser omentum

1087. Which of these is not a feature of the mucosa of the gastrointestinal tract?
A. Lamina propria B. Goblet cells
C. Myenteric plexus D. Plicae circulares

1088. Adults have ________ true molars teeth.
A. 4 B. 8 C. 12 D. 16

1089. Teeth are composed of a number of substances, the bulk of which is ________.
A. Enamel B. Gingiva
C. Cementum D. Dentin

1090. Which of these is not one of the three pairs of extrinsic salivary glands?
A. Parotid B. Palatine
C. Submandibular D. Sublingual

1091. Within the stomach lining, _______________ cells secrete hydrochloric acid.
A. Parietal B. Goblet
C. Principal D. Argentaffin

1092. During which phase of gastric secretion is gastric juice released?
A. Cephalic phase B. Gastric phase
C. Intestinal phase D. All of the Above

1093. Which of these is a structural modification unique to the small intestine?
A. Plicae circulares
B. Villi
C. Microvilli
D. All of these are unique to the small intestine.

1094. The longitudinal muscle layer of the large intestine forms three distinct muscle bands called _______________.
A. Sigmoid colon
B. Taeniae coli
C. Haustra
D. Epiploic appendages

1095. Within the liver, bile is produced by _______________ and secreted into bile canaliculi.
A. Kupffer cells B. Liver lobules
C. Hepatocytes D. Acinar cells

1096. The condition in which the liver becomes infused with fibrous tissue and is unable to repair itself is known as _______________.
A. Hepatitis B. Cirrhosis
C. Jaundice D. Hepatoma

1097. This is the job of the digestive system.
A. To give the body shape
B. To take in and break down food for use by the body
C. To take in oxygen and give off carbon dioxide
D. All of the Above

1098. A long tube that carries food from the mouth to the stomach.
A. Trachea B. Esophagus
C. Urethra D. All of the Above

1099. Stores the liver's digestive juices until they are needed by the intestines.
A. Pancreas B. Gall bladder
C. Villi D. All of the Above

1100. An organ that produces a bodily juice called bile.
A. Liver B. Pancreas
C. Gallbladder D. All of the Above

1101. The place where digested molecules of food, water and minerals are absorbed.
A. Small intestine B. Large intesine
C. Mouth D. All of the Above

1102. This organ produces a digestive juice that contains a wide array of enzymes to break down fat, carbohydrate and protein in food.
A. Pancreas B. Liver
C. Large intestine D. All of the Above

1103. This part of the digestive system removes solid wastes such as feces from the body.
A. Large intestine B. Small intestine
C. Esophagus D. All of the Above

1104. This organ stores swallowed food and liquid, mixes up digestive juices with the food and liquid and sends it to the small intestine.
A. Small intestine B. Large intestine
C. Stomach D. All of the Above

1105. Tiny fingerlike projections in the small intestine.
A. Villi B. Anus
C. Rectum D. All of the Above

1106. This contains tiny glands that produce juices to digest food, found in the mouth, stomach and small intestine.
A. Villi B. Mucosa
C. Anus D. All of the Above

1107. Composed of the teeth, tongue, salivary glands and muscles, this part takes in food to begin the process of digestion.
A. Mouth B. Anus
C. Esophagus D. All of the Above

1108. The final portion of the large intestine.
A. Esophagus B. Rectum
C. Gallbladder D. All of the Above

1109. The opening at the end of the digestive tract in which solid wastes are eliminated?
A. Anus B. Mucosa
C. Liver D. All of the Above

1110. The place where digested molecules of food, water and minerals are absorbed?
A. Small intestine B. Large intestine
C. Mouth D. All of the Above

1111. Which of the following is the correct order of tissue from the outer to the inner layer in the wall of the digestive system?
A. Submucosa, serous membrane, smooth muscle, mucous membrane
B. Smooth muscle,serous membrane, mucous membrane, submucosa
C. Serous membrane, smooth muscle, submucosa, mucosa
D. Mucous membrane, submucosa, smooth muscle, smooth muscle

1112. The parotid salivary gland is located?
A. Inferior and anterior to the ear
B. Under the tongue
C. In the cheek
D. In the oropharynx

1113. Which of the following is NOT a portion of the peritoneum?
A. Mesocolon B. Mesentery
C. Hiatus D. Greater omentum

1114. The active ingredients in gastric juice are
A. Amylase and pepsin
B. Pepsin and HCl
C. Maltase and secretin
D. Bile and trypsin

1115. An instrument used to examine the lower portion of the colon is called:
A. Sigmoidoscope B. Bronchoscope
C. Catheter D. EKG

1116. In an adult, fats are digested in the:
A. Mouth B. Stomach
C. Small interstine D. All of the Above

1117. Which of the following is an enzyme except?
A. Bile B. Gastrin
C. Trypsin D. Secretin

1118. What is the digestive system?
A. The body's breathing system
B. The body's system of nerves
C. The body's food-processing system
D. The body's blood-transporting system

1119. Digestion begins in the mouth. Which of the following statement is INCORRECT?
A. The tongue aids in the digestion of the food.
B. The saliva changes some of the starches in the food to sugar.
C. The tongue keeps the food in place in the mouthwhile the food is being chewed.
D. The digestive juices can react more easily with the food when chewed.

1120. Where does food pass through between the mouth and the stomach?
A. The gullet B. The rectum
C. The small intestine D. The large intestine

1121. Our throat divides into two separate tubes: the windpipe and the gullet. What prevents food from entering the windpipe?
A. The uvula B. The tongue
C. The trachea D. The epiglottis

1122. What is normal stroke volume ?
A. 100 ml B. 90 ml
C. 70 ml D. 50 ml.

1123. What happens when food reaches the stomach?
A. Nothing. No digestion occurs in the stomach.
B. The food moves quickly into the small intestine.
C. Juices mix with the food and stomach muscles squeeze it.
D. The food is completely digested and is absorbedby tiny blood vessels in the walls of the stomach.

1124. What is The formula of Cardiac Output ?
A. CO = (stroke volume) x (heart rate).
B. CO = stroke volume
C. CO = stroke volume + heart rate
D. CO = stroke volume - heart rate

1125. Where does the partly-digested food (in liquid form) go after it leaves the stomach?
A. The gullet B. The appendix
C. The small intestine D. The large intestine

1126. What is Stroke volume?
A. Pressure exerted by blood on blood vessels.
B. Total amount of blood ejected by heart
C. Amount of blood ejected by each con-traction of the right atrium
D. Amount of blood ejected by each contraction of the left ventricles

1127. How does digested food finally reach the bloodstream?
A. It passes through the gullet into the blood.
B. It is absorbed into the blood through blood vessels.
C. It is absorbed into the blood through the walls of the lungs.
D. It passes from the small intestine into the largeintestine, then into the blood.

1128. What is normal period of one cardiac cycle ?
A. 0.4 sec B. 1.8 sec
C. 0.8 sec D. 2 sec

1129. Solid waste leaves the body through the rectum then the anus. Liquid waste leaves the body after passing through the ...
A. Kidneys and bladder
B. Blood vessels and lungs
C. Large intestine and bowel
D. Small intestine and large intestine

1130. The liver is located in the abdomen and performs many functions. Which of the following is NOT a function of the liver?
A. Storing food
B. Manufacturing insulin
C. Producing digestive juices
D. Healing itself when it is damaged

1131. Which of the following valve situated between a left atrium and ventricle in the heart?
A. Bicuspid valve B. Monocuspid valve
C. Mitral valve D. A & C

1132. The function of the hepatic portal circulation is to?
A. Carry toxins to the venous system for disposal through the urinary tract
B. Collect absorbed nutrients for metabolic processing or storage
C. Distribute hormones
D. Return glucose to the general circulation when blood sugar is low

1133. The Tricuspid valve is situated on:
A. Bicuspid valve
B. Mitral valve
C. Right atrioventricular valve
D. None of them

1134. The main functions of the digestive system are
A. Ingestion and digestion
B. Propulsion and secretion
C. Absorption and elimination
D. All of the Above

1135. Which of the following centre is found in medulla oblongata?
A. Cardiovascular centre.
B. Respiratory centre
C. Reflex centres of vomiting
D. All of the Above

1136. The movement of digestion products, electrolytes, vitamins, and water across the GI tract epithelium and into the underlying blood and lymphatic vessels is called
A. Ingestion B. Absorption
C. Digestion D. Secretion

1137. The part of the neuron that receive messages from other cells is called:
A. Axon B. Soma
C. Schwann cell D. Dendrites

1138. All of the following are organs of the digestive system except the
A. Spleen B. Liver
C. Tongue D. Esophagus

1139. Which sensory area is found in Temporo-Perietal lobe of cerebrum?
A. Olfactory B. Auditory
C. Speech D. All of the Above

1140. Which selection includes only accessory digestive organs?
A. Salivary glands, thyroid gland, pancreas, liver
B. Stomach, duodenum, pancreas, gall bladder
C. Gall bladder, liver, pancreas, salivary glands
D. Liver, thyroid gland, gall bladder, spleen

1141. When glucose if found in urine it is called _____.
A. Glucosuria
B. Uremia
C. Ureteritis
D. Glucose intolerance

1142. Movements in the small intestine that churn the materials being digested and mix them with intestinal secretions are called
A. Peristalsis B. Pendular motility
C. Segmentation D. Haustral churning

1143. Which term describes the wave of muscular contraction that moves material through the GI tract toward the anus?
A. Peristalsis B. Pendular motility
C. Segmentation D. Haustral churning

1144. Cardiac contractibility regulate by?
A. Medulla oblongata B. Pituitary
C. Hypothalamus D. Cerebellum

1145. Digestive functions of the tongue include
A. Manipulating and mixing ingested materials during chewing
B. Helping compress partially digested food to form a bolus
C. Assisting in the swallowing process
D. All of the Above

1146. Which of the following is the largest part of brain?
A. Cerebellum B. Midbrain
C. Medulla oblongata D. Cerebrum

1147. The three pairs of multicellular salivary glands that secrete into the oral cavity are the __________ glands.
A. Alpha, beta, and gamma
B. Parotid, submandibular, and sublingual
C. Palatine, lingual, and pharyngeal
D. Serous, mucous, and mixed

1148. Cerebro Spinal Fluid is present in?
A. Arachnoid space
B. Epidural space
C. Subarachnoid space
D. None of the Above

1149. What is the mineralized matrix, similar to bone but harder, that forms the primary mass of each tooth?
A. Enamel B. Dentin
C. Cementum D. Pulp

1150. Brain stem is formed by:
A. Pons B. Midbrain.
C. Medulla oblongata D. All of the Above

1151. Which mesentery covers most of the abdominal organs, extending inferiorly like an apron from the greater curvature of the stomach?
A. Mesentery proper B. Lesser omentum
C. Greater omentum D. Mesocolon

1152. Total volume of CSF secreted in a day:
A. 100ml. B. 1000 ml
C. 500 ml D. 150-200 ml

1153. From deep to superficial, what are the tunics of the intraperitoneal portions of the GI tract?
A. Serosa, muscularis, submucosa, and mucosa
B. Mucosa, submucosa, muscularis, and serosa
C. Adventitia, muscularis, submucosa, and mucosa
D. Mucosa, submucosa, muscularis, and adventitia

1154. Which of The following inner most layer covers the brain?
A. Duramater B. Arachnoid
C. Myometrium D. Piamater

1155. In which of the following selections are the GI tract organs or regions correctly matched with the type of epithelium that lines them?
A. Oral cavity and esophagus; stratified cuboidal
B. Stomach and small intestine; stratified squamous
C. Cecum, colon, and rectum; simple columnar
D. All of the Above

1156. A place where the nerve impulse transfer from one neuron to another is called as:
A. Synapse. B. Tendon
C. Myelin sheath D. Node of Ranvier

1157. The esophagus enters the abdominal cavity through an opening in the diaphragm, the ________, before it connects to the stomach.
A. Diaphragmatic foramen
B. Thoracic canal
C. Cardiac orifice
D. Esophageal hiatus

1158. What are the three phases of the swallowing process?
A. Mastication, eruption, and dentition
B. Oral, cranial, and pharyngeal
C. Voluntary, pharyngeal, and esophageal
D. Cardiac, gastric, and pyloric

1159. Which of the following hormone is responsible for fight or flight response?
A. Corticosterone B. Cortisol
C. Adrenaline D. Gama.

1160. Which digestive organ mechanically and chemically transforms a food bolus into chyme?
A. Esophagus B. Stomach
C. Small intestine D. Large intestine

1161. Which list proceeds from the superior to the inferior end of the stomach?
A. Pylorus, fundus, cardia, body
B. Cardia, body, fundus, pylorus
C. Cardia, fundus, body, pylorus
D. Body, cardia, pylorus, fundus

1162. Which of the following gland plays a vital role in responding to stress?
A. Adrenal. B. Pancreas
C. Parathyroid D. Pituitary

1163. From the superior end downward, the three segments of the small intestine are the
A. Ileum, duodenum, and jejunum
B. Duodenum, jejunum, and ileum
C. Jejunum, ileum, and duodenum
D. Duodenum, ileum, and jejunum

1164. What is the function of the villi in the small intestine?
A. To decrease the amount of exposed surface
B. To facilitate enzyme retention and dispersal
C. To increase the surface area for absorption and secretion
D. To sweep particles across the surface with wavelike actions

1165. Which sequence lists the regions of the large intestine in order, from the end of the ileum to the anus?
A. Cecum, rectum, anal canal, colon
B. Colon, rectum, anal canal, cecum
C. Cecum, colon, rectum, anal canal
D. Colon, cecum, rectum, anal canal

1166. Which of The following smallest functional unit of the body ?
A. Liver B. Organ
C. Cell D. Mitochondria

1167. Arrange the segments of the colon in the sequence through which digested material passes prior to defecation: (1) sigmoid (2) transverse (3) descending (4) ascending
A. 4, 2, 3, 1 B. 2, 1, 4, 3
C. 1, 3, 4, 2 D. 3, 1, 2, 4

1168. Which of the following is the example of ECF?
A. CSF B. Blood
C. Interstitial fluid D. All of the Above

1169. The mucosa of the large intestine is characterized by
A. Lack of intestinal villi
B. Numerous goblet cells and intestinal glands
C. Many lymphatic nodules and cells in the lamina propria
D. All of the Above

1170. What is the Percentage of ECF in total body fluid ?
A. 50-60%. B. 60-70%
C. 38-40% D. 10-20%

1171. Age-related changes in the digestive system include which of the following?
A. Reduced secretion of mucin, enzymes, and acid
B. Decreased replacement of epithelial cells
C. Diminished muscular tone and GI tract motility
D. All of the Above

1172. Which of the following affects the function of other endocrine glands:
A. Thyroid B. Hypothalamus
C. Adrenal D. Pituitary

1173. Which hormones stimulate the production of pancreatic juice and bicarbonate?
A. Angiotensin and epinephrine
B. Gastrin and insulin

C. Cholecystokinin and secretin
D. Insulin and glucagon

1174. What are the Functions of skin?
A. Maintaining body temperature.
B. Excretion of urea when functions of kidneys are impaired
C. Vitamin D synthesis
D. All of the Above

1175. Which of the following nerves innervates the teres minor muscle?
A. Subscapular nerve
B. Suprascapular nerve
C. Axillary nerve
D. Pectoral nerve

1176. Which of the following nerves innervates the pronator teres muscle?
A. Radial B. Median
C. Musculocutaneous D. Ulnar

1177. Which of the following supplies the muscles of the perineum?
A. Pudendal nerve B Sciatic nerve
C. Femoral nerve D. Tibial nerve

1178. Which of the following eye muscles rotates the eye downward and away from midline?
A. Inferior oblique B. Superior oblique
C. Inferior rectus D. Superior rectus

1179. Which of the following eye muscles rotates the eye upward and toward midline?
A. Inferior oblique B. Superior oblique
C. Inferior rectus D. Superior rectus

1180. Coracoid process is on:
A. Humerus B. Scapula
C. Femur D. Pelvic girdle

1181. The primary function of the descending loop of Henle in the kidney is?
A. Reabsorption of sodium ions
B. Reabsorption of water by osmosis
C. Secretion of hydrogen ions
D. Secretion of potassium ions

1182. Location and secretion of Leydig cells are
A. Liver-cholestrol
B. Ovary-estrogen
C. Testis-testosterone
D. Pancreas-glucogen

1183. Olfactory nerve is:
A. Both Sensory and Motor
B. Purely Sensory
C. Mainly Motor
D. None of the Above

1184. Gonads develop from embryonic
A. Ectoderm B. Endoderm
C. Mesoderm D. Both B & C

1185. Cranial nerves supplying eyes are:
A. 3. 4, 5 B. 4, 6, 7
C. 4, 5, 6 D. 3, 4, 6

1186. Damage to __________ cranial nerve results in inability to shrug and weak head movement.
A. Vagus nerve
B. Accessory nerve
C. Glossopharyngeal nerve
D. Facial nerve

1187. Acromion process is located on:
A. Ilium B. Scapula
C. Humerus D. Ulna

1188. Fourth cranial nerve is:
A. Trigeminal B. Abducens
C. Trochlear D. Facial

1189. Which one is produced by mesoderm?
A. Heart and notochord
B. Heart and brain
C. Spinal cord and notochord
D. Brain

1190. A cranial nerve with maximum branches in the body is:
A. Vagus B. Auditaory
C. Facial D. Trigeminal

1191. What is Acalculia?
A. Inability to do mathematical calculations
B. Inability to recognize sensory input
C. Visual aphasia
D. Inequality in size of the pupils

1192. What instruction is most appropriate in patient with trigeminal neuralgia to prevent triggering the pain?
A. Drink iced foods
B. Avoid oral hygiene
C. Apply warm compresses
D. Chew on the unaffected side

1193. Which cranial nerve Innervates the lateral rectus muscle of the eye?
A. Occulomotor B. Trochlear
C. Trigeminal D. Abducens nerve

1194. The cranial nerve which innervates superior oblique muscle is:
A. Optic B. Trochlear
C. Facial D. Abducens nerve

1195. Trochlear nucleus of the trochlear cranial nerve is located in:
A. Frontal lobe B. Medulla oblongata
C. Mid brain D. Pons

1196. The receptors with which norepinephrine, epinephrine, or other adrenomimetic drugs combine are called :
A. Adrenoreceptors
B. Cholenergic receptors
C. Nicotinic receptors
D. None of the Above

❑❑❑

Answer Sheet

1. B.	2. B.	3. C.	4. D.	5. B.	6. C.	7. C.	8. D.	9. B.	10. C.
11. B.	12. A.	13. .B	14. D.	15. B.	16. C.	17. A.	18. A.	19. D.	20. B.
21. B.	22. A.	23. B.	24. B.	25. A.	26. A.	27. A.	28. D.	29. D.	30. B.
31. B.	32. D.	33. C.	34. D.	35. A.	36. A.	37. C.	38. D.	39. C.	40. A.
41. A.	42. A.	43. A.	44. A.	45. A.	46. C.	47. D.	48. B.	49. D.	50. B.
51. A.	52. A.	53. D.	54. C.	55. A.	56. A.	57. D.	58. C.	59. A.	60. C.
61. B.	62. B.	63. B.	64. C.	65. D.	66. B.	67. D.	68. D.	69. B.	70. D.
71. D.	72. C.	73. A.	74. C.	75. A.	76. C.	77. D.	78. D.	79. D.	80. A.
81. A.	82. B.	83. B.	84. C.	85. D.	86. B.	87. C.	88. A.	89. D.	90. A.
91. A.	92. C.	93. D.	94. C.	95. A.	96. C.	97. C.	98. A.	99. D.	100. A.
101. B.	102. D.	103. D.	104. C.	105. A.	106. B.	107. C.	108. B.	109. B.	110. C.
111. B.	112. B.	113. D.	114. A.	115. B.	116. D.	117. C.	118. A.	119. D.	120. C.
121. B.	122. A.	123. C.	124. B.	125. A.	126. A.	127. A.	128. B.	129. C.	130. A.
131. .C	132. .B	133. .C	134. .A	135. .A	136. .D	137. .D	138. .D	139. .B	140. C.
141. A.	142. A.	143. C.	144. D.	145. A.	146. D.	147. D.	148. C.	149. B.	150. B.
151. C.	152. D.	153. B.	154. A.	155. C.	156. A.	157. A.	158. B.	159. A.	160. .D
161. B.	162. C.	163. A.	164. C.	165. C.	166. C.	167. C.	168. A.	169. B.	170. B.
171. C.	172. C.	173. B.	174. C.	175. C.	176. A.	177. D.	178. B.	179. D.	180. B.
181. D.	182. A.	183. B.	184. B.	185. C.	186. C.	187. D.	188. A.	189. C.	190. A.
191. C.	192. A.	193. C.	194. D.	195. D.	196. A.	197. A.	198. D.	199. C.	200. B.
201. C.	202. D.	203. D.	204. C.	205. D.	206. C.	207. B.	208. C.	209. A.	210. D.
211. A.	212. A.	213. A.	214. C.	215. A.	216. C.	217. B.	218. D.	219. C.	220. B.
221. B.	222. C.	223. C.	224. B.	225. B.	226. D.	227. D.	228. B.	229. D.	230. B.
231. A.	232. C.	233. B.	234. A.	235. D.	236. C.	237. C.	238. B.	239. B.	240. C.
241. D.	242. A.	243. C.	244. C.	245. D.	246. D.	247. D.	248. B.	249. A.	250. C.
251. C.	252. B.	253. B.	254. D.	255. B.	256. D.	257. D.	258. A.	259. B.	260. C.
261. A.	262. D.	263. A.	264. D.	265. B.	266. C.	267. B.	268. A.	269. B.	270. B.
271. B.	272. B.	273. C.	274. C.	275. B.	276. D.	277. C.	278. B.	279. B.	280. C.
281. B.	282. C.	283. C.	284. B.	285. C.	286. B.	287. A.	288. D.	289. B.	290. A.
291. A.	292. D.	293. D.	294. C.	295. B.	296. C.	297. A.	298. C.	299. C.	300. B.
301. A.	302. C.	303. B.	304. A.	305. A.	306. B.	307. D.	308. B.	309. D.	310. D.
311. C.	312. C.	313. A.	314. D.	315. A.	316. D.	317. B.	318. B.	319. C.	320. C.

321. B.	322. C.	323. D.	324. C.	325. B.	326. B.	327. A.	328. C.	329. C.	330. D.
331. C.	332. B.	333. A.	334. D.	335. A.	336. A.	337. B.	338. A.	339. A.	340. D.
341. D.	342. D.	343. B.	344. D.	345. D.	346. C.	347. B.	348. B.	349. C.	350. B.
351. D.	352. A.	353. B.	354. B.	355. A.	356. D.	357. C.	358. D.	359. A.	360. B.
361. B.	362. B.	363. D.	364. B.	365. B.	366. A.	367. A.	368. B.	369. B.	370. D.
371. B.	372. D.	373. D.	374. A.	375. D.	376. B.	377. C.	378. D.	379. C.	380. B.
381. A.	382. B.	383. D.	384. A.	385. B.	386. C.	387. B.	388. A.	389. A.	390. D.
391. B.	392. D.	393. B.	394. B.	395. B.	396. C.	397. D.	398. C.	399. D.	400. D.
401. B.	402. A.	403. D.	404. A.	405. A.	406. C.	407. B.	408. D.	409. D.	410. A.
411. B.	412. A.	413. C.	414. A.	415. D.	416. C.	417. D.	418. B.	419. B.	420. C.
421. D.	422. B.	423. C.	424. C.	425. B.	426. D.	427. B.	428. D.	429. C.	430. A.
431. B.	432. B.	433. C.	434. C.	435. A.	436. D.	437. C.	438. A.	439. B.	440. C.
441. B.	442. B.	443. B.	444. D.	445. A.	446. A.	447. B.	448. A.	449. B.	450. A.
451. B.	452. A.	453. D.	454. A.	455. B.	456. C.	457. B.	458. B.	459. C.	460. A.
461. A.	462. C.	463. D.	464. A.	465. A.	466. D.	467. B.	468. C.	469. D.	470. D.
471. A.	472. A.	473. A.	474. B.	475. B.	476. D.	477. A.	478. B.	479. A.	480. C.
481. A.	482. B.	483. A.	484. A.	485. D.	486. C.	487. A.	488. C.	489. C.	490. D.
491. .C	492. .C	493. .C	494. .D	495. .C	496. .A	497. .B	498. .C	499. .C	500. .B
501. .D	502. .A	503. .A	504. .A	505. .A	506. .B	507. .A	508. .D	509. .A	510. .D
511. .A	512. .C	513. .A	514. .A	515. .A	516. .D	517. .D	518. .B	519. .A	520. .B
521. .A	522. .B	523. .B	524. .C	525. .B	526. .B	527. .C	528. .B	529. .A	530. .A
531. .D	532. .A	533. .B	534. .C	535. .B	536. .C	537. .A	538. .A	539. .C	540. .D
541. .A	542. .C	543. .B	544. .B	545. .C	546. .A	547. .C	548. .B	549. .C	550. .D
551. .A	552. .D	553. .D	554. .D	555. .D	556. .C	557. .D	558. .A	559. .A	560. .A
561. .D	562. .B	563. .A	564. .B	565. .C	566. .D	567. .A	568. .A	569. .D	570. .D
571. .B	572. .D	573. .A	574. .B	575. .C	576. .A	577. .B	578. .A	579. .D	580. .D
581. .D	582. .C	583. .B	584. .A	585. .B	586. .A	587. .C	588. .D	589. .C	590. .B
591. .C	592. .D	593. .B	594. .C	595. .C	596. .C	597. .C	598. .A	599. .D	600. .A
601. .C	602. .A	603. .A	604. .A	605. .B	606. .B	607. .A	608. .D	609. .A	610. .A
611. .A	612. .A	613. .C	614. .D	615. .A	616. .D	617. .B	618. .D	619. .D	620. .D
621. .C	622. .B	623. .D	624. .B	625. .D	626. .B	627. .C	628. .B	629. .C	630. .D
631. .B	632. .B	633. .C	634. .B	635. .C	636. .D	637. .A	638. .D	639. .B	640. .B
641. .D	642. .C	643. .C	644. .C	645. .A	646. .B	647. .D	648. .D	649. .A	650. .D
651. .A	652. .C	653. .B	654. .D	655. .D	656. .C	657. .B	658. .C	659. .B	660. .A

661. .D	662. .B	663. .A	664. .A	665. .C	666. .B	667. .B	668. .C	669. .D	670. .B
671. .D	672. .A	673. .D	674. .C	675. .B	676. .D	677. .A	678. .C	679. .B	680. .A
681. .B	682. .B	683. .A	684. .D	685. .C	686. .D	687. .B	688. .C	689. .B	690. .C
691. .A	692. .C	693. .B	694. .C	695. .A	696. .C	697. .D	698. .A	699. .D	700. .A
701. .D	702. .D	703. .B	704. .D	705. .D	706. .B	707. .C	708. .D	709. .C	710. .D
711. .D	712. .A	713. .D	714. .C	715. .D	716. .D	717. .D	718. .D	719. .D	720. .D
721. .B	722. .C	723. .C	724. .C	725. .A	726. .A	727. .A	728. .D	729. .D	730. .C
731. .D	732. .C	733. .D	734. .B	735. .C	736. .C	737. .B	738. .D	739. .D	740. .A
741. .D	742. .D	743. .D	744. .C	745. .A	746. .A	747. .D	748. .D	749. .B	750. .C
751. .A	752. .A	753. .D	754. .C	755. .D	756. .A	757. .C	758. .A	759. .C	760. .C
761. .B	762. .C	763. .B	764. .D	765. .A	766. .A	767. .C	768. .D	769. .C	770. .A
771. .A	772. .C	773. .A	774. .D	775. .B	776. .C	777. .B	778. .B	779. .C	780. .D
781. .B	782. .B	783. .D	784. .C	785. .D	786. .C	787. .C	788. .C	789. .A	790. .C
791. .A	792. .C	793. .C	794. .A	795. .A	796. .C	797. .D	798. .D	799. .A	800. .D
801. .A	802. .B	803. .D	804. .D	805. .B	806. .D	807. .A	808. .D	809. .D	810. .A
811. .B	812. .C	813. .C	814. .A	815. .B	816. .D	817. .D	818. .B	819. .B	820. .B
821. .D	822. .D	823. .A	824. .C	825. .B	826. .D	827. .D	828. .B	829. .C	830. .A
831. .B	832. .A	833. .A	834. .A	835. .B	836. .B	837. .C	838. .A	839. .D	840. .C
841. .C	842. .B	843. .C	844. .C	845. .A	846. .D	847. .D	848. .A	849. .B	850. .A
851. .B	852. .A	853. .D	854. .D	855. .D	856. .B	857. A	858. .A	859. .C	860. .D
861. .C	862. .A	863. .A	864. .B	865. .D	866. .D	867. .B	868. .A	869. .A	870. .D
871. .D	872. .D	873. .C	874. .B	875. .C	876. .D	877. .C	878. .B	879. .D	880. .D
881. .B	882. .C	883. .A	884. .A	885. .D	886. .A	887. .A	888. .C	889. .C	890. .D
891. .C	892. .C	893. .D	894. .A	895. .D	896. .A	897. .D	898. .B	899. .B	900. .C
901. .C	902. .C	903. .C	904. .C	905. .A	906. .C	907. .A	908. .C	909. .C	910. .C
911. B	912. .B	913. .A	914. .D	915. .A	916. .C	917. .C	918. C	919. .B	920. C
921. C	922. .D	923. .B	924. .C	925. .B	926. .A	927. .C	928. A	929. .C	930. D
931. C	932. .B	933. .B	934. .C	935. .B	936. .B	937. .D	938. D	939. .D	940. A
941. C	942. .C	943. .B	944. .B	945. .A	946. .A	947. .A	948. D	949. .A	950. C
951. D	952. .C	953. .A	954. .B	955. .A	956. .D	957. .B	958. D	959. .C	960. B
961. D	962. .A	963. .D	964. .C	965. .A	966. .A	967. .C	968. A	969. .A	970. D
971. A	972. .A	973. .A	974. .C	975. .D	976. .A	977. D.	978. C	979. .D	980. C
981. C	982. .D	983. .D	984. .C	985. .B	986. .C	987. A	988. B	989. D	990. C
991. D	992. .D	993. A	994. B	995. .D	996. B	997. B	998. A	999. D	1000. D

1001. .B	1002. .D	1003. .B	1004. .C	1005. .A	1006. .D	1007. .D	1008. .C	1009. .C	1010. .D
1011. .D	1012. .D	1013. .B	1014. .B	1015. .B	1016. .C	1017. .D	1018. .D	1019. .C	1020. .C
1021. .D	1022. .D	1023. .C	1024. .A	1025. .A	1026. .A	1027. .D	1028. .C	1029. .A	1030. .C
1031. .D	1032. .A	1033. .A	1034. .B	1035. .D	1036. .C	1037. .C	1038. .D	1039. .C	1040. .B
1041. .A	1042. .C	1043. .A	1044. .C	1045. .B	1046. .C	1047. .D	1048. .D	1049. .D	1050. .B
1051. .C	1052. .D	1053. .D	1054. .D	1055. .B	1056. .A	1057. .D	1058. .A	1059. .A	1060. .B
1061. .C	1062. .C	1063. .C	1064. .B	1065. .C	1066. .B	1067. .B	1068. .A	1069. .C	1070. .B
1071. .B	1072. .C	1073. .B	1074. .B	1075. .B	1076. .D	1077. .B	1078. .B	1079. .A	1080. .B
1081. .C	1082. .D	1083. .A	1084. .C	1085. .C	1086. .D	1087. .C	1088. .C	1089. .D	1090. .B
1091. .A	1092. .D	1093. .D	1094. .B	1095. .B	1096. .C	1097. .B	1098. .B	1099. .B	1100. .A
1101. .A	1102. .A	1103. .A	1104. .C	1105. .A	1106. .B	1107. .A	1108. .B	1109. .A	1110. .A
1111. .C	1112. .A	1113. .A	1114. .B	1115. .A	1116. .C	1117. .A	1118. .C	1119. .A	1120. .A
1121. .D	1122. .C	1123. .C	1124. .A	1125. .C	1126. .D	1127. .B	1128. .C	1129. .A	1130. .B
1131. .D	1132. .B	1133. .C	1134. .D	1135. .D	1136. .B	1137. .D	1138. .A	1139. .D	1140. .C
1141. .A	1142. .A	1143. .A	1144. .A	1145. .D	1146. .D	1147. .B	1148. .C	1149. .A	1150. .D
1151. .C	1152. .C	1153. .B	1154. .D	1155. .D	1156. .A	1157. .D	1158. .C	1159. .C	1160. .B
1161. .C	1162. .A	1163. .B	1164. .D	1165. .C	1166. .C	1167. .A	1168. .D	1169. .D	1170. .C
1171. .D	1172. .B	1173. .C	1174. .D	1175. .C	1176. .B	1177. .A	1178. .B	1179. .D	1180. .B
1181. .B	1182. .C	1183. .B	1184. .C	1185. .D	1186. .B	1187. .B	1188. .C	1189. .A	1190. .D
1191..A	1192..D	1193..D	1194..B	1195..C	1196..B				

3. Nursing Education (MCQ)

1. **In teaching - learning lesson plan method means:**
   A. Eating plan
   B. Walking plans
   C. Plan imposed by a trained person
   D. Freedom to choose own plan

2. **Which teaching method would be most appropriate to teach to a group of parents to change their attitude towards female feticide?**
   A. Lecture
   B. Role play
   C. Panel discussion
   D. Group Discussion

3. **Self understanding is facilitated by the study of:**
   A. Newman's window
   B. Kothari window
   C. Johari window
   D. Bohari window

4. **Which of the following curriculum is known as problem solving curriculum?**
   A. Core curriculum
   B. Basic curriculum
   C. Integral curriculum
   D. Co-relational curriculum

5. **What is most important Objective of nursing education except?**
   A. Provide nursing information to society
   B. To prepare nurses who will be able to work as an important member of health team
   C. To provide opportunities for development of the personality of each nurse
   D. To prepare nurses who will provide qualitative nursing care

6. **Which of the following components of cognitive domain ?**
   A. Knowledge B. Application
   C. Analysis D. All of the Above

7. **Internalization is a component of which domain of educational objective**
   A. Affective B. Formative
   C. Summative D. Cognitive

8. **Which of the learning activities are planned and guided by the school, wheather they are carried out in groups or individually, inside and outside the school, known as -**
   A. Lesson plan B. Demonstration
   C. Curriculum D. Symposium

9. **Which of the following components of learning objective?**
   A. Activity B. Condition
   C. Content D. All of the Above

10. **Which of the following is a principle of curriculum?**
    A. Principle of individual difference
    B. Creativity
    C. Principle of forward looking
    D. All of the Above

11. **Nurse should be SMART, in this 'A' means**
    A. Achievable B. Answerable
    C. Affordable D. Angry

12. **Which of the stage of curriculum in which overall design of the curriculum take place?**
    A. Evaluative B. Self assessment
    C. Formative D. Directive

13. **What is Master rotation plan?**
    A. Rotation of students in clinical
    B. Planning of course for one year
    C. Planning of one year's vacation and examination
    D. Complete course planning of all years

14. **The curriculum should be:**
    A. Student centred
    B. Knowledge centered
    C. Institution centred
    D. Subject centred

15. **Planning of practical & theory of a particular or specific subject is known as:**
    A. Master plan B. Subject plan
    C. Unit plan D. Course plan

16. **Overall plan of rotation of all students in a particular educational institution, showing the placement of the students in both theory and practical area, is termed known as:**
    A. Curriculum
    B. Lesson plan
    C. Master rotation plan
    D. Clinical rotation plan

17. **Which of the following is a component of course planning?**
    A. Assignments
    B. Evaluation criteria
    C. Teacher-learning methods
    D. All of the Above

18. The blue print which is prepared by the teacher to teach student in the classroom is known as:
A. Lesson plan B. Course plan
C. Unit plan D. None

19. What is the ideal duration or time of a lesson-plan ?
A. 10 min. B. 60 min.
C. 40 min. D. 120 min.

20. Non-projected teaching aids are also known as -
A. Audio aids B. Aids
C. Visual aids D. Graphic aids

21. What is time used by nursing educator for The introductory part of lesson-plan?
A. 1 min B. 10 min
C. 8 min D. 5 min

22. Most commonly used teaching method is
A. Lecture B. Discussion
C. Demonstration D. Role-play

23. The periodic evaluation of a programme is known as?
A. Summative evaluation
B. Systematic evaluation
C. Formative evaluation
D. None of them

24. Which of the following Examples of 3 dimensional teaching aids include?
A. Models B. Specimen
C. Puppets D. All of the Above

25. Who introduce the Inductive model of teaching?
A. Hilda Taba B. B.F. Skinner
C. Jean Piaget D. Maslow

26. Cognitive model of teaching was given by
A. Jean Piaget B. B.F. Skinner
C. Sigmund Freud D. Walpe

27. A supposition or system of ideas that is proposed to explain a given phenomenon best defines:
A. Paradigm B. Concept
C. A theory D. Abstraction

28. Which of following method of teaching can be presented to a large group at one time?
A. Lecture B. Discussion
C. Workshops D. Conference

29. It is a meeting of a teacher with a small number of students as a group for the discussion of a problem or selected situation before or after an observation visit known as:-
A. Workshop B. Symposium
C. Demonstration D. Conference

30. A method of teaching which is a simulated experience where participants an act interpersonal problems typical of real life situations?
A. Role playing B. Problem Solving
C. Brain storming D. Simulation

31. A problematic act carried out to completion in its natural setting?
A. Demonstration B. Problem solving
C. Case study D. Project method

32. Example of sensory learning is:-
A. Case study exercise
B. Simulation exercise
C. Seminar
D. Demonstration

33. A method of teaching which provide first hand experience in a natural setting?
A. Simulation B. Project method
C. Case study D. Problem solving

34. Buzz session is also known as:-
A. Class discussion B. Panel discussion
C. Group discussion D. Simulation

35. Which of the following visual aid fix in book to summarize the topic?
A. Flashcard B. Leaflet
C. Pamphlet D. Handout

36. A student nurse is preparing for a health talk on AIDS for community people, how many cards she should prepare for a flashcard presentation
A. 3-7 B. 12-15 C. 10-12 D. 18-20

37. What is systematic presentation of various aspect of a topic by a group of two or more persons with a special knowledge of the subject?
A. Seminar B. Discussion
C. Symposium D. Panel discussion

38. How many members can participate in panel discussion?
A. 4-8 members B. 10-12 members
C. 15-20 members D. 25-30 members

39. Micro teaching is an education technique for:-
A. Learner
B. Teacher
C. Large group of students
D. None of the Above

40. Following are forms of education, except?
A. Formal B. Informal
C. Non formal D. Vocational

41. It is a device for displaying study material or current news in a visualization form known as:-
A. Felt board B. Bulletin board
C. Flash card D. Model

42. All statements are true about anecdoial record. EXCEPT
A. A factual record of an observation of a single, significant incident in the behaviour of students

B. It is a verbal snapshot of an observed
C. It is a brief description of an observed behaviour that appears significant for evaluation purpose.
D. It also includes records of two or more incident

43. Sending information through test is an example of:-
A. Oral communication
B. Written communication
C. Non-verbal communication
D. None of the Above

44. All statement about philosophy is true. EXCEPT
A. Philosophy is a search for a comprehensive view of nature, an attempt at universal explanation of nature of things.
B. Philosophy describes what the school faculty believes about the education of nursing.
C. Philosophy of nursing education determines the aims objective, content, method of teaching and evaluation.
D. Philosophy is not the essential components in the structural hierarchy of nursing curriculum.

45. All statement about MICRO TEACHING is true. EXCEPT.
A. Its teaching of teachers to improve teaching skills.
B. Self improvement of teachers in teaching skills
C. Teaching is evaluated by students, peers and supervisor using checklist and feedback is given in both positive and negative aspect
D. Time limit 5-10 is not boundation.

46. When considering philosophy of education, John Dewey was a proponent of
A. Existentialism B. Pragmatism
C. Idealism D. Realism

47. Cognitive domain in Bloom's Taxonomy includes all the following, except
A. Evaluation and Application
B. Synthesis and Knowledge
C. Analysis and Comprehension
D. Criticism

48. A type of educational assessment which is generally carried out throughout a course or project is
A. Summative assessment
B. Formative assessment
C. Criterion-referenced assessment
D. Ipsative assessment

49. Which of the following is an example of Criterion-referenced assessment ?
A. Driving test
B. Wechsler Intelligence Scale for Children (WISC)
C. SAT
D. Graduate Record Examination (GRE)

50. Who stated "Education is not a preparation for life; education is life itself"?
A. Mahatma Gandhi
B. Bertrand Russell
C. Helen Keller
D. John Dewey

51. Trained Nurses Association of Indian (TNAI) was formed in the year
A. 1916 B. 1947 C. 1908 D. 1888

52. In India, first MSc Nursing programme was started in RAK college in the year
A. 1959 B. 1947 C. 1946 D. 1968

53. Characteristics of Problem Based Learning include all, EXCEPT:
A. Learning is driven by challenging, open-ended, ill-defined and ill-structured problems.
B. Students generally work in collaborative groups.
C. The teacher is the authority
D. Teachers take on the role as "facilitators" of learning

54. In India, the first four year basic Bachelor Degree nursing program was established in
A. 1910 B. 1940 C. 1946 D. 1880

55. "Democracy and Education" (1916) was authored by
A. Sigmond Freud
B. Jean Piaget
C. John Dewey
D. Ravindra Nadh Tagore

56. The type of discussion where a group of 6-8 qualified experts discuss a topic in front of an audience is called:
A. Group discussion B. Symposium
C. Panel discussion D. Workshop

57. Who proposed that education be designed on the basis of a theory of experience?
A. Socrates B. John Dewey
C. Bertrand Russell D. Jean Piaget

58. Which of the following is not a 2-way communication?
A. Lectures B. Group discussion
C. Panel discussion D. Symposium

59. To increase awareness of rural population towards small family norm, the best method is
A. Film show B. Charts and exhibits
C. Role playing D. Television

60. Which of the following is Socratic method of teaching?
A. Lecture B. Film
C. Exhibition D. Panel discussion

61. When giving health education to a community, the most important step is:
A. Contact doctors
B. Community discussion
C. Health education
D. Knowing of local needs

62. In a education programme, a group of 10 people are speaking on a topic of common interest is called as:
A. Workshop
B. Panel discussion
C. Group discussion
D. Symposium

63. The following statements are true about group discussion, except:
A. It is a two-way communication
B. An effective group is composed for 6-20 people
C. The leader initiates and guides the discussion
D. Each member prepares a topic for speech

64. Which of the following is NOT a feature of mass media education?
A. Deals with local problem of the community
B. Easily understandable
C. Widely approachable
D. Rapid and controlled

65. Andragogy refers to:
A. Adult learning
B. Action Learning
C. Experiential learning
D. Child learning

66. All that is learnt during school/college activities that is not a designated part of official curriculum is
A. The vocational curriculum
B. The hidden curriculum
C. The observed curriculum
D. The curriculum-as-experienced

67. Which of the following is NOT a feature of Process Model of curriculum?
A. Emphasis on means rather than ends
B. Learner should have part in deciding nature of learning activities
C. More individualized atmosphere
D. Makes assessment more precise

68. The International Council of Nurses (ICN) was established in the year:
A. 1867 B. 1899 C. 1950 D. 1962

69. The International Council of Nurses (ICN) is headquartered in:
A. New York, US
B. London, UK
C. Geneva, Switzerland
D. Toronto, Canada

70. Areas of philosophical inquiry include
A. Metaphysics concerned with questions about the nature of reality
B. Epistemology concerned with the nature of knowledge
C. Axiology concerned with the nature of values
D. All of the Above

71. Behavioral objectives model is also referred as:
A. Product model B. Process model
C. Classical model D. Competence model

72. The concepts of curriculum include:
A. He official curriculum
B He hidden curriculum
C He observed curriculum
D. All of the Above

73. Hich philosophical thought states that ultimate reality is spiritual rather than physical, mental rather than material?
A. Dealism B. Ealism
C. Ragmatism D. Onstructivism

74. A common data collecting instrument in nursing research is :-
A. Interview B. Questionnaire
C. Critical incident D. Q. short

75. A questionnaire item that allows the respondent complete freedom is:-
A. Open ended B. Closed ended
C. Indirect D. Direct

76. An advantage of the interview is that:-
A. Data from each interview are usable
B. Depth of response can be assured
C. Greater flexibility is provide
D. All of the Above

77. A study describing the evolution of using education in India would be which type of study?
A. Longitudinal B. Descriptive
C. Historical D. Evaluative

78. The most powerful research method for establishing casual relationship is the -
A. Experimental method
B. Casual comparative method
C. Correlation method
D. Descriptive method

79. Survey is:-
A. Used to obtain demographic data
B. Used to obtain information about people's behaviour
C. Frequently conducted by mail, telephone or interview
D. All of the Above

80. A factor that prohibits a direct study of total population is :-
A. Cost
B. Limited time
C. Lack of accessibility
D. All of the Above

81. Those restrictions that the nurse researcher place on the study before gathering are called:-
A. Assumptions B. Statistic
C. Delimitation D. Limitation

82. Facts generally accept as true are known as:-
A. Assumptions B. Limitation
C. Statistic D. Evaluation

83. A hypothesis usually identifies:
A. Measurement to be used
B. Variable to be used
C. Sample to be studied
D. Problem solution that has been selected

84. When establishing rapport an interviewer should:-
A. Identify himself and give the purpose of the study
B. Assure confidentiality of information
C. Create a friendly free atmosphere
D. All of the Above

85. Validity of a tool means it:-
A. Measures what is supported to be measured
B. Measures consistency
C. Is feasible and applicable
D. Is standardized

86. Reliability of an instrument means it;
A. Measures what is intended to measure
B. Measures consistently
C. Is feasible and applicable
D. None of these

87. Which of following is step of data analysis? .EXCEPT
A. Collection of data
B. Organization of data
C. Presentation of data
D. Interpretation of data

88. Nursing has used theories from :
A. Sociology B. Psychology
C. Anthropology D. All of the Above

89. An academically poor student may work hard and may show his abilities in dramatics or a person with a physical handicap may strive hard to excel in his studies? It is an example of:-
A. Rationalization B. Compensation
C. Projection D. Displacement

90. All are characteristics of research design. EXCEPT?
A. Objectivity and generality
B. Reliability
C. Validity
D. Experimental

91. Which of following terms is not synonymous with independent variable?
A. Casual variable
B. Stimulus or treatment
C. Experimental variable
D. Response or acutance variable

92. Which of following types of studies is considered a qualitative study?
A. Correlation B. Ethnographic
C. Comparative D. Methodological

93. When both qualitative and quantitative research methods are used simultaneously in the same study, the techniques is called?
A. Triangulation
B. Meta-analysis
C. Multitrait / multi method
D. Methodological plurality

94. A researcher wants to determine future priorities for research in maternal nursing . The participants will be clinical specialists in maternal nursing. Which of the following data collection methods would probably be used?
A. Projective techniques
B. Observation
C. Delphi Techniques
D. Semantic differential

95. Which of the following data collection methods is most likely to prevent subjects from providing socially acceptable response to question?
A. Attitude scale
B. Projective techniques
C. Self report questionnaire
D. Interview

96. A researcher will probebly receive a monetary reward for which of the following methods of presenting research?
A. Journals articles B. Research paper
C. Poster D. All of the Above

97. The conclusion of a study are based on the :
A. Finding of the study
B. Review of the literature
C. Implication of the study
D. Generalizations of the finding

98. What is the mode of the mode of the following group of vision test results? 20/20; 20/30; 20/40; 20/100; 20/30
A. 20/20 B. 20/30
C. 20/40 D. 20/50

99. Which of the following measures of central tendency would be appropriate to describe the average pulse rates of a group of surgical patients?
A. Mode B. Median
C. Mean D. All of the Above

100. The standards deviation is a measures of
A. Skewness B. Correlation
C. Central tendency D. Variability

101. The most objective means of obtaining nursing knowledge is through:
A. Trial and error
B. Tradition
C. Scientific research
D. Authority

102. One of main purposes of conducting a review of the literature before carrying out a research project is to:
A. Determine existing knowledge of the topic
B. Help select an optimum sample size.
C. Discover an instrument for date collection that has been used many times.
D. Prevent duplication of research

103. Assumptions are:
A. Beliefs that are thought to the be true but have not necessarily been proven
B. False beliefs help by the researcher
C. Expectations for study results.
D. None of the Above

104. Which of the following is not one of the common concepts that is included in nearly all of the nursing conceptual models?
A. Person B. Environment
C. Death D. Health

105. Which of the following is a both audio and visual teaching aid?
A. Bulletin-board B. Computer
C. Speaker D. Specimen

106. A combination of pictorial, graphic, numerical or vertical material can be displayed in:
A. Chart B. Map
C. Globe D. Diagram

107. Bulletin board is an example of :
A. Audio teaching aid
B. Projected teaching aid
C. Audio visual aid
D. Visual teaching aid

108. Which of the following graphic presentation is most suitable to represent the causes of maternal mortality?
A. Bar graph B. Map
C. Diagram D. Pie-chart

109. The teaching method in which nursing educator shows the various steps of doing procedure in systematic way in front of students is known as:
A. Lecture B. Symposium
C. Panel discussion D. Demonstration

110. The metaphorical presentation of reality can be displayed in form of:
A. Cartoons B. Graph
C. Histogram D. Puppets

111. How many members or Number of experts are involved in panel discussion?
A. 1-2 B. 4-6 C. 2-4 D. 4-10

112. What is The duration of micro-teaching ?
A. < 5 min. B. 10-15 min
C. 5-10 min. D. > 15 min.

113. How many members or Number of experts are involved in symposium ?
A. 1-2 B. 2-3 C. 7-8 D. 3-5

114. Which of the component of microteaching under 5 'R' ?
A. Recording B. Review
C. Redoing D. All of the Above

115. Field trip is a:
A. Natural learning
B. Inspirational learning
C. Expository learning
D. Individual learning

116. Which is not a Essential elements of communication?
A. Source
B. Message
C. Sender
D. Communication barriers

117. Which of the following method of teaching that includes both exhibition & explanation?
A. Demonstration B. Lecture
C. Discussion D. Learning by doing

118. Which of the following type of communication where the message is passed from one person to another like a chain is known as?
A. Interpersonal B. Two-way
C. Serial D. Mock up

119. The latest technology used by nursing educator in teaching is:
A. OHP presentation
B. Word presentation
C. Power point presentation
D. Verbal presentation

120. Way of Communication through facial expressions, gestures or body movements is an example of:
A. Verbal communication

B. One way communication
C. Dumb communication
D. Non verbal communication

121. Which of the following effective method nursing educator will select to teach his students?
A. Lecturer cum demonstration
B. Demonstration
C. Discussion
D. Lecturer

122. Chalk and talk method of teaching is also known as:
A. Demonstration B. Lecture
C. Symposium D. Discussion

123. The method of clinical teaching is based on:
A. Demonstration
B. Group discussion
C. Chalk board method
D. Panel discussion

124. Which of following the traditional type of curriculum is mostly centered on:
A. Subject centered
B. Students centered
C. Environment centered
D. Teacher centered

125. The numbers of members in the group discussion should be:
A. 6 - 12 B. 3 - 6 C. 8 - 18 D. 16-20

126. Which of the following sentence is incorrect regarding symposium method?
A. It is a series of speeches on a selected subject
B. All the members discuss on the given topic
C. In the end audience may ask questions
D. None of them

127. Which of the following sentence is regarding panel discussion?
A. The success of the panel depends upon the chairman
B. All the members discuss on the given topic
C. The chairman introduces the panel speakers
D. All of the Above

128. Which of the following is not a method of teaching?
A. Evaluation B. Demonstration
C. Seminar D. Lecture

129. Which of the following is not the element of communication?
A. Message B. Attention
C. Sender D. Feed back

130. Which of the following is the most commonly method of teaching used by nursing educator?
A. Seminar B. Lecture
C. Demonstration D. Discussion

131. Which of the following example of one way communication?
A. Workshop B. Group discussion
C. Panel discussion D. Lecture

132. Which of the following example of Three dimensional aid ?
A. Bulletin board B. Book
C. Model D. Black board

133. Which of the following method of teaching are most effective to teach the procedure about NG tube insertion?
A. Demonstration method
B. Lecture cum discussion
C. Lecture method
D. Discussion

134. Which of the following stage of curriculum except?
A. Evaluative B. Formative
C. Directive D. Summative

135. The effective Teaching is based on:
A. Intellectual capacity
B. Social capacity
C. Physical and mental capacity
D. Spiritual capacity

136. While grading of curriculum 'D' reflect that contents should be
A. Desirable B. Distance
C. Development D. Democratic

137. Which of the following is the important aim of nursing education?
A. Mental and intellectual development
B. Physical development
C. Vocation development
D. All of the Above

138. Which of the following activity involve in curriculum?
A. Laboratory activity
B. Play and clinical activity
C. Class room activity
D. All of the Above

139. Which of the following role of the teacher is most important?
A. Motivating students
B. Plan and organise course
C. Instructing students
D. All of the Above

140. Which of the following is not a phase of curriculum?
A. Implement B. Diagnosis
C. Evaluate D. Development

141. Which of the following important phase of communication?
A. Message B. Sender
C. Feedback D. Channel

142. Response from a receiver to sender is known as :
A. Feedback B. Message
C. Stimulus D. Answer

143. Which does not comes under 'C' of curricular planning
A. Comprehensive B. College
C. Concrete D. Continuous

144. Which of the following philosophy emphasizes upon learning by doing is?
A. Realism B. Pragmatism
C. Idealism D. Naturalism

145. When a learner learns through his own active response this is known as:
A. Purposive learning
B. Self active learning
C. Individual learning
D. Creative learning

146. Who is the father of pragmatism?
A. BF skinner
B. Florence Nightingale
C. M. Gandhi
D. William James

❑❑❑

Answer Sheet

1.D.	2.B.	3.C.	4.D.	5.A.	6.D.	7.A.	8.C.	9. D.	10. D.
11. A.	12. C.	13. D.	14. A.	15. D.	16. C.	17. D.	18. A.	19. C.	20. D.
21.D.	22. A.	23. C.	24. D.	25. A.	26. A.	27. C.	28. A.	29. D.	30. A.
31. D.	32. B.	33. B.	34. C.	35. B.	36. C.	37. C.	38. A.	39. B.	40. D.
41. B.	42. D.	43. B.	44. D.	45. D.	46. B.	47. D.	48. B.	49. A.	50. D.
51. C.	52. A.	53. C.	54. C.	55. C.	56. C.	57. B.	58. A.	59. C.	60. D.
61. D.	62. C.	63. D.	64. A.	65. A.	66. B.	67. D.	68. B.	69. C.	70. D.
71. A.	72. D.	73. A.	74. D.	75. A.	76. D.	77. C.	78. A.	79. D.	80. D.
81. D.	82. A.	83. D.	84. D.	85. A.	86. A.	87. D.	88. D.	89. B.	90. D.
91. D.	92. B.	93. A.	94. C.	95. C.	96. D.	97. A.	98. B.	99. C.	100. C.
101. C.	102. A.	103. A.	104. C.	105. B.	106. A.	107. D.	108. D.	109. D.	110. A.
111. C.	112. C.	113. D.	114. D.	115. A.	116. D.	117. A.	118. C.	119. C.	120. D.
121. A.	122. B.	123. A.	124. A.	125. A.	126. B.	127. D.	128. A.	129. B.	130. B.
131. D.	132. C.	133. A.	134. D.	135. A.	136. A.	137. D.	138. D.	139. D.	140. B.
141. C.	142. A.	143. B.	144. B.	145. B.	146. D.				

4. MEDICAL SURGICAL NURSING (MCQ)

1. **Congestive Heart Failure is best described as**
   A. Collection of the fluid in the tissue
   B. Inability of the heart to meet the body's demands
   C. Reduced body needs as opposed to increased heart activity
   D. Venousreturn retardation by a compensatory heart
2. **A nurse can decontaminate the HIV contaminated waste products with all the following, except**
   A. Sodium hypo-chlorite
   B. Formaldehyde
   C. Methanol
   D. Glutaraldehyde
3. **Physician wants central venous catheterization. Nurse has to know which vein he should make use of**
   A Cephalic vein B. Radial vein
   C. Femoral vein D. Basilic vein
4. **Pre renal failure occurs in**
   A. Glomerulonephritis
   B. Heart failure
   C. Nephrolithiasis
   D. Toxic nephropathy
5. **Twenty five yrs old male patient had sweating, palpitations and found to have blood sugar of 45 mg/dl. Multiple similar episodes had been recorded in the past, corrected with glucose. Nurse caring for this patient should consider which one of the following diagnosis?**
   A. Glucaganoma B. VIP oma
   C. Insulinoma D. Gastrinoma
6. **An accurate picture of the effectiveness of diuretic therapy is ascertained through ?**
   A. Daily weight measurement
   B. Intakeoutput records every hour
   C. Testing for pedal edema daily
   D. Type of diuretic administered
7. **Nurse is about to catheterize bladder of a pregnant lady. She should be aware that all the following facts about female urethra are true, except**
   A. It is straight and offers minor resistance for catheterization
   B. It is about 1.5 inches in length
   C. It's posterior to vaginal orifice
   D. It pierces through urogenital diaphragm
8. **The postoperative patient who exhibits ,pyrexia, purulent drainage and congestion around the incision may be said to have**
   A. Exudation
   B. Resolution
   C. Postoperative infection
   D. Rubor
9. **All the following cancers have infective etiology except**
   A. Kaposi's sarcoma
   B. Squamous carcinoma of penis
   C. Squamous carcinoma of lung
   D. Burkit's lymphoma
10. **Which one of the following cancer does not metastasize commonly to liver?**
    A. Prostate B. Breast
    C. Lung D. Colon
11. **Direct action of parathyroid hormone include everything except**
    A. Increased production of 1,25 ` dihydroxy Vita-min D
    B. Increased resorption of calcium from bone
    C. Increased absorption of calcium from intes-tine
    D. Increased reabsorption of calcium from kid-ney
12. **Gastric resections may result in the following**
    A. Diabetes insipidus
    B. Dumping syndrome
    C. Esophageal varices
    D. Thrombocytopenia
13. **What is the best way to be adapted by a nurse to avoid hematoma, formation when undertaking venipuncture?**
    A. Apply heparin containing ointment after pro-cedure
    B. Choose a vein that is soft and refills fast
    C. Tap the vein hard before venipuncture
    D. Apply firm pressure for 1 minute after proce-dure
14. **Nurse giving oxygen therapy should know that it has to be humidified because**
    A. Oxygen is easily absorbed because humidification add H-ion to it
    B. Oxygen is a hot air and it may burn trachea
    C. Oxygen is a dry gas and thickens the mucus
    D. Oxygen gets cleaned of pathogens by humidification

15. For the patient with otitis media nursing care is centered on reducing the severity or alleviating problems ?
A. Dizziness and decreased hearing
B. Fever and tinnitus
C. Pain and pressure in the ear
D. Nausea and vomiting

16. A nurse observes palmar erythema and she understands that it is met within
A. Adrenal failure B. Cardiac failure
C. Renal failure D. Hepatic failure

17. The diagnostic study to assess left ventricular dysfunction is:
A. Echocardiography
B. Angiogram
C. Catheterisation
D. ECG

18. Absolute glaucoma is a condition that result in
A. Detachment of the retina
B. Hypertrophy of the conjunctiva
C. Severe pain and loss of vision
D. Temporary loss of vision

19. Acid base imbalance that develops in acute renal failure is:
A. Metabolic alkalosis
B. Metabolic acidosis
C. Respiratory acidosis
D. Respiratory alkalosis

20. Clay coloured stool is suggestive of:
A. Obstructive jaundice
B. Amoebic dysentery
C. Typhoid
D. Ulcerative colitis

21. Surgery done for myasthenia gravis is:
A. Thymectomy B. Pallidotomy
C. Hypophysectom D. Sympathectomy

22. What is the effect of cyclosporine in a patient undergone renal transplantation?
A. Diuretic
B. Immunosuppressant
C. Anti-inflammatory
D. Antibacterial

23. Mrs. A is scheduled for pneumoencephalography. This procedure, done in the xray department, consists of an injection of
A. Air directly into the ventricles
B. A dye into the lumbar subarachnoid space
C. A radioactive substance intravenously
D. Air into the lumbar subarachnoid space

24. Carpel tunnel syndrome is caused by:
A. Injury to wrist joint
B. Pressure on cephalic nerve
C. Damage to lower motor neuron
D. Pressure on median nerve

25. Surgical fusion of a joint is known as:
A. Nailing B. Arthrodesis
C. Arthroplasty D. Arthrotomy

26. It is suspected that a patient has meningococcal meningitis and should therefore, be isolated
A. For his entire hospitalization
B. For the first 48 hours
C. Until his culture are negative
D. For 24 hours after initiating antibiotic therapy

27. The most common site of occurring peptic ulcers in stomach:
A. Body of the stomach
B. Pyloric portion
C. Cardiac portion
D. Esophageal junction

28. Parenteral preparation of potassium should be administered slowly to prevent:
A. Over load B. Acidosis
C. Cardiac arrest D. Respiratory arrest

29. Tumor of blood vessel of brain is:
A. Astrocytoma B. Glioma
C. Meningioma D. Hemangioma

30. Emergency nursing care of the patient suspected of a spinal cord injury will be to A.Place in semiFowler's position to stabilize the vertebral column B.Keep flat with head and neck stabilized C.Logroll onto a stretcher for transport D.Place in orthopneic position to facilitate respiration
A. A and C B. B and C
C. B and D D. C and D

31. Hemiplegia involves:
A. Paresis of upper and lower extremities
B. Paresis of both lower extremities
C. Paralysis of one side of the body
D. Paralysis of both lower extremities

32. To promote postburn hydration and kidney function, the nurse should
A. Keep accurate intake and output, weight daily, and maintain IV fluids
B. Reverse isolation and measure urine specific gravity
C. Reposition frequently and administer analgesics
D. Note depth of respirations and measure intake and output accurately

33. Palliative care means:
A. General care B. Pain relief
C. Symptom relief D. Ostomy care

34. Invertogram is one of the diagnostic test in:
A. Diverticulum
B. Pyloric stenosis
C. Intussusception
D. Anorectal anomalies

35. Important point to remember in instructing a mastectomy patient before discharge are
A. Frequent changing of dressings and good nutrition
B. Promotion of rest
C. Prevention of infection and phlebitis
D. Teaching of good posture and prescribed exercise

36. Bronchiolitis is commonly seen in which age group?
A. 65–85 years B. 6 –12 years
C. <6 –12 years D. 2–3 years

37. Respiratory center is located at:
A. Spinal cord
B. Cerebrum
C. Pons
D. Medulla oblongata & pons

38. Underproduction of thyroxin produces:
A. Myxedema
B. Grave's disease
C. Cushing's disease
D. Acromegaly

39. All the following hormones are secreted by anterior pituitary except
A. FSH B. GH
C. GRH D. TSH

40. Glyeated haemoglobin (HbAIC.tests, mean glucose levels
A. Over 90 days B. Over 2 days
C. Over 14 days
D. Over 30 days

41. How do you know that intercostal drainage tube is functioning?
A. Continuous bubbling in waterseal bottle
B. Continuous bubbling from suction tube
C. Oscillation of water column in drainage bottle
D. No bubbling in the drainage bottle

42. Which of the following is not a parameter for "Glasgow Coma Scale"?
A. Motor response
B. Eye opening
C. Pupillary response
D. Verbal response

43. The cardiotonic dose of dopamine is:
A. 25 to 50 mg/kg/minute
B. 1 to 5 mg/kg/minute
C. 5 to 15 mg/kg/minute
D. 15 to 25 mg/kg/minute

44. In a case of hypothyroidisrn, which of the following is increased?
A. T3 B. T4
C. TSH D. All of the above

45. In hemolytic jaundice the following are true EXCEPT
A. Liver function test is normal
B. Unconjugated bilirubin level increases
C. Anemia is common
D. Serum alkaline phosphatase level increases

46. Persistent generalized lymph-adenopathy, is caused by
A. HIV B. HST
C. HIB D. AST

47. Which one of the following viruses cause post transfusion hepatitis?
A. Hepatitis D B. Hepatitis A
C. Hepatitis B D. Hepatitis C

48 Cancer of epithelial tissue is called
A. Hodgkin's disease
B. Carcinoma
C. Sarcoma
D. Lukemia

49. Thirty yr old female complained of wetting her dress while coughing. Which one of the following conditions a nurse should suspect?
A. Urethrocele B. Cystocele
C. Rectocele D. Enterocele

50. Antigen is a substance which:
A. It is used as an antidote to poison
B. Lowers body temperature
C. Destroys harmful substances
D. Triggers the immune system

51. Goiter occurs due to the deficiency of:
A. Chloride B. Iodine
C. Calcium D. Potassium

52. The break in the continuity of bone is referred as:
A. Inflammation B. Wound
C. Arthritis D. Fracture

53. Klinefelter syndrome is indicated by:
A. Chromosome 46XY
B. Chromosome 47XXY
C. Chromosome 23XY
D. Chromosome 47X

54. All the factors aid in venous return to the heart except
A. Squeezing action of major muscle
B. Negative intrathoracic pressure
C. One way valves in the veins
D. Left ventricular contraction

55. All the following enzymes are secreted by gastrointestinal system except
A. Angiotensin B. Ptyalin
C. Pepsin D. Chymotrypsin

56. The complaint of oligomenorrhea, obesity and Hirsultism in a 20-year-old lady indicates:
A. Pregnancy
B. PCOD
C. Cancer of edometrium
D. Prolactenoma

57. BMI greater than 30 is considered as:
A. Stout B. Overweight
C. Bulimia D. Obese

58. While recording Intake Output nurse has to consider Insensible water loss from human body and the normal is
A. 1000 ml B. 200 ml
C. 400 ml D 800 ml

59. Stimulation of vagus nerve results in Expect:
A. Dilatation of coronary artery
B. Increase in heart rate
C. Decrease in heart rate
D. Dilatation of bronchioles

60. Pain in appendicitis is experienced:
A. Meburney's point
B. Above umbilicus
C. Left iliac fossa
D. Below umbilicus

61. Positive Homan's sign is indicative of:
A. Renal calculi
B. Pulmonary embolism
C. Varicose vein
D. Deep vein thrombosis

62. Surgery involving renal pelvis is:
A. Pyeloplasty B. Pyloroplasty
C. Urethroplasty D. Lithotripsy

63. A cataract is:
A. Opacity of conjunctiva
B. Crystallization of the pupil
C. Opacity of lens
D. Thin film over the cornea

64. Symptoms that may be experienced by patient in diabetic coma are
A. Sweating, hunger and trembling
B. Pallor, headache and weakness
C. Slow pulse and difficulty in breathing
D. Hot dry skin, nausea, vomiting and drowsiness

65. The purpose of peritoneal dialysis is to:
A. Provide fluid
B. Clean the peritoneal cavity
C. Reestablish kidney function
D. Remove the toxins and metabolic waste

66. Lumbar sympathectomy relieves:
A. Spondylosis
B. Spinal cord compression
C. POVD
D. Trigeminal neuralgia

67. The presence of synovial fluid in joints reduces:
A. Speed of movements
B. Efficiency
C. Workload
D. Friction in joints

68. Which of the following nursing measures should be avoided in a patient with increased in cranial pressure?
A. Catheterization
B. Suctioning for prolonged time
C. Oral feeding
D. Fowler's position

69. In an adult, the skeleton comprises around:
A. 10-20% of the total body weight
B. 40-50% of the total body weight
C. 30-40% of the total body weight
D. 60-70% of the total body weight

70. Aphonia would lead one to suspect
A. Hemorrahge
B. Hysteria
C. Injury to esophagus
D. Injury to the recurrent laryngeal nerve endings

71. Which of the following is most dangerous complication during induction of spinal anesthesia?
A. Hypotension B. Hyperthermia
C. Bradypnea D. Tachycardia

72. Which of the following is the earliest sign of poor respiratory function?
A. Faintness B. Fast thready pulse
C. Restlessness D. Cyanosis

73. ELISA test is used to detect:
A. Cholera infection B. HIV infection3
C. Malaria infectionD. Lung infection

74. Tetany, postoperatively, may be caused by
A. Invasion by the bacillus tetany
B. An increase in the amount of calcium in the blood

C. Decrease of phosphorus in the blood
D. A decrease in the amount of calcium in the blood

75. The instrument used to measure blood pressure is:
A. Sphygmomanometer
B. Electrocardiograph
C. Stethescope
D. Rotameter

76. When the patient vomits, the most important nursing objective is to prevent:
A. Aspiration
B. Dehydration
C. Metabolic Alkalosis
D. None of them

77. Homologous Serum Hepatitis (Hepatitis B.is contacted byHindi
A. Exposure to infection
B. Parental inoculation
C. Physical damage to the liver
D. Improper utilization of bile salts

78. Oxygen therapy is recommended in:
A. Severe trauma
B. Acute myocardial infarction
C. Severe respiratory distress
D. All the above

79. The symptoms indicative of benign proatatic hypertrophy areHindi
A. Frequency, hesitancy, straining and hematuria
B. Nocturia, hesitancy, straining and nuria
C. Frequency, pyuria, straining and hematuria
D. Hesitancy, straining, suppression and urgency

80. Nursing responsibilities for either external or internal radiation therapy include:
A. Provide emotional support
B. Carefully assess and manage any complications, in collaboration with the radiation oncologist
C. Assist in documenting the results of therapy
D. All the above

81. The number of pairs of cranial nerves are:
A. 12 B. 14
C. 16 D. 10

82. The symptoms associated with the type of fracture would probably be
A. Shock, pain and adduction with hip and knee
B. Pain, external rotation and lengthening of the extremity
C. Pain, external rotation and shortening of the extremity
D. Shock, internal rotation and shortening of the extremity

83. Contraction of the abdominal muscles is important in:
A. Forced (maximum)
B. Normal (quiet) expiration
C. Forced (maximum) expiration
D. Normal (quiet) inspiration

84. To diagnosis meningitis which type of sample is collected:
A. Urine B. CSF
C. Bone-marrow D. Stool

85. Visual acuity may be assessed by using a snellen's chart: If a patient has acuity of 6/12 in both eyes, this means:
A. The patient has normal vision
B. The patient can see twice as well as normal
C. The patient has less than normal vision
D. The patient has double vision

86. Guillian Barre syndrome is a disease of which of the following:
A. Brain
B. Spinal cord
C. Peripheral nerve
D. All of the above

87. Which type of burn is painless?
A. Third degree
B. Second degree
C. First degree
D. None of the above

88. Which of the following is not a parameter for "Glasgow coma scale"
A. Eye opening
B. Pupillary response
C. Verbal response
D. Motor response

89. The most likely side effect of external radiation to the neck for cancer of larynx is:
A. Constipation B. Dyspnea
C. Sore throat D. Diarrhoea

90. Most dangerous complication of venous thrombus is:
A. Gangreous development of veins
B. Chronic occlusion of the vein
C. Pulmonary embolism
D. Formation of venous ulcers

91. Eye padding is applied on unconscious patients to prevent:
A. Dryness of eye
B. Blinking of eyes
C. Corneal ulcer
D. Eye movement

92. A nurse is watching the cardiac monitor and notices that the rhythm suddenly changes, there are no P waves, the QRS complexes are wide and the ventricular rate is regular but over 100, the nurse determines that the patient is experiencing:

A. Sinus tachycardia
B. Ventricular tachycardia
C. Ventricular fibrillation
D. Premature ventricular contractions

93. What is the cause of anaemia in chronic renal failure:

A. Decreased erythropoietin
B. Hemolysis
C. Production of immature RBCs
D. Inappropriate renal functioning.

94. Infection of middle ear is called:

A. Otitis media B. Labyrinthitis
C. Sinusitis D. Mastoiditis

95. In following which is not a cause of hypokalemia:

A. Vomitting
B. Potassium wasting diuretics
C. Aldosteronism
D. Renal failure

95. A patient is scheduled for a IVP using a radio-opaque dye, which of the following assessment is most critical before the procedure:

A. Measurement of heights and weight
B. Measurement of baseline peripheral pulse rates
C. History of intake and output
D. History of allergy to iodine

96. Which of the following formula is correct for calculating Body Mass Index (BMI):

A. Weight in Kg. + (Height in meter)2
B. Weight in Kg. - (Height in meter)2
C. Weight in Kg. x (Height in meter)2
D. Weight in Kg. / (Height in meter)2

97. Nephrotic syndrome is characterized by:

A. Pyuria, oliguria, hematuria
B. Hematuria, Azotemia, hypertension
C. Proteinuria, Edema, Hyperlipidemia
D. Hematuria, proteinuria, hypertension

98. Which organ is most at risk for dysfunction in a patient with a potassium level of 6.2 M.Eq/L

A. Lungs B. Kidney
C. Liver D. Heart

99. Shock which is resulting from severe allergic reaction is:

A. Anaphylactic shock
B. Distributive shock
C. Septic shock
D. Neurogenic shock

100. Each normal heart beat is initiated by which of the following ?

A. Sino Atrial Node
B. Bundle of His
C. Cardiac Center of Medulla
D. Sympathetic nerves

101. When the nurse is assessing a patient who has cirrhosis of the liver, which of the following findings would indicate that the patient's condition is worsening?

A. Positive babinski sign
B. Bilateral basal lung crepts
C. Visual field loss
D. Flapping hand tremors

102. When blood pressure falls, which of the following is secreted by kidney to raise it ?

A. Renin B. Epinephrine
C. Aldosterone D. Erythropoetin

103. Which of the following infections agent can be transmitted by blood transfusion?

A. Plasmodium B. HIV
C. Hepatitis D. All of the above

104. Permanent pacemaker is indicated in which of the following dysrhythmias ?

A. Ventricular fibrillation
B. Asymptomatic bradycardia
C. Atrial fibrillation
D. Third degree heart block

105. Glasgow coma scale has all, axcept:

A. Sensory response
B. Eye opening
C. Verbal response
D. Motor response

106. Which of the following structure covers the larynx during swallowing?

A. Hydroid Cartilage
B. Vocal cords
C. Soft palate
D. Epiglottis

107. In which surgery part of stomach is removed and remaining portion is anastomosed to duodenum?

A. Gastrectomy
B. Endoscopic mucosal resection
C. Gastrojejunostomy
D. Gastroduodenostomy

108. Which of the following is not a risk factor for gallbladder disease

A. Male
B. Obese

C. Multiple pregnancies
D. Age 40 or above

109. Exophthalmos of the eyes is a characteristic sign of:
A. Grave's disease
B. Gushing's disease
C. Myxedema
D. Cretinism

110. Urea is a waste product of which of the following the metabolism?
A. Nucleic acid B. Amino acid
C. Muscle tissue D. Carbohydrate

111. Abnormal sensitivity to light is known as:
A. Aphasia B. Photophobia
C. Hydorphobia D. Diplopia

112. Which of the following is restricted for a patient scheduled for an intravenous pyelogram?
A. Salt intake
B. Fluid intake
C. Use of tobacco
D. Physical Activities

113. The blood contains:
A. 95% of water B. 60% of water
C. 90% of water D. 80% of water

114. Which of the followings are signs and symptoms of tetany?
A. Numb fingers, muscle cramps
B. Weakness, muscle fatigue
C. Hallucinations, delusions
D. Dyspnoea and tachycardia

115. Which one of the following is the most appropriate addition to the care plan for the patient with Bell's palsy?
A. Inspect the buccal pouch for food after eating
B. Advise the patient to drink liquids from a cup
C. Discourage the patient from looking in a mirror
D. Reduce the amount of light with in the room

116. When neurologist asks a patient to smile which cranial nerve is being tested?
A. Optic B. Facial
C. Vagus D. Accessary

117. Which of the following statement is false?
A. Untreated HFV infection can remain in the ealy chronic stage for a decade or more
B. Infection with HIV results in a chronic disease with acute exacerbations
C. Late stage detection is called AIDS
D. Opportunistic disease occur more often when the CD4+ T cells count is high and viral load is low

118. When testing Visual fields, the nurse is assessing which of the following parts of vision?
A. Peripheral vision B. Near vision
C. Distance vision D. Central vision

119. Anisometropia is a condition, there is:
A. Variation in the refractive power of two eyes
B. The ideal refractive condition
C. Differences in the image sizes
D. None of them

120. Which of the following rule to be applied while estimating surface area of burns in adults?
A. Rule of thumb B. Rule of 9
C. Rule of 5 D. Rule of 1

121. The cells involved in the specific immune response are derived from:
A. Spleen
B. Bone marrow
C. Lymphatic tissues
D. Immunoglobulins

122. According to WHO , the blindness is defined as visual acquity is less than
A. 6/6 B. 6/60
C. 1/60 D. 18/60

123. Which one of the following is a function of liver?
A. Secretion of cholecytokinin
B. Elimination of carbohydrates
C. Concentration of bile
D. Synthesis of plasma proteins

124. Which of the following test is used for diagnosis of scarlet fever?
A. Widal test B. MGIT
C. TestDucrey test D. Dick test

125. Which patient is at risk for respiratory acidosis?
A. The patient who overuses antacids
B. The patient with chronic pulmonary disease
C. The patient with uncontrolled diabetes mellitus
D. The patient who is very anxious

126. Deficiency of Iron in children causes which of the following diseases?
A. Goiter B. Rickets
C. Beriberi D. Anaemia

127. A butterfly rash is a classic symptom of .... Which of the following disorder?
A. Osteo sarcoma
B. Lupus erythematous
C. Pagef s disease
D. Rhumatoid arthritis

128. **Which of the following microorganism causes the most prevalent form of meningitis among the children aged 2 months to 3 years?**
A. Streptococcus pneumoniae
B. Vibrio cholerae
C. Staphylococcal Pneumoniae
D. Neisseria meningitides

129. **The largest part of the brain is:**
A. Cerebellum B. Hypothalamus
C. Cerebrum D. Medulla

130. **What is the total lung capacity of an adult male?**
A. Six liters B. Four liters
C. Three liters D. Two liters

131. **The most common clinical finding associated with cancer of the urinry bladder:**
A. Suprapubic pain
B. Dysuria
C. Urinary retention
D. Pain less haematuria

132. **Which one of the following is popularly known as Dry ice?**
A. Frozen Nitrogen
B. Frozen distilled water
C. Solid carbon dioxide
D. Moisture frozen in the air

133. **The best treatment for an allergy is:**
A. Prevent the person from coming in contact with the sensitizing allergens
B. Live in a room free of dust
C. Use an electrostatic filter
D. Use antihistamines

134. **Which one of the following chemicals could be an alternative to petrol for automobiles and yet is likely to be a not pollutant?**
A. Formalin B. Acetylene
C. Formaldehyde D. All of the above

135. **Cigarette smoking can affect the cirulation by:**
A. Extravasation of blood
B. Blocking of the blood vessels
C. Narrowing of the blood vessels
D. Over expanding of the blood vessels

136. **Myasthenia gravis is an example of**
A. Viral diseases
B. Immuno deficient diseases
C. Autoimmune diseases
D. Allergic reactions

137. **A client at risk for increased intracranial prssure which of the following would be the priority for the nurse of monitor:**
A. Decreasing systolic blood pressure
B. Unequal pupil size
C. Tachycardia
D. Increasing body temperature

138. **HIV Selectively targets**
A. Bmemory cells B. Thelper cells
C. Beffector cells D. TCytotoxic cells

139. **Which symptom is an early indicator of hypoxia in an unconscious client?**
A. Hypertension
B. Cyanosis
C. Restlessness
D. Deceased respiration

140. **The term "molecular scissors"generally refers to**
A. DNA Polymerases
B. RNA Polymerases
C. Restriction endonucleases
D. DNA ligases

141. **A patient with cirrhosis of the liver has a serum bilirubin level of 30 mg/dl. In order to evaluate these laboratory results you need to know that the normal serum bilirubin level is:**
A. 20 to 30 mg/dl
B. 0.2 to 1.0 mg/dl
C. 10 to 20 mg/dl
D. 3 to 10 mg/dl

142. **The product of which of the following organisms has been commercialized as blood cholesterol lowering agent**
A. Trichoderma polysporum
B. Monascus purpureus
C. Saccharonyces cerevisiae
D. Aspergillus niger

143. **Which of the following is an initial sign of parkinson's disoase?**
A. Tremor B. Rigidity
C. Akinesia D. Bradykinesia

144. **Malignant malaria is caused by**
A. Plasmodium vivax
B. Plasmodium ovale
C. Plasmodium falciparum
D. Plasmodium malaria

145. **Peripheral blood flow is dependent on:**
A. Pressure differences in the arterial and venous system and resistance
B. Force of contraction of heart and resistance of vessels
C. Blood viscosity and diameter of vessels
D. Diameter and resistance of vessels

146. **The major phagocytic cells are**
A. Lymphocytes B. Mastcells
C. Macrophages D. Plasma cells

147. **The goal on Nursing care for a cient with acute myeloid-leukaemia is to prevent:**
A. Renal failure

B. Haemorrhage
C. Cardiac arrhythmia
D. Liver failure

148. Aedes aegypti is a vector of
A. both dengue and yellow fever
B. dengue fever
C. yellow fever
D. Japanese encephalitis

149. Inpresbyopia the individual needs to hold the reading material:
A. Very closs to the eyes
B. At arm's length
C. Not too close to the eyes
D. So distant to the eyes

150. Which of the following is a covalent solid?
A. Fe B. Diamond
C. Sodium chloride D. Cu

151. Which of the following clients is at risk for varicose veins?
A. A client who has had thrombo phlebitis
B. A client who had C.V.A
C. A client who has had anaemia
D. A client who has had transient ischemic attacks

152. Which of the following is a strong electrolyte?
A. Acetic Acid
B. Ammonium Hydroxide
C. Sodium Chloride
D. Carbonic Acid

153. The pain associated with migraine headache s caused by:
A. Sustained contraction of muscles around the scalp of face
B. Dilatation of the cranial arteries
C. A temporary decrease in intracranial pressure
D. Irritation and inflammation of the opening of sinuses

154. Which of the following is strongly acidic:
A. Acetic acid B. Formic acid
C. Propionic acid D. Butyric acid

155. A client with pneumonia is experiencing peurite chest pain, he describes:
A. Muscle spasm pain that accompanies coughing
B. Severe media sternal pain
C. Moderate pain that worsens on inspiration
D. A mild but constant aching in the chest

156. Which of the following compound is highly basic:
A. Ethyl amine B. Diethyl amine
C. Aniline D. Ammonia

157. Which of the following systems is not blocked by spinal anaesthesia?
A. The Parasympathetic system
B. The sympathetic nervous system
C. The sensory nervous system
D. The motor system

158. Which of the following is not addition polymer:
A. Polyethene B. Teflon
C. Nylon66 D. Polyvinyl chloride

159. Meniere's disease affects:
A. EAR B. EYE
C. NOSE D. SKIN

160. Which concentration term is not affected by temperature:
A. Normality B. Molarity
C. Molality D. Formality

161. The pressure exerted by a fluid with in a closed system is:
A. Hydrostatic pressure
B. Osmotic pressure
C. Oncotic pressure
D. Hydrolic pressure

162. Which of the following compound does not contain asymmetric carbon atom:
A. Lactic acid B. Isopentane
C. Tartaric acid D. 2Butanol

163. Treadmill test done for a cardiac patient is to plan:
A. His discharge from the hospital
B. Progressive physical activity
C. Dietary regime for the patient
D. Drug adjustment

164. Which of the following is water soluble vitamin:
A. A B. C
C. E D. D

165. A closed sac or pouch which consist of semi solid, solid or liquid material is a:
A. Vesicle B. Nodule
C. Pustule D. Cyst

166. Which of the following is not an example of reducing sugar:
A. Sucrose B. Maltose
C. Lactose D. Glucose

167. Normal pacemaker of the heart is:
A. Lymph node B. S.A. node
C. Bundle of his D. A.V. node

168. Which of the following act as an strong oxidizing agent:
A. Chlorine B. Bromine
C. Iodine D. Fluorine

169. Downwards displacement of the kidney is:
A. Nephrotosis
B. Nephrotic syndrome

C. Nephrosclerosis
D. Hydronephrosis

170. Principles underlying radio therapy is:
A. Malignant cells are more sensitive radiation than normal cells
B. Resistance to normal cells is incresed
C. Radiation may cause metasisis
D. Radiation kills the orgnisms

171. A patient with haemorrhoids asks the nurse the cause of the problem. The nurse explains that it generally results from :
A. Eating spicy foods
B. Diabetes
C. Hypertension
D. Constipation

172. Most important objective during the post burn phase is to:
A. Relieve pain
B. Prevent infection
C. Replace blood loss
D. Replace fluid volume

173. During the first 24 hours of treating a patient for burns,you can assist in assessing fluid replacement needs by monitoring hourly:
A. Urine specific gravity
B. 2 I/V fluid rate
C. Vital signs
D. I/V fluid intake

174. Oedema is most effectively controlled in patients with heart failure by:
A. Restriction of sodium
B. Proper positioning
C. Fluid restriction
D. Medication

175. The physician considers performing a magnetic resonance imaging (MRI) tests on the elderly client with cirrhosis. Before the MRI is performed, which nursing action is essential?
A. The nurse administers a pretest sedative
B. The nurse records the client's body weight
C. The nurse removes the client's dental bridge
D. The nurse inserts a Foley retention catheter

176. A client is receiving radiation to the neck for cancer of the larynx. The most likely side effects to be expected is :
A. Sore throat B. Constipation
C. Diarrhoea D. Dyspnoea

177. The test that is most specific for myocardial damage is :
A. CK MB B. Myoglobin
C. Troponin I D. CK

178. A patient is admitted with a suspected bladder cancer .A nurse assesses the patient for which of the following earliest manifestation of the disease?
A. Protienuria and dysuria
B. Haematuria and no pain
C. Painful urinations and haematuria
D. Pyuria and palpable abdominal mass

179. A patient has been admitted in the hospital with gastroenteritis .During assessment, the nurse is expected to find:
A. Hypoactive bowel sounds
B. Hyperactive bowel sounds
C. Rigid and broad like abdomen
D. Rebound tenderness

180. The nurse while taking care of a patient with cervical level spinal cord injury should give priority to the following nursing diagnosis
A. Risk for hypertension
B. Ineffective airway clearance
C. Ineffective thermoregulation
D. Impaired physical mobility

181. A client with cancer develops pleural effusion . During chest auscultation ,the following breath sounds should be expected to hear :
A. Cackles
B. Rhonchi
C. Diminished breath sounds
D. Wheeze

182. A 35 - year old male has been an Insulin dependentdiabetic for last 5 years and is now unable to urinate. The following is most likely to suspect:
A. Atherosclerosis
B. Diabetic nephropathy
C. Autonomic neuropathy
D. Somatic neuropathy

183. The following problem does not typically result from uncontrolled gestational diabetes mellitus:
A. Maternal hyperglycemia
B. Fetal demise
C. Insufficient amniotic fluid
D. Maternal hypertension

184. When disposing plastic bags, tubings, syringes and gloves used to administer antineoplastic drugs, the nurse should implement which nursing intervention?
A. Avoiding contact with the equipment by allowing housekeeping to remove it
B. Discarding all used equipment in a container marked "Isolation"

C. Dispose all equipment in a container marked " Bio health Hazard"
D. Disposing all used equipment in the regular trash receptacles

185. The client with a rectovaginal fistula is at risk of Infection. The intervention, most important in preventive aspect of nursing care is :
A. Administering antibiotics
B. Ensuring adequate rest to enhance healing
C. Monitoring temperature and WBC count
D. Performing perineal care

186. A client is presented with embolic stroke. Which of the following condition places the client at the risk of thrombo embolic stroke?
A. Atrial fibrillation
B. Bradycardia
C. superficial vein thrombosis
D. History of myocardial infarction

187. The following is the most frequent classic site of internal bleeding associated with hemophilia :
A. Brain tissue B. tract
C. Joint cavities D. Spinal cord

188. The nurse should anticipate which immediate treatment for a patient experiencing pulseless ventricular tachycardia?
A. Transcutaneous pacing
B. Electrical counter shock
C. Transvenous pacing
D. Intravenous bolus of Lidocaine 100mg

189. Which of the following can cause hypovolaemic shock?
A. Allergic reaction of medication
B. Third- space shifting of fluid into the abdominal cavity
C. Sepsis
D. Profound bradycardia

190. What measurement can best be used to monitor the respiratory status of a patient with pulmonary oedema?
A. Arterial blood gas analysis
B. Pulse oximetry
C. Skin color assessment
D. Lung sounds

191. Which body system most commonly is affected in patients with electrolyte imbalances?
A. Cardiovascular system
B. Neuromuscular system
C. Renal system
D. Endocrine system

192. A patient with colonic obstruction should be observed for which potential complication?
A. Hepatitis B. Cirrhosis
C. Bowel Necrosis D. Pancreatitis

193. Which drug is preferred for prophylactic therapy of mild tomoderate asthma?
A. Formoterol
B. Montelukast
C. Ipratropium bromide
D. Theophy line

194. The disease Athelete's Foot is caused by ?
A. Bacteria B. Fungi
C. Protozoa D. Nimatod

195. White blood cells act:
A. As a defense against infection
B. As source of energy
C. For clotting blood
D. As a medium for oxygen transport from lungs to tissues

196. Development of Goitre (Enlarged thyroid glanD.is mainly due to deficiency of ?
A. Sodium B. Iodine
C. Calcium D. Iron

197. Warm, dry, pink skin is seen in?
A. Hypovolemic shock
B. Cardiogenic shock
C. Anaphylactic shock
D. Neurogenic shock

198. The medicine given during acute anaphylactic reaction is :
A. Atropine B. Aminophyline
C. Deriphyl ine D. Adrenaline

199. Which sign or symptom you will find in an infant with pyloric stenosis?
A. Vomiting of bile
B. Lethargy
C. Diarrhea
D. Projectile vomiting

200. Excessive exercise without rest results in accumulation of carbon dioxide and lactic acid and this causes fatigue in muscles. Therefore, nurse advise patients to:
A. Sit and take rest
B. Breath inbetween exercise
C. Sit and breath
D. Breathe deeply after exercise

201. Renin catalyzes the synthesis of angiotensins which causes vasoconstriction in the kidneys thereby:
A. Causing water and electrolyte excretion
B. Causing water and electrolyte retention
C. Stimulate synthesis of minerals
D. Affect melatonin synthesis

202. Antibodies that cause pathogens to dissolve or break up are known as:
A. Antitoxins B. Lysine
C. Agglutinins D. 4 Precipitins

203. When the body is able to make its own antibodies by having disease & recovering or by vaccination, it is known as:
A. Acquired immunity
B. Passive immunity
C. Active immunity
D. Passive acquired immunity

204. Extra space or room in between the patient's room and main corridor of hospital will help in:
A. Less contamination of room articles
B. Reduced flow of airborne pathogens
C. Patient will be less disturbed
D. Nurse will have place for things

205. Cardiovascular insufficiency is caused due to atherosclerotic plaque/thrombosis and:
A. Decrease intracranial pressure and PCO2 and increase PO2
B. Decrease intracranial pressure and increase PO2, PCO2
C. Increase intracranial pressure and PCO2 and decrease PO2
D. Increase intracranial pressure and increase PO2, PCO2

206. Which of the following pathophysiological changes are seen in patient with pleurisy:
A. Inflammation of pleura stimulates nerve endings causing pain
B. Decrease of absence of inflammation
C. Increase pulmonary vascular resistance
D. Increase pulmonary arterial pressure

207. Atherosclerotic plaque formation causing narrowing, ischemia lead to thromboembolism, which results in cadio or cerebro vascular disease in patient with:
A. Infective endocarditis
B. Cardiogenic shock
C. Hyperlipidemia
D. Myocardial infarction

208. Genetic disorders are classified under following EXCEPT:
A. Chromosomal abnormalities
B. Genetic abnormalities
C. Unifactoral diseases
D. Multifactoral diseases

209. G6PD deficiency is classified in the following trait:
A. Autosomal dominant
B. Dominant x linked
C. Autosomal recessive
D. Recessive sex linked

210. One of the following disorders in which an abnormal haemoglobin leads to chronic haemolytic anaemia with other clinical manifestations due to point mutation of DNA is:
A. Thalassemia B. Haemophilia
C. Haemoglobinopathy
D. Sickle cell anaemia

211. Disorders like Cancer, CHD, Schizophrenia, IHD, Mental retardations are examples of:
A. Unifactoral disorders
B. Multifactoral disorders
C. Chromosomal disorders
D. Genetic disorders

212. In myocardial infarction, thrombolytic agents such as tissue plasminogens activators, streptokinase are given to:
A. Prevent fibrogen from adhering to platelets
B. Improve oxygen supply and dissolve thrombus
C. Reestablishing blood flow by dissolving thrombus
D. Decrease ventricular irritability

213. Patient with pulmonary embolism is given heparin I/V as an anti coagulant and antithrombotic agent to:
A. Extend prothombin time
B. Interrupt the coagulation mechanism
C. Neutralize heparin in case of bleeding
D. Extend clotting time and stop further thrombus formation

214. Hepatic cirrhosis patient is given diuretic therapy because it will:
A. Maintain osmotic pressure
B. Decrease osmotic pressure
C. Inhibit the action of aldosterone
D. Inhibit action of rennin

215. What will nurse do if she receives a patient with status asthamaticus manifest with tachypnea, laboured respiration with effort on exhalation, tachycardia, elevated blood pressure and is irritable:
A. Administer treatment as prescribed
B. Monitor i/v therapy and give bronchodilators
C. Start oxygen check vital signs
D. Provide comfortable position and check vital signs

216. What will nurse do in case patient have seizures if alcohol is withdrawn suddenly:
A. Make patient comfortable and restrain
B. Take blood sample for ethanol level
C. Monitor vital signs
D. Prevent patient from injury

217. The glomerular Filteration Rate (GFR) of normal healthy adult is

A. 60ml/min B. 100ml/min
C. 125ml/min D. 160ml/min

218. Which of the following is unmatched according to their sensory functions?

A. Nose - Olfactory nerve
B. Tongue and nose - Chemosensory
C. Ears - Organ of corti
D. Eyes – Extra sensory nerve

219. What assessment is carried out by a nurse in case patient had heat stroke:

A. Take history and record
B. Assess airway, breathing and circulation
C. Perform neurological assessment
D. Inform doctor

220. Which of the ones wrongly matched:

A. Hiatal hernia- Herniation of the por-tion of the stomach area esophagus
B. Achalaria-Foul smelling breath
C. Zeuker's diverticula - Pharyngeal pouches
D. Haliton's- Absent peristalsis of distal esophagus

A. A and B B. B and C
C. C and D D. C and D

221. Why active exercises are encouraged if traction is applied:

A. To improve the condition of patient
B. To prevent foot drop
C. To improve circulation
D. To avoid pressure sores

222. A patent with hepatic encephalopathy is prescribed lactulose. The nurse knows that the purpose of this medication is to

A. Decrease the bacterial flora, decreasing for-mation of ammonia
B. Decrease the gastric acidity
C. Prevent reabsorption of Na+ and water
D. Acidification of feces and trapping of ammo-nia, causing its elimination in feces

223. Reed Sternberg cell is the Hallmark in which disease

A. Burkitt's Lymp
B. Hodgkin's disease
C. Non Hodgkin's Lymphoma
D. Multiple Myeloma

224. The clinical features of Portal Hypertension are the following:

A. Splenomegaly
B. Caput medusae
C. Fruit breath odour
D. Thrombocytopenia

A. a, b, c and d B. a, b and c
C. a, c and d D. a, b and d

225. Nurse should be alert for following complications after patient has undergone bronchoscopy:

A. Bronchitis B. Haemoptysis
C. Pneumonitis D. Pneumothorax

226. Which of the following is the precursor of Vitamin D?

A. Cephalins B. Glycolipid
C. Cholesterol D. Ergosterol

227. match the list of symptoms with the list on particular electrolyte imbalance.

List I	Litst II
A.Hypocalcemia	1. Paralysis
B.Hypomagnesemia	2. diarrhoea
C.Hypokalemia	3. Leg and foot cramp
D.Hyperkalemia	4. Tatany

A.B.C.D

A. 2 3 1 4 B. 3 1 4 2
C. 3 1 2 4 D. 4 3 1 2

228. Which of the following rule will be used to determine the extent of body surface after burn:

A. Rule of eleven B. Rule of nine
C. Rule of eight D. Rule of four

229. Find the odd one out in case of co-factors and metabolic factors of enzymes?

A. Mo B. $Zn^{2}+$
C. Mg^{2+} D. COA

230. Which of the following hormones promotes the glycogen metabolism?

A. Mineralo corticoids
B. Epinephrine
C. Non-epinephrine
D. Gluco corticoids

231. One of the complication of hypertension is:

A. Myocardial infarction
B. Accelerated hypertension
C. Acute arterial occlusion
D. Irreversible ischemia

232. Raising the foot end of the bed of the patient with chronic venous insufficiency will 0013056 help in:

A. Preventing oedema
B. Improve circulation
C. Provide comfort
D. Venous drainage by gravity

233. The function of B Lymphocyte is

A. Removal of antigens in acute inflammation
B. Provide cell mediated immunity
C. Humoral immunity
D. Rejection of transplanted organs

234. Which molecule cannot cross the blood-brain barrier?

A. Urea B. Glucose
C. Protein D. Potassium

235. Patient with acute pulmonary oedema should be provided with:

A. Ventilator in ICU
B. High concentrated oxygen
C. Position and rest
D. Comfort and with upright position

236 Which of the statements given below is/are true about Antigen — specific immunoglobulin E (IgE) in allergic Rhinitis?

A. Causes infiltration of inflammatory cells into the nasal tissue
B. Releases histamine and prostaglandins
C. Maintains the inflammatory response
D. Produced as a result of initial exposure to an allergen

237. An immediate interventions during an injury to muscle or joint include the following

A. Rest to affected part
B. Applying ice compress to the injured area
C. Compressing the involved extremity
D. Elevating the extremity
A. A, B and C B. B, C and D
C. A, C and D D. A, B, C and D

238. Hemophilia is a _ ___________disorder.

A. Autosomal recessive
B. X linked dominant
C. X linked recessive
D. Autosomal dominant

239. In which condition the number of eosinophils is increased?

A. Increase in the level of potassium
B. Allergic conditions
C. Increase in the level of calcium
D. Decrease in the level of sodium.

240. Aspirin prolongs bleeding time by inhibiting the synthesis of

A. Thromboxane A2 in platelets
B. Clotting factors in liver
C. Prostacyclin in vascular endothelium
D. Cyclic AMP in platelets

241. One of the complication of chronic otitis media is:

A. Acute and chromic mastoiditis
B. Irreversible hearing loss
C. Infection
D. Internal injury

242. A student used the formula to calculate the daily protein requirements of a patient. It describes the following category of cognitive domain.

A. Synthesis B. Comprehension
C. Application D. Analysis

243. Clinical manifestation of patient with gastrointestinal bleeding are:

A. Collapsed with low feeble pulse
B. Low blood pressure, bright red blood in vomiting
C. Acute bright red hematemasis, rapid pulse, drop in BP
D. Fatigue, normal BP, pulse rapid

244. Which of the statements regarding epistaxis is not true?

A. Maxillary or ethmoidal surgical artery ligation
B. Posterior source of epistaxis is Kisselbach's plexes
C. Cauterization is by silver nitrate application
D. Nasal packing for 48 to 72 hrs

245. Patient with appendicitis complains of pain, nurse can reduce pain by:

A. Giving analgesics
B. Applying ice bag
C. Giving rest and medicine
D. Giving position and comfort

246. In the elderly, the respiratory system undergoes the following changes EXCEPT:

A. Increasing cough
B. Decreased number of alveoli
C. Decreased chest wall size
D. Increased rigidity of trachea

247. What is the diagnosis if the ABG's values are pH-7.2 $PaCO_2$-55mm of hg,HCO_3-24 meq/L,PaO_2 - 65 mm

A. Mixed acid-base
B. Respiratory acidosis
C. Metabolic acidosis
D. Compensated resp. acidosis

248. Hook worms are otherwise termed as:

A. Teniasis B. Oxyruriasis
C. Ancylostomiasis D. Ascariasis

249. Hernia protrusion of the meninges through a midline defect in the posterior vertebral arch is known as

A. Menigomyelocele
B. Meningocele
C. Spina bifida
D. Spina Bifida cocculta

250. Match List I correctly with List II anu select your answer using the codes given below.

List I		List II
A. Craniotomy capacity	1.	To enlarge the pelvic
B. Cleidotomy head	2.	Perforation on the fetal

C.	Symphysiotomy		3. Removal of abdominal con-tents thoracic and	
D.	Evisceration		4. Reduction in the bulk of the shoulder girdle	

	A.	B	C.	D
A.	1	2	3	4
B.	3	4	2	1
C.	4	3	1	2
D.	2	4	1	3

251. A man swallowed a safety pin which is stuck in the eosophagus. Which one of the following is the correct treatment measure?
A. Prepare and administer polyethylene glycol
B. Emergent endoscopy
C. Ask the man to drink clear until the repeat X-ray shows pin has moved down to stomach
D. Discharge the patient with the instruction to check the stool for the elimination of pin

252. Withhold oral feeding in patient with acute pancreatitis to:
A. Maintain alkaline gastric PH
B. Relieve gastric statsis
C. Relieve distension
D. Reduce pancreatic secretions

253. The destruction of donor red cells by and D antibodies formed from previous exposure is called
A. Agglutination reaction in coomb's test
B. Rh incompatibility
C. Hemolytic anemia
D. Erythroblastosis fetals

254. Which one of the following is a functionally active form of vitamin D?
A. Calcitriol
B. Gholecalciferol
C. Ergocalciferol
D. Dehydrocholesterol

255. In prolonged hyperglycemia,____ accumulates in the tissues, resulting in microvascular complications
A. Glucose B. Ketons
C. lactic acid D. Sorbitol

256. Thr inhibition of glycolysis by oxygen is known as
A. Pasteur effect B. Bohr effect
C. Crab tree effect D. Leubering effect

257. Azotemia is a symptom seen in
A. Scurvy
B. Diabetes mellitus
C. Acute renal fail-ure
D. PEM

258. Which one of the following anticoagulant binds with Ca2+ and prevents blood clotting?
A. Warfarin B. Heparin
C. Oxalate D. Protein C

259. Salivary amylase becomes inactive in the stomach primarily due to
A. Inhibition by peptides
B. Inactivation by low pH
C. Degradation by gastric pepsin
D. Inhibition by CI-

260. Anorexia nervosa complications are:
A. Hypokalemia, dehydration anaemia, electrolyte imbalance
B. Obesity, electrolyte imbalance, anaemia
C. Protein deficiency, dehydration, anaemia
D. Vitamin and protein deficiency with anaemia

261. Obesity places patients at an increased surgical risk because of which of the following factors?
A. Metabolic demands are increaed
B. Risk for bleeding is increased
C. Ventilatory capacity is reduced
D. Fatty tissue has a poor blood supply

262. Lateral movement of the eyeball is controlled by the following nerve
A. Abducens B. Auditory
C. Optic D. Facial

263. Which diet is given to patient with nephritic syndrome:
A. Fluid restriction and high calorie and high protein
B. Protein supplement with calorie restriction
C. Protein supplement, sodium and fluid restriction
D. Fluid and sodium and potassium restriction

264. An immunoglobulin which crosses the placenta is:
A. IgG B. IgE
C. IgM D. IgA

A. B and D B. A and E
C. A only D. A and D

265. Which of the following statement is not true?
A. Transistors were used in radio and other ele-ments
B. Transistors and much smaller
C. Transistors produce low heat
D. Transistors were fast in conducting electricity

266. One of the following is a universally accepted indicator of health status and socio economic condition of a country:
A. Materral mortality rate
B. Life expectancy
C. Under 5 proportionate rate
D. Infant mortality rate

267. Benign skin tumors include the following
A. Warts
B. Angiomas
C. Kaposi's sarcoma
D. Keloids
A. A, B and C B. B, C and D
C. A, B and D D. A, B, C and D

268. 'Barrel chest' is the manifestation found in the following form of chronic airflow limitation
A. Chronic obstructive bronchitis
B. Bronchial asthma
C. Bronchitis
D. Emphysema
A. A B. B C. C D. D

269. Inflammatory disease of the skin characterized by well-defined erythematous plaques and salivary scales is
A. Rosacea
B. Psoriasis
C. Acne vulgaris
D. Pemphigus vulgaris

270. Which is the microvascular complication of diabetes mellitus?
A. Cerebro vascular disease
B. Diabetic nephropathy
C. Coronary artery disease
D. Peripheral arterial disease

271. Reye's syndrome is the complication of
A Diphtheria B. Polio myelitis
C. Chickenpox D. Pertusis

272. AIDS can be confirmed by
A. Western blot test
B. Antigen detection test
C. ELISA test
D. Kampass test

273. Which of the following urinary stone is formed by the bacterial enzyme, urease?
A. Struvite stone B. Uric acid stone
C. calcium stone D. Oxalate stone

274. Identify the odd one out
A. Fentanyl B. Morphine
C. Phenobarbital D. Noradrenaline

275. A burns victims with 90% burns in a multi-storeyed shopping complex fire accident is categorized to the following code in triaging
A. Orange B. Black
C. Red D. Yellow

276. The cardinal signs of parkinson's disease are
A. Tremor, bradykinesia and muscles rigidity
B. Paresis, anaesthesia and muscles spasticity :
C. Chorea and muscles hypotonia ;
D. Tremor, ataxia and muscle hypotonia

277. A man who met with a motor vehicle accidents i reveals bone fragemtns in the X-ray of femur. What type of fracture it is?
A. Avulsion B. Compressed
C. Comminuted C. Open

278. When planning health teaching for a patient with hiatus hernia the nurse should be share to include instruction to
A. Eat frequent, small soft solids with low fiber content
B. Eat three large meals per day with no restric-tions
C. Lie down immediately following a meal
D. Eat frequent, small blend meals with high fi-ber content

279. Among the following which is matched correctly
A. Acute illness - Short term symptoms
B. Etiology - Process of changes
C. Adaptation - Health maintenance
D. Holistic health - Self care
A. A B. B C. C D C.

280. In the post operative period following a hip replacement, the patient should perform whichof the following exercises to prevent DVT
A. Leg raising
B. Dorsiflexion and extension of the foot
C. Flexion and extension of the knee joint
D. Quadriceps-sothing
A. A B. B C. C D. D

281. Baroreceptors are located in the
A. Right atrium B. Carotid artery
C. Left atrium D. Aortic arch
A. A, B,C, B. B,C,D,
C. A,C,D, D. A, B, C, D

282. Levels of prevention in pathogenesis phase of natural history of disease are:
A. Primary and secondary prevention
B. Secondary and tertiary prevention
C. Preprimary and primary prevention
D. Primary and tertiary prevention

283. A patient has sustained burns to anterior chest and anterior abdomen. Using rule of nine how much of patient's body surface area has been affected?
A. 36% B. 8% C. 18% D. 27%

284. A 30 year old lady with normal systolic blood pressure, increased heart rate, slightly delayed capillary refill and cool, pale skin. What is the stage of shock is the lady in?

A. Progressive stage
B. Decompensate stage
C. Compensatory stage
D. Hypotensive stage

285. A client taking cyclophosphamids (cytoxan) for treatment of lymphom. The nurse should be vary cautious in administering the medication because this drug pores the fatal side effect of
A. Haemorrhagic cyst
B. Alopacia
C. Myeloma
D. Central nervous system toxicity

286. Method by which search for unrecognized diseases in healthy individuals is done is known as:
A. Screening B. Surveys
C. Health camp D. Health check ups

287. Full thickness (third degree) burns involves
A. Fascia and bones
B. Subcutaneous tis-sue
C. Nerve endings
D. Epidermis and dermis
A. A,B,C, B. A,B,D,
C. B,D,C, D A,C,D,

288. Malignant tumor of bone arising in medullary tissue is called
A. Genu valgum B. Osteosarcoma
C. Ewing's tumor D. Osteomylitis

289. A positive reinforcer
A. Has nothing to do with modifying behaviour
B. Increasest he probability that a behavior will recur
C. Decreaes the probability that a behavior will recur
D. Always results in positive behaviour

290. In case child of 2 years manifest with chest indrawing, wheezing, fever, nurse will:
A. Give antibiotics and advice home care
B. Do assessment and give antibiotics
C. Give treatment for fever and advice home care
D. Treat for fever, wheezing, give antibiotics and refer

291. The type of written report used in clinical practice is
A. Dispatch index ledger
B. Intake and output chart
C. Interdepartmental report
D. Sponge book

292. Anemia which is caused by lack of absorption of vitamin B12 due to lack of intrinsic factor is
A. Sickle cell anaemia
B. Addisonian pernicious anaemia
C. Dimorphic anaemia
D. Aplastic anaemia

293. The disease in which the patients blood does not clot easily is:
A. Diabetes
B. Sickle cell anaemia
C. Haemophilia
D. Rabies

294. Radio active cobalt and radium are used for the treatment of-diseases.
A. Sickle cell anae-mia
B. Cholera
C. Haemophilia
D. Cancer

295. Tobacco contains a poisonous substance called
A. Caffeine B. Nicotine
C. Narcotics D. Alcohol

296. A disease caused by allergic disease is called
A. Gastroenteritis B. Asthma
C. Tuberculosis D. Cancer

297. An adult has ...... litres of blood in his body.
A. 2-3 B. 7-8
C. 5-6 D. 9-10

298. Several persons in a town got the attack of leukemia. Which of the following can be possible reason for that?
A. Breathing in impure air
B. Exposed to radiation
C. Drinking polluted water
D. Smoking

299. The characteristic of enantiomers is
A. Only that they are mirror images of each other
B. Only that they are chemically identical
C. Both A and B
D. None of these

300. Atmospheric pressure is important in the process of____.
A. Breathing B. Blood Flow
C. Micturition D. Reproduction

301. The encysted blood so collected in the pouch of douglas is called
A. Pelvic hematocele
B. Intra ligamentary hematoma
C. Diffuse intraperitoneal hemorrhage
D. Secondary abdominal pregnancy

302. Deficiency of thyroxin in adults leads to a condition called:
A. Graves diseases B. Tetani
C. Cretinism D. Myxoedema

303. Principal electrolyte of intracellular fluid compartment is
A. Calcium B. Sodium
C. Potassium D. Magnesium

304. Of the following, which is the most common site for metastasis in lung cancer ?
A. Spleen B. Kidney
C. Stomach D. Liver

305. The goal of management of Glaucoma is :
A. Only to increase the production of aqueous humor
B. Only to increase the inflow of aqueous humor
C. Only to increase the outflow of aqueous hu-mor
D. Decrease the pain in eye

306. Which is the best test for detecting Liver dysfunction?
A. Prothrombine time
B. Serum albumin
C. Serum bilirubin
D. SGPT

307. Abnormal communication between the urinary and genital tract is called Geneto Urinary_____
A. Prolapse B. Fistula
C. Tumour D. Atresia

308. What is the main reason for angina pectoris?
A. Cardiac disease
B. Neurological disease
C. Gastric disease
D. Respiratory disease

309. The destruction of alveolar walls is called:
A. Lung abcess B. Emphyma
C. Bronchitis D. Emphysema

310. Process that draws the solvent from a less concentrated solute through a selectively permeable membrane into a more concentrated solute till the point of equalization is called
A. Osmosis B. Diffusion
C. Ultrafiltration D. Filtration

311. If gut motility is increased then:
A. Nothing definite can be said
B. Drug absorption is decreased
C. Drug absorption is increased
D. Drug absorption is not affected

312. An energy consuming process by which cells of the human body absorb molecules (such as proteins) by engulfing them is called _____.
A. Endocytosis B. Lipid diffusion
C. Aqueous diffusion
D. Exocytosis

313. The process of taking food into the digestive system is:
A. Elimination B. Ingestion
C. Propulsion
D. Digestion

314. Space between the parietal and visceral pericardium is
A. Virtual B. Absolute
C. Essential D. Virtuous

315. Which of these is an example of a neurotransmitter ?
A. Only Acetylcholine
B. Only Dopamine
C. Only Norepinephrine
D. All of these

316. The reason why lip tick and nail-polish is removed before surgery is:
A. Cyanosis is checked
B. Surgery becomes easier
C. Surgery becomes more successful
D. Psychological benefits to the patient

317. Which of the following nursing intervention can be used to prevent increased intracranial pressure (ICP) in an child?
A. Lower the position of head
B. Avoid activities that cause pain or crying
C. Provide environmental stimulation
D. Turn head left side every hourly

318. Which of layer of the artery contains smooth muscles?
A. Tunica interna B. Tunica media
C. Tunica alba D. Tunica externa

319. Which one of the following is a non-modifiable risk factor for atherosclerosis?
A. Sedentary lifestyle
B. Cigarette smoking
C. Hyperlipidemia
D. Female over 55 years of age

320. The symptoms of severe dehydration in adult include all of the following except:
A. Palpitations B. Decreased thirst
C. Dizziness D. Weakness

321. Doctor has advised the nurse to prepare the room for a patient with a spinal cord injury (at C7 level). Which one of the following is most essential to be kept ready for this patient?
A. The spinal kinetic bed
B. The halo brace device
C. A catheterization tray
D. A ventilator on stand by

322. Which of the following symptoms is most characteristic of a patient with a cancer of the lung?
A. Persistent or intense coughing

B. Air hunger
C. Exertion Dyspnea
D. Cough with night sweats

323. Alpha cells of pancreas secretes
A. Insulin B. Somatostatin
C. Somatotropin D. Glucagon

324. Mr. Pramod has been diagnosed to have Parkinson's disease. He complains that the resting tremors he is experiencing in his right hand are very frustrating. What advice to be given to him by the attending nurse?
A. To give diazepam as needed
B. To take a warm bath
C. To hold an object
D. To practice deep breathing

325. A patient has just returned from the post anaesthesia care unit (PACU) after haemorrhoidectomy. His postoperative orders include site baths every morning. The nurse understands that site bath is necessary to:
A. Promote healing
B. Reduce pain
C. Relieve tension
D. Lower body temperature

326. Platelets get activated when they come in contact with
A. Heparin B. Collagen
C. Fibrinogen D. Endothelium

327. A child in postoperative ward under observation after tonsillectomy is suspected to have postoperative haemorrhage when the child:
A. Swallows frequently
B. Snores noisily
C. Complains of thirst
D. Become pale

328. A hypertensive patient has been admitted in a ward for observation. He informs the attending nurse about squeezing pain in the chest even at rest. Which of the following action is necessary for this patient?
A. Rest to the patient and call the attending doc-tor
B. Give ibuprofen tablet to reduce pain
C. Inform the patient that he is fine nothing to worry
D. Advise the patient to move out for fresh air

329. White monitoring an unconscious child admitted with a history of fall, nurse notices that the child suddenly has a fixed and dilated pupil. This indicates
A. Increased parasympathetic activity
B. Neurosurgical emergency
C. Eye trauma
D. indication of brain death

330. In a patient hospitalized with acute glomerulonephritis, nursing care include all of the following except:
A. Recording fluid intake and output every 8 hourly
B. Recording the weight of the patient twice weekly
C. Recording vital signs every 4 hourly
D. Recording BP 4 hourly

331. Which of the following disease is produced by dog bite?
A. Influenza B. Yellow fever
C. Rabies D. Herpes

332. Cyanosis in a child be seen in all the places mentioned below except:
A. Lips B. Nainbeds
C. Sclera D. Tongue

333. The child with acute glomerulonephritis is under treatment in a ward. The nurse should look for following as an indicator for acute renal failure..
A. Glycosuria B. Polyuria
C. Hematuria D. Oliguria

334. A tracheoesophageal fistula should be suspected in a neonate immediately after birth if one of the following is present?
A. Bile-stained vomitus
B. Jaundice
C. Absence of sucking
D. Excessive amount of frothy saliva in the mouth

335. All of the following are symptoms of head injury except
A. Headache B. Sweating
C. Sleepiness D. Vomiting

336. Lipid profile does not include:
A. LDL B. SCOT
C. HDL D. VLDL

337. Increase in number of cells in a tissue is called
A. Aplasia B. Hypertrophy
C. Hypoplasia D. Hyperplasia

338. Which is the most lethal arrhythmia?
A. Sinus arrhythmia
B. Atrial fibrillation
C. Ventricular fibrillation
D. Ventricular tachycardia

339. Lactulose is prescribed for patients with hepatic ancephalopathy to

A. Decrease the serum ammonia level
B. Increase the protein level
C. Decrease the bilirubm level
D. Increase the glucose level

340. The corrective surgery for hirchsyprung's Disease is:

A. Pyeloplasty
B. Pyloroplasty
C. Kosai's procedure
D. Duhanvel procedure

341. Which of the following is used in the management of hyperkalemia?

A. Sodium bicarbonate
B. Insulin with glucose
C. Potassium chloride
D. Magnesium sulphate

342. Which of the following is most important to prevent the progress of disease in thromboangiitis obliterans (Buerger's disease)?

A. Smoking cessation
B. Controlling diabetes
C. Weight reduction
D. Controlling blood pressure

343. The normal intraocular pressure is

A. 20-35 mmHg B. 16-25 mmHg
C. 8-21 mmHg D. 19-38 mmHg

344. After a radical mastectomy with lymph node removal, which of the following measures help to prevent lymphoedema?

A. Placing arm close to body in sling
B. Warm moist heat application
C. Restricting all movements of the arm
D. Raising arm above heart on pillows

345. Which of the following is a cyanotic heart disease?

A. Tetralogy of fallot
B. Carctation of aorta
C. Patent ductus arteriosus
D. Atrial septal defect

346. Currect jelley stool is a manifestation of:

A. Anorectal malformation
B. Trachea oesophageal fistula
C. Intussusception
D. Oesophageal atresia

347. A 36 year old female complains of headache and neck pain. Examination by a nurse reveals painful flexion of the neck of the chest (nuchal rigidity), This could be due to:

A. Subdural hematoma
B. Brain tumour
C. Meningitis
D. Cerebro-vascular accident

348. Which of the following is a fracture in which bone is shattered into numerous fragments?

A. Spiral fracture
B. Displaced fracture
C. Avulsion fracture
D. Comminuted fracture

349. After tow house th of the radio active isotope remains undecayed. Half life of the isotope is:

A. 30 minutes B. One hour
C. 12 minutes D. 45 minutes

350. Which among the following is an indication of portal hypertension?

A. Confusion
B. Elevated blood pressure
C. Asterixis
D. Hematemesis

351. Which, of the following procedure is used to correct otosclerosis?

A. Myringoplasty B. Myringotomy
C. Mastoidectomy D. Stapedectomy

352. The surgical procedure done to relieve pressure in compartment syndrome is

A. Meniscectomy
B. Fasciotomy
C. Open reduction with internal fixation (ORIF)
D. Arthroplasty

353. Removal of an entire lung is called as

A. Lobectomy
B. Pneumonectomy
C. Segmental resection
D. Wedge resection

354. Goniometer is used to assess

A. Range of motion of joints
B. Muscle strength
C. Visual acuity
D. Auditory acuity

355. Potassium intake is restricted in:

A. Lung failure B. Cardiac failure
C. Liver failure D. Renal failure

356. Fractures of the distal radius is called

A. Galeazzi fracture
B. Monteggia fracture
C. Hume fracture
D. Colles fracture

357. Which of the following is a risk factor for development of breast cancer?
A. Early first pregnancy
B. Late menarche
C. Earlymenopause
D. No pregnancies

358. Buck's extension traction is
A. Skin traction to the lower leg
B. Skeletal traction to the lower leg
C. Applied as cervical head halter
D. Tongs applied to the head

359. Small painful nodes on fingers and toes called osier's nodes are seen in:
A. Myocarditis
B. Cardiomyopathy
C. Pericarditis
D. Infective endocarditis

360. A patient who is on sengstaken-Blakemore tube, Suddenly experiences difficulty in breathing. Which of the following actions should the nurse take first?
A. Cut and remove the tube
B. Elevate the head of the bed
C. Listen to the client's lungs
D. Administer oxygen with a nasal Cannula

361. A good insulator of heat is:
A. Iron B. Copper
C. Mercury D. Trapped air

362. Which of the following is a neural tube defect?
A. Encephalitis B. Meningitis
C. Meningocoele D. Scoliosis

363. After thyroid surgery (thyroidectomy) patient shows carpo-pedal spasm. This sign indicates:
A. Hypocalcemia tetany
B. Very low thyroid hormone levels
C. Severe postoperative bleeding
D. Decreased metabolism and hypothemia

364. During the delivery, the perineal tear extends through the sphincter of the rectum but the rectal mucosa in intact. How would you classify this type of perineal tear?
A. Third-degree B. Second-degree
C. First-degree D. Fourth-degree

365. All-of the following are signs of anaemia in a patient except:
A. Lethargy
B. Yellowness of the sclera
C. Dyspnoea on exertion
D. Tachycardia pale skin

366. Kaposi's sarcoma is associated with
A. Human immunodeficiency virus
B. Epstein-Barr virus
C. Human T cell lymphotropic virus type I (HTLV-I)
D. Human papilloma virus

367. Cell concentration techniques include all of the following exxept:
A. Filtration
B. Centrifugation
C. Cell block preparation
D. Cytospin

368. BUN used for kidney function tests stand for:
A. Blood Urine acid nitrogen
B. Blood Urea nitrogen
C. Blood Urine nitrogen
D. Blood Urea nitrogen

369. Cell with a horse-shoe shaped nucleus and abundant cytoplasm in a peripheral blood smear is:
A. Eosinophil B. Monocyte
C. Lymphocyte D. Neutrophil

370. A disease condition caused by bacteria and characterized by fluid filled alveoli and inflammation is
A. SARS B. Amyloidosis
C. ARDS D. Pneumonia

371. Which of the following cannot be corrected by dialysis?
A. Hyperkalemia
B. Elevated creatinine
C. Hypernatremia
D. Decreased hemoglobin

372. ECG change in myocardial infarction is
A. ST segment elevation
B. Wide QRS complex
C. Presence of U wave
D. Prolonged PR interval

373. Tissue injury followed by acute inflammation and marked neutrophil reaction leads to
A. Resolution
B. Fibrosis
C. Supporation
D. Chronic inflammation

374. The normal cholesterol level is
A. 150-200 mg/dl B. 200-250 mg/dl
C. 250-300 mg/dl D. 100-150 mg/dl

375. Inflammation of tissues surrounding the nail is known as
A. Onycholysis B. Koilonychia
C. Paronychia D. Clubbing

376. A disease condition characterized by excessive mucus collection with collapse of alveoli is
A. Asthma B. Atelectasis
C. Bronchiectasis D. Lung abscess

377. The normal mean pulmonary artery pressure is
A. 25-30 mm Hg B. 20-25 mm Hg
C. 10-15 mm Hg D. 15-20 mm Hg

378.ECG changes seen in hypocalcaemia are
A. Widened QT interval
B. prominent U wave
C. Widened T wave
D. Shortened QT interval

379. Which of the following condition of manifested by increased intraocular pressure?
A. Dacryocystitis B. Conjunctivitis
C. Glaucoma D. Cataract

380. The most commonly affected heart valve in RHD is
A. Aortic B. Mitral
C. Pulmonary D. Tricuspid

381. Which of the following is a manifestation of pyloricstenosis?
A. Tenesmus
B. Steatorrhea
C. Regurgitation
D. Projectile vomiting

382. Which of the following is NOT a clinical manifestation of diabetes mellitus?
A. Hyperglycemia B. Polyphagia
C. Glycosuria D. Hypernatremia

383. Which of the following is not the risk factor for the development of duodenal ulcers?
A. Smoking B. Stress
C. Alcohol D. Antibiotics

384. Which of the following is a specific investigation to detect seizures?
A. MRI B. CTscan
C. EEC D. X-ray

385. A patient with Dumping Syndrome should be given
A. High protein, high fat and low carbohydrate diet
B. Low protein, low fat and low carbohydrate diet
C. Normal protein, high fat and high carbohydrate diet
D. Low protein, low fat and low carbohydrate diet

386. Lead poisoning is known as
A. Plumbism
B. Plummer version syndrome
C. Asterixis
D. Parder willis syndrome

387. Chronic ulcerative colitis is characterized by muscular hypertrophy of bowel with its
A. Widening B. Shortening
C. Thinning D. Fibrosis

388. Diabetes insipidus is due to the deficiency of
A. Insulin
B. Glucagon
C. Glucose
D. Anti diuretic hormone

389.An acute condition characterized by diminished production and increased destruction of RBC. triggered by viral infection or folic acid deficiency is
A. Adrenal crisis
B. Aplastic crisis
C. Vasoocclusive crisis
D. Splenic crisis

390. Which of the following is a complication o[f] splenectomy?
A. Pancreatitis B. Appendicitis
C. Cholecystitis D. Gastritis

391. A brain tumor located within the anterio[r] twothirds of brain mainly cerebrum is called
A. Supratetntorial
B. Inferior tentorial
C. Posterior tentorial
D. Middle tentorial

392. Classic symptoms of deep vein thrombosi[s] include all of the following Except
A. Homanssign B. Swelling
C. Muscle pain D. Redness

393. Distended abdomen and absence of bowe[l] sounds after abdominal surgery indicates
A. Ruptured colon B. Hemorrhage
C. Intussusception D. Paralytic ileus

394. Which of the following is an indicator of AIDS?
A. CD4 count lower than 600 cells/mm3
B. CD4 count lower than 1000 cells/mm3
C. CD4 count lower than 200 cells/mm^3
D. CD4 count more than 400 cells/mm^3

395. Which of the following is NOT the sign o[f] meningitis
A. Kernig's sign B. Bebinski's Sign
C. Brudzinski's sign D. Battle's sign

396. A patient who is receiving antibiotic therap[y] complaints of ringing in the ears. Th[e] ototoxicity is damage to
A. 7th CN B. 8th CN
C. 4th CN D. 9th CN

397. Parkinson's disease is caused by
A. Demyelination of the nerve cells
B. Impairment of dopamine producing cells [in] the brain

C. Death of brain cells due to old age
D. Hereditary factors

398. Features of brain stem being affected during the surgical removal of brain tumor is
A. Inability to swallow
B. Elevated temperature
C. Altered hearing ability
D. orthostatic hypotension

399. While measuring central venous pressure the zero point of the manometer is adjusted to
A. Anterior axillary line
B. Midaxillary line
C. Posterior axillary line
D. Shoulder level

400. The causative organism for peptic ulcer is
A. Eschericia coli
B. Staphylococci
C. Helicobacter pylori
D. Streptococci

401. Which of the following ECG findings indicate the presence of hypokalemia?
A. Prologed PR interval
B. Widening of QRS complex
C. Tall, peak T wave
D. ST segment depression

402. What is the percentage of a large burn area to total body surface area?
A. More than 10% B. More than 25%
C. More than 35%. D. More than 50%

403. Fever, headache and nuchal rigidity are classic symptoms seen in
A. Meningitis
B. Alzheimer's disease
C. Brain abscess
D. Parkinson's disease

404. Nursing assessment for neurovascular status of the extremity with a cast include the following Except
A. Paresthesia B. Range of motion
C. Pallor D. Pain

405. Distant vision is assessed by using
A. Jaeger card B. Confrontation test
C. Hirschbergs test D. Snellen chart

406. Which is a wrong statement about Acne Vulgaris
A. A chronic multifactorial disease
B. Requires active treatment
C. Has androgenic influence on sebaceous glands
D. Heat, humidity and perspiration increases it

407. Dumping syndrome is a complication of
A. Histrectomy
B. Nephrectomy
C. Colectomy
D. Subtotal gastrectomy

408. While instilling car drops, the ear of an adult is straightened by pulling the pinna
A. Up and back B. Straight down
C. Down and back D. Straight back

409. A patient's GRBS is 40mg%. the immediate management is to administer
A. Normal saline
B. 10 units' human act rapid insulin
C. 5% dextrose and ns
D. 50% dextrose

410. When helping a stroke patient nurse should assist
A. From back B. On weak side
C. On strong side D. From behind

411. Highly toxic nerve gas that can cause death within seconds following exposure is
A. Sarin B. Furin
C. Diaoxine D. Metformin

412. Which one of the following nursing measures would be most appropriate in the care of the patient who has acute epistaxis?
A. Place warm compresses on the patient's nasal bridge
B. Tilt the patient's head back
C. Place the patient's head between his legs
D. Pinch the nose and have the patient lean for-ward

413. Other name of Herpes Zoster infection is
A. Shigella B. Shingles
C. Varicella D. Variolla

414. An active 'male patient who weighs 81kg has undergone dietary instruction. The patient reports that his current diet consists of 60 g of fat, 200 mg of cholesterol, and 5 g of sodium per day. What a nurse advises the patient to do?
A. Decrease his sodium
B. Increase his cholesterol
C. Increase his sodium
D. Decrease his cholesterol

415. Bleeding time is prolonged in all the following except
A. Von-Will brand disease
B. Viper bite
C. Idiopathic thrombocytopenia
D. Haemophilia A

416. A lethargic patient has fever, vomiting, headache and the nurse has to prepare him for which one of the following procedure?
A. Ultra sound exam
B. Urine culture
C. Lumbar puncture
D. CAT scan

417. **A 7 weeks old child who has diarrhea for 14 days but has no sign of dehydration, is classified as?**
A. Persistent diarrhea
B. Dysentery
C. Severe dysentery
D. Severe persistent diarrhea

418. **Which nursing- diagnosis is most appropriate for a patient with chronic venous insufficiency?**
A. Skin Integrity, impaired
B. Activity Intolerance
C. Body Image, disturbed
D. Fluid Volume, deficient

419. **A old male patient who is diagnosed with an evolving myocardial infarction (MI) insists on going home. The nurse encourages the patient to be admitted, because the greatest risk within the first 24 hours of sustaining an MI is**
A. Ventricular aneurysm
B. Heart failure
C. Sudden death
D. Pulmonary embolism

420. **Maximum period of infectivity in Mumps is in**
A. Incubation period
B. Onset of swelling
C. After swelling appear
D. Prodromal period

421. **Modifiable risks factors for Hypertension are EXCEPT**
A. Age B. Obesity
C. Salt intake D. Alcohol intake

422. **Which of the antibiotics is likely to impair hearing**
A. Streptomycin B. Neomycin
C. Erythromycin D. Gentamycin

423. **Which of the following complications can be seen in patients receiving total parenteral nutrition (TPN) at the time of tube change**
A. Pneumothorax B. Hypervolemia
C. Air embolism
D. Metabolic derangement

424. **Which of the following is a hereditary hemolytic anemia?**
A. Aplastic anemia
B. Pernicious anemia
C. Megaloblastic anemia
D. Thalassemia

425. **When caring for a patient who has intermittent claudication, nurse advises the patient to**
A. Apply graduated compression stockings
B. Elevate the legs when sitting
C. Refrain from vigorous exercise
D. Walk as much as tolerated

426. **Which of the following is not a precipitating factor related to pain crisis in the child witl sickle cell anemia**
A. Stress B. Trauma
C. Infection D. Fluid overload

427. **Which of the following actions would a nurs take first when caring for a patient experiencin a cardiac arrest?**
A. Obtain a pulse oximetry reading
B. Initiate cardiac monitoring
C. Provide intravenous access
D. Establish an open airway

428. **The nurse understands that hemiplegi involves:**
A. Paresis of both lower extremities
B. Paralysis of one side of the body
C. Paralysis of both lower extremities
D. Paresis of upper and lower extremities

429. **Ketone bodies appear in the blood and urin when fats are being oxidized in great amounts The condition is associated with:**
A. Starvation
B. Bone healing
C. Alcoholism
D. Positive nitrogen balance

430. **A test that should be included in the yearl physical examination of men during the lat middle and older adult years is:**
A. PSA
B. ELISA
C. Western blot
D. Serum Triglycerides

431. **Cretinism is due to deficiency of:**
A. Thyroxine B. Estrogen
C. Epinephrine D. Renin

432. **Fasting blood sugar is done to detect:**
A. Amount of insulin in blood
B. Amount of glucose in blood
C. Course of diabetes
D. Treatment of diabetes

433. **Excessive albuminuria is associated with:**
A. Dehydration B. Bruising
C. Infection D. Oedema

434. **The mother's blood pressure climbs to 170/10 mmttg. Which of the following symptoms woul suggest to the nurse that the patient may l about to convulse:**
A. Increased fetal movements
B. Decreased temperature
C. Epigastric pain
D. Urine output of 40 ml/hour

435. The commonest cause of death in women with cancer cervix is:

A. Septicaemia B. Renal failure
C. Haemorrhage D. Cachexia

436. Which of the sign and symptoms would be an early indication that the patients serum potassium level is below usual:

A. Sticky mucous membrane
B. Diarrhoea
C. Muscle weakness in the legs
D. Tingling in the fingers

437. The "Rule of Nine" in patients with burns helps to assess:

A. The amount of body surface burned
B. Rehabilitation needs
C. Ventilatory assistance needs
D. Types of intravenous infusion required

438. A patient is suspected to have hepatitis, which diagnostic test will confirm the diagnosis?

A. Elevated haemoglobin level
B. Elevated serum bilirubin level
C. Elevated blood urea nitrogen level
D. Decreased erythrocyte sedimentation rate

439. Cystolithotomy means removal of stones from:

A. Bladder B. Gallbladder
C. Kidney D. Ureter

440. Anesthesia machine is used in general anesthesia for:

A. Pumping oxygen into lung
B. Removing exhaled gases from lung
C. Pumping anesthetic gases into lung
D. All of these

441. Bagassosis is an occupational disease of the lung caused by an inhalation of

A. Cotton B. Jute
C. Sugarcane dust D. Coal

442. Long arm cast type of plaster cast is used in the treatment of

A. Fracture of the carpal and metacarpal bones
B. Fracture of radius and ulna bones
C. Fracture of metatarsal bones
D. Fracture of tibia and fibula bones

443. When helping a stroke patient nurse should assist:

A. On weak side B. On strong side
C. From behind D. From back

444. Immunity means

A. Antibodies and antigens reaction
B. Transfer of maternal antibodies across the placenta
C. Level of resistance of a person to a particular disease
D. Acquired immunity by immunization

445. Hemophilia A is

A. Christmas disease
B. Factor VIII deficiency
C. Factor IX deficiency
D. Von Willebrand disease

446. Floating tip of the iceberg represents

A. Clinical cases
B. Apparent cases
C. Latent cases
D. Undiagnosed cases

447. Mastication is ---------------------

A. Digestion B. Absorption
C. Assimilation D. Chewing

448. Cardinal signs of inflammation are all except

A. Pain B. Redness
C. Swelling D. Hypothermia

449. Exposure to sun without appropriate protection may cause

A. Skin Cancer B. Blood Cancer
C. Bone Cancer D. Mouth Cancer

450. Which part of the eye is transplanted from the eyes that are donated

A. Retina B. Cornea
C. Entire eyeball D. Iris

451. The commonest site of thrombosis is

A. Vein B. Artery
C. Heart D. Capillary

452. Ossification centre of Medial epicondyle appears in

A. 5th year B. 7th year
C. 9th Year D. 11th Year

453. Kupffer cells in liver are

A. Phagocytic B. Lytic
C. Secretory D. Excretory

454. Absorption of iron occurs better

A. On empty stomach
B. With meal
C. After break fast
D. All of the Above

455. Koplik's spot is seen in

A. Chickenpox B. Measles
C. Mumps D. Variola

456. Which of the following condition may require fluid restriction

A. Fever
B. Chronic obstructive pulmonary disease
C. Renal failure
D. Dehydration

457. A patient is admitted with dehydration as a result of prolonged watery diarrhea. Which intervention ordered by the physician should the nurse question

A. Parenteral albumin
B. Psyllium
C. Potassium supplements
D. Half Normal saline solution

458. Which of the following is true about benign prostatic hypertrophy (BPH)

A. It is a congenital abnormality
B. It usually becomes malignant
C. It causes an elevated acid phosphatase
D. It predispose to hydronephrosis

459. Glucose is

A. Filtered , reabsorbed and secreted
B. Filtered , and reabsorbed , but not secreted
C. Filtered , and secreted, but not reabsorbed
D. Filtered , and neither secreted not reabsorbed

460. Increased blood sugar level is found in

A. Diabetes mellitus
B. Pancreatitis
C. Hyperpara-thyroidism
D. All of the Above

461. Primary prevention for cervical cancer include except

A. Raising the age of marriage
B. Use of condom during early intercourse
C. Effective therapy of STDs
D. Radiotherapy

462. Winging of scapula is due to paralysis of

A. Axillary B. Long thoracic
C. Radial D. Median

463. Find out the odd one

A. Brain B. Vertebral canal
C. Spinal cord D. Stomach

464. Using the rule of nines, percent of both lower extremity that is burned is

A. 4.5 % B. 18 % C. 36% D. 22.5%

465 A predisposing factor for oral cancer

A. Tabacco use
B. Taking hot fluids
C. Taking cold fluids
D. Taking spicy food

466. Painless hematuria may be a sign of

A. Renal stones
B. Urolithiasis
C. Cancer of bladder
D. Acute renal failure

467. The most effective way of preventing tetanus is

A. Surgical debridement and toilet
B. Hyperbaric oxygen
C. Antibiotics
D. TT

468. Potts' fracture is fracture of

A. Tibia B. Radius
C. Fibula D. Ulna

469. Pink frothy sputum is a clinical sign of

A. Myocardial infarction
B. Angina pectoris
C. Pulmonary edema
D. Cardiac arrhythemia

470. Oral thrush is caused by

A. Neisseria gonorrhea
B. Candida albicans
C. Entamoeba
D. Varicella

471. When positioning a patient in preparation for surgery , the nurse understands that injury to the patient is most likely to occur as a result of

A. Incorrect musculoskeletal alignment
B. Loss of perception of pain or pressure
C. Pooling of blood in peripheral vessels
D. Disregarding the patient's need for modesty

472. Referred pain from ureteric colic is felt in the groin due to the involvement of the following nerve:

A. Subcostal B. Iliohypogastric
C. Ilioinguinal D. Gentiofemoral

473. Invasion of the body by the pathogenic organism

A. Inflammation B. Infection
C. Sepsis D. Carrier

474. Anterior cruciate ligament prevents

A. Ant. dislocation in tibia
B. Post dislocation of tibia
C. Ant. Dislocation of femur
D. Post dislocation of femur

475. A 38 years old patient's vital sign at 8 a.m. are axillary temperature 99.6F (37.6 C); pulse rate 80 ; respiratory rate , 30. Which finding should be reported

A. Respiratory rate only
B. Temperature only
C. Pulse rate and temperature
D. Temperature and respiratory rate

476. Cigarette smoking can cause which of the following cancer

A. Stomach cancer B. Lungs cancer
C. Blood cancer D. Bone cancer

477. TB is very often seen amongst patients with

A. HIV B. Blindness
C. Renal infection D. Heart Diseases

478. The HIV affects the

A. Growth and development

B. Nervous system
C. Immune system
D. Heart functioning

479. Hypertension are of which types
A. Phase 1 and Phase 2
B. Stage 1 and Stage 2
C. Primary and Secondary
D. Type A and Type B

480. The removal of a compound that the body no longer requires is called ....
A. Secretion B. Excretion
C. Movement D. Digestion

481. A sexual pain disorder reported in females
A. Anorgasmia
B. Vaginismus
C. Peyronie`s disease
D. Impotence

482. Excessive thirst is called:
A. Polyphagia B. Polyuria
C. Polydypsia D. Oliguria

483. Right ventricular enlargement due to pulmonary problem is called
A. Cardiac temponade
B. Corpulmonale
C. Cardiomyopathy
D. Emphysema

484. Sinus bradycardia is heart rate less than:
A. 80 beats per minute
B. 60 beats per minute
C. 70 beats per minute
D. 72 beats per minute

485. Tetany is a classical finding in
A. Hyponatremia B. Hypernatremia
C. Hypokalemia D. Hypocalcemia

486. Most common causes of Esophagitis is
A. Myasthenia Gravis
B. Glossoplegia
C. Duodenal ulcer
D. Reflux esophagitis

487. A patient with low T3, T4, will have:
A. Irritability B. Profuse diaphoresis
C. Tachycardia D. Cold intolerance

488. A decrease in blood glucose that causes the inhibition of insulin is an example of ....
A. Positive Feedback
B. Negative Feedback
C. Abnormal function
D. The action of glucagon

489. Staging of cervical cancer is primarily based on
A. Severity of symptoms
B. Age of female
C. Clinical examination
D. All of the Above

490. The transportation of heat in the body is mainly a property of the ....it contains
A. Food B. Oxygen
C. Water D. Pressure

491. To Decrease G1 irritability, the nurse should suggest the patient to minimize the use of
A. Sugar product
B. Milk Product
C. Cola drink and coffee
D. Both b and C

492. Creatinine is a
A. Chemical that is typically not secreted
B. Substance typically found in greater amounts in renal arteries than in renal veins
C. Building block for complex carbohydrates
D. 2 of the above are correct

493. Which of the following patient is at greater risk for contracting an infection
A. A patient with Leukopenia
B. A patient receiving broad –Spectrum antibiotic
C. A post operative patient who has undergone orthopedic surgery
D. A newly diagnosed diabetic patient

494. Increased blood volume in a tissue is known as
A. Hyperaemia B. Edema
C. Congestion D. Purpura

495. What is the full from of ELISA
A. Enzyme Lyses Immuno Solutions activity
B. Enzyme Linked Immune Sorbent Assay
C. Enzyme Lined Integrated Solutions Activity
D. Enzyme Lysis Immuno Solutions Assay

496. Keeping the frequency of normal illness within acceptable limits is best described by
A. Elimination B. Eradication
C. Control D. Surveillance

497. Anabolic steroid are ....versions of testosterone
A. Effective B. Synthetic
C. Natural D. Ineffective

498. Which of the following is not a neurotransmitter
A. Epinephrine
B. Dopamine
C. Gamma-aminobutyric acid
D. Troponin

499. In human immunodeficiency virus (HIV) what kind of immunity is lost
A. Active immunity
B. Passive immunity
C. Humoral immunity
D. Cellular immunity

500. Kupffer cells are a type of
A. Dendritic cells B. Macrophages
C. B cells D. T cells

501. Signs of pulmonary consolidation are all except
A. Dullness B. Increased fremitus
C. Ecophony D. Cystic fibrosis

502. Peptic ulcer disease particularly gastric ulcer is thought to be caused by which of the following micro-organisms
A. E. Coli B. H. pylori
C. S. aureus D. K. pneumonia

503. The symptoms of positive "Montoux test "includes
A. Erythema B. Edema
C. Induration D. All

504. Which of the following is most important to prevent the progress of disease in the thromboangitis obliterans (Buerger's disease)
A. Controlling blood pressure
B. Controlling diabetes
C. Weight reduction
D. Smoking

505. A method used to assist a patient to achieve highest level of independence is called
A. Restorative care
B. Reconciliation
C. Rehabilitation
D. Recreation

506. Any disturbance that blocks the transmission of nerve impulse from SA node downwards is known as:
A. Cardiac arrhythmias
B. Heart block
C. Heart attack
D. Nerve block

507. The erosion of mucosal layer of stomach muscle is termed:
A. Diverticulitis B. Duodenal ulcer
C. Gastric ulcer D. Crohn's disease

508. The inflammation and degeneration of liver parenchyma is referred as:
A. Cystitis B. Cirrhosis
C. Jaundice D. Cooley's

509. Which of the following can lead to infertility in adult males
A. German measles B. Orchitis
C. Chickenpox D. Rubella

510. The procedure which involves giving a synchronized counter-shock to convert an undesirable rhythm to stable rhythm is
A. Cardio version
B. Defibrillation
C. Cardiac Stimulator
D. Pacemaker

511. Nurse is caring for a patient with active upper GI bleeding. What should be prescribed for this client during the first 24 hrs after admission
A. Regular diet
B. Skimmed milk
C. Nothing by mouth
D. Clear liquids

512. In chronic Renal Failure all the following noticed except:
A. Hypokalemia B. Anemia
C. Hypocalcemia D.Metabolic Acidosis

513. Diseases transferred through contact are called
A. Communicable Disease
B. Infectious Disease
C. Contagious Disease
D. Epidemic Disease

514. The complaint of Insulin secretion is noticed in:
A. Type I diabetes
B. Type II diabetes
C. Secondary diabetes
D. Diabetes insipidus

515. The inability to read small words held at usual distance is a primary feature of:
A. Myopia B. Astigmatism
C. Presbyopia D. Cataract

516. Moon face with central obesity is noticed in:
A. Turner's syndrome
B. Addison's disease
C. Cushing's syndrome
D. Down's syndrome

517. Chovstek's sign is an indication of:
A. Hypocalcaemia B. Hypernatremia
C. Hypercelcemia D. Hyponatramia

518. Thalassemia is
A. Iron deficiency anemia
B. Vit-12 deficiency anemia
C. Hereditary haemolytic anaemia
D. Respiratory disorder

519. Breaking down of big molecules in small molecules in known as
A. Anabolism B. Catabolism
C. Absorption D. Metabolism

520. Kerning's sign is a striking feature of:
A. Meningitis B. Turner's syndrome
C. Neuritis D. down's syndrome

521. Celle's fracture refers to the injury of:
A. Elbow joint B. Shoulder joint
C. Knee joint D. Wrist joint

522. The lack of oxygen supply to myocardium of heart leads to:
A. Infarction B. Fibrillation
C. Heart failure D. Angina

523. What are the risk factors after coronary artery bypass graft (CABG)
A. Depression B. Ankle Edema
C. Memory Lapses D. Dizziness

524. Which suture separates occipital and parietal bones
A. Lambdoid suture B. Frontal Suture
C. Coronal Suture D. Sagittal Suture

525. The Centre to control body temperature is -
A. Medulla B. Hypothalamus
C. Cerebral Cortex D. Pons

526. Hyperkalemia leads to what changes in ECG?
A. Wide QRS complex
B. Inverted T waves
C. Tall T waves
D. Prolonged QT interval

527. The amount of protein intake to be maintained during renal failure is:
A. 60to8Og/day B. 40 to 60g/day
C. 80to100g/day D. 20 to 40g/day

528. The enzyme level which is found elevated after myocardial infarction is:
A. Creatine kinase B. Serum creatine
C. Amylase D. Phosphokinase

529 A New born baby weighs 2.5 Kg. The weight in pounds will be
A. 1 Pound B. 5.5 Pound
C. 7 Pound D 9.5 Pound

530 Acute pancreatitis is manifested by an elevated
A. Serum Bilirubin
B. Serum Amylase
C. Serum Alkaline Phosphatase
D. Serum Cretinine

531. A Nurse is assessing a coma patient by using glassgow coma scale, the score of scale is
A. 7 B. 9 C 11 D. 13

532. Most important care of an unconscious patient includes
A. Breathing
B. Blood Circulation
C. Patency of Airway
D. Eye Care

533. Which is not found in hypo secretion of thyroid gland
A. Anorexia B. Fatigue
C. Weight gain D. Diarrhea

534. A Child admitted with the diagnosis of rheumatic fever. He may give the history of-
A. Cholera
B. Sore throat
C. Subcutaneous nodes
D. Headache

535. SARS is a
A. Bacterial Infection
B. Viral Infection
C. Fungal Infection
D. Protozoal Infection

536. Loss of hair is
A. Alopecia B. Anorexia
C. Apnea D. Amnesia

537. Tuberculosis of the spine is also called
A. Ostecmalacia
B. Charcot's Disease
C. Erving's Disease
D. Pott's Disease

538. Newborn with neonatal tetanus shows
A. Risus Sardonious
B. Opisthotonus
C. Poor Feeding and rigidity
D. Trismus and lock jaw

539. Formation of blood cells is known as
A. Haemostasis B. Haemopoesis
C. E rythropoesis D. H aemocytosis

540. Hydrophobia is related to which disease
A. Swine Flu B. Chikungunya
C. Rabies D. None of above

541. Which serum potassium level require no immediate nursing intervention for an adult:
A. 3.2 mEq/litre B. 4 mEq/litre
C. 5.7 mEq/litre D. 6 mEq/litre

542. A second year nursing student has just suffered a needlestick while working with a patient that is positive for AIDS. Which of the following is die most important action that nursing student should take?
A. Immediately see a social worker
B. Start prophylactic AZT
C. Start prophylactic pentamide treatment
D. Seek counseling

543. A nurse is making rounds taking vital signs. Which of the following vital signs is abnormal?
A. 11-year-old male-90 b.p.m, 22 resp/min., 100/70 mm Hg
B. 13-year-old female-10 b.p.m., 22 resp/min., 105/60 mm Hg
C. 5-year-old male-102 b.p.m., 24 resp/min., 90/65 mm Hg
D. 6-year-old female 100 b.p.m., 26 resp/min., 90/70 mm Hg

544. A .... occurs when the atria and the ventricles are beating independently.
A. First degree block
B. Second degree block
C. Third degree block
D. Ventricular flutter

545. Which of the following conditions is most closely associated with weight gain, nausea, and a decrease in urine output?
A. Angina pectoris
B. Cardiomyopathy

C. Left-sided heart failure
D. Right-sided heat failure

546. Diabetic foot is an example of:
A. Dry gangrene
B. Wet gangrene
C. Gas gangrene
D. Gangrenous inflammation

547. Most frequently and severely involved joints in rheumatoid arthritis are:
A. Knees
B. Elbows
C. Interphalangeai
D. Sacroiliac

548. A client is receiving chemotherapy with several antineoplastic agents. The side effects of chemotherapy is:
A. Slow slurred speech
B. Increased leukocytes on CBC
C. Gingivitis and oral cancer
D. Sinus dysrhythmias bradicardia

549. The most common area for finding cancer in women is the:
A. Ovaries B. Failopiantubes
C. Cervix D. Urinary bladder

550. A nurse is watching the cardiac monitor and a client rhythm. There are no P waves: instead there are wavy lines. The QRS complexes measures 0.08 seconds but they are very irregular. The muse interpret that the rhythm is:
A. Sinus tachycardia
B. Atrial fibrillation
C. Ventricular tachycardia
D. Ventricular fibrillation

551. A nurse is caring for a client with a right sided cerebral venous accident, (CVA.what activity is to be included in the care of this client:
A. Passive ROM exercises to affected side, active on unaffected side
B. Place food on the affected side of the client's mouth
C. Hot packs to right leg to decrease muscle spasm
D. Turn every 2 hours and maintain position on the right side for 2 hours

552. A woman had been OTC antacids for relief of gastric upset. She is on renal dialysis three times a week, the nurse should carefully monitor the client for the development of what condition:
A. Hypomagnesemia
B. Hyperkalemia
C. Hypermagnesemia
D. Hyponatremia

553. A client is admitted with duodenal ulcer. What will the nurse anticipate the history to include:
A. Recent weight loss
B. Increasing indigestion after meal
C. Awaking with pain at night
D. Episodes of vomiting

554. The Nurse explains to the patient undergoing ostomy surgery that the procedure that maintains the most normal functioning of the bowels is:
A. A sigmoid colostomy
B. A transverse colostomy
C. A decending colostomy
D. An ascending colostomy

555. The most common type of Leukaemia in older adult is:
A. Acute myelocyticleukemia
B. Acute Lymphocytic leukemia
C. Ch. Lymphocytic leukemia
D. Ch. Myelocytic leukemia

556. Asthma is best characterized as:
A. An inflammatory
B. A steady progressive disease
C. An obstructive disease with loss of alveolar walls
D. A chronic obstructive disorder characterized mucus production

557. The most important needs of the newborn at birth are:
A. Hugging and kissing
B. Bathing and wrapping the child
C. Clear child's airway and maintain temperature
D. Keep the child in close contact with the moth-er

558. The nurse is evaluating the client response to haemodialysis which lab values would not reflects changes from the haemodialysis:
A. Serum creatinine levels
B. Dissolved pressure of carbon dioxide
C. Serum potassium level
D. Haemoglobin level

559. When plasma enters the tissue it is called:
A. Interstitial fluid B. Blood
C. Lymph D. Capillary fluid

560. Haemoglobin is a type of:
A. Carbohydrate
B. Respiratory pigment
C. Skin pigment
D. Vitamin

561. Nails, claws and hoofs are formed by:
A. Bone
B. Skin muscles
C. Stratum corneum of skin
D. Cartilage

562. Bile is acidic in:
A. Rabbit B. Cow
C. Horse D. Cats and Dogs

563. Vitamin A is produced from carotin:
A. Blood B. Skin
C. Intestinal tract D. Liver

564. When a person eats glucose the process that does not take place is:
A. Ingestion B. Digestion
C. Absorption D. Assimilation

565. A stigmatism can be corrected by:
A. Bifocal lenses
B. Cylindrical lenses
C. Concavelenses
D. Piano convex lenses

566. What type of a chemical reaction take place with the evolution of heat?
A. Reversible B. Irreversible
C. Exothermic D. Endothermic

567. Root of the hair is:
A. Multi cellular B. Uni cellular
c. Both of above D. none of them

568. Glaucoma is characterized by the following features except
A. Optic nerve atrophy
B. Increased intraocular pressure
C. Inflammation of cornea
D. Peripheral visual field loss

569. After adrenelectomy for pheochromocytoma, the patient is likely to experience
A. Hyperkalemia
B. Marked variation in BP
C. Sodium and fluid retention
D. Hypokalaemia

570. All of the following are classical features of nephritic syndrome except
A. Hypotension
B. Proteinuria
C. Hyperlipidemia
D. Hypoalbuminaemia

571. The suffix used for making an opening?
A. Otomy B. Raphy
C. Ostomy D. Ectomy

572. In increased ICP manifestations of Cushings triad include all of the following except
A. Tachycardia
B. Bradycardia
C. Increased systolic BP
D. Irregular respiratory pattern

573. Following kidney transplantation, signs of rejection include
A. Fever, weight gain, reduced urine output and increased BP
B. Fever, weight loss, increased urine output and increased BP
C. Fever, weight gain, increased urine output and increased BP
D. Fever, weight loss, increased urine output and reduced BP

574. All of the following are adventitious breath sounds except
A. Fremitus B. Crackles
C. Rhonchi D. Wheeze

575. Enlargement of the right ventricle secondary to disease of the lung, thorax or pulmonary circulation is
A. Corpulmonale
B. Cachexia
C. Cardiac tamponade
D. CCF

576. An elevation of—has a strong and direct association with CAD
A. LDL B. HDL
C. Serum sodium D. Serum Creatinine

577. A client with dysphagia experience difficulty in
A. Writing B. Swallowing
C. Walking D. Comprehension

578. It is most important for the nurse to observe a client with tetanus for
A. Muscular rigidity
B. Respiratory tract spasm
C. Restlessness and irritation
D. Spastic voluntary contraction

579. The most lethal arthythmia among the following is
A. Sinus tachycardia
B. First degree heart block
C. Ventricular fibrillations
D. Atrial fibrillations

580. The normal value of RBS is
A. 90-130 mg B. 80-120 mg
C. 60-80 mg D. 100-140 mg

581. Dumping syndrome may occur in
A. Colostomy B. Pneumonectomy
C. Gastrostromy D. Gastrectomy

582. After IVP for a patient, the most important nursing responsibility is
A. Observe urine for contrast material
B. Keep nil orally for 6 hours
C. Assess for flank pain
D. Advice to take increased oral fluids

583. The quantity of fluid intake allowed for a patient with renal failure is
A. Previous day's urine output+ 500 ml
B. Equal to the amount of previous day's urine output
C. Previous day's urine output + 100ml
D. One litre

584. The higher the RBC count
A. The lesser the hematocrit
B. The greater the viscosity
C. The higher the blood pH
D. Immunity will be less

585. In a patient affected with HIV, the organism will be present in all of the following except
A. Blood B. Sperm
C. Semen D. vaginal secretions

586. The majority of the body's water is contained in which of the following fluid compartments
A. Intracellular B. Extracellular
C. Interstitial D. Intravascular

587. Vitamin K is essential for normal blood clotting because if promotes
A. Platelet aggregation
B. Prothrombine formation by liver
C. Lonization of blood calcium
D. Fibrinogen formation by liver

588. In nephritic syndrome oedema results from
A. Increased sodium retention
B. Decreased glomerular filtration
C. Reduced aldosterone secretion
D. Reduced osmotic pressure caused by the loss of serum proteins

589. The disadvantage of ileal conduct is
A. Peristalsis greatly reduced
B. Absorption of nutrients is decreased
C. Stool continuously oozes from it
D. Urine continuously drains from it

590. Polydipsia means excessive
A. Thirst B. Peristalsis
C. Hunger D. Sweating

591. In obstructive jaundice there will be
A. Clay coloured stools
B. Dark urine and stools
C. Fever and pruritus
D. Elevated urinary Urobillinogen

592. Lack of intrinsic factor in the stomach results in failure of absorption of vitamin
A. Bl B. B12 C. B6 D. B2

593. Is an auto immune disease of the neuromuscular junction characterized by fluctuating weakness of certain skeletal muscles
A. Dementia
B. Myasthenia gravis
C. Alzheimer's disease
D. Scleroderma

594. An increase in number of cells resulting from increased cellular division is known as:
A. Hyperplasia B. Hypertrophy
C. Atrophy D. Dysplasia

595. The arterial blood gases cf a child is deteriorating and respiratory failure is impending, nurse first assess for:
A. Cyanosis B. Distended neck
C. Bradycardia D. Confusion

596. The major rcle in the maintaining fluid balance in the body is performed by the
A. Kidney B. Liver
C. Lungs D. Heart

597. Antinuclear antibody (ANA.may be positive in
A. Pneumonia
B. Autoimmune disease
C. Myocardial infarction
D. Syphilis

598. The nurse must assess a client experiencing excessive production of ADH for
A. Hyponatramia B. Hypoglycaemia
C. Dysuria D. Dehydration

599. Lipid profile test consists of the following except
A. LDL B. Total cholesterol
C. SCOT D. HDL

600. Widal test is used to diagnose
A. Typhoid fever B. Tuberculosis
C. Hepatitis D. Leptospirosis

601. A coin placed at the bottom of a container appears to rise as the container is slowly filled with water. This is due to:
A. Deflection of light
B. Polarisation of light
C. Refraction of light
D. Reflection of light

602. Osteoporosis is disease of:
A. Brain B. Muscles
C. Skin D. Bones

603. The most common cause of coronary artery disease is:
A. Hyperglycemias
B. Atherosclerosis
C. Vasospasm of coronary artery
D. Stress

604. A nurse is expected to find all the symptoms in GB syndrome, except:
A. Parathesia B. Urinary retention
C. Hypertonia D. Areflexia

605. Qiole cryptography is performed to:
A. Diagnose stone in the gall bladder

B. Detect obstruction in the duodenum
C. Detect conditions of the stomach
D. None of these

606. Electrocardiogram is:
A. Recording of peristalsis
B. Recording of brain wave activity
C. Recording of heart activity
D. None of the above

607. Glycosylated haemoglobin is determined to diagnose:
A. Diabetes mellitus
B. Gout
C. Hypothyroidism
D. All of the above

608. An important nursing responsibility for a patient after an invasive cardiovascular diagnostic study is:
A. Discourage fluid intake and place the patient in prone position
B. Limit motion of the affected extremity and assess the puncture site
C. Restrict fluid intake and encourage ambulation
D. Apply heat to the puncture site and passively exercise the involved extremity

609. A necessary safety precaution when ambulating a patient is to:
A. Have family members
B. Have at least two persons
C. Have patient wear well fitted shoes
D. None of the Above

610. Which of the following methods of intracranial pressure monitoring provides most accurate results:
A. Intraventricular catheter
B. Epidural catheter
C. Subarachnoid catheter
D. Intravertebral catheter

611. The code of ethics is composed and published by the:
A. National league of nursing
B. American medical association
C. National institute of health
D. American nursing association

612. Fasting blood sugar is done to detect:
A. Amount of glucose in blood
B. Amount of insulin in blood
C. Course of diabetes
D. Treatment of diabetes

613. Renal threshold for glucose is decreased in:
A. Insulinoma
B. Diabetes mellitus
C. Renal glycosuria
D. Alimentary glycosuria

614. A nurse assesses the patient's respiratory status. Which of the following symptoms be an early indicator of hypoxia in a patient:
A. Decreased respiration
B. Restlessness
C. Hypotension
D. Cyanosis

615. Serum lipase level increases in:
A. Paget's disease
B. Acute pancreatitis
C. Diabetes mellitus
D. Gaucher's disease

616. In the diet of a diabetic patient, the recommended carbohydrate intake should preferably be in the form of:
A. Polysaccharides B. Disaccharides
C. Monosaccharide D. All of these

617. Alpha-Keratin is a protein present in:
A. Blood B. Skin
C. Wool D. Eggs

618. Which of the following would most likely be a major nursing diagnosis for a patient with acute pancreatitis?
A. Altered nutrition less than body requirement
B. Ineffective airway clearance
C. Fluid volume excess
D. Impaired swallowing

619. Which portion of the heart receives oxygenated blood:
A. Left auricle B. Left ventricle
C. Right ventricle D. Right auricle

620. Which part of body is affected in typhoid:
A. Liver B. Pancreas
C. Lungs D. Intestines

621. Retention of abnormal amount of fluid in the body is due to:
A. Chloride B. Sodium
D. Potassium D. Calcium

622. Cretinism is due to deficiency of:
A. Epinephrine B. Renin
C. Thyroxin D. Estrogen

623. For assessing range of joint movement the nurse will ask the patient to move away from the body evaluating the movement of:
A. Abduction B. Adduction
C. Flexion D. Extinction

624. The sources of wound infection are:
A. Poor hygiene in nurses or patients
B. Cross infection from other wounds
C. Infected droplets from mouths and noses
D. All of the above

625. Oedema is:
A. Vitamin deficiency
B. Depression or deficiency of the quality of blood
C. Excess of fluid in tissue
D. Malnutrition and dehydration

626. Septicaemia is:
A. Spread of organism in blood stream
B. Spread of toxic product in blood stream
C. Invasion and multiplication of bacteria blood stream
D. Process of pus formation

627. An excessive vomiting and haemorrhage leads to:
A. Fluid overload B. Hypovolamia
C. Hypervolaemia D. Oedema

628. 1 dioptre of power of a lens:
A. Whose focal length is 10 meters
B. Whose focal length is 0.01 meter
C. Whose focal length is 100 meters
D. Whose focal length is 1 meter

629. Vomiting of blood is called:
A. Epistaxis B. Haemothorax
C. Haemoptysis D. Haematemesis

630. The sign and symptoms of retinal detachment include the following except:
A. Light flashes in the visual field of vision
B. Sudden severe pain in eye
C. A curtain failing across the field of vision
D. Floaters in the field of vision

631. The earliest signs of the postoperative shock is monitored by nurse by observing the:
A. Pulse rate
B. Pulse pressure
C. Body temperature
D. Urine output

632. Pathogens means:
A. Microorganism which causes disease
B. Organisms which are found in animals
C. Organisms which are beneficial for us
D. Organisms which are found in plants

633. Addison's disease is caused by insufficiency of hormone:
A. Thyroid hormone
B. Parathyroid hormone
C. Corticosteroid hormone
D. Insulin

634. Osteoporosis is caused by deficiency of:
A. Vitamin-A B. Vitamin-B
C. Vitamin-C D. Vitamin-D

635. Which is the most common occupational hazard of computer worker?
A. Cancer
B. Lung disease
C. Cataract
D. Carpel tunnel syndrome

636. A promising treatment for some children suffering from Thalassemia is:
A. Bone marrow transplantation
B. Chemotherapeutic agents
C. Radiation therapy
D. Steroidal therapy

637. A major priority of nursing care of a child suspected of having meningitis is to:
A. Check the temperature and give the cold sponging
B. Isolate the child immediately
C. Administer the antibiotics as soon as it is or-dered
D. Restrain the child to prevent accidents

638. The child's apical pulse is always checked before administering digoxin, the drug is not given if the pulse rate is:
A. Below 90 to 110 beats/minute
B. Above 90 to 110 beats/minute
C. Less than 60 beats/minute
D. More than 150 beats/minute

639. Typhoid fever is a:
A. Bacterial disease
B. Skin disease
C. Parasitic disease
D. Viral disease

640. The most likely side effect of external radiation to the neck for cancer of larynx is:
A. Constipation B. Dyspnea
C. Sore throat D. Diarrhoea

641. A patient is scheduled for ileostomy to treat ulcerative colitis. This is done to:
A. Prevent possible perforation from colitis
B. Decrease liquid faces
C. Control the order from diarrhoea
D. Prevent intestinal obstruction

642. Following an injury the nurse should assess for fat embolism:
A. During 1st 24 hrs
B. During 1st 48 hrs.
C. History of chronic respiratory disease
D. Patient on skeletal traction

643. The vaccine for Meningococcal meningitis provides immunity that lasts for about:
A. 5 years B. 2 years
C. 3 years D. 4 years

644. Immunity means:
A. Antibodies and antigens reaction
B. Transfer of maternal antibodies across theplacenta
C. Level of resistance of a person to a particular disease
D. Acquired immunity by immunization

645. Trichomonal infection is caused by:
A. Protozoa B. Fungus
C. Yeast D. Bacteria

646. Community Health Nurse explains a new diagnosed diabetes mellitus patient that the purpose of medication is to treat:
A. Hypoglycemia
B. Hyperglycemia
C. Hypocalcemia
D. Hyperbilirubinaemia

647. Early ambulation in the postpartum period is encouraged to:
A. Promote respiration
B. Increase peripheral vasomotor activity
C. Increase tone of bladder
D. Increase tone of abdominal muscles

648. The hormone controlling the use of glucose by the cell is:
A. Thyroxin B. Growth hormone
C. Steroids D. Insulin

649. The most important nursing action in the first 48 hours of hospitalization of a patient with full thickness burns over 30% of the body is directed towards preventing:
A. Contactures B. Pneumonia
C. Shock D. Hypertension

650. Which of the following would predispose a patient to the occurrence of diabetic ketoacidosis?
A. Doing too much exercise
B. Taking too much insulin
C. Running a fever with infection
D. Eating less calories

651. Hemiplegic means:
A. Paralysis of both lower extremities
B. Paralysis of upper and lower extremities
C. Paralysis of one side of the body
D. Paresis of one side of the body

652. The first aid treatment for a patient who had been bitten by a dog involves:
A. Administering ant rabies vaccine
B. Applying a wound dressing
C. Cleaning the wound with soap and water
D. Applying tourniquet proximal to the wound

653. Which of the following is a blood borne infection?
A. Hepatitis B B. Chikungunya
C. Weil's disease D. Plague

654. The best recommended body mass index for adult is:
A. 15-19 B. 20-25
C. 26-30 D. 31-35

655. Causative organism of infectious mononucleosis (Classical) is:
A. Varicella zoster virus
B. Toxoplasma
C. Cytomegalo virus
D. Epstein-Barr virus

656. The risk for tetanus infection is high in:
A. Large cut wounds
B. Abrasions
C. Deep penetrating wounds
D. Lacerations

657. Nephrotic syndrome is characterized by all of the following except:
A. Massive edema
B. Massive proteinuria
C. Hyperlipidemia
D. hyper albuminemia

658. Which of the following assessment would be most appropriate before adding potassium chloride of the IV fluid of a child with severe gastroenteritis?
A. Ability to void
B. Passage of stool on the day
C. Serium calcium level
D. Baseline electro cardiogram

659. A child with insulin dependent diabetes mellitus will have the following test done to assess the effectiveness of treatment:
A. Haemoglobin electrophoresis
B. Postprandial blood sugar test
C. Glycosylalid haemoglobin level
D. Glucose tolerance test

660. Pulse polio immunization is usually planned in winter months because:
A. Poliomyelitis incidence is more during winter months
B. The vaccine will be more stable during winter
C. Low incidence of enteric viral infections favouring take of vaccine virus
D. Implementation of the program is more effec-tive during winter

661. Which of the following is a long-term complication of hypertension?
A. Renal insufficiency and failure
B. Valvular heart disease
C. Endocarditis
D. Peptic ulcer

662. The goal of nursing care to a patient with acute myeloid leukemia is to prevent:
A. Cardiac arrhythmia
B. Liver failure
C. Renal failure
D. Haemorrhage

663. A primary risk factor for development of cancer larynx is:
A. Chronic allergy
B. Chewing Tobacco
C. Exposure to dusty environment
D. Smoking

664. The priority care after nasal surgery is:
A. Assessing pain
B. Inspecting for per orbital edema ;
C. Assessing respiratory status
D. Checking Melaena

665. The most common complication following inguinal hernia repair is:
A. Inability to void
B. Hypostatic pneumonia
C. Wound dehiscence
D. Deep vein thrombosis

666. The most possible cause for peptic ulcer is:
A. A diet high in fat
B. A genetic predisposition
C. Work related stress
D. Infection with helicobacter pylori

667. Which of the following complication the nurse has to watch in a patient after spinal anesthesia?
A. Convulsion
B. Cardiac arrest
C. Renal failure
D. Respiratory paralysis

668. A patient with fracture femur is at risk of developing fat embolus. The nurse should watch for:
A. Oliguria B. Confusion
C. Dyspnea D. Petechia

669. A conscious client with a history of consuming acid should have:
A. Stomach wash given
B. Vomiting induced
C. Plenty of water to drink
D. Nil orally status maintained

670. Ketone bodies are found in urine of patients with uncontrolled diabetes due to:
A. Increased metabolism of fat
B. Decomposition of excess sugar in blood
C. Increased metabolism of protein
D. Impaired kidney function

671. Ulceration and cracking of the lips and angles of the mouth is:
A. Sordes B. Glossitis
C. Cheilosis D. Gingivitis

672. In status epilepticus:
A. Patient will have confusion and paranoid de-lusion
B. Seizures are episodic disturbances of con-sciousness
C. Patient passes from one seizure to another without recovering consciousness
D. Patient develop only momentary loss of con-sciousness

673. Thyrotoxicosis is indicated by the following laboratory values:
A. Elevated Thyroid hormone level and normal TSH
B. Elevated TSH and normal Thyroid hormone level
C. Decreased Thyroid hormone level and elevat-ed TSH
D. Elevated Thyroid hormone level and de-creased TSH

674. Inflammation of cornea is:
A. Conjunctivitis B. Keratitis
C. Uveitis D. Blepharitis

675. A disease of the inner ear characterized by vertigo nausea vomiting deafness tinnitus is:
A. Otosclerosis
B. Meniere's disease
C. Hunt's syndrome
D. Vestibular neuronitis

676. The most common cause epistaxis in elderly is:
A. Nasal allergy B. Nose picking
C. Hypertension D. Injury

677. Soft tissue X-ray of the breast is:
A. Mammoplasty B. Mammography
C. Mastopexy D. Cholangiography

678. Passive immunity against tetanus is obtained by the administration of:
A. DPT
B. DT
C. TT
D. Tetanus immunoglobulin

679. A nurse observes that the fingers of the casted forearm of a patient with fractured ulna are pale, cool, and capillary refill is delayed. She has to interpret it as:
A. Nerve impairment is developing in the fin-gers
B. Arterial blood supply to the fingers is re-duced
C. A normal finding
D. Venous stasis occurring in the fingers

680. Normal value of serum blood urea is:
A. 20-40 mg/dL B. 40-60 mg/dL
C. 10-20 mg/dL D. 70-80 mg/dL

681. The ringing sound in the ear:
A. Otitis media B. Petit mat
C. Tinnitus D. Pharyngitis

682. Temporary paralysis of intestinal wall:
A. Erb's paralysis B. Monoplegia
C. Paralytic ileus D. Bell's palsy

683. Loss of appetite is:
A. Anemia B. Apnea
C. Anorexia D. Alopacia

684. Liver stores glucose in the form of:
A. Carbohydrate B. Glucolysis
C. Glycogen D. Glycodin

685. Hemoptysis is:
A. Blood from stomach
B. Blood from lungs
C. Blood from hearts
D. Blood from brain

686. Absence of hydrochloric acid in stomach is:
A. Hyperchlohydria
B. Hypochlorhydria
C. Achlorhydria
D. Hypochondriasis

687. Bad breath from mouth is:
A. Stomatitis B. Glossitis
C. Halitosis D. Gingivitis

688. Anemia is caused by:
A. Malabsorption
B. Deficient food intake
C. Excessive blood loss
D. All of the above

689. Health is:
A. The absence of illness
B. A state of rehabilitation
C. A condition between illness and wellness
D. A state of complete physical, mental and so-cial well-being

690. The inflammation of the nail bed is:
A. Paroncychia B. Clubbing
C. Pruritus D. Eczema

691. Drooping of the eyelid is:
A. Otitis B. Entropion
C. Ptosis D. Pterygium

692. Ideal weight loss for an obese patient to achieve weight reduction is:
A. 1 kg/week
B. 2 kg/week
C. 3 kg/week
D. More than 3 kg/week

693. Parenteral nutrition is used when the patient is:
A. Nil per oral
B. Critically ill
C. Recovering from abdominal surgery
D. Experiencing gastro intestinal dysfunction

694. A complication of leprosy is:
A. Exomphalos B. Omphalocele
C. Exomphthalmos D. Xerophthalmia

695. Father of Indian surgery is:
A. Charaka B. Vagbhata
C. Atreya D. Sushruta

696. The most important sign of heat stroke is:
A. Hot dry skin
B. Hot moist skin
C. Cold dry skin
D. Cold and clammy skin

697. Which one of the following in food can increase the risk of cancer?
A. High fat
B. High carbohydrate
C. Low CHO
D. Low protein

698. The most common complication occurring after cardiac surgery:
A. Hypertension B. Tamponade
C. Dysrrthymias D. Bleeding

699. Which mineral is necessary for blood clothing?
A. Iron B. Sodium
C. Potassium D. Calcium

700. Surgical removal of the stomach:
A. Gastrostomy
B. Gastrotomy
C. Gastrectomy
D. Gastrojejunostomy

701. Discharge from the ear is termed as:
A. Otorrhea B. Octalgia
C. Ototoxic D. Otitis media

702. Common cause of peptic ulcer is:
A. Alcoholism
B. Smoking
C. Hyperchlorhydria
D. None of the above

703. Hepatitis B can be prevented by giving:
A. HBSAG vaccine B. BCG vaccine
C. DTP vaccine D. HIB vaccine

704. Influenza is a:
A. Waterborne disease
B. Fomite borne disease
C. Vector borne disease
D. Airborne disease

705. The typical sign of anaphylactic shock is:
A. Chest pain B. Hot, dry skin
C. Dyspnea D. Fever

706. Urination at night is:
A. Polyuria B. Dysuria
C. Nocturia D. Pyuria

707. Continuous asthma is termed as:
A. Allergic asthma
B. Cardiac asthma
C. Status asthmatic us
D. Bronchial asthma

708. Cholelithiasia means:
A. Inflammation of gallbladder
B. Inflammation of bile duct
C. Stone in the gallbladder
D. Stone in the bile duct

709. A postoperative complication of appendicat:
A. Perimetritis B. Pericarditis
C. Peritonitis D. Pneumonitis

710. The most common complication during the first 24 hours following an amputation:
A. Infection
B. Flexion
C. Haemorrhage
D. Sloughing of the sutures

711. The most serious complication fracture is:
A. Infection B. Fat embolism
C. Haemorrhage D. Air embolism

712. Buck's extension is a method of:
A. Skin traction B. Skin grafting
C. Skeletal traction D. Born grafting

713. The normal serum bilirubin is:
A. 0.1-1 mg/dl B. 2-4mg/di
C. 1.5-3.5 mg/dl D. 10-12 mg/dl

714. The symptom of enlarged prostrate include:
A. Pyuria
B. Difficulty in micturition
C. Ototoxicity
D. Visual disturbance

715. A degenerative disease of the brain associated with liver failure:
A. Uremia B. Diabetic coma
C. Septicemia D. Hepatic coma

716. Severe pain occur in the right quadrant of the abdomen radiating the back right shoulder:
A. Renal colic B. Internal colic
C. Biliary colic D. Abdominal colic

717. Diabetes mellitus is usually recognized by:
A. Albuminuria B. Lack of appetite
C. Glycosuria D. Urea in the urine

718. The cause of ascites in cirrhosis of the liver is:
A. General fluid imbalance
B. Portal obstruction
C. Kidney trouble
D. All of the Above

719. Dr Salk discovered a vaccine for the prevention of:
A. Measles B. Poliomyelitis
C. Smallpox D. Tetanus

720. Pneumathorax is the condition in which there is:
A. Water in the visceral space
B. Air in the visceral space
C. Water in the pleural space
D. Air in the pleural space

721. The cause of anemia in renal failure is
A. Erythropoietin deficiency
B. Repeated hemodialysis
C. Excessive use of diuretics
D. Restriction of protein in the diet

722. Best therapeutic measure for empyema is:
A. Chest drainage
B. Postural drainage
C. Breathing exercise
D. Fowler's position

723. Allergen causes:
A. Bronchitis B. Asthma
C. Bronchiectasis D. Pneumonia

724. Serum cholesterol level will be elevated in case of:
A. Hypothyroidism B. Hyperthyroidism
C. Cretinism D. Diabetes

725. Normal bleeding time is:
A. 1-3 mts B. 6-10 mts
C. 2-6 mts D. 10-12 mts

726. Excessive salivation and drooling is seen in:
A. Esophageal atresia
B. Diaphragmatic hernia
C. Omphalocele
D. Tracheoesophageal fistula

727. The bilirubin encephalopathy due to high concentration of indirect bilirubin on brain and basal ganglia in the neonatal period is:
A. Status epileptics B. Kerning's sign
C. Kernicterus D. Jaundice

728. Diabetes insipidus is caused by:
A. Growth hormone
B. Insulin metabolism
C. Ant diuretic hormone
D. Carbohydrate metabolism

729. Liver enzymes which converts lipid soluble bilirubin:
A. Low density lipoprotein
B. Acetyle choline
C. Glucoronyl transferase
D. High density lipoprotein

730. A substance which suppress or neutralize bad odors is called:

A. Deodorant B. Antiseptic
C. Disinfectant D. Antibiotic

731. Tobacco is not only is cigarettes but is chewed by many people. Which poisons alkaloid is present in tobacco?

A. Lead C. Alcohol
B. Nicotine D. Caffeine

732. When the lens of the eyes become cloudy and opaque, the condition is known as:

A. Glaucoma B. Long sightedness
C. Cataract D. Short sightedness

733. Paralysis of the lower half of the torso and of both legs:

A. Quadriplegia
B. Hemiplegia
C. Paraplegia
D. Paralysis of lower extremity

734. Cardiac muscle differ from skeletal muscle by

A. It contains actin and myosin
B. It has automaticity and conductivity
C. It needs calcium for contraction
D. It thrives without oxygen

735. The nurse explains to the mother of a neonate diagnosed with erythroblastosis fetalis, that the exchange transfusion is necessary to prevent damage to

A. Liver B. Lungs
C. Kidneys D. Brain

736. What should be the position of the limb, a nurse should maintain in a patient who had undergone right hip prosthesis surgery?

A. Adduction B. Abduction
C. Flexion D. Neutral

737. A post operative patient develops evisceration what a nurse should do?

A. Provide moral support
B. Ask patient to drink more water
C. Push the protruding organs inside
D. Cover the protruding organs

738. A nurse is caring for an old lady with osteoarthritis and all the following facts are true regarding osteoarthritis except:

A. Pain on moving the joint
B. Crepitus
C. Tophi
D. Subcutaneous nodules

739. How a nurse will teach breathing exercise for a patient with chronic bronchitis?

A. Use deep inhalation breathing
B. Use chest breathing
C. Use diaphragmatic breathing
D. Use open mouth breathing

740. Which joint movement is restricted in a patient with pericapsulitis of shoulder?

A. Extension B. Adduction
C. Abduction D. Flexion

741. A nurse caring for a head injury comatose patient. Which intervention he/she should implement to prevent increased intracranial pressure?

A. Elevate the head end of the patient
B. Maintain well lit room
C. Maintain round the clock suctioning
D. Change the position round the clock

742. Before giving blood transfusion a nurse must note the date, time of collection and must be aware that Packed RBC's can be stored up to

A. 55 days B. 25 days
C. 35 days D. 45 days

743. A nurse was called to see a patient with noisy breathing. She suspects laryngospasm with strider and it occurs commonly with

A. Hypocalcemia B. Hyperkalemi
C. Hypercalcemia D. Hypokalemia

744. Nurse working in an operation theatre must know, the risk of HIV infection with needle stick injury is about

A. 1400 B. 1:100
C. 1:200 D. 1 :300

745. What recommendation a nurse should give to 55 yr old patient with blood pressure of 150/90 mmHg?

A. Recheck your BP after 1 year
B. It is normal BP for your age
C. Recheck your BP 2 weeks later
D. Recheck your BP after 6 months

746. Which one of the following is a DNA Virus?

A. Hepatitis D B. Hepatitis A
C. Hepatitis B D. Hepatitis

747. Nurse is about to insert Kyle's Tube for a patient. Before this act she must be aware of the distance between incisor teeth and Castro esophageal junction. Which of the following is correct distance?

A. 60 cm B. 30 cm
C. 40 cm D. 50 cm

748. A nurse is taking care of a patient with DVT and she must be aware that venous emboli will be lodged in

A. Kidneys B. Heart
C. Lungs D. Liver

749. Hyaline membrane disease of an infant is due and the source of to deficiency of surfactant pulmonary surfactant is
A. Pneumonocytes type 2
B. Alveolar macrophages
C. Capillary endothelium
D. Pneumonocytes type 1

750. A nurse is caring an anemic patient. What finding should suggest her that it is acute blood loss anemia?
A. Postural hypotension
B. Exertional dyspnea
C. Easy fatigue on exertion
D. Bradycardia at rest

751. All are true regarding H. Pylori infection except
A. Is gram positive bacteria
B. Is eradicated by triple therapy
C. Produces urease enzyme
D. Causes Maltoma tumor

752. When assessing a patient with appendicitis how a nurse must initiate to get information?
A. Tell me whether cough aggravates pain
B. Tell me how you are feeling
C. Tell me where is the pain
D. Tell me relief of pain with what

753. Which one of the following statements by a patient with backache should alert the nurse?
A. Pain on movement
B. Pain radiating the leg
C. Perineal anaesthesia
D. Pain sensation lost in feet

754. Before endotracheal intubation some facts about trachea a nurse has to understand and all the following are true regarding trachea except
A. It ends at the level of sternal angle of Louis
B. It's about. 13 cm long
C. It bifurcates into two major bronchi
D. It starts at the level of 7th cervical vertebra

755. The purpose of lymph nodes is to trap
A. RBC's B. Antigens
C. Macrophages D. Hormones

756. Which one of the following indices a nurse has to consider as an indicator of good nutrition?
A. Total lymphocytes 1900/microliter
B. Albumin level 2.5 gm/dl
C. Pre-albumin level 18 mg/dl
D. Transferrin level 244 mg/dl

757. Cytokines are chemical messengers, which
A. Produce antibodies
B. Kill microorganisms
C. Promote inflammation
D. Cause severe pain

758. Obstruction of the artery or vein by a clot of blood:
A. Thrombosis
B. Embolism
C. Thrombophlebitis
D. Phlebitis

759. "Mask like fades" is a typical features of:
A. Tetanus
B. Hypothyroidism
C. Parkinson disease
D. Down's syndrome

760. The thymus related T cells
A. Recognize body's own cells
B. Produce antibodies
C. Produce NK cells
D. Recognize B cells

761. A nurse caring a patient on pancreatic enzyme replacement therapy should assess them for
A. GIT irritation B. Weight gain
C. Hypertension D. Arrhythmias

762. Guillain Barre syndrome is a disease of which of the following?
A. Peripheral nerve
B. Brain
C. Spinal cord
D. All of the above

□□□

Answer Sheet

1. B	2. C.	3. D.	4 . B.	5. C.	6.A.	7.C.	8.C.	9.C.	10.A.
11.C.	12.B.	13.B.	14.C.	15.C.	16.D.	17.B.	18.C.	19.B.	20.A.
21.A.	22.B.	23.D.	24.D.	25.B.	26.C.	27.B.	28.C.	29.B.	30.B.
31.C.	32.A.	33.B.	34.A.	35.D.	36.C.	37.D.	38.A.	39.C.	40.A.
41.C.	42.C.	43.C.	44.C.	45.A.	46.A.	47.D.	48.B.	49.B.	50.D.
51.B.	52.D.	53.B.	54.D.	55.A.	56.B.	57.D.	58.D.	59.B.	60.A.
61.D.	62.A.	63.C.	64.D.	65.D.	66.B.	67.D.	68.C.	69.C.	70.D.
71.A.	72.C.	73.B.	74.D.	75.A.	76.A.	77.B.	78.D.	79.A.	80.D.
81.A.	82.C.	83.C.	84.B.	85.C.	86.C.	87.A.	88.B.	89.C.	90.C.
91. C.	92. B.	93. A.	94. A.	95. D.	96. D.	97. C.	98. D.	99. A.	100. A.
101. D.	102. A.	103. D.	104 D.	105. A.	106. D.	107. D.	108. A.	109. A.	110. B.
111. B.	112. B.	113. B.	114 A.	115. D.	116. B.	117. D.	118 A.	119. A.	120. B.
121. B.	122. B.	123. D.	124. D.	125. B.	126. D.	127. B.	128 A.	129. C.	130. A.
131. D.	132. C.	133. A.	134. B.	135. C.	136. C.	137. B.	138 B.	139. B.	140. C.
141. .B	142. B.	143. A.	144. C.	145. A.	146. C.	147. B.	148 A.	149. B.	150. B.
151. A.	152. C.	153. B.	154. A.	155. C.	156. B.	157. A.	158. C.	159. A.	160. C.
161. A.	162. B.	163. B.	164. B.	165. D.	166. A.	167. B.	168. D.	169. A.	170. A.
171. D.	172. D.	173. A.	174. A.	175. C.	176. A.	177. C.	178. B.	179. B.	180. B.
181. C.	182. C.	183. B.	184. C.	185. D.	186. A.	187. C.	188. B.	189. B.	190. A.
191. B.	192. C.	193. .B	194. B.	195. A.	196. B.	197. D.	198. D.	199. D.	200. C.
201. B.	202. B.	203. A.	204. B.	205. C.	206. A.	207. B.	208. B.	209. D.	210. D.
211. B.	212. C.	213. A.	214. C.	215. C.	216. D.	217. C.	218. D.	219. B.	220. C.
221. B.	222. D.	223. B.	224. D.	225. D.	226. C.	227. D.	228. B.	229. D.	230. B.
231. A.	232. D.	233. C.	234. A.	235. B.	236. D.	237. D.	238. C.	239. B.	240. A.
241. A.	242. C.	243. C.	244. B.	245. B.	246. A.	247. B.	248. C.	249. B.	250. D.
251. B.	252. D.	253. B.	254. A.	255. D.	256. A.	257. C.	258. C.	259. B.	260. A.
261. C.	262. A.	263. C.	264. C.	265. A.	266. D.	267. C.	268. D.	269. B.	270. B.
271. C.	272. A.	273. A.	274. D.	275. B.	276. A.	277. C.	278. D.	279. .A	280. .B
281. .D	282. B.	283. C.	284. C.	285. A.	286. A.	287. .C	288. C.	289. B.	290. D.
291. B.	292. B.	293. C.	294. D.	295. B.	296. B.	297. C.	298. B.	299. C.	300. A.
301. A.	302. D.	303. C.	304. D.	305. C.	306. C.	307. B.	308. A.	309. D.	310. A.
311. B.	312. A.	313. B.	314. A.	315. D.	316. A.	317. B.	318. B.	319. D.	320. B.
321. D.	322. A.	323. D.	324. C.	325. A.	326. B.	327. A.	328. A.	329. B.	330. B.
331. C.	332. C.	333. D.	334. D.	335. B.	336. B.	337. D.	338. C.	339. A.	340. D.
341. B.	342. A.	343. C.	344. D.	345. A.	346. C.	347. C.	348. D.	349. A.	350. D.
351. D.	352. B.	353. B.	354. A.	355. D.	356. D.	357. D.	358. A.	359. D.	360. A.
361. D.	362. C.	363. A.	364. A.	365. B.	366. A.	367. D.	368. D.	369. D.	370. D.
371. D.	372. A.	373. C.	374. A.	375. C.	376. B.	377. D.	378. A.	379. C.	380. B.
381. D.	382. D.	383. D.	384. C.	385. A.	386. A.	387. B.	388. D.	389. B.	390. A.
391. A.	392. D.	393. D.	394. C.	395. D.	396. B.	397. B.	398. B.	399. B.	400. C.
401. D.	402. B.	403. A.	404. B.	405. D.	406. A.	407. D.	408. A.	409. D.	410. B.
411. A.	412. D.	413. B.	414. A.	415. D.	416. C.	417. D.	418. A.	419. C.	420. B.
421. A.	422. A.	423. C.	424. D.	425. D.	426. D.	427. D.	428. B.	429. A.	430. A.

431. A.	432. B.	433. D.	434. C.	435. C.	436. C.	437. A.	438. B.	439. A.	440. D.
441. C.	442. B.	443. A.	444. C.	445. B.	446. A.	447. D.	448. D.	449. A.	450. B.
451. A.	452. A.	453. A.	454. B.	455. B.	456. C.	457. A.	458. D.	459. B.	460. D.
461. D.	462. B.	463. D.	464. C.	465. A.	466. C.	467. D.	468. C	469. C.	470. B.
471. A.	472. D.	473. B.	474. A.	475. D.	476. B.	477. A.	478. C.	479. C.	480. B.
481. B.	482. C.	483. B.	484. B.	485. D.	486. D.	487. D.	488. B.	489. C.	490. C.
491. D.	492. B.	493. A.	494. A.	495. B.	496. C.	497. B.	498. D.	499. D.	500. B.
501. D.	502. B.	503. D.	504. D.	505. C.	506. B.	507. C.	508. B.	509. B.	510. A.
511. C.	512. A.	513. C.	514. A.	515. C.	516. C.	517. A.	518. C.	519. B.	520. A.
521. D.	522. A.	523. D.	524. A.	525. B.	526. C.	527. B.	528. A.	529. B.	530. B.
531. A.	532. C.	533. D.	534. B.	535. B.	536. A.	537. D.	538. D.	539. B.	540. C.
541. B.	542. B.	543. B.	544. C.	545. D.	546. B.	547. C.	548. C.	549. C.	550. B.
551. A.	552. C.	553. D.	554. A.	555. C.	556. A.	557. C.	558. B.	559. A.	560. B.
561. A.	562. B.	563. C.	564. B.	565. B.	566. B.	567. A.	568. C.	569. A.	570. A.
571. C.	572. A.	573. A.	574. A.	575. A.	576. A.	577. B.	578. B.	579. C.	580. B.
581. D.	582. D.	583. A.	584. B.	585. B.	586. A.	587. B.	588. D.	589. D.	590. A.
591. C.	592. B.	593. B.	594. A.	595. D.	596. A.	597. B.	598. A.	599. C.	600. A.
601. C.	602. D.	603. B.	604. C.	605. A.	606. C.	607. A.	608. B.	609. C.	610. C.
611. D.	612. A.	613. C.	614. B.	615. B.	616. A.	617. B.	618. A.	619. A.	620. D.
621. B.	622. C.	623. A.	624. D.	625. C.	626. C.	627. B.	628. B.	629. D.	630. B.
631. A.	632. A.	633. C.	634. D.	635. D.	636. A.	637. B.	638. C.	639. A.	640. C.
641. A.	642. A.	643. C.	644. C.	645. A.	646. B.	647. B.	648. D.	649. C.	650. D.
651. C.	652. C.	653. A.	654. B.	655. D.	656. C.	657. D.	658. A.	659. C.	660. C.
661. A.	662. D.	663. D.	664. C.	665. A.	666. D.	667. D.	668. D.	669. C.	670. A.
671. C.	672. C.	673. D.	674. B.	675. B.	676. C.	677. B.	678. D.	679. B.	680. A.
681. C.	682. C.	683. C.	684. C.	685. B.	686. C.	687. C.	688. D.	689. D.	690. A.
691. C.	692. A.	693. D.	694. D.	695. D.	696. B.	697. D.	698. C.	699. D.	700. C.
701. A.	702. C.	703. A.	704. D.	705. B.	706. C.	707. C.	708. C.	709. C.	710. C.
711. B.	712. A.	713. A.	714. B.	715. D.	716. C.	717. C.	718. B.	719. B.	720. D.
721. A.	722. B.	723. B.	724. D.	725. C.	726. A.	727. C.	728. C.	729. C.	730. A.
731. B.	732. C.	733. C.	734. B.	735. D.	736. B.	737. D.	738. C.	739. C.	740. C.
741. A.	742. C.	743. A.	744. D.	745. C.	746. C.	747. C.	748. C.	749. A.	750. A.
751. A.	752. C.	753. C.	754. D.	755. B.	756. A.	757. C.	758. A.	759. C.	760. A.
761. B.	762. A.								

❑❑❑

5. Nutrition & Biochemistry (MCQ)

1. Deficiency of the following substance causes hypo chromic microcytic anaemia
A. Niacin B. Vitamin B_{12}
C. Folate D. Iron

2. Which of the following is not a feature of niacin deficiency
A. Diarrhoea
B. Red tongue
C. Psychosis
D. Conjunctival congestion

3. A patient who has undergone gastrectomy is likely to develop deficiency of
A. Vitamin A B. Vitamin B_{12}
C. Vitamin B_1 D. Vitamin K

4. Which of the form of hemoglobin stored in body?
A. Ferritin. B. Transferring
C. Heame. D. All of the Above.

5. For the repair of body tissues which nutrient is required
A. Fats B. Protein
C. Carbohydrate D. Vitamin C

6. Which is the following disease caused by vitamin A deficiency?
A. Night blindness.
B. Depression.
C. Pernicious anemia.
D. Magaoblastic anemia.

7. The patient who is immobilized because of spinal cord injuries, should have a diet rich in:
A. Calories B. Carbohydrates
C. Fats D. Proteins

8. What is the normal calcium serum level in a client.?
A. 20-30 mg. B. 45-50 mg.
C. 9-11 mg/dl D. 1-2 mg.

9. Often the baby, who is given only milk during infancy, develops iron deficiency anemia because:
A. The number of red blood cells is destroyed during infancy
B. Milk interferes with the absorption of iron
C. Milk is a poor source of iron
D. It impairs or decreases rate of production of Red Blood Cells

10. Which of the following is not considered a fat soluble vitamin?
A. Vitamin A B. Vitamin B
C. Vitamin K D. Vitamin E

11. Which of the vitamin found in citrus fruits?
A. Vitamin A B. Vitamin K
C. Vitamin C D. Vitamin D

12. Which is disease caused by Vitamin B_1?
A. Beri- Beri. B. Glossitis
C. Pellagra. D. Paresthesia

13. Which of the following is not considered a water soluble vitamin?
A. Vitamin B B. Vitamin C
C. Vitamin D D. Vitamin B_{12}

14. Which is disease caused by Vitamin B_3?
A. Beri- Beri. B. Glossitis.
C. Pellagra. D. Paresthesia.

15. Priya, a 5year old girl is suffering from acute respiratory infection. She could be given:
A. Plenty of fluids and food
B. Restricted food and fluids
C. Milk only
D. Only intravenous fluids

16. The extra energy allowances needed per day during pregnancy is:
A. 150 K calories B. 200 K calories
C. 300 K calories D. 550 K calories

17. In comparison to cow's milk, which one of the following is more in human milk:
A. Lactose B. Proteins
C. Minerals D. Iron

18. Best test to detect iron deficiency in community is:
A. Transferrin B. Serum Ferritin
C. Serum Iron D. Hemoglobin

19. The Vitamin A supplements administered in 'Prevention of nutritional blindness in children programme" contain:
A. 25000 I.U/ml B. 1 lakh I.U/ml
C. 3 lakh I.U/ml D. 5 lakh I.U/ml

20. All the following are a good source of omega 3 PUFA except:
A. Mustard Oil B. Groundnut Oil
C. Corn Oil D. Fish Oil

21. Food cooked in copper utensils lose ascorbic acid quickly because it:
A. Oxidise in presence of copper and iron
B. Oxidise in presence of copper and aluminium
C. Is destroy by alkalise
D. Is stable due to acidic action

22. Which of the following is not an underlying cause of hypercalcemia?
A. Paget's disease
B. Hyperparathyroidism
C. Hartnup disease
D. Sarcoidosis

23. Which of the following is caused by a B_5 deficiency?
A. Ectopic pregnancy B. Nausea
C. Dermatitis D. Fever

24. Which of the following is caused by a B_6 deficiency?
A. Excessive irritability
B. Non-productive cough
C. Dry mouth
D. Depression

25. What is the other name of Vitamin B_2?
A. Thiamine B. Rivoflavin
C. Niacin D. Pantothenic acid

26. What is the other name of Vitamin B_3?
A. Thiamine B. Rivoflavin.
C. Niacin D. Pantothenic acid

27. In which cycle pyrubic acids oxidise in CO_2 and H_2O?
A. Krebs cycle B. Glycolysis cycle
C. Glucose cycle D. None of the Above

28. Glossitis is due to the deficiency of
A. Niacin B. Thiamine
C. Riboflavin D. Vitamin B_{12}

29. The first clinical sign of Vitamin-A deficiency is
A. Conjunctival xerosis
B. Corneal xerosis
C. Bitot's spots
D. Keratomalcia

30. Lipids can be stored in the body as a food resource because they are:
A. Insoluble in aqueous solution
B. Soluble in aqueous solution
C. Rich in fatty acids
D. Fat soluble

31. One of the following organism causes food intoxication in milk, meat and cheese:
A. Streptococcus
B. Salmonella
C. Clostridium botulinum
D. Staphylococcus

32. Which of the following is caused by a B_2 deficiency?
A. Glossitis B. Fever
C. Hypertension D. Edema

33. Which of the following is caused by a Vitamin C deficiency?
A. Fever B. Anemia
C. Headaches D. Nausea

34. Which of the following is caused by a Vitamin D deficiency?
A. Edema B. Anemia
C. Lupus D. Rickets

35. Which of the following is caused by a Vitamin K deficiency?
A. Bruising
B. Optic Nerve degeneration
C. Anemia
D. Hemorrhage (infants)

36. Another name for Vitamin B1 is :
A. Thiamine B. Riboflavin
C. Pyridoxine D. Cobalamin

37. Which of the following foods is not high in potassium?
A. Oranges B. Bananas
C. Tomatoes D. Turnips

38. 1 gram of protein is equal to ____ of energy.
A. 3 kcals B. 4 kcals
C. 5 kcals D. 6 kcals

39. A protein restricted diet requires only ____ grams/day.
A. 20-40 B. 30-50
C. 40-60 D. 50-70

40. Which of the following is not considered a food reaction for infants?
A. Diarrhea B. Hypertension
C. Skin rash D. Difficulty breathing

41. Which of the following vitamins will be the most common in: oils from cereal seeds, salad oils, margarine and shortenings?
A. Vitamin A B. Vitamin D
C. Vitamin E D. Vitamin K

42. Which of the following vitamins will be the most common in: leafy green vegetables, egg yolk and soy oil?
A. Vitamin A B. Vitamin D
C. Vitamin E D. Vitamin K

43. Which of the following vitamins will be the most common in: fish liver oils, milk, and egg yolk?
A. Vitamin A B. Vitamin D
C. Vitamin E D. Vitamin K

44. **Another name for Vitamin B_{12} is :**
A. Pantothenic Acid
B. Cyanocobalamin
C. Niacin
D. Riboflavin

45. **Which of the following disease condition where weight loss occur drastically and sub contentious fat is reduced on body?**
A. Marasmus B. Kwashiorkor
C. Goiter D. Anemia

46. **Which of the state iron absorbed in the body?**
A. Ferrous state B. Ferric state
C. Both A and B D. None of the Above

47. **Which nutrient needs to be assessed by nurse in case patient has infective endocarditis:**
A. Protein and fat intake
B. Calorie protein intake and record weight
C. Calorie intake and record weight
D. Fat and calorie intake

48. **Which of the following is iodine deficiency disease EXCEPT?**
A. Goitre
B. Mental retardation
C. Deaf mute condition
D. Night blindness

49. **Which of the following is VitaminA deficiency disease?**
A. Xerophthalmia. B. Bitot spot.
C. Keratomalcia. D. All of the Above.

50. **Which is the energy malnutrition?**
A. Marasmus B. Kwashiorkor
C. Both A & B D. None of the Above

51. **Which of the following does not contain a high concentration of Niacin?**
A. Yeast B. Meat
C. Liver D. Corn

52. **Which of the following does not contain a high concentration of Vitamin A?**
A. Strawberries B. Oranges
C. Green Vegetables D. Yellow Vegetables

53. **When was the Prevention of food and adulteration act passed in parliament?**
A. 1947 B. 1952 C. 1954 D. 1960

54. **Which of the following disease condition required purine reduced food?**
A. Hypertension B. Gout
C. Renal failure D. Hepatitis

55. **How much calories required by a infant?**
A. 200 Kilo calorie/ Kg
B. 500 Kilo calorie/ Kg
C. 300 Kilo calorie/ Kg
D. 120 Kilo calorie/ Kg

56. **A patient with prolonged protein deficiency will manifest with low plasma proteins which will affect the maintenance of:**
A. Osmotic pressure
B. Blood pressure
C. Circulatory blood volume
D. Total blood volume

57. **Dietician will prescribe one of the following diet for the patient with emphysema:**
A. Low protein low calorie
B. High protein high calorie
C. High calorie normal diet
D. High calorie soft diet

58. **In which of the condition patient is indicated to take milk initially with small amount of easily digested diet:**
A. Gastritis
B. Indigestion
C. Peptic ulcer
D. Malabsrption syndrome

59. **Food exchange list will help the diabetic patient to:**
A. Avoid certain food items
B. Plan menu
C. Select food items and amount of food for a day
D. Select food items if sugar level is low

60. **Which of the condition where edema occur on the child's body?**
A. Miasmas B. Kwashiorkor
C. Goitre D. Anemia

61. **Which of the following diet plans would be appropriate for the nurse to discuss with the family of a child with acute renal failure?**
A. Low in carbohydrate and fat
B. Low fat and protein
C. High fat and carbohydrate
D. High carbohydrate and protein

62. **Feed given to the infant in the absence of breast feeding is called as:**
A. Supplementary food
B. Artificial food
C. Weaning
D. All of the Above

63. **Which of the following deficiency disease is caused by deficiency of Thiamine (B1):**
A. Angular stomatitis B. Pellagra
C. Glosittis D. Beriberi

64. **Mid day meal supplement diet provides following nutrients:**
A. 200 calories 6-8 gms protein
B. 200 calories 7-10 gms protein
C. 300 calories 8-12 gms protein
D. 300 calories 14-16 gms protein

65. Weaning should start in a child at the:
A. 10 months B. 6 months
C. 2 months D. 8 months

66. Worm that is transmitted through meat is:
A. Hookworm B. Tapeworm
C. Pinworm D. Roundworm

67. Which is the effect of Vitamin B_7 deficiency?
A. Alopecia
B. Depression
C. Pernicious anemia
D. Magaoblastic anemia

68. Germination of seeds increases:
A. Digestive enzymes
B. Vitamin C
C. Vitamin B_1
D. Both A and B

69. Which is the main component of CHO to provide energy?
A. Hexose B. Ribose
C. Lyxose D. Glucose

70. Which of the following is a clinical manifestation associated with imperforate anus?
A. Child Failure to pass me conium stool in the first 24 hours after birth
B. Child passage of currant jelly-like stools
C. Sausage-shaped mass palpated in the upper right abdominal quadrant
D. Bile-stained faecal emesis

71. Which of the following is the major sugar in milk?
A. Glucose B. Fructose
C. Sucrose D. Lactose

72. Most sensitive test for detection of Argimone oil.
A. Nitric Acid Test
B. Nitrate Acid Test
C. Gel Chromatography
D. Paper Chromatography

73. Following is included in daily meals to supplement the protein:
A. Vegetables B. Daal
C. Potatoes D. Ghee

74. Maximum amount of Vitamin D is present in which of the following:
A Milks B. Eggs
C. Fish fat D. Cod liver oil

75. National Nutrition Policy was adopted by Government of India in:
A. 1975 B. 1990 C. 1993 D. 1999

76. IYCF (Infant and young child feeding) is related to which of the following:
A. Initiation of breastfeeding within one hour of birth
B. Exclusive breastfeeding for the first six months
C. Complementary feeding starting on completion of 6 months of age
D. All the of Above

77. Which food nutrient is required more in pregnant woman in India :
A. Iron B. Calcium
C. Potassium D. Zinc ftad

78. Iron Sucrose is given to :
A All women
B. All anemic women
C. Pregnant women who are highly anemic
D. Lactating mothers who are anemic

79. Which sugar called as table sugar?
A. Glucose B. Fructose
C. Sucrose D. Lactose

80. This nutrient is needed for a healthy immune system and strong connective tissue :
A. Fiber B. Vitamin K
C. Vitamin C D. Fluoride

81. Keratomalacia is :
A. Toad skin
B. Phernoderma
C. Corneal disease due to deficiency of Vitamin-A
D. Weak bones due to deficiency of Calcium

82. Which of the enzyme in saliva convert starch in maltose?
A. Maltase B. Isomaltase
C. Sucrose D. Amylase

83. Deficiency of Vitamin A causes :
A. Beri-Beri B. Scurvy L
C. Night Blindness D. Rickets

84. Which of the following cycle glycogen convert in glucose and glucose in pyrubic acids?
A. Krebs cycle B. Glycolysis cycle
C. Glucose cycle D. All of the Above

85. Proteins and carbohydrates are classified as :
A. Macromolecule B. Microbes
C. Organelles D. Atoms

86. ....is the body's primary source of energy:
A. Iron B. Sucrose
C. Fructose D. Glucose

87. Whole wheat is an excellent source of:
A. Vitamin D B. Vitamin C
C. Vitamin A D. Thiamine

88. A person suffering from swollen spongy and bleeding gums is mostly deficient in

A. Vitamin A B. Vitamin B_1
C. Vitamin C D. Vitamin D

89. This vitamin is needed to prevent a birth defect called Spina Bifida :

A. Vitamin D B. Vitamin A
C. Folate D. Vitamin E

90. The best way to retain nutrient while cooking vegetables is :

A. First wash then peel vegetables
B. Soaking in water
C. Drain water after cooking
D. Use shortest cooking time

91. A nurse provides home care instructions to the parents of a child with celiac disease. The nurse teaches the parents to include which food item in the child's diet?

A. Oatmeal B. Rice
C. Wheat bread D. Rye toast

92. Which is a rich source of Iron :

A. Potato B. Lemon
C. Jaggery D. Papaya

93. Bitot spot is caused by deficiency of :

A. Vitamin A B. Vitamin B
C. Vitamin D D. Vitamin E

94. "Pellagra" is caused by a deficiency of :

A. Niacin B. Riboflavin
C. Vitamin B_{12} D. Thiamin

95. Which edible oil contains highest quantity of PUFA :

A. Coconut oil B. Soyabeen oil
C. Sunflower oil D. Groundnut oil

96. What should be in diet of an anemic child :

A. Milk, Banana, Sweet lime
B. Apple, Pomegranate, Green Leafy Vegetable
C. Cereals, Meat, Fish
D. Papaya, Potato, Onion, Bread

97. Which of the following is a water soluble Vitamin:

A. Vitamin A B. Vitamin C
C. Vitamin D D. Vitamin K

98. Which of the following is the high rich source of Omega- 9?

A. Mustered oil B. Ground nut oil
C. Olive oil D. Soya oil

99. Which oral dose is given to the infant at 9 months of age :

A. Iron B. Vitamin A
C. Polio D. None of the Above

100. A nurse advises a patient to reduce the dietary intake of sodium by:

A. Increasing the use of dairy products
B. Voiding the use of carbonated beverages
C. Using an artificial sweetener in tea
D. Using vinegar for cooking and flavouring foods

101. Which of the following lipid had highest associated with atherosclerosis?

A. Triglycerides
B. Very high density lipoproteins
C. Low density lipoproteins
D. High density lipoproteins

102. The increased calorie need during puerparium is :

A. 1000 kcals B. 800 kcals
C. 500 kcals D. 300 kcals

103. Which of the following nutrients restriction in a child with chronic renal failure?

A. Phosphorus B. Magnesium
C. Calcium D. Ascorbic acid.

104. Which is the primary source of energy for the brain?

A. Glucose. B. Fatty acids.
C. Xylose. D. All. of the Above

105. 1 gm of protein gives ..... kcals.

A. 10 B. 5. C. 4 D. 7

106. Diet prescribed for patient having malabsorption syndrome is:

A. Corticotrophin B. Folk acid
C. Vitamin B_{12} D. A gluten free diet

107. Which vitamin is called alpha tecopherol?

A. Vitamin K B. Vitamin A
C. Vitamin B D. Vitamin E

108. Which of the following is called as fruit sugur?

A. Levulose B. Fructose
C. Both A & B D. None of the Above

109. Which of the following disaccharides required for absorption of lactose and maltose?

A. Glucose B. Fructose
C. Sucrose D. Lactose

110. Prophylactic ally how many IFA tablets are given to pregnant and lactating mothers for prevention of Anaemia?

A. 3 times a day for 110 days
B. 3 times a day for 90 days
C. 3 times a day for 100 days
D. 3 times a day for 120 days

111. The daily requirement of calcium that an adult must take is:

A. 40-50 mg B. 4.0-5.0 mg
C. 400-500 mg D. 4000-5000 mg

112. **The first indicator of Protein Energy Malnutrition (PEM) in children is:**
A. Overweight for age
B. Weak and lethargic child
C. Underweight for age
D. Child having less intake of food

113. **For Severe Mal Nutrition according Sakir tab.**
A. < 13.5 cm B. < 12.5 cm
C. < 11.5 cm D. < 10 cm

114. **Amount of sodium in body :**
A. 100 gm B. 250 gm
C. 400-500 gm D. None

115. **The deficiency which can cause Skin rashes:**
A. Selenium B. CU
C. Ca^{+} D. Zn

116. **4 Feb. is celebrate as :**
A. World Cancer Day
B. World Health Day
C. World Hypertension Day
D. World Breast Feeding Day.

117. **% of alcohol in Bear.**
A. 40-50 B. 30-40
C. 5-8 D. 10-20

118. **Value of BMI above which person is considered obese -:**
A. 20 B. 25 C. 30 D. 40

119. **Most Sensative test for diagnosis of Iron deficiency anemia in our Community.**
A. Serum Feritin Level
B. Serumtrans Transferase Saturation
C. Serum Iron Level
D. Hemoglobin Level

120. **According to WHO Normal Hb level for pregnant women.**
A. 12 gm/dL B. 11 gm/dL
C. 13 gm/dL D. 10 gm/dL

121. **Which of the following foods would be appropriate for a 12 month old child with celiac disease?**
A. Waffles B. Rice Chex
C. Pancakes D. Cheerios

122. **Which of the following foods would be recommended for a client who suffer from the disease "Beri-Beri"?**
A. Tuna and chicken.
B. Broccoli and grapefruits
C. Meats and sunflower seeds
D. Milk products and oranges.

123. **Which food is naturally rich in Vitamin C?**
A. Chicken B. Banana
C. Orange D. Milk

124. **One gram of fat provides:**
A. 4 calories B. 6 calories
C. 8 calories D. 9 calories

125. **The diet should be followed by a patient with colostomy is:**
A. Rich in protein
B. Higher in carbohydrate
C. Low in fiber
D. As close to normal as possible

126. **The nutrients essential to prevent nutritional anemia include proteins, iron, vitamin B_{12} and:**
A. Iodine B. Calcium
C. Thiamine D. Folic acid

127. **Which of the following is Anti-sterility vitamin?**
A. Vitamin-A B. Vitamin-B
C. Vitamin-E D. Vitamin-K

128. **Which of the following disease is associated with a deficiency of Vitamin C?**
A. Pellagra B. Neural tube defects
C. Scurvy D. Pitted edema

129. **Which of Vitamin is responsible for rickets?**
A. Vitamin A B. Vitamin B
C. Vitamin C D. Vitamin D

130. **The daily protein requirement for an adult is:**
A. 1 gm/kg body weight
B. 2 gm/kg body weight
C. 0.5 gm/kg body weight
D. 3 gm/kg body weight

131. **Mottling of teeth may be produced by drinking water with excess:**
A. Bromide B. Chloride
C. Iodine D. Fluoride

132. **A patient with microcytic hypo chromic anemia is advised to include the following in the diet:**
A. Citrus fruits B. Sprouted pulses
C. Milk products D. Egg

133. **A patient with viral hepatitis should be provided with:**
A. High fat and low protein diet
B. High carbohydrate and high calorie diet
C. Low sodium low fat diet
D. High protein and low carbohydrate diet

134. **When a child diagnosed with diarrhoea due to Salmonella, for which of the following possible sources would the nurse be alert during history taking?**
A. Undercooked eggs
B. Cold water intake
C. Unwashed fruit
D. Non-refrigerated custard.

135. Which of the following is the effect of vitamin B_6 deficiency?
A. Alopecia
B. Depression
C. Pernicious anemia
D. Magaoblastic anemia

136. Which of the following is not an essential amino acid?
A. Threonine B. Arginine
C. Alanine D. Tryptophan

137. The normal supplement of IFA during antenatal period is for:
A. One tablet throughout period
B. Only one tablet for 100 days
C. 2 tablet for 100 days
D. 3 tablets for 90 days

138. Which of the following is the effect of vitamin B_9 deficiency?
A. Alopecia
B. Depression
C. Pernicious anemia
D. Magaoblastic anemia

139. Which of the following is the effect of vitamin B_{12} deficiency?
A. Alopecia
B. Depression
C. Pernicious anemia
D. Magaoblastic anemia

140. Which of the following is the precursor of Vitamin D?
A. Glycolipid B. Cholesterol
C. Ergosterol D. Cephalins

141. Find the odd one out in case of co-factors and metabolic factors of enzymes?
A. Zn^{2+} B. Mg2+
C. COA D. MO

142. Which one of the following is a functionally active form of Vitamin D?
A. Gholecalciferol
B. Ergocalciferol
C. Dehydrocholesterol
D. Calcitriol

143. A nurse provides feeding instructions to a mother of an infant diagnosed with gastroesophageal reflux disease.To assist in reducing the episodes of emesis, the nurse tells the mother to:
A. Burp the infant less frequently during feedings
B. Provide less frequent, larger feedings
C. Thicken the feedings by adding rice cereal to the formula
D. Thin the feedings by adding water to the formula.

144. What is the other name of Vitamin-B_6?
A. Biotin B. Pyridoxine
C. Folate D. Cyanocobalamin

145. A child with type 1 diabetes mellitus has football practice. The school nurse provides instructions regarding how to prevent hypoglycaemia during practice. The school nurse tells the child to:
A. Eat normally food at lunch time
B. Take half the amount of prescribed insulin on practice days
C. Drink a cup of orange juice before practice
D. Take the prescribed insulin at practice time.

146. When planning health teaching for a patient with hiatus hernia the nurse should be share to include instruction to
A. Eat three large meals per day with no restrictions
B. Lie down immediately following a meal
C. Eat frequent, small blend meals with high fibre content
D. Eat frequent, small soft solids with low fibre content

147. Protein requirement for a pregnant woman per day:
A. 50 grams B. 55 grams
C. 60 grams D. 65 grams

148. What is the other name of Vitamin-B_7?
A. Biotin B. Pyridoxine
C. Folate D. Cyanocobalamin

149. Which is the fatty acids body can synthesize?
A. Omega-3. B. Omega-6.
C. Omega-9 D. Omega 12.

150. What is the other name of the omega-3 ?
A. Linoleic acid. B. Linolenic acids.
C. Oleic acids. D. Polylinolenic acids

151. The energy value of .... is more than that of others
A. Fats B. Starch C. Protein D. Sugar

152. The product formed when amino acid molecules combine together is called
A. Nucleic acid B. Starch
C. Carbohydrate D. Proteins

153. Which nutrient is not found in eggs ?
A. Carbohydrate and Vitamin-C
B. Protein and calcium
C. Fat and Vitamin-D
D. Protein and Iron

154. Which one of the following is an essential amino acid?
A. Alanine B. Tryptophan
C. Glutamic acid D. Serine

155. Lactose present in a milk is a:
A. Polysaccharide
B. Heteropolysaccharide
C. Monosaccharide
D. Disaccharide

156. Which one of the following is a major protein present in human milk?
A. Lactglobulin B. Lactalbumin
C. Lactoferrin D. Casein

157. Lactulose is prescribed for patients with hepatic ancephalopathy to
A. Increase the protein level
B. Decrease the bilirubm level
C. Increase the glucose level
D. Decrease the serum ammonia level

158. Which one of the following indices a nurse has to consider as an indicator of good nutrition?
A. Albumin level 2.5 gm/dl
B. Pre-albumin level 18 mg/dl
C. Transferrin level 244 mg/dl
D. Total lymphocytes 1900/microliter

159. All are true regarding Vitamin A except :
A. It is found in green leafy vegetables
B. High dose in pregnancy is teratogenic
C. Supplementation reduce mortality in measle
D. Supplementation reduce morbidity in diarrhoea

160. A nurse must be aware that eating Maize alone may lead onto :
A. Beri-Beri B. Pellagra
C. Scurvy D. Phrynoderma

161. Prolonged use of Khesari dhal can lead to:
A. Lathyrism B. Gastric upset
C. Gout D. Cesophagitis

162. Optimum level of fluoride in drinking water per liter is:
A. l-2mg B. 0.05-0.08 mg
C. 05-0.8g D. 0.5-0.8rl

163. Bone deformation can occur due to lack of:
A. Calcium B. Vitamin D
C. Phosphorus D. All of these

164. The Process by which proteins are broken down to their amino acids is also called:
A. Proteolysis B. Glycogenolysis
C. Glycolysis D. All of the Above

165. The breakdown products of hemoglobin is:
A. Phospholipids B. Bile pigments
C. Fibrin D. Prothrombin

166. A compound within a cell nucleus that consists of a protein bound to a nucleic acid is called:
A. Nucleoprotein B. Albumin
C. Glycoprotein D. All of the Above

167. Aspartate aminotransf erase enzyme
A. Plays a role in processing proteins
B. Plays a role in metabolism, the process that converts food into energy
C. Both A and B
D. None of the Above

168. The nurse should instruct a patient who has a diagnosis of folic acid deficienty anaemia to increase intake of which of the following foods?
A. Green leafy vegetables
B. Dairy products
C. Citrus juices
D. Fish and poultry

169. Milk sugar is:
A. Lactose B. Glucose
C. Sucrose D. Cellulose

170. The antibodies are:
A. Proteins B. Carbohydrates
C. Lipids D. Germs

171. To reduce the risk of osteoporosis the nurse should advice :
A. Eat red meat
B. Drink plenty of water
C. Eat dairy product
D. Perform weight bearing exercise

172. What type of diet is restricted in renal Failure :
A. Protein B. Carbohydrates
C. Vitamins D. Iron supplements

173. Which of the following is rich in Protein :
A. Orange B. Fish
C. Soyabean D. Wheat

174. Who can take a food sample under the PFA Act :
A. Consumer B. Sanitary Inspector
C. Police inspector D. None of the Above

175. Which one of the following is not a bodybuilding Food:
A. Meat
B. Fruits
C. Pulses and Legumes
D. Egg

176. What is the other name of the omega-6 ?
A. Linoleic acid B Linolenic acids
C. Oleic acids D. Poly linolenic acids

177. What is the other name of the omega-9 ?
A. Linoleic acid B. Linolenic acids
C. Oleic acids D. Poly linolenic acids

178. What is the best time to ask a woman to start taking folic acid supplements?
A. Second half of menstrual cycle
B. When she consult for a missed period

C. When pregnancy is confirmed
D. Once she plans a pregnancy

179. For absorption of calcium essential is :
A. Vitamin A B. Vitamin B
C. Vitamin C D. Vitamin D

180. What is the other name of vitamin B_5?
A. Thiamine B. Rivoflavin
C. Niacin D. Pantothenic acid

181. Which of the following is disease caused by Vitamin B_5?
A. Beri- Beri B. Glossitis
C. Pellagra D. Paresthesia

182. Factor affecting nutrition :
A. Religion B. Culture
C. Economic D. All of the Above

183. The agent responsible for catalyzing chemical and physical changes within the cells is :
A. Hormone B. Enzyme
C Microorganism D. Acid

184. What is the other name of Vitamin-B_9?
A. Biotin B. Pyridcxine.
C. Folate d Cyanocobalamin.

185. What is the other name of Vitamin-B_{12}?
A. Biotin B. Pyridoxine
C. Folate D. Cyanccobalamin

186. Bland diet is used for patients with :
A. Diabetes mellitus
B. Gastrointestinal disturbances
C. Hypertension
D. Cardiac disease

187. Balance diet means :
A. Protein rich diet
B. Carbohydrate rich diet
C. Fat rich diet
D. Mixure of all necessary elements of diet in proper proportion

188. Yellow orange fruits and vegetables are rich in :
A. Carotenes B. Vitamin D
C. B –complex D. Zinc

189. The functions of Vitamin C includes :
A. It helps in the absorption of iron from food
B. It helps in wound healing
C. It acts as an antioxidant
D. All of the Above

190. The process that provides main pathway for the metabolism of fructose and galactose derived from diet is :
A. Glycolysis B. Gluconeogenesis
C. Glycogenolysis D. Glycogenesis

191. What types of compounds Purines and Pyrimidines are?
A. Homocyclic B. Metacyclic
C. Hetrocyclic D. Monocyclic

192. Which of vitamin could be deficient in vision in dim light?
A. Vitamin A B. Vitamin B
C. Vitamin C D. Vitamin D

193. Number of ATPs released at the end of glycolysis from glucose to lactate is :
A. One B. Two
C. Three D. Four

194. Which of the following is the most preferred source of energy?
A. Protein B. Fat
C. Carbohydrate D. Vitamins

195. Which of the following diet prescribed for a cardiac patient?
A. Low fat, low sodium, and high carbohydrates
B. Low fat, high prctein, and carbohydrates
C. Low fat, low sodium, and low carbohydrates
D. Liquids for several days, progressing to a soft and then a regular diet

196. Adverse effect of Thiazides does not include :
A. Hypercalcemia B. Hypouricemia
C. Hyperlipidemia D. Hypomagnesaemia

197. Which of the kind of fat shows space available for hydrogen atoms to bond?
A. Saturated fat B. Unsaturated fat
C. Trans fats D. Unitrans fat

198. Which kind of the fat called as good fats?
A. Saturated fat B. Unsaturated fat
C. Trans fats D. Unitrans fat

199. The most common ionized mediator of hormone action in our body is :
A. Calcium B. Magnesium
C. Iron D. Potassium

200. Adenine in DNA structure pairs with :
A. Thymines B. Cytosine
C. Guanines D. Pyrimidine

201. How many carbon double bond are in monounsaturated fatty acids?
A. Only one carbon atom of double bond.
B. More than two carbon atoms of double bond.
C. More than one carbon atoms of double bond.
D. More than four carbon atoms of double bond

202. What is the advantage of the monounsaturated fatty acids?
A. Increase rancidity
B. Increase insulin resistance
C. Bad for health
D. Lowering the low density protein

203. Which of the following food item is low in potassium :
A. Apple B. Carrots
C. Spinach D. Pear

204. A patient with Dumping Syndrome should be given :
A. High protein, high fat and low carbohydrate diet
B. Low protein, low fat and low carbohydrate diet
C. Normal protein, high fat and high carbohydrate diet
D. Low protein, low fat and low carbohydrate diet

205. Which of the fat prepared by hydrogenated fats?
A. Saturated fat B. Unsaturated fat
C. Trans fats D. Unitrans fat

206. An acute condition characterized by diminished production and increased destruction of RBC, triggered by viral infection or folic acid deficiency is :
A. Adrenal crisis
B. Aplastic crisis
C. Vasoocclusive crisis
D. Splenic crisis

207. A patient with gout should follow which type of diet :
A. Potassium modified diet
B. Renal diet
C. Low purine diet
D. High calcium diet

208. A patient ask you what vitamin is best for eye sight :
A. Vitamin B_6 B. Vitamin C
C. Vitamin B_{12} D. Vitamin A

209. Knowing that malnutrition is a frequent community health problem, you decided to conduct nutritional assessment. What population is particularly susceptible to protein energy malnutrition (PEM)?
A. Pregnant women and the elderly
B. 5 year old children
C. 1-4 year old children
D. School age children

210. Inadequate intake by the pregnant woman of which vitamin may cause neural tube defects?
A. Niacin B. Riboflavin
C. Folic Acid D. Thiamine

211. The richest natural source of Vitamin A is:
A. Carrot B. Fish
C. Peas D. Cod liver oil

212. Ascorbic acid is a:
A. Protein B. Vitamin
C. Enzyme D. Lipid

213. Which of the following is not a known source of Vitamin C?
A. Indian gooseberry (Amla)
B. Orange
C. Tomato
D. Sweet potato

214. How much dose of Vitamin A is administered every 6 months to pre-school :
A. 1,00,000 IU B. 1,50,000 IU
C. 2,00,000 IU D. 2,50,000 IU

215. Which of the carbohydrate food that would provide the quickest source of energy is a:
A. Glass of milk
B. Slice of bread
C. Snicker
D. Glass of orange juice

216. Which of the following is an Essential amino acid :
A. Alanine B. Serine
C. Tryptophan D. Glutamic Acid

217. Example of water soluble Vitamin is :
A. Vitamin A B. Vitamin B
C. Vitamin D D. Vitamin E

218. Which is the purpose of TPN is to:
A. To provide short term nutrition after surgery
B. Assist in providing supplemental nutrition for the client
C. Provide total nutrition when GI function is questionable
D. Assist people who are unable to eat but have active GI function

219. Type of diet recommended for a patient having difficulty in chewing and swallowing due to dry mouth is:
A. Soft diet B. Liquid diet
C. Low fibre diet D. Low residue diet

220. Which of the nutrition therapy for hypertension includes?
A. A low residue diet
B. Reduction in kilocalories, increase amounts of fat, sodium, and cholesterol
C. Decreased sodium intake
D. A high fibre diet

221. Which patients should receive calcium from non dairy sources :
A. Phenylketonuria B. Lactose intolerance
C. Osteopenia D. Gout

222. Which of the following vitamin have Blood clotting function?
A. Vitamin A B. Vitamin D
C. Vitamin E D. Vitamin K

223. A child with leukemia having nausea should be offered :
A. Cold clear fluid B. Warm clear fluid
C. Low protein diet D. Low calorie diet

224. Which of the following food should be avoided in celiac disease?
A. Rice B. Milk
C. Wheat D. Chicken

225. What is the important mineral lost during a haemorrhage?
A. Potassium B. Iron
C. Sodium D. Phosphorus

226. Which of the following is rich source of folic acid :
A. Spinach B. Banana
C. Carrots D. Papaya

227. Which of the following foodstuff in the richest source of Vitamin C:
A. Amla B. Guava
C. Orange D. Apple

228. Among the commonly used nuts, the richest source of iron is:-
A. Cashew nuts B. Almonds
C. Pistachio D. Ground nut

229. With reference to balanced diet the full form of RDA is :
A. Recommended Dietary Allowance
B. Rules for Diet Allowance
C. Routine Diet Average
D. Recommended diet for adults

230. Sunlight is a good source of which Vitamin :
A. Vitamin A B. Vitamin K
C. Vitamin D D. Vitamin E

231. The average daily iodine requirement of an adult is :
A. 150 micrograms a day
B. 200 milligrams a day
C. 100 micrograms a day
D. 175 milligrams a day

232. To address high diarrhoeal morbidity and mortality among children ,which Tablet has been added with ORS :
A. Zinc B. Vitamin A
C. Vitamin K D. Iron-Folic

233. Iodine deficiency can cause a disease called :
A. Goitre B. Cancer
C. Kidney stones D. Arthritis

234. Which of the following is a good source of Vitamin C:
A. Fish B. Guava
C. Papaya D. Milk

235. Which of the following mineral element causes pathological changes in bones and teeth in its deficiency as well as in excess :
A. Chlorine B. Zinc
C. Iodine D. Fluorine

236. The recommended energy requirement in reference to Indian woman (45 kg, moderate work) :
A. 1900 kacl B. 2200 kacl
C. 3000 kacl D. 2800 kacl

237. What is the source of Vitamin C :
A. Goose berry B. Peas
C. Carrot D. Coconut

238. Small Pox is also known as:
A. Badi Mata B. Chorion
C. Badi ANT D. Amnion

239. Macro Nutrients also known as:
A. Bulk of Diet
B. Proximate Principle
C. Both A & B
D. None of the Above

240. Most sensitive test for detection of Argimone oil.
A. Nitric Acid Test
B. Nitrate Acid Test
C. Gel Chromatography
D. Paper Chromatography

241. Concentrated Source of energy :
A. Carbohydrate B. Fat
C. Protein D. All of the Above

242. Reserved Food in over body :
A. Carbohydrate B. Protein
C. Fat D. Vitamins

243. Energy Source for Heart :
A. Carbohydrate B. Fat
C. Protein D. Vitamins

244. Energy Source for Brain :
A. Carbohydrate B. Fat
C. Protein D. Minerals

245. 1 Cup Tea energy given :
A. 100 KCal B. 69 Kcal
C. 75 KCal D. 50 KCal

246. 1 Cup Coffee energy given:
A. 97 KCal B. 75 KCal
C. 100 KCal D. 10 KCal

247. Higher Protein (In per 100 gm) is present in :
A. Milk B. Egg
C. Pules D. Ground Nets

248. Protein requirement in gm/day :
A. 10 gm / day B. 0.7 gm / day
C. 0.7 gm / day D. 1 gm / day

249. Net Protein Utilization for Rice:
A. 96 B. 55 C. 65 D. 50

250. All are true for Net Protein utilization except : -
A. Best Marker
B. Ratio of N_2 retain to N_2 Intake
C. Higest for ECG
D. 1 gm Protein in equalient to 1 gm Nitrogen.

251. Which Amino acid is absent in Soyabin :
A. Glycine B. Phenyalanine
C. Cysteine D. Tryptophan

252. In Maize Stable population disease occur :
A. Beri-Beri
B. Pallegra
C. Nural tube defect
D. Megloblastic anemia

253. ASHA / ANM detects a case of PEM in field, which instrument is used :
A. Salter tap B. Shakir's tap
C. Infanto Meter D. Gluco meter

254. Daily Requirement of fat in Lactation mother:
A. 20 gm / day B. 45 gm / day
C. 30 gm / day D. 25 gm / day

255. Atherogenic Lipids are :
A. VLDL B. LDL
C. HDL D. Both A & B

256. Vegetables Milk is :
A. Ground Nuts B. Soyabine
C. Both A & B D. None of the Above

257. Phrynoderma is caused by:
A. EFA Decrease
B. Decrease Protein
C. Increase vitamin Toxicity
D. Decrease Glucose

258. Normal Blood Cholesterol (mg%) :
A. 50-100 B. 100-200
C. 150-250 D. 250-300

259. Denaturizatin all structure of protein are destroyed except :
A. Primary B. Secondary
C. Tertiary D. Quaterly

260. Continous Breast feeding upto 6 month:
A. Classical B. Excellent
C. Exclusive D. Important

261. Vitamin which Incrase Iron absorption.
A. Vitamin D B. Vitamin A
C. Vitamin E D. Vitamin C

262. Most sensitive tool for growth & development of child :
A. Height B. Weight
C. Age D. None of the Above

263. Drug of choice for vomiting in pregnancy :
A. Domperidone
B. Meta colimide
C. Ondesterone
D. Doxylemine Sccinate

264. Kissing Disease Cause by :
A. CMV
B. HPV
C. HIV
D. Infecious Mono Nucleosis

265. All are seen in Vitamin A Deficiency except.
A. Night Blindness
B. Biots Spots
C. Conjunctiva Xerosis
D. Pipily Edema

266. Ist week of August is celebrate as:
A. Immunization Week
B. World Health Week
C. World Tobacco Prevention Week
D. Breast Feeding Promotion Week

267. Iodized salt is example of:
A. Mixing
B. Adulteration
C. Fortification
D. Chemical Reaction

268. Most common Carcinoma in Indian Male:
A. Lungs B. Prostate
C. Skin D. Bone

269. Vitamin Responsible for Maturation of RBC.
A. Vitamin A B. Vitamin D
C. Vitamin B_1 D. Vitamin B_9

270. EFA is also known as (In-past).
A. Vitamin A B. Vitamin B_2
C. Vitamin F D. Biotin

271. Highest amount of Iron in found in:
A. Pista B. Soya bin
C. Spinach D. Cabbage

272. Month & amount of Milk produce (maximum).
A. 4th Month = 500 ml
B. 5th Month – 650 ml
C. 6th Month = 750 ml
D. 3th Month – 540 ml

273. Protein present in Breast Milk.
A. Desmin B. Kinin
C. Casein D. Myosin

274. Cow milk is deficient in.
A. Fe B. Vitamin C
C. Both A & B D. None of the Above

❑❑❑

Answer Sheet

1.D.	2. D.	3. B.	4. D.	5. B.	6. A.	7. D.	8. C.	9. C.	10. B.
11. C.	12. A.	13. C.	14. C.	15. A.	16. C.	17. A.	18. B.	19. B.	20. A.
21. A.	22. C.	23. C.	24. A.	25. B.	26. C.	27. A.	28. C.	29. A.	30. A.
31. D.	32. A.	33. B.	34. D.	35. D.	36. A.	37. D.	38. B	39. C.	40. B.
41. C.	42. D.	43. B	44. B	45. A.	46. A.	47. C.	48. D.	49. D.	50. A.
51. D.	52. C.	53. C.	54. B.	55. D.	56. A.	57. D.	58. C.	59. C.	60. B.
61. C.	62. B.	63. D.	64. C.	65. B.	66. B.	67. A.	68. D.	69. D.	70. A.
71. D.	72. B.	73. B.	74. D.	75. C.	76. D.	77. A.	78. C.	79. C.	80. C.
81. C.	82. A.	83. C.	84. B.	85. A.	86. D.	87. D.	88. C.	89. C.	90. A.
91. B.	92. C.	93. A.	94. A.	95. C.	96. B.	97. B.	98. C.	99. B.	100. D.
101. C.	102. C.	103. A.	104. A.	105. C.	106.D.	107.D.	108.B.	109. C.	110. C.
111. C.	112. C.	113. B.	114. A.	115. D.	116. A.	117. C.	118. C.	119. A.	120. B.
121.B.	122. C.	123. C.	124. D.	125.A.	126. B.	127. C.	128. C.	129.D.	130. A.
131. D.	132.D.	133. B.	134. A.	135. B.	136. C.	137. B.	138. D.	139. C.	140. B.
141. C.	142. D.	143. C.	144. B.	145. C.	146. C.	147. B.	148. A.	149. C.	150. B.
151. A.	152. D.	153.A.	154.B.	155. D.	156. D.	157. D.	158. D.	159. A.	160. B.
161. A.	162. C.	163. D.	164. A.	165. B.	166. A.	167. C.	168. A.	169. A.	170. A.
171. C.	172. A.	173. C.	174. D.	175. B.	176. A.	177. C.	178. D.	179. D.	180. D.
181. D.	182. D.	183. B.	184. C.	185. D.	186. B.	187. D.	188. A.	189. D.	190. A.
191. C.	192. A.	193. B.	194. C.	195. A.	196. B.	197. B.	198. B.	199. A.	200.A.
201. A.	202. D.	203. A.	204. A.	205. C.	206. B.	207. C.	208. D.	209. C.	210. C.
211. D.	212. B.	213. D.	214. C.	215. D.	216. C.	217. B.	218. C.	219. A.	220. C.
221. B.	222. D.	223. A.	224. C.	225. B.	226. A.	227. A.	228. C.	229. A.	230. C.
231. A.	232. A.	233. A.	234. B.	235. D.	236. B.	237. A.	238. A.	239. C.	240. D.
241. B.	242. A.	243. B.	244. A.	245. B.	246. A.	247. C.	248. A.	249. C.	250. D.
251. C.	252. B.	253. B.	254. B.	255. D.	256. C.	257. C.	258. C.	259. A.	260. C.
261. D.	262. B	263. C.	264. D.	265. D.	266. D.	267. C.	268. A.	269. D.	270. C.
271. D.	272. C.	273. C.	274. C.						

6. Pharmacology (MCQ)

1. **Which drug is responsible for "Red men syndrome"?**
A. Vancomycin B. Linezolid
C. Chloramphenicol D. Cefadroxyl

2. **Which of these used in multidrug resistant tuberculosis?**
A. Ciprofloxacin B. Penicillin
C. Metronidazole D. Linezolide

3. **Which of the following is not typical anti-psychotic and does not have marked extra pyramidal side effects?**
A. Cblorpromazine B. Flupbenazine
C. Clozapine D. Haloperidol

4. **The first drug of choice for a patient admitted with status epilepticus is -**
A. Phenytoin B. Carbamezepine
C. Diazepam D. Sodium valproate

5. **When teaching an adolescent with a seizure disorder who is receiving valproic acid (Depakene) which of the following would the nurse instruct the client to report to the health care provider?**
A. Sore throat
B. Jaundice
C. Loss of appetite
D. Three episodes of diarrhea.

6. **Nurse should recognize that a patient has coronary artery disease is receiving acetylsalicyclic acid (aspiring.) to:**
A. Relieve pain
B. Decrease platelet adhesion
C. Reduce fever
D. Diminish inflammation

7. **Which substance increases the amount of urine produced**
A. Caffeine containing drinks, such as coffee and cola
B. Beets
C. Urinary analgesics
D. Kaolin with pectin (Kaopectate).

8. **The injectable contraceptive is**
A. Mala D B. Mala N
C. DMPA D. CuT

9. **A drug can:**
A. Diagnose disease B. Cure disease
C. Prevent disease D. All of the Above

10. **Clotrimazole is:**
A. Antiprotozoal drug B. Antibacterial drug
C. Antiviral drug D. Antifungal drug

11. **Nurse is to administer sublingual nitroglycerin to the newly admitted patient. Immediately afterward, the patient may experience**
A. Throbbing headache or dizziness
B. Nervousness cr paresthesia
C. Drowsiness or blurred vision
D. Tinnitus or diplopia

12. **Which of the following drug is not available as metered dose inhaler (MDI)?**
A. Albuterol B. Salbutamol
C. Aminophylline D. Terbutaline

13. **A patient is scheduled for an IVP using a radio-opaque dye, which of the following assessment is most critical before the procedure:**
A. Measurement of baseline peripheral pulse rates
B. History of intake and output
C. History of allergy to iodine
D. Measurement of heights and weight

14. **Generally associated with:**
A. Slurred speech
B. Impairment in attention and speech
C. Uncoordinated motor movements
D. All of the Above

15. **Streptomycin is used in treatment of infections. The nurse should observed for?**
A. Agranulocytosis
B. Edema, especially of the face
C. Impairment of hearing and equilibrium
D. Oliguria

16. **ALT exceeds AST in:**
A. Viral hepatitis B. Cholestatic hepatitis
C. Toxic hepatitis D. All the Above

17. **Test for hypersensitivity is called:**
A. Patch test B. Post-coital test
C. Patrick's test D. None of the Above

18. **An example of a synthetic narcotic include all the following except.**
A. Dilaudid B. Leritine
C. Morphine D. Talwin

19. **A drug order states 'Nembutal, gr 3 h.s. and the nurse has on hand 100 mg capsules.The nurse gives**
A. ½ capsule B. 1 capsule
C. 2 capsule D. 3 capsule

20. The nurse should check carefully to make certain the eye drops administered to the glaucoma patient are
A. Mydriatics
B. Sterile
C. Miotics
D. Warmed before administration

21. The most serious complication of a major tranquilizera
A. Parkinsonian symptoms
B. Photosensitivity
C. Agranulocytosis
D. Hypotension

22. Morphine is contraindicated in:
A. Angina B. Bronchial asthma
C. Pancreatitis D. M.I.

23. Librium is a:
A. Antimanic drug
B. Antidepressant drug
C. Antiparkinson drug
D. Tranquilizer drug

24. A child with eczema complains of itching.Which drug can be ordered by the doctor to relieve this symptom?
A. Ecotrin B. Benadryl
C. Wydase D. Epinephrine

25. Antitussive drugs are drugs that inhibit:
A. Cough B. Excessive tears
C. Sweating D. Itching

26. Ability of the drug to cause foetal abnormality when administered during pregnancy is known as:
A. Therapeutic effect
B. Idiosyncratic reaction
C. Teratogenic effect
D. Toxic effect

27. A patient has orders to receive 1 L (one litre). of 5% dextrose to be infused over 8 hours. How many ml to be infused per hour?
A. 80 ml B. 100 ml C. 125 ml D. 150 ml

28. A patient has order to receive 50 ml of an antibiotic to be infused over 1 hour. The tubing drip factor of 60. How many drops/minute should be set?
A. 66 B. 17 C. 50 D. 100

29. Which of the following is an indication of mild shock?
A. Blood Pressure: 88/50 mm Hg
B. Pulse: 110/minute
C. Lethargy
D. Urine output 18ml/hr

30. Which of the following medications would the nurse anticipate the physician would order to increase the blood pressure for a patient with septic shock?
A. Atropin B. Dopamine
C. Digoxine D. Nitroglycerine

31. Psycho tropic medications that block the acetyl choline receptor may result in which of the following side effects?
A. Dry mouth B. Sexual dysfunction
C. Nausea D. Priapism

32. Which of the following medications is the physician most likely to order for a client experiencing alcohol withdrawal syndrome?
A. Haloperidol (Haldol)
B. Chlordiazepoxide (Librium)
C. Methodone (Dolophine)
D. Phenytoin (Dilantin)

33. The drug of choice for the management of gestational Diabetes mellitus is
A. Troglitazone B. Glipizide
C. Metformin D. Insulin

34. Which of the following need serum level monitoring?
A. Lorazepam B. Lithium
C. Amitryptylline D. Haloperidol

35. The drug of choice for eclampsia is
A. $MgSo_4$
B. Prostodin
C. Timolol
D. Beta adrenergic blocker

36. Drug of Choice for induction of abortion is
A. Prostaglandin B. Ergometrine
C. Methotrexate D. Clomiphene citrate

37. Which tablet is given under Deworming programme?
A. Paracetamol B. Cetrizine
C. Amoxycilline D. Albandazol

38. Which of the following drug is the choice of treatment in drug induced anaphylactic shock?
A. Dopamine B. Adrenaline
C. Digoxin D. Protamine sulphate

39. The local anesthetic which also acts as an antiarrythmic agent
A. Cocaine B. Lidocaine
C. Bupivacaine D. Ropivacaine

40. In a patient of head injuries with rapidly increasing intracranial tension without haematoma, the drug of choice of initial management would be
A. Lasix B. Steroids
C. Mannitol D. Glycine

41. Nephrotoxicity is seen with
A. Doxycycline B. Aminoglycosides
C. Erythromycin D. Rifampicin

42. What would you monitor in a patient taking high doses of Acetaminophen over a prolonged period?
A. GI irritation B. Kidney function
C. Liver function D. Prothrombin time

43. The drug most widely tried against AIDS virus is?
A. Zidovudine (azido thymidine).
B. Miconazole
C. Nonoxynol-9
D. Virazole

44. During hemodialysis, which of the following drug is used to prevent blood clotting?
A. Aspirin B. Warfarin
C. Heparin D. Protamine

45. Calcium channel blocking agents of use in the treatment of hypertension include:
A. Prazosin B. Lidoflazin
C. Captropril D. Nifedipine

46. Major side effect of haloperidol:
A. Drowsiness
B. Dry mouth
C. Extrapyramidal reactions
D. Anorexia

47. Hypertensive patient is given diuretics because it lowers blood pressure by:
A. Excretion of water and potassium
B. Excretion of sodium, water and potassium
C. Excretion of water and sodium
D. Excretion of sodium and potassium

48. In which of the following situation nurse should inform doctor immediately if patient is on antipsychotic drugs and blood pressure falls by:
A. 40-50mm of Hg B. 20-30mm of Hg
C. 10-20mm of hg D. 80-100mm of hg

49. In case psychiatric patient is having liver or cardio vascular disorder; Nurse should take precautions while administering:
A. Antidepressants B. Antihistamines
C. Anticholinergics D. Antipsychotic

50. Adverse effect of Thiazides does not include
A. Hypercalcemia B. Hypouricemia
C. Hyperlipidemia D. Hypomagnesaemia

51. Drug used in the treatment of migraine is
A. Ergotamine B. Histamine
C. Mephensin D. Baclofen

52. Decrease in response with a particular amount of drug is called
A. Resistance B. Addiction
C. Tolerance D. Dependence

53. Drugs that bind the ions of heavy metals to form a stable nontoxic compound which can be easily excreted by kidney is
A. Antimetabolite B. Chelating agent
C. Antibodies D. TNF agent

54. Action of magnesium sulphate is
A. CNS depressant and anticonvulsant
B. Dietary supplement
C. Muscle relexant and anticonvulsant
D. CNS stimulant

55. Nifedipine used in the treatment of eclampsia is
A. Betablocker
B. Prostaglandin inhibitor
C. Calcium channel blocker
D. Adrenergic antagonist

56. For mother receiving magnessium sulphate for symptoms of hypomagresimia an important sign for the nurse to note first is:
A. Cool skin temperature
B. Rapid pulse rate
C. Tingling in the toes
D. Decreased deep tendon reflex

57. Which of the test must be done before the patient starts taking imipramine?
A. Electrocardiogram
B. Urine Protein
C. Thyroid scan
D. Creatinine clearance test

58. Which of the following clinical features alert the nurse to lithium toxicity?
A. Increasingly agitated behaviour
B. Marked increased food intake
C. Sudden increase in blood pressure
D. Anorexia with nausea and vomiting

59. Which are the drugs to be avoided for a hemophilic child?
A. Acetyl salicylic acid
B. Magnesium hydroxide
C. Acetaminophen
D. Poly-Vi-Sol

60. Digoxin is administered intravenously to the patient as drug acts to:
A. Dilate coronary arteries
B. Increase myocardial contractility
C. Decrease electrical conductivity to heart
D. Decrease cardiac dysrrhythmias

61. A patient has undergone mitral valve replacement having persistent bleeding from surgical incision in the early postoperative period, which drug will be administered:
A. Protamine sulfate B. Vitamin C
C. Quinidine sulphate D. Warfarin sodium

62. A patient receiving aminoglycosides antibiotics need to undergo which investigation positively:
A. Serum sodium
B. Serum potassium
C. Red blood cell count
D. Serum creatinine

63. Which of following is muscle relaxant?
A. Thiopentone
B. Ketamine
C. Epontol
D. Pancuronium bromide

64. Drug used in the treatment of pediatric AIDS
A. Procaine penicillin B. Nevirapine
C. Azithromycin D. Acyclovir

65. Multi Drug therapy (MDT) is treatment for:
A. TB B. Leprosy
C. HIV D. All of the Above

66. Which of the following anti tuberculosis drug is not given in Pregnancy?
A. Streptomycin B. INH
C. Ethambutol D. Rifampicin

67. Antidote of morphine is
A. Protamine sulfate B. Naloxone
C. BAL D. N-acetyl cystine

68. A patient is to be given phenytoin 100 mg orally at 6 PM but is having difficulty in swallowing capsules. The nurse should
A. Open the capsule and sprinkle the powder in a cup of water
B. Insert a rectal suppository containing 100 mg of phenytoin
C. Administer 4 ml of phenytoin suspension containing 125 mg /5 ml
D. Obtain a change in the prescribed administration route to allow IM administration

69. Which of the following drug is to be infused fast?
A. Aminophylline B. Mannitol
C. Dopamine D. Potassium chloride

70. Cimetidine is administered 6 hourly to a patient with burn in order to
A. Prevent infection
B. Restore electrolyte balance
C. Promote renal function
D. Prevent curling's ulcers

71. Ototoxicity is seen with:
A. Tetracyclines B. Penicillins
C. Aminoglycosides D. Chloramphenicol

72. Which of the following is a shortest acting local anaesthetic agent?
A. Lidocaine B. Procaine
C. Bupivacaine D. Amithocaine

73. Which drug is given to prevent HIV transmission from mother to child?
A. Nevirapine B. Lamivudine
C. Stavudine D. Abacavir

74. Paracetamol is
A. Anti pyretic B. Anti tussive
C. Anti asthmatic D. Anti emetic

75. The discovery that lead to the development of first antibiotic was made by
A. Robert Koch B. Alexander Fleming
C. Joseph Lister D. William Harvey

76. An emergency treatment for an acute asthmatic attack is Adrenaline 1:1000 given hypodermically. This is given to
A. Increase BP
B. Decrease mucosal swelling
C. Relax the bronchial smooth muscle
D. Lower third of the sternum

77. Side effect of Oxytocine use
A. Uterine rupture B. Renal Failure
C. Cervical cancer D. None of the Above

78. Which in the most common side effect associated with chemotherapy?
A. Pain B. Infertility
C. Alopecia D. Dysphagia

79. A pregnant women in second trimester is suffering from UTI, which is the drug of choice for treatment
A. Co- trimoxazole B. Ampicilline
C. Ciprofloxacin D. Pheynytoin

80. Which of the following drugs is NOT used as antiemetic after recovery from anesthesia?
A. Avomine B. Largactil
C. Stemetil D. Pethidine

81. What drugs are given to the client with Meniere's disease?
A. Antihypertensive B. Diuretic
C. Antibiotic D. Vasoconstrictor

82. The hypertensive patient is being given propranol What is the action of drugs?
A. Vasodilatation occurs resulting in a decrease in the cardiac after load
B. Decrease in cardiac output
C. Decrease in cardiac rate with a resulting in the cardiac output
D. Pericardial fluid is decreased, thus decreasing the cardiac workload

83. A client with Parkinoson's disease s experiencing anorexia and vomiting since beginning of levodop. What will be the initial activity?
A. Assess his food preference
B. Monitor his blood pressure
C. Hold his medication
D. Administer his medication with food

84. Many bacteria are now resistant to penicillin, because:
A. Penicillin causes gene mutations, some of which are beneficial
B. Previously resistant forms survived and reproduced better than non-resistance forms
C. The hospital environment inhibits competitions among bacteria
D. Penicillin triggers the synthesis of resistant proteins

85. Bark of which plant yield famous durgs of Malaria:
A. Cinchona B. Quercus
C. Betula D. Eucalyptus

86. Should not be given when the baby is in uterus
A. Oxytocin B. Prostaglandin
C. Ergometrine D. Duvadilan

87. Vincristine is an example of
A. Mustard B. Antibiotics
C. Plant alkaloid D. Hormone

88. .... are antipsychotics except
A. Chlorpromazine B. Prochloroperazine
C. Trifluroperazine D. Promethazine

89. DOTS is related with
A. Leprosy B. Well's disease
C. HIV infection D. Tuberculosis

90. Mydriatics are drugs that
A. Dilate pupil
B. Reduce BP
C. Constrict pupil
D. Reduce intraocular pressure

91. When a patient is receiving anticoagulants, this drag is contraindicated as
A. Chlorpromazine
B. Phenytoin sodium
C. Acetylsalicylic acid
D. Frusemide

92. Propanolol is included under
A. Calcium channel blockers
B. ACE inhibitors
C. Beta adrenergic blockers
D. Anti platelet agents

93. The antidote for $MgSO_4$ is
A. Nacl B. NAHCO3
C. Calcium gluconate D. Kcl

94. Tocolytics act on uterus to produce
A. Contraction B. Constriction
C. Relaxation D. Retraction

95. A patient with CCF is getting digoxine therapy and loop diuretic in order to prevent complication the nurse needs to
A. Monitor serum potassium levels
B. Maintain 1/0 chart
C. Restrict intake of potassium
D. Stop digoxine if heat rate is above 100

96. .... must be checked prior to administration of digoxine
A. Respiration B. Heart rate
C. BP D. Temperature

97. Nevirapine is given in pregnancy
A. To prevent measles
B. To reduce viral load in HIV infection
C. To prevent hepatitis
D. To prevent rubella

98. Chickenpox can be fatal to children who are receiving
A. Antibiotics B. Steroids
C. Anticonvulsants D. Bronchodilators

99. When providing care to patients with thrombocytopenia the nurse must avoid aspirin because if
A. Interferes with platelet aggregation
B. Produce haemolysis
C. Destroy thrombocytes
D. Reduces circulation

100. .... must be taken in empty stomach
A. Refampicin B. Paracetamol
C. INH D. Ampicillin

101. Important side effect of cisplatin is
A. Liver failure B. Nephrotoxicity
C. Bleeding tendencies D. Hypotension

102. Terbutaine is
A. Analgesic B. Antispasmodic
C. Vasodilator D. Bronchodilator

103. Captoprilis is
A. Antipyretics B. Diuretics
C. Antihypertensive D. Antipsychotic

104. A patient has undergone mitral valve replacement having persistent bleeding from surgical incision in the early postoperative period, which drug will be administered:
A. Vitamin C B. Protamine sulfate
C. Quinidine sulphate D. Warfarin sodium

105. A patient received codeine sulphate for severe back pain, which of the following observation must be done by the nurse:
A. Monitor fluid balance
B. Monitor peripheral pulses
C. Monitor bowel activity
D. Monitor for hypertension

106. Analgesics are given:
A. To relieve pain
B. To give rest
C. To induce sleep
D. To destroy pathogenic microorganisms

107. Paracetamol medicine/drugs are:
A. Antipyretic B. Antitussive
C. Antiasthemetic D. Antiemetic

108. Abrupt withdrawal of barbiturate use could cause a person to experience:
A. Ataxia B. Urticaria
C. Diarrhea D. Seizures

109. The therapeutic effective serum lithium:
A. 12-24 hrs. B. 24-48 hrs.
C. 3-5 days D. 10-14 days

110. One of the hazards during induction of Pitocin is:
A. Elevation in blood pressure
B. Infection
C. Rupture of uterus
D. Early rupture of membrane

111. Which of the following is an antiretroviral agent?
A. Nevirapine B. Cifran
C. Acyclovir D. Both A & C

112. Scheduled dose of digoxine is withheld and notify physician when the adult patient's pulse rate drop below:
A. 50/min B. 60/min
C. 80/min D. 70/min

113. One ounce is:
A. 30 g B. 10 g C. 20 g D. 40 g

114. The action of ranitidine is
A. Increase gastric motility
B. Increase histamine release
C. Inhibit gastric acid secretion
D. Neutralize gastric acidity

115. Which of the following side effect should be monitored in a patient on Refampicin?
A. Skin rashes B. Headach
C. Jaundice D. Giddiness

116. The specific treatment of filariasis is by administration of:
A. Diethylcarbamazine
B. Chloroquin
C. Dapsone
D. Carbamazepine

117. The purpose of administering streptokinase to a patient experiencing MI is to:
A. Keep him well hydrated
B. Prevent infection
C. Prevent renal failure
D. Dissolve clot he may have

118. Imipramine is:
A. Antidepressant B. Antimanic
C. Anticholinergic D. Antimanic

119. Anticholinergic effects of Tricyclic antidepressants results in:
A. Respiratory depression and convulsions
B. Sedation and delirium
C. Cardiac arrhythmias
D. Blurred vision and urinary retention

120. Drugs used to induce vomiting is:
A. Emetic B. Antiemetic
C. Pyretics D. Antipyretics

121. To lower the acidity of gastric secretion gives:
A. Gelusil
B. Beuadona
C. Aspirin
D. Carminative mixture

122. Nitroglycerine is given sublingually to relieve pain by vasodilatation of:
A. Pulmonary artery B. Coronary artery
C. Aortic artery D. Carotid artery

123. Which of the following is recommended along with intravenous administration of Quinine sulphate for treatment of malaria?
A. Hydrocortisone B. Multivitamin
C. Glucose D. Calcium gluconate

124. Which out of the following drugs should be given first in a patient of acute myocardial infarction?
A. Statin
B. Calcium channel blocker
C. Aspirin
D. ACE inhibitor

125. In premature labour, which of the following medicines is useful for the newborn?
A. Magnesium sulphate
B. Oxytocin
C. Betamethasone
D. Testosterone

126. Which of the following drug is given to increase uterine contraction?
A. Methargine B. Oxytocin
C. Pethedine D. Phenergan

127. The drug used by health workers in the management of acute respiratory illness is:
A. Clotrimoxazole B. Chloramphenicol
C. Benzyl penicillin D. Gentamicin

128. The main drug of choice for Heart Failure is:
A. Decadron B. Digoxin
C. Morphine D. Efcorlin

129. The reasons for using the parenteral route to administer Medications include
A. Parenteral Medication lasts longer than an oral medication
B. It is the least expensive method
C. It is easier to measure an accurate dose
D. The parenteral route allows more rapid, absorption than the oral route

130. While instilling eye drops, instruct your patient to
A. Look down and away
B. Look up and away
C. Look straight a head
D. Look up and directly at the dropper

131. Aspirin prolongs bleeding time by inhibiting the synthesis of
A. Clotting factors in liver
B. Prostacyclin in vascular endothelium
C. Cyclic AMP in platelets
D. Thromboxane A2 in platelets

132. An effective anti TB drug against intracellular as well as extracelluar bacilli is:
A. INH B. Streptomycin
C. Rifampicin D. Pyrazinamide

133. Certain code drugs which can be administered through tube for children in an emergency
A. Dopamine, Dobutamine, Adenosine, Atropine
B. Naloxone, Dopamine, Glucose, Adenosine
C. Glucose, Atropine, Ipecac, Charcoal
D. Lidocaine, Epinephrine, Atropine, Naloxone

134. Which statement by a person clearly with paranoid schizophrenia most clearly indicates the antipsychotic medication is effective?
A. I used to hear scanty voices but now I don't hear them anymore
B. My medicine is working fine. F m not having any problems
C. Sometimes it's hard for me to fall asleep, but I usually sleep all night
D. I think some of the staff members don't like me. They're mean to me

135. A newborn born for a HIV infected mother is treated with
A. Zidovudine syrup 2 mg/kg
B. Zidovudine syrup 1 mg/kg
C. Zidovudine syrup 3 mg/kg
D. Zidovudine syrup 4 mg/kg

136. Clotting can be prevented by using
A. Antiemitics B. Antibiotics
C. Anticoagulants D. Analgesics

137. Which one of the following anticoagulant binds with Ca2+ and prevents blood clotting?
A. Heparin B. Oxalate
C. Protein C D. Warfarin

138. Match list I with list II and select the correct answer using the codes given below the list

List I	List II
A. Allopurinol	1. Immune suppres-sion
B. 5 thiorouraril	2. AIDS
C Didanosin	3. Gout
D. Azothioprine	4. Cancer

	A.	B.	C	D.
A.	2	3	4	1
B.	4	3	2	1
C.	3	4	2	1
D.	4	3	1	2

139. Cortisone is used as an effective anti-inflamatory drug in the treatment of ……...
A. High blood pressure
B. Arteroisderosis
C. Arthritis
D. Diabetes

140. If gut motility is increased then:
A. Drug absorption is decreased
B. Drug absorption is increased
C. Drug absorption is not affected
D. Nothing definite can be said

141. The rate of drug absorption is greatest in the _____.
A. Large intestine B. Stomach
C. Gall bladder D. Small intestine

142. Benzodiazepines reduce anxiety by acting on which neurotransmitter?
A. Dopamine B. GABA
C. Serotonin D. Noradrenaline

143. Opioids are obtained from:
A. Erythroxylum coca
B. Claivceps purpurea
C. Cannabis sativa
D. Papaver somniferum

144. After tow house of the radio active isotope remains undecayed. Half life of the isotope is:
A. One hour B. 12 minutes
C. 45 minutes D. 30 minutes

145. Severe allergic reaction to a drug is known as
A. Adverse B. Toxicity
C. Anaphylactic D. Interaction

146. All of the following are side effects of phenytoin, Except?
A. Gum hypertrophy B. Hirsuitism
C. Ataxia D. Hypoglycemia

147. Sensitivity and reaction is tested by administering the drug
A. Subcutaneously B. Intramuscularly
C. Intradermally D. Intravenously

148. Which of the following listed drug is a proton pump inhibitor?
A. Sucraifate B. Pantoprazole
C. Famotidine D. Ranitidine

149. If 500 ml of ringer lactate is to be administered in four hours, how many drops per minute is would be (drop factor= 20 drops/ml)?
A. 42 B. 20 C. 60 D. 35

150. Which of the following drug is contraindicated in pancreatitis?
A. Spasmoproxyvon B. Meperidine
C. Diclofenac D. Morphine

151. Which of the following drug is withheld if the patient's pulse is less than 60/minute?
A. Dobulamine B. Digoxin
C. Phenytoin D. Dopamine

152. H_2 blacker of choice, in liver disease is
A. Cimetidine B. Ranitidine
C. Famotidine D. Nizatidine

153. A nurse is caring for a patient with 'Swine Flu' and she has to give the Drug of choice for 'Swine Flu' and it is
A. Acyclovir B. Adefovir
C. Cidofovir D. Oseltamivir

154. Drug of choice for treatment and prevention of further episodes of bipolar mood disorder is:
A. Amitryptiline B. Lithium
C. Fluoxetine D. Chlordiazepoxide

155. Which of the following is used in the management of hyperkalemia?
A. Insulin with glucose
B. Potassium chloride
C. Magnesium sulphate
D. Sodium bicarbonate

156. Prescription is inj. Dopamine 200 mg in 250 cc D5 W to infuse at 5 mcg/kg/min. The patient's weight is 50 kg. How many cc/hour would this be on an infusion pump?
A. 28 B. 19 C. 30 D. 22

157. Physician prescribed to administer Tablet, Digoxin 0.125 mg OD orally. Tablet Diagoxin is available in 0.25 mg. The nurse should administer
A. 4 tablets B. 1/4 tablet
C. 2 tablets D. 1/2 tablet

158. Ondansetron IV given before chemotherapy is to prevent
A. Fatigue B. Pain
C. Alopecia D. Vomiting

159. Patient on enalepril and diuretic therapy for heart failure. Nurse should notify the Physician that the therapy is not effective when she finds
A. Dry cough B. Skin rash
C. Edema legs D. Postural fall in B.P.

160. Rifampicin is used for prophylaxis of:
A. Gonorrhoea
B. Malaria
C. Leprosy
D. Meningococcal Meningitis

161. Varapamil is:
A. Beta adrenergic Blocker
B. Hz receptor antagonist
C. Cardiac glycoside
D. Calcium channel blocker

162. The drug of choice for treatment of leptospirosis is:
A. Gentamycin and kanamycin
B. Sulfonamides with cotrimaxazole
C. Penicillin and tetracyclines
D. Tobramycin and cephalosporin

163. Match

	List I	List II
A.	Levodapa	1. Sulfide metabolite
B.	Sulindac acid	2. 5-amino salicydic
C.	Dipivefrine	3. Dopamine
D.	Sulfasalazine	4. Epinephrine

	A.	B.	C.	D.
A.	3	1	4	2
B.	1	2	3	4
C.	4	3	2	1
D.	1	4	3	2

164. The most important observation for a patient in labor in Pitocin augmentation is:
A. Monitoring FHS
B. Monitoring TPR
C. Preparing for emergency CS
D. Monitoring and recording the length of contraction

165. How much will be the drop rate/mt if 500 ml of fluid is to be administered over 24 hours via ordinary drip set with drop factor 15 drops/ml.
A. 3 drops/mt B. 5 drops/mt
C. 24 drops/mt D. 50 drops/mt

166. Use of Carbameapine in psychiatry is as a:
A. Mood stabilizer B. Antidote
C. Antipsychotic D. Neuroleptic

167. The important nursing intervention prior to administration of pre-anesthetic medication is:
A. Ask patient to empty the bladder
B. Do deep breathing and coughing exercises
C. Shave the skin
D. Regulate IW accurately

168. What is the effect of cyclosporine in a patient undergone renal transplantation?
A. Immunosuppressant
B. Anti-inflammatory
C. Antibacterial
D. Diuretic

169. Dose of acetyl salicylic acid is:
A. 10 mg/kg/dose B. 500mg/dose
C. 100 mg/kg/dose D. 50 mg/kg/dose

170. Drug of choice for rheumatic fever is:
A. Cephalosporin B. Penicillin
C. Streptomycin D. Gentamycin

171. What is Saline Purgative?
A. Isabgol B. Phenolphthalein
C. Castor oil D. Magnesium sulfate

172. In a prescription 'post cibos' means
A. Before food B. After food
C. As directed D. Occasionally

173. What is ter in die-in prescription?
A. Once in three days
B. Three tablets at a time
C. Three times a day
D. Two or three times a day

174. Penicillinase resistant penicillin is
A. Amoxycillin B. Ampicillin
C. Penicillin V D. Methicillin

175. Effect of injecting hypotonic saline intravenously
A. Damage to venous walls
B. Raise in the blood pressure
C. Hemolysis
D. Dieresis

176. BCG vaccines are prepared from the
A. M. tuberculosis B. M. bovis
C. M. microti D. M. africanum

177. Drugs of choice for grandmal epilepsy are
A. Phenytoin and sodium valproate
B. Sodium valproate and carbamazepin
C. Carbamazepin and phenobarbital
D. Phenobarbital and phenytoin

178. Sucralftate is used in the treatment of
A. Vomit B. Constipation
C. Duodenal ulcer D. Diarrhoea

179. U.S.P. stands for
A. United states pharmacopoeia
B. United nations pharmacopoeia
C. Unsaturated solutions and powders
D. United states National plan

180. Antihypertensive agent
A. Amphetamine B. Adrenaline
C. Salbutamol D. Propranolol

181. One quart is equal to
A. 250 ml B. 500 ml
C. 750 ml D. 1000 ml

182. What is strophanthus?
A. Diuretic B. Antianemic
C. Cardiac glycoside D. Antianginal

183. Centrally acting muscle relaxant
A. Halothane B. 2-tubocurarine
C. Mephenesin D. Succinyl choline

184. Drugs useful in peptic ulcer are all except
A. Aluminium hydroxide gel
B. Magnesium sulfate
C. Magnesium trisilicate
D. Magnesium hydroxide

185. Broad spectrum antihelminthic
A. Piperazine citrate B. Albendazole
C. Niclosamide D. Tetrachloro thylene

186. Long term use of cemetidine may cause
A. Gynecomastia
B. Cardiac failure
C. Rebound acidity
D. Parietal cell blockade

187. Drugs classified under narcotic drugs and psychotropic agents include all except
A. Ephedrine B. Cocaine
C. Heroin D. Hashish

188. Analgesic from opium poppy
A. Diazepam B. Morphine
C. Aspirin D. Diclofenac

189. The mechanism of action of penicillin is
A. By inhibition of protein synthesis
B. By interference with ribosome function
C. By anti metabolite action
D. By interference with cell wall synthesis

190. Drug obtained from animal source
A. Dicoumarol B. Heparin
C. Insulin-human D. Cocaine

191. The dose for children can be calculated on the basis of body weight by
A. Young's rule or Dilling's rule
B. Young's rule or Catzel rule
C. Dilling's rule or Catzel rule
D. None of the Above

192. Anti-anxiety agent
A. Imipramine B. Chlorpromazine
C. Thiopentone D. Diazepam

193. International pharmacopoeia is published by
A. UNCTAD B. WHO
C. UNESCO D. UNICEF

194. Ciprofloxacin is drug of choice in
A. Tonsillitis
B. Urinary tract infections
C. Fungal infections
D. Scabies

195. In leprosy, the MDT refers to
A. Multi Drug Therapy
B. Multi Drug Treatment
C. Multiple Diagnostic Treatments
D. Multiple Diagnostic Therapies

196. In emergency contraception which progesterone is used
A. Norethisterone
B. Medroxy Progesterone
C. Desogestrel
D. Levonorgestrel

197. Vasopressin hormone is also known as
A. Thyroxin hormone
B. Parathyroid haromone
C. Anti-diuretic hormone
D. Prolactin hormone

198. Which drug is not an antiamoebic?
A. Metronidazole B. Tinidazole
C. Secnidazole D. Pentoprazole

199. Drug used for lung maturation in premature baby:
A. Mineralo - corticoid drugs
B. Gluco-Corticoid drugs
C. Amino glycoside drugs
D. Erogmetrine Maleate

200. In order to administer a drug safely, the nurse should know to read which of the following fact in the drug order
A. Name of the patient and name of the drug
B. Dose of the drug and route of administration
C. Date and signature of doctor
D. All of the above

201. What is rectified sprit?
A. 75 % ethanol B. 100% ethanol
C. 90% ethanol D. 50% ethanol

202. Site of action for anti emetics
A. Basal ganglia
B. Spinal chord
C. Chemoreceptor trigger zone
D. Cerebral hemispheres

203. In a prescription "QID" means
A. One fourth B. One quart
C. Once in four days D. Four times a day

204. What is the meaning of 'ou' in a prescription?
A. One unit B. Once a day
C. Orally D. Both eyes

205. One kilogram is equal to
A. 2.2 pounds B. 3.0 pounds
C. 3.3 pounds D. 4 pounds

206. What advise will you give to the patient while giving tetracycline?
A. To take with milk
B. Not to take with milk
C. To take with fatty diet
D. To take in evening

207. Which of the following drug is used in medical method of abortion
A. Mifepristone
B. Mifepristone & Misoprostol
C. Clomiphene & Misoprostol
D. All of the Above

208. Which of the following hormone is present in Mala-N
A. Levonorgestrel B. Ethinyloestradiol
C. None of these D. Both 1 and 2

209. Which of the following drugs is used to decrease uterine contractions and increase the duration of the labour?
A. Oxytocics B. Tocolytics
C. Anticonvulsants D. Anticoagulants

210. The following is a selective COX-2 inhibition :
A. Paracetamol B. Aspirin
C. Celecoxib D. Indomethacin

211. Methadone is used in the management of morphine addiction because:
A. It causes euphoria
B. It is orally effective and longer acting
C. Faster and shorter acting
D. Blocks the opioid receptors

212. The following is true about paracetamol :
A. A selective COX-2 inhibitor
B. A good-inflammatory agent
C. A good uricosuric
D. A good analgesic and antipyretic

213. Ibuprofen is:
A. Pyrazolon derivative
B. Indole acetic acid derivative
C. Propionic acid derivative
D. Antharanillic acid derivative

214. The following are narrow spectrum antibiotics:
A. Aminoglycosides and tetracyclines
B. Penicillins and tetracyclines
C. Chloramphenicol
D. Pencillin G and aminoglycosides

215. An ointment:
A. May be absorbed from the skin
B. Is a semisolid preparation
C. Contains greasy base
D. All of the above are true

216. The following statement about liniments is correct:
A. It is a soothening agent
B. It is a liquid preparation for application on skin
C. To be applied without friction
D. Meant for oral use

217. Lotions have the following properties:
A. Soothening and protective effects
B. Irritant effects
C. Counter irrihant actions
D. None of the above

218. Selection of a flavoring agent is a difficult task because:
A. Some tastes are difficult to mask
B. Individual tastes differ
C. After prolonged used the person maydislike
D. All of the above

219. The standard unit of weight in metric system is:
A. Pound B. Kilogram
C. Milligram D. Gram

220. The symbol of grain is :
A. Gm B. G C. Gr D. Grm

221. The standard unit of weight in apothecaries system is :
A. Pound B. Gram
C. Kilogram D. Grain

222. The standard unit of weight in avoirdupois system is:
A. Pound B. Kilogram
C. Grain D. Gram

223. 1 gallon is equal to:
A. 40 fl. Oz B. 160 fluid ounces
C. 100 fluid ounces D. 30 fl. Oz

224. 1 kilogram is equal to:
A. 2.2 pounds B. 2 Pounds
C. 1.2 pounds D. 10 pounds

225. 3 Pints is equal to:
A. 1800 ml B. 2500 ml
C. 1000 ml D. 1500 ml

226. 1 fl. ounce is same as:
A. 100 ml B. 20 ml
C. 60 ml D. 30 ml

227. Quantity of adrenaline present in 100 ml of 1 in 1000 solution is:
A. 100 grams B. 1 gram
C. 0.1 gram D. 10 grams

228. All these are disease modifying agents used in rheumatoid arthritis :
A. Prednisolone, Paracetamol, Indomethacin
B. Aspirin, Gold, Methotrexate
C. Gold, Chloroquine, Cyclophosphamide
D. Ibuprofen, Methotrexate, Sulphasalazine

229. This drug used in Gout inhibits the synthesis of uric acid:
A. Sulphinpyrazone B. Allopurinol
C. Colchicine D. Probenecid

230. Colchicine is useful in the treatment of:
A. Sulphinpyrazone
B. Goutic arthritis
C. Osteoarthritis
D. Ankylosing spondylitis

231. Haloperidol is an:
A. Antiarrthymic B. Antipsychotic
C. Antiseptic D. Antidepressant

232. The following is an example of a neuroleptic:
A. Citalopram B. Fluoxetine
C. Droperidol D. Imipramine

233. Buspirone is:
A. An antiepileptic
B. A CNS stimulant
C. An analgesic
D. An antianxiety agent

234. The following is an atypical antipsychotic:
A. Venlafaxine B. Risperidone
C. Fluoxetine D. Trazodone

235. The following is an atypical antidepressant:
A. Trazodone B. Chlorpromazine
C. Olanzapine D. Trifluperidol

236. The following is a selective serotonin reuptake inhibitor (SSRI):
A. Phenelzine B. Imipramine
C. Fluoxetine D. Trazodone

237. Olanzapine is an:
A. Antiamoebic B. Antidepressant
C. Antianxiety agent D. Antipsychotic

238. Risperidone is an:
A. Antiepileptic
B. Atypical neuroleptic
C. Anxiolytic
D. Antidepressant

239. Extrapyramidal symptoms can be produced by:
A. Chlorpromazine B. Haloperidol
C. Olanzapine D. All of these

240. Diazepam has the following therapeutic actions:
A. Antianxiety, hypnotic, muscle relaxant
B. Antipsychotic, hypnotic, CNS stimulant
C. Anticonvulsant, antiarrhythmic, antidepressant
D. Antipsychotic, analgesic, antipar-kinsonian

241. Safer analgesic for peptic ulcer patient-
A. Paracetamol B. Diclofenec
C. Ibuprofen D. Indomethacin

242. Enalapril is used in the treatment of:
A. Myocardial infarction
B. Congestive cardiac failure
C. Hypertension
D. All of the Above

243. Nor adrenaline prefer for-
A. Cardiac resuscitation
B. Hypotension
C. Both
D. None of the Above

244. Digoxin (Cardiac glycoside) is used in:
A. Shock
B. Congestive cardiac failure
C. Angina pectoris
D. Hypertrophy

245. Antipsychotic that also use as antiemetic -
A. Ondensetron B. Metaclopramide
C. Hyoscine D. Chlorpromazine

246. The following is true of warfarin:
A. It is an oral anticoagulant
B. The action is antagonized by Protamine sulfate
C. The duration of action is a low
D. It acts immediately

247. Choice of drug for chemotherapy induced vomiting-
A. Ondensetron B. Metaclopramide
C. Hyoscine D. Chlorpromazine

248. The type of cough that should be suppressed with an antitussive is :
A. Cough in tuberculosis
B. Productive cough
C. Cough due to infection
D. Dry irritant cough

249. Use of digoxine-
A. Anti hypertensive
B. Positive inotropic agent
C. Positive chronotropic agent
D. None of the above

250. This anthelmintic acts probably by blocking glucose uptake in the parasite, depleting its glycogen stores and by binding to the tubulin to inhibit its polymerization:
A. Praziquantel
B. Diethyl carbamazine
C. Mebendazole
D. Niclosamide

251. Side effect of atropine-
A. Dry mouth B. Tachycardia
C. Photophobia D. All of the Above

252. Pharmacodynamics is the study of:
A. Absorption of the drug
B. What the drug does to the body
C. What the body does to the drug
D. What the body and the drug do to each other

253. Organophosphate poisoning treated with-
A. Atropine B. Pralidoxime
C. Both A or B D. None of the Above

254. Rickets is due to deficiency of:
A. Riboflavin B. Vitamin D
C. Retinoic acid D. Alpha tocopherol

255. Choice of drug for motion sickness-
A. Ondensetron B. Metaclopramide
C. Hyoscine D. Chlorpromazine

256. Fentanyl is:
A. An antiemetic
B. A synthetic opioid
C. A benzodiazepine antagonist
D. A non-steroidal anti-inflammatory drug

257. Barbiturate use as -
A. Anaesthetic B. Anti epileptic
C. Both A & B D. None of the above

258. Opioids can produce:
A. Cough, vomiting and diarrhea
B. Sedation, euphoria and respiratory depression
C. Euphoria, diarrhea and CNS stimulation
D. Vomiting, respiratory stimulation and fever

259. Choice of anticholinergic for urinary spas-
A. Atropine B. Flavoxate
C. Dicyclomine D. Drotaverine

260. The following are synthetic opioids:
A. Papaverine, Noscapine
B. Morphine, Pethidine
C. Pethidine, Methadone
D. Codiene, Pethidine

261. Use of betadine tablet through intra vaginal route comes under-
A. Local route B. Systemic route
C. Both D. None of the above

262. Morphine is contraindicated in head injury because it causes:
A. Vomiting, miosis and mental clouding
B. Increased intracranial tension
C. Respiratory depression
D. All of the above

263. In all of these which is the use of dicyclomine
A. Anti spasmodic B. Anti hypertensive
C. Glaucoma D. Asthma

264. Douche is -
A. A solid preparation made of sugar and gum
B. A sweet liquid preparation
C. An aquesous solution for rinsing a body cavity
D. Meant for application to the skin

265. Uses of opoids except-
A. Analgesic B. Antitussive
C. Anti diarrhoeal D. Anti psychotic

266. The following is/are true about linctuses
A. Cough remedies are available as linctuses
B. May have glycerine as a vehicle
C. Are sweet viscous liquids
D. All of the Above

267. Drug metabolism mainly occurs in-
A. Liver B. Kidney
C. Intestine D. Lungs

268. The following is a prodrug:
A. Chlorthalidone B. Penicillin
C. Levodopa D. Insulin

269. Preferred route for insulin is-
A. Sub cuteneous B. Sub lingual
C. Oral D. Topical

270. Vomiting should not be induced in the treatment of :
A. Paracetamol poisoning
B. Poisoning with corrosives
C. Aspirin poisoning
D. Atropine poisoning

271. Which vitamin should be avoided with anti coagulant-?
A. Vitamin A B. Vitamin B
C. Vitamin D D. Vitamin K

272. Mifepristone is:
A. Sweating releasing factor
B. Progesterone antagonist
C. Oestrogen antagonist
D. Androgen antagonist

273. Patient receiving iron therapy should be advised-
A. Sedation
B. Dizziness
C. Vertigo
D. Blackening of stools

274. The following is a short acting glucocorticoid:
A. Hydrocortisone B. Paramethasone
C. Dexamethasone D. Betamethasone

275. Side effect of thiazide diuretics-
A. Hypokalemia B. Hypercalcemia
C. Both A & B D. None of the Above

276. The following is true about activated charcoal:
A. Can destroy all poisons
B. Can absorb poisons on to its surface
C. Chemically reacts with poisons
D. None of the Above

277. Mannitol contraindicated in-
A. Severe anemia
B. Pulmonary edema
C. Congestive heart failure
D. All of the Above

278. Beri-Beri results from deficiency of:
A. Pyridoxine B. Riboflavin
C. Niacin D. Thiamine

279. Anti diuretic contraindicated in hyperkalemia-
A. Frusemide B. Thizide
C. Spiranolactone D. None of the Above

280. The following drug is used in malaria
A. Methotrexate B. Ciprofloxacin
C. Mefloquine D. Metronidazole

281. Drugs uses for parkinsonism treatment-
A. Dopamine agonist
B. Dopamine antagonist
C. Cholinergic agonist
D. None of the above

282. Chloroquine is used in the treatment of:
A. Rheumatoid arthritis B. Malaria
C. Amoebiasis D. All of these

283. Sudden withdrawal of phenobarbitone may cause-
A. Seizures B. Sedation
C. Weakness D. None of the above

284. Rabies immunoglobulin is indicated in :
A. In dog bite cases instead of rabies vaccine
B. Post exposure prophylaxis along with rabies vaccine
C. All people having a dog at home
D. All of the Above

285. Preffered drug for status epilepticus-
A. Diazepam B. Phenobarbitone
C. Phenytoin D. Carbamazepine

286. The drug which can cause dangerous bone marrow depression is one of the following:
A. Chloramphenicol B. Sulfonamides
C. Penicillins D. Aminoglycosides

287. Antibiotic which damage to VIII cranial nerve-
A. Streptomycin B. Gentamycin
C. Amikacin D. All of the above

288. The drug which inhibits protein synthesis:
A. Erythromycin B. Tetracyclines
C. Chloramphenicol D. All of the above

289. Side effect of alpha blockers -
A. Reflex tachycardia B. Hypotension
C. Diarrhea D. All of the Above

290. Pellagra is due to deficiency of:
A. Niacin B. Biotin
C. Ascorbic acid D. Folic acid

291. Non selective beta blockers contraindicated in –
A. Hypotension B. Bradycardia
C. Asthma D. All of the Above

292. An antitubercular drug which is responsibility for peripheral neuritis and is treated with pyridoxine is one of the following:
A. Streptomycin B. Rifampin
C. Isoniazid D. Ethambutol

293. Dry coughs mainly ocurrs with-
A. Lisinopril B. Atenolol
C. Propanolol D. Prazocin

294. Which one of the antifungal agent has been known to cause to cause gynecomastia, infertility, decreased androgen production and reduced libido:
A. Flucytosine B. Ketoconazole
C. Grisiofulvin D. Terbinafine

295. Which is thrombolytic agent -?
A. Streptokinase B. Aspirin
C. Atorvastain D. Vitamin K

296. A child on antitubercular regimen developed deafness. The drug given to her is likely to be:
A. INH B. Rifampicin
C. Streptomycin D. Pyrazinamide

297. Use of lignocaine-
A. Antiarrthymic B. Local anaesthetic
C. Both D. None of the above

298. The drug which inhibits the bacterial DNA gyrase is :
A. Doxycycline B. Bacitracin
C. Cotrimoxazole D. Ciprofloxacin

299. Digoxin contraindicated in-
A. Bradycardia
B. Myocardial infraction
C. Hypokalemia
D. All of the above

300. The antagonist used in Benzodiazepine overdosage is :
A. Naloxone B. Physostigmine
C. Flumazenil D. Atropine

301. Physiological coagulant-
A. Vitamin K B. Heparin
C. Fibrinogen D. Iron

302. The drug of choice in filariasis is :
A. Piperazine
B. Mebendazole
C. Albendazole
D. Diethyl carbamazine citrate

303. Anti coagulant should be avoided in-
A. Bleeding disorder
B. Severe hypertension
C. Chronic alcoholics
D. All of the Above

304. The following is/are lactam antibiotic:
A. Aztreonam B. Cephalexin
C. Imipenem D. All of these

305. Rice polishing is rich in:
A. Vitamin D B. Vitamin K
C. Vitamin C D. Vitamin A

306. Diuretic that increase digoxin toxicity-
A. High efficiancy B. Medium efficacy
C. Both A & B D. None of the Above

307. Damage to growing cartilage and tendinitis can be caused by
A. Penicillin G B. Ciprofloxacin
C. Chloramphenicol D. Ethambutol

308. Choice of route of to produce a local effect is:
A. Topical B. Oral
C. Parenteral D. Sublingual

309. The following is generally the drug of first choice in typhoid:
A. Ciprofloxacin B. Amoxicillin
C. Tetracycline D. Chloramphenicol

310. Route of administration of a drug to provide a systemic effect are:
A. Topical B. Oral
C. Parenteral D. Both B & C

311. Cotrimoxazole has trimethoprim and sulfamethoxazole in the following ratio:
A. 1: 9 B. 1: 20 C. 1: 5 D. 1: 7

312. Parenteral administration of drug includes-
A. Orally B. Intramuscularly
C. Intravenously D. Both B & C

313. The following are topical sulfonamides:
A. Sulfasalazine and sulfadoxine
B. Sulfacetamide and mefenide
C. Sulfadoxine and sulfamethoxazole
D. All of the above

314. Antibiotic that is used in the treatment of malaria.
A. Doxycycline B. Ciprofioxacin
C. Amikacin D. Clindamycin

315. The following is an example where a combination of antibiotics is used to obtain synergistic effect:
A. Amoxicillin with clavulinic acid in hospital acquired infections
B. Penicillin and gentamicin in bacterial endocarditis
C. Carbenicillin and gentamicin in pseudomonas infections
D. All of the Above

316. Pharmacokinetics considers:
A. The way in which the body affects a drug by the processes of absorption, distribution, metabolism and excretion
B. The effects of the drug on the body and the mode of drug action
C. Both A & B
D. None of the Above

317. A pregnant lady complains of non-specific urethritis. The doctor prescribed her certain drugs. Later the child was born and when its teech erupted, it was observed that milk teeth were affected, they had brownish discoloration and the teeth were ill formeD. The drug given during pregnancy is likely to be:
A. Erythromycin B. Ciprofloxacin
C. Amikacin D. Tetracyclines

318. If peristalsis movement is increased then:
A. Drug absorption is decreased
B. Drug absorption is increased
C. Both A & B
D. None of the Above

319. Co-trimoxazole is a combination of:
A. Sulfamethoxazole + sulfadoxine
B. Trimethoprim + Sulfamethoxazole
C. Trimethoprim + dapsone
D. Trimethoprim + sulfadoxine

320. Drug absorption is higher in:
A. The small intestine B. The large intestine
C. The stomach D. None of the above

321. Megaloblastic anemia results from deficiency of:
A. Vitamin E B. Vitamin C
C. Folic acid D. Vitamin D

322. Drug distribution may depend on:
A. Vascularity
B. Lipid solubility of drug
C. Plasma protein binding
D. All of the Above

323. Drugs that inhibit cell wall synthesis:
A. Penicillins B. Tetracyclines
C. Dapsone D. Aminoglycosides

324. Most drugs excreted through:
A. Urine B. Stools
C. Exhaled Air D. Saliva and tears

325. Suprainfection is more likely to develop following the use of:
A. Very short course of antibiotics
B. Narrow spectrum antibiotics
C. Broad spectrum antibiotics
D. All antibiotics

326. Pharmacodynamics considers:
A. The way in which the body affects a drug
B. The effects of the drug on the body and the mode of drug action
C. Drug metabolism
D. Biotransformation

327. The following is/are true about powders -
A. Hygroscopic drugs can be given as powders
B. Absorbed faster
C. Absorption is slow
D. All of the Above

328. Drug that binds to a cell receptor and causes a response is called an:
A. Agonist B. Antagonist
C. Receptor blocker D. None of the Above

329. The following is/are true of Schedule H drugs:
A. Warning-to be sold on prescription of a RMP only-should be given
B. Includes drugs to be sold under prescription only
C. Symbol Rx should be printed on the left hand top corner of the table
D. All of the Above

330. A drug allergy occurs:
A. When too much drug has accumulated in an individual
B. When the drug act as an antigen
C. An unwanted but predictable response to a drug
D. None of the Above

331. Retinoic acid used in acne (pimples) is a form of:
A. Vitamin E B. Vitamin C
C. Vitamin D D. Vitamin A

332. Factors affecting response to a drug include:
A. Body weight B. Sex
C. Disease condition D. All of the Above

333. The Dangerous Drugs Act prohibits:
A. Sale of opium products
B. Manufacture of opium products
C. Cultivation of opium products
D. All of the above

334. Each of the following is an effective antidepressant drug except:
A. Chlorpromazine B. Imipramine
C. Fluoxetine D. Desipramine

335. The poison ACT was passed in:
A. 1945 B. 1878 C. 1919 D. 1985

336. Side effects of which of the following may include salivation and sweating:
A. Physostigmine B. Neostigmine
C. Both D. Neither

337. Paracetamol can be grouped under:
A. Over the counter drugs
B. Dangerous drugs
C. Prescription drugs
D. All of the Above

338. Which of the following is the most lethal and dose limiting adverse effect of morphine?
A. Extreme sedation
B. Increased intracranial pressure
C. Decreased respiration
D. Decreased myocardial conductivity

339. Transdermal adhesive units are made in order to deliver the drug:
A. Constantly over a long period
B. Intermittently
C. For immediate action
D. None of the Above

340. Which one of the following is not a route of administration?
A. Intravenous (IV) B. Oral
C. Topical D. Dissolution

341. Intra-articular route of administration involves injection into the:
A. Atria B. Arteries
C. Joints D. Auricles

342. A rectal suppository is used to treat fever, this would represent what type of drug delivery?
A. Parenteral B. Systemic
C. Topical D. Dissolution

343. The following is true about plastic syringes:
A. Can be easily sterilized
B. Allow proper emptying of the syringe
C. Can break easily
D. Have higher risk of air embolism

344. Which one of the following medicines does not rely on topical drug delivery?
A. Nasal spray of decongestant
B. Anti-dandruff shampoo
C. Amikacin
D. Xylocaine jelly

345. The following drug is used in the treatment of cancers:
A. Cyclopropane
B. Cyclophosphamide
C. Carbamazepine
D. Captopril

346. Which one of the following is not a common dosage form for gentamycin?
A. Tablet B. Injection
C. Cream D. None of the above

347. The following is/are disadvantage of intravenous route:
A. Only aqueous solutions can be given
B. Thrombophlebitis
C. Self medication is difficult
D. All of the Above

348. In pregnancy, all of the following drugs are contraindicated except
A. ACE Inhibitors
B. Angiotensin Receptor Blockers
C. Paracetamol
D. Thalidomide

349. The preferred route of administration in an unconscious patient is:
A. Nasal B. Sublingual
C. Oral D. Intravenous

350. A newborn baby was born with absence of limb It is teretogenic effect of -
A. Tetracycline B. Thalidomide
C. Heparine D. Alcohol

351. Intravenous regional anesthesia can be used to anesthetize:
A. The head and the neck
B. The upper and lower limbs
C. The abdomen
D. The thorax

352. Local anesthetics produce:
A. Analgesia, amnesia & loss of consciousness
B. Blocking pain sensation without loss of consciousness
C. Alleviation of anxiety and pain with an altered level of consciousness
D. Convulsion

353. The drug which acts on slowly dividing bacilli or persisters is:
A. Streptomycin B. INH
C. Ethambutol D. Rifampicin

354. A good local anesthetic agent shouldn't cause:
A. Local irritation and tissue damage
B. Systemic toxicity
C. Vasodilatation
D. All of the Above

355. Which of the following agents is the precursor of dopamine?
A. Bromocriptine B. Levodopa
C. Acetylcholine D. Amantadine

356. Why use levodopa, the precursor of dopamine, instead of dopamine is:
A. Dopamine does not cross the blood-brain barrier
B. Dopamine may induce acute psychotic reactions
C. Dopamine is intensively metabolized in humans
D. All of the Above

357. Which is peripheral dopa decarboxylase inhibitor?
A. Tolcapone B. Clozapine
C. Carbidopa D. Selegiline

358. Sodium Valproate is effective against:
A. Absence seizures
B. Myoclonic seizures
C. Generalized tonic-clonic seizures
D. All of the Above

359. The drug of choice in the treatment of petit mal (absence seizures) is:
A. Phenytoin B. Ethosuximide
C. Phenobarbital D. Carbamazepin

360. Which of the following antiseizure drugs is also effective in treating trigeminal neuralgia?
A. Zonisamide B. Topiramat
C. Carbamazepine D. Lamotrigine

361. The most effective drug for status epilepticus in adults is:
A. Phenytoin B. Ethosuximide
C. Diazepam D. Zonisamide

362. Hypnotic drugs are used to treat:
A. Depression
B. Sleep disorders
C. Narcolepsy
D. Parkinsonian disorders

363. Which of the following barbiturates is an ultra-short-acting drug?
A. Pentobarbital B. Amobarbital
C. Thiopental D. Phenobarbital

364. Competitive antagonist of BDZ receptors use in benzodiazepine poisoning:
A. Flumazenil B. Picrotoxin
C. Zolpidem D. Temazepam

365. Barbiturates are being replaced by hypnotic benzodiazepines because of:
A. Low therapeutic index
B. More respiratory & cardiovascular depression
C. High potential of physical dependence and abuse
D. All of the Above

366. Which of the following hypnotic drugs is used intravenously as anesthesia?
A. Thiopental B. Phenobarbital
C. Flurazepam D. Alprazolam

367. Which of the following local anesthetics is also use as antiarrhythmic agent?
A. Cocaine B. Lidocaine
C. Bupivacaine D. Dibucaine

368. The symptoms of Atropine poisoning include:
A. Salivation, lacrimation, nausea, vomiting
B. Dryness of mouth, hyperpyrexia, tachycardia
C. Headache, abcominal colic
D. Bradycardia, hypotension and shock

369. Effect of Parasympathomimetic drugs:
A. Bronchodilation B. Mydriasis
C. Bradycardia D. Constipation

370. Paraympathomimetics that is commonly used in the treatment of glaucoma?
A. Pilocarpine B. Lobeline
C. Acethylcholine D. Neostigmine

371. Chronic long-term therapy of myasthenia is involve:
A. Edrophonium B. Neostigmine
C. Physotigmine D. Carbachol

372. Paraympathomimetics that is used in the treatment of atropine intoxication?
A. Neostigmine B. Carbochol
C. Physostigmine D. Lobeline

373. Anticholinergic drugs that is, especially use in motion sickness?
A. Atropine B. Ipratropium
C. Hyoscine D. Homatropine

374. Which of the following agents is used as an inhalation anti asthma?
A. Atropine B. Ipratropium
C. Hyoscine D. Homatropine

375. Anticholinergics are used in the treatment of the following EXCEPT:
A. Motion sickness B. Glaucoma
C. Urinary spas D. Asthma

376. Receptor present on bronchial smooth muscle:
A. Alfa1 receptor B. Alfa 2 receptor
C. Beta 1 receptor D. Beta 2 receptor

377. Stomach wash is contraindicated in:
A. Foreign body ingestion
B. Poisoning with corrosive
C. Poisoning with petroleum products
D. All of the Above

378. Noradrenaline produces:
A. Vasoconstriction
B. Vasodilatation
C. Bronchodilation
D. Decresed potassium concentration in the plasma

379. The following is/are true about stomach wash:
A. The patient is put in left lateral position
B. Should be done in a conscious patient
C. Warm water or saline should be used
D. All of the Above

380. Which is long-acting topical nasal decongestant?
A. Epinephrine B. Norepinephrine
C. Phenylephrine D. Xylometazoline

381. The antidote in morphine overdosage is:
A. Naloxone B. Dextrose
C. Buprenorphine D. Promethazine

382. Which of the following sympathomimetics is used in the therapy of bronchial asthma?
A. Salmeterol B. Norepinephrine
C. Methoxamine D. Dobutamine

383. 'Coma cocktail' used in comatose patients consists of:
A. Ethyl alcohol + Naloxone + Buprenorphine
B. Promethazine + Thiamine + Chlorpromazine
C. Nalorpromazine + Thiamine + Dextrose
D. Thiamine + Riboflavine + Dextrose

384. Indicate the agent of choice in the emergency therapy of anaphylactic shock:
A. Methoxamine B. Terbutaline
C. Norepinephrine D. Adrenaline

385. Centchroman (SAHELI) is:
A. Long acting
B. A nonsteroidal contraceptive
C. Developed by CDRI Lucknow
D. All of the above

386. Example of nonselective beta receptor antagonist?
A. Metoprolol B. Atenolol
C. Propranolol D. Acebutolol

387. The following are used as postcoital contraceptive except:
A. Combined pill B. Minipill
C. Diethyl stilbestrol D. Mifepristone

388. Example of beta1 selective antagonist:
A. Propranolol B. Metoprolol
C. Carvedilol D. Sotalol

389. Which of these is not an inhalational glucocorticoid?
A. Fluticasone B. Beclomethasone
C. Prednisolone D. Budesonide

390. Example of nonselective alfa, beta antagonist?
A. Labetalol B. Phentolamine
C. Metoprolol D. Propranolol

391. Bone resorption can be prevented by :
A. Vitamin D B. Calcium
C. Estrogens D. All of the above

392. Alpha receptor antagonists such as tamsulosin, terazosin are efficacious in:
A. Hyperthyroidism
B. Cardiac arrhythmias
C. Benign prostatic hyperplasia (BPH)
D. Asthma

393. Bisphosphonates can be used in:
A. Postmenopausal osteoporosis
B. Paget's disease of the bone
C. Hypercalcemia
D. All of the Above

394. Propranolol is used in the treatment all of the following EXCEPT:
A. Hypertension B. Angina pectoris
C. Migraine headache D. Bronchial asthma

395. Which of these has selective glucocorticoid actions without mineralocorticoid activity?
A. Fludrocortisone B. Prednisolone
C. Dexamethasone D. Hydrocortisone

396. Alcohol may induce:
A. CNS depression B. Vasodilatation
C. Hypoglycemia D. All of the above

397. Which of these is insulin analog?
A. Regular insulin B. Insulin Lispro
C. Isophane insulin D. None of the above

398. Which of the following agents may be used as an antidote for ethylene glycol and methanol poisoning?
A. Disulfiram B. Fomepizol
C. Naltrexone D. Flumazenil

399. Nandrolone decanoate is:
A. An oral contraceptive
B. An anabolic steroid
C. An anti oestrogen
D. An anti progestin

400. Which of the following opioid analgesics is used in the treatment of left ventricular failure?
A. Morphine B. Codeine
C. Fentanyl D. Loperamide

401. Norplant, a hormonal contraceptive is:
A. Subcutaneous implant
B. A combiner pill
C. Mini pill
D. Intramuscular injection

402. Non-narcotic analgesics agents can cause:
A. Respiratory depression
B. Antipyretic effect
C. Euphoria
D. Physical dependence

403. Which of these is a sulfonylurea derivate used in diabetes mellitus?
A. Glargine B. Glipizide
C. Phenformin D. Troglitazone

404. Choose the non-narcotic analgesic, which lacks an anti-inflammatory effect:
A. Naloxone B. Paracetamol
C. Metamizole D. Aspirin

405. Neuroleptics are used to treat:
A. Neurosis B. Psychosis
C. Narcolepsy D. Depresion

406. Which of these is a long acting insulin?
A. Semilente insulin B. Regular insulin
C. Lente insulin D. Ultra lente insulin

407. Lithium carbonate is useful in the treatment of:
A. Petit mal seizures B. Bipolar disorder
C. Neurosis D. Neuralgia

408. Carbimazole is:
A. An antimoebic drug
B. An antithyroid drug
C. An antifungal drug
D. An antihelminthic drug

409. Which of the following antidepressants is a selective serotonin reuptake inhibitor?
A. Phenelzine B. Desipramine
C. Imipramine D. Fluoxetine

410. Cetrimide and benzalkonium chloride are:
A. Dyes B. Surfactants
C. Oxidising agents D. Aldehydes

411. Anxiolytics are used to treat:
A. Neurosis B. Psychosis
C. Mania D. Bipolar disorders

412. Hydrogen peroxide is:
A. A dye A halogen
B. An aldehyde
C. An oxidizing agent
D. All of the above

413. Effects of "general anesthesia" usually includes:
A. Analgesia
B. Loss of consciousness, inhibition of sensory and autonomic reflexes
C. Amnesia
D. All of the above

414. Which of the following is a surfactant?
A. Benzoyl peroxide
B. Glutaradehyde
C. Sodium lauryl sulfate
D. Chlorhexidine

415. Indicate the anesthetic, which is prefer in children's:
A. Thiopental B. Halothane
C. Ketamine D. Sevoflurane

416. Formaldehyde:
A. Is a carcinogen
B. Has a pungent odour
C. Is a gas at room temperature
D. All of the above are true

417. Anesthetic, which is used intravenously:
A. Propofol B. Halothane
C. Desflurane D. Nitrous oxide

418. Cresol, Lysol and chloroxylenol are:
A. Aldehydes B. Halogens
C. Phenols D. Acids

419. Intravenous anesthetic, which is belong to ultra-short-acting barbiturate:
A. Fentanyl B. Thiopental
C. Midazolam D. Ketamine

420. Hyaluronidase is a:
A. Viral enzyme
B. Mammalian enzyme
C. Bacterial enzyme
D. Plant enzyme

421. Intravenous anesthetic, which is a benzo diazepine derivative:
A. Midazolam B. Thiopental
C. Fentanyl D. Propofol

422. The antidote in warfarin overdosage is:
A. Vitamin K-oxide B. Vitamin C
C. Protamine sulfate D. Vitamin P

423. Intravenous anesthetic, which produces dissociative anesthesia:
A. Midazolam B. Ketamine
C. Fentanyl D. Propofol

424. The preferred antidote in methanol poisoning is:
A. Flumazenil B. Ethanol
C. Oxygen D. Fomepizole

425. Which of these groups of drugs is used for asthma treatment?
A. Methylxanthines
B. Anti cholinergic agents
C. Beta2 – agonist
D. All of the above

426. The antidote in atropine poisoning is:
A. Naloxone B. Penicillamine
C. Warferin D. Physostigmine

427. Choose the drug belonging to proton pump inhibitors:
A. Pirenzepine B. Ranitidine
C. Omeprazole D. Trimethaphan

428. The antidote of choice in lead poisoning is:
A. D-penicillamine
B. Dimercaprol
C. Calcium disodium acetate
D. Desferrioxamine

429. Choose the drug which is a H2-receptor antagonist:
A. Omeprazole B. Propantheline
C. Carbenoxolone D. Ranitidine

430. The drug of choice in arsenic poisoning is:
A. N-acetylcystiene B. Dimercaprol
C. D-penicillamine D. Desferioxamine

431. Choose the anticholinergic use in peptic ulcer treatment:
A. Cimetidine B. Ranitidine
C. Pirenzepin D. Omeprazole

432. The drug of choice in insulin overdosage is:
A. Desferrioxamine B. Glucagon
C. Adrenaline D. Glucose

433. Anta acid that causes diarrhoea
A. Sodium bicarbonate
B. Aluminium hydroxide
C. Calcium carbonate
D. Magnesium Hydroxide

434. The preferred antidote in copper poisoning is :
A. Glucose B. Dimercaprol
C. Desferrioxamine D. D-penicillamine

435. Choose an emetic drug of action:
A. Hyoscine
B. Promethazine
C. Ddicyclomine
D. Apomorphine hydrochloride

436. Atropine poisoning is treated with:
A. Adrenaline B. Dimercaprol
C. Physostigmine D. Adrenaline

437. All of the following drugs are antiemetics EXCEPT:
A. Metoclopramide B. Ondansetron
C. Chlorpromazine D. Emetine

438. The following drug is used in the treatment of organophosphorous poisoning:
A. Pilocarpine B. Physostigmine
C. Atropine D. N-acetylcystiene

439. Indicate an antiemetic agent which is related to neuroleptics:
A. Metoclopramide B. Nabilone
C. Tropisetron D. Chlorpromazine

440. The following is/are true of trypsin:
A. May be used topically or intramuscularly
B. Is a proteolytic enzyme
C. Digests dead tissue
D. All of the above

441. Select the drug which decreases bowel tone:
A. Castor oil B. Bisacodyl
C. Loperamide D. Sorbitol

442. Following drugs use in anemia EXCEPT:
A. Iron dextran B. Vitamine B_{12}
C. Methotrexate D. Folic acid

443. In all of the following which increases absorption of iron from intestine:
A. Cyanocobalamin B. Folic acid
C. Ascorbic acid D. Erythropoetin

444. The following preparation of iron can be given both IM and IV:
A. Iron carbohydrate complex
B. Iron sorbital citric acid
C. Iron Dextran
D. Ferrous gluconate

445. Pernicious anemia is developed due to deficiency of:
A. Erythropoetin B. Vitamin B_{12}
C. Magnesium D. Vitamin B_6

446. The following is injected deep IM by 'Z' technique:
A. Iron B. Calcium
C. Zinc D. Vitamin A

447. An adverse effect of oral iron therapy is:
A. Fever B Thrombocytopenia
C. Headache D. Constipation

448. Milk is a very poor source of:
A. Phosphorus B. Calcium
C. Zinc D. Iron

449. Choose the drug which contains cobalt atom:
A. Folic acid B. Ascorbic acid
C. Cyanocobalamine D. Ferrous gluconate

450. The chief cation in the cell is:
A. Calcium B. Magnesium
C. Potassium D. Sodium

451. Which of the following is low-molecular weight heparine?
A. Dicumarol B. Enoxaparin
C. Phenprocoumon D. Heparin

452. The following minerals are absolutely essential for the formation of bones and teeth:
A. Manganese and magnesium
B. Calcium and phosphorus
C. Sodium and Potassium
D. Potassium and iron

453. Which are antagonists of heparin?
A. Aspirin B. Dicumarol
C. Dalteparin D. Protamine sulfate

454. Tender coconut water is rich in this mineral:
A. Magnesium B. Calcium
C. Iron D. Potassium

455. Choose the drug used as an oral anticoagulant:
A. Heparin B. Daltreparin
C. Warferine D. Enoxaparin

456. Active immunization is administration of:
A. Antitoxic sera to the host
B. Antigen to the host
C. Antibodies to the host
D. Both antigen and antibodies

457. All of these drugs are antiplatelet agents EXCEPT:
A. Aspirin B. Streptokinase
C. Ticlopidine D. Clopidogrel

458. The following are all mammalian enzymes:
A. Collagenase, trypsin, chymotrypsin
B. Chymotrypsin, hyaluronidase, pancreatic dornase
C. Streptokinase, hyaluronidase, papain
D. Trypsin, a chymotrypsin, papain

459. In all of the following Which is fiibrinolytic agent?
A. Ticlopidine B. Streptokinase
C. Aspirin D. Warfarin

460. Serratiopeptidase is obtained from:
A. Palavers somniferous
B. Streptococci
C. Serratia species
D. Staphylococci

461. Which is an example of cardiac glycoside?
A. Digoxin B. Amiadarone
C. Dobutamine D. Amrinone

462. The most useful drug in amoebic dysentry is:
A. Clotrimazole B. Albendazole
C. Metronidazole D. Miconazole

463. Drug that is use in supraventricular tachycardias:
A. Digoxin B. Dobutamine
C. Amrinone D. Dopamine

464. Albendazole is used in the treatment of infestation with :
A. Roundworm B. Pinworm
C. Hookworm D. All of these

465. Drug of choice for acute treatment of ventricular tachycardias:
A. Amlodipine B. Sotalol
C. Lidocaine D. Verapamil

466. In rickettsial infections the following is the drug of choice:
A. Ciprofloxacin B. Penicillin
C. Tetracyclines D. Metronidazole

467. Calcium channel blocker that is not useful in the treatment of cardiac arrhythmias
A. Losartan B. Diltiazem
C. Verapamil D. Nifedipine

468. The following is a macrolide antibiotic:
A. Clarithromycin B. Streptomycin
C. Tobramycin D. Clindamycin

469. Duration of nitroglycerin action (sublingual) is:
A. 10-30 minutes B. 6-8 hours
C. 1-5 minutes D. 1.5-2 hours

470. Toxicity like ototoxicity, nephrotoxicity and neuromuscular blockade can result from the use of:
A. Pct B. Sulfonamides
C. Cephalosporins D. Aminoglycosides

471. Which of the following antianginal agents is a calcium channel blocker?
A. Nitroglycerin B. Dipyridamole
C. Minoxidil D. Amlodipine

472. The following is an aminoglycoside:
A. Erythromycin B. Azithromycin
C. Gentamicin D. Tramadol

473. Clinical use of calcium channel blockers includes:
A. Angina pectoris B. Hypertension
C. Antiarrhythmic D. All of the above

474. The drug which is ionized, not absorbed orally, excreted unchanged in the urine and needs parenteral administerion is:
A. Erythromycin B. Chloramphenicol
C. Streptomycin D. Cloxacillin

475. Which beta-adrenoceptor-blocking drug use as a antianginal agent:
A. Dipyridamole B. Validol
C. Atenolol D. Amlodipine

476. 'Gray Baby syndrome' can be produced by:
A. Chloramphenicol B. Gentamicin
C. Erythromycin D. Azithromycin

477. Vasodialator that is also use in the treatment of alopecia:
A. Dipyridamole B. Propanolol
C. Atenolol D. Minoxidil

478. The following is an antibiotic:
A. Sulfamethoxazole B. Tetracycline
C. Ciprofloxacin D. Streptomycin

479. Choose the selective beta1 receptor blocker:
A. Labetalol B. Prazosin
C. Atenolol D. Propranolol

480. Frusemide (LASIX) is the preferred diuretic in the treatment of:
A. Acute pulmonary edema
B. Forced diuretisis in poisoning
C. Congestive cardiac failure
D. All of the Above

481. Drugs that inhibits angiotensin-converting enzyme:
A. Captopril B. Enalapril
C. Ramipril D. All of the Above

482. The anticoagulant that should be given only SC/IV is:
A. Phenindione B. Heparin
C. Warfarin D. Nicoumalone

483. Pick out the diuretic agent for hypertension treatment:
A. Losartan
B. Hydrochlorthiazide
C. Captopril
D. Prazosin

484. The following is a cough suppressant acting on the CNS:
A. Cough drops B. Codeine
C. Bromhexine D. Potassium cloride

485. Anti hypertenive drug that is contraindicated in patients with bronchial asthma:
A. Propranolol B. Clonidine
C. Enalapril D. Nifedipine

486. Mebendazole is used in:
A. Pinworm B. Amoebiasis
C. Infection D. Filariasis

487. This drug routinely produces reflex tachycardia:
A. Propranolol B. Atenolol
C. Verapamil D. Nifedipine

488. The following is extended spectrum penicillin:
A. Penicillin V1 B. Piperacillin
C. Clavulanic acid D. Methicillin

489. Antihypertensive effect of beta-blockers is due to:
A. Peripheral vasodilatation
B. Diminishing of blood volume
C. Decreasing of cardiac work
D. Depression of vasomotor center

490. The main adverse effects of salbutamol are :
A. Diarrhea and hypotension
B. Bradycardia and heart block
C. Palpitation and muscle tremors
D. Nausea and diarrhoea

491. Diuretic agent that is aldosterone antagonist:
A. Furosemide B. Spironolactone
C. Dichlothiazide D. Captopril

492. Salbutamol (Asthalin) and terbutalin used in bronchial asthma are:
A. Antimicrobial
B. Mast cell stabilizers
C. Adrenergic agonists
D. Anticholinergic drugs

493. Example of high efficacy diuretic agent:
A. Furosemide B. Spironolactone
C. Dichlothiazide D. Aldoteron

494. The following is a bulk laxative:
A. Castor oil B. Ispagula
C. Magnesium sulfate D. Liquid paraffin

495. The following Ergot derivative is used for treatment of acute migraine attack:
A. Paracetamol B. Sulindac
C. Ergotamine D. Metoclopramide

496. Loperamide is useful in the treatment of:
A. Diarrhoea B. Vomiting
C. Peptic ulcer D. Pain

497. Hormonal drug which is a steroidal derivative:
A. Gonadotropine B. Insulin
C. Levothyroxine D. Hydrocortisone

498. Sucralfate is:
A. A proton pump inhibitor
B. An ulcer protective agent
C. An antacid
D. A receptor blocker

499. Which of the following hormone is secreted from hypothalamus?
A. Growth hormone-releasing hormone (GHRH)
B. Follicle-stimulating hormone (FSH)
C. Aldosterone
D. Estradiol

500. The following drugs are useful in the treatment of peptic ulcer:
A. Prednisolone and phenylbutazone
B. Ranitidine and paracetamol
C. Ranitidine and Omeprazole
D. Omeprazole and phenylbutazone

501. Hormone that is produced by the anterior lobe of the pituitary?
A. Thyrotropin-releasing hormone (TRH)
B. Corticotropin-releasing hormone (CRH)
C. Growth hormone (somatotropin, GH)
D. Growth hormone-releasing hormone (GHRH)

502. The drug of choice in anaphylactic shock is:
A. Atropine B. Acetylcholine
C. Adrenaline D. Physostigmine

503. Hormone that's posterior pituitary does NOT secret:
A. Vasopressin B. Oxytocin
C. Growth hormone D. All of the Above

504. Fluconazole is an:
A. Antiamoebic drug
B. Antifungal drug
C. Antibiotic
D. Antiarrythmic drug

505. Prolactin hormone act on?
A. Liver B. Adrenal cortex
C. Thyroid D. Mammary gland

506. The following are azole antifungal drugs:
A. Cotrimoxazole, Metronidazole
B. Clotrimazole, miconazole
C. None of them
D. Mebendazole, thiabendazole

507. Indication of vasopressin:
A. Diabetes mellitus
B. Hypertension
C. Neurogenic diabetes insipidus
D. Abortificient

508. The following is the most useful in the treatment of HIV infection:
A. Cotrimoxazole B. Amantadine
C. Acyclovir D. Zidovudine

509. hormone that is produced by the thyroid gland?
A. Thyroid-stimulating hormone
B. Thyrotropin-releasing hormone
C. Triiodothyronine
D. Thyroglobulin

510. Acyclovir is used in:
A. Staphylococcal infections
B. Bacterial endocarditis
C. Herpes simplex infections
D. Influenza

511. Hormone that is secrete from pancreatic cells:
A. Glucagon
B. Insulin
C. Somatostatin
D. Pancreatic Polypeptide (PP)

512. Ototoxicity and nephrotoxicity are the most common adverse effects of all:
A. Tetracyclines B. Cephalosporins
C. Acyclovir D. Aminoglycosides

513. Insulin is a polypeptide hence:
A. It is resistant to destruction by gastric juice
B. It is destroyed by gastric juice
C It is metabolized immediately by cellular enzymes
D. All of the Above

514. Tapeworm infestation can be treated with:
A. Niclosamide B. Albendazole
C. Praziquantel D. All of the above

515. Insulin is not effective when administered through:
A. Oral route
B. Intravenous route
C. Subcutaneous route
D. Intramuscular route

516. Excess administration of the following vitamin is a waste because it is not stored in the body and gets excreted :
A. Vitamin K
B. Vitamin B complex
C. Vitamin D
D. Vitamin A

517. Complications of insulin therapy includes the following:
A. Hypoglycemia
B. Insulin allergy
C. Lipodystrophy at an injection site
D. All of the Above

518. The following statement about vitamin A is correct :
A. Deficiency results in haemolytic anemia
B. It is a water soluble vitamin
C. Gooseberry is rich in Vitamin A
D. Deficiency results in night blindness and rough skin

519. Progesterone is secreted by:
A. Ovarian follicles B. Corpus luteum
C. Adrenal medulla D. All of the Above

520. Which of the following is true of polio vaccine (OPV) :
A. It is a live viral vaccine used only for post exposure prophylaxis
B. It is a live viral vaccine given orally
C. It is a bacterial vaccine given orally
D. All of the above

521. Indication of glucocorticoids is:
A. Anti Asthmatic
B. Organ transplants (prevention and treatment of rejection – immunosuppression)
C. Inflammatory conditions of bones and joints (arthritis, bursitis, tenosynovitis).
D. All of the above

522. Booster dose of DPT vaccine is given at:
A. 12 months
B. 18 weeks
C. 18 months and at 4-6 yrs
D. Every 2 months

523. Which of the following NSAIDs is a selective COX-2 inhibitor?
A. Piroxicam B. Indomethacin
C. Etoricoxib D. Diclofenac

524. The following is used in roundworm infestation:
A. Fluconazole B. Metronidazole
C. Albendazole D. Clotrimazole

525. Which of histamine H1 antagonists is used as appetite stimulant?
A. Brompheniramine B. Cyproheptadine
C. Cyclizine D. Cetrizine

526. The following drugs are used in leprosy:
A. Penicillin and isoniazid
B. Rifampicin and dapsone
C. Pyrazinamide and chloroquine
D. Cotrimoxazole and metronidazole

527. Plasma volume expander contra indicated in
A. Severe anemia
B. Pulmonary edema
C. Renal insufficiency
D. All of the Above

528. The first line drugs in tuberculosis are :

A. Cycloserine, Isoniazid, Para-amino salicylic acid (PAS)
B. Isoniazid, Rifampicin, Pyrazinamide
C. Isoniazid, Dapsone, Thiacetazone
D. Isoniazid, Ethionamide, Amikacin

529. Which of the following vitamins is given along with isoniazide in treatment of tuberculosis?

A. Nicotinic acid B. Thaimine
C. Pyridoxine D. Ascorbic acid

530. The following drug is used in malaria:

A. Mebendazole B. Metronidazole
C. Clotrimazole D. Chloroquine

531. In all of the following which vitamin is also known as an antisterility factor?

A. Vitamin E B. Vitamin C
C. Vitamin B_1 D. Vitamin D

532. The drug used for both intestinal and extraintestinal amoebiasis is:

A. Tetracyclines B. Chloroquine
C. Diloxanide furoate D. Metronidazole

533. Bone marrow depression may be produced by:

A. Daunorubicin
B. Cyclophosphamide
C. Methotrexate
D. All of the Above

534. Route of administration of Vitamin D3 is:

A. Subcutaneous B. Oral
C. Intravenous D. Intradesmal

535. The following is an alkylating agent:

A. Methotrexate
B. Etoposide
C. Vincristine
D. Cyclophosphamide

536. Diuretic drug can cause ototoxicity:

A. Furosemide B. Acetazolamide
C. Spiranolactone D. All of the Above

537. The common adverse effects of most anticancer drugs are :

A. Vomiting, weight gain, psychosis
B. Vomiting, otoxicity, nephrotoxicity
C. Vomiting, alopecia, bone marrow depression
D. Nausea, renal failure, pulmonary edema

538. The drug should never be administered to patients taking potassium supplements:

A. Hydrochlorothiazide
B. Spiranolactone
C. Furosemide
D. Neither of the Above

539. Methotrexate is used in:

A. Acute leukemia B. Choriocarcinoma
C. Breast cancer D. All of these

540. Diuretic use to decrease intra cranial pressure:

A. Furosemide B. Acetazolamide
C. Triamterene D. Mannitol

541. Which one of the following is a newer macrolide?

A. Clindamycin B. Clarithromycin
C. Amikacin D. Netilmycin

542. All of the following drugs are antibiotics, EXCEPT:

A. Streptomycin B. Cefixime
C. Co-trimoxazole D. Chloramphenicol

543. The following are both bacteriostatic:

A. Erythromycin, Gentamicin
B. Sulfadoxine, Doxycycline
C. Amoxicillin, Streptomycin
D. Chloramphenicol, Ampicillin

544. Antibiotic belonging to tetracyclines:

A. Doxycycline B. Streptomycin
C. Clarithromycin D. Ampicillin

545. The first line antitubercular drug is:

A. Ethambutol D. Thiacetazone
C. Ofloxacin B. Ethinomide

546. All of are aminoglycosides, EXCEPT:

A. Gentamycin B. Streptomycin
C. Clindamycin D. Neomycin

547. The following antibiotics acts/act by inhibiting protein synthesis:

A. Chloramphenicol B. Erythromycin
C. Gentamicinm D. All of these

548. Antibiotics act by inhibiting the bacterial cell wall synthesis are:

A. Penicillines B. Tetracyclines
C. Aminoglycosides D. Macrolide

549. A patient was on an antitubercular regimen. He consults a physician and complains of loss of visual acuity and impaired color vision. The drug responsible for this adverse effect could be:

A. Streptomycin B. Rifampicin
C. Ethambutol D. INH

550. Example of beta-lactamase inhibitor:

A. Clavulanic acid B. Sulbactam
C. Tazobactam D. All of the Above

551. The drug which inhibits tetrahydrofolate synthesis by inhibiting dihydrofolate reductase:

A. Rifampicin B. Trimethaprim
C. Tetracyclines D. Streptomycin

552. Unwanted effects of tetracyclins are:

A. Phototoxicity
B. Hepatotoxicity
C. Yellowish coloration of teeth
D. All of the Above

553. The advantage/advantages of giving a drug intravenously are:
A. Irritants can be given
B. Useful in emergencies
C. Large volumes can be injected
D. All of the Above

554. Chloramphenicol has the following unwanted effects:
A. Nephrotoxicity
B. Bone marrow depression
C. Hepatotoxicity
D. Ototoxicity

555. The process/processes involved in elimination of drugs through the kidneys is/are:
A. Passive tubular reabsorption
B. Glomerular filtration
C. Active tubular secretion
D. All of the above

556. Combination of sulfonamides with trimethoprim:
A. Decreases the unwanted effects of sulfonamides
B. Bacteriocidal activity
C. Decreases the antimicrobial activity
D. Bacteriostatic activity

557. The following is a third generation cephalosporin :
A. Cefoxitin B. Ceftrioxone
C. Cefazolin D. Cefachlor

558. Choose the anti mycobacterial drug belonging to first-line drugs:
A. PAS B. Pyrazinamide
C. Kanamycin D. Ciprotoxoacin

559. The following is a first generation cephalosporin:
A. Cephalexin B. Cefotaxime
C. Cefepime D. Cefuroxime

560. Choose the anti mycobacterial drug, belonging to second-line drugs:
A. Isoniazid B. Amikacin
C. Rifampin D. Streptomycin

561. The following is contraindicated in children below 8 years of age:
A. Gentamicin B. Tetracyclines
C. Chloramphenicol D. PCT

562. Choose the anti mycobacterial drug, belonging to aminoglycosides:
A. Isoniazid B. PAS
C. Ethambutol D. Streptomycin

563. Hypervitaminosis due to excess can result due to administration of the following:
A. Vitamin D B. Vitamin A
C. Folic acid D. Riboflavin

564. Side effect of Isoniazid includes:
A. Nephrotoxicity
B. Hepatotoxicity, peripheral neuropathy
C. Loss of hair
D. Immunotoxicity

565. Vitamin B-12 is also called :
A. Niacin B. Biotin
C. Cyanocobalamin D. Adenine

566. Which prostaglandin helps in cervical ripening?
A. PGI2 B. PGF2
C. PGE2 D. PGD2

567. .... must be taken in empty stomach
A. Refampicin B. Paracetamol
C. INH D. Ampicillin

568. .... is the movement of solutes from an area of greater concentration to an area of lesser concentration-
A. Osmosis B. Diffusion
C. Ultrafiltration D. Conduction

569. Important side effect of cisplatin is
A. Liver failure B. Nephrotoxicity
C. Bleeding tendencies D. Hypotension

570. Terbutaine is
A. Analgesic B. Antispasmodic
C. Vasodilator D. Bronchodilator

571. There are .... pair of cranial nerves
A. 12 B. 10 C. 8 D. 14

572. The nurse must assess a client experiencing excessive production of ADH for
A. Hyponatraemia B. Hypoglycaemia
C. Dysuria D. Dehydration

573. Captoprilis
A. Antipyretics B. Diuretics
C. Antihypertensive D. Antipsychotic

574. Intravenous heparin therapy is prescribed for a client. While implementing this prescription, a nurse ensures that which of the following medications is available on the nursing unit?
A. Protamine sulfate B. Potassium chloride
C. Aminocaproic acid D. Vitamin K

575. Which laboratory study will be prescribed to monitor the therapeutic effect of heparin?
A. Hematocrit
B. Hemoglobin
C. Prothrombin time
D. Activated partial thromboplastin time

576. A nurse is caring for a client who receiving digoxine. Which commonest side effect observed by nurse?
A. Ataxia
B. Nausea and vomiting
C. Tinitus
D. Insomnia

577. Lithum toxicity happens at serum lithium level of:
A. 0.8 mEq/L B. >2 mEq/L
C. 0.6 mEq/L D. >0.1 mEq/L

578. Vitamin K1 is administered as an antidote for poisoning with:
A. Heparin B. Warfarin
C. Diphenoxalate D. Aminocaproic acid

579. Commonest side effect of the following drugs can cause liver failure;
A. Acetaminophen B. Ibuprofen
C. Piroxicam D. Ketorelac

580. The most useful drug in enuresis, is:
A. Haloperidol B. Diazepam
C. Imipramine D. Chloprromazine

581. An accurate picture of the effectiveness of diuretic therapy is ascertained through?
A. Daily weight measurement
B. Intakeoutput records every hour
C. Testing for pedal edema daily
D. Type of diuretic administered

582. Which of the following is a first-line drug used for pain management?
A. Acetaminophen B. Clonidine
C. Morphine D. Tramadol

583. The physician ordered: ranitidine A.c, what does A.c means?
A. As desired B. Before meals
C. After meals D. Before bed time

584. Which of the following drug can crossed by Blood brain barrier ?
A. Dopamine B. Propanolol
C. Glycopyrrolate D. Betadine

585. Tactile sensations over the body are characteristics of which poisoning?
A. Cocaine B. Opium
C. Cannabis D. Barbiturate

586. A client is diagnosed with diabetic ketoacidosis. Which insulin should the nurse expect the physician to order?
A. Human NPH insulin
B. Human Regular insulin
C. Insulin lispro injection
D. Insulin glargine injection

Explaination: Regular insulin is rapid acting and should be used for diabetic coma

587. Imipramine is a
A. Tricyclic antidepressant (TCA)
B. Selective serotonin reuptake inhibitor antidepressant
C. Monoamine oxidase inhibitor antidepressant (MAOI)
D. Antimanic drug

588. Which of the following antitubercular drug causes red orange discoloration of urine and other body secretions?
A. Isoniazid B. Ethambutol
C. Rifampicin D. Streptomycin

589. The anti dote of Warfarin is:
A. Protamine sulfate B. Vitamin K
C. Vitamin C D. Vitamin D

590. Which of the following adverse effect of insulin?
A. Edema B. Lipodystrophy
C. Allergy D. All of the Above

591. Dapsone is used in all except:
A. Dermatitis herpetiformis
B. Leprosy
C. Pneumocystis pneumonia
D. TB

592. Drugs used for detrusor instability are all except
A. Flavoxate B. Solifenacin
C. Duloxetine D. Tiaperetide

593. If osfamide belongs to which class?
A. Alkylating agent B. Anti metabolite
C. Taxanes D. Antibiotics

594. DOC for refractory histiocytosis
A. Cladarabine
B. Fludarabine
C. Cytosine arabinoside
D. High dose methotrexate

595. TNF alpha inhibitors are contraindicated in
A. SLE
B. Seronegative spondyloarthritis
C. Rheumatoid arthritis
D. None of the above

596. True about acarbose are A/E?
A. Controls both pre and post prandial hyperglycemia
B. It decreases fibrinogen level
C. Its an alpha glucosidase inhibitor
D. It delays progression of diabetes

597. A female has hypopigmented leison on centre of forehead. Drug responsible is
A. Hydroquinone
B. Ether metabolite of hydroquinone
C. Para tetra butyl catechol
D. Para tetra butyl phenol

598. Which of the following does not contribute to Digoxin toxicity?

A. Hyperkalemia B. Hypercalcemia
C. Renal failure D. All of the Above

599. Which drug used in treatment of osteoporosis causes both bone formation and decreased bone resorption?

A. Bisphosphonate
B. Strontiun ranoxalate
C. Terapeptide
D. Calcitonin

600. A girl on Sulphonamides developed abdominal pain and presented to emergency with seizure.What is the probable cause?

A. Acute intermittent porphyria
B. Congenital erythropoietic porphyria
C. INF mononcleosis
D. Kawasakis DS

601. Which of the following drug is a xantine oxidase inhibitor use in the treatment of Gout?

A. Physostigmine B. Allopurinol
C. Aminocaproic acid D. Acetazolamide

602. Which of the following agency is responsible for socialization?

A. School B. Peer group
C. Family D. All of the Above

603. Neuro transmitter which is sympathetic

A. Acetylcholine B. Nor-adrenaline
C. Glutamine D. Glycine

604. Anti viral drug that also use in the treatment of Parkinsonism.

A. Amantidine B. Cimentidine
C. Ranitidine D. Diphenhydramine

605. The following drug is used in acute angina pectoris :

A. Salbutamol B. Adrenaline
C. Nitroglycerin D. Acnomycin

❑❑❑

Answer Sheet

1. A	2. A	3. D	4. D	5. B	6. B	7. A	8. C	9. D	10. D
11.A	12.C	13.C	14.C	15.C	16.D	17.A	18.C	19.C	20.C
21. C	22. B	23. D	24. B	25. A	26. C	27. C	28. C	29. B	30. B
31. A	32. B	33. D	34. B	35. A	36. A	37. D	38. B	39. B	40. C
41. B	42. C	43. A	44. C	45. D	46. C	47. C	48. B	49. A	50. B
51. A	52. C	53. B	54. A	55. C	56. D	57. A	58. D	59. A	60. B
61. A	62. D	63. D	64. B	65. D	66. A	67. B	68. C	69. B	70. D
71. C	72. B	73. A	74. A	75. B	76. C	77. A	78. C	79. B	80. D
81. A	82. A	83. B	84. B	85. A	86. C	87. C	88. D	89. D	90. A
91. C	92. C	93. C	94. C	95. A	96. B	97. B	98. B	99. A	100. A
101. B	102. D	103. C	104. B	105. C	106. A	107. A	108. D	109. A	110. C

111.D	112.B	113.A	114.C	115.C	116.A	117.D	118.A	119.D	120.A
121. A	122. B	123. C	124. C	125. C	126. B	127. A	128. B	129. D	130. B
131. D	132. C	133. D	134. A	135. A	136. C	137. B	138. C	139.C	140. A
141. B	142. B	143. D	144. D	145. C	146. D	147. C	148. B	149. A	150. D
151. B	152. D	153. D	154. B	155. A	156. B	157. D	158. D	159. C	160. C
161. D	162. C	163. A	164. D	165. B	166. C	167. A	168. A	169. A	170. B
171. D	172. B	173. C	174. D	175. C	176. B	177. A	178. C	179. A	180. D
181. D	182. C	183. C	184. C	185. B	186. A	187. A	188. B	189. A	190. B
191. A	192. D	193. B	194. B	195. A	196. D	197. C	198. D	199. B	200. D
201. C	202. C	203. D	204. D	205. A	206. B	207. B	208. D	209. B	210. C
211.B	212.D	213.C	214.D	215.D	216.B	217.A	218.D	219.B	220.C
221. D	222. A	223. B	224. A	225. D	226. D	227. C	228. C	229. B	230. B
231. B	232. C	233. D	234. C	235. A	236. C	237. D	238. B	239. D	240. A
241. A	242. D	243. B	244. B	245. D	246. A	247. A	248. D	249. B	250. C
251. D	252. B	253. C	254. B	255. C	256. B	257. C	258. B	259. B	260. C
261. A	262. D	263. A	264. C	265. D	266. D	267. A	268. C	269. A	270. B
271. D	272. B	273. D	274. A	275. C	276. B	277. D	278. D	279. C	280. C
281. A	282. D	283. A	284. B	285. A	286. A	287. D	288. D	289. D	290. A
291. D	292. C	293. A	294. B	295. A	296. C	297. C	298. D	299. D	300. C
301. A	302. D	303. D	304. D	305. C	306. C	307. B	308. A	309. A	310. D
311.C	312.D	313.B	314.A	315.D	316.A	317.D	318.A	319.B	320.A
321. C	322. D	323. A	324. A	325. C	326. D	327. B	328. A	329. D	330. B
331. D	332. D	333. D	334. A	335. C	336. C	337. A	338. C	339. A	340. D
341. C	342. B	343. B	344. C	345. B	346. A	347. D	348. C	349. D	350. B
351. B	352. B	353. D	354. D	355. B	356. A	357. C	358. D	359. B	360. C
361. C	362. B	363. C	364. A	365. D	366. A	367. B	368. B	369. C	370. A

371. B	372. C	373. C	374. B	375. B	376. D	377. D	378. A	379. D	380. D
381. A	382. A	383. C	384. D	385. D	386. C	387. B	388. B	389. C	390. A
391. D	392. C	393. D	394. D	395. C	396. D	397. B	398. B	399. B	400. A
401. A	402. B	403. B	404. B	405. B	406. D	407. B	408. B	409. D	410. B
411.A	412.C	413.D	414.C	415.C	416.D	417.A	418.C	419.B	420.B
421. A	422. A	423. B	424. D	425. D	426. D	427. C	428. C	429. D	430. B
431. C	432. D	433. D	434. D	435. D	436. C	437. D	438. C	439. D	440. D
441. C	442. C	443. C	444. C	445. B	446. A	447. D	448. D	449. C	450. C
451. B	452. B	453. D	454. D	455. C	456. B	457. B	458. B	459. B	460. C
461. A	462. C	463. A	464. D	465. C	466. C	467. D	468. A	469. A	470. D
471. D	472. C	473. D	474. C	475. C	476. A	477. D	478. D	479. C	480. D
481. D	482. B	483. B	484. B	485. A	486. A	487. D	488. B	489. C	490. C
491. B	492. C	493. A	494. B	495. C	496. A	497. D	498. B	499. A	500. C
501. C	502. C	503. C	504. B	505. D	506. B	507. C	508. D	509. C	510. C
511.B	512.D	513.B	514.D	515.A	516.B	517.D	518.D	519.B	520.B
521. D	522. C	523. C	524. C	525. B	526. B	527. D	528. B	529. C	530. D
531. A	532. D	533. D	534. B	535. D	536. A	537. C	538. B	539. D	540. D
541. B	542. C	543. B	544. A	545. A	546. C	547. D	548. A	549. C	550. D
551. B	552. D	553. D	554. B	555. D	556. B	557. B	558. B	559. A	560. B
561. B	562. D	563. B	564. B	565. C	566. C	567. A	568. B	569. B	570. D
571. A	572. A	573. C	574. A	575. D	576. B	577. B	578. B	579. A	580. C
581. A	582. A	583. B	584 B	585. A	586. C	587. A	588. C	589. B	590. D
591. D	592. C	593. A	594. D	595. A	596. A	597. D	598. A	599. B	600. A
601. B	602.D	603. B	604. A	605. C					

7. Community Health Nursing (MCQ)

1. **Infective hepatitis virus is present in**
   A. Saliva B. Sputum
   C. Faces & Blood D. All of the Above
2. **Coal dirt causes**
   A. Anthracosis B. Silicosis
   C. Bagassosis D. Byssinosis
3. **The stools of cholera are**
   A. Green B. Yellow
   C. Rice water D. Normal
4. **Rabies is transmitted by the bite of**
   A. Anopheles mosquito
   B. Culex mosquito
   C. Flies
   D. A rabid dog
5. **Vaccine produces**
   A. Passive immunity
   B. Active immunity
   C. Active and passive immunity
   D. All of the Above
6. **Important objectives of health services are**
   A. Prevention of diseases
   B. Promotion of health
   C. Cure from the diseases
   D. All of the Above
7. **Audio visual aids are classified in to**
   A. Auditory B. Visual
   C. Combined D. All of the Above
8. **Year of 1981 was declares as year of**
   A. Immunization B. Handicapped
   C. Youth D. Nurses
9. **Copper T is contra indicated during**
   A. Pregnancy B. Pelvic infections
   C. Heart diseases D. All of the Above
10. **When is the most appropriate time for a women to perform breast self examination?**
    A. The first day of the menstrual period
    B. One week after the start of the menstrual period
    C. Just before the time of intercourse
    D. Any convenient time of the month
11. **A client receiving recieving rifampicin should be taught that the effect of the drug could cause;**
    A. Reddish orange color of urine, saliva and sputum
    B. Eighth cranial nerve damage
    C. Brain
    D. Vestibular dysfunction
12. **SOS means**
    A. Once a day B. 4 times a day
    C. If necessary D. At night
13. **Elements of primary health care**
    A. Promotion of food supply & proper nutrition
    B. Adequate supply of safe water & sanitation
    C. Maternal and child health care
    D. All of the Above
14. **Gerontology is the study of**
    A. Old age
    B. Care of old
    C. Diseases related to aging
    D. Aging process
15. **Intelligent quotient (IQ) level of 20-34 indicates?**
    A. Mild mental retardation
    B. Moderate mental retardation
    C. Profound mental retardation
    D. Severe mental retardation
16. **Who Established the Red Cross in the United States in 1882?**
    A. Dorothia Dix
    B. Clara Barton
    C. Florence Nightingale
    D. Jane Addams
17. **An organism which transfers infection by being ingested is known as a;**
    A. Vector B. Paratenic Host
    C. Transform Host D. Fomite
18. **Which one is not a responsibility of a supervisor?**
    A. Divide work B. Policy making
    C. Training D. Evaluation
19. **Which one of the following is not a nursing care unit?**
    A. ICU B. ICCU
    C. PCI D. PICU
20. **Family planning programme was launched in india in:**
    A. 1967 B. 1952
    C. 1969 D. 1983
21. **Which disease is not included in water born diseases?**
    A. Cholera B. Weil's disease
    C. Hydatid disease D. Siderosis
22. **Which drug is not part of DOT's treatment?**
    A. Rifampicin B. Streptomycin
    C. Penicilin D. Ethambutol

23. In India UNICEF procured ORS formula was launched in:
A. January 2004 B. April 2004
C. June 2004 D. November 2004

24. Which vaccine is not included in National Immunization Schedule?
A. Hepatitis B B. Hib
C. Diphtheria D. Measles

25. Who was the chairman of "Committee on integration of Health Services":
A. Mr. Kartar Singh B. Dr. N. Jangalwala
C. Dr. M.S. Chadah D. Sir Joseph Bhore

26. Causes of blindness includes
A. Vitamin A deficiency
B. Trachoma
C. Squint
D. All of the Above

27. Small pox is a
A. Bacterial disease B. Viral disease
C. Fungal disease D. Protozoal disease

28. Chicken pox is a
A. Bacterial disease B. Viral disease
C. Fungal disease D. Protozoal disease

29. Measles is a
A. Bacterial disease B. Viral disease
C. Fungal disease D. Protozoal disease

30. Mumps is a
A. Bacterial disease B. Viral disease
C. Fungal disease D. Protozoal disease

31. Influenza is a
A. Bacterial disease B. Viral disease
C. Fungal disease D. Protozoal disease

32. Diphtheria is a
A. Bacterial disease B. Viral disease
C. Fungal disease D. Protozoal disease

33. Pertusis is a
A. Bacterial disease B. Viral disease
C. Fungal disease D. Protozoal disease

34. Tuberculosis is a
A. Bacterial disease B. Viral disease
C. Fungal disease D. Protozoal disease

35. Polio is a
A. Bacterial disease B. Viral disease
C. Fungal disease D. Protozoal disease

36. Typhoid fever is a
A. Bacterial disease B. Viral disease
C. Fungal disease D. Protozoal disease

37. Yellow fever is a
A. Bacterial disease B. Viral disease
C. Fungal disease D. Protozoal disease

38. Leishmaniasis is a
A. Bacterial disease B. Viral disease
C. Fungal disease D. Protozoal disease

39. Tetanus is a
A. Bacterial disease B. Viral disease
C. Fungal disease D. Protozoal disease

40. Leprosy is a
A. Bacterial disease B. Viral disease
C. Fungal disease D. Protozoal disease

41. AIDS is a
A. Bacterial disease B. Viral disease
C. Fungal disease D. Protozoal disease

42. Cholera is a
A. Bacterial disease B. Viral disease
C. Fungal disease D. Protozoal disease

43. In following which is not a communicable disease
A. TB B. Leprosy
C. Cancer D. Measles

44. In following which is a communicable disease
A. Head injury B. Fracture
C. Renal tumor D. Mumps

45. In following which is not a communicable disease
A. Polio B. Tetanus
C. Angina pectoris D. Diphtheria

46. In following which is a communicable disease
A. MI B. CVA
C. Leprosy D. Peptic ulcer

47. Causitive organism of small pox is
A. Vericella zoster virus
B. Variola virus
C. Myxovirus
D. HIV

48. Causitive organism of chicken pox is
A. Vericella zoster virus
B. Variola virus
C. Myxovirus
D. HIV

49. Causitive organism of measles is
A. Vericella zoster virus
B. Variola virus
C. Myxovirus
D. HIV

50. Causative organism of AIDS is
A. Varicella zoster virus
B. Variola virus
C. Myxovirus
D. HIV

51. India was declared smallpox free in
A. April 1977 B. May 8, 1980
C. July 1987 D. May 1982

52. World was declared smallpox free by WHO on
A. April 1977 B. May 8, 1980
C. July 1987 D. May 1982

53. Rashes of chicken pox first appears on
A. Trunk B. Face
C. Arm D. Legs

54. Characteristics of rashes of chicken pox are
A. Rash is symmetrical
B. Evolution is rapid
C. Rashes are pleomorphism
D. All of the Above

55. Disease rubella is also known as
A. Rubella B. German measles
C. Pertusis D. Hepatitis

56. Other name of whooping cough is
A. Rubella B. German measles
C. Pertusis D. Hepatitis

57. Rashes of measles first occur on
A. Trunk B. Face
C. Hands D. Legs

58. Measles is a disease of mainly
A. Childhood B. Adult age
C. Old age D. All of the Above

59. The disease characterized by enlargement and tenderness of parotid gland is
A. Measles B. Mumps
C. Rubella D. Chickenpox

60. The disease characterized by lymphadenopathy is
A. Measles B. Mumps
C. Rubella D. Chickenpox

61. Rashes of rubella first occur on
A. Face B. Abdomen
C. Trunk D. Legs

62. Influenza is a
A. Respiratory tract infection
B. Urinary tract infection
C. Digestive infection
D. Neurological infection

63. Diphtheria is caused by
A. Corynebacterium diphtheria
B. Clostridium tetani
C. Bordetella pertusis
D. Mycobacterium tuberculoses

64. Tetanus is caused by
A. Corynebacterium diphtheria
B. Clostridium tetani
C. Bordetella pertusis
D. Mycobacterium tuberculoses

65. Whooping cough is caused by
A. Corynebacterium diphtheria
B. Clostridium tetani
C. Bordetella pertusis
D. Mycobacterium tuberculoses

66. Tuberculosis is caused by
A. Corynebacterium diphtheria
B. Clostridium tetani
C. Bordetella pertusis
D. Mycobacterium tuberculoses

67. Diphtheria mainly affects
A. Respiratory system
B. Cardiovascular system
C. Neurological system
D. Reproductive system

68. Schick test is done to identify
A. Diphtheria B. Tuberculosis
C. Polio D. Mumps

69. Mantoux test is done to diagnose
A. Diphtheria B. Tuberculosis
C. Polio D. Mumps

70. Diphtheria is mainly disease of
A. Childhood B. Adulthood
C. Old age D. All of the Above

71. Pertusis is mainly disease of
A. Childhood B. Adulthood
C. Old age D. All of the Above

72. Most important form of TB is
A. Pulmonary TB B. Bone TB
C. Intestine TB D. Skin TB

73. Tuberculosis is the disease of
A. Childhood B. Infancy
C. Old age D. Affects all ages

74. Tuberculin test was discussed by
A. Jackson B. Van Pirquet
C. Aristotle D. Khurana

75. Tuberculosis is mainly transmitted by
A. Droplet infection
B. Infected blood
C. Polluted water
D. Contaminated food

76. Investigations done for TB are
A. Sputum exam B. Chest X-ray
C. Tuberculin test D. All of the Above

77. In DOTS diagnosis of TB is made on the basis of report of
A. MRI and sonography
B. Chest x-ray & sputum exam
C. Skull x-ray and sputum exam
D. Blood and urine exam

78. Bactericidal drug given to treat TB is
A. Ethambutol B. Thioacetazone
C. Paracetamol D. Rifampicin

79. Bactericidal drug given during TB is
A. Rifampicin B. INH
C. Streptomycin D. All of the Above

80. DOTS is given to treat
A. Polio B. TB
C. Leprosy D. AIDS

81. MDT is given to treat
A. Polio B. TB
C. Leprosy D. AIDS

82. In DOTS
A. All the drugs during intensive phase of treatment are given under direct supervision of health worker
B. Diagnosis of TB is made on the basis of chest x-ray and sputum exam report
C. Medicines are given to treat TB
D. All of the Above

83. In DOTS patient are categorized in
A. 1 B. 2
C. 3 D. 4

84. The patients that come in category I of DOTS are
A. New sputum smear positive cases
B. Relapse cases
C. Sputum smear negative but not seriously ill cases
D. All of the Above

85. The patients that come in category II of DOTS are
A. New sputum smear positive cases
B. Relapse cases
C. Sputum smear negative but not seriously ill cases
D. All of the Above

86. The patients that come in category Ist of DOTS are
A. New sputum smear positive cases
B. New cases
C. Sputum smear negative but not seriously ill cases
D. All of the Above

87. The patients that come in category I of DOTS are exclude
A. New sputum smear positive
B. Seriously ill sputum smear negative
C. Seriously ill extra pulmonary
D. Sputum smear positive failure

88. The patients that come in category II of DOTS are exclude
A. Relapse cases
B. Failure of treatment cases
C. Extra pulmonary seriously ill
D. Default of treatment

89. Treatment given during intensive phase of category I of DOTS is
A. $2(HRZE)_3$
B. $2(HRZES)_3+1(HRZE)_3$
C. $2(HRZ)_3$
D. $4(HR)_3$

90. Treatment given during intensive phase of category II of DOT is
A. $2(HRZE)_3$
B. $2(HRZES)_3+1(HRZE)_3$
C. $2(HRZ)_3$
D. $4(HR)_3$

91. Treatment given during intensive phase of category 6(KOCZEE$_d$) + 18 (OCEE$_d$) of DOT is
A. $2(HRZE)_3$
B. $2(HRZES)_3+1(HRZE)_3$
C. $2(HRZ)_3$
D. $4(HR)_3$

92. Treatment given during continuous phase of category I of DOT is
A. $2(HRZE)_3$
B. $2(HRZES)_3+1(HRZE)_3$
C. $2(HRZ)_3$
D. $4(HR)_3$

93. The category of TB patient in which streptomycin is given
A. Category I B. Category II
C. Category III D. All category

94. Duration of treatment in DOTS for the I category patients is
A. 6 months B. 8 months
C. 5 months D. 4 months

95. Duration of treatment in DOTS for the II category patients is
A. 6 months B. 8 months
C. 5 months D. 4 months

96. Duration of treatment in DOTS for the IVth category patients is
A. 6 months B. 8 months
C. 5 months D. 24 months

97. Treatment of II category patients of TB in DOTS is 2(HRZES)3. Here 2 means
A. These medications are given twice in a day
B. These medications are given for 2 months
C. These medications are given for 2 days
D. These medications are given to 2 patients

98. Treatment of II category patients is 2(HRZES)3. Here 3 means
A. These medications are given thrice in a day
B. These medications are given 3 times in a week
C. These medications are given for 3 days
D. These medications are given for 3 months

99. Treatment of II category TB patient is 2(HRZES)3. Here H means

A. Isoniazide B. Pyrazinemide
C. Rifampicin D. Ethambutol

100. Treatment of II category TB patient is 2(HRZES)3. Here Z means

A. Isoniazid B. Pyrazinemide
C. Rifampicin D. Ethambutol

101. Single dose amount of isoniazide in DOTS is

A. 600 mg B. 450 mg
C. 1500 mg D. 1200 mg

102. Single dose amount of Rifampicin in DOTS is

A. 600 mg B. 450 mg
C. 1500 mg D. 1200 mg

103. Single dose amount of pyrazinemide in DOTS is

A. 600 mg B. 450 mg
C. 1500 mg D. 1200 mg

104. Single dose amount of ethambutol in DOTS is

A. 600 mg B. 450 mg
C. 1500 mg D. 1200 mg

105. Single adult dose of streptomycin in DOTS is

A. 750 mg B. 1200 mg
C. 600 mg D. 900 mg

106. Polio is the primarily infection of

A. Urinary tract B. Respiratory tract
C. Alimentary canal D. Nervous system

107. More than half cases of polio are reported in

A. Infancy B. Childhood
C. Adulthood D. Old age

108. Most common route of transmission of polio is

A. Faecal-oral route B. Droplet
C. Sexual contact D. All of the Above

109. Most common mode of transmission of diphtheria is

A. Faecal-oral route B. Droplet
C. Sexual contact D. All of the Above

110. Flaccid paralysis, fever, sore throat, constipation are the manifestations of

A. Diphtheria B. Tuberculosis
C. Polio D. Renal tumor

111. Skin rashes, fever, anorexia, respiratory difficulty are the features of

A. Diphtheria B. Tuberculosis
C. Polio D. Renal tumor

112. Fever, chest pain, hemoptysis are the symptoms of

A. Diphtheria B. Tuberculosis
C. Polio D. Renal tumor

113. Causative organism of cholera is

A. Vibrio cholera B. Salmonella typhi
C. Mosquito D. Clostridium tetani

114. Causative organism of enteric fever

A. Vibrio cholera B. Salmonella typhi
C. Mosquito D. Clostridium tetani

115. Causative organism of malaria is

A. Vibrio cholera B. Salmonella typhi
C. Mosquito D. P.Vivax

116. Causative organism of tetanus is

A. Vibrio cholera B. Salmonella typhi
C. Mosquito D. Clostridium tetani

117. Enteric fever also known as

A. Dengue fever B. Typhoid fever
C. Pertusis D. Measles

118. Stepladder fever, sore throat, abdominal pain, cough are the features of

A. Polio B. Meningitis
C. Typhoid fever D. MI

119. Malaria is a

A. Bacterial disease B. Viral disease
C. Protozoal D. Fungal

120. Trachoma is a infectious disease of

A. Ear
B. Conjunctiva and cornea
C. Nose & pharynx
D. Cervix

121. Characteristic features of tetanus is

A. Skin rashes B. Lock jaw
C. Fever D. Anorexia

122. Leprosy is also known as

A. Fever B. Addison's disease
C. Hensen's disease D. Whooping cough

123. Leprosy is caused by

A. Mycobacterium leprae
B. M. tuberculosis
C. Salmonella
D. Clostridium

124. Highest incidence of pertusis is found among age group

A. 0-5 years B. 6-9 years
C. 10-17 years D. Old age

125. Whooping cough and diphtheria mainly spread by

A. Deficiency of vitamins
B. Virus
C. Droplet infections
D. Polluted water

126. The chief complications of pertusis are

A. Bronchitis
B. Bronchopneumonia
C. Bronchiectasis
D. All of the Above

127. Control measures of whooping cough includes

A. Isolation of patient
B. Disinfection of discharges
C. DPT vaccines
D. All of the Above

128. Control measures of diphtheria includes
A. Isolation of patient
B. Disinfection of discharges
C. DPT vaccines
D. All of the Above

129. Control measures of tetanus includes
A. Isolation of patient
B. Disinfection of discharges
C. DPT vaccines
D. All of the Above

130. Clinical features of Tuberclosis are except
A. Chest pain B. Abdominal pain
C. Cough D. Hemoptysis

131. No. of sputum specimen collected to diagnosis Tuberclosis in DOTS is
A. 1 B. 2
C. 3 D. 4

132. Serum hepatitis is also known as
A. Hepatitis A B. Hepatitis B
C. Hepatitis C D. Hepatitis D

133. Latest name of infections hepatitis is
A. Hepatitis A B. Hepatitis B
C. Hepatitis C D. Hepatitis D

134. The major route of transmission of hepatitis A is
A. Faecal oral B. Parenteral
C. Sexual D. Per anal

135. Hepatitis B is
A. Water borne disease
B. Bacteria borne
C. Blood borne
D. Both A & C

136. Mode of transmission of cholera is
A. Faecal contaminated water
B. Contaminated food
C. Contaminated hands
D. All of the Above

137. Profuse watery diarrhoea followed by vomiting is the manifestation of
A. Measles B. Polio
C. Cholera D. Hepatitis

138. Rice water stool is the manifestation of
A. Measles B. Polio
C. Cholera D. Hepatitis

139. Sunken eyes, hollow cheeks, sub normal temperature, decrease urine output washer man's hands are the features of
A. Measles B. Dehydration
C. Over hydration D. Polio

140. Causative organism of amoebiasis is
A. E.histolytica B. Lumbricoides
C. Medinensis D. Plasmodium

141. Causative organism of ascariasis is
A. E.histolytica B. Lumbricoides
C. Medinensis D. Plasmodium

142. Causative organism of dracunculiasis is
A. E.histolytica B. A.lumbricoides
C. Medinensis D. Plasmodium

143. Amoebiasis is a common infection of
A. Gastrointestinal tract
B. Respiratory tract
C. Circulatory system
D. Urinary tract

144. Ascariasis is the infection of
A. Gastro intestinal tract
B. Respiratory tract
C. Circulatory system
D. Urinary tract

145. Most common mode of transmission of ascariasis is
A. Sexual B. Faecal-oral
C. Droplet D. Infected needles

146. Most common mode of transmission of amoebiasis is
A. Sexual B. Faecal-oral
C. Droplet D. Infected needles

147. Preventive measures of amoebiasis includes except
A. Safe disposal of human excreta
B. TAB vaccine
C. Protection of water supplies from contamination
D. Food hygiene

148. Preventive measures of ascariasis are except
A. Safe disposal of human excreta
B. TAB vaccine
C. Protection of water supplies from contamination
D. Food hygiene

149. In following which is not a respiratory infection
A. Chickenpox B. Diphtheria
C. Mumps D. Polio

150. In following which is a respiratory infection
A. Measles B. Rubella
C. Influenza D. All of the Above

151. In following which is not a respiratory infection
A. Tuberculosis B. Measles
C. Chickenpox D. Cholera

152. In following which is an intestinal infection
A. Tuberculosis B. Measles
C. Chickenpox D. Cholera

153. In following which is not an intestinal infection
A. Cholera B. Diarrhea
C. Ascariasis D. Dengue syndrome

154. In following which is an arthropod borne infection
A. Cholera B. Diarrhea
C. Ascariasis D. Dengue syndrome

155. In India most of malaria cases are reported to be due to
A. P. falcifarum B. P. malariae
C. P. vivax D. P. ovale

156. Sexual cycle of malaria parasite occure in
A. Man B. Mosquito
C. Dog D. Both A & B

157. Maximum prevalence of malaria in India occurs during
A. Winter B. Rainy season
C. Summer D. Spring

158. The stage of malaria parasite enters in the man during asexual cycle is
A. Sporozoites B. Schizonts
C. Merozoites D. Gametocytes

159. Vector of malaria is
A. Plasmodium B. Female anopheles
C. Vivax D. All of the Above

160. Filariasis is transmitted by the biting of
A. Dog B. Rat
C. Mosquito D. House-fly

161. Rabies is transmitted by the biting of
A. Dog B. Rat
C. Mosquito D. House-fly

162. The disease that is also known as hydrophobia is
A. Dengue B. Rabies
C. Plague D. Measles

163. Hydrophobia means
A. Fear of water B. Fear of air
C. Fear of height D. Fear of pain

164. First successful human anti rabies vaccine was discovered by
A. Jacobson B. Pasteur
C. Hargovind Khurana D James

165. Yellow fever is caused by
A. Flavivirus fibricus B. Yerisinia pestis
C. Coxiella burnetti D. Leishmania

166. Causative organism of Kala Azar is
A. Flavivirus fibricus B. Yerisinia pestis
C. Coxiella burnetti D. Leishmania

167. Causative organism of plague is
A. Flavivirus fibricus B. Yerisinia pestis
C. Coxiella burnetti D. Leishmania

168. Natural reservoirs of plague are
A. Field mice B. Gerbils
C. Shunks D. All of the Above

169. Kala Azar is transmitted by the biting of
A. Rat B. House fly
C. Sand fly D. Mosquito

170. Leprosy may be transmitted by
A. Droplet infection B. Direct contact
C. Fomites D. All of the Above

171. Incubation period of leprosy is about
A. 3 to 5 yrs. B. 6-10 days
C. 45-180 days D. 2-6 days

172. Incubation period of tetanus is about
A. 3 to 5 yrs. B. 6-10 days
C. 45-180 days D. 2-6 days

173. Incubation period of hepatitis B is
A. 3 to 5 yrs. B. 6-10 days
C. 45-180 days D. 2-6 days

174. Incubation period of diphtheria is
A. 3 to 5 yrs. B. 6-10 days
C. 45-180 days D. 2-6 days

175. MDT is used for the treatment of
A. Leprosy B. TB
C. Diphtheria D. Malaria

176. The drugs used in MDT are
A. Rifampicin B. Dapsone
C. Clafazimine D. All of the Above

177. Leprosy containing only one skin lesion is known as
A. Paucibacillary single lesion leprosy
B. Paucibacillary leprosy
C. Multibacillary leprosy
D. All of the Above

178. Leprosy containing (2-5) skin lesions in known as
A. Paucibacillary single lesion leprosy
B. Paucibacillary leprosy
C. Multibacillary leprosy
D. All of the Above

179. Leprosy containing more than five skin lesions is known as
A. Paucibacillary single lesion leprosy
B. Paucibacillary leprosy
C. Multibacillary leprosy
D. All of the Above

180. Lepromin test is used to diagnose
A. Diphtheria B. Leprosy
C. TB D. Malaria

181. Drugs for treatment of multibacillary cases of leprosy are
A. Rifampicin - 600 mg once monthly, dapsone 100 mg daily and clofazimine 300 mg once monthly supervised and 50 mg daily self administered
B. Rifampicin 600 mg once a month and dapsone 100 mg daily for 6 months

C. Single dose of a combination of 600 mg
D. None of these

182. Drugs given for treatment of paucibacillary leprosy is
A. Rifampicin - 600 mg once monthly, dapsone 100 mg daily and clofazimine 300 mg once monthly supervised and 50 mg daily self administered
B. Rifampicin 600 mg once a month and dapsone 100 mg daily for 6 months
C. Single dose of a combination of 600 mg
D. None of these

183. Drugs given for treatment of single lesion paucibacillary leprosy is
A. Rifampicin - 600 mg once monthly, dapsone 100 mg daily and clofazimine 300 mg once monthly supervised and 50 mg daily self administered
B. Rifampicin 600 mg once a month and dapsone 100 mg daily for 6 months
C. Single dose of a combination of 600 mg
D. None of these

184. In following which is a sexually transmitted disease
A. Measles B. Polio
C. Tuberclosis D. Syphilis

185. In following which is not a STD
A. Gonorrhoea B. Chancroid
C. Syphilis D. Diphtheria

186. Causative organism of gonorrhoea is
A. Neisseria gonorrhoea
B. Traponema pallidum
C. Haemophilus decreyi
D. Colymmato bacterium

187. Causative organism of syphilis is
A. Neisseria gonorrhoea
B. Traponema pallidum
C. Haemophilus decreyi
D. Colymmato bacterium

188. Causative organism of AIDS is
A. Neisseria gonorrhoea
B. Herpes simplex virus
C. HIV
D. Trichomonas vaginalis

189. Social factors responsible for spread of STDs are
A. Prostitution
B. Sexual disharmony
C. Broken homes
D. All of the Above

190. HIV found in greatest concentration in
A. Blood B. Semen
C. CSF D. All of the Above

191. Mode of transmission of AIDS are except
A. Sexual transmission B. Blood transfusion
C. Mother to child D. Mosquito biting

192. Clinical features of AIDS includes
A. Weight loss B. Lymphadenopathy
C. Fever D. All of the Above

193. Lab investigation done to diagnose HIV is
A. ELISA test
B. Western blot
C. Complete blood count
D. All of the Above

194. Preventive measures of AIDS includes
A. Use of condom
B. Strict aseptic technique in hospitals
C. Examination of blood before transfusion
D. All of the Above

195. Preventive measures of STDs includes
A. Education
B. Use of condom
C. Prevention of prostitution
D. All of the Above

196. Nosocomial infections are also known
A. Bacteria borne infection
B. Viral infections
C. Hospital acquired infection
D. None of these

197. Source of nosocomial infection are except
A. Patients
B. Community health nurse
C. Hospital staff
D. Environment

198. Preventive measures of nosocomial infection includes
A. Isolation of the patient
B. Keep away the hospital staff that has infections disease
C. Hand washing
D. All of the Above

199. BCG vaccine is a
A. Live attenuated vaccine
B. Killed vaccine
C. Toxoid
D. Antisera

200. OPV is a
A. Live attenuated vaccine B. Killed vaccine
C. Toxoid D. Antisera

201. Polio (Salk) type vaccine is a
A. Live attenuated vaccine
B. Killed vaccine
C. Toxoids
D. Antisera

202. Hepatitis B vaccine is a
A. Live attenuated vaccine
B. Killed vaccine
C. Toxoid
D. Antisera

203. In following which is not a live attenuated vaccine
A. BCG B. Measles
C. Hepatitis B D. OPV

204. In following which is a killed vaccine
A. BCG B. Measles
C. Hepatitis B D. OPV

205. Typhoid and cholera vaccines are example of
A. Live attenuated vaccine
B. Killed vaccine
C. Combined vaccine
D. None

206. When more than one immunizing agent may be included in the vaccine, this is known as
A. Live vaccine B. Killed vaccine
C. Combined vaccine D. Toxoid

207. Cold chain is used for
A. Storage of vaccines
B. To treat pyrexia
C. To maintain room temperature
D. All of the Above

208. BCG vaccine was discovered in
A. 1921 B. 1957
C. 1923 D. 1927

209. The vaccine given at birth is
A. BCG B. DPT
C. Measles D. MMR

210. The vaccine given at 6th week of age is
A. BCG B. DPT
C. Measles D. MMR

211. The vaccine given at 9th months of age is
A. BCG B. DPT
C. Measles D. MMR

212. The vaccine given at 15-18 months of age is
A. BCG B. DPT
C. Measles D. MMR

213. The vaccine given intradermaly is
A. BCG B. DPT
C. Measles D. MMR

214. The vaccine given intramuscularly is
A. BCG B. DPT
C. Measles D. MMR

215. Route of DPT vaccine is
A. IM B. SC
C. Orally D. ID

216. Route of hepatitis vaccine is
A. IM B. SC
C. Orally D. ID

217. Route of TT vaccine is
A. IM B. SC
C. Orally D. ID

218. Route of measkes vaccine is
A. IM B. SC
C. Orally D. ID

219. Route of MMR vaccine is
A. IM B. SC
C. Orally D. ID

220. Route of typhoid vaccine is
A. IM B SC C. Orally D. ID

221. Dose of BCG vaccine at birth is
A. 0.05 ml B. 0.5 ml
C. 2 drops D. 0.1 ml

222. Dose of BCG vaccine if given at one month is about
A. 0.05 ml B. 0.5 ml
C. 2 drops D. 0.1 ml

223. Dose of Hepatitis B vaccine is
A. 0.05 ml B. 0.5 ml
C. 2 drops D. 0.1 ml

224. Dose of DPT vaccine is
A. 0.05 ml B. 0.5 ml
C. 2 drops D. 0.1 ml

225. Dose of MMR vaccine is
A. 0.05 ml B. 0.5 ml
C. 2 drops D. 0.1 ml

226. Dose of measles vaccine is
A. 0.05 ml B. 0.5 ml
C. 2 drops D. 0.1 ml

227. Dose of OPV is
A. 0.05 ml B. 0.5 ml
C. 2 drops D. 0.1 ml

228. Dose of TT is
A. 0.05 ml B. 0.5 ml
C. 2 drops D. 0.1 ml

229. No. of doses of hepatitis B vaccine is
A. 1 B. 2 C. 3 D. 4

230. No. of doses of TT in pregnant lady is
A. 1 B. 2 C. 3 D. 4

231. Booster dose of DPT is given at
A. 10 weeks B. 14 weeks
C. 16-24 month D. 5-6 years

232. The immunity develops following clinical infection is known as
A. Active immunity B. Passive immunity
C. Natural immunity D. None of these

233. In India Birth and Death Registration Act was passed in
A. 1973 B. 1880 C. 1897 D. 1911

234. The vaccination act was passed in
A. 1973 B. 1880 C. 1897 D. 1911

235. The Epidemic disease act was passed in
A. 1973 B. 1880 C. 1897 D. 1911

236. The lady reading health school Delhi was established in
A. 1918 B. 1940 C. 1948 D. 1952

237. The drugs act was passed in
A. 1918 B. 1940 C. 1948 D. 1952

238. ESI Act was passed in
A. 1918 B. 1940 C. 1948 D. 1952

239. Central Council of Health was constituted in
A. 1918 B. 1940 C. 1948 D. 1952

240. The national malaria control programme was launched in
A. 1958 B. 1953 C. 1954 D. 1955

241. A nation wide family planning programme was started in
A. 1958 B. 1953 C. 1954 D. 1955

242. The national water supply and sanitation programme was started in
A. 1958 B. 1953 C. 1954 D. 1955

243. The prevention of food adulteration act was passed in
A. 1958 B. 1953 C. 1954 D. 1955

244. National filarial control programme was started in
A. 1958 B. 1953 C. 1954 D. 1955

245. National leprosy control programme was started in
A. 1958 B. 1953 C. 1954 D. 1955

246. NMCP was converted as national malaria eradication programme in
A. 1958 B. 1953 C. 1954 D. 1955

247. The school health programme was initiated in
A. 1962 B. 1963 C. 1972 D. 1977

248. The district TB programme was started in
A. 1962 B. 1963 C. 1972 D. 1977

249. Applied nutrition programme was launched in
A. 1962 B. 1963 C. 1972 D. 1977

250. Medical termination of pregnancy act came into force in
A. 1962 B. 1963 C. 1972 D. 1977

251. Rural health scheme was launched in
A. 1962 B. 1963 C. 1972 D. 1977

252. National health policy was launched in
A. 1983 B. 1984 C. 1985 D. 1987

253. Bhopal gas tragedy occurred in
A. 1982 B. 1984 C. 1985 D. 1987

254. Universal immunization programme was launched in
A. 1982 B. 1984 C. 1985 D. 1987

255. National cancer control programme initiated in
A. 1982 B. 1984 C. 1975 D. 1987

256. National AIDS control programme was initiated
A. 1982 B. 1984 C. 1985 D. 1987

257. CSSM programme was launched in
A. 1992 B. 1993
C. 1997 D. 1988-99

258. Revised national TB programme with DOTS introduced in
A. 1992 B. 1993
C. 1997 D. 1988-99

259. RCH programme was launched in
A. 1992 B. 1993
C. 1997 D. 1988-99

260. National anti malaria programme was started in
A. 1992 B. 1993
C. 1997 D. 1988-99

261. First phase of pulse polio immunization programme was took place on
A. 09 Dec. 1995 & 20 Jan. 1996
B. 07 Dec. 1996 & 18 Jan. 1997
C. 20 Jan. 1996 & 09 Dec. 1997
D. 20 Dec. 1995 & 09 Jan. 1996

262. Second phase of pulse polio immunization programme was took place on
A. 09 Dec. 1995 & 20 Jan. 1996
B. 07 Dec. 1996 & 18 Jan. 1997
C. 20 Jan. 1996 & 09 Dec. 1997
D. 20 Dec. 1995 & 09 Jan. 1996

263. Special nutrition programme was launched in
A. 1970 B. 1961 C. 1975 D. 1993

264. Integrated child development service (ICDS) programme was launched in
A. 1970 B. 1961 C. 1975 D. 1993

265. Mid day meal programme was started in
A. 1970 B. 1961 C. 1975 D. 1993

266. DOTS programme was started in
A. 1970 B. 1961 C. 1975 D. 1993

267. Duration of GNM course is
A. 3 years B. 4½ years
C. 5 years D. 2 years

268. In following which is water borne disease
A. Rheumatoid B. Tuberculosis
C. Typhoid D. Tetanus

269. In following which is not water borne disease
A. Dysentery B. Typhoid
C. Leprosy D. Cholera

270. The chemical used for household purification of water is
A. Na Cl B. Potassium chloride
C. Bleaching powder D. Urea

271. **The chemical which is not used for the household purification of water is**
A. Bleaching powder B. Alum
C. Benedict's solution D. Chlorine tablets

272. **The chemical used for well disinfection is**
A. Benedict's solution B. Bleaching powder
C. Alum D. All of the Above

273. **Noise is measured in**
A. Meter B. Kilogram
C. Inch D. Decibels

274. **The recommended maximum noise level is**
A. 30 db B. 50 db
C. 120 db D. 85 db

275. **The noise level best for normal conversation is**
A. 30 db B. 60 db
C. 120 db D. 85 db

276. **Noise level of motor car horn is**
A. 30 db B. 60 db
C. 120 db D. 85 db

277. **Noise level of train passing station is**
A. 30 db B. 60 db
C. 110 db D. 85 db

278. **Noise level that may cause mechanical damage is**
A. 30 db B. 60 db
C. 160 db D. 85 db

279. **Effects of noise pollution includes**
A. Deafness
B. Inability to concentrate
C. Disturbance to sleep
D. All of the Above

280. **The best method of refuse disposal is**
A. Burning B. Dumping
C. Composting D. All of the Above

281. **Examples of house fly borne diseases are except**
A. Diarrhoea B. Cholera
C. Gastroenteritis D. French fever

282. **In following with is a louse borne disease**
A. Diarrhoea B. Cholera
C. Gastroenteritis D. French fever

283. **The time period between the entry of disease agent in the body and occurrence of clinical signs and symptoms of that disease is known as**
A. Incubation period B. Fastigium
C. Defervescence D. Defection

284. **The stage of the disease cycle represents the height of the disease is**
A. Incubation period B. Fastigium
C. Defervescence D. Defection

285. **The stage of disease cycle in which signs and symptoms are clear cut is**
A. Incubation period B. Fastigium
C. Defervescence D. Defection

286. **The stage of disease cycle in which patients starts to feel better is**
A. Incubation period B. Fastigium
C. Defervescence D. Defection

287. **The stage of disease in which patient completely recovers from the disease is**
A. Incubation period B. Fastigium
C. Defervescence D. Defection

288. **The level of prevention in which actions are taken prior to the onset of the disease is**
A. Primary B. Secondary
C. Tertiary D. All of the Above

289. **Immunization is the level of prevention**
A. Primary B. Secondary
C. Tertiary D. All of the Above

290. **The level of prevention to which actions are taken to inhibit the progress of a disease at its incipient stage is**
A. Primary B. Secondary
C. Tertiary D. All of the Above

291. **The level of prevention in which action are taken to reduce or limit impairments and disabilities and to promote patient's adjustment to irremediable condition is**
A. Primary B. Secondary
C. Tertiary D. All of the Above

292. **Example of tertiary prevention is**
A. Immunization B. Early diagnosis
C. Proper treatment D. Rehabilitation

293. **Example of primary prevention is**
A. Immunization B. Early diagnosis
C. Proper treatment D. Rehabilitation

294. **A sudden outbreak of disease in a community in excess of normal expectation is known as**
A. Epidemic B. Endemic
C. Pandemic D. Isolation

295. **The constant presence of disease with in a geographical area is known as**
A. Epidemic B. Endemic
C. Pandemic D. Isolation

296. **An epidemic which spreads from country to country or over the world is known as**
A. Epidemic B. Endemic
C. Pandemic D. Isolation

297. **A person who harbors the disease agent without having any outward signs and symptoms is known as**
A. Patient B. Carrier
C. Isolation D. Vector

298. **The separation of a person with infections disease from contact with other human beings is known as**
A. Patient B. Carrier
C. Isolation D. Vector

299. In following which is not a direct mode of transmission of communicable
A. Droplet infection
B. Transplacental
C. Inoculation into skin or mucosa
D. Vector borne transmission

300. Most of respiratory infections are transmitted by
A. Droplet infection
B. Transplacental
C. Inoculation into skin or mucosa
D. Vector borne transmission

301. The mode of transmission in which diseases are transmitted due to coughing, sneezing or talking of infected person, is
A. Droplet infection
B. Transplacental
C. Inoculation into skin or mucosa
D. Vector borne transmission

302. Transmission of infection disease from mother to foetus is known as
A. Droplet
B. Vehicle borne
C. Fomite borne
D. Vertical transmission

303. The articles that convey infection is known as
A. Arteries B. Fomite
C. Autoclave D. All of the Above

304. An agent which kills the infections agent outside the body is known as
A. Disinfectant B. Deodorant
C. Disinfection D. Bacteriostatic

305. An agent which suppress bad odour is
A. Disinfectant B. Deodorant
C. Disinfection D. Bacteriostatic

306. Killing of infections agents outside the human body by direct exposure to chemical or physical agents is
A. Disinfectant B. Deodorant
C. Disinfection D. Bacteriostat

307. The application of disinfective measures as early as possible after the discharge of infections material from the body of an infected person is known as
A. Concurrent disinfection
B. Terminal disinfection
C. Prophylactic
D. All of the Above

308. The application of disinfective measures after a patient has died or has been discharged from the hospital is
A. Concurrent disinfection
B. Terminal disinfection
C. Prophylactic
D. All of the Above

309. The multipurpose worker's scheme was launched in
A. 1970 B. 1974 C. 1990 D. 1985

310. The ovum is released from the ovary on which day of menstrual cycle
A. 10 B. 14 C. 20 D. 5

311. The care provided a during pregnancy is known as
A. Antenatal B. Intranatal
C. Postnatal D. All of the Above

312. The care which is provided at the time of delivery is known as
A. Antenatal B. Intranatal
C. Postnatal D. All of the Above

313. Post natal period is
A. 5 weeks B. 6 weeks
C. 7 weeks D. 8 weeks

314. The prenatal examinations includes
A. Record of vital signs
B. Urine examination for sugar and albumin
C. HIV test
D. All of the Above

315. Method for calculating expected date of delivery is
A. Ist day of last menstrual period + 280 days
B. Ist day of last menstrual period + 200 days
C. Last day of last menstrual period + 280 days
D. Last day of first menstrual period + 280 days

316. Examples of high risk pregnancies are except
A. Elderly primi
B. Multiple pregnancy
C. No H/O previous caesarian
D. Ante partum haemorhage

317. Every pregnant lady should be visited at least
A. 3 times B. 2 times
C. 1 times D. 4 times

318. Prenatal advices includes
A. Encourage the mother to take additional calorie & protein
B. Encourage the mother to take iron folic acid tabs
C. Encourage the mother to maintain proper personal hygiene
D. All of the Above

319. Warning signs of pregnancy are except
A. Swelling of feet B. Fits
C. Blurring of vision D. Increase appetite

320. Objectives of family planning includes
A. To avoid unwanted births
B. To bring about wanted births
C. To regulate the interval between two pregnancies
D. All of the Above

321. Contraception means
A. Preventing the union of sperm and ovum
B. Suppressing ovulation
C. Interfering with implantation of fertilized ovum in the uterus
D. All of the Above

322. In following which is not a spacing contraceptive method
A. Condom B. Vasectomy
C. Copper-T D. Mala-N

323. In following which contraceptive method is used by males
A. Vasectomy B. Condom
C. Mala-N D. Withdrawal

324. In following which contraceptive method is used by females
A. Vasectomy B. Condom
C. Mala-N D. Withdrawal

325. In following which is a male contraceptive method
A. Copper-T B. Mala-N
C. Tubectomy D. Vasectomy

326. In following which contraceptive method is used by female
A. Nirodh B. Withdrawal
C. Copper-T D. Vasectomy

327. In following which is a permanent method of contraception used by males
A. Tubectomy B. Vasectomy
C. Copper-T D. Oral pills

328. Method of female permanent contraception is
A. Tubectomy B. Vasectomy
C. Copper-T D. Oral pills

329. The contraceptive device that prevents the deposition of sperm in the vagina is
A. Condom B. Copper-T
C. Mala-N D. Tubectomy

330. The contraceptive device that interfere with the implantation of fertilized ovum in the uterus is
A. Condom B. Copper-T
C. Mala-N D. Tubectomy

331. The contraceptive device that suppress ovulation is
A. Condom B. Copper-T
C. Mala-N D. Tubectomy

332. In following which is not an advantage of condom
A. It is easy to use
B. Has no side effects
C. A new condom must be used each time
D. Protects from unwanted pregnancy

333. The natural method of contraception is
A. Condom B. NSV
C. Withdrawal D. Copper-T

334. Oral contraceptive pills contain
A. Only oestrogen B. Only progesterone
C. Both A & B D. None of these

335. Total no. of tablets contained by a packet of oral contraceptive pills is
A. 25 B. 28 C. 30 D. 31

336. A packet of oral contraceptive pills contains
A. 28 contraceptive pills
B. 21 contraceptive + 7 iron tablets
C. 7 contraceptive + 21 iron pills
D. All 28 iron pills

337. The first course of oral contraceptive pills should be started on
A. 1st day of menstrual cycle
B. 3rd day of menstrual cycle
C. 5th day of menstrual cycle
D. 14th day of menstrual cycle.

338. Contraindications for oral contraceptive pills includes
A. Pregnancy
B. Women over 35 years of age
C. Medical conditions such as hypertension, DM etc.
D. All of the Above

339. Example of injectable contraceptives is
A. Condom B. Copper-T
C. Mala-N D. DMPA

340. Injectable contraceptives such as DMPA and NET-EN contains
A. Only progesterone
B. Only oestrogen
C. Both Progesterone & oestrogen
D. None of the Above

341. Injectable contraceptives are administered
A. IM B. IV
C. SC D. ID

342. Safe period is defined as
A. A week before and a week after the menstrual cycle
B. A week before ovulation and a week after ovulation
C. 2 weeks before and 2 weeks after menstrual cycle
D. It is a period when diseases can not occur in human being

343. Sources of vital and health statistics are
A. Census
B. Registration of births, deaths and manages
C. Health survey
D. All of the Above

344. No. of live birth during a year per 1000 estimated mid year population is known as
A. Birth rate B. Under 5 birth rate
C. General fertility rate D. Death rate

345. No. of live births during a year per 1000 women in reproductive age group is known as
A. Birth rate B. Under 5 birth rate
C. General fertility rate D. Death rate

346. The no. of deaths per 1000 estimated mid year population is known as
A. Death rate
B. IMR
C. MMR
D. Neonatal mortality rate

347. IMR & MMR are always calculated on
A. Live births
B. Total births
C. Estimated midyear population
D. Total no. of females

348. Germ theory of disease was propounded by
A. Aristotle B. LouisPasteur
C. Henri D. Abdul Kalam

349. Health for all by year 2000 was adopted by WHO in
A. 1977 B. 1981
C. 1983 D. 1985

350. Goals of Health For All by 2000 AD are except
A. Reduction of infant mortality rate from 125 to below 60
B. To reduce the birth rate from 32 to 21
C. To reduce death rate from 12 to 9
D. To reduce expectation of life from 64 years to 52 years

351. In following which is not a principle of primary health care
A. Community involvement
B. Unequal distribution
C. Appropriate technology
D. Multisectoral approach

352. In recent years well baby clinics has been replaced as
A. Antenatal clinic
B. Under five clinic
C. Child clinic
D. Homeopathic clinic

353. The apex of the triangle of under five clinic represents
A. Care and treatment of sick children
B. Family planning
C. Healthy teaching
D. Immunization

354. Border that presents around the whole symbol of under five clinic and touches all the other areas represents
A. Care and treatment of sick children
B. Family planning
C. Healthy teaching
D. Immunization

355. The center of the symbol of under five clinics which is a triangular area and red in colour represents
A. Care and treatment of sick children
B. Family planning
C. Healthy teaching
D. Immunization

356. Components of under five clinic includes
A. Immunization
B. Nutritional surveillance
C. Oral rehydration therapy
D. All of the Above

357. Road to health card is used for
A. Measuring the size of road
B. Growth monitoring in children
C. Growth monitoring in adults
D. All of the Above

358. In following which is not included in six killer diseases
A. Diphtheria B. Pertusis
C. Cholera D. Polio

359. A sub centre is situated over population of
A. 3000-5000 B. 20000-30000
C. 30000-120000 D. 2 lac

360. A primary health centre is situated over population of
A. 3000-5000 B. 20000-30000
C. 30000-120000 D. 2 lac

361. A community health centre is situated over population of
A. 3000-5000 B. 20000-30000
C. 30000-120000 D. 2 lac

362. Total number of staff of PHC is
A. 5 B. 15 C. 25 D. 10

363. Total number of staff at CHC is
A. 5 B. 15 C. 25 D. 10

364. In charge of the PHC is
A. Nurse grade Ist
B. Nurse grade IInd
C. Medical officer
D. Health assistant female

365. Functions of PHC includes
A. MCH & family planning services
B. Implementation of national health programmes
C. School health services
D. All of the Above

366. Geriatric nursing means nursing care given to
A. Infants B. Pregnant ladies
C. Old people D. All patients

367. World health day is celebrated on
A. 15 March B. 7 April
C. 1 December D. 10 March

368. World AIDS day is celebrated on
A. 15 March B. 7 April
C. 1 December D. 10 March

369. Headquarter of WHO is situated in
A. London B. Geneva
C. Washington D. Delhi

370. Constitution of WHO can into force on
A. 9th April 1948 B. 7th April 1950
C. 7th April 1947 D. 7th April 1946

371. Head quarter of UNICEF is situated at
A. Geneva B. New Delhi
C. London D. New York

372. Activities of UNICEF includes
A. Education B. Immunization
C. Nutrition D. All of the Above

373. In following which is not a international health agency
A. WHO B. UNICEF
C. CHC D. FAO

374. Tools of measurement in epidemiology are
A. Rates B. Ratio
C. Proportions D. All of the Above

375. Epidemiology means
A. Study of diseases
B. Study of bacteria
C. Study of community health nursing
D. All of the Above

376. The no. of new cases occurring in a defined population during a specific time period is known as
A. Incidence B. Prevalence
C. Rate D. Proportion

377. The no. of all cases (old+new) is known as
A. Incidence B. Prevalence
C. Rate D. Proportion

378. Measles vaccine is stored at
A. 0°C temp B. 4-8°C temp
C. -4 to -8°C temp D. 10-12°C temp

379. DPT vaccine is stored at
A. 0°C temp B. 4-8°C temp
C. -4 to -8°C temp D. 10-12°C temp

380. The syringe used for BCG vaccination is
A. 2 cc syringe B. 5 cc syringe
C. Tuberculin syringe D. All of the Above

381. Complications of BCG vaccinations are
A. Severe and prolonged ulceration at the site of administration
B. Osteomyelitis
C. Suppurative lymphadenitis
D. All of the Abcve

382. Today is a
A. Vaccine
B. Drug
C. Contraceptive method
D. Type of anti body

383. Copper IUDs comprise the
A. First generation B. Second generation
C. Third generation D. Forth generation

384. Hormone releasing IUCDs comprise the
A. First generation B. Second generation
C. Third generation D. Forth generation

385. Lippes loop is a
A. Male contraceptive method
B. Female contraceptive method
C. Comfort device
D. Surgical instruments

386. The most wide used hormonal IUDs is
A. Progestasert B. Cu-T-200
C. Lippes loop D. TODAY

387. IUDs provide protection against pregnancy for about
A. 3-5 months B. 1-2 years
C. 3-5 years D. Life time

388. The commonest side effect of IUDs is
A. Bleeding B. Pain
C. PID D. Pregnancy

389. Components of school health services are
A. Health appraisal
B. Immunization
C. Healthful school environment
D. All of the Abcve

390. Waste sharp such as needles, syringes, scalpels, blades are kept in
A. Red bag B. Yellow bag
C. Blue bag D. Black bag

391. Human anatomical waste, such as human tissue and body parts and animal waste are kept in
A. Red bag B. Yellow bag
C. Blue bag D. Black bag

392. Non infections material is kept in
A. Red bag B. Yellow bag
C. Blue bag D. Black bag

393. Waste rubber goods are kept in
A. Red bag B. Yellow bag
C. Blue bag D. Black bag

394. ESI act protects the rights of
A. Children
B. Pregnant ladies
C. Old men
D. All industrial employee

395. In following which is not a group approach of health communication
A. Demonstration B. Lectures
C. Symposium D. Home visits

396. In following which is a individual approach of health education
A. Demonstration B. Lectures
C. Symposium D. Home visits

397. Mass approach of health communication is
A. TV B. Radio
C. Posters D. All of the Above

398. Role play, seminars, panel discussion are the example of
A. Individual approach of health communication
B. Group approach of health communication
C. Mass approach of health communication
D. All of the Above

399. Personal contacts and home visits are the examples of
A. Individual approach of health communication
B. Group approach of health communication
C. Mass approach of health communication
D. All of the Above

400. New paper, radio, posters, TV are the examples of
A. Individual approach of health communication
B. Group approach of health communication
C. Mass approach of health communication
D. All of the Above

401. Goals of National Health Policy-2002 are
A. Eradicate polio by 2005
B. Achieve zero level of growth of HIV by 2007
C. Reduce MMR to 100/lakh by 2010
D. All of the Above

402. Health survey and development committee also known as
A. Bhore Committee
B. Mudaliar Committee
C. Kartar Singh Committee
D. Srivastav Committee

403. Health survey and planning committee also known as
A. Bhore Committee
B. Mudaliar Committee
C. Kartar Singh Committee
D. Srivastav Committee

404. The committee on MPWs under health and family planning is also known as
A. Bhore Committee
B. Mudaliar Committee
C. Kartar Singh Committee
D. Srivastav Committee

405. "Group on medical education and support manpower" popularly known as
A. Bhore Committee
B. Mudaliar Committee
C. Kartar Singh Committee
D. Srivastav Committee

406. Bhore committee was appointed in
A. 1943 B. 1946 C. 1973 D. 1975

407. Bhore Committee submitted report in
A. 1943 B. 1946 C. 1973 D. 1975

408. Kartar Singh Committee submitted report in
A. 1943 B. 1946 C. 1973 D. 1975

409. Srivastav Committee submitted report in
A. 1943 B. 1946 C. 1973 D. 1975

410. The committee appointed to study the arrangements necessary for the maintenance phase of NMEP, was
A. Chadah Committee
B. Mudaliar Committee
C. Kartar Singh Committee
D. Srivastav Committee

411. The committee that appointed to survey the progress made in the field of health since submission of Bhore Committee's report, was
A. Chadah Committee
B. Mudaliar Committee
C. Kartar Singh Committee
D. Srivastav Committee

412. Replacing of ANMs by the female health workers, basic health workers, vaccinator's health education assistant by the male health workers were the recommendations of
A. Chadah Committee
B. Mudaliar Committee
C. Kartar Singh Committee
D. Srivastav Committee

413. There should be one PHC for a population of 50,000 and each PHC should be divided into 16 sub-centers this was the recommendation of
A. Chadah Committee
B. Mudaliar Committee
C. Kartar Singh Committee
D. Srivastav Committee

414. Chairman of health survey and development committee was
A. Sir Joseph Bhore B. Dr. A.L. Mudaliar
C. Kartar Singh D. Srivastav

415. Chairman of health survey and planning committee was
A. Sir Joseph Bhore
B. Dr. A.L. Mudaliar
C. Kartar Singh
D. Srivastav

416. Ninth five year plan began in
A. 1996 B. 1997 C. 1998 D. 1999

417. Three tier system of health care delivery in rural area based on the recommendations of
A. Bhore Committee
B. Mudaliar Committee
C. Kartar Singh Committee
D. Srivastav Committee

418. An anganwadi worker is appointed over a population of
A. 500 B. 1000 C. 2000 D. 5000

419. In following which is not a Indian voluntary health agency
A. Indian Red Cross Society
B. Hind Kusht Nivaran Sangh
C. TB Association of India
D. Indian Nursing Council

420. The voluntary health agency that provides services in case of earth quakes, floods, epidemics is
A. Indian Red Cross Society
B. Hind Kusht Nivaran Sangh
C. TB Association of India
D. Indian Nursing Council

421. The voluntary health agency the provides financial support to various leprosy homes and clinics and health education is
A. Indian Red Cross Society
B. Hind Kusht Nivaran Sangh
C. TB association of India
D. Indian Nursing Council

422. The voluntary health agency whose main objective is to improve condition of women, is
A. Red Cross Society
B. Kasturba Memorial Fund
C. Bharat Sevak Samaj
D. TB Association of India

423. The Indian Red Cross Society was established in
A. 1920 B. 1950 C. 1939 D. 1926

424. Hind Kusht Nivaran Sangh was formed in
A. 1920 B. 1950 C. 1939 D. 1926

425. TB Association of India was formed in
A. 1920 B. 1950 C. 1939 D. 1926

426. All India Women's conference was set up in
A. 1920 B. 1950 C. 1939 D. 1926

427. UNICEF was established in
A. 1946 B. 1945
C. 1948 D. 1950

428. Food and agriculture organization (FAO) was formed in
A. 1946 B. 1945 C. 1948 D. 1950

429. Florence Nightingale is known as
A. Lamp with lady
B. Lady with the lamp
C. Mother of nursing
D. Mother of fundamental

430. Florence Nightingale was born on
A. 12 May 1820 B. 12 June 1822
C. 30 May 1820 D. 12 May 1920

431. The non verbal communication following except
A. Facial expression B. Body posture
C. Spoken words D. Eye contact

432. In communication posture the person who wishes to convey a message to another is known as
A. Receiver B. Message
C. Sender D. Channel

433. The person who receives the message from sender is
A. Receiver B. Message
C. Sender D. Channel

434. The place of information passed from one person to another is known as
A. Receiver B. Message
C. Sender D. Channel

435. The route by which information are send from a person to another is known as
A. Receiver B. Message
C. Sender D. Channel

436. Barriers of communication are except
A. Lack of privacy B. Speech defects
C. Peaceful environment D. Lack of interest

437. Communication may be blocked by except
A. Changing the subject
B. Lack of interest
C. Lack of listening
D. Proper use of knowledge

438. Cross infection occurs usually in
A. Community B. Home
C. Hospital D. Schools

439. The entry and development of a disease producing agent in the body is known as
A. Infection B. Immunity
C. Antigen D. Disease

440. The pathway by which the pathogens enter the body are all called as
A. Portal of entry B. Carrier
C. Portal of exit D. Infection

441. The pathways by which the pathogens leave the body are called as
A. Portal of entry B. Carrier
C. Portal of exit D. Infection

442. The infection of the body by pus forming bacteria is known as
A. Disease B. Immunity
C. Sepsis D. Inflammation

443. The small animals with strong sharp teeth such as rats, mice, rabbits are examples of
A. Arthropods B. Fungi
C. Rodents D. Insects

444. The technique which is used to prevent cross infection is known as
A. Nursing care B. Barrier nursing
C. Actual nursing care D. Preventive nursing

445. The type of isolation technique used in situation when the pathogens are spread by droplet mode of transmission is
A. Respiratory isolation B. Enteric isolation
C. Skin isolation D. Blood isolation

446. Respiratory isolation includes
A. Use of mask B. Use of gown
C. Hand washing D. All of the Above

447. The type of isolation techniques used in the condition when the pathogens are transmitted in faeces, is
A. Respiratory isolation B. Enteric isolation
C. Skin isolation D. Blood isolation

448. Ghon's foci is seen in:
A. Rheumatic fever B. Measles
C. Renal tumor D. Tuberculosis

449. Dose of BCG vaccination is:
A. 0.5ml sc B. 0.5 ml ID
C. 0.1 ml ID D. 1 ml IM

450. Which of the following is tertiary level of prevention?
A. Disability limitation
B. Health promotion
C. Specific protection
D. Early diagnosis and treatment

451. First AIDS case in India was reported in the year:
A. 1987 B. 1982
C. 1992 D. 2002

452. Only human beings are reservoir for:
A. Rabies B. Smallpox
C. Influenza D. Salmonella

453. 3- tier system of Local Self Govt, at block level is:
A. Grama panchayat
B. Panchayath samithi
C. Zilla parishad
D. Panchayath Raj

454. As per the latest WHO guidelines which dehydration status required ORS?
A. Any form of dehydration
B. Mild dehydration
C. Moderate dehydration
D. Severe dehydration

455. The composition of Pentavalent vaccine is
A. Diphtheria, Pertusis, Tetanus, Cholera and OPV
B. Measles, Mumps, Rubella, Typhoid and Cholera
C. Diphtheria, Pertusis, Tetanus, Haemophillus influenza and Hepatitis B
D. Typhoid, Chickenpox, Measles, Rubella and Hepatitis B

456. Match the following :

Part I	Part II
A. Live Vaccine	1. Typhoid
B. Killed Vaccine	2. Rubella
C. Toxoids	3. Rabies
D. Antisera	4. Diphtheria

	A.	B.	C.	D.
A.	2	1	4	3
B.	4	2	3	1
C.	3	4	2	1
D.	2	4	1	3

457. Optimum level of fluoride in drinking water per liter is:
A. 1-2 mg B. 0.05-0.08 mg
C. 05-0.8g D. 0.5-0.8 rl

458. Vande Mataram Scheme is an integral part of
A. 20 point programme
B. Minimum needs programme
C. RCH programme
D. Nutritional programme

459. Hardness of water is expressed as:
A. OZ/L B. mg
C. mg % D. mEq/L

460. NRHM was launched in the year of
A. 2004 B. 2005
C. 2006 D. 2007

461. Tuberculosis is caused by polluted:
A. Food B. Fomites
C. Air D. Water

462. The occupational disease caused by inhalation of sugar-cane dust is
A. Silicosis B. Anthracosis
C. Byssinosis D. Bagassosis

463. A person with no sign of disease but may transmit, it is called:
A. An allergic person B. Immune person
C. A resistant person D. A carrier person

464. Primordial prevention means prevention of
A. Infections B. Complications
C. Diseases D. Risk factors

465. Polio is transmitted through:
A. Food B. Insects
C. Water D. Air

466. Viruses are
A. One-cell microorganisms with a simple cellular organization whose nucleus lacks a membrane.
B. Pieces of nucleic acid (DNA or RNA) wrapped in a thin coat of protein that replicate only within the cells of living hosts
C. Multicelluar organisms that live in or on a host to obtain nourishment with out providing any benefit to the host
D. None of the Above

467. Cornea and conjunctiva will become dry in
A. Keratomalacia B. Bitot's Spot
C. Xerophthalmia D. Night Blindness

468. Following is a contagious disease:
A. Filaria
B. Tuberculosis
C. Malaria
D. Hookworm infestation

469. Arrange the Demographic cycle
I. High stationary stage
II. Early expanding stage
III. Late expanding stage
IV. Low stationary stage
V. Decline stage
A. I, II, III,IV, V B. I, III, II, IV, V
C. I, V, IV, III, II D. IV, III, II, I, V

470. VDRL test is performed to diagnose
A. Syphillis B Pregnancy
C. Myasthenia gravis D. All of the Above

471. The most common early symptom of hepatitis 'A' is:
A. Loss of appetite
B. Abdominal distention
C. Shortness of breath
D. Ecchymosis

472. Malaria is a
A. Zoonotic Disease
B. Viral Disease
C. Bacterial Disease
D. Protozoal Disease

473. Common cold is caused by:
A. Rhinovirus
B. Staphylococcus aureus
C. Shigella
D. Escherichia coil

474. Point out the wrong one in the following measurements in epidemiology
A. Measurement of mortality
B. Measurement of disability
C. Measurement of nurse-patient ratio
D. Measurement of natality

475. Most common cause of post measles death:
A. SSPE B. RTI
C. Weakness D. Diarrhea

476. Find the cdd one in the following responses. Following are the examples of live vaccines
A. BCG B. Measles
C. Oral Polio D. Tetanus

477. Congenital varicella is related with which disease?
A. Mumps B. Germen measels
C. Measels D. Chicken pox

478. An effective anti TB drug against intracellular as well as extracelluar bacilli is:
A. INH B. Streptomycin
C. Rifampicin D. Pyrazinam

479. Maximum maternal mortality is seen:
A. Hepatitis A B. Hepatitis E
C. Hepatitis C D. Hepatitis B

480. Varicella vaccine is
A. Killed vaccine
B. Live attenuated vaccine
C. Immunoglobulin
D. None of the Above

481. Which vaccine is contraindicated in pregnancy?
A. Hepatitis B. OPV
C. BCG D. Rubella

482. In polio transmission, easy block can be applied by acting on:
A. Agent B. Reservoir
C. Susceptible host D. Feco-oral route

483. One PHC is located for a population of
A. 5000 B. 30,000
C. 100,000 D. 500

484. Poliomyelitis is caused by-
A. Bacteria B. Protozoa
C. Virus D. Rickettsiac

485. Vaccine which is given at the earliest:
A. MMR B. BCG
C. DPT D. DT

486. Eligible couple register is maintained at
A. Sub centre
B. CHC
C. PHC
D. District headquarters

487. BCG vaccine is administered to children:
A. Intradermally C. Intramuscularly
B. Subcutaneously D. Orally

488. 'Monday morning fever' is a common name for:
A. Asbestosis
B. Bagassosis
C. Byssinosis
D. Mad Hatter's disease

489. Tuberculin test is read after:
A. 72 hours B. 24 hours
C. 78 hours D. 12 hours

490. Example of acid fast bacilli?
A. E coli B. Myobacterium
C. Chlostrideium D. None of the Above

491. What is true of primary facilities?
A. They are usually governmentrun
B. Their services are provided on an outpatient basis
C. They have training facilities for health professionals
D. A community hospital is an example of this level of health facilities

492. Prevalence of tuberculosis infection is measured by:
A. Sputum culture B. Chest X-ray
C. Sputum AFB D. Tuberculin test

493. Which of the following diseases is known as "Barometer of social welfare"?
A. Leprosy B. Tuberculosis
C. Cholera D. Malaria

494. Malaria is transmitted to man by which mosquito?
A. Female anopheles B. Culin
C. Culex D. Aedes

495. Continuous scrutiny of factors that determine the occurrence and distribution of disease and other condition of ill health is the definition of
A. Disease control B. Monitoring
C. Surveillance D. System analysis

496. Identify the waterborne disorder:
A. Malaria B. Dengue
C. Cholera D. AIDS

497. Yellow plastic bags containing biomedical wastes are treated by
A. Microwaving B. Autoclaving
C. Shredding D. Incineration

498. The procedure of removal and ligation of fallopian tube is referred as:
A. Tubectomy B. Mastectomy
C. Vasectomy D. Appendectomy

499. Three remarkable components of Integrated Management and Childhood Illness (IMNCI)are
1. Improvement of case management skills of health care providers
2. Provision of essential supplies
3. Integration of child health services
4. Optimization of family and community prac-tices in relation to child health

A. 1,2,3 B. 2,3,4
C. 1,3,4 D. 1,2,4

500. Decrease in the incidence of a disease to a level where it ceases to be a pubic health problem is
A. Elimination B. Control
C. Surveillance D. Eradication

501. For education of measles, immunization coverage should be at least
A. 80% B. 85% C. 96% D. 100%

502. Period of maximum infectivity in mumps is during
A. Incubation period
B. Onset of swelling
C. After swelling appears
D. Prodromal period

503. Major epidemics of influenza A occur at intervals of
A. 1 year B. 2-3 years
C. 10-15 years D. 20-25 years

504. The most common source of infection for diphtheria is a
A. Case B. Sub clinical case
C. Carrier D. All of the Above

505. Shick test is done in
A. Meningitis B. Diphtheria
C. Pertussis D. Polimyelitis

506. Adjuvant present in DPT vaccine is
A. Aluminium phosphate
B. Aluminium hydroxide
C. Zinc phosphate
D. Magnesium phosphate

507. Recommended site of administration of DPT in infants is
A. Gluteal
B. Deltoid
C. Lateral aspect of thigh
D. Forearm

508. The most severe complications following DPT are due to …….. component
A. Diphtheria B. Pertussis
C. Tetanus D. Adjuvant

509. The vaccine usually given to pilgrims to the Middle East is
A. DPT B. Influenza
C. Yellow fever D. Meningitis

510. Best index to estimate case load of T.B. in a community is
A. Incidence of infection
B. Prevalence of infection
C. Incidence of disease
D. Prevalence of disease

511. Prevalence of T.B. infection in a community is estimated by
A. Tuberculin test
B. Sputum microscopy
C. Culture
D. Chest X-ray

512. The amount of PPD used in mantoux test in India is
A. 1 TU B. 5 TU
C. 25 TU D. 250 TU

513. Result of mantoux test is read after
A. 6 hours B. 24 hours
C. 48 hours D. 72 hours

514. Present day BCG vaccine is supplied as
A. Liquid vaccine
B. Freeze dried vaccine
C. Both A & B
D. None of the Above

515. The diluent used for reconstituting BCG vaccine is
A. Normal saline B. Distilled water
C. Dextrose D. None of the Above

516. Reconstituted BCG vaccine should be used with in
A. 3 hours B. 6 hours
C. 18 hours D. 24 hours

517. The age for BCG vaccination is recommended at
A. Birth or at 6th week
B. Only 6th week
C. 6-8 weeks
D. Within 1 year

518. At the village level sputum for AFB is collected and fixed by
A. Anganwadi worker
B. Village health guide
C. Health worker male
D. Health worker female

519. Source of most polio infections are
A. Clinical cases B. Sub clinical cases
C. Carrier D. Both B & C

520. Risk factors for development of paralytic polio include
A. 1/M injections B. Tonsillectomy
C. DPT D. All of the Above

521. Major route of transmission of Hepatitis A is
A. Facco oral route
B. Parentral route
C. Sexual transmission
D. Perinatal transmission

522. Vaccine vial monitor is present on which of these vaccines
A. BCG B. DPT
C. OPV D. Measles

523. Immunity after Hepatitis A lasts for
A. 6 months B. 1 year
C. 6 years D. Life long

524. Following methods destroy vibrio cholerae except
A. Boiling
B. Drying
C. Bleaching powder 1 mg/L
D. Cresol

525. Best method of collecting choleric stools for diagnosis is by
A. Rectal catheter B. Rectal swab
C. Disinfected stool D. All of the Above

526. All are vaccines included under the Universal Immunization Programme except
A. Diphtheria B. Pertussis
C. Measles D. MMR

527. The MTP act was passed in the year
A. 1975 B. 1971
C. 1986 D. 2000

528. All are Anti Rabies vaccine currently used in Kerala except
A. Chick embryo cell vaccine
B. Human diploid cell vaccine
C. Vero cell vaccine
D. Neural tissue vaccine

529. Annual Parasitic incidence is used to measure the problem of
A. Filariasis
B. Dengue fever
C. Malaria
D. Japanese encephalitis

530. The causative organism of plague is
A. Y pestis B. R. Prowazeki
C. Coryne bacterium D. Arbovirus

531. Which of these is a Conventional Contraceptive
A. Combined pill B. IUD
C. Condom D. Mini pill

532. Which of these insecticides is used as a space spray
A. Paris green B. Abate
C. Pyrethrum D. Mineral oil

533. Chemical ideally used for disinfecting sputum is
A. Cresol B. Dettol
C. Savlon D. Phenol

534. Census is carried out at regular intervals of
A. 5 years B. 10 years
C. 7 years D. 15 years

535. Vaccine carrier should ideally have number of ice packs
A. 1 B. 2 C. 3 D. 4

536. The dose of elemental iron in Folifer tablet given to pregnant women under the RCH programme is
A. 60 mg B. 80 mg
C. 50 mg D. 100 mg

537. Sanitary latrine should be located at least .... feet from source of contamination
A. 15 B. 25 C. 50 D. 75

538. For calculating Bacterial index in Leprosy a minimum of ..... sites should be examined
A. 4 B. 6 C. 7 D. 9

539. Number of Tetanus toxoid doses to be given to an antenatal mother with last child birth 2 years back is
A. 2 B. 1 C. 3 D. None

540. As per the Birth and Deaths Registration Act all births are to be registered with in a period of
A. 7 days B. 14 days
C. 21 days D. 1 month

541. Dengue fever is transmitted by the bite of .... mosquito
A. Anopheles B. Aedes
C. Mansonia D. Culex

542. Route of administration of BCG vaccine is
A. Intramuscular B. Intradermal
C. Subcutaneous D. Intrathecal

543. Pasteurisation of milk kills all organisms except
A. Anthrax B. M. Tuberculosis
C. Streptococcus D. Brucella

544. Prevalence of hook worm infection in a community is assessed by
A. Pearl index B. Breteaux index
C. Chandler index D. None of the Above

545. The level of iodisation of iodised salt at the consumer level as specified under the IDD control programme is
A. 40 ppm B. 30 ppm
C. 15 ppm D. 50 ppm

546. All are steps in Primary Prevention of diseases except
A. Promotion of healthy life styles
B. Good nutrition
C. Immunization
D. Treatment

547. Communicability of measles declines
A. After onset of fever
B. During prodromal period
C. At the time of eruption
D. After appearance of rash

548. After effective chlorination of water free residual chlorine shoul not be less than
A. 0.5 mg/L B. 1 mg/L
C. 50 mg/L D. 200 mg/L

549. All are side effects of oral contraceptives except
A. Hypertension
B. Cervical cancer risk
C. Gall bladder disease
D. Iron deficiency anameia

550. World AIDS day is observed on
A. December 1st B. January 31st
C. May 1st D. October 1st

551. Highest source of vitamin A is seen in
A. Cod liver oil
B. Green leafy vegetables
C. Papaya
D. Carrot

552. Which is a live vaccine
A. Hepatitis B vaccine
B. Hepatitis A vaccine
C. Oral polio vaccine
D. DPT vaccine

553. Scurvy is a deficiency disease due to
A. Vitamin A B. Vitamin D
C. Vitamin C D. Vitamin B_{12}

554. Number of sputum smears to be taken for confirmation of tuberculosis under the Revised National Tuberculosis control programme is
A. 1 B. 2 C. 3 D. 4

555. The target population under the Universal Immunization Programme is
A. Infants and antenatal mothers
B. Infants
C. Under fives
D. Under fives and antenatal mothers

556. RCH programme was launched in the year
A. 1997 B. 1992 C. 1990 D. 1998

557. Additional energy requirement to be supplemented for a lactating mother is
A. 200 calories B. 550 calories
C. 350 calories D. 100 calories

558. Dental caries is caused due to deficiency of
A. Iodine B. Iron
C. Fluorine D. Copper

559. Most ideal equipment for vaccine storage in a PHC is
A. Domestic refrigerator
B. Ice lined refrigerator
C. Cold box
D. Vaccine carrier

560. Village Health Guide is present in all these states except
A. Uttar Pradesh B. Bihar
C. Orissa D. Kerala

561. Route of transmission of pneumonic plague is
A. Vector B. Droplet
C. Formite D. Food

562. Most simple way of data presentation to a common man is
A. Bar chart B. Line diagram
C. Pictogram D. Histogram

563. The best method for operation theatre disinfection is
A. Dettol B. Phenol
C. Lysol D. Fromaldehyde

564. Primary schedule of hepatitis B immunization is
A. 0,1,6 months B. 1,3,6 months
C. 1,2,12 months D. 0,1,5 years

565. The control of ..... has led to the eradication of guinea worm disease
A. Mosquito B. Rat flea
C. Sand fly D. Cyclops

566. The confirmatory test for paralytic poliomyelitis is a
A. Stool examination B. CSF examination
C. Blood examination D. Nerve examination

567. The drug given to peripheral health worker under the Actute Respiratory infection Control Programme is
A. Tetracycline B. Cotrimoxazole
C. Doxy cycline D. Chloroquine

568. The fitration technique in modern water treatment plant is
A. Slow sand filter
B. Rapid sand filter
C. Activated sludge process
D. Double pot method

569. World Health Day is observed every year on
A. May 9th B. July 11th
C. April 7th D. July 1st

570. Health education technique most suited for introducing the correct use of O.R.S. among Rural mothers is
A. Group discussion B. Flash card
C. Demonstration D. Flannel graph

571. All are anti scabies preparations except
A. BHC B. Permethrin
C. Benzyl benzoate D. Malathion

572. All are tests used for bacteriological quality testing of drinking water except
A. Multiple tube method
B. Membrane filtration technique
C. Colony court
D. Biological oxygen demand

573. During an epidemic of cholera, wells should be disinfected ideally
A. Every day B. 2 days
C. 3 days D. 1 week

574. All are components of under five clinic except
A. Immunization
B. Growth monitoring
C. Oral rehydration
D. Referral treatment

575. All are true of prevention of Food Adulteration Act except
A. Prescribes minimum standards
B. Is not mandatory
C. Punishment includes imprisonment
D. Latest amendment was in the year 1986

576. Physical quality of life index includes all except
A. Infant mortality
B. Life expectancy at age one
C. Per capita GNP
D. Literacy

577. Incubation period is less than 3 days in all the following except
A. Influenza
B. Cholera
C. Mumps
D. Staphylococcal food poisoning

578. The type of influenza virus causing epidemics every year is
A. A B. B
C. C D. One of the Above

579. The incubation period of Rabies in men is determined by
A. Site of bite B. Severity of bite
C. Number of wounds D. All of the Above

580. Nosocomial infection means
A. Infection of nose
B. Hospital acquired infection
C. Notifiable disease
D. New disease

581. All of the following are mosquito borne diseases except
A. Malaria
B. Filaria
C. Kysanur forest disease
D. Dengue fever

582. Which is not true of small pox
A. No animal reservoir
B. No carrier stage
C. No sub-clinical infection
D. No air borne transmission

583. ORS contains all except
A. Sodium chloride
B. Potassium sulphate
C. Trisodium citrate
D. Glucose

584. The danger zone for bacterial growth in food is
A. 10-49 degree C B. 20-49 degree C
C. 10-60 degree C D. 20-60 degree C

585. Aldehyde test is used for the diagnosis of
A. Malaria
B. Kala Azar
C. Japanese encephalitis
D. Typhus fever

586. The period from disease initiation to disease detection in chronic disease is called
A. Incubation period B. Serial interval
C. Latent period D. Median period

587. Herd immunity does not protect an individual in
A. Diphtheria B. Poliomyelitis
C. Small pox D. Tetanus

588. Vaccines which should not be frozen include
A. Typhoid B. DPT
C. TT D. All of the Above

589. ILR stands for
A. Income Literacy Ratio
B. Illiteracy- Literacy Ratio
C. Ice Lined Refrigerator
D. Infant Living Rate

590. Cold chain equipment used at out reach sites is
A. Cold box B. Vaccine carrier
C. Ice pack D. Freezer

591. Most heat sensitive vaccine is
A. BCG B. Polio
C. Measles D. DPT

592. Zero dose of polio vaccine means
A. No vaccination
B. Dose before first dose
C. No antibody response
D. Vaccination at mobile camps

593. Pasteurisation of milk is an example disinfection
A. Pre current B. Con current
C. Terminal D. Absolute

594. Boiling for 5-10 minutes kills
A. Bacteria B. Spores
C. Virus D. None of the Above

595. All of the following can be sterilized by Auto claving except
A. Gloves B. Culture media
C. Plastics D. Linen

596. All are suitable for disinfection of faces and urine except
A. 8% bleaching powder
B. 1% crude phenol
C. 5% cresol
D. 1-2% formalin

597. Ideally bed pans and urinals are sterilized using
A. 1% cresol B. Bleaching powder
C. Steam D. All of the Above

598. Sputum is best disposed by
A. Burning B. Boiling
C. 5% cresol D. Any of the Above

599. Immunity conferred by an attack of small pox is for
A. 10 years B. 15 years
C. 20 years D. Life long

600. Which is not true regarding measles
A. Source of infection is a case
B. Secondary attack rate is 80%
C. Carries do not occur
D. Sub clinical measles not known

601. A sub-center is meant to be there for every …… population in Hilly areas
A. 1000 B. 3000
C. 5000 D. 10000

602. One primary health center should be there for every ……. rural population in the plains
A. 10000 B. 20000
C. 30000 D. 40000

603. Hind Kusht Nivaran Sangh is a voluntary agency related to the disease:
A. Tuberculosis B. Leprosy
C. Malaria D. Filaria

604. The colour of the center square in the vaccine vial monitor in a well stored polio vaccine should be:
A. White B. Violet
C. Blue D. Pink

605. The world Health Day is celebrated on
A. March 1st B. April 7th
C. July 1st D. December 1st

606. GOBI campaign of the UNICEF includes all except:
A. Growth monitoring B. Observation
C. Breast feeding D. Immunization

607. The international agency providing support for the National Blindness Control Programme is:

A. DANIDA B. SIDA
C. USAID D. CARE

608. Major symptoms of an AIDS patient is:
A. Weight loss B. Diarrhea
C. Fever D. All of the Above

609. The ideal weight for an adult person is calculated on the basis of his:
A. Age B. Height
C. Economic status D. All of the Above

610. Risk factors for developing coronary heart disease include:
A. Smoking B. Hypertension
C. Serum Cholesterol D. All of the Above

611. The salt intake per day should be kept to a limit of:
A. 1 gm daily B. 5 gm daily
C. 10 gm daily D. 15 gm daily

612. A normal blood pressure is said to be about:
A. 300 / 200 B. 200 / 150
C. 120 / 80 D. 70 / 40

613. Pulse rate of babies is:
A. More than adults B. Less than adults
C. Same as adults D. No fixed pattern

614. Normal respiratory rates in adults is about:
A. 5/ min B. 10/min
C. 17/min D. 27/min

615. Streptococcal throat infection can later lead to:
A. Tuberculosis
B. Leprosy
C. Rheumatic heart Disease
D. Malaria

616. India's population at present is about:
A. Ten Thousand B. One Million
C. One Billion D. Ten Billion

617. While calculating birth rates the denominator used is:
A. Live births
B. Mid-year population
C. Census population
D. None of the Above

618. The objective of National population policy is to bring the total fertility rates to replacement level by:
A. 2005 B. 2010
C. 2015 D. 2020

619. A woman is expected to attend the antenatal clinic at least ..... / month during the first 7 months:
A. One B. Twice
C. Thrice D. Four times

620. On an average a normal healthy woman should gain about ..... kg of weight during pregnancy
A. 5 kg B. 12 kg
C. 20 kg D. 30 kg

621. An unimmunised mother should be given ..... doses of Tetanus toxoid during pregnancy
A. One B. Two
C. Three D. Four

622. The extra amount of calories required during pregnancy is:
A. 300 Kcal B. 440 Kcal
C. 550 Kcal D. 600 Kcal

623. At one year of age a baby should weigh around:
A. 5 kg B. 10 kg
C. 15 kg D. 20 kg

624. As per Baby friendly hospital initiative breast feeding by the mother after normal delivery should be started within:
A. One hour B. Five hours
C. 10 hours D. 24 hours

625. Under the ICDS programme the amount of protein provided for children between 1-6yrs is:
A. 5 gms B. 10 gms
C. 15 gms D. 20 gms

626. Father of medicine is:
A. Hippocrates
B. Aesculapius
C. Susrutha
D. Thomas Syndenham

627. James Lind is related to the disease:
A. Small pox B. Scurvy
C. Scabies D. Scoliosis

628. DPT vaccination is related to the disease:
A. Polio B. Measles
C. Pertussis D. All of the Above

629. Chicken pox is caused due to a:
A. Virus B. Bacteria
C. Fungus D. Protozoa

630. Measles vaccine is given under the National Immunization Programme
A. 1 month B. 6 months
C. 9 months D. 15 months

631. The classical triad of Rubella include:
A. Cataract
B. Cardiac Malformation
C. Deafness
D. All of the Above

632. BCG vaccination is given to protect against:
A. Tuberculosis B. Meningitis
C. Chicken pox D. All of the Above

633. Oral polio vaccine:
A. Live vaccine
B. Killed vaccine
C. Freeze dried vaccine
D. Recombinant vaccine

634. Hepatitis A virus is mainly transmitted through:
A. Faeco-oral route
B. Parental route
C. Sexual transmission
D. Blood transmission

635. Rice water stools is seen in:
A. Cholera B. Typhoid
C. Salmonellosis D. Botulism

636. DOTS is related to the disease:
A. Leprosy B. Tuberculosis
C. Hepatitis D. Malaria

637. Ancylostomiasis is the other name for
A. Hook worm B. Round worm
C. Tape worm D. Guinea worm

638. The worm infestation eliminated from India is:
A. Hook worm B. Round worm
C. Tape worm D. Guinea worm

639. Dengue fever is transmitted by:
A. Aedes B. Culex
C. Anopheles D. Mansonia

640. Malaria is caused by:
A. Bacteria B. Protozoan
C. Virus D. Fungus

641. The disease not present in India is
A. Dengue
B. Yellow fever
C. Japanese encephalitis
D. Kyasanur forest disease

642. Leptospirosis is transmitted through:
A. Rat urine B. Rat bite
C. Mosquito D. Dog bite

643. Beef tape worm is:
A. Taenia saginata
B. Taenia solium
C. Echinococcus granulosis
D. Guenia worm

644. Trachoma is a disease related to:
A. Eyes B. Ears
C. Nose D. Throat

645. Leprosy should be treated for a minimum period of:
A. Life long B. 20 yrs
C. 5 yrs D. 6-12 months

646. Gonorrhea is a disease transmitted through
A. Food B. Needle prick
C. Blood transfusion D. Sexually

647. Modifiable risk factors in case of hypertension include all except
A. Age B. Obesity
C. Salt intake D. Alcohol intake

648. Rheumatic heart disease is related to the condition:
A. Throat infection B. Ear infection
C. Eye infection D. Leg infection

649 Goiter is related to the gland:
A. Pancreas B. Thyroid
C. Parotid D. Adrenals

650. Diabetes is caused due to deficiency of:
A. Insulin B. Ptyalin
C. Thyroxin D. Glucagon

651. Most common cause of blindness in India is:
A. Cataract
B. Glaucoma
C. Refractive index
D. Vitamin A deficiency

652. Barrier method of contraception is:
A. Condom
B. Intraoeuterine device
C. Oral pills
D. Injectables

653. One gram of protein will give .... Kcal/gm
A. 4 B. 9 C. 12 D. 15

654. The reference protein is:
A. Egg B. Milk
C. Meat D. Fish

655. Limiting Amino acid in plus is:
A. Lysine B. Threonine
C. Methionine D. Valine

656. The amount of protein required by an Indian adult is ...... grm protein/kg body wt.
A. 0.5 B. 1 C. 5 D. 10

657. Saturated fatty acids are all except
A. Auric B. Palmitic
C. Stearic D. Oleic

658. Deficiency of vitamin D causes
A. Rickets B. Scurvy
C. Night blindness D. All of the Above

659. Pellagra is a deficiency disease caused due to the deficiency of
A. Riboflavin B. Thiamine
C. Niacin D. Folate

660. Rich source of vitamin A is
A. Ripe papaya
B. Ripe mango
C. Green leafy vegetables
D. All of the Above

661. The mineral that is associated with anemia is:
A. Calcium B. Iron
C. Magnesium D. Sodium

662. Infections primarily of animals that can be transmitted through milk is all except
A. Tuberculosis B. Brucellosis
C. Q fever D. Malaria

663. The addition of colouring agents to food is called
A. Food additives B. Food adulteration
C. Food fortification D. None of the Above

664. As per the Mid-day meal programme the meals should supply at least ...... of the total energy requirement
A. 1/3rd B. 1/4th
C. 1/2 D. 3/4th

665. The type of learning relating to skills is:
A. Cognitive B. Affective
C. Psychomotor D. All of the Above

666. The average population of a village in India is estimated to be:
A. 5000 B. 2500
C. 1500 D. 550

667. The amount of bleaching powder required to disinfect 1000 liters of water is
A. 1.5 gms B. 2.5 gms
C. 3.5 gms D. 4.5 gms

668. Hardness of water can be caused due to
A. Chlorides B. Sulphates
C. Nitrates D. All of the Above

669. Free and combined chlorine in water can be determined using:
A. Orthotoludine test
B. Methylene blue test
C. Phosphatase test
D. All of the Above

670. In a house window area should be at least .... of the floor area
A. 1/20th B. 1/10th
C. 1/5th D. 1/2

671. Overcrowding is said to exist if .... no of persons over 9 yrs of age not husband and wife, of opposite sexes are obliged to sleep in the same room
A. 2 B. 3 C. 4 D. 5

672. The method of waste disposal in which waste is disposed along with night soil is known as
A. Dumping B. Tipping
C. Composting D. Incineration

673. The mosquito which lays its eggs on the leaves of certain aquatic plants is
A. Aedes B. Anopheles
C. Mansonia D. Culex

674. The tiger mosquito is
A. Anopheles. B. Culex
C. Aedes D. Mansonia

675. Biological control of mosquitoes is by using
A. Minerals oils B. Fishes
C. Insecticides D. All of the Above

676. Lindane is a:
A. DDT B. BHC
C. Malathion D. Fention

677. Zinc phosphide is an efficient
A. Rodenticide B. Insecticide
C. Bactericide D. Disinfectant

678. Bird flu is caused by:
A. Virus B. Bacteria
C. Fungus D. Protozoa

679. The normal human body contains
A. 20 chromosomes B. 25 chromosomes
C. 36 chromosomes D. 46 chromosomes

680. Among the blood groups the blood group considered as the universal donor is
A. A group B. B group
C. AB group D. O group

681 The sex chromosome composition of XO is related to
A. Turners syndrome
B. Klienfelters syndrome
C. Super female
D. None of the Above

682 Erythroblastosis foetalis is a disease related to
A. Blood groups B. Red blood cells
C. White blood cells D. Platelets

683 Births and deaths should be registered with in
A. 7 days B. 14 days
C. 21 days D. 30 days

684 The census is taken at intervals of
A. 5 yrs B. 10 yrs
C. 15 yrs D. 20 yrs

685 The diseases notifiable to the WHO under the international Regulation Act are all except
A. Cholera B. Plague
C Yellow fever D. Diphtheria

686. The best method to present data to the man on the street is:
A. Bar chart
B. Pie chart
C. Pictogram
D. Frequency polygon

687. When a set of numbers is arranged in ascending or descending order and the center number is taken it is called a:
A. Mean B. Median
C. Mode D. Range

688. Socratic method of communication is
A. One-way B. Two-way
C. Verbal D. Non-verbal

689. The recommended illumination required for casual reading is
A. 50 lux B. 100 lux
C. 300 lux D. None of the Above

690. A daily exposure of.... dB is about the limit people can tolerate without substantial damage to bearing
A. 35 B. 55 C. 65 D. 85

691. The best method that can be used to teach mothers on how to use oral rehydration solution is
A. Lecture B. Flash cards
C. Demonstration D. Panel discussion

692. Message in a poster created for health education should be
A. Short B. Simple
C. Direct D. All of the Above

693. Resource for health planning are:
A. Man power B. Money
C. Material D. All of the Above

694. The committee that visualized the development of primary health center is:
A. Bhore Committee
B. Mukerji Committee
C. Chadah Committee
D. Shrivastav Committee

695. Zila parishad is at the:
A. Village level B. Town level
C. Block level D. District level

696. The drug used for tuberculosis include all except
A. Dapsone B. Rifampicin
C. Ethambutol D. Isoniazid

697. Crude death rate in India as per the latest population statistics is:
A. 25 B. 20 C. 15 D. 8

698. Infant mortality rate in Kerala is about ..... / 1000 live births
A. 67 B. 50 C. 25 D. 14

699. Sex ratio in Kerala is ...... / 1000 males
A. 850 B. 933
C. 1000 D. 1058

700. As per the ICDS scheme an Anganwadi worker is meant to be there for every....population
A. 500 B. 1000
C. 3000 D. 5000

701. Mode of transmission of Pertussis:
A. Vector transmission
B. Through contaminated water
C. Droplet infection
D. Faecoaral

702. Time required to measure the Mantaux test:
A. 24 to 48 hrs B. 48 to72 hrs
C. 10 to12 hrs D. 2 to 4 hrs

703. Name of the oral Polio Vaccine:
A. BCG B. TAB
C. Salk D. Sabin

704. The following are the standard tuberculosis drug except:
A. Chloromycin B. Streptomycin
C. INH D. PAS

705. Combination of Tripple Antigen:
A. DPT B. BCG
C. TAB D. ECG

706. The time interval between infection of suspected person and the appearance of signs and symptom of the disease is called
A. Quarrentine B. Recovery period
C. Incubation D. Isolation period

707. Route of transmission of Hepatitis B:
A. Oral
B. Parenteral
C. Faeco oral
D. Contaminated water

708. Mode of transmission of typhoid fever:
A. Intravenous B. Oro faceal
C. Respiratory D. Droplet

709. Causative organism of diphtheria:
A. Mycobacteria
B. Streptococcus
C. Coryne Bacterium diphtheria
D. Staphylococcus

710. Incubation period of measles:
A. 1-7 days B. 7-14 days
C. 14-21 days D. 21-28 days

711. Site for mantaux test:
A. Outer and upper quadrant of gluteus maximus
B. Deltoid region
C. Posterior left forearm
D. Anterior left forearm

712. Media of transmission of bovine type of tubercle bacili:
A. Milk B. Water
C. Air D. Food

713. Painful Micturition:
A. Eneuresis B. Dysuria
C. Rentention of urine D. Diarrhoea

714. Amount of solution used for evacuant enema in adults:
A. 100-250 ml B. 250-350 ml
C. 500-1000 ml D. 1000-1500 ml

715. Drugs used to relieve pain:
A. Anti inflammatory B. Antipyretics
C. Antibiotics D. Analgesics

716. Hormone secreted by the testes:
A. Oestrogen B. Pitocin
C. Androgens D. Progesterone

717. One teaspoon contains .... ml

A. 2 ml B. 5 ml
C. 10 ml D. 15 ml

718. One ml contains .... drops

A. 5 drops B. 10 drops
C. 15 drops D. 20 drops

719. Average weight of a new born baby:

A. 2 kg B. 4 kg
C. 3 kg D. 5 kg

720. How much salt must be added to one litre of water to make a solution of normal saline?

A. 2 grams B. 5 grams
C. 6 grams D. 9 grams

721. Number of vertebra in the sacrum:

A. 5 B. 3 C. 4 D. 1

722. Number of chromosome in a cell:

A. 23 B. 44 C. 46 D. 40

723. A trial septal defect occurs due to the persistence of:

A. Formen ovale B. Ductus arteriosis
C. Ductus venosus D. Mitral valve

724. .... is a water soluble vitamin:

A. Vitamin A B. Vitamin K
C. Vitamin B D. Vitamin D

725. Quickening means:

A. Hearing of the fetal heart sound
B. Sudden cessation of Menstruation
C. The movement of the feuts in the uterus felt by the mother
D. Nausa and vomiting in the morning

726. Cholera is caused by a kind of bacterium called:

A. Tubercle bacillus
B. Vibrio cholerae
C. Protozoa
D. Entamoeba histolytica

727. Drinking of alcohol will severely effects the

A. Kidney B. Brain
C. Stomach D. Liver

728. The disease in which the patients blood does not clot easily is:

A. Sickle cell anaemia B. Haemophilia
C. Rabies D. Diabetes

729. Discolouration of teeth is caused by a kind of antibiotics called

A. Streptomycin B. Neomycin
C. Tetracycline D. Penicillin

730. .... is caused by the fungus

A. Malaria B. Athletes foot
C. Filariasis D. Typhus fever

731. The Filariasis is transmitted by ....

A. Anopheles female mosquito
B. Anopheles male mosquito
C. Culex female mosquito
D. Culex male mosquito

732. The blood group contain no antibodies:

A. A B. B C. O D. AB

733. The disease that spread through sexual contact is ....

A. Leprosy B. AIDS
C. Itches D. Scabies

734. Typhoid is transmitted through –

A. Water and food B. Air
C. Touch D. Personal contact

735. .... is example for the disease caused by bacteria:

A. Cold B. Typhoid
C. Typhus fever D. Chicken pox

736. .... is the immunity get by the body after the first attack of disease.

A. Natural immunity
B. Passive immunity
C. Artificial immunity
D. Acquired immunity

737. The cells that are responsible for the production of antibodies are ....

A. Red blood cells B. Platelets
C. Plasma D. White blood cells

738. A healthy person can donate blood ...... or ..... times a year.

A. Six or seven B. Five or six
C. Three or four D. Two or three

739. Radio active cobalt and radium are used for the treatment of –diseases.

A. Cholera
B. Haemophilia
C. Cancer
D. Sickle cell anaemia

740. World health day is on ......

A. May 12th B. April 7th
C. April 30th D. December 18th

741. To relieve from dyspnoea the appropriate position to be used is:

A. Prone position B. Supine position
C. Side lying position D. Fowler's position

742. Protein requirement for a pregnant woman per day:

A. 50grams B. 55 grams
C. 60 grams D. 65 grams

743. The findus is at the level of umbilicus during .... week pregnancy

A. 16 B. 20 C. 24 D. 28

744. Total weight gain during pregnancy is

A. 7-8 kg B. 10-11 kg
C. 13-14 kg D. 15-16 kg

745. The birth weight of the baby doubles at the age of

A. 3 months B. 6 months
C. 9 months D. 12 months

746. Infancy period is from

A. Birth to one month
B. One month to 1 year
C. 1 years to 3 years
D. 3 years to 5 years

747. The following are the signs of dehydration except:

A. Sunken tearless eyes
B. Loss of skin elasticity
C. Diuresis
D. Depressed fintenelle

748. The following are the contests of ORS except:

A. Sodium chloride
B. Sugar
C. Potassium Chloride
D. Calcium Carbonate

749. The most common from of malnutrition are the following except

A. Beri-Beri
B. Protein energy malnutrition
C. Marasmus
D. Kwashiorkor

750. The first course of oral pills should be stared on the ..... day of menstrual cycle.

A. 2nd B. 7th C. 5th D. 10th

751. The following are the natural method of contraception except:

A. Foam tablet
B. Basal metabolic temperature
C. Rhythm method
D. Safe period

752. .... is the permanent method of sterilization.

A. MTP B. Diaphragm
C. Tubectomy D. D & C

753. The following organs are situated in the abdominal cavity except:

A. Stomach B. Oesophagus
C. Liver D. Spleen

754. The system of body which helps for the removal of waste matter from body:

A. Digestive system
B. Endocrine system
C. Respiratory system
D. Excretory system

755. Total number of bones in human body:

A. 306 B. 206 C. 106 D. 406

756. Eruption of teeth starts at the age of .... month

A. 4 months B. 6 months
C. 8 months D. 10 months

757. The never, which carries messages from the brain and spinal cord muscles and glands:

A. Motor nerve B. Sensory nerve
C. Mixed nerve D. Autonomic nerve

758. Speech centre is situated in:

A. Perietal lobe B. Frontal lobe
C. Occipital lobe D. Temporal lobe

759. Largest gland in the body:

A. Pituitary gland B. Adrenal gland
C. Liver D. Gall bladder

760. Head control of the infant occurs at the age of ...... month

A. 2 B. 3 C. 5 D. 6

761. Peurparium is the period begins:

A. As soon as the placenta is expelled and last for 6 to 8 weeks
B. As soon as the baby is expelled and last for 6 to 8 weeks
C. As soon as the membrane ruptures and last for 6 to 8 weeks
D. As soon as the placenta is expelled and last for 10 to 12 weeks

762. When the umbilical cord lies in front of the presenting part and the membranes are intact it is known as:

A. Cord prolapse B. Cord presentation
C. Cord pulsation D. Cord delivery

763. Starting of menstrual cycle is called:

A. Ovulation B. Menstruation
C. Menarche D. Menopause

764. Normal blood urea level is:

A. 40-60 mg% B. 20-40 mg%
C. 10-20 mg% D. 80-120 mg%

765. One gram of carbohydrate yields:

A. 4 calories B. 8 calories
C. 9 calories D. 1 calorie

766. A method of making the victim to breath passively

A. Artificial respiration
B. Spontaneous respiration
C. Deep breathing
D. Kusmal breathing

767. Minute, this walled blood vessels between the ends of the arteries and beginning of veins is called:

A. Arteries B. Veins
C. Capillaries D. Alveoli

768. A waste gas produced by the body and exhaled through the lungs is:

A. Carbon dioxide B. Carbon monoxide
C. Nitrogen peroxide D. Oxygen

769. A condition characterized by moving of bones out joint:
A. Fracture B. Sprain
C. Strain D. Dislocation

770. A tube of muscular tissue carrying ingested food from the mouth to stomach:
A. Oesophagus B. Duodenum
C. Trachea D. Pharynx

771. A red pigment in the blood cells which combines with oxygen and carbon dioxide for carrying them:
A. Red blood cells B. Haemoglobin
C. Platelet D. Plasma

772. Information given by the sufferer about his illness:
A. Sign B. Symptom
C. Observation D. Diagnosis

773. Normal respiratory rate in adults is:
A. 20–40 breath/mint
B. 40 – 60 breath/mint
C. 16 – 20 breath/mint
D. 10 – 15 breath/mint

774. The normal body temperature is .... 0C.
A. 35ºC B. 37ºC
C. 40ºC D. 42ºC

775. Characteristic of the blood flow due to arterial bleeding is the following except:
A. Bright red in colour
B. Spunts at each contraction of the heart
C. Flow is pulsatile
D. Dark red in colour

776. An agent that has power to kill Micro-organism:
A. Bacteriostat B. Bacteriocide
C. Antiseptic D. Bacteriostasis

777. Strength of savlon forcleaning of wounds:
A. 1:10 B. 1:100
C. 1:1000 D. 1:10000

778. Inflammation of the tongue:
A. Glossitis B. Gingivitis
C. Stomatitis D. Parotitis

779. Following are predisposing cause for bedsore except:
A. Impaired circulation B. Lowered vitality
C. Emaciation D. Anorexia

780. Inability to sleep is termed as:
A. Dyspepsia B. Dyspnaea
C. Anorexia D. Insomnia

781. Tobacco contains a poisonous substance called
A. Nicotine B. Narcotics
C. Alcohol D. Caffeine

782. A disease caused by allergic disease is called
A. Asthma B. Tuberculosis
C. Cancer D. Gastroenteritis

783. An adult has ...... litres of blood in his body.
A. 7-8 B. 5-6
C. 9-10 D. 2-3

784. Several persons in a town got the attack of leukemia. Which of the following can be possible reason for that?
A. Exposed to radiation
B. Drinking polluted water
C. Smoking
D. Breathing in impure air

785. The energy value of .... is more than that of others
A. Fats B. Starch
C. Protein D. Sugar

786. The product formed when amino acid molecules combine together is called
A. Nucleic acid B. Starch
C. Carbohydrate D. Proteins

787. Women having normal limbs may sometimes give birth to babies with deformed limbs. This must be due to:
A. Spontaneous generation
B. Mutation
C. Inheritance of acquired character
D. Natural selection

788. Hormones are transported to all parts of the body through the
A. Nerves B. Blood
C. Lymph D. Muscles

789. Deficiency of ...... in food causes simple goiter.
A. Sodium B. Iron
C. Iodine D. Calcium

790. Cortisone is used as an effective anti-inflamatory drug in the treatment of ....
A. High blood pressure
B. Arteroisclerosis
C. Arthritis
D. Diabetes

791. Deficiency of thyroxin in adults leads to a condition called:
A. Tetani B. Cretinism
C. Myxoedema D. Graves diseases

792. The hormone that is injected to pregnant women at the time of delivery is
A. Vasopressin B. Oxytocin
C. Androgen D. Oestrogen

793. The outer layer of the eye ball is
A. Sclera B. Choroids
C. Retina D. Conjunctiva

794. The smallest bone in the human body is
A. Malleus B. Incus
C. Stapes D. Sternum

795. Central nervous system includes:
A. The brain and cranial nerves
B. The cranial nerves and spinal cord
C. The spinal nerves and brain
D. The spinal nerves and brain

796. Short sightedness can be corrected by using spectacles with ..... lens.
A. Concave B. Convex
C. Cylindrical D. Opaque

797. Normal sugar level in our blood is:
A. 95-125 mg/100ml B. 65-130 mg/100ml
C. 80-120 mg/100ml D. 90-140 mg/100 ml

798. Labour takes place after ...... days of last menstrual period
A. 300 B. 280
C. 365 D. 240

799. Signs of true labour are the following except:
A. Painful rhythmic uterine contraction
B. Dilatation of the OS
C. Fetal movement
D. Show

800. Signs of separation of placenta are the following except:
A. Lengthening of the cord at vulva
B. Gush of blood is seen
C. Fundus risas upto umbilicus
D. Temperature rises

801. Spot the correct statement in terms of "Epispadias". It is an abnormal urethral opening on the
A. Ventral aspect of the penis
B. Urethral serotal junction
C. Shaft of the penis
D. Dorsal aspect of the penis

802. To achieve net reproduction rate of 1, the couple protection rate should be?
A. 50% B. 65% C. 55% D. 60%

803. The causative organism for Varicella is
A. Corynebacterium diphtheriae
B. C. tetani
C. Bordetella pertusis
D. Varicella zoster virus

804. Best indicator of fertility
A. GFR (General fertility rate)
B. TFR (Total fertility rate)
C. CBR (Crude birth rate)
D. NRR (Net reproductive rate)

805. "Universal children is day" November 14th was initiated by
A. WHO B. UNICEF
C. ICDS D. NGO

806. Very wide gap between the birth and death rates is celled as
A. Life expectancy gap
B. Age gap
C. Population gap
D. Dempgraphic gap

807. The procedure of 'Quarantine' was introduced to protect against importation of:
A. Yellow fever B. Cholera
C. Leprosy D. Plague

808. The census count is taken only once in_____ years
A. 5 B. 10 C. 15 D. 20

809. Among the following which is matched wrongly
A. Domestic refuse — Vegetable peel-ings
B. Street refuse — Markets
C. Stable refuse — Metal scrapping
D. Constructional refuse — Stone pieces

810. Who is the president of trainad nurses association of india?
A. Mrs. Anitha Malik B. Sr. (Prof.) Gilbert
C. Mrs. Shiela Seda D. Mrs. Gracy Mathai

811. Point out the wrong option in the following Indicators helping for monitoring progress towards health for all
A. Health policy indicators
B. Social and economic indicators
C. Health status indicators
D. Environmental indicators

812. Basic unit of health care delivery service is:
A. District hospitals
B. Sub centres situated in the village
C. Primary health centres
D. Community Health centres

813. What is the housing standards prescription of floor space area for one person?
A. 100 sqft B. 150 sqft
C. 200 sqft D. 250 sqft

814. Reproductive and child health programme (R.C.H.) launched in 1997, is a continuation and modification of...... ..programme.
A. C.S.S.M B. M.C.H
C. I.C.D. S D. F.H.I

815. Measles is otherwise called as
A. Rubeola B. Rubella
C. Small pox D. Varicella

816. Government of India re-designated national family planning programme as national family welfare programme in the year:
A. 1975 B. 1977 C. 1953 D. 1969

817. Three tier structure of rural local government in India is
A. Community development block
B. Taluks
C. Town
D. Panchayat raj

818. Nosocomial infection means:
A. Infection acquired from hospital
B. Infection from animal source
C. Infection from mosquito bite
D. Infection acquired from home care

819. The specific instructions that has to be followed by the community health nurse during 'Home visit is called as
A. Prescription B. Job description
C. Standing orders D. Procedure manual

820. The best time for 1UD insertion is between which days of menstruation cycle?
A. Within 1 days B. 3 to 7 days
C. 8 to 12 days D. 13 to 14 days

821. The nucleus of health service in rural area is:
A. Sub centres
B. Primary health centre
C. Community health centre
D. Rural hosptials

822. The metal which is commonly used for family planning is:
A. Silver B. Iron
C. Aluminium D. Copper

823. The objective of W.H.O. is:
A. To promote the well being of mankind through out the world
B. To help the poorer nations
C. Assist for the development of countries
D. The attainment by all people of the highest level of health

824. Mala D is an example of:
A. Foam tablet
B. Pill form
C. Inject able contraceptive
D. Vaginal diaphragm

825. Which committee is known as the health surgery and planning committee?
A. Bhore committee
B. Mudaliyar committee
C. Kartar committee
D. Shrivastar committee

826. The multipurpose worker in general serves a rural population of:
A. 5000 B. 500
C. 1000 D. 3000

827. Religion is an important institution of
A. Social process B. Social control
C. Community D. Modernization

828. The system of storing and transporting vaccines is termed:
A. Vaccination B. Cold chain
C. Freezer chain D. Cool chain

829. Tertiary prevention is needed in which stage of the natural history of disease?
A. Prepathogenesis B. Pathogenesis
C. Predromal D. Terminal

830. Keratomalacia is associated with:
A. Chickenpox B. Measles
C. Mumps D. Rubella

831. Match the following and write the code given as below

A.	Typhoid fever	1. Pharyngeal paral-ysis
B.	Whooping cough	2. Intestinal perfora-tion
C.	Diphtheria	3. Atelectasis
D.	Mumps	4. Deafness

	A.	B.	C.	D.
A.	3	2	1	4
B.	2	3	4	1
C.	2	4	3	1
D.	2	3	1	4

832. The PHN bag is an important tool in providing nursing care during a home visit. The most important principle in bag technique states that it;
A. Should save time and effort
B. Should minimize if not totally prevent the spread of infection
C. Should not overshadow concern for the patient and his family
D. May be done in variety of ways depending on the home situation,etc.

833. Incubation period for mumps is:
A. 31 days B. 18 days
C. 7 days D. 3 days

834. The back bone of public health nursing is:
A. Immunization
B. School health programme
C. Nutritional programme
D. Home visiting

835. Which of the following gives lifelong immunity after an attack?
A. Diphtheria B. Typhoid
C. Mumps D. Tetanus

836. Central births and death registration act came into force on:
A. 7th April 1980
B. 1st April 1970
C. 12th May 1990
D. 10th November 1990

837. Communication period of chickenpox is:
A. Only up to fever lasts
B. Till last scab falls off
C. 4-5 days after rash
D. Only during incubation period

838. Which of the following is a function of epidemiology?
A. Identifying the disease condition based on manifestations presented by a client
B. Determining factors that contributed to the occurrence of pneumonia in a 3 year old
C. Determining the efficacy of the antibiotic used in the treatment of the 3 year old client with pneumonia
D Evaluating the effectiveness of the implementation of the Integrated Management of Childhood Illness

839. Rice water stools are observed in:
A. Amoebic dysentery B. Typhoid
C. Cholera D. Food poisoning

840. Government of india launched national health mission (NRHM) on:
A. 7th April 1977
B. 14th November 1953
C. 5th April 2005
D. 1st December 1975

841. The infection which is acquired from animals to human is:
A. Malaria B. Plague
C. Polio D. Pertrussis

842. The most important diagnostic test in malaria:
A. Erythrocyte sedimentation rate
B. Smear of peripheral blood
C. Blood leucocyte count
D. Splenic puncture

843. The most common cause of Urinary Tract Infection (UTI) in community is:
A. E. coli B. Shigella
C. Vibrio cholera D. Proteus Vulgaris

844. The key for effective communication is:
A. Hearing B. Listening
C. Talking D. Sharing

845. Hookworm penetrates into the body by penetrating the skin of:
A. Head B. Foot
C. Arm D. Hand

846. The universal immunization launched on:
A. 14th November 1985
B. 4th July 1987
C. 2nd October 1987
D. 19th November 1985

847. The common cause for bacterial sore throat is:
A. Mycobacterium
B. Streptococcus pyogenes
C. Mycoplasma pneumonia
D. Corynebacterium

848. The number of cases of Dengue fever usually increases towards the end of the rainy season. This pattern of occurrence of Dengue fever is best described as;
A. Epidemic occurrence
B. Cyclical variation
C. Sporadic occurrence
D. Secular occurrence

849. Malaria infection can be transmitted by:
A. Blood transfusion
B. Bite of infected female anopheles mosquito
C. Vertical transmission through placental defect
D. All of the Above

850. Primary health care is a total approach to community development. Which of the following is an indicator of success in the use of the primary health care approach ?
A. Health services are provided free of charge to individuals and families
B. Local officials are empowered as the major decision makers in matters of health
C. Health workers are able too provide care based on identified health needs of the people
D. Health programs are sustained according to the level of development of the community

851. The immunoglobulin found in mother's breast milk is:
A. IgA B. IgM
C. IgD D. IgE

852. Weils disease otherwise called:
A. Leukoderma B. Leprosy
C. Lyphoma D. Leptospirosis

853. Schick's test indicates the infection of:
A. Rubella B. Measles
C. Mumps D. Diphtheria

854. You are computing the crude rate of your municipality, with a total population of about 18,000 for last year. There were 94 deaths. Among those who died, 20 died because of diseases of the heart and 32 were aged 50 years or older. What is the crude death rate?
A. 4.1/1000 B. 5.2/1000
C. 6.3/1000 D. 7.3/1000

855. Widal test is performed for identifying:
A. Meningococcal B. Clostridium
C. Salmonella D. Staphylococcus

856. Time required to measure the Mantaux test:
A. 24 to 48 hrs B. 48 to 72 hrs
C. 10 to 12 hrs D. 2 to 4 hrs

857. Endemic disaese refer to those occur:
A. Generally throughout the entire population
B. Sporadically throughout the entire population
C. In a large population in a localized geographical area
D. In a limited population in a localized geographical area

858. Name of the oral Polio Vaccine:
A. BCG B. TAB
C. Salk D. Sabin

859. The following are the standard tuberculosis drug except:
A. Chloromycin B. Streptomycin
C. INH D. Rifampicin

860. Combination of Tripple Antigen:
A. DPT B. BCG
C. TAB D. ECG

861. The time interval between infection of suspected person and the appearance of signs and symptom of the disease is called
A. Quarrentine B. Recovery period
C. Incubation D. Isolation period

862. Route of transmission of Hepatitis B:
A. Oral
B. Parenteral
C. Faecooral
D. Contaminated water

863. Mode of transmission of typhoid fever:
A. Intravenous B. Oro faceal
C. Respiratory D. Droplet

864. Causative organism of diphtheria:
A. Mycobacteria
B. Streptococcus
C. Coryne Bacterium diphtheria
D. Staphylococcus

865. Incubation period of measles:
A. 1-7 days B. 7-14 days
C. 14-21 days D. 21-28 days

866. Site for mantaux test:
A. Outer and upper quadrant of gluteus maximus
B. Deltoid region
C. Posterior left forearm
D. Anterior left forearm

867. Media of transmission of bovine type of tubercle bacilli:
A. Milk B. Water
C. Air D. Food

868. Fever with relative bradycardia is seen in:
A. Malaria B. Diphtheria
C. Typhoid D. Filaria

869. Which one of the following is not a oral contraceptive pill?
A. Cortisol only pill
B. Estrogen only, mini pill
C. Estrogen and progesterone, combined pill
D. Estrogen followed by progesterone, sequen-tial pill

870. The age of administration of measles vaccine is:
A. 18 months B. 6 months
C. 3 months D. 9 months

871. The back bone of public health nursing is:
A. Primary health care
B. Primary health centre
C. Home visiting
D. Bag technique

872. Which of the following is observed malaria month?
A. December B. May
C. June D. January

873. Causative organism of yellow fever is:
A. Myxovirus B. Rhabdovirus
C. Enterovirus D. Arbo virus

874. The goal of "Health for all by 2000 AD" was mooted in world health assembly in the year:
A. 1966 B. 1948
C. 1957 D. 1978

875. Which of the following is the medication of choice for patient with an open contaminated injury and no recent history of tetanus immunization?
A. Tetanus antitoxin
B. DPT vaccine
C. Tetanus toxoid
D. Tetanus immunoglobulin

876. Nurse caring for a retro positive patient with Molluscum Contagiosum. This secondary infection is caused by
A. Pox Virus
B. Papilloma Virus
C. Epstein Barr Virus
D. Herpes Simplex Virus

877. Malarial transmission occurs by:
A. Vector
B. Air borne
C. Fomite (inanimate object)
D. Food and water

878. The three tier system of local self government at block level is:
A. Panchayath samithi
B. Gramasabha
C. Nyaya panchayat
D. Zilla parishad

879. In the prevention of communicable diseases, the primary prevention results from:
A. Early diagnosis
B. Immunizations
C. Treatment of disease
D. Strict isolation

880. Widal test is used for the diagnosis of:
A. Cholera B. Malaria
C. Enteric fever D. Plague.

881. The vaccination was first performed by:
A. Jonas salk B. Edward jenner
C. Louis pasteur D. Alexander fleming

882. Which one of the health service is not available in rural health unit?
A. Cancer treatment facility
B. Maternal and child health work
C. Communicable disease control work
D. Environmental sanitation work

883. Filaria is caused by
A. Bacteria B. Fungus
C. Protozoa D. Virus

884. Which of the following method of contraception can prevent sexually transmitted diseases?
A. Oral pills B. Cervical cap.
C. Condom D. Copper-T

885. .... is caused by the fungus
A. Malaria B. Athletes foot
C. Filariasis D. Typhus fever

886. The Filariasis is transmitted by ....
A. Anopheles female mosquito
B. Anopheles male mosquito
C. Culex female mosquito
D. Culex male mosquito

887. The disease that spreads through sexual contact is ....
A. Leprosy B. AIDS
C. Itches D. Scabies

888. Typhoid is transmitted through -
A. Water and food B. Air
C. Touch D. Personal contact

889. .... is example for the disease caused by bacteria:
A. Cold B. Typhoid
C. Typhus fever D. Chicken pox

890. Which of the following women should be considered as special targets for family planning?
A. Those who have two children or more
B. Those with medical conditions such as anemia
C. Those younger than 20 years and older than 35 years
D. Those who just had a delivery within the past 15 months

891. Among the following diseases, which is airborne?
A. Viral conjunctivitis
B. Acute poliomyelitis
C. Diphtheria
D. Measles

892. A client was diagnosed as having Dengue Fever. You will say that there is slow capillary refill when the color of the nailbed that you pressed does not return within how many seconds?
A.. 3 B. 5 C. 8 D. 10

893. Which is an example of the school nurse's health care provider function?
A. Requesting for BCG from the RHU for school entrance immunization
B. Conducting random classroom inspection during measles epidemic
C. Taking remedial action on an accident hazard in the school playground
D. Observing places in the school where pupils spend their free times

894. Isolation of a child with measles belongs to what level of prevention?
A. Primary B. Secondary
C. Intermediate D. Tertiary

895 Which of the following is an advantage of a home visit?
A. It allows the nurse to provide nursing care to a greater number of people
B. It provides an opportunity to do first hand appraisal of the home situation
C. It allows sharing of experience among people with similar health problems
D. It develops the family's initiative in providing for health needs of its members

896. Which type of familynurse contact will provide you with the best opportunity to observe family dynamics?
A. Clinic consultation
B. Group conferences
C. Home visit
D. Written communication

897. Which step in community organizing involves training of potential leaders in the community?
A. Integration
B. Community organization
C. Community study
D. Core group formation

898. In which step are plans formulated for solving community problems?
A. Mobilization
B. Community organization
C. Follow up/ extension
D. Core group formation

899. CHN is a communitybased practice. Which best explains this statement?
A. The service is provided in the natural environment of people
B. The nurse has to conduct community diagnosis to determine nursing needs and problems
C. The service are based on the available resources within the community
D. Priority setting is based on the magnitude of the health problems identified

900. Medication management offers the client the possibility of a reduction in levels of:
A. Distress and disability associated with the acute symptoms of a psychiatric disorder
B. Hormones
C. Happiness
D. Employment

901. Thermophilic bacteria grow at following minimum temperature:
A. 20°C B. 35°C C. 55°C D. 85°C

902. Life cycle of malarial parasite was first described by:
A. Ronald Ross B. Robert Koch
C. Louis Pasterur D. Banting and Best

903. HIV virus belongs to which of the following groups?
A. Flavivirus B. Retrovirus
C. Rhabdovirus D. Hepadnavirus

904. In following which is a vector borne disease:
A. Diptheria B. Dengue
C. Tetanus D. Measles

905. Platelet count decreases in:
A. Malaria B. Filaria
C. Dengue D. Typhoid

906. Hepatitis-A is caused:
A. Due to infected blood transfusion
B. Due to use of contaminated water
C. Due to addiction of drug
D. Due to dialysis

907. Which of the following disease is not transmitted by airborne droplets?
A. Measles B. Chickenpox
C. Poliomyelitis D. Tuberculosis

908. WHO was established on;
A. 14th April, 1948 B. 7th April, 1948
C. 7th April, 1945 D. 7th April, 1947

909. What is the full form of UNDP:
A. United Nation's Development Programme
B. Unique Nursing Developmental Programme
C. United Nation Developmental Project
D. United Nurses'Development Project

910. Typhoid fever is a:
A. Bacterial disease
B. Skin disease
C. Parasitic disease
D. Viral disease

911. Polio vaccine is prepared from:
A. Live attenuated organism
B. Killed organisms
C. Toxoid
D. Aerobic bacteria

912. The full form of abbreviation ICDS is:
A. Indian Child Development Scheme
B. Internal Committee of Development Scheme
C. International Children Development Scheme
D. Integrated Child Development Service

913. Community Health Nurse explains a new diagnosed diabetes mellitus patient that the purpose of medication is to treat:
A. Hypoglycemia
B. Hyperglycemia
C. Hypocalcemia
D. Hyuperbilirubinaemia

914. Which is the most appropriate time of IUD insertion?
A. During or within 10 days of menstruation
B. About the midst of the cycle
C. Just before menstruation
D. At any time of menstruation

915. The type of BCG vaccine is :
A. Killed vaccine B. Triple vaccine
C. Live attenuated D. Combined vaccine

916. WHO-ORS packet includes following except:
A. Sodium Chloride
B. Potassium Chloride
C. Sodium Bicarbonate
D. Calcium Carbonate

917. Infant mortality rate is expressed in terms of:
A. Rate per 100 live birth
B. Rate per 1000 live birth
C. Rate per 1000 total birth
D. Rate per 100 total birth

918. On which day International AIDS day is celebrated every year:
A. 1st May B. 7th April
C. 11th April D. 1st December

919. In following which disease is caused by Varicella Zoster:
A. Diphtheria B. Small pox
C. Symphilis D. Chicken Pox

920. Treatment therapy which is used for T.B. :
A. MDT B. BCG vaccination
C. ORS D. DOT's

921. Polio is the mainly infection of:
A. Respiratory tract
B. Central nervous system
C. Alimentary tract
D. Reproductive system

922. What do you mean by incidence:
A. New cases of any disease
B. Old cases of any disease
C. Total cases of any disease
D. All of the Above

923. In following which disease has been eradicated from all over world:
A. Chicken pox B. Small pox
C. Cholera D. Pertusis

924. AIDS is a:
A. Bacterial disease B. Viral disease
C. Fungal disease D. Protozoal disease

925. The richest natural source of Vitamin A is:
A. Carrot B. Fish
C. Peas D. Cod liver oil

926. The target "Health for All by 2000 AD" was declared by:
A. WHO B. UNICEF
C. Red Cross Society D. TNAI

927. Best method of teaching in a community set up about ORS would be
A. Demonstration B. Role play
C. Lecture D. Discussion

928. Census are done every
A. 1 year B. 2 years
C. 5 years D. 10 years

929. Registration of birth to be done within
A. 7 days B. 15 days
C. 21 days D. 30 days

930. Which of the following Health program provides Supplementary Nutrition and non formal education services as two major components?
A. Universal immunization program
B. ICDS
C. RCH program
D. NRHM

931. Which one of the following is not a functions of the sub center ?
A. Maternal and Child Health
B. Refferal
C. National Health programs
D. Training

932. The National rural Health Mission (NRHM) was launched with the aim of further improving health in rural areas. The main functionary or health care provider in this programe is :
A. Auxillary Nurse Midwife
B. Public Health Nurse
C. ASHA
D. Lady Health visitor

933. Population norm for a PHC is
A. 5000 at plain area and 3000 at hilly area
B. 30,000 at plain area and 50, 000 at hilly area
C. 20,000at hilly area and 30, 000 at plain area
D. 3000 at plain area and 5000 at hilly area

934. Universal immunization programe included,
A. Immunisation of pregnant mothers
B. Immunization of children under 5 years
C. Immnisation of pregnant mothers and children
D. All kind of immunisation

935. Which one of the following is the First Referral unit (FRU) for Tehsil, Taluk/Block population?
A. District Hospital/divisional
B. Sub district/Subdivisional Hospital
C. Community Center
D. Rural Hospital

936. First Five year plan for all round development of rural areas was formulated during:
A. 1946 B. 1950 C. 1951 D. 1952

937. Which of the following committee recommended multipurpose workers for ensuring proper coverage of health services?
A. Shrivastav Committee
B. Mudaliar Committee
C. Kartar Singh Committee
D. Bhore Committee

938. First National Health policy was formulated in which of the following year?
A. 1973 B. 1983 C. 1993 D. 2003

939. Which of the following NRHM program has an objective to improve health care at household level through the village level health workers
A. Strengthening existing PHC
B. Integrating vertical health and family welfare program at all levels
C. Introduction of ASHA scheme
D. Introduction of one additional ANM at Sub centre

940. The First Referral Unit as per NRHM guideline is :
A. Community Health Centre
B. District Hospital
C. Rural Hospital
D. Rural Health Institutes

941. **Which of the following is not a major nutritional programme in India?**
A. ICDS
B. Mid day Meal Scheme
C. National Nutritional program
D. Water Supply and sanitation program

942. **All of the following diseases are preventable through immunisation except**
A. Mumps B. Measles
C. Diphtheria D. Influenza

943. **All of the following are negative health indicators except**
A. Death rate
B. IMR
C. Perinatal Mortality rate
D. Life expectancy at birth

944. **When a group of 68 qualified experts discuss a topic in front of an audience is said to be**
A. Panel discussion B. Group discussion
C. Seminar D. Workshop

945. **Conducting Pap smear examination to detect cancer cervix is**
A. Primary prevention
B. Secondary prevention
C. Tertiary prevention
D. Specific protection

946. **MMR vaccine is given at the age of**
A. 9-12 months B. 6 weeks
C. 1 1/2 year D. 5 years

947. **Neonatal mortality rate is calculated by estimating the number newborn death within ...... days**
A. 24 hrs B. One week
C. 28 days D. One year

948. **Incidence of a disease is defined as**
A. Number of old cases present during given period
B. Number of cases existing in a given population at a given time
C. Number of cases existing at a given period
D. Number of new cases occurring in a specific period

949. **The process of restriction of movement of persons who have come in contact of diseased person is called as**
A. Active surveillance B. Quarantine
C. Isolation D. Passive surillance

950. **Mid day meal supplement diet provides following nutrients feM**
A. 200 Calories and 6-8 gms proteins
B. 200 Calories and 7-10 gms proteins
C. 300 Calorie and 8-12 gms protein
D. 300 Calories and 14-16 gms proteins

951. **Final Stage of disaster management is**
A. Reconstruction
B. Preparedness
C. Rehabilitation
D. Identification of dead

952. **Which of the following in known "Backbone" of community Health -**
A. Home Visit B. Family
C. Economy D. Individual

953. **Sexually transmitted Diseases can**
A. Spread HIV B. Can be treated
C. Can be prevented D. All of the Above

954. **Which among the following vaccine should be stored at 20 °C -**
A. DPT B. T.T.
C. BCG D. Polio

955. **"ELISA Test" is a test for detecting**
A. HIV Infection B. Hepatitis A
C. Hepatitis B D. Hepatitis C

956. **An Example of protein energy malnutrition is**
A. Anemia B. Scurvy
C. Marasmus D. Rickets

957. **The infant mortality rate is assessed**
A. By per 100 live birth
B. By per 1000 live birth
C. By per 1,00,000 live birth
D. None of the Above

958. **Refuse along with human excreta is disposed of by a method known as**
A. Controlled Tipping B. Composting
C. Dumping D. Incineration

959. **The headquarters of World Health Organization is**
A. Geneva B. New York
C. New Zealand D. Canada

960. **The System of storing and transporting vaccine is termed as -**
A. Cold Chain B. Freezer Chain
C. Cool Chain D. Vaccination

961. **Global Alliance on Vaccines Initiative (GAVI) is associated with**
A. Immunization B. Nutrition
C. Health D. Nourishment

962. **The members of VHSC are**
A. Sarpanch B. ASHA
C. Teachers D. All of the Above

963. **Condom protects from**
A. Sexually Transmitted Infections
B. Reproductive Tract Infection
C. Pregnancy
D. All of the Above

964. Which country has the highest TB burden in the world
A. Nigeria B. South Africa
C. India D. Bangladesh

965. When is Maternal and Child Health and Nutrition day celebrated
A. Every Thursday B. 2nd Friday
C. 3rd Wednesday D. 2nd Saturday

966. Under HBPNC ASHA makes how many visits to a woman who had institutional delivery
A. 6 B. 7 C. 5 D. 4

967. Leprosy is transmitted by
A. Bacteria B. Hand holding
C. Eating together D. Kissing

968. What is the benefit given in urban areas under JSY scheme
A. Rs.1400 is paid to the delivered mother
B. Rs.1100 is paid to the delivered mother
C. Rs.2000 is paid to the delivered mother
D. Rs. 1000 is paid to the delivered mother

969. Zika virus has been declared as Public Health Emergency of International Concern by
A. United Nations
B. International Institute for Public Health
C. SEARO
D. WHO

970. Sterilization method for males
A. Tubectomy B. Laproscopy
C. Vasectomy D. Bronchoscopy

971. Which is the most cost effective Family planning method
A. Condom B. Pills
C. Sterilization D. IUCD

972. What is the minimum educational qualification for being selected as ASHA
A. 10th pass B. 5th pass
C. Literate D. Graduation

973. IUCD 380 A is valid for how many years IUCD 380 A
A. 5 years B. 10 years
C. 8 years D. 7 years

974. What is the aim of Kushal Mangal Karyakram
A. Identifying all eligible couples through community survey
B. Bringing down MMR in the state by identifying high-risk pregnancies
C. Promoting health of families through Primary Health.
D. Giving health benefits to elderly.

975. BCG vaccine is
A. Killed B. Live attenuated
C. Toxoid D. Cellular fraction

976. The first sign of chickenpox in the children is
A. Fever B. Rashes
C. Shivering D. Malaise

977. Which communicable disease is also known as "German measles"
A. Mumps B. Rubella
C. Diphtheria D. Pertusis

978. Spread of a disease among a large population of world is called as
A. Endemic B. Epidemic
C. Episodic D. Pandemic

979. Who discovered vibrio cholera
A. Robert Koch
B. Ronald Ross
C. Necholaier
D. Alexander Flaming

980. Immunization is
A. Primary prevention
B. Secondary prevention
C. Tertiary prevention
D. Disability limitation

981. As per the RCH, first referral unit (FRU) is
A. Sub Center
B. Primary Health Center
C. Community Health Center
D. District Hospital

982. Cold chain is used for
A. Storage of vaccines
B. To treat pyrexia
C. To maintain room temperature
D. All of the Above

983. Prevalence is a
A. Rate B. Ratio
C. Proportion D. Mean

984.' Ek Mein Paanch Ka Dum' is the tag line of
A. Pentavalent Vaccine
B. Panchamrit Scheme
C. Mission Indradhanush
D. Pulse Polio

985. What is true in context of HIV infection
A. Females are more prone to HIV infection
B. Males are more prone to HIV infection
C. Some particular blood group persons are more prone to HIV infection
D. None of the Above

986. With context to diarrhea in children which of the following is incorrect
A. Children die due to dehydration in diarrhea
B. As soon as diarrhea starts, it is essential that child be given extra fluid
C. Breast feeding cannot help to prevent diarrhea
D. ORS can help to recover from diarrhea

987. Incentive given to ASHA for promoting a couple for opting sterilization method on one/two children is
A. Rs. 100/- B. Rs. 250/-
C. Rs. 500/- D. Rs. 1000/-

988. ASHA soft can be used for
A. Providing counselling to ASHA
B. Monitoring progress of ASHA
C. Giving directions to ASHA
D. All of the Above

989. World Tobacco Day is on
A. May 31 B. June 30
C. July 31 D. August 31

990. Under NUHM program, those cities have been selected which have a population of
A. More than 10,000
B. More than 50,000
C. More than 5,00,000
D. More than 1,00,000

991. For calcium requirement during pregnancy and lactation, ASHA should counsel for
A. 1 glass of milk everyday
B. Exposure to morning sunlight
C. Eating green leafy vegetables
D. All of the Above

992. Who is responsible for referral of malnourished children to MTC at the community level
A. Anganwadi Worker
B. ASHA
C. Anganwadi Sahayika
D. Teacher

993. Sunita asks ASHA Sahyogini, "When will ANM visit our village?" ASHA replies:
A. On MCHN Day
B. On second Saturday
C. On full moon day
D. On third Friday

994. Indoor patient services are not available at
A. PHC B. District Hospital
C. CHC D Sub-Center

995. IUCD is
A. Permanent family planning method
B. Temporary spacing method under family planning
C. Temporary spacing method which can also protect from HIV
D. Permanent spacing method which protects from HIV

996. 24x7 PHC should provide
A. 24 hr delivery services
B. 24 hr emergency services
C. Both A and B
D. 24 types of services

997. Mission Indradhanush program was launched to cover the dropouts and left out beneficiaries of
A. Tuberculosis B. Leprosy
C. Immunization D. Malnutrition

998. During MCHN day what are the major responsibilities of ANM
A. Vaccination B. Counselling
C. ANC D. All of the Above

999. The most critical time for a newborn just after birth is
A. First 48 hrs B. 7 days
C. 15 days D. 28 days

1000. Which microorganism causes Hepatitis B ?
A. Virus B. Protozoa
C. Bacteria D. Fungi

1001. Insects that can transmit diseases to human are referred to as ?
A. Carriers B. Reservoirs
C. Vectors D. Incubators

1002. The disease Filaria is caused by?
A. Ascaris
B. Wuchereria bancrofti
C. Peasmodium
D. Tinea soleum

1003. Community health centre :
A. Has 100 beds
B. Covers a population of approx. 1 Lakh
C. Has X-rays and laboratory facilities
D. Acts as a referral hospital for the community block

1004. All are water borne diseases except:
A. Leptospirosis B. Schistosomiasis
C. Fish Tape worm D. Brucellosis

1005. Vector of Kala azar is:
A. Flea B. Tsetse fly
C. Sand fly D. Mosquito

1006. The time interval between the invasion by an infectious agent and just appearance of the just signs and symptoms of the disease:
A. Latent period
B. Quarantine
C. Incubation period
D. Termination period

1007. All are gross root level workers except:
A. Anganwadi workers
B. Traditional birth attendant
C. Village health guide
D. Health assistants

1008. Which of the following person is present in subcenter?
A. Multi purpose health worker
B. Laboratory technician
C. Health educator
D. Medical officer

1009. Case finding in RNTCP is based on:
A. Sputum culture
B. Sputum microscopy
C. X-ray chest
D. Mantoux test/PCR

1010. ASHA (Accredited Social Health Activist) work at :
A. Community level
B. Village level
C. PHC Level
D. District Level

1011. Five clean practices' under strategies for elimination of neonatal tetanus includes all except :
A. Clean surface of delivery
B. Clean hand of attendant
C. New blade for cutting the cord
D. Clean airway

1012. Diluent used for BCG is :
A. Distilled water
B. Normal Saline
C. Dextrose Solution
D. Ringer lactate

1013. Commonest complication of mumps is :
A. Orchitis and oopheritis
B. Encephalitis
C. Pneumonia
D. Myocarditis

1014. Which committee is known as health survey and development committee?
A. Bhore Committee
B. Mudalier Committee
C. Shrivastav Committee
D. Mukharji Committee

1015. Pertusis is known as:
A. Enteric fever
B. Whooping cough
C. German measles
D. Rubella

1016. The 2- way process of exchange of information between individuals through a common system can be termed as:
A. Interaction
B. Interpersonal relationship
C. Communication
D. Sharing

1017. Which type of channel is considered as thebest one for effective communication?
A. Combined B. Visual
C. Auditory D. Tactile

1018. Line of authority is followed under:
A. Symbolic communication
B. Informal communication
C. Formal communication
D. Therapeutic communication

1019. Who gave the theory of interpersonal relations?
A. Dorothy Orem
B. Martha Rogers
C. Florence Nightingale
D. Hildegard Peplau

1020. Change in relationship, economic independence, small family, marriage settled by partners is an features of:
A. Single family
B. Joint family
C. Traditional family
D. Modern family

1021. Group in which people are not married if having blood relations but are married outside the group is termed as;
A. Endogamy B. Exogamy
C. Caste exogamy D. Caste endogamy

1022. The phenomenon in society in which people move up and down and vice versa on social scale is known as:
A. Social status
B. Social class
C. Social classification
D. Social mobility

1023. Following are the features of social control in society:
A. Influence by specific group for welfare
B. Influence by society for welfare
C. Opinion by family and religious group for welfare
D. Suggestions by formal and informal groups for welfare

1024. Concept of one to one relationship between agent and disease is explained by;
A. Germ theory of disease
B. Multifactoral disease causation
C. Epidemiological triad
D. Web of causation of disease

1025. Nurse will advise the mother to isolate the child with measles for:
A. 3 days B. 5 days
C. 7 days D. 9 days

1026. Mode of transmission of Pertussis:
A. Vector transmission
B. Through contaminated water
C. Droplet infection
D. Faecoaral

1027. Which test is undertaken to measure the amount actively replicating HIV virus which help to know the progress and relapse of ART drugs:
A. HIV viral load test
B. CD4 count
C. CD4 percentage
D. Western blot test

1028. Which of the following prepacked STI/RTI kit is for the treatment of vaginitis:
A. Grey colour B. White colour
C. Green colour D. Yellow colour

1029. One difference between human beings and animals is the
A. Shared beliefs
B. Common territory
C. Division of work
D. Persistence in time

1030. Social structure of a society is a network of
A. Institutional relations
B. Value system
C. Traditions
D. Compliance to norms

1031. Gerontology is the study of
A. Human beings
B. Animals
C. Earths
D. Aged and aging process

1032. Disease that affects many people at different countries is termed as
A. Sporadic B. Pandemic
C. Epidemic D. Endemic

1033. B.C.G. vaccine is given to protect the child against:
A. Diphtheria B. Tetanus
C. Typhoid D. Tuberculosis

1034. Diluent used for BCG vaccine is
A. Distilled water
B. Normal saline
C. Dextrose solution
D. Ringer lactate

1035. The first dose of Hepatitis B vaccine is to be given to a baby
A. At 6 weeks B. At 10 weeks
C. At birth D. At 8 week

1036. The causative organism of dengue fever is
A. Enteric Virus B. Arbovirus
C. Variola virus D. Influenza virus

1037. Cholera is caused by a
A. Retrovirus
B. Viron
C. Bacteria and virus
D. Bacteria

1038. Poliomyelitis is transmitted through
A. Water B. Air
C. Blood D. Vectors

1039. Hepatitis virus that spreads by faecal-oral route
A. Hepatitis A B. Hepatitis B
C. Hepatitis C D. Hepatitis D

1040. Which of the following virus is rarely transmitted through parenteral route
A. Hepatitis A B. Hepatitis B
C. Hepatitis C D. None of the Above

1041. What is the colour coding of bag in hospitals to dispose off human anatomical waste such as body part
A. Yellow B. Black
C. Red D. Blue

1042. Staining technique used in RNTCP
A. Zeihl Nielson stain
B. Gram stain
C. Giemsa stain
D. PAS

1043. Severe joint pain is associated with which of the following
A. Malaria B. Flu
C. Chikungunya D. Dengue

1044. March 8 is celebrated as
A. Rajasthan Day
B. World Women's Day
C. WHO day
D. UN Day

1045. The Millennium Development Goal 6 was associated with
A. Reduce Child Mortality
B. To improve Maternal health
C. Combat HIV/AIDS, Malaria and other diseases
D. Develop a Global Partnership for Development

1046. District level authority of health department is
A. BCMO B. Joint Director
C. CM&HO D. All of the Above

1047. The national program - RNTCP is related to which disease
A. Neonatal Tetanus
B. Measles

C. T.B.
D. HIV

1048. The primary health Centre is managed by
A. Health Inspector
B. ANM
C. Medical officer
D. BCMO

1049. What is the measure of health status of children in the community
A. MMR B. CDR
C. CBR D. IMR

1050. Infant mortality rate (IMR) is defined as number of deaths of infants under age one per
A. 1000 births
B. 1000 live births
C. 1000 mid year population
D. 1000 women of reproduction age group

1051. Most heat sensitive vaccine is
A. Measles B. DPT
C. OPV D. Hepatitis B

1052. Cu T 380 IUD should be replaced in
A. 4 years B. 6 years
C. 8 years D. 10 years

1053. What is the population based norm for selection of rural ASHA.
A. 1000 B. 1500
C. 800 D. 5000

1054. Which of the following will protect infants against most common childhood diseases
A. Exclusive Breastfeeding, Immunization
B. Nutrition, kangaroo Mother care
C. Early identification, care
D. Supplementary nutrition, referral

1055. Malaria is a .... disease –
A. Bacterial B. Protozoal
C. Viral D. Fungal

1056. The National Maternity Benefit Scheme (NMBS) has been modified into:
A. JSSK B. RKSK
C. JSY D. RBSK

1057. Red Ribbon Express is related to
A. Malaria awareness
B. AIDS awareness
C. Cancer awareness
D. Polio awareness

1058. Which amongst the following is the most authentic source of obtaining population data
A. Census B. NFHS
C. SRS D. DLHS

1059. Presently which phase of National AIDS Control Program is running –
A. I B. II
C. III D. IV

1060. Non-Communicable diseases are also called as
A. Lifestyle Diseases
B. Permanent Diseases
C. Long-Term Diseases
D. Costly Diseases

1061. Who are the beneficiaries of JSY Scheme?
A. Women having institutional delivery at government and accredited hospitals
B. Lactating Mothers
C. Children up to 5 yrs of age
D. All Diabetic women

1062. AFHS program comes under
A. Maternal Health
B. Child Health
C. Adolescent health
D. Family Welfare

1063. The national program for leprosy is –
A. National Program for Leprosy Control
B. National Leprosy Eradication Program
C. National Program for Prevention and Control of Leprosy
D. National Program for Prevention of Leprosy

1064. Spermicide used contraceptive TODAY is :
A. Norethisterone
B. 9-Nanoxynol
C. Prostaglandin F-2
D. MPA

1065. Maternal mortality rate is
A. Maternal death per 100 thousand live birth
B. Maternal death per 10 thousand live birth
C. Maternal illness per 100 thousand live birth
D. Maternal illness per 10 thousand live birth

1066. ICDS was launched in
A. 1955 B. 1968
C. 1975 D. 2005

1067. Disease eradicated from world:
A. Small pox B. Malaria
C. Polio D. Diphtheria

1068. MCH service includes
A. Prenatal and postnatal care
B. Under fives care
C. Family planning service
D. All of the Above

1069. Sterilization method for males
A. Tubectomy B. Laproscopy
C. Vasectomy D. Bronchoscopy

1070. Giobal Alliance on Vaccines Initiative (GAVI) is associated with
A. Immunization B. Nutrition
C. Health D. Nourishment

1071. Which virus causes chicken pox
A. Varicella B. Variola
C. Vaccinia D. Cytomegalovirus

1072. What is the most dangerous species of plasmodium
A. P.Ovale B. P.Vivax
C. P.Falciparum D. P.Malarie

1073. An organism which takes its food from another organism without giving anything in return is called as
A. Host B. Parasite
C. Carrier D. Agent

1074 ………… Is caused by the fungus
A. Malaria B. Athlete's foot
C. Filariasis D. Typhus fever

1075. The window period in HIV infection is
A. 1 Month B. 2 Months
C. 3 Months D. 6 Months

1076. Eradication of disease from a particular geographic region is called
A. Elimination B. Transmission
C. Surveillance D. Infestation

1077. Recently which health facilities have been taken up under PPP mode:
A. PHC B. CHC
C. DH D. SDH

1078. What is the color of the coat of Yashoda
A. Blue B. Pink
C. Green D. Yellow

1079. Surakshit Matratva Diwas is organized
A. Once in a month
B. Once in two months
C. Once in three months
D. Once in nine months

1080. Incentive given to ASHA for ensuring birth of first child after two years of marriage
A. 100/- B. 250/-
C. 500/- D. 700/-

1081. The counselling on HIV/AIDS is given at…….in the government hospitals
A Integrated counselling and testing centre
B HIV testing centre
C HIV counselling centre
D Integrated counselling centre

1082. Maternal death is
A. Death of a female between the day of her conception to 42 days of her delivery due to any cause related to pregnancy or delivery
B. Ratio of deaths of Women to Men
C. Rate of deaths of pregnant women during labor
D. All of the Above

1083. Which of the following is related to mosquito control
A. Jogging B. Fogging
C. Plantation D. Fishing

1084. Which of the following are the symptoms of Tuberculosis
A. Cough for two weeks with weight loss and fever
B. Cough for two weeks with weight loss, loss of appetite and fever at night
C. Cough for two weeks and fever at night
D. Cough for two weeks with fever and loss of appetite

1085. OCP, IUCD and Male condom are OCP, IUCD
A. Temporary family planning methods
B. Permanent family planning methods
C. Family planning methods used by males
D. None of the Above

1086. Central Government has launched a program for eradication of which disease from India on April 23, 2015
A. Tuberculosis B. Measles
C. Polio D. Leprosy

1087. Which of the following program is related with child health screening and early intervention and services under NHM
A. RKSK B. RBSK
C. NSSK D. JSSK

1088. Pulse Polio Vaccination Started in India
A. December 1994 B. December 1995
C. January 1994 D. November 1996

1089. Which vaccine can be given intramuscularly (IM)
A. BCG B. OPV
C. DPT D. MMR

1090. Schick's test is done in
A. Tuberculosis B. Diphtheria
C. Polio D. Mumps

1091. World Health Day is celebrated on
A. March 24 B. December 1
C. April 7 D. January 1

1092. Out of following which policy was implemented in 2002 in India
A. National Ayush policy

B. National Nutrition Policy
C. National Population Policy
D. National Health Policy

1093. Which vaccination is given to the infant at 9 months of age
A. TT B. DPT
C. Measles D. Polio

1094. Goli Ki Hamjoli Campaign is associated with
A. Immunization B. Child care
C. Maternal care D. Family Planning

1095. The Millennium Development Goal 4 was associated with
A. To improve Maternal health
B. Reduce Child Mortality
C. Combat HIV/AIDS, Malaria and other diseases
D. Develop a Global Partnership for Development

1096. Kayakalp program is related to
A. Health Management in Hospitals
B. Information Management in Hospitals
C. Communication Management in Hospitals
D. Cleanliness and Waste Management in Hospitals

1097. When is National Deworming Day organized
A. 7 March B. 19 April
C. 10 February D. 12 July

1098. What is the full form of LHV
A. Lady Health Volunteer
B. Lady Health Visitor
C. Lady House Volunteer
D. Lady House Visitor

1099. Generally, an Anganwadi serves a population of
A. 2000 B. 3000
C. 1500 D. 1000

1100. AFHS program is for
A. Mothers
B. Infants
C. Adolescent boys and girls
D. Lactating mothers

1101. What is the full form of AYUSH
A. Ayurveda, Youth, Unani, Siddha and Homeopathy
B. Ayurveda, Yoga and Naturopathy, Unani, Siddha and Homoeopathy
C. Ayurveda, Yoga, Unani, Siddha and Homeopathy
D. Allopathy, Yoga, Unani, Siddha and Homoeopathy

1102. Which of the following is not covered under '4D' of RBSK
A. Defect at birth
B. Deficiency
C. Development delay
D. Dietary delay

1103. What is the time period of post delivery care
A. 6 months B. 4 months
C. 42 days D. 40 days

1104. MCH Services includes
A. Pre natal & postnatal care
B. Family planning
C. Care of Children below 5 years
D. All of the Above

1105 Regarding cholera vaccine all are correct except that:.
A. It is given at interval of 6 months
B. Long-lasting immunity
C. Not useful in epidemics
D. Not given orally

1106. AIDS was first detected in India in the year:
A. 1985 B. 1981
C. 1986 D. 1991

1107. Incubation period of mumps is:
A. 18 days B. 10 days
C. 14 days D. 5 days

1108. Which of the following diseases gives life-long immunity after the attack?
A. Typhoid B. Tetanus
C. Mumps D. Diphtheria

1109. Which state has lowest infant mortality rate:
A. Kerala B. West Bengal
C. Tamil Nadu D. Madhya Pradesh

1110. Posting of midwives in the areas under PHCs is influenced by:
A. The birth rate prevalent in the area
B. The infant mortality rate prevalent in the area
C. The maternal mortality rate prevalent in the area
D. The crude death rate prevalent in the area

1111. Typhoid fever is an example of:
A. Acute inflammation
B. Chronic non-specific inflammation
C. Chronic granulomatous
D. Chronic suppurative inflammation

1112. The nurse epidemiologist:
A. Is responsible for doing cultures of all infec-tions and drainages
B. Works in the laboratory to identify bacteria causing infection

C. Decides what antibiotics should be prescribed for infections
D. Helps providers of care to control infections

1113. On which day International AIDS. Day is celebrated every year?
A. 1 May B. 7 April
C. 11 April D. 1 December

1114. The family includes relatives in addition to the nuclear family is:
A. Joint family
B. Extended family
C. Blended family
D. Single parent family

1115. Family functioning involves:
A. The process used by the family to achieve goals
B. The patterns of people who are considered to be family members
C. The ongoing membership of the family
D. The pattern of relationships

1116. Family structure is:
A. The process used by the family to achieve goals
B. The patterns of people who are considered to be family members
C. The ongoing membership of the family and the pattern of relationship
D. Intra familiar system of support

1117. The relationship that is of extreme importance in the formation of the personality is the:
A. Peer B. Sibling
C. Parent-child D. Heterosexual

1118. Communication process is influenced by except:
A. Motivation B. Attitude
C. Anger D. Culture difference

1119. Polio vaccine is prepared from:
A. Live attenuated organism
B. Killed organism
C. Toxoids
D. Aerobic bacteria

1120. The most often cells from blood infected by HIV is:
A. CD4 (Helper) T. Lymphocyte B
B. Lymphocyte
C. CDS (Suppressor) T. Lymphocytes
D. Polymorph

1121. The most important complication of mumps in post pubertal males is:
A. Decrease in libido
B. Decrease in androgens
C. Hypo pituitartism
D. Sterility

1122. Which of the following is a zoonosis?
A. Chikungunya B. Malaria
C. AIDS D. Rabies

1123. Outbreak of a diseases in the community in excess of normal expectation is:
A. Epidemic B. Sporadic
C. Endemic D. Pandemic

1124. Which of the following waterborne disease is caused by protozoa?
A. Poliomyelitis B. Shigellosis
C. Ascariasis D. Amebiasis

1125. When an infectious disease is spread over the whole world it is referred?
A. Epidemic B. Endemic
C. Pandemic D. Sporadic

1126. TAB vaccination prevents:
A. Cholera B. Meningitis
C. Typhoid D. Influenza

1127. Swine fever is caused by:
A. Corona virus B. Rota virus
C. H1N1 virus D. Retrovirus

1128. Dengue fever is transmitted by the mosquito:
A. Aedes aegypti B. Anopheles
C. Culex D. Mansonoides

1129. Cerebral malaria is caused by the following parasite:
A. Plasmodium vivax
B. Plasmodium quart an
C. Plasmodium falciparum
D. Plasmodium ovale

1130. The causative organism of Koch's disease is:
A. Mycobacterium diphtheria
B. Mycobacterium tuberculosis
C. Mycobacterium leprae
D. Streptococcus aureus

1131. The functional unit of the community:
A. Head of the family
B. The infant
C. The family
D. IPR

1132. The first five year plan was started in the year:
A. 1947 B. 1955
C. 1951 D. 1949

1133. The following are examples of live vaccine except:
A. Typhoid B. Oral polio
C. BCG D. Measles

1134. Poliomyelitis is:
A. Bacterial infection
B. Viral infection

C. Fungal infection
D. Spirochetal infection

1135. Rabies is a fatal viral disease of:
A. Cardiovascular system
B. Muscular system
C. Central nervous system
D. Skeletal system

1136. In hospital waste management, plastic bag of which colour is not used?
A. Green B. Blue
C. Yellow D. Red

1137. Which of the following is not a species of plasmodium parasite?
A. Hasmodium ovale
B. Hasmodium mexicana
C. Plasinodium malariae
D. Hasmodium vivax

1138. Life cyle of malarial parasite was first described by:
A. Ronald Ross B. RoberKoch
C. Lous Pasteur D. Banting and Best

1139. "MMR vaccine" provides protection against all of the following diseses except:
A. Mumps
B. Meningococcal meningitis
C. Rubella
D. Rubeola

1140. HIV virus belongs to which of the following groups?
A. Flavivirus B. Retrovirus
C. Rhabdovirus D. Hepadnavirus

1141. Which of the following diseases is not transmitted by airborne droplets?
A. Measles B. Chickenpox
C. Poliomyelitis D. Tuberculosis

1142. Which infecting serotype of dengue virus is most dangerous?
A. Type 1 B. Type 2
C. Type 3 D. Type 4

1143. Maximum maternal mortality is seen:
A. Hepatitis B B. Hepatitis E
C. Hepatitis A D. Hepatitis C

1144. Which vaccine is contraindicated in pregnancy?
A. Rubella B. OPV
C. BCG D. Hepatitis

1145. In polio transmission, easy block can be applied by acting on:
A. Reservoir B. Susceptible host
C. Feco-oral route D. Agent

1146. Oral vaccine
A. Hepatitis-A B. Hepatitis-B
C. Salk's vaccine D. Sabin's vaccine

1147. Copper carrying contraceptive devices acts by
A. Preventing Ovulation
B. Prevent spermatozoa coming in contact with ovum
C. Destruction of Spermatozoa
D. Making cervical mucus thick to prevent penetration of spermatozoa

1148. Which biological used in Expanded Program on Immunization (EPI) should NOT be stored in the freezer?
A. DPT
B. Oral polio vaccine
C. Measles vaccine
D. MMR

1149. Which of the following severe conditions DOES NOT always require urgent referral to a hospital? Mastoiditis
A. Severe dehydration
B. Severe pneumonia
C. Severe febrile disease
D. All of the Above

1150. A client was diagnosed as having Dengue fever. You will say that there is slow capillary refill when the color of the nailbed that you pressed does not return within how many seconds?
A. 3 B. 5 C. 8 D. 10

1151. Which is the most appropriate measure that the PHN may carry out to prevent Dengue shock syndrome?
A. Insert an NGT and give fluids per NGT.
B. Instruct the mother to give the child Oresol.
C. Start the patient on intravenous fluids STAT.
D. Refer the client to the physician for appropriate management.

1152. The pathognomonic sign of measles is Koplik's spot. You may see Koplik's spot by inspecting the _____.
A. Nasal mucosa
B. Buccal mucosa
C. Skin on the abdomen
D. Skin on the antecubital surface

1153. Among the following diseases, which is airborne?
A. Viral conjunctivitis
B. Acute poliomyelitis
C. Diphtheria
D. Measles

1154. Among children aged 2 months to 3 years, the most prevalent form of meningitis is caused by which microorganism?
A. Hemophilus influenzae
B. Morbillivirus
C. Steptococcus pneumoniae
D. Neisseria meningitidis

1155. Human beings are the major reservoir of malaria. Which of the following strategies in malaria control is based on this fact?
A. Stream seeding
B. Stream clearing
C. Destruction of breeding places
D. Zooprophylaxis

1156. Which of the following is NOT appropriate for malaria control?
A. Use of chemically treated mosquito nets
B. Seeding of breeding places with larva-eating fish
C. Destruction of breeding places of the mosquito vector
D. Use of mosquito-repelling soaps, such as those with basil or citronella

1157. A 3-year old client was brought to the health centre with the chief complaint of severe diarrhea and the passage of "rice water" stools. The client is most probably suffering from which condition?
A. Giardiasis B. Cholera
C. Amebiasis D. Dysentery

1158. Which is the BEST control measure for AIDS?
A. Being faithful to a single sexual partner
B. Using a condom during each sexual contact
C. Avoiding sexual contact with commercial sex workers
D. Making sure that one's sexual partner does not have signs of AIDS

1159. Complications to infectious parotitis (mumps) may be serious in which type of clients?
A. Pregnant women
B. Elderly clients
C. Young adult males
D. Young infants

1160. Which immunization produces a permanent scar?
A. DPT
B. BCG
C. Measles vaccination
D. Hepatitis B vaccination

1161. A 4-week old baby was brought to the health centre for his first immunization. Which can be given to him?
A. DPT1
B. OPV1
C. Infant BCG
D. Hepatitis B vaccine 1

1162. You will not give DPT 2 if the mother says that the infant had
A. Seizures a day after DPT 1.
B. Fever for 3 days after DPT 1.
C. Abscess formation after DPT 1.
D. Local tenderness for 3 days after DPT 1.

1163. A pregnant woman had just received her 4th dose of tetanus toxoid. Subsequently, her baby will have protection against tetanus for how long?
A 1 year B. 3 years
C. 10 years D. Lifetime

1164. Which of the following signs will indicate that a young child is suffering from severe pneumonia? Dyspnea
A. Wheezing B. Fast breathing
C. Chest indrawing D. All of the Above

1165. During the physical examination of a young child, what is the earliest sign of xerophthalmia that you may observe?
A. Keratomalacia
B. Corneal opacity
C. Night blindness
D. Conjunctival xerosis

1166. To prevent xerophthalmia, young children are given Retinol capsule every 6 months. What is the dose given to preschoolers?
A. 10,000 IU B. 20,000 IU
C. 100,000 IU D. 200,000 IU

1167. The major sign of iron deficiency anemia is pallor. What part is best examined for pallor?
A. Palms
B. Nailbeds
C. Around the lips
D. Lower conjunctival sac

1168. Management of a child with measles includes the administration of which of the following?
A. Gentian violet on mouth lesions
B. Antibiotics to prevent pneumonia
C. Tetracycline eye ointment for corneal opacity
D. Retinol capsule regardless of when the last dose was given

1169. Secondary prevention for malaria includes
A. Planting of neem or eucalyptus trees
B. Residual spraying of insecticides at night

C. Determining whether a place is endemic or not
D. Growing larva-eating fish in mosquito breeding places

1170. Scotch tape swab is done to check for which intestinal parasite?
A. Ascaris B. Pinworm
C. Hookworm D. Schistosoma

1171. Which of the following signs indicates the need for sputum examination for AFB?
A. Hematemesis
B. Fever for 1 week
C. Cough for 3 weeks
D. Chest pain for 1 week

1172. Which clients are considered targets for DOTS Category I?
A. Sputum negative cavitary cases
B. Clients returning after a default
C. Relapses and failures of previous PTB treatment regimens
D. Clients diagnosed for the first time through a positive sputum exam

1173. Diagnosis of leprosy is highly dependent on recognition of symptoms. Which of the following is an early sign of leprosy?
A. Macular lesions
B. Inability to close eyelids
C. Thickened painful nerves
D. Sinking of the nose bridge

1174. Which of the following clients should be classified as a case of multi bacillary leprosy?
A. 3 skin lesions, negative slit skin smear
B. 3 skin lesions, positive slit skin smear
C. 5 skin lesions, negative slit skin smear
D. 5 skin lesions, positive slit skin smear

1175. A woman, 6 months pregnant, came to the center for consultation. Which of the following substances is contraindicated?
A. Tetanus toxoid
B. Retinol 200,000 IU
C. Ferrous sulfate 200 mg
D. Potassium iodate 200 mg. capsule

1176. You are in a client's home to attend to a delivery. Which of the following will you do first?
A. Set up the sterile area.
B. Put on a clean gown or apron.
C. Cleanse the client's vulva with soap and water.
D. Note the interval, duration and intensity of labor contractions.

1177. You explain to a breastfeeding mother that breast milk is sufficient for all of the baby's nutrient needs only up to ____.
A. 3 months B. 6 months
C. 1 year D. 2 years

1178. What is given to a woman within a month after the delivery of a baby?
A. Malunggay capsule
B. Ferrous sulfate 100 mg. OD
C. Retinol 200,000 I.U., 1 capsule
D. Potassium iodate 200 mg, 1 capsule

1179. Which biological used in Expanded Program on Immunization (EPI) is stored in the freezer?
A. DPT
B. Tetanus toxoid
C. Measles vaccine
D. Hepatitis B vaccine

1180. Unused BCG should be discarded how many hours after reconstitution?
A. 2
B. 4
C. 6
D. At the end of the day

1181. Tertiary prevention is needed in which stage of the natural history of disease?
A. Pre-pathogenesis B. Pathogenesis
C. Prodromal D. Terminal

1182. Isolation of a child with measles belongs to what level of prevention?
A. Primary B. Secondary
C. Intermediate D. Tertiary

1183. Which of the following is an advantage of a home visit?
A. It allows the nurse to provide nursing care to a greater number of people.
B. It provides an opportunity to do first hand appraisal of the home situation.
C. It allows sharing of experiences among people with similar health problems.
D. It develops the family's initiative in providing for health needs of its members.

1184. To maintain the cleanliness of the bag and its contents, which of the following must the nurse do?
A. Wash his/her hands before and after providing nursing care to the family members.
B. Put on an apron to protect her uniform and fold it with the right side out before putting it back into the bag.
C. At the end of the visit, fold the lining on which the bag was placed, ensuring that the contaminated side is on the outside.
D. None of them

1185. **Which of the following is an epidemiologic function of the nurse during an epidemic?**
A. Teaching the community on preventive measures against the disease
B. Monitoring the condition of the cases affected by the communicable disease
C. Participating in the investigation to determine the source of the epidemic
D. Teaching the community on preventive measures against the disease

1186. **The primary purpose of conducting an epidemiologic investigation is to**
A. Identify geographical location of cases of the disease in the community
B. Delineate the aetiology of the epidemic
C. Encourage cooperation and support of the community
D. None of them

1187. **The midwife teaches that the most frequent side effect associated with the use of IUDs is:**
A. Rupture of uterus
B. Excessive menstrual flow
C. Expulsion of IUD
D. Ectopic pregnancy

□□□

Answer Sheet

1. D	2. A	3. C	4. D	5. B	6. D	7. D	8. A	9. D	10. B
11. A	12. C	13. D	14. D	15. D	16. B	17. A	18. B	19. C	20. B
21. D	22. C	23. C	24. B	25. B	26. D	27. B	28. B	29. B	30. B
31. B	32. A	33. A	34. A	35. B	36. A	37. B	38 D	39. A	40. A
41. B	42. A	43. C	44. D	45. C	46. C	47. B	48. A	49. C	50. D
51. A	52. B	53. A	54. D	55. B	56. C	57. B	58. A	59. B	60. C
61. A	62. A	63. A	64. B	65. C	66. D	67. A	68. A	69. B	70. A
71. A	72. A	73. D	74. B	75. A	76. D	77. B	78. D	79. D	80. B
81. C	82. D	83. C	84. A	85. B	86. D	87. D	88. C	89. A	90. B
91. A	92. D	93. B	94. A	95. B	96. D	97. B	98. B	99. A	100. B
101. A	102. B	103. C	104. D	105. A	106. C	107. A	108. A	109. B	110. C
111. A	112. B	113. A	114. B	115. D	116. D	117. B	118. C	119. C	120. B
121. B	122. C	123. A	124. A	125. C	126. B	127. D	128. D	129. D	130. B
131. B	132. B	133. A	134. A	135. C	136. D	137. C	138. C	139. B	140. A

141. B	142. C	143. A	144. A	145. B	146. B	147. B	148. B	149. D	150. D
151. D	152. D	153. D	154. D	155. C	156. B	157. B	158. A	159. B	160. C
161. A	162. B	163. A	164. B	165. A	166. D	167. B	168. D	169. C	170. D
171. A	172. B	173. C	174. D	175. A	176. D	177. A	178. B	179. C	180. B
181. A	182. B	183. D	184. D	185. D	186. A	187. B	188. C	189. D	190. A
191. D	192. D	193. D	194. D	195. D	196. C	197. B	198. D	199. A	200. A
201. B	202. B	203. C	204. C	205. B	206. C	207. A	208. D	209. A	210. B
211. C	212. D	213. A	214. B	215. A	216. A	217. A	218. B	219. B	220. B
221. A	222. D	223. B	224. B	225. B	226. B	227. C	228. B	229. C	230. B
231. C	232. C	233. A	234. C	235. B	236. A	237. B	238. C	239. D	240. B
241. B	242. C	243. C	244. D	245. D	246. A	247. A	248. A	249. B	250. C
251. D	252. A	253. B	254. C	255. C	256. D	257. A	258. B	259. C	260. D
261. A	262. C	263. A	264. C	265. B	266. D	267. A	268. C	269. C	270. C
271. C	272. B	273. D	274. D	275. B	276. C	277. C	278. C	279. D	280. A
281. C	282. D	283. A	284. B	285. B	286. C	287. D	288. A	289. A	290. B
291. C	292. D	293. A	294. A	295. B	296. C	297. B	298. C	299. D	300. A
301. A	302. D	303. B	304. A	305. B	306. C	307. A	308. B	309. B	310. B
311. A	312. B	313. B	314. D	315. A	316. C	317. D	318. D	319. D	320. D
321. D	322. B	323. B	324. C	325. D	326. C	327. B	328. A	329. A	330. B
331. C	332. C	333. C	334. C	335. B	336. B	337. C	338. D	339. D	340. A
341. A	342. A	343. D	344. A	345. C	346. A	347. B	348. B	349. B	350. D
351. B	352. B	353. D	354. C	355. B	356. D	357. B	358. C	359. A	360. B
361. C	362. B	363. C	364. C	365. D	366. C	367. B	368. C	369. B	370. D

371. D	372. D	373. C	374. D	375. A	376. A	377. B	378. B	379. B	380. C
381. D	382. C	383. B	384. C	385. B	386. A	387. C	388. A	389. D	390. C
391. B	392. D	393. A	394. D	395. D	396. D	397. D	398. B	399. A	400. C
401. D	402. A	403. B	404. C	405. D	406. A	407. B	408. C	409. D	410. A
411. B	412. C	413. C	414. A	415. B	416. B	417. C	418. B	419. D	420. A
421. B	422. B	423. A	424. B	425. C	426. D	427. A	428. B	429. B	430. A
431. C	432. C	433. A	434. B	435. D	436. C	437. D	438. C	439. A	440. A
441. C	442. C	443. C	444. B	445. A	446. D	447. B	448. D	449. C	450. B
451. A	452. D	453. B	454. A	455. C	456. A	457. C	458. C	459. B	460. B
461. C	462. D	463. D	464. D	465. C	466. B	467. C	468. B	469. A	470. A
471. A	472. D	473. A	474. C	475. D	476. D	477. D	478. C	479. B	480. B
481. D	482. A	483. B	484. C	485. B	486. A	487. B	488. C	489. A	490. B
491. B	492. D	493. B	494. A	495. C	496. C	497. D	498. A	499. D	500. B
501. B	502. A	503. D	504. B	505. A	506. C	507. C	508. D	509. C	510. C
511. A	512. A	513. D	514. B	515. A	516. B	517. A	518. A	519. C	520. D
521. A	522. B	523. A	524. D	525. A	526. C	527. B	528. C	529. A	530. A
531. C	532. C	533. A	534. B	535. C	536. C	537. D	538. C	539. B	540. C
541. B	542. B	543. B	544. C	545. C	546. D	547. D	548. A	549. A	550. A
551. A	552. C	553. C	554. C	555. C	556. B	557. B	558. C	559. B	560. C
561. B	562. C	563. D	564. A	565. D	566. A	567. B	568. A	569. C	570. C
571. D	572. D	573. A	574. D	575. B	576. D	577. C	578. B	579. D	580. D
581. C	582. C	583. B	584. C	585. B	586. A	587. B	588. D	589. C	590. D
591. B	592. B	593. A	594. D	595. C	596. D	597. B	598. C	599. D	600. B

601. B	602. C	603. B	604. A	605. B	606. B	607. A	608. D	609. B	610. D
611. D	612. C	613. A	614. C	615. C	616. C	617. B	618. B	619. A	620. B
621. B	622. A	623. B	624. A	625. D	626. A	627. B	628. C	629. A	630. C
631. D	632. A	633. A	634. A	635. A	636. B	637. A	638. D	639. A	640. B
641. B	642. A	643. A	644. A	645. D	646. D	647. A	648. A	649. B	650. A
651. A	652. A	653. A	654. A	655. C	656. B	657. D	658. A	659. C	660. D
661. B	662. D	663. A	664. A	665. C	666. D	667. B	668. D	669. A	670. C
671. A	672. C	673. C	674. C	675. B	676. B	677. A	678. A	679. D	680. D
681. A	682. A	683. C	684. B	685. D	686. C	687. B	688. B	689. B	690. D
691. C	692. D	693. D	694. A	695. D	696. A	697. D	698. D	699. D	700. B
701. C	702. B	703. C	704. A	705. A	706. C	707. B	708. B	709. C	710. B
711. D	712. A	713. B	714. C	715. D	716. C	717. B	718. C	719. C	720. D
721. A	722. C	723. A	724. C	725. C	726. B	727. D	728. B	729. C	730. B
731. C	732. D	733. B	734. A	735. B	736. D	737. D	738. C	739. C	740. B
741. D	742. B	743. C	744. B	745. B	746. B	747. C	748. D	749. A	750. C
751. A	752. C	753. B	754. D	755. B	756. B	757. A	758. A	759. C	760. C
761. A	762. B	763. C	764. B	765. A	766. A	767. C	768. A	769. D	770. A
771. B	772. B	773. C	774. B	775. D	776. B	777. A	778. A	779. D	780. D
781. A	782. A	783. B	784. A	785. A	786. D	787. B	788. B	789. C	790. C
791. C	792. B	793. D	794. C	795. C	796. A	797. C	798. B	799. C	800. D
801. D	802. D	803. D	804. D	805. B	806. D	807. D	808. B	809. C	810. B
811. D	812. B	813. A	814. D	815. A	816. B	817. D	818. A	819. C	820. B
821. B	822. D	823. D	824. B	825. B	826. A	827. B	828. B	829. D	830. D

831. D	832. B	833. B	834. D	835. C	836. B	837. C	838. D	839. C	840. C
841. B	842. B	843. A	844. B	845. B	846. A	847. B	848. B	849. D	850. D
851. A	852. D	853. D	854. B	855. C	856. B	857. D	858. D	859. A	860. A
861. C	862. B	863. B	864. C	865. B	866. D	867. A	868. C	869. A	870. D
871. C	872. C	873. D	874. D	875. C	876. A	877. A	878. A	879. B	880. C
881. B	882. A	883. C	884. C	885. B	886. C	887. B	888. A	889. B	890. D
891. D	892. A	893. B	894. A	895. B	896. C	897. D	898. B	899. B	900. A
901. C	902. A	903. B	904. B	905. C	906. B	907. C	908. B	909. A	910. A
911. A	912. D	913. B	914. A	915. C	916. D	917. B	918. D	919. D	920. D
921. C	922. A	923. B	924. B	925. D	926. A	927. A	928. D	929. C	930. B
931. D	932. C	933. C	934. C	935. B	936. C	937. C	938. B	939. C	940. A
941. D	942. D	943. D	944. A	945. A	946. A	947. C	948. D	949. B	950. C
951. C	952. A	953. D	954. D	955. A	956. C	957. B	958. D	959. A	960. A
961. A	962. D	963. D	964. C	965. A	966. A	967. A	968. D	969. D	970. C
971. C	972. A	973. B	974. B	975. B	976. A	977. B	978. D	979. A	980. A
981. C	982. A	983. C	984. A	985. A	986. C	987. D	988. B	989. A	990. B
991. D	992. B	993. D	994. D	995. B	996. C	997. C	998. D	999. A	1000. A
1001. C	1002. B	1003. B	1004. D	1005. C	1006. C	1007. D	1008. A	1009. B	1010. B
1011. D	1012. B	1013. A	1014. A	1015. B	1016. C	1017. A	1018. C	1019. D	1020. D
1021. B	1022. D	1023. B	1024. A	1025. C	1026. C	1027. A	1028. C	1029. A	1030. D
1031. D	1032. A	1033. D	1034. B	1035. C	1036. B	1037. D	1038. A	1039. A	1040. A
1041. A	1042. A	1043. C	1044. B	1045. C	1046. C	1047. C	1048. C	1049. D	1050. B
1051. C	1052. D	1053. A	1054. A	1055. B	1056. C	1057. B	1058. A	1059. D	1060. A

1061. A	1062. C	1063. B	1064. B	1065. A	1066. C	1067. A	1068. D	1069. C	1070. A
1071. A	1072. C	1073. B	1074. B	1075. C	1076. A	1077. A	1078. B	1079. A	1080. C
1081. A	1082. A	1083. B	1084. B	1085. A	1086. A	1087. B	1088. B	1089. C	1090. B
1091. C	1092. D	1093. C	1094. D	1095. B	1096. D	1097. C	1098. B	1099. D	1100. C
1101. B	1102. D	1103. C	1104. D	1105. B	1106. C	1107. C	1108. C	1109. A	1110. A
1111. A	1112. D	1113. D	1114. B	1115. A	1116. C	1117. C	1118. A	1119. A	1120. A
1121. D	1122. D	1123. A	1124. D	1125. C	1126. C	1127. C	1128. A	1129. C	1130. B
1131. C	1132. C	1133. A	1134. B	1135. C	1136. A	1137. B	1138. A	1139. B	1140. B
1141. C	1142. B	1143. B	1144. A	1145. D	1146. D	1147. D	1148. A	1149. A	1150. A
1151. B	1152. B	1153. D	1154. A	1155. D	1156. C	1157. B	1158. A	1159. C	1160. B
1161. C	1162. A	1163. A	1164. C	1165. D	1166. D	1167. A	1168. D	1169. C	1170. B
1171. C	1172. D	1173. C	1174. D	1175. B	1176. D	1177. B	1178. C	1179. C	1180. B
1181. D	1182. A	1183. B	1184. A	1185. C	1186. B	1187. B	.	.	.

□□□

8. Psychology & Mental Health Nursing (MCQ)

1. **When rehabilitating a client addicted to alcohol. The most important factor is.**
   A. The client's emotional or motivational readiness
   B. The qualitative level; Of the client's physical state
   C. The accepting attitude of the clinical family
   D. The availability of community resources
2. **The most important assessment data for the nurse to gather from a client in crisis would be:**
   A. Any significant physical health data
   B. The specific circumstances surrounding the "perceived" crisis situation
   C. A past history of any emotional problems in the family
   D. The client's work habits
3. **Projection: Rationalization, denied by a client with hallucinations and delusions are examples of disturbance:**
   A. The thought process B. Reality testing
   C. Logic D. Association
4. **Disulfiram (Antabuse) is prescribed for a client with a problem related to alcohol. The nurse understand that this medication works on the principle of which of the following therapies ?**
   A. Desensitization
   B. Self- Control Therapy
   C. Milieu Therapy
   D. Aversion therapy
5. **An elderly confused client with socially aggressive behaviour needs an environment that**
   A. Allows freedom of expression
   B. Provides control by setting limits
   C. Can be manipulated
   D. Is mainly group oriented
6. **If a patient asks you to pray with him you should?**
   A. Summon the hospital chaplain or minister of the patient faith
   B. Ask him about his faith because you may not agree with his religious belief
   C. Comply with his reuest, asking him if he has any special prayer he would like to say
   D. Ignore his reuest, realizing that illness after causes a patient concern about spiritual welfare
7. **An example of a synthetic narcotic include all the following except**
   A. Talwin B. Leritine
   C. Dilaudid D. Morphine
8. **If a group therapy has been successful, an individual will most likely be expected to**
   A. Gain personal insights into his or her own behaviour
   B. Be more understanding of the behaviour of others
   C. Be free from all emotional problems
   D. Be free from anxiety
9. **In planning nursing care for the elevated patient, a primary aim is**
   A. Providing a no stimulating environment
   B. Demanding that the patient follow rules
   C. Accepting and understanding behaviour
   D. Encouraging interpersonal contact
10. **A client frequently is seen a ghost when no one is present. She is most likely experiencing a**
    A. Delusion B. Illusion
    C. Hallucination D. Obsession
11. **A primary goal of nursing care for a withdrawn patient would be directed towards**
    A. Encouraging numerous group activities
    B. Gradually develop trust and one-to-one relationship
    C. Insisting on patient's own management
    D. Building his trust in all the staff initially
12. **The most serious complication of a major tranulizer.**
    A. Photosensitivity
    B. Agranulocytosis
    C. Parkinsonian symptoms
    D. Hypotension
13. **As a nurse you will know if the person has mood disorder if:**
    A. Has a flight of ideas B. Has flat affect
    C. Has a paranoia D. Has an illusion
14. **Which of the following is an appropriate nursing action to a patient with a delusion?**
    A. Isolate the patient as he or she may harm other people.
    B. Do not challenge the patient in proving the delusion
    C. Promise that antipsychotic drugs in order to improve the though content
    D. Make it to a point to challenge the patient in proving the delusion

15. Disorders like Cancer, CHD, Schizophrenia, IHD, Mental retardations are examples of:
A. Unifactoral disorders
B. Multifactoral disorders
C. Chromosomal disorders
D. Genetic disorders

16. Retaining permanent change in behaviour that occurs as a result of prior experiences is known as:
A. Education B. Aptitude
C. Learning D. Intelligence

17. One of the following experiments by Pavlov had shown an association between stimulus and response i.e. through pairing of conditional stimulus with an unconditional stimulus which gave response:
A. Operant con conditioning
B. Classical conditioning
C. Conditional reinforcement
D. Autonomic responses

18. Repulsion, curiosity, self assertion, construction are examples of:
A. Needs B. Drives
C. Incentives D. Instincts

19. Psychological changes during emotional arousal results from activation of the sympathetic division of the:
A. Autonomic nervous system
B. Parasympathetic system
C. Central nervous system
D. Peripheral nervous system

20. One of the stages as per Freud's psychosocial development theory emphasized that an infant in first year of life derives pleasure by nursing and sucking, putting finger or things in mouth:
A. Anal stage B. Phallic stage
C. Oral stage D. Latency stage

21. What will nurse do in case patient have seizures if alcohol is withdrawn suddenly:
A. Make patient comfortable and restrain
B. Take blood sample for ethanol level
C. Monitor vital signs
D. Prevent patient from injury

22. Anorexia nervosa complications are:
A. Hypokalemia, dehydration anaemia, electrolyte imbalance
B. Obesity, electrolyte imbalance, anaemia
C. Protein deficiency, dehydration, anaemia
D. Vitamin and protein deficiency with anaemia

23. Erikson theory of emotional development emphasized that 6-12 years of child wants adults to recognize him/her, have strong sense of duty and engage in many tasks; this is known as:
A. Sense of initiative B. Sense of identity
C. Sense of intimacy D. Sense of industry

24. In which of the following situation nurse should inform doctor immediately if patient is on antipsychotic drugs and blood pressure falls by:
A. 50mm of Hg B. 30mm of Hg
C. 20mm of hg D. Varies frequently

25. Psychological treatment for the personality problems, adjustment is done by:
A. Milieu therapy B. Family therapy
C. Individual therapy D. Psycho therapy

26. When patient expresses his/her feeling freely it is known as:
A. Persuasion B. Emotional catharsis
C. Ventilation D. Discussion

27. 50 years patient shows severe brain and mental deterioration, emotional distress, over activity; patient can be diagnosed to be suffering with:
A. Alzheimer's disease B. Picks disease
C. Parkinson's disease D. Huntington's disease

28. Which of the following disorder have symptom like persecution, grandeur, idea of reference, incoherence:
A. Disorder of activity
B. Disorder of attention
C. Disorder of thought
D. Disorder of perception

29. In case you find any patient is pre occupied with repeated thought that his/her hands are dirty and wash frequently for long time; it is an example of:
A. Phobia B. Obsession
C. Hallucination D. Delusion

30. Which of the following personality person will have in case he is having rigid behaviour and feels uncomfortable if anything is changed:
A. Hysterical
B. Paranoid
C. Obsessive compulsive
D. Schizoid

31. In case psychiatric patient is having liver or cardio vascular disorder; nurse should take precautions while administering:
A. Antidepressants B. Antihistamines
C. Anticholinergics D. Antipsychotic

32. What will be the diagnosis of the patient in case nurse found patient is giving silly smile, giggling,had hallucinations, fantasy delusions,do not maintain daily personal hygiene:
A. Hebephrenic schizophrenia
B. Simple schizophrenia
C. Catatonic schizophrenia
D. Paranoid schizophrenia

33. Which of the following is not one of the steps in the grief process?
A. Bargaining B. Denial
C. Anger D. Repression

34. Which of the following months matches with an infant first having the ability to sit-up independently?
A. 4 months B. 6 months
C. 8 months D 10 months

35. Which mechanism used by student when a student blaming to his teacher about failure in exam?
A. Compensation B. Projection
C. Denial D. Rationalization

36. A client justification of his behaviour using reason other than the real reason known as?
A. Compensation B. Rationalization
C. Delusion D. Projection

37. Severe emotion stress resulting in involuntary disturbance of physical functions is known as?
A. Alzheimer's disease
B. Conversion disorder
C. Depressive reaction
D. Bipolar disorder

38. Which of the following reflexes is not found at birth?
A. Flexion B. Babinski
C. Palmar D. Moro

39. Parallel play for toddlers develops in this age range?
A. 24-48 months B. 5-10 months
C. 10-14 months D. 12-24 months

40. Which of the following is not a sign of anxiety?
A. Moist mouth B. Dry Mouth
C. Hyperventilation D. GI symptoms

41. Which of the following best describes a person that is completely awake falling asleep spontaneously?
A. Somnambulism B. Cataplexy
C. Narcolepsy D. Transitional sleep

42. Which of the following is not a characteristic of a panic disorder?
A. Chest pain
B. Nausea
C. Excessive perspiration
D. Urination

43. Which of the following categories would a 72 year old adult be placed in?
A. Longevity vs. Guilt
B. Intimacy vs. Isolation
C. Generativitiy vs. Stagnation
D. Integrity vs. Despair

44. Which of the following categories would a 58 year old adult be placed in?
A. Longevity vs Guilt
B. Intimacy vs. Isolation
C. Generativitiy vs. Stagnation
D. Integrity vs. Despair

45. Which of the following categories would a 22 year old adult is placed in?
A. Autonomy vs. Doubt
B. Intimacy vs. Isolation
C. Generativitiy vs. Stagnation
D. Integrity vs. Despair

46. Which of the following term where a person using words that have no known meaning?
A. Erotic Delusion B. Neologisms
C. Neolithic D. Verbalism

47. Which treatment approach would be most therapeutic for a hospitalized client with antisocial behaviour?
A. Providing an unstructured environment
B. Participation in group therapy
C. Negotiating the treatment plan with the client
D. None of them

48. A client with paranoid delusions believes the hospital food is being poisoned by the staff. What is the most effective method of encouraging nutritional intake is to serve:
A. Appoint nutritional therapist
B. The client's favourite foods in an attractive arrangement
C. Only warm foods that arrive from the kitchen with lids in place
D. Individual items that are pre-packaged and sealed

49. Which will the nurse expect to be ordered to manage a client's withdrawal from alcohol?
A. Promethazine B. Chlordiazepoxide
C. Haloperidol D. Disulfiram

50. Initially the nurse would expect a client to react to a diagnosis of cancer with:
A. Anger B. Denial
C. Acceptance D. Fear

51. The nurse would judge that a client might be developing Wernicke-Korsakoff syndrome when the client exhibits:
A. Mood swings and suicidal ideation
B. Suspicion and fearfulness
C. Short term memory loss and disorientation
D. Aggression and impulsiveness

52. A priority nursing intervention for a client experiencing an acute manic episode?
A. Discourage the client's use of vulgar language
B. Protect the client from impulsive behaviour
C. Maintain the client's contact with his/her family
D. Redirect excessive energy to creative tasks

53. A client who is taking chlorpromazine hydrochloride is experiencing extra pyramidal side effects (EPS). The nurse understands that EPS is:
A. Dysfunction of the cardiovascular system
B. Involuntary muscle movement's
C. Similar to a seizure disorder
D. A toxic reaction of the liver

54. A client is being prepared to receive electroconvulsive therapy (ECT) when the nurse realizes the client has not signed an informed consent. What provides the Rational for the appropriate nursing action needed to address this issue?
A. Permission is assumed since the client is an involuntary admission
B. Failure to obtain informed consent can result in a law suit
C. A physician is needed to witness the consent form
D. Verbal consent by the client is sufficient

55. A female patient with paranoid schizophrenia runs to the nurse and says, "Why are you poisoning me? How should the nurse respond?
A. "I'm a nurse, I'm not poisoning you. It's against the nursing code of ethics."
B. "I'm a nurse, and you're a patient in the hospital. I'm not going to harm you."
C. "I'm not poisoning you. And how could I possibly steal your soul?"
D. "I sense anger, Are you feeling angry today?"

56. The nurse formulates a nursing diagnosis of "impaired verbal communication" for a male patient with schizotypal personality disorder. Based on this nursing diagnosis, which nursing intervention is most appropriate?
A. Helping the patient to participate in social interactions
B. Establishing a one-on-one relationship with the patient
C. Establishing alternative forms of communication
D. Allowing the patient to decide when he wants to participate in verbal communication with you

57. A female patient with obsessive-compulsive disorder tells the nurse that he must check the lock on his apartment door 5 times before leaving for an appointment. The nurse knows that this behaviour represents the patient's attempt to:
A. Pt forget about lock
B. Control his thoughts
C. Maintain the safety of his home
D. Reduce anxiety

58. Which nursing intervention is most important when restraining a violent male patient?
A. Reviewing hospital policy regarding how long the patient can be restrained
B. Preparing a p.r.n. dose of the patient's psychotropic medication
C. Checking that the restraints have been applied correctly
D. Asking if the patient needs to use the bathroom or is thirsty

59. Mental health laws in each state specify when restraints can be used and which type of restraints are allowed. Most laws tell that restraints can be used:
A. For a maximum of 2 hours
B. As necessary to control the patient
C. If the patient poses a present danger to self or others
D. Only with the patient's consent

60. The nurse is aware that the Hormonal effects of the antipsychotic medications include which of the following?
A. Retrograde ejaculation and gynecomastia
B. Dysmenorrhea and increased vaginal bleeding
C. Polydipsia and dysmenorrheal
D. Akinesia and dysphasia

61. The nurse is caring for a female client in the manic phase of bipolar disorder that's ready for discharge from the psychiatric unit. As the nurse begins to terminate the nurse-client relationship, which client response is most appropriate?
A. Expressing feeling of anxiety
B. Displaying anger, shouting, and banging the table
C. Withdrawing from the nurse in silence
D. Rationalizing the termination, saying that "everything comes to an end"

62. The nurse is caring for a male client with schizophrenia. Which outcome is the least desirable?
A. The client spends more time by himself

B. The client doesn't engage in delusional thinking
C. The client doesn't harm himself or others
D. The client demonstrates the ability to meet his own self-care needs

63. The nurse is assigned to care for a recently admitted female client who has attempted suicide. What should the nurse do?
A. Search the client's belongings and room carefully for items that could be used to attempt suicide
B. Express trust that the client won't cause self-harm while in the facility
C. Respect the client's privacy by not searching any belongings
D. Remind all staff members to check on the client frequently

64. The person with generalised anxiety disorder:-
A. Worries about everyday routine events
B. Does not worry about everyday routine events
C. Has no routine everyday events to worry about
D. Is carefree and settled in mood

65. Which theory views that people have free-will and potential for self-actualization?
A. Behaviourism
B. Psychodynamic theory
C. Cognitive theory
D. Humanism

66. Operant conditioning was proposed by:-
A. Ivan Pavlov B. BF Skinner
C. Sigmond Freud D. Abraham Maslow

67. A Neurotic disorder in which person has two more personalities or which only one is being manifest at a time:
A. Dissociative fuge
B. Dissociative Amnesia
C. Dissociative Identity Disorder
D. Hysterical Fits

68. The Most important dependence producing opoid Derivates are?
A. Codeine and Papaverine
B. Morphine and Heroine
C. Heroine and Methadone
D. Pethidine and Nolaptrine

69. In following which is not a characteristic of disulfiram ethanol reaction?
A. Tachycardia B. Hypotension
C. Hypertension D. Headache

70. The drug which is used for managing withdrawal symptoms of opoid?
A. Clonidine B. Naltrxone
C. Mathadone D. All of the Above

71. In following which statement is true:-
A. Onset of dementia is acute while onset of delirium is chronic
B. During dementia sleep wake cycle is grossly disturbed while during delirium it is normal
C. Attention and Concentration during delirium grossly disturbed while during dementia it is normal.
D. All of the Above

72. A disorder in which attempt is made to counteract the effects of overeating by self induced vomiting, after period of starvation etc.
A. Anorexia Nervosa B. Bulimia Nervosa
C. Hypermnesia D. Anorexia

73. The nurse employed in a psychiatric unit is as signed to care for a client admitted to the unit 2 days ago. On review of the client's record. The nurse notes that the admission was an informal voluntary admission. Based on this type of admission, the nurse expects which of the following?
A. The client will be very resistant to treatment measures
B. The client's family will be very resistant to treatment measures
C. The client will be angry and will refuse care
D. The client will participate in the treatment plan

74. The nurse is planning care for a client admitted to the psychiatric unit with a diagnosis of paranoid schizophrenia. Which nursing diagnosis should receive the highest priority?
A. Risk for violence toward self or others
B. Imbalanced nutrition: Less than body requirements
C. Ineffective family coping
D. Impaired verbal communication

75. A client is admitted to the psychiatric unit of a local hospital with chronic undifferentiated schizophrenia. During the next several days, the client is seen laughing, yelling, and talking to herself. This behaviour is characteristic of:
A. Delusion
B. Looseness of association
C. Illusion
D. Hallucination

76. The definition of nihilistic delusions is:
A. A false belief about the functioning of the body
B. Belief that the body is deformed or defective in a specific way

C. False ideas about the self, others, or the world
D. The inability to carry out motor activities

77. A client with schizophrenia hears a voice telling him he is evil and must die. The nurse understands that the client is experiencing:
A. A delusion B. Flight of ideas
C. Ideas of reference D. A hallucination

78. The characteristic manifestation that will differentiate bulimia nervosa from anorexia nervosa is that bulimic individuals
A. Have episodic binge eating and purging
B. Have repeated attempts to stabilize their weight
C. Have peculiar food handling patterns
D. Have threatened self-esteem

79. A psychotic client reports to the evening nurse that the day nurse put something suspicious in his water with his medication. The nurse replies, "You're worried about your medication?" The nurse's communication is:
A. An example of presenting reality
B. Reinforcing the client's delusions
C. Focusing on emotional content
D. A non-therapeutic technique called mind reading

80. A nurse is performing an assessment on a client with dementia. Which data gathered during the assessment indicate a manifestation associated with dementia?
A. Confabulation
B. Improvement in sleeping
C. Absence of sundown syndrome
D. Presence of personal hygienic care

81. A nurse is caring for a client with anorexia nervosa. The nurse is monitoring the behaviour of the client and understands that a client with anorexia nervosa manages anxiety by:
A. Engaging in immoral acts
B. Always reinforcing self-approval
C. Observing rigid rules and regulations
D. Having the need always to make the right decision

82. A client reports losing his sight in both eyes. He's diagnosed as having conversion disorder and is admitted to the psychiatric unit. Which nursing intervention would be most appropriate for this client?
A. Not focusing on his blindness
B. Providing self-care for him
C. Telling him that his blindness isn't real
D. Teaching eye exercises to strengthen his eyes

83. A nurse places a female client in full leather restraints. How often must the nurse check the client's circulation?
A. Once per hour
B. Once per shift
C. Every 15 to 30 minutes
D. Every 2 hours

84. Which is the best indicator of success in the long term management of the client?
A. His symptoms are replaced by indifference to his feelings
B. He participates in diversionary activities.
C. He learns to verbalize his feelings and concerns
D. He states that his behaviour is irrational.

85. The client said "I can't even take care of my baby. I'm good for nothing." Which is the appropriate nursing diagnosis?
A. Ineffective individual coping related to loss
B. Impaired verbal communication related to inadequate social skills
C. Low esteem related to failure in role performance
D. Impaired social interaction related to repressed anger

86. Dissociation is present in all, EXCEPT:-
A. Fugue B. Delirium
C. Multiple personality D. Somnambulism

87. A client on Lithium has diarrhea and vomiting. What should the nurse do first?
A. Recognize this as a drug interaction
B. Give the client Cogentin
C. Reassure the client that these are common side effects of lithium therapy
D. Hold the next dose and obtain an order for a stat serum lithium level

88. Which of the following best describes a therapeutic milieu?
A. A therapy that rewards adaptive behaviour
B. A cognitive approach to change behaviour
C. A living, learning or working environment.
D. A permissive and congenial environment

89. At what age can medical treatment be withdrawn?
A. 65 B. 80
C. 100 D. No age

90. Mutism is NOT associated with?
A. Hysteria
B. Catatonic stupor
C. Depressive stupor
D. Korsakoff's psychosis

91. In following which is not included in the 4 " A" S of Schizophrenia ?
A. Ambivalence
B. Autism

C. Anxiety
D. Association Disorder

92. In ICD-10 Classification the disease that are classified in group F70-79 are-:
A. Neurotic Stress Related and Somatoform Disorder
B. Mood (Affective) Disorder
C. Disorder of Adult Personality.
D. Mental Retardation

93. Nursing care for improving sleep pattern of Schizophrenic patient include except?
A. Switch off the main light
B. Give a glass of hot milk before sleeping
C. Avoid day time activities
D. Provide calm and cool environment

94. Tertiary prevention of mental retardation includes-:
A. Training and Education level
B. Autism
C. Early detection of presence of mental Retardation
D. Immunization of children with DPT, BCG, OPV and MMR

95. Confabulation is commonly observed in patients with:-
A. Obsessive-compulsive disorders
B. Delusional disorders
C. Personality disorders
D. Amnestic syndrome

96. After ingestion of alcohol by a person who is on disulfiram, disulfiram ethanol reaction occurs within:-
A. 10 min B. 30 min
C. 60 min D. 120 min

97. A five year old Mohan diagnosed as rectal cancer and his response to the diagnosis is that " Nothing is wrong it is just hemorrhoids" which defensive mechanism he used :–
A. Projection B. Repression
C. Denial D. Displacement

98. The factor which is responsible to cause schizophrenia :-
A. Genetic Factor
B. Psychosocial Factor
C. Socio-cultural Factor
D. All of the Above

99. Another term for superego is:
A. Self B. Ideal self
C. Conscience D. Subconscious

100. The therapy in which harmony between husband and wife may achieved or established by efforts of experts :-
A. Family therapy B. Marital therapy
C. Cognitive therapy D. Group therapy

101. Nursing care in electroconvulsive therapy includes:
A. Preparing and monitoring the patient during the actual procedure
B. Providing educational and emotional support
C. Pre-treatment planning and assessment
D. All of the Above

102. Electroencephalogram is:
A. Recording of brain wave activity
B. Recording of peristalsis
C. Recording of heart activity
D. None of the above

103. A patient has adequate speech amount but content provides little information, the patient is suffering from:
A. Poverty of speech B. Echolalia
C. Poverty of idea D. Mutism

104. Catatonic behaviour in schizophrenia is characterized by which of the following:
A. Resisting attempts to be moved
B. Maintaining rigid, immobile postures
C. Decrease in reactivity to the environment
D. All of the above

105. Which of the following are risk factors for childhood psychiatric disorders?
A. Harsh or inadequate parents
B. Parental psychopathology
C. Repeated early separation from parents
D. All of the Above

106. Excessive sleep is termed as:
A. Insomnia B. Asomnia
C. Somnambulism D. Hypersomnia

107. The nurse is planning to formulate apsychotherapy group; several clients are interested in attending the session. The nurse plans the group, knowing that the maximum number of group members to include in this group is:
A. 16 B. 10 C. 12 D. 14

108. Parents of the hospitalized infants should be encouraged to stay with their child to help decrease:
A. Problem with attachment
B. Risk for injury
C. Separation anxiety
D. Failure of thrive

109. The primary physical effect of alcohol in the body is to:
A. Stimulates the cerebral cortex
B. Decrease the irritability of muscle cells
C. Depress the central nervous system
D. Increase activirty on gastro-intestinal system

110. The mental disorder know as "Split personality"
A. Psychosis B. Schizophrenia
C. Paranoia D. Psychoneurosis

111. Growth retardation can be identified by
A. Blood examination B. Feeding pattern
C. Apgar score D. Weight recording

112. In Maslow's hierarchy of needs, which considered as the most basic:
A. Love and belonging needs
B. Esteem needs
C. Self actualization needs
D. Physiological needs

113. Which One of the best form of controlled thinking?
A. Reasoning B. Imagination
C. Day dreaming D. Memorizing

114. Repeated small movement of a habitual kind:
A. Mannerism B. Tics
C. Compulsion D. Over activity

115. The IQ. of a person with normal intelligence is
A. 50-69 B. 70-80
C. 110-119 D. 90-109

116. "Sour grape mechanism" is a form of:
A. Rationalization B. Projection
C. Substitution D. Sublimation

117. Filling the gap of memory with fabrication:
A. Par amnesia B. Amnesia
C. Dejvu D. Hyperamenesia

118. Ego works based on the:
A. Reality B. Pleasure
C. Perfection D. Conscience

119. Gradual disappearance of conditioned response to stimuli is referred as:
A. Negative conditioning
B. Extinction
C. Delayed conditioning
D. Elimination

120. A defence mechanism that allows to convert our unacceptable behaviour into acceptable form is:
A. Introjection B. Sublimation
C. Projection D. Displacement

121. Father of Intelligence test is:
A. Alfred Binet B. Erick Erickson
C. Alfred Adler D. Carljung

122. The stage which keeps an individual physically alert to face the danger arising out of stress is termed:
A. Adjustment reaction
B. Stage of resistance
C. Exhaustion stage
D. Alarm reaction

123. Elevated mood with increased psychomotor activity is a characteristic feature of:
A. Mania B. Euphoria
C. Bipolar Disorder D. Dysthymia

124. Irrational fear related to closed spaces is referred as:
A. Acrophobia B. Agoraphobia
C. Claustrophobia D. Nosophobia

125. Loss of personal identity and wandering away from psychiatric hospital is referred as:
A. Fugue B. Split personality
C. Possession state D. Trance state

126. The voltage needed to produce seizures while giving ECT is:
A. 180 to 220 volts B. 40 to 70 volts
C. 150 to 180 volts D. 70 to 150 volts

127. The emotional state an individual experience to the loss of loved object is:
A. Grief B. Mourning
C. Ereavement D. Agony

128. Release of feelings that takes place by talking about an emotionally charged areas is:
A. Clarification B. Abreaction
C. Suggestion D. Exploration

129. Temporary discharge of the patient from the psychiatric hospital is referred as:
A. Parole B. Abscond
C. Termination D. Escape

130. The drug which is used to create aversion of the Alcohol Dependence:
A. Apomorphine B. Propanolol
C. Diazepam D. Disulphiram

131. Serene is an example of:
A. Antipsychotic B. Antidepressant
C. Mood stabilizer D. Anxiolytic

132. The recording of conversation between the nurse and patient in a psychiatric set up is termed:
A. Therapeutic communication
B. Interview technique
C. Process recording
D. Case study

133. Which of the brain regulates NREM sleep?
A. Pons B. Hypothalamus
C. Basal forebrain D. Amygdale

134. The teaching directed towards creating/ promoting an interest in learning is known as
A. Principle of creativity
B. Principle of motivation
C. Principle of training
D. Principle of reinforcement

135. Major approaches in problem solving are

A. Inductive, Deductive, Active, Analytic
B. Inductive, Deductive, Analytic, Synthetic
C. Inductive, Deductive, Initiative, Synthetic
D. Inductive, Deductive, Purposive, Synthetic

136. Normal coping strategies are activated in the following phase of crisis

A. Phase I- Establishing relationship
B. Phase II - Assessment
C. Phase IV - Intervention
D. Phase V - Termination

137. A child with typical facial features such as low nasal bridge with short upturned nose, flattened mid face, long philtrum with narrow upper lip is diagnosed to have

A. Fetal Alcohol syndrome
B. Autism spectrum disorder
C. Down syndrome
D. Tourette syndrome

138. Identify the wrong answer behavioral problems of childhood includes

A. Breath-holding spell
B. Temper Tantrums
C. Thumb sucking
D. Failure to thrive

139. Match the developmental stage with their psycho social development according to Eric Ericksol

A	B
A. Infancy	A. Sense of industry
B. School age	B. Sense of intimacy
C. Early adolescence	C. Sense of trust
D. Late adolescence	D. Sense of identity

	1.	2.	3.	4.
A.	C	B	A	D
B.	C	B	D	A
C.	C	A	D	B
D.	C	D	B	A

140. Which statement by a person clearly with paranoid schizophrenia most clearly indicates the antipsychotic medication is effective?

A. I used to hear scany voices but now I don't hear them anymore
B. My medicine is working fine. I am not having any problems
C. Sometimes it's hard for me to fall asleep, but I usually sleep all night
D. I think some of the staff members don't like me. They're mean to me

141. Following are the dysfunctional behaviours associated with substance abuse

A. Manipulation B. Impulsiveness
C. Anger D. Acceptance

A. B,C,D B. A,B,C
C. A,B,D D. D,C,A

142. The Misinterpretation of a real stimuli within the environment is called as

A. Hallucination B. Delusion
C. Illusion D. Obsession

143. A nurse suggests activities for a 7-yr old child with autistic disorder. Which activity is most likely to engage this child?

A. Playing checkers with another child
B. Building with blocks alone
C. Playing kickball with a small group of chil-dren
D. Having a birthday party with 6 to 8 other children

144. Roarschah ink blot test, thematic apperception test are based on the phenomenon of

A. Projection B. Identification
C. Transference D. Observation

145. Individuals rate attitudes using a pair of opposite adjective in the

A. Thurstone scale
B. Semantic differential scale
C. Interview method
D. Likert scale

146. Which of the following is an example of a primary prevention programme in mental health?

A. Efforts to make the disorders less debilitating
B. Improving the study skills of school drop out
C. Genetic counselling
D. Telephone counselling for those contemplating suicide

147. Consider the following stages of personality by freud

1. Oral 2. Anal
3. Latency 4. Phallic
5. Genital

What is the correct order of stages by freud?

A. 1-2-3-4-5 B. 2-1-3-4-5
C. 1-2-4-3-5 D. 2-1-4-5-3

148. The concept used for father - dominated family

A. Patrilocal family B. Patriarchal family
C. Patrilineal family D. Conjugal family

149. Find the odd statement

A. Casual, conventional, expressive
B. The contagion theory, the emergent theory
C. Mob, crowd, public
D. Active crowd, audience, public opinion

A. C and D are odd statements
B. A and B are odd statements
C. B and D are odd statements
D. Only B odd statement

150. Sociology is important for nursing practice because nurses are, except
A. Critically involved in making sense and giving purpose to life, illness and death
B. Able to discriminate people by culture
C. Confronting problems which is controversial in society
D. Engaged in the study of human societies

151. The form of marriage in which one man marries more than one woman at a given time
A. Fraternal polyandry B. Polyandry
C. Polygony D. Monogamy

152. The causes of population growth are except
A. Widening gap between birth and death rates
B. Low age at marriage
C. High literacy
D. Religious attitude towards family planning

153. The most useful therapy in treating children with psychiatric disorder is
A. Behaviour therapy B. Psycho therapy
C. Cognitive therapy D. Pharmaco therapy

154. Spot the incorrect statement regarding principles of learning according to JTFSL (Joint Task force on student learning)
A. Learning is an active process
B. Learning is an outcome of stimulation and motivation of the learner
C. Learning is an act of self-awareness
D. Learning is an act of self-identification

155. The function of gland which is affected in lithium toxicity is:
A. Thyroid B. Parathyroid
C. Pituitary D. Adrenal

156. A behavioural therapy of sudden, direct and maximum exposure to the fear producing stimulus:
A. Response prevention
B. Bio feed back
C. Flooding
D. Desensitization

157. Ms. 'M' is diagnosed with an obsessive compulsive disorder. She is consistently late for duty as a result of repetitively checking whether appliances are unplugged before leaving home. The most appropriate nursing diagnosis for Ms. 'M' is:
A. Anxiety
B. Social isolation
C. Situational low self esteem
D. Deficient knowledge

158. Patient: "I cannot study. My mind keeps wandering"
Nurse: "You have trouble concentrating"
The above statements are example of the following therapeutic communication technique:
A. Focusing B. Restating
C. Exploring D. Reflecting I

159. An adult with major depression complains of severe sleep disturbances, daytime drowsiness and fatigability. How would the nurse classify this sleep problem?
A. Dyssomnia
B. Parasomnia
C. Secondary sleep disorder
D. Primary sleep disorder

160. A client says to the nurse, "Life doesn't have any joy in it anymore. Things I once did for pleasures aren't fun". How would the nurse document this complaint?
A. Dysthymia
B. Anhedonia
C. Euphoria
D. Psychomotor retardation

161. The drugs used in schizophrenia are:
A. Olanzapine
B. Risperidone
C. Imipramine
D. Clozapine
Choose the correct code:
A. A, B and C only B. A, B and D only
C. C, B and A only D. C, D and B only

162. Drinking of alcohol severely effects the
A. Kidney B. Brain
C. Stomach D. Liver

163. Psychoanalytic therapy was developed by:
A. Sigmund Freud B. Jacobson
C. Franklin D. Aristotle

164. Hallucination is caused by:
A. Gastro-intestinal disorder
B. Mental illness
C. Disorder of reproductive organs
D. Infectious disease

165. Which of the following is not a symptom of depression?
A. Loss of interest in daily Activities
B. Delusion of guilt
C. Suicidal ideas
D. Delusion of grandiosity

166. If the IQ. of a child is 45, in which category of Mental Retardation will he be categorised?
A. Mild mental retardation
B. Moderate mental retardation
C. Severe mental retardation
D. Profound mental retardation

167. Nurse attending to a patient receiving electroconvulsive therapy (ECT) in a psychiatry department should ensure the compliance of the following except:
A. Patient's hair should be kept clean and dry
B. Emptying of bladder and bowel is not necessary.
C. Hairpins, bracelets, body piercing should be removed
D. Take the informed consent from a patient.

168. A person seeing a design on the floor thought it was a fossil. It is an example of:
A. Illusion B. Delusion
C. Hallucination D. Idea of reference

169. Mr. Santosh, 18 year old student, is admitted to the ward with a diagnosis of epilepsy. He tells the nurse that be is experiencing a generalized tingling sensation and sinell of roses. These complaints indicate:
A. An olfactory hallucination
B. Acute neuritis
C. An aura
D. Acute cerebro-vascular accident

170. All of the following are signs of anorexia nervosa, except:
A. Fatigue
B. Frequent eating habits
C. Dry hair and skin
D. Anxious and hopeless look

171. All of the following are true about nursing care for a patient with delirium except:
A. Allow the client to wear his/her own clothes
B. Refrain family members to stay with the patient
C. Avoid room changes, especially at night
D. Avoid physical restraint whenever possible

172. Benzodiazepines reduce anxiety by acting on which neurotransmitter?
A. Dopamine B. GABA
C. Serotonin D. Noradrenaline

173. The most effective psychotherapy for a 9 year old child diagnosed with Attention Deficit hyperactivity Disorder (ADHD) is:
A. Family therapy B. Milieu therapy
C. Play therapy D. Behaviour therapy

174. Aphasia refers to:
A. Loud speech
B. Increased rate of speech
C. Inability to speak
D. High pitch speech

175. A special kind of therapy in which the total structure of the treatment unit is involved as part of the helping process is called:
A. Milieu therapy
B. Psychotherapy
C. Gestalt therapy
D. Cognitive behaviour therapy

176. Fear of high places is known as:
A. Acrophobia B. Algophobia
C. Claustrophobia D. Xenophobia

177. A false memory that the patient believes to be true is:
A. Confabulation B. Fugue
C. Cataplexy D. Anxiety

178. Most severe alcohol withdrawal syndrome is:
A. Alcoholic hallucinosis
B. Hang over
C. Alcoholic seizures
D. Delirium tremors

179. A condition in which person maintaining the body posture into which it is placed is:
A. Anxiety B. Echopraxia
C. Cataplexy D. Catalepsy

180. Abnormal involuntary movement which occurs suddenly, repetitively and purposeless is:
A. Mannerism B. Compulsion
C. Cataplexy D. Tic

181. Common risk of severe depression is
A. Thought block B. Fatigability
C. Hallucinations D. Suicide

182. In which defence mechanism the person transfers his anger on others:-
A. Conversion B. Delusion
C. Projection D. Repression

183. Mania is a
A. Mood disorder
B. Thought disorder
C. Anxiety related disorder
D. Dissociative disorder

184. Which condition places a patient with cardiac illness at increased risk of sudden death?
A. Depression B. Anxiety
C. Bulimia D. Chest pain

185. The ability to tolerate frustration is an example of one of the functions of the:
A. Superego B. ID
C. Ego D. Unconscious

186. The Cause of suicide is :-
A. Worthlessness B. Hopelessness
C. Helplessness D. All of the Above

187. Flight of ideas refers to:
A. Pattern of rapid transition from topic to topic
B. Repetition of words heard
C. New words invented by patient
D. Use of rhyming words

188. Hallucinations and social behaviours are typical symptoms of:
A. Paranoid schizophrenia
B. Disorganized type of schizophrenia
C. Catatonic schizophrenia
D. Undifferentiated schizophrenia

189. When a client requires increasingly larger doses to obtain the desired effect of a drug it is referred to as:
A. Tolerance B. Dependence
C. Habituation D. Addiction

190. The nursing actions recommended for a client experiencing alcohol withdrawal include all the following except one:
A. Using short concrete statements
B. Assessing vital signs
C. Monitoring intake output
D. Ambulating the client

191. A person with cyclothyamiacs personality has:
A. Alternating periods of elation and depression
B. Rigid behaviour
C. A feeling of helplessness and pessimism
D. Emotionality and aggressiveness

192. Aggression turned inwardly on the individual himself, it is referred to as:
A. Sadism B. Obsession
C. Masochism D. Compulsion

193. Mental retardation is due to;
A. Birth injuries
B. Infection of the brain
C. Delayed milestone
D. All of the Above

194. A childhood behaviour problem is:
A. Temper tantrum B. Enuresis
C. Encopresis D. Incontinence

195. Loss of reality is the typical sign of:
A. Obsessive compulsive neurosis
B. Hysteria
C. Schizophrenia
D. Anxiety Neurosis

196. Physical symptoms in psychosomatic disorders are caused by:
A. Emotional factors
B. Physical factors
C. Environmental factors
D. Genetic factors

197. Individual difference is interest, ability and capacity in a specific field is measured by applying one of the following test:
A. Attitude test
B. Aptitude test
C. Intelligence quotient test
D. Mental ability test

198. Thinking is a mental process that deals with:
A. Thoughts and ideas
B. Motives and movements
C. Actions and reactions
D. Feeling and emotions

199. Significant components of personality as described by Sigmond Freud are:
A. Conscious, preconscious and subconcious
B. Id, ego and supergo
C. Dream interpretation
D. Defense mechanism

200. When a person retreat or revert to an infantile of childish level of behaviour is called:
A. Suppression B. Repression
C. Regression D. Sublimation

201. The family plays an important role in the emotional development of the individual because it?
A. Provides support for the young
B. Gives reward and punishment
C. Helps one to learn identity and roles
D. Reflects the mores of a larger society

202. Unsatisfied needs create anxiety that motivate and individual to act. The action is brought about mainly to
A. Reduce tension
B. Deny the situation
C. Remove the problem
D. Relieve the physical discomfort

203. Causes of delirium are:-
A. Head Trauma B. Infection
C. Metabolic Disorder D. All of the Above

204. In ECT, The intensity of Electric Current is between:
A. 70-130 Volts B. 130-220 Volts
C. 220-440 Volts D. None of the above

205. Projection: Rationalization, denied and distortion by a client with hallucinations and delusions are examples of disturbance in
A. Logic B. Association
C. Reality testing D. The thought process

206. The main personality problem for clients who needs props to blur reality is usually?
A. Mistrust B. Ego ideal
C. Dependency D. Role blurring

207. An elderly confused client with socially aggressive behaviour needs an environment that
A. Can be manipulated
B. Is mainly group oriented
C. Allows freedom of expression
D. Provides control by setting limits

208. Which of the following is not symptom of Schizophrenia?
A. Delusion B. Hallucination
C. Excessive Anxiety D. None of the above

209. In planning nursing care for the elated patient, a primary aim is
A. Encouraging interpersonal contact
B. Providing a non-stimulating environment
C. Demanding that the patient follow rules
D. Accepting and understanding behaviour

210. When a nurse patient relationship is ending the patient may react by
A. Rejecting the nurse
B. Becoming angry
C. Regression and withdrawal
D. Acceptance

211. Mrs A frequently is seen to lean her head to one side, cup her ear and move her lips when no one is present. She is most likely experiencing a
A. Illusion B. Hallucination
C. Delusion D. Obsession

212. A primary goal of nursing care for a withdrawn patient would be directed towards
A. Building his or her trust in all the staff initially
B. Gradually building trust by means of a one to one relationship
C. Encouraging numerous group activities
D. Insisting on patient's own management

213. Increased dopamine neurotransmitter receptors in the Brain could be responsible for the onset of
A. Depression B. Narcissism
C. Schizophrenia D. None of the Above

214. Hebephrenic Schizophrenia is known as:-
A. Disorganized Schizophrenia
B. Undifferentiated Schizophrenia
C. Residual Schizophrenia
D. None of the Above

215. In following which is the major indication of ECT:
A. Severe depression with suicidal risk
B. Severe mania
C. Phobia
D. Hysteria

216. What is the main side effect of ECT:
A. Retrograde amnesia B. Fracture
C. Hypotension D. Seizure

217. Which one of the following is not a part of the group structure?
A. Role B. Status
C. Norm D. Obedience

218. Learning is defined as:
A. Any change in behaviour
B. Acquisition of information
C. Maturational change
D. Relatively permanent change in behaviour accused by experience

219. "Classical conditioning" is a learning process. Which of the following action is taking place in that process?
A. Some response is shaped by its consequences
B. People follow what they observe other people doing
C. Reflexive response is associated with a new stimulus
D. Behaviour is controlled using punishment

220. As per the IQ. formula, a normal child is one for whom:
A. Mental age less than chronological age
B. Mental age greater than chronological age
C. Mental age is equivalent to chronological age
D. Mental age is not related to chronological age

221. The ability to produce a novel and unique ideas is called as:
A. Intelligence B. Aptitude
C. Prudence D. Creativity

222. Redirecting feelings from a threatening target to a less threatening target is known as:
A. Reaction formation B. Displacement
C. Regression D. Projection

223. A teenager who required lengthy rehabilitation after an accident decides to become a physical therapist as a result of his experience is an example for
A. Introjections B. Projection
C. Identification D. Displacement

224. Which one of the following is not a component of nonverbal communication?
A. Physical Appearance and dress
B. Touch
C. Facial expression
D. Language

225. In Psychiatry, therapy involving environment is called as
A. Group therapy B. Family therapy
C. Behaviour therapy D. Milieu therapy

226. The nurse identifies the primary nursing diagnosis for a patient admitted in psychiatric ward as risk for suicide related to feelings of hopelessness from loss of relationship. Which of the following outcome criterion would be most accurate for the client?
A. The client has experienced no physical harm
B. The client sets realistic goals for herself
C. The client expresses some optimism and hope for the future
D. The client has reached a stage of acceptance in the loss of the relationship

227. The psychotic persons invents new words, that are meaningless to others but have symbolic meaning to the psychotic person is called as
A. Associative looseness
B. Neologism
C. Clang association
D. Word salad

228. Revised name of the Multiple Personality is :-
A. DID B. MDP
C. OCD D. None of the Above

229. The diurnal (24 hour rhythm of our body) such as the sleep wake cycle is regulated by which of the following hormones?
A. Thyroxin B. Melatonin
C. Gonadotrophin D. Relaxin

230. Play for the preschool age child is necessary for the emotional development of :
A. Projection B. Competition
C. Introjection D. Independence

231. The stage of growth and development basically concerned with role identification is the :
A. Oral stage B. Oedipal stage
C. Latency stage D. Genital stage

232. Agitated depression is NOT characterized by?
A. Depressed mood
B. Increased motor activity
C. Restless and purposeless movements
D. Elevated mood

233. A client expresses the belief that the C.B.I is out to kill him. This is an example of:
A. A hallucination
B. A self-accusatory delusion
C. A delusion of persecution
D. An error in judgement

234. Mr. James is withdrawn and non-communicative; to encourage him to talk, the best plan of nursing intervention would be to:
A. Ask simple questions that require answers
B. Focus on non-threatening subjects
C. Try to get him to discuss his feelings
D. Sit and look through magazines with him

235. The most accurate definition of 'depression', as used in psychiatry, is:
A. A disturbance in mood as a reaction to the loss of a love object
B. A total loss of control over emotional impulses
C. An inability to make decisions or function
D. A disturbance in mood as a result of frustration of instinctual strivings.

236. The affect most commonly found in client with schizophrenia is one of:
A. Happiness and elation
B. Apathy and flatness
C. Sadness and depression
D. Anger and hostility

237. Imaginary perceptions are called:
A. Delusions B. Hallucinations
C. Illusions D. Magical thinking

238. Electroconvulsive therapy (ECT) may be used to treat :
A. Dysthymic disorder
B. Major depressive disorder
C. Cyclothymic disorder
D. Bipolar I disorder

239. The personality disorder that is characterized primarily by mistrust is:
A. Paranoid personality disorder
B. Antisocial personality disorder
C. Dependent personality disorder
D. Schizotypal personality disorder

240. The most serious complication of anorexia nervosa:
A. High risk of mortality
B. Coexisting depression
C. Poor family relationships
D. Ocial isolation

241. The test for assessing patient's orientation and recall:
A. Beck depression inventory
B. Thematic appreciation test
C. Mini-mental status examination
D. Millon clinical multiaxial inventory

242. Which of the following is not included in psychosomatic disorder:
A. Essential Hypertension B. Epilepsy
C. Anorexia Nervosa D. None of them

243. "Flight of Body" is known As
A. Amnesia
B. Fugue
C. Depersonalization Disorder
D. None of the Above.

244. Another name of conversion disorder:-
A. Hysteria B. Epilepsy
C. Hypochondriasis D. None of them

245. Irrational Fear from public places is known as :-
A. Specific phobia B. Agoraphobia
C. Social Phobia D. None of the above

246. An idea or a thought that is silly, absured or appartly meaningless. Yet a person can't get rid of is known as :-
A. Obsession B. Agoraphobia
C. Both of the above D. None of the above

247. Following are examples of groups in which members identify themselves with the whole group with sense of belonging, mutual respect, sympathy and attitude:
A. Family college
B. Family, club members
C. College, religious group
D. Club and religious groups

248. All of following are neurotic disorders except?
A. Mania B. Conversion Disorder
C. Neurotic Depression D. Phobias

249. The essential features of obsessional thoughts in OCD (Lewis, 1938) are all, except?
A. A feeling of subjective compulsion
B. A resistance to subjective compulsion
C. Preservation of insight
D. Presence of primary delusions

250. When thought are too quick without association it is called ?
A. Flight of ideas B. Catalepsy
C. Mannerisms D. Clang Association

251. Morphine belongs to one of the following group of drugs :-
A. Balldona Alkaloids B. Anticholinergics
C. Opiate D. Barbiturates

252. Fear of going outside to open space is called as:-
A. Algo Phobia B. Agro Phobia
C. Acro Phobia D. Claustro phobia

253. Patient with mania with having all of the following symptoms expects:
A. Elated and Unstable mood
B. Sluggish & Fatigue
C. Increase Pressure of Speech
D. Increased Motor Activity

254. Which of the following is not the example of emotion:-
A. Love B. Fear
C. Hunger D. None of these

255. Illusion is the
A. Distortion of existing stimuli
B. Same as hallucination
C. Result of innate mechanism
D. Not based on external reality

256. The tendency to group together objects that are the same size, shape and colour is known as
A. Closure B. Continuation
C. Similarity D. Nearness

257. Deceased perceptual response to a repeated stimulus is known as
A. Habituation
B. Selective attention
C. Undivided attention
D. Hallucination

258. The information surrounding a stimulus is
A. Adaptation B. Context
C. Aura D. Internal frame

259. The unconscious contains
A. Material that can be brought to awareness
B. Everything that we are aware of
C. Repressed emotions
D. Thoughts and perceptions

260. A personality disorder in which an individual suspects of other people harming him is
A. Paranoid B. Melancholic
C. Hypomaniac D. Cyclothymic

261. A disorder in which patient maintains a fixed posture without any movement is
A. Mannerism B. Cataplexy
C. Negativism D. Preservation

262. A therapy which provides a safe environment to meet the patient's treatment need is
A. Psychotherapy B. Behaviour therapy
C. Milieu therapy D. Microtherapy

263. The Important phase of interpersonal relationship is
A. Identification B. Exploitation
C. Orientation D. Resolution

264. Preoccupation with fears of having a serious disease is called
A. Somatization B. Conversion
C. Hypochondriasis D. Dissociation

265. Best nursing intervention for a delusion patient with confusion at night time is to
A. Keep patient next to nursing station
B. Use indirect light source
C. Keep TV on
D. Play soft music on

266. A patient not willing to go outside alone with the fear of doing something crazy in public is
A. Agoraphobia B. Social phobia
C. Claustrophobia D. Hydrophobia

267. The Indian Mental Health Act was passed during the year
A. 1992 B. 1987
C. 1947 D. 1942

268. Behaviourism, " the science of behaviour" was proposed by
A. Sigmond freud B. Erik Erickson
C. JB Watson D. Ivan Pavlov

269. The most common deficiency seen in alcoholics is
A. Riboflavin B. Thaimine
C. Pyridoxine D. Pantothenic acid

270. An IQ. is a ratio of
A. Chronological age to mental age
B. Mental age to Chronological age
C. Present and Past age
D. Self and Parent's age

271. The proponent of psychoanalysis theory is
A. Sigmund Freud B. Ivan Pavlov
C. BF skinner D. Eric bernec

272. False unshakable belief exhibited by patients with psychosis is
A. Delusions B. Illusion
C. Hallucination D. Confabulation

273. Senseless repetition of same words or phrases over and over again is termed as
A. Neologism B Verbigeration
C. Echolalia D Perseveration

274. Loss of power of expression of speech is
A. Aphonia B Aphasia
C. Apraxia D Aplasia

275. Which one represents people themselves?
A. Self-concept B. Self-esteem
C. Self-realize D. Self-identity

276. Emotional evaluation of self-worth is the:
A. Self-concept B. Self-esteem
C. Self-realize D. Self-identity

277. The components of self-concept is the following except:
A. Self-esteem B. Body image
C. Role D. Behaviour

278. The basic emotional task for the toddler is:
A. Trust B. Industry
D. Independence C. Identification

279. Which of the following will influence An individual's perception?
A. Previous Experiences
B. Individual Needs
C. Sensory Limitations
D. All of the above

280. The nurse understands that one of the most difficult tasks for the depressed client is the:
A. Remorse and guilt
B. Need for comforting
C. Anger towards others
D. Feeling of low self-esteem

281. All of the following are types of delusions except?
A. Grandisoity B. Persecution
C. Wrong Perception D. Ideas of Reference

282. A person who deliberately pretends an illness is usually through to be:
A. Neurotic
B. Malingering
C. Out of concept with reality
D. Using conversion defences

283. The client with antisocial personality:
A. Suffers from a great deal of anxiety
B. Is generally unable to postpone gratification
C. Rapidly learns by experience and punishment
D. Has a great sense of responsibility towards others

284. The emotional experience in childhood becomes traumatic when:
A. Parents are harse and restrictive
B. The superego has not been internalised
C. The child is unable to verbalise own feeling
D. The ago is overwhelmed by anxiety it cannot handle

285. Group therapy can best help those who:
A. Are emotionally ill
B. Are dependent on others
C. Feel they have a problem
D. Have no one to listen to them

286. Self help group such as Alcoholic Anonymous are successful because they meet the clients need to:
A. Grow B. Belong
C. Be trusted D. Be independent

287. Mentally healthy individual can be defined as those who:
A. Lack of insight into their own problems
B. Are able to meet their own basic needs
C. Are not exhibiting pathological symptom
D. Are free from both physical and emotional problems

288. Which is not the element of communication?
A. Message B. Sender
C. Attention D. Channel

289. All behaviour can be said to be:
A. A response to stimulus
B. A conditioned response
C. An intellectual response
D. An emotional response

290. La Bella indifference is related to which of the following neurosis?
A. Phobic anxiety
B. Anxiety disorder
C. Obsessive compulsion disorder
D. Conversion reaction

291 Gustatory hallucination affects the:
A. Nose B. Taste buds
C. Ears D. Skin

292. Exclusive of unwanted or unpleasant experience, emotions or ideas from conscious awareness is:
A. Denial B. Repression
C. Regression D. Projection

293. Electro convulsive therapy is most commonly given in the following condition:-
A. Neurosis B. Obsession
C. Substance Abuse D. Depression

294. Hydrophobia is a sing observed in a patient with:
A. Ant bite B. Dog bite
C. Snakebite D. Mosquito bite

295. Ability to recall signs and symptoms of a disease by a student belongs to:
A. Affective domain
B. Cognitive domain
C. Psychomotor domain
D. Receiving domain

296. Which teaching method would be most appropriate to teach to a group of women to change their attitude towards female child?
A. Role play B. Lecture
C. Discussion D. Symposium

297. A client was admitted to a medical unit with acute blindness. Many tests are performed and three seems to be no organic reason why this client cannot see. The nurse later learns that the client become blind after witnessing a hit-and-run car accident , when a family of three was killed. The nurse suspects that the client may be experiencing a :-
A. Psychosis
B. Conversion Disorder
C. Dissociative Disorder
D. Repression

298. The nurse is preparing a client for electroconvulsive therapy (ECT). Which is scheduled for the following morning. Which of the following is not a component of the plan of care ?
A. Withhold food and fluids for 4 hours prior to the treatment
B. Have the client void before the procedure
C. Remove dentures and contact lenses prior to the procedure
D. Administer tap water enemas on the evening before the procedure

299. The nurse is assigned to care for a client at risk for alcohol withdrawal. Which of the following symptoms alerts the nurse to the potential for delirium tremors (DTs)?
A. Fever, hypertension, changes in level of consciousness and hallucinations
B. Hypotension, Stupor , agitation , headache and auditory hallucinations
C. Vomiting, ataxia, muscular rigidity, and tactile hallucinations
D. Coarse hand tremor , agitation , hallucinations and hypotension

300. Which of the following is not typical anti-psychotic and does not have marked extra pyramidal side effects ?
A. Chlorpromazine B. Fluphenazine
C. Clozapine D. Haloperidol

301. Which of the following is the most accurate in regard to dementia?
A. Impairment of memory
B. Reversible
C. Auditory hallucination
D. Primary delusions

302. The most common cause of dementia is
A. Multiple sclerosis
B. General infection
C. Alzheimer's disease
D. Multi infarct lesion

303. Visual hallucinations, illusions, fugue, disorientation are typical features of
A. Delirium
B. Dementia
C. Schizophrenia
D. Dissociative disorders

304. A delirium associated with glossitis, stomatitis, and dermatitis is suggestive of
A. Porphyria
B. Myxoedema
C. Pellagra
D. Wernicke's syndrome

305. The most common post-operative psychiatric condition is
A. Delusional disorder B. Delirium
C. Depression D. Mania

306. Disorientation and visual hallucinations are hallmark of
A. Delirium
B. Schizophrenia
C. Mania
D. Depersonalization syndrome

307. Impaired consciousness, visual hallucinations, hyperactivity and fragmentary delusions are typically seen in
A. Dementia B. Delirium
C. Schizophrenia D. Delusional disorder

308. Korsakoff's psychosis is due to intake of
A. Cannabis B. Opium
C. Amphetamine D. Alcohol

309. Korsakoff's psychosis is due to the deficiency of
A. Thiamine B. Vitamin B_{12}
C. Riboflavin D. Biotin

310. Astasia-Abasia is seen in
A. Alzeihmer's disease
B. Parkinsonism
C. Hysterical conversion disorder
D. Schizophrenia

311. Alzeihmer's disease is associated with
A. Chromosome 19 B. Chromosome 21
C. Chromosome 220 D. Chromosome 22

312. Eugen Bleuler renamed dementia precox as
A. Autism
B. Schizophrenia
C. Bipolar affective disorder
D. Parkinsonism

313. Melancholia Bizarre and childish thinking, speech, and very disordered motor actions are characteristics of:
A. Catatonic schizophrenia
B. Paranoid schizophrenia
C. Undifferentiated schizophrenia
D. Disorganized/hebephrenic schizophrenia

314. First rank symptoms of schizophrenia (FRSS) include all the following, EXCEPT:
A. Auditory hallucinations
B. Delusional perception
C. Passivity phenomenon
D. Mood disturbances

315. Fundamental symptoms of schizophrenia include all the following, EXCEPT:
A. Ambivalence
B. Autism
C. Affective disturbances
D. Apraxia

316. The first effective antipsychotic drug was:
A. Chlorpromazine B. Thioridazine
C. Haloperidol D. Trifluperazine

317. Which of the following drugs is most safe in pregnant patients with acute schizophrenia?
A. Haloperidol B. Chlorpromazine
C. Trifluperazine D. Thioridazine

318. Clozapine is associated with a higher risk of ______________ than other antipsychotics.
A. Extrapyramidal symptoms
B. Seizures
C. Neuroleptic malignant syndrome
D. Anticholinergic side effects

319. Systematic desensitization consist of following steps, except:
A. Relaxation training
B. Hierarchy construction
C. Desensitization of stimulus
D. Resolving unconscious conflicts

320. The patient should try and say everything that comes into his mind without self-control or censure, is a fundamental rule in
A. Interpersonal psychotherapy
B. Cognitive behavioural psychotherapy
C. Long-term psychodynamic psychotherapy
D. Acceptance and commitment therapy

321. Which of the following therapy is based on learning theory?
A. Logotherapy
B. Psychoanalysis
C. Behaviour therapy
D. Interpersonal therapy

322. Which of the following is considered to be most effective and treatment of choice for phobic disorders?
A. Behaviour therapy
B. Interpersonal psychotherapy
C. Family therapy
D. Psychoanalysis

323. A psychotherapy technique effective in obsessive ruminations is
A. Exposure B. Thought stopping
C. Flooding D. Sensitization

324. Socratic questioning' as a tool for therapeutic process is employed in
A. Psychodynamic psychotherapy
B. Logotherapy
C. Behaviour therapy
D. Cognitive psychotherapy

325. 'Enmeshment, homeostasis, circular causality' are concepts related to
A. System approach to couple therapy
B. Psychodynamic couple therapy
C. Behaviour approach to couple therapy
D. Cognitive behavioural approach to couple therapy

326. Which of the following is a direct pharmacological antagonist?
A. Methadone B. Morphine
C. Naltrexone D. Disufiram

327. Benzodiazepines primarily act on:
A. GABA receptors
B. 5HT receptors
C. Dopamine receptors
D. Mu receptors

328. Which of the following is an antagonist of benzodiazepines:
A. Flumazenil B. Naloxone
C. Flupenthixol D. N-acetyl cystine

329. Extrapyramidal symptoms include all, except:
A. Psuedoparkinsonism
B. Dytonia
C. Tardive dyskinesia
D. Agnosia

330. A drug which is commonly associated with orthostatic hypotension is:
A. Chlorpromazine B. Fluoxamine
C. Buproprion D. Lithium

331. The first psychotropic drug introduced in the treatment of depression was:
A. Clorpromazine B. Lithium
C. Dothipin D. Imipramine

332. Dry mouth, blurred vision, constipation and urinary retention are side effects due to blocked of:
A. HA histaminic receptors
B. 5HTA serotoninergic receptors
C. Dopaminergic receptors
D. Muscarinic-cholinergic

333. Tricyclic antidepressants act by blocking:
A. Dopaminergic receptors
B. GABA receptors
C. Reuptake of serotonin and norepinephrine
D. Cholinergic receptors

334. Therapeutic effects of typical antipsychotics are predominantly due to blocked of:
A. Dopaminergic receptors
B. GABA receptors
C. Serotoninergic receptors
D. Norepinephrine receptors

335. Pharmacokinetics refers to:
A. The processes of absorption, transport, distribution, metabolism and excretion
B. Action of drug on the body
C. Selective action of the drug on the receptors
D. The adverse effects caused by a drug on the body

336. The nurse is caring for a client who is scheduled for electroconvulsive therapy (ECT). The nurse notes that an informed consent has not been obtained for the procedure. Based on this information, the nurse determines that:-
A. An informed consent does not need to be obtained
B. An informed consent should be obtained from the family
C. An informed consent need to be obtained from the client.
D. The physician will obtain the informed consent.

337. Naltrexone occupies which of the following opiod receptors?
A. Sigma B. Kappa
C. M(μ) D. Beta

338. All are side effects of valproic acid, except:
A. Ataxia
B. Tremor
C. Fulminant hepatitis
D. Polycystic Disease

339. Hypersalivation is a paradoxical adverse effect observed in treatment with
A. Chlorpromazine B. Clozapine
C. Trihexyphenidyl D. Ziprazidone

340. A common adverse effect shared by clozapine, olanzapine and risperidone is:
A. Seizures B. Sialorrea
C. Agranulocytosis D. Weight gain

341. Benzodiazepines have the following effects except:
A. Suppress REM sleep
B. Produces respiratory depression
C. Produce tolerance and dependence
D. Induces seizures

342. Visual hallucinations are seen in
A. Delirium tremors B. Mania
C. Depression D. Phobia

343. Tactile hallucinations are associated with
A. Schizophrenia
B. Cocaine psychosis
C. Temporal lobe epilepsy
D. All of the Above

344. Auditory hallucinations are NOT seen in
A. Schizophrenia
B. Manic episode with psychosis
C. Dissociative disorders
D. Amphetamine toxicity

345. Verbigeration (repetition of words and phrases without reference to their meaning and without apparently signifying anything) may be seen in:
A. Catatonic schizophrenia
B. Dementia
C. Paranoid schizophrenia
D. Delusional disorders

346. Dissociation is present in all, EXCEPT:
A. Fugue B. Delirium
C. Multiple personality D. Somnabulism

347. Persevaration is:-
A. Repeating persistently the words of his own or others
B. Using strange words
C. Using real words strung together oddly
D. Persistent thinking from which patient can't get rid of himself

348. Deja vu may be seen in all of the following, EXCEPT:
A. Temporal lobe epilepsy
B. Hysteria
C. Drug intoxication
D. Obsessional thoughts

349. Pseudo-hallucinations are NOT considered as typical symptoms of
A. Dissociative disorders
B. Hysteria
C. Schizophrenia
D. Malingering

350. In DSM-IV, Cluster A personality includes all, except
A. Paranoid B. Schizoid
C. Schizotypal D. Anankastic

351. As per ICD-10, features of anorexia nervosa includes all, except:
A. Body-image distortion
B. Body weight at least 15% below the expected
C. Amenorrhea
D. Early puberty

352. "A subjective feeling of ugliness or physical defect which the patient feels noticeable to others, although his appearance is within normal limits" is termed as
A. Delusional Dysmorphobia
B. De Clearmalt's syndrome
C. Megalomania
D. Othello syndrome

353. Most freuent content of delusion is
A. Persecution B. Jealousy
C. Love D. Misidentification

354. WAIS and WISC are intelligence tests based on:
A. Mental age
B. Chronological age
C. Verbal and performance abilities
D. Personality and aptitude

355. The term used to designate a peculiar change in the awareness of self, in which the individual feels 'as if' he is unreal is:
A. Derealization B. Depersonalization
C. Jamais Vu D. Dissociation

356. The association of hypochondriacal delusion and nihilistic delusions with depressive psychosis in the elderly is called:
A. Cotard's syndrome
B. Ganser syndrome
C. Landau–Kleffner syndrome
D. Korsakoff 's syndrome

357. 'Mirage' is an example of
A. Illusion B. Delusion
C. Hallucination D. Phantasy

358. "Phantom limb" is an example of
A. Delusion B. Illusion
C. Phi phenomenon D. Hallucination

359. Illusion is a
A. False perception
B. Misinterpretation of stimuli
C. Increased intensity of stimuli
D. Confusional state

360. The drug of choice in the management of alcohol withdrawal is
A. Barbiturates B. Benzodiazepines
C. Disulfiram D. Acamprosate

361. The drug of choice in alcohol-induced psychosis is
A. Disulfiram B. Haloperidol
C. Diazepam D. Imipramine

362. Narcissistic personality disorder is characterized by
A. Callous unconcern for feelings of others
B. Self-dramatization, theatricality
C. Ideas of grandiosity and inflated sense of self-importance
D. Significant and persistent disturbances of identity of self.

363. Which condition is characterised by the flow of speech or fluency is disrupted by involuntary speech motor events?
A. Stuttering
B. Laryngeal webbing
C. Functional dysphonias
D. Organic dysphonias

364. DSM-IV-TR Criteria for Mental Retardation include all, except
A. Significantly sub average intellectual functioning: an IQ. of appx. 70 or below on an individually administered IQ. test.
B. Concurrent deficits or impairments in present adaptive functioning.
C. The onset is before age 18 years.
D. Presence of third person auditory hallucinations.

365. Cold Turkey" is a term associated with dependence of:
A. Cocaine B. Cannabis
C. Alcohol D. Opioid

366. Hippocrates classified mental disorders in to:
A. Major and minor mental illness
B. Psychosis and neurosis
C. Schizophrenia, mania and depression
D. Mania, melancholia and phrenitis

367. A client expresses the belief that armed forces are out to kill him. This is an example of:
A. Hallucinations
B. Delusion of persecution
C. Delusion of infidelity
D. Derealization

368. A patient perceives that his face is distorted and his hand are becoming long. The term used to explain this condition is:
A. Dejavu B. Depersonalization
C. Derealization D. Jamais vu

369. Nurse must observe one of the following side effects in a patent who is on Antipsychotic
A. Arrythmia
B. Hypertension
C. Extra pyramidal symptom
D. Anorexia

370. What nursing action would be most effective in changing the behaviour of a child diagnosed with attention deficit hyperactivity disorder (ADHA)?
A. Reward appropriate behaviour
B. Sedate the child for acting out
C. Use aggressive punishment to control undesired behaviour
D. Use lengthy time out session

371. During psychiatric interview patient retains a constellation of ideas long after they have ceased to be appropriate. E.g. "where do you live?", "INDIA", "How old are you", "INDIA.The term used to explain the condition is:
A. Perseveration B. Mannerisms
C. Ambivalence D. Echopraxia

372. Omega sign is noticed in patients with:
A. Dementia B. Schizophrenia
C. Depression D. OCD

373. Which is not a negative symptom of schizophrenia:
A. Asociality B. Anhedonia,
C. Avolition D. Delusion

374. "A false perception, which is not a sensory distortion or a misinterpretation which occurs at the same time as real perception occurs" - This definition refers to:
A. Delusion
B. Hallucination
C. Illusion
D. Delusional perception

375. A term used to explain a disorder of thought in which thinking proceeds slowly with many unnecessary trivial details, but finally the point is reached is:
A. Flight of ideas B. Prolixity
C. Tangentiality D. Circumstantiality

376. Bizarre somatic hallucinations are typical features of
A. Generalized anxiety disorder
B. Multiple personality
C. Hebephrenic schizophrenia
D. Simple schizophrenia

377. According to Freud, the term used for "that force by which the sexual instinct is represented in the mind" is:
A. Narcissism B. Condensation
C. Libido D. Dispositions

378. The phase of peaking of sexual pleasure, with release of sexual tension and rhythmic contraction of the perineal muscles and pelvic reproductive organs, observed in male sexual cycle, is termed as
A. Desire B. Excitement
C. Orgasm D. Resolution

379. A sexual pain disorder reported in females is
A. Anorgasmia B. Vaginismus
C. Peyronie's disease D. Impotence

380. Persistant or recurrent tendency to observe unsuspecting persons, naked disrobing or engaged in sexual activity is termed as
A. Exhibitionism B. Sadism
C. Voyeurism D. Frotteurism

381. Excessive sexual desire in women is termed as
A. Satyriasis B. Frigidity
C. Vaginismus D. Nymphomania

382. Sildenafil citrate is administered in
A. Impotence
B. Erectile dysfunction
C. Paraphilias
D. Premature ejaculation

383. Sexual gratification by rubbing against or touching a nonconsenting person is termed as
A. Frotteurism B. Fetishism
C. Exhibitionism D. Voyeurism

384. Getting sexual gratification by inflicting injuries to opposite partner is
A. Masichism B. Sadism
C. Voyerism D. Transvestism

385. Which of the following is an objective method for determining daytime sleepiness?
A. Polysomnography
B. Multiple Sleep Latency Test (MSLT)
C. Electromyogram (EMG)
D. PLMS index

386. Kleine-Levin syndrome is characterized by the following features, EXCEPT
A. Male predominance B. Hypersomnia
C. Hypersexuality D. Hyperphagia

387. Defence mechanism in obsessive compulsive disorders is
A. Reaction formation B. Displacement
C. Projection D. Sublimation

388. A defence mechanism typical of obsessive compulsive disorders is
A. Denial B. Undoing
C. Projection D. Displacement

389. All of the following are features of obsessive compulsive disorders, except
A. Anxiety relieved by doing the act
B. Sense of guilt
C. Magical thought
D. Patient is aware of helplessness

390. Which of the following technique is found to be effective in obsessive ruminations?
A. Psychoanalysis
B. Interpersonal therapy
C. Logo therapy
D. Thought stopping

391. Morphine is extracted from
A. Cajanus cajan
B. Cannabis sativa
C. Papaver somniferum
D. Rauwolfia serpentina

392. Which of the following statements about marijuana TRUE?
A. Marijuana is not physically addictive
B. It is safe to drive under the influence of pot.
C. Marijuana is healthier than tobacco.
D. Short-term memory is enhanced by smocking marijuana.

393. Lacrimation, rhinorrhea, pin-point pupils, sweating, diarrhoea, and muscle cramps are charecteristic of:
A. Alcohol withdrawal syndrome
B. Cannabis withdrawal syndrome
C. Opium withdrawal syndrome
D. Cocaine withdrawal syndrome

394. In opium over dose, naloxone is administered as
A. 10 mg IM B. 2 mg IV
C. 100 mg orally D. 5 mg s/c

395. Detoxification of opium is done with
A. Methadone B. Chlordiazeproxide
C. Diazepam D. Disulfiram

396. The CAGE questionnaire consists of
A. 10 questions B. 14 questions
C. 4 questions D. 20 questions

397. Slow respiration, slow pulse, and constriction o pupil occurs due to drug addiction of
A. Morphine and opium
B. Cocaine and heroin
C. Alcohol and thalidomide
D. Nicotine and caffeine

398. Dypsomania" is related to
A. Compulsion to drink alcohol
B. Impulsive stealing
C. Compulsion to drink water
D. Compulsive smocking

399. Disulfiram(aversion) therapy is indicated in
A. Acute alcohol intoxication
B. Acute opium intoxication
C. Alcohol dependence
D. Cannabis dependence

400. Which is NOT a positive sign seen i schizophrenia:-
A. Hallucinations B. Delusions
C. Thought disorder D. Flat affect

401. A common drug causing Disulfiram-ethano reaction (DER) is
A. Chlorouine B. Metronidazole
C. Ciprofloxacin D. Metaprolol

402. Claustrophobia means fear of
A. Open spaces B. Closed spaces
C. Height D. Lizards

403. Agoraphobia is characterized by
A. Fear of lifts and heights
B. Association with schizophrenia
C. Often associated open space with panic attacks
D. Fear of closed spaces

404. Sudden "loss of memory" or "blackouts" related to painful or humiliating experience i seen in
A. Generalized anxiety disorders
B. Obsessive compulsive disorders
C. Dissociative disorders
D. Bipolar affective disorders

405. La belle indifference may be seen in
A. Dissociative disorders
B. Phobic anxiety disorders
C. Schizophrenia
D. Bipolar affective disorders

406. Which of the following may clearly differentiate attacks of pseudoseizures and epileptic seizures?
A. Tongue biting
B. EEG recording
C. Preceding emotional disturbance
D. Leg movements

407. Drug-induced parkinsonism is most commonly presents in
A. Schizophrenia
B. Mania
C. Obsessive compulsive disorders
D. Phobia

408. Classical depression is characterised by all, except
A. Psychomotor retardation
B. Loosening of association
C. Retardation of thinking process
D. Pervasive mood of sadness

409. Resperidone is a:-
A. Atypical Antidepressant
B. Atypical Antipsychotic
C. Benzodiazipine
D. Mood Stabilizer

410. Treatment of choice in depression with suicidal tendencies is
A. Tricyclic antidepressants
B. Lithium therapy
C. MAO inhibitors
D. ECT

411. Librium is:
A. Antimanic Drug B. Antidepressant Dru
C. Antiparkinson Drug D. Tranuilizer Drug

412. Who authored the book "Interpersonal Relations in Nursing"?
A. John Hopkins B. Hildegard Peplau
C. Linda Richards D. Maxwell Jones

413. Which law in India has deemed the attempt to commit suicide is a punishable offence?
A. Section 309 of the IPC
B. Section 114 of the IPC
C. Mental Health Act
D. Sections 328-339 of the IPC

414. The Narcotic Drugs and Psychotropic Substances Act (NDPSA) was passed in the year
A. 1982 B. 1985
C. 1995 D. 2000

415. The theory of operant conditioning was proposed by:
A. Ian Pavlov
B. Watson
C. Burrhus Frederick Skinner
D. Harry Stock Sullivan

416. Which of the following area of brain is known to be associated with OCD?
A. Reticular system
B. Nigrostraital pathway
C. Basal ganglia
D. Corpus callosum

417. Charecteristics of OCD include all the folowing, EXCEPT:
A. Obsessive thoughts
B. Compulsive acts
C. Cosiderable degree of anxiety
D. Ordered flight of ideas

418. Which of the following is most effective in OCD management?
A. Psychodynamic psychotherapy
B. Interpersonal psychotherapy
C. Cognitive behaviour therapy
D. Supportive psychotherapy

419. Common side effect of ECT is impairment of
A. Judgement B. speech
C. Thought D. Retrograde amnesia

420. According to Hildegard Peplau, one of the sub role of a nurse is -
A. Priest B. Academician
C. Builder D. Mother surrogate

421. Voluntary agreement, compliance or permission is called -
A. Competence B. Preamble
C. Confidentiality D. Consent

422. Multiple referrals between psychiatrists and other professionals is known as -
A. Steering B. Ping Ponging
C. Ganging D. Touting

423. A technique in which producing unpleasant sensation in the patient in association with stimulus is called as -
A. Aversion B. Modelling
C. Flooding D. Abreaction

424. Professional Negligence also known as -
A. Malpractice B. Euthanasia
C. Maloccurrence D. Torticollis

425. In standard form of modified ECT, short acting muscle relaxant used is -
A. Pancronium Bromide
B. Succinyl choline
C. Thiopentone
D. Atropine

426. Spaces between Schwann cells of neurons are called;
A. Nodes of Ranvier B. Synapse
C. Nissl Bodies D. Ventricles

427. The term which refers to muscular hypertonicity with increased resistance to stress:
A. Akinesia B. Ataxia
C. Myoclonus D. Spasticity

428. The brain area involved in receptive language functions that are localized to the left hemisphere is called:
A. Wernicke's area B. Broca's area
C. Cuadate Nucleus D. Hippocampus

429. Average dose of electric current to obtain adeuate seizure response is ----- in ------ seconds.
A. 100 volts in 0.6 seconds
B. 150 volts in 0.2 seconds
C. 90 volts in 1. 2 seconds
D. 180 volts in 0.8 seconds

430. Which theory views that people have free-will and potential for self-actualization?
A. Behaviourism
B. Psychodynamic theory
C. Cognitive theory
D. Humanism

431. Which of the following specialization in psychology deals with diagnosis and treatment of mental disorders?
A. Clinical B. Developmental
C. Experimental D. Personality

432. A dissociative disorder characterized by a period of almost complete amnesia, during which a person actually flees from an immediate lite situation and begins a different life pattern is termed as:
A. Neurasthenia
B. Dissociative amnesia
C. Dissociative fugue
D. Trance

433. An unconscious defence mechanism in which unacceptable mental contents are banished or kept out of consciousness is:
A. Sublimation B. Suppression
C. Rationalization D. Sepression

434. Psychopathological repeating of words or phrases of one person by another; tends to be repetitive and persistent is termed as:
A. Echopraxia B. Echolalia
C. Verbigeration D. Mannerism

435. An elimination disorder in which the patient suffers from incontinence of urine during sleep is termed as:
A. Enuresis B. Encopresis
C. Dyspareunia D. Pseudocyesis

436. Craving and eating of nonfood substances, such as paint and clay observed in some mental illness is termed as:
A. Binge eating B. Verbigeration
C. Polyphagia D. Pica

437. Symptoms such as sleep disturbance (especially early morning awakening), decreased appetite, constipation, weight loss, and loss of sexual response usually observed in depression are collectively called as:
A. Negative signs B. Vegetative signs
C. Positive signs D. Cardinal signs

438. A kind of delusion in which the patient believes one's thoughts are being removed from one's mind by other people or forces is termed as:
A. Delusional perception
B. Thought broadcasting
C. Thought blocking
D. Thought withdrawal

439. Therapeutic blood level of lithium is:
A. 11 to 10 Meq./ ltr B. 15 to 2 Meq./ ltr
C. 0.8 to 1.2 Meq./ ltr D. 150 to Meq./ ltr

440. ECT is indicated in which of the following conditions?
A. Severe depression B. Hypomania
C. Autistic disorders D. Tourette ssyndrome

441. What is the main side effect of ECT:-
A. Retrograde B. Fracture
C. Hypotension D. Seizure

442. Which is the best unit for quantification of ECT stimuli?
A. Millicoulombs (mC) B. Joules
C. Watts D. Volt

443. What is the best accepted placement of electrodes in unilateral ECT?
A. Bifrontotemporal B. Paritotemporal
C. Occipital D. D'Elia position

444. The first therapeutic use of electrically induced seizures in the treatment of mental disorders is related to
A. Harold Sackeim
B. Luigi Bini and Ugo Cerletti
C. D. Goldman
D. G. Holmberg and S. Thesieff

445. Less memory disturbance is seen with
A. Bilateral ECT B. Unilateral ECT
C. Direct ECT D. Modified ECT

446. Use of succinylecholine in ECT is
A. Safer than curare
B. May cause prolonged apnea
C. Reduces possibility of fractures
D. All are true

447. Absolute contraindication for ECT is
A. Pregnancy
B. Lactation

C. Old gae
D. Raised intracranial pressure

448. Best response to ECT is seen in
A. Catatonic schizophrenia
B. Paranoid schizophrenia
C. Hebiphreniac Schizophrenia
D. Simple schizophrenia

449. Which of the following is TRUE about electroconvulsive therapy?
A. Contraindicated in brain tumor
B. Reuires more than 70 volts
C. Treatment of major depression
D. All are true

450. Freud used the case of "Little Hans", a 5-year-old boy to explain
A. Isolation
B. Behavior Problems
C. Inferiority complex
D. Oedipus complex

451. Absence of feeling is
A. Apathy B. Anhedonia
C. Euphoria D. Neuroticism

452. Melancholia literally means
A. Yellow bile B. Black bile
C. Blunting D. Flattening

453. Difficulties in the capacity to verbalize affect and elaborate fantasies " is termed as
A. Cyclothymia B. Neuroticissm
C. Alexithymia D. Narcissism

454. Important phase in the following
A. Pre-interaction phase B. Orientation phase
C. Working phase D. Terminatory phase

455. Morbid fear of open places or leaving the familiar setting of the home is called:
A. Claustrophobia B. Xenophobia
C. Zoophobia D. Agoraphobia

456. Inability or difficulty in describing or being aware of one's emotions or moods is termed as:
A. Apraxia B. Alexithymia
C. Agnosia D. Anomia

457. Anhedonia
A. Loss of interest in and withdrawal from all regular and pleasurable activities.
B. Inability to recall the names of objects.
C. Loss or decrease in appetite.
D. Inability to recognize a physical deficit in oneself.

458. Inability to perform a voluntary purposeful motor activity is termed as:
A. Apraxia B. Alogia
C. Aphasia D. Anhedonia

459. Thinking in which the thoughts are largely narcissistic and egocentric, with emphasis on subjectivity rather than objectivity, and without regard for reality is termed as:
A. Abstract thinking B. Logical thinking
C. Concrete thinking D. Autistic thinking

460. Unconscious defense mechanism by which the emotional component of an unacceptable idea or object is transferred to a more acceptable one is called:
A. Dissociation B. Denial
C. Displacement D. Devaluation

461. A kind of aphasia characterized by difficulty in giving the correct name of an object is :
A. Nominal aphasia B. Amnestic aphasia
C. Sensory aphasia D. Receptive aphasia

462. A patient with OCD freuency washes his hands, what is the reason behind this?
A. He protect himself from infection
B. He protect himself from dirt
C. Hand washing relieves anxiety
D. It is the part of treatment suggested by psychiatrist

463. What is the term used to explain the phenomenon seen in the following context?
Examiner: "What is the colour of sky?"
Patient: "Green"
Examiner: "What is the colour of snow?"
Patient: "Black"
A. Transitory thinking B. Ganser syndrome
C. Drivelling thinking D. Neologisms

464. In following which is not an example of opioid:-
A. Morphine B. Heroin
C. Pethidine D. Naloxone

465. A delusion in which the patient denies the existence of his body, mind, his loved ones, and the world around him is:
A. Persecutory delusion
B. Nihilistic delusion
C. Extracampine delusion
D. Delusion of reference

466. In following which is the major indiction of ECT:-
A. Servere Deressicn with Suicidal
B. Servere Mania
C. Phobia
D. Hysteria

467. The response that was appropriate to a first stimulus being given inappropriately to a second different stimulus is termed as:
A. Conditioning B. Confabulation
C. Circumstantiality D. Perseveration

468. Which of the following is a technique used in hypnosis?
A. Flooding B. Socratic questioning
C. Suggestion D. Desensitization

469. Sleep walking is also termed as
A. Sleep terror
B. Somnabulism
C. Pickwickian syndrome
D. Bruxism

470. Which of the following type of hallucination is NOT considered as a first rank symptoms of schizophrenia?
A. Audible thoughts
B. Voices hearing arguing
C. Voices hearing running commentary
D. Vissle blowing

471. A phenomenological term which refers to the subjective experience of dissatisfaction with body shape or form is:
A. Unilateral neglect
B. Dissociation
C. Dysmorphophobia
D. Obtundation

472. Imipramine is a :-
A. Antimanic Drug
B. Antipsychotic Drug
C. Antidepressant Drug
D. Antianxeity Drug

473. Pseudo hallucinations are a type of
A. Illusions
B. functional hallucination
C. True perception
D. Mental imagery

474. Mentally Healthy Individual can be defined as those who?
A. Have insight into their own problems
B. Are able to meet their own basic needs
C. Are not exhibiting pathological symptoms
D. Are free from both physical and emotional problems

475. Perception of any object in the absence of actual stimulus is termed as:
A. Illusion B. Hallucination
C. Delusion D. Dementia

476. In which year Mental health Act was passed:-
A. 1995 B. 1982 C. 1987 D. 1975

477. In following which therapy is used for treating Phobia:
A. Aversion therapy
B. Ect
C. Systematic Desensitization
D. Hypnosis

478. Nurse is caring for a female client who has suicidal tendency. When accompanying the client to the restroom, Nurse should...
A. Give her privacy
B. Allow her to urinate
C. Open the window and allow her to get some fresh air
D. Close Observe to client

479. Nurse is developing a plan of care for a female client with anorexia nervosA.Which action should the nurse include in the plan?
A. Provide privacy during meals
B. Set-up a strict eating plan for the client
C. Encourage client to exercise to reduce anxiety
D. Restrict visits with the family

480. The client with Antisocial Personality :-
A. Suffers From a Great Deal of Anxiety
B. Is generally unable to postpone gratification
C. Rapidly learns by experience and punishment
D. Has a great sense of responsibility towards others

481. The emotional experience in childhood becomes traumatic when ?
A. Parents are harse and restrictive
B. The Superego has not been internalized
C. The child is unable to verbalized own feeling
D. The ego is overwhelmed by Anxiety it cannot be handled

482. A 20 year old client was diagnosed with dependent personality disorder. Which behaviour is not most likely to be evidence of ineffective individual coping?
A. Recurrent self-destructive behaviour
B. Avoiding relationship
C. Showing interest in solitary activities
D. Inability to make choices and decision without advise

483. A male client is diagnosed with schizotypal personality disorder. Which signs would this client exhibit during social situation?
A. Paranoid thoughts
B. Emotional affect
C. Independence need
D. Aggressive behavior

484. Nurse Claire is caring for a client diagnosed with bulimia. The most appropriate initial goal for a client diagnosed with bulimia is?
A. Encourage to avoid foods
B. Identify anxiety causing situations
C. Eat only three meals a day
D. Avoid shopping plenty of groceries

485. Which is the example of antianxiety drug ?
A. Promazine B. Diazepalm
C. Lethium carbonate D. Perinorm

486. Nurse Trish is working in a mental health facility; the nurse priority nursing intervention for a newly admitted client with bulimia nervosa would be to?
A. Teach client to measure I & O
B. Involve client in planning daily meal
C. Observe client during meals
D. Monitor client continuously

487. A 39 year old mother with obsessive-compulsive disorder has become immobilized by her elaborate hand washing and walking rituals. Nurse Trish recognizes that the basis of O.C.Disorder is often:
A. Problems with being too conscientious

B. Problems with anger and remorse
C. Feelings of guilt and inadequacy
D. Feeling of unworthiness and hopelessness

488. A Client with borderline personality disorder who is to be discharge soon threatens to "do something" to herself if discharge. Which of the following actions by the nurse would be most important?
A. Ask a family member to stay with the client at home temporarily
B. Discuss the meaning of the client's statement with her
C. Request an immediate extension for the client
D. Ignore the clients statement because it's a sign of manipulation

489. To establish open and trusting relationship with a female client who has been hospitalized with severe anxiety, the nurse in charge should?
A. Encourage the staff to have frequent interaction with the client
B. Share an activity with the client
C. Give client feedback about behaviour
D. Respect client's need for personal space

490. Nurse recognizes that the focus of environmental (MILIEU) therapy is to:
A. Manipulate the environment to bring about positive changes in behavior
B. Allow the client's freedom to determine whether or not they will be involved in activities
C. Role play life events to meet individual needs
D. Use natural remedies rather than drugs to control behaviour

491. Nurse would expect a child with a diagnosis of reactive attachment disorder to:
A. Have more positive relation with the father than the mother
B. Cling to mother & cry on separation
C. Be able to develop only superficial relation with the others
D. Have been physically abuse

492. When teaching parents about childhood depression Nurse should say?
A. It may appear acting out behaviour
B. Does not respond to conventional treatment
C. Is short in duration & resolves easily
D. Looks almost identical to adult depression

493. Nurse Perry is aware that language development in autistic child resembles:
A. Scanning speech B. Speech lag
C. Shuttering D. Echolalia

494. A 60 year old female client who lives alone tells the nurse at the community health center "I really don't need anyone to talk to". The TV is my best friend.
The nurse recognizes that the client is using the defense mechanism known as?
A. Displacement B. Projection
C. Sublimation D. Denial

495. When working with a male client suffering phobia about black Rat, Nurse should anticipate that a problem for this client would be?
A. Anxiety when discussing phobia
B. Anger toward the feared object
C. Denying that the phobia exist
D. Distortion of reality when completing daily routines

496. A client is pacing the floor and appears extremely anxious. The duty nurse approaches in an attempt to alleviate patient's anxiety. The most therapeutic question by the nurse would be?
A. Would you like to watch TV?
B. Would you like me to talk with you?
C. Are you feeling upset now?
D. Ignore the client

497. Nurse is aware that the symptoms that distinguish post traumatic stress disorder from other anxiety disorder would be:
A. Avoidance of situation & certain activities that resemble the stress
B. Depression and a blunted affect when discussing the traumatic situation
C. Lack of interest in family & others
D. Re-experiencing the trauma in dreams or flashback

498. Nurse is communicating with a male client with substance-induced persisting dementia; the client cannot remember facts and fills in the gaps with imaginary information. Nurse is aware that this is typical of?
A. Flight of ideas
B. Associative looseness
C. Confabulation
D. Concretism

499. A Patient who is diagnosed with bipolar disorder and acute mania, states the nurse, "Where is my daughter? I love Liza. Rain, rain go away. Dogs eat dirt." The nurse interprets these statements as indicating which of the following?
A. Echolalia B. Neologism
C. Clang associations D. Flight of ideas

500. A patient has been hospitalized for major depression and suicidal ideation. Which of the following statements indicates to the nurse that the client is improving?
A. "I'm of no use to anyone anymore."
B. "I know my kids don't need me anymore since they're grown."
C. "I couldn't kill myself because I don't want to go to hell."
D. "I don't think about killing myself as much as I used to."

501. Nurse invites new client's parents to attend the psycho educational program for families of the

chronically mentally ill. The program would be most likely to help the family with which of the following issues?

A. Developing a support network with other families
B. Feeling guiltier about the client's illness
C. Recognizing the client's weakness
D. Managing their financial concern and problems

502. To assess a client's suicidal potential. Nurse should be especially alert to the client expression of:

A. Frustration & fear of death
B. Anger & resentment
C. Anxiety & loneliness
D. Helplessness & hopelessness

503. A nursing care plan for a male client with bipolar IQ. disorder should include:

A. Providing a structured environment
B. Designing activities that will reuire the client to maintain contact with reality
C. Engaging the client in conversing about current affairs
D. Touching the client provide assurance

504. Nurse recognizes that paranoid delusions usually are related to the defence mechanism of:

A. Projection B. Identification
C. Repression D. Regression

505. Within a few hours of alcohol withdrawal, nurse should assess the male client for the presence of:

A. Disorientation, paranoia, tachycardia
B. Tremors, fever, profuse diaphoresis
C. Irritability, heightened alertness, jerky movements
D. Yawning, anxiety, convulsions

506. A 23 year old client has been admitted with a diagnosis of schizophrenia says to the nurse "Yes, its Monday, Monday is little woman". That's literal you know". These statements illustrate:

A. Neologisms
B. Echolalia
C. Flight of ideas
D. Loosening of association

507. A long term goal for a paranoid male client who has unjustifiably accused his wife of having many extramarital affairs would be to help the client develop:

A. Insight into his behaviour
B. Better self control
C. Feeling of self worth and self Respect
D. Faith in his wife

508. A male client who is experiencing disordered thinking about food being poisoned is admitted to the mental health unit. The nurse uses which communication technuie to encourage the client to eat dinner?

A. Focusing on self-disclosure of own food preference
B. Using open ended question and silence
C. Offering opinion about the need to eat
D. Verbalizing reasons that the client may not choose to eat

509. Nurse is aware that the defence mechanism commonly used by clients who are alcoholics is:

A. Displacement B. Rationalization
C. Projection D. Compensation

510. When A Person Retreat or Revert To an infantile or Childish level of Behaviour is called ?

A. Suppression B. Repression
C. Regression D. None of the Above

511. Nurse should first discuss terminating the nurse-client relationship with a client during the:-

A. Termination phase when discharge plans are being made.
B. Working phase when the client shows some progress.
C. Orientation phase when a contract is established
D. Working phase when the client brings it up.

512. During electroconvulsive therapy (ECT) the client receives oxygen by mask via positive pressure ventilation. The nurse assisting with this procedure knows that positive pressure ventilation is necessary because?

A. Anaesthesia is administered during the procedure
B. Decrease oxygen to the brain increases confusion and disorientation
C. Grand mal seizure activity depresses respirations
D. Muscle relaxations given to prevent injury during seizure activity depress respirations.

513. A Client who has just experienced her second spontaneous abortion expresses anger towards her physician, the hospital and the "rotten nursing care". When assessing the situation, the nurse recognizes that the client may be using the coping mechanism of:-

A. Projection B. Displacement
C. Denial D. Reaction formation

514. Nurse is caring for a client with depression who has not responded to antidepressant medication. The nurse anticipates that what treatment procedure may be prescribed?

A. Neuroleptic medication
B. Short term seclusion
C. Psychosurgery
D. Electroconvulsive therapy

515. Mira is admitted to the emergency room with drug-included anxiety related to over ingestion of prescribed antipsychotic medication. The most important piece of information the nurse In- charge should obtain initially is the:-

A. Length of time on the med.
B. Name of the ingested medication & the amount ingested
C. Reason for the suicide attempt
D. Name of the nearest relative & their

516. Significant Components of personality as described by sigmund freud Are:-
A. Conscious, Preconscious and subconscious
B. Id, Ego & Supergo
C. Dream Interpretation
D. Defense Mechanism

517. A five year old Mohan diagnosed as rectal cancer and his response to the diagnosis is that "Nothing is wrong it is just hemorrhoids" which defensive mechanism he used:
A. Projection B. Repression
C. Denial D. Displacement

518. Delusion is a disorder of:-
A. Denial B. Derailment
C. Repression D. Undoing

519. Preoccupation with a fear of having a serious physical illness, not based on real or organic pathology is :-
A. Hypoesthesia
B. Hypochondriasis
C. Psychosomatic Disorder
D. Hypertonicity

520. Common form of ECT used in the hospital is:
A. Direct ECT B. Modified ECT
C. Both of the above D. None of the above

521. Catatonic Behaviour in Schizophrenia is characterized by which of the following:-
A. Resisting attempts to be moved
B. Maintaining rigid, immobile postures
C. Decrease in reactivity to the environment
D. All of the Above

522. With Barbiturate and Benzodiazepine abuse and dependency, sedative intoxication is generally associated with:
A. Slurred speech
B. Uncoordinated motor movements
C. Impairment in attention and speech
D. All of the Above

523. Which of the following are risk factors for childhood Psychiatric Disorders?
A. Parental Psychopathology
B. Repeated early separation from parents
C. Harsh or inadequate parents
D. All of the Above

524. Autism is:-
A. Neuro Developmental Disorders
B. Social and Language Communication Problem
C. Mainly due to Hypothalamic Damage
D. Metabolic Disease

525. A patient who decides to leave that hospital against medical advice (LAMA) must sign a form. What is the purpose of this form?
A. To indicate the patient`s wishes
B. To use in the event of readmission
C. To release the physician and hospital from legal responsibility for the patient's health status.
D. To ethicaly illustrate that the patient has control of his or her own care and treatment

526. A Comprehensive Health Assessment of an older person includes:-
A. Functional assessment
B. Clinical assessment
C. Psychosocial Assessment
D. All of the Above

527. Abnormal Sensitivity to light is known is :-
A. Hydrophobia B. Diplopia
C. Aphasia D. Photophobia

528. The antidote of Morphine overdoes is:-
A. N-acetyl cysteine B. Naloxone
C. Atropine sulphate D. Esmolol

529. Drug of choice in breast carcinoma:-
A. Methotrexate B. Chlorambucil
C. Tamoxifen citrate D. Co- trimoxazole

530. Thinking is mental process that deals with:-
A. Thoughts & Ideas
B. Motives & Movements
C. Action & Reaction
D. Feelings & Emotions

531. The part of the mind that distinguishes right from wrong and acts as a censor or behaviour is called:-
A. Ego B. Id
C. Libido D. Super ego

532. Persecutory Delusion is more common in:-
A. Schizophernia
B. Paranoid Schizophernia
C. Manic Depressive Psychosis
D. Biploar Affative Disorder

533. The Most common type of Dementia is:-
A. Pick's Disease B. Parkinson's Disease
C. Aizhelmer's Disease D. Tics Disease

534. In following which is a thought disorder:-
A. Mannerism B. Compulsion
C. Automatism D. Delusion

535. A mental disorder in which a person feels that lice are crawling on his arm, But actually there are no lice on his skin, the person is suffering from :-
A. Auditory illusion
B. Auditory hallucination
C. Tactile illusion
D. Tactile hallucination

536. A false belier in which the patient thinks that he is being talked about by other people is known as:-
A. Delusion of reference
B. Delusion of guilt
C. Delusion of grandeur
D. Delusion of self accusation

537. **What is a sociological definition of the word drug ?**
A. Substance that changes mood, behaviour or consciousness
B. A dysfunction
C. A chemical
D. Ecology

538. **Hypnotherapy is least effective on people suffering from**
A. Anxiety B. Hypertension
C. Pain D. Schizophrenia

539. **Which one of these is used in bed wetting in children?**
A. Imipramine B. Chlorpromazine
C. Levodopa D. Tacrine

540. **During the initial care of rape victims the following are to be considered by a nurse except:-**
A. Maintain a non-judgmental approach.
B. Assure privacy
C. Touch the client to show acceptance and empathy.
D. Accompany the client in the examination room.

541. **The first drug of choice for a patient admitted with status epilepticus is:-**
A. Phenytoin B. Carbamezepine
C. Diazepam D. Sodium valproate

542. **A 55-year-old man was admitted after a motor vehicle accident with multiple injuries. His friend reported that he had been seeing a psychiatrist for an unknown diagnosis. He stated that the patient sometimes gets "hyper" for no reason, and becomes violent and sometimes is depressed of the following, which general psychiatric disorder is characterized by a pattern of aggression or violence which includes irritability, agitation, and violent behavior during manic or psychotic episodes ?**
A. Schizophrenia B. Bipolar disorder
C. Delusional disorder D. Depression

543. **"Mask Like Faces" is a Typical Feature of :-**
A. Tetanus B. Hypothyroidism
C. Parkinson Disease D. Down Syndrone

544. **Alfred Binet is associated with :-**
A. Personality Testing B. Intelligence Testing
C. Aptitude Testing D. Value Testing

545. **Emotion can be expressed by which of following**
A. Language B. Gesture
C. Facial Expression D. All of the above

546. **Physical Symptoms in Psychosomatic Disorders Are caused by :-**
A. Emotional Factors
B. Physical Factors
C. Environmental Factors
D. Genetic Factors

547. **The part of Mind that distinguish right from wrong and Acts as censor of Behaviour is called:-**
A. Ego B. ID
C. Libido D. Superego

548. **A patient keeps repeating the last few words of what he heard the condition is known as:-**
A. Neologism B. Echopraxia
C. Echolalia D. Thought Insertion

549. **La Bella indifference is related to which of the following neurosis?**
A. Phobic Anxiety Disorder
B. Anxiety Disorder
C. Obesessional Compulsion Disorder
D. Conversion Reaction

550. **Gustatory Hallucination Affects The:-**
A. Nose B. Taste Buds
C. Ears D. Skin

551. **The Therapeutic Effective Serum Lithium concentration level is monitored:-**
A. 12-24 Hrs B. 24-48 Hrs
C. 3-5 days D. 10-14 days

552. **Intellectual uotient (i) Tells about:-**
A. Intellectual Maturity
B. Mental Age in Relation to Chronological Age
C. Academic Achievement
D. Mental Growth

553. **Best agent for premenstrual syndrome management is?**
A. Progesterone B. Anxiolytic
C. SSRI D. Vitamin E

554. **A female treatment for depression took a massive dose of amitriptyline for suicide. Which of the following statement regarding her management is WRONG?**
A. Gastric lavage should be done
B. Sodium bicarbonate should be administered to treat acidosis
C. Atropine sulphate should be administered as an antidote
D. Diazepam should be injected to control seizures.

555. **Antidepressant drug that can be used in nocturnal enuresis is?**
A. Imipramine B. Fluvoxamine
C. Phenelzine D. Bupropion

556. **A patient on lithium therapy was found to be hypertensive also. Which of the following antihypertensive drugs is contraindicated in a patient on lithium therapy in order to prevent toxicity?**
A. Clonidine
B. Beta blockers
C. Calcium channel blockers
D. Diuretics

557. **A schizophrenic patient started on haloperidol days back, comes with complaints of torticollis and orofaciolingual movements. What is the diagnosis?**
A. Acute dystonia B. Tardive dyskinesia
C. Parkinsonism D. Akathisia

558. A womentreated with lithium during pregnancy, the fetus should be tested for :
A. Neural tube defects
B. Cardic malformations
C. Urogenitlabnormalities
D. Scalp defects

559. What is the drug of choice for obsessive compulsive disorder?
A. Imipramine B. Fluoxetine
C. Benzodiazepines D. Alprazolam

560. Which of the following has highest potential to cause metabolic syndrome?
A. Clozapine B. Risperidone
C. Quetiapine D. Aripiprazole

561. All of the following can result in serotonin syndrome when combined with MAO inhibitors except
A. Tricyclic antidepressants
B. Selective serotonin reuptake inhibitors
C. Carbamazepine
D. Tyramine containing foods

562. Buspirone is used as a/an:
A. Anxiolytic B. Sedative
C. Muscle relaxant D. Anticonvulsant

563. Increased suicidal tendency is associated with alteration in the brain levels of:
A. Noradrenaline B. Serotonin
C. Dopamine D. GABA

564. In depression , there is deficiency of :
A. 5 HT B. Acetylcholine
C. Dopamine D. GABA

565. Lithium is used in the prophylactic treatment of
A. Schizophrenia
B. Mdp
C. Acute depression
D. Conversion reaction

566. As a side effect the metabolic syndrome is most commonly associated with which of the following group of medications ?
A. Anti anxiety drugs
B. Anti depressant drugs
C. Anti psychotic drugs
D. Anti cholinergic drugs

567. Which of the following is the most common side effect seen with fluoxetine therapy?
A. Seizure B. Anxiety
C. Hypotension D. Loose stools

568. Antipsychotic drug induced parkinsonism is treated by:
A. Anticholinergics B. Levodopa
C. Selegiline D. Amantadine

569. Prolactin secretion is inhibited
A. Dopamine antagonist
B. GABA
C. Neurophysin
D. Bromocriptine

570. A 30 year old manic patient was prescribed haloperiod 3 months back. For last two days, he has become restless and kept pacing in the room for a day. On examination he was found to have tremors of hand. He is most likely to be suffering from :
A. Anhedonia
B. Dystonia
C. Restless leg syndrome
D. Akathisia

571. A patient ingested some unknown substance and presented with myoclonic jerks, seizures, tachycardia and hypotension. ECG shows a heart rate of 120/min. the arterial blood revealed a pH of 7.25, pCO_2 of 30 mm hg and bicarbonate ions are 15 mmo I/L. the most likely poisonous agent is :
A. Amanita phylloids
B. Ethylene glycol
C. Imipramine
D. Phencyclidine

572. Which of the following diuretics decreases the renal lithium clearance?
A. Acetazolamide B. Mannitol
C. Furosemide D. Spironolactone

573. Lithium is used in a pregnant woman. Which of the following congenital anomaly occurs in the fetus ?
A. Tetralogy of fallot
B. Bicuspid atresia
C. Ebstein's anomaly
D. Pulmonary stenosis

574. A psychotic female on phenothiazine therapy complains of sudden onset of high grade fever, muscle rigidity and altered sensorium. The diagnosis is :
A. Malignant hyperthermia
B. Neuroleptic malignant syndrome
C. Tardive dyskinesia
D. Akathisia

575. Which of the following drugs is both effective and safe to use in a pregnant patient suffering from bipolar disorder?
A. Carbamazepine B. Lithium
C. Olanzapine D. Valproic acid

576. Which of the following effects is unlikely to occur during treatment with imipramine ?
A. Elevation of seizure threshold
B. Mydriasis
C. Sedation
D. Urinary retention

577. The secretion of which of the following hormones increases with chlorpromazine therapy?
A. Prolactin
B. Gonadotropin
C. Corticotropin
D. Antidiuretic hormone

578. A patient ,hari has been diagnosed to have schizophrenia. Which of the following acts as a

limiting factor in the use of clozapine as an antipsychotic drug in this patient ?
A. Its potential to cause agranulocytosis
B. Its inability to benefit negative symptoms of schizophrenia
C. High incidence of extrapyramidal side effects
D. Production of hyperprolactinemia

579. Propanolol is useful in the management of which of the following side effects of typical neuroleptic ?
A. Parkinsonism
B. Acute muscle dystonia
C. Tardive dyskinesia
D. Akathisia

580. Now – a- days, the selective serotonin reuptake inhibitors are the preferred drugs for which of the following psychiatric disorder apart from their role in the treatment of depression :
A. Phobias
B. Obsessive compulsive disorder
C. Post traumatic stress disorder
D. All of the above

581. A psychiatric patient taking medication develops a tremor, thyroid enlargement and leukocytosis. Drug implicated is :
A. Clomipramine B. Haloperidol
C. Lithium D. Olanzapine

582. A patient presents in your psychiatry OPD with complaints of diminished vision. Ophthalmological examination revealed corneal and lenticular opacities. He had been prescribed some antipsychotic drug during his last visit. Which of the following it can be ?
A. Thioridazin B. Haloperiodol
C. Flupenthixol D. Pimozide

583. After starting your patient on imipramine, his heart rate rises to 120/min and he has blurred vision. These effects can be explained by the fact imipramine :
A. Is a muscarinic antagonist
B. Potentiates epinephrine
C. Is a ganglionic blocker
D. Is a potent a adrenergic blocker

584. Drug of choice in intractable hiccups is :
A. Metoclopramide
B. Fluoxetine
C. Selegiline
D. Chlorpromazine

585. Prophylactic plasma concentration range of lithium inmEq does not include :
A. 0.5 B. 0.8
C. 0.6 D. 1.0

586. Which among the following medications has been found to be effective in smoking cessation ?
A. Bupropion B. Buspirone
C. Paroxetine D. Venlafaxine

587. Akathisia is seen with the use of :
A. Clozapine B. Propranolol
C. Benztropine D. Haloperiodol

588. Which of the following drug may cause hypertensive crisis in patient on MAO inhibitor therapy
A. Tyramine
B. Guanethidine
C. Phenobarbitone
D. Nor – epinephrine

589. Extrapyramidal symptoms are a complication of treatment with following drugs :
A. Antipsychotics
B. Anti anxiety drugs
C. Anti depressants
D. Anti malarial drugs

590. Drug useful in malignant hyperthermia is :
A. Halothane B. Succinyl choline
C. Dantrolene D. Haloperiodol

591. Neuroleptic malignant syndrome is cused by :
A. Carbamazepine B. Clonazepam
C. Haloperiodol D. Fluoxetine

592. Half – life of lithium is :
A. 8 hours B. 16 hours
C. 24 hours D. 36 hours

593. The apeutic levels of lithium (in meq/l) in a patient of acute mania is :
A. 0.4 – 0.8 B. 0.8 – 1.2
C. 1.2 – 1.6 D. 1.6 – 2.0

594. Which of the following drugs should not be given with tyramine as it may result in dangerous reaction ?
A. Selegiline
B. Meperidine
C. Tranylcypromine
D. Dextromethorphan

595. Anti depressant drug that can be safely used in children is :
A. Imipramine B. Fluoxetine
C. Dothiepin D. Respiridone

596. Galactorrhoea is caused by :
A. Phenothiazines B. Bromocriptine
C. Pyridoxine D. None

597. Long term antipsychotic use may cause :
A. Depression B. Mania
C. Schizophrenia D. Tardive dyskinesia

598. Drug of choice for the treatment of negative symptoms of schizophrenia is :
A. Chlorpromazine B. Haloperiodol
C. Clozapine D. Doxepin

❑❑❑

Answer Sheet

1..A	2..B	3..B	4..D	5..B	6..C	7..D	8..A	9..A	10.. C
11. .B	12. .B	13. .B	14. .B	15. .B	16. .C	17. .B	18. .D	19. .A	20. .C
21. .D	22. .A	23. .D	24. .B	25. .D	26. .C	27. .A	28. .C	29. .B	30. .C
31. .A	32. .A	33. .D	34. .C	35. .B	36. .B	37. .B	38. .A	39. .A	40. .A
41. .B	42. .D	43. .D	44. .C	45. .B	46. .B	47. .B	48. .D	49. .B	50. .B
51. .C	52. .B	53. .B	54. .B	55. .B	56. .B	57. .D	58. .C	59. .C	60. .D
61. .A	62. .A	63. .A	64. .A	65. .D	66. .B	67. C.	68. .B	69. .B	70. D.
71. .C	72. .B	73. .D	74. .A	75. .D	76. .C	77. .D	78. .A	79. .C	80. .A
81. .C	82. .A	83. .C	84. .C	85. .C	86. .B	87. .D	88. .C	89. D.	90. .D
91. .C	92. .D	93. C.	94. .B	95. .D	96. .B	97. .C	98. .D	99. .C	100. .B
101. .D	102. .A	103. .C	104. .D	105. .D	106. .D	107. .C	108. .C	109. .A	110. .B
111. .D	112. .D	113. .A	114. .A	115. .D	116. .A	117. .A	118. .A	119. .B	120. .B
121. .A	122. .D	123. .A	124. .C	125. .A	126. .D	127. .A	128. .B	129. .A	130. .D
131. .A	132. .C	133. .C	134. .B	135. .B	136. .A	137. .A	138. .D	139. .C	140. .A
141. .B	142. .C	143. .B	144. .A	145. .B	146. .C	147. .C	148. .B	149. .D	150. .B
151. .C	152. .C	153. .A	154. .D	155. .A	156. .C	157. .A	158. .B	159. .C	160. .B
161. .B	162. .D	163. .A	164. .B	165. .D	166. .B	167. .B	168. .A	169. .C	170. .B
171. .B	172. .B	173. .D	174. .C	175. .A	176. .A	177. .A	178. .D	179. .D	180. .D
181. .D	182. .C	183. .A	184. .A	185. .C	186. .D	187. .A	188. .D	189. .A	190. .D
191. .A	192. .C	193. .D	194. .A	195. .C	196. .A	197. .B	198. .A	199. .B	200. .C
201. .C	202. .A	203. .D	204. .A	205. .C	206. .C	207. .D	208. .C	209. .B	210. .B
211. .B	212. .B	213. .C	214. .A	215. .A	216. .A	217. .D	218. .D	219. .C	220. .C
221. .D	222. .B	223. .C	224. .D	225. .D	226. .A	227. .B	228. .A	229. .B	230. .C
231. .D	232. .D	233. .C	234. .B	235. .A	236. .B	237. .B	238. .B	239. .A	240. .A
241. .C	242. .B	243. .B	244. A	245. .C	246. .A	247. .A	248. .A	249. .B	250. .A
251. .C	252. .B	253. .B	254. .C	255. .A	256. .C	257. .A	258. .B	259. .A	260. .A
261. .B	262. .C	263. .C	264. .C	265. .B	266. .A	267. .B	268. .C	269. .B	270. .B
271. .A	272. .A	273. .B	274. .B	275. .D	276. .B	277. .A	278. .D	279. .D	280. .A
281. .C	282. .D	283. .B	284. .A	285. .D	286. .B	287. .B	288. .C	289. .A	290. .D
291. .B	292. .B	293. .D	294. .B	295. .B	296. .A	297. .B	298. .D	299. .C	300. .C

301. .A	302. .C	303. .A	304. .C	305. .B	306. .A	307. .B	308. .D	309. .A	310. .C
311. .B	312. .B	313. .D	314. .D	315. .D	316. .A	317. .A	318. .B	319. .D	320. .C
321. .C	322. .A	323. .B	324. .D	325. .A	326. .C	327. .A	328. .A	329. .D	330. .A
331. .D	332. .D	333. .C	334. .A	335. .A	336. .C	337. .C	338. .D	339. .B	340. .D
341. .D	342. .A	343. .D	344. .C	345. .A	346. .B	347. .A	348. .D	349. .C	350. .D
351. .D	352. .A	353. .A	354. .C	355. .B	356. .A	357. .A	358. .D	359. .B	360. .B
361. .B	362. .C	363. .A	364. .D	365. .D	366. .B	367. .B	368. .B	369. .C	370. .A
371. .A	372. .C	373. .D	374. .B	375. .D	376. .C	377. .C	378. .C	379. .B	380. .C
381. .D	382. .B	383. .A	384. .B	385. .B	386. .C	387. .A	388. .B	389. .B	390. .D
391. .C	392. .C	393. .C	394. .B	395. .A	396. .C	397. .A	398. .A	399. .C	400. .D
401. .B	402. .B	403. .C	404. .C	405. .A	406. .B	407. .B	408. .B	409. .B	410. .D
411. .D	412. .B	413. .A	414. .B	415. .C	416. .C	417. .D	418. .C	419. .D	420. .D
421. .D	422. .B	423. .A	424. .A	425. .B	426. .A	427. .D	428. .A	429. .A	430. .D
431. .A	432. .C	433. .D	434. .B	435. .A	436. .D	437. .B	438. .D	439. .C	440. .A
441. .A	442. .A	443. .D	444. .B	445. .B	446. .D	447. .D	448. .A	449. .D	450. .D
451. .A	452. .B	453. .C	454. .B	455. .D	456. .B	457. .A	458. .A	459. .D	460. .C
461. .A	462. .D	463. .B	464. .D	465. .B	466. .A	467. .D	468. .C	469. .B	470. .D
471. .C	472. .C	473. .D	474. .A	475. .B	476. .C	477. .C	478. .D	479. .B	480. .B
481. .C	482. .D	483. .A	484. .B	485. .B	486. .D	487. .C	488. .B	489. .D	490. .A
491. .C	492. .D	493. .D	494. .D	495. .A	496. .B	497. .D	498. .C	499. .D	500. .D
501. .C	502. .D	503. .A	504. .A	505. .C	506. .D	507. .C	508. .B	509. .B	510. .D
511. .C	512. .D	513. .B	514. .D	515. .B	516. .B	517. .C	518. .A	519. .B	520. .B
521. .B	522. .D	523. .D	524. .B	525. .C	526. .B	527. .D	528. .B	529. .C	530. .A
531. .D	532. .B	533. .C	534. .D	535. .D	536. .A	537. .A	538. .D	539. .A	540. .D
541. .C	542. .B	543. .C	544. .B	545. .D	546. .A	547. .D	548. .C	549. .D	550. .B
551. A	552. B	553. C	554. C	555. A	556. D	557. A	558. B	559. B	560. A
561. D	562. A	563. B	564. A	565. B	566. C	567. B	568. A	569. D	570. D
571. C	572. C	573. C	574. B	575. C	576. A	577. A	578. A	579. B	580. D
581. C	582. A	583. A	584. D	585. D	586. A	587. D	588. A	589. A	590. C
591. C	592. C	593. B	594. C	595. B	596. A	597. D	598. C		

❑❑❑

9. Nursing Research (MCQ)

1. **Which of the following techniques includes Random sampling or probability sampling?**
   A. Simple random sampling
   B. Stratified random Sampling
   C. Cluster sampling
   D. All of the Above Sampling
2. **Gender, age-class, religion, type of disease, and blood group are measured on:**
   A. Nominal scale of measurement
   B. Ordinal scale of measurement
   C. Interval scale of measurement
   D. Ratio scale of measurement
3. **Which of the following scale of measurement has an absolute zero?**
   A. Nominal B. Ordinal
   C. Interval D. Ratio
4. **Which of the following variable is influenced by the intervention of the researcher?**
   A. Independent B. Dependent
   C. Discrete D. Extraneous
5. **The statistical approach which helps the investigator to decide whether the outcome of the study is a result of factors planned within design of the study or determined by chance is called:**
   A. Descriptive statistics
   B. Inferential statistics
   C. Normal distribution
   D. Standard deviation
6. **Which of the following methods is a form of graphical presentation of data?**
   A. Line Diagram B. Pie diagram
   C. Bar diagram D. Histogram
7. **Which of the following are measures of central tendency?**
   A. Mean B. Median
   C. Mode D. All of the Above
8. **Which measure of central tendency is Influenced by extreme scores and skewed distributions?**
   A. Mean B. Median
   C. Mode D. Range
9. **Which of the following measure of central tendency is calculated by numbers arranging in numerical order?**
   A. Standard deviation
   B. Range
   C. Median
   D. Mode
10. **What is the mode in statistics?**
    A. Value of middle observation
    B. Arithmetic mean
    C. Most commonly occurring value
    D. Difference between the highest and lowest value
11. **Which of the following indices used to measure variation or dispersion?**
    A. Range
    B. Variance
    C. Standard deviation
    D. All of the Above
12. **A measure of dispersion of a set of observations in which it is calculated by the difference between the highest and lowest values produced is called:**
    A. Standard deviation
    B. Variance
    C. Range
    D. Mode
13. **Shape of a normal curve is:**
    A. Symmetrical B. Curvilinear
    C. Linear D. Parabolic
14. **The Median value is the:**
    A. 25th percentile B. 50th percentile
    C. 75th percentile D. 95th percentile
15. **Large standard deviations suggest that:**
    A. Scores are probably widely scattered.
    B. There is very little deference among scores.
    C. Mean, median and mode are the same
    D. The scores not normally distributed.
16. **The formula given below is computational formula for:**

$$\sqrt{\frac{\sum\left(X-\overline{X}\right)^2}{(n-1)}}$$

    A. Variance
    B. Mean
    C. Standard deviation
    D. t-statistic
17. **The squire of the standard deviation is the:**
    A. Variance. B. Standard error
    C. Z-score D. Variance

18. Which is a characteristic of normal distribution?
A. Symmetric
B. Beil-shaped
C. Mean = median = mode
D. All of the Above

19. Skewness is a measure:
A. Of the asymmetry of the probability distribution
B. Decides the distribution may have high or low variance
C. Of central tendency
D. None of the Above

20. The formula given below is used to calculate:

$$\sum\frac{(O-E)^2}{E}$$

O= Observed frequency E= Expected frequency
A. t-test statistic
B. Chi-squire statistic
C. Correlation coefficient
D. Standard deviation

21. Which of the following variable didn't change in experiment?
A. Dependent variable.
B. Extraneous variable.
C. Independent variable.
D. Confounding variable.

22. Square root of deviation is called:
A. Standard deviation
B. Standard error
C. Mean deviation
D. Range

23. Which is true about cluster sampling?
A. Every month case is chosen fro study
B. A natural group is taken as sampling unit
C. Stratification of population
D. Involves use of random numbers

24. The information that an investigator collects from the subjects or participants in a research study is usually called:
A. Hypothesis B. Data
C. Variable D. Concept

25. The degree of flatness or peakedness of a graph of a frequency distribution is termed as:
A. Standard deviation
B. Kurtosis
C. Skewness
D. Mode

26. In a negatively skewed distribution, the mean generally falls to:
A. The left of the median and the median usually lies to the left of the mode.
B. The right of the median and the median usually lies to the right of the mode.
C. The middle of median and mode.
D. The centre of the distribution.

27. Sum of all squares of deviation from the mean is called:
A. Mean B. Mode
C. Variance D. Standard Error

28. A measure used to standardize the central tendency away from the mean across different samples is:
A. Skewness B. Range
C. Z-score D. Mode

29. Probability values fall on scale between:
A. -1 to +1 B. 0 and 1
C. -3 to + 3 D. 0.05 to 0.01

30. Standard error is calculated by:
A. Dividing standard deviation by the square root of the sample size.
B. Dividing number of nominated outcome by number of possible outcome.
C. Adding all the numbers and then dividing by the numbers of observations.
D. Arranging the numbers in numerical order, then taking the middle one.

31. When explaining the direction of the linear association between two numerical paired variables, a positive correlation is stated when:
A. One variable increases and the other variable decreases or vice versa.
B. Dependent variable increases and independent variable decreases
C. Both variables increase and decrease at the same time.
D. Correlation coefficient is stated close to 0.

32. A type of graphical presentation data used to explain correlation between dependent and independent variable is:
A. Histogram B. Frequency polygon
C. Frequency curve D. Scatter plot

33. Correlation coefficient ranges from:
A. 0.01 to 0.05 B. 0 to 1
C. -1 to +1 D. -3 to +3

34. A contingency table (2x2) is used to calculate:
A. t-statistic
B. Correlation coefficient
C. Variance
D. Chi-squire statistic

35. Normal distribution curve is explained using:
A. Mean and sample
B. Mean and median
C. Median and standard deviation
D. Mean and standard deviation

36. **In a highly skewed distribution central tendency is better explained by:**
A. Mode
B. Median
C. Standard deviation
D. Mean

37. **A tentative explanation/statement of a declaration of the expected outcome of a research study based on observations is called:**
A. Relationships B. Analysis
C. Variables D. Hypothesis

38. **In a naturalistic observation, the phenomenon in which the behaviour of the subjects being observed changes because they are being watched is called:**
A. Observer bias
B. Observer effect
C. Participant observation
D. Representative sampling

39. **The entire group of people or animals in which the researcher is interested is called:**
A. Sample B. Experiment group
C. Sample D. Controls

40. **In the scientific investigation, the first step is:**
A. Reporting your results
B. Perceiving a question
C. Drawing conclusion
D. Testing hypothesis

41. **Which of the following is a method of quantitative research?**
A. Experimental Research
B. Correlational Research
C. Quasi-Experimental Research
D. All of the Above

42. **The grounded theory approach was developed by**
A. Heidegger B. Glaser and Strauss
C. Husserl D. Denzin

43. **Deductive Reasoning is applied in:**
A. Qualitative research
B. Quantitative research
C. Action research
D. Applied research

44. **Which of the following is a qualitative research design where lived experiences of individuals are examined in their "life-world"?**
A. Ethnography B. Ethology
C. Phenomenology D. Grounded theory

45. **Which of the following is a characteristic of qualitative research?**
A. Deductive process
B. Control over the context
C. Fixed research design
D. Inductive process

46. **Qualitative research design involves**
A. Emergent design
B. Correlative design
C. Experimental design
D. Cohort design

47. **Which of the following features involve in Phenomenological study?**
A. Bracket out B. Description
C. Analysis D. All of the Above

48. **Which of the following qualitative methods focuses on description and interpretation of cultural behaviour?**
A. Phenomenology
B. Grounded theory
C. Ethnography
D. Symbolic interactionism

49. **The area of inquiry in grounded theory approach is**
A. Holistic view of culture
B. Lived experiences
C. Behaviour observed over time in natural context
D. Social structural processes with in social setting

50. **The research design in which the area inquiry is the manner by which people make sense of social interactions:**
A. Grounded theory
B. Phenomenology
C. Symbolic interactionism
D. Ethnography

51. **The term triangulation was given by:**
A. Denzin
B. Leininger
C. Glaser and Strauss
D. Heidegger

52. **In qualitative research, a guiding principle in deciding sample size is:**
A. Effect size B. Number of variables
C. Data saturation D. Sub-group analysis

53. **The term refers to the use of multiple referents to draw conclusions about what constitutes the truth:**
A. Item analysis
B. Factor analysis
C. Error measurement
D. Triangulation

54. Characteristics of qualitative research design are
A. Flexible and elastic design
B. Use of mixed methodologies
C. Ongoing analysis to formulate subsequent strategies
D. All of the Above

55. The tendency in qualitative research to derive a complex array of data from a variety of sources, using variety of methods is termed as:
A. Triangulation B. Bricolage
C. Cross-tabulation D. Confirmability

56. Another name for a bar graph is:
A. Polygon B. Histogram
C. Normal curve D. Line graph

57. A table that shows how often different scores appear in a set of scores is called a frequency:
A. Polygon B. Histogram
C. Normal curve D. Distribution

58. Analysis of Variance (ANOVA) test is used to
A. Test the difference between two independent group means
B. Test the difference between two related group means
C. Test the difference among the means of 3+ independent groups
D. Test the difference in ranks of scores of 3+ independent groups

59. Kruskal-Wallis test is used to:
A. Test the difference between two independent group means
B. Test the difference among the means of 3+ related groups
C. Test the difference among the means of 3+ independent groups
D. Test the difference in ranks of scores of 3+ independent groups

60. Chi-square test is used to test:
A. Difference in proportions
B. Difference in means of two independent variables
C. Relationship between two bivariate variables
D. Difference in means of three or more set of variables

61. Which of the following is a criteria for Fisher's exact test?
A. When proportions derived from independent groups are compared
B. When there are cells with a value of 0
C. Sample size is small (less than 30)
D. All of the Above

62. The type of research focused on finding a solution to an immediate practical problem is termed as:
A. Basic research
B. Applied research
C. Explanatory research
D. Descriptive research

63. Which of the following methods allows the use of any group of research subject?
A. Purposive sampling
B. Convenience sampling
C. Snow-ball sampling
D. Quota sampling

64. Which of the following is TRUE about features of quasi-experimental research design?
A. Manipulation. control group, randomization
B. Manipulation, but no control group or randomization
C. No manipulation of independent variable
D. Use of correlational approach

65. Which of the following data collection method has better subjectivity?
A. Self-reports
B. Observation
C. Biophysiologic measures
D. Questionnaires

66. Basic principles that are accepted as being true on the basis of logic or reason, without proof or verification is termed as:
A. Assumptions B. Hypothesis
C. Constructs D. Propositions

67. A fundamental ethical principle that seeks to prevent harm and exploitation of, to maximize benefits for, study participants is:
A. Justice B. Beneficence
C. Nonmalificence D. Coercion

68. The degree of consistency with which an instrument measures the attribute it is supposed to be measuring is called:
A. Validity B. Reliability
C. Sensitivity D. Objectivity

69. The reliability of a measuring tool has following aspects, except:
A. Stability B. Internal consistency
C. Efficiency D. Equivalence

70. The extent to which the same results are obtained on repeated administrations of the instrument is termed as:
A. Internal consistency
B. Validity
C. Stability
D. Sensitivity

71. The Spearman's-Brown formula is used to estimate:
A. Test-retest reliability
B. Internal consistency
C. Equivalence
D. Validity

72. The degree to which an instrument measures what it is supposed to be measuring is its:
A. Validity
B. Internal consistency
C. Sensitivity
D. Equivalence

73. Multi-trait-multi-matrix is a procedure developed to establish:
A. Internal consistency
B. Interrater reliability
C. Construct validity
D. Content validity

74. Which of the following is a procedure for establishing construct validity of an instrument?
A. Known-group technique
B. Factor analysis
C. MTMM
D. All of the Above

75. Which of The following most common type of composite scale?
A. Likert scale B. Visual analog scale
C. Checklists D. Thurstone scale

76. For a two-group comparison study, standardized measure of effect size is:
A. Square of the Pearson correlation coefficient.
B. Eta squired value
C. Chi-squire value
D. The difference between the two means, divided by the average of the standard deviations.

77. Kappa coefficient of reliability is related to:
A. Ratio scale of measurement
B. Interval scale of measurement
C. Nominal scale of measurement
D. Continuous variables

78. The sum of the values of a variable for a set of observations, divided by the number of the observations in the set refers to:
A. Mode
B. Standard deviation
C. Median
D. Mean

79. The number of new cases that occur within a specific population within a defined time interval is:
A. Point Prevalence
B. Incidence
C. Period prevalence
D. Lifetime Prevalence

80. The phi coefficient is used for correlations between
A. Two continuous variables
B. Two set of means
C. Two dichotomous variables
D. Two rating scales

81. A systematic method for continuous monitoring of diseases in a population, in order to be able to detect changes in disease patterns and then to control them is:
A. Conditional probability
B. Screening
C. Prevalence
D. Surveillance

82. A hypothesis which a researcher tries to disprove is:
A. Research hypothesis
B. Null hypothesis
C. Alternate hypothesis
D. Positive hypothesis

83. Number of births divided by total population includes men women and children (1000s) are:
A. Crude birth rate
B. General fertility rate
C. Age-specific fertility rates
D. Total period fertility rate

84. Which of the following diagrams can be draw from quantitative data?
A. Frequency curve B. Scatter diagram
C. Histogram D. All of the Above

85. Best graph for demonstration of relationship between ages and weight is:
A. Bar Diagram B. Histogram
C. Scatter D. Pie diagram

86. Age and sex representation is best represented by:
A. Histogram B. Pie chart
C. Bar diagram D. Sketch of photos

87. Quantitative data can be best represented by:
A. Pie chart B. Pictogram
C. Histogram D. Bar diagram

88. Percentage of data can be shown in:
A. Graph presentation
B. Pie chart
C. Bar diagram
D. Histogram

89. The average birth weights in a hospital are to be demonstrated by statistical representation. This is best done by:
A. Frequency curve B. Pictogram
C. Histogram D. Bar diagram

90. The two important values necessary for describing the frequency distribution of a series of observation are:
A. Mean and standard deviation
B. Mean and range
C. Median and range
D. Median and standard deviation

91. Arrangement of values in a serial order is to determine:
A. Mean B. Mode
C. Median D. Range

92. A scatter diagram shows:
A. Trends of events with the passage of time
B. Relationship between two variables
C. Proportion of an event
D. Positive relationship between two variables

93. In 11 babies born in a hospital is 5 above 3.5 kg and 5 below 3.5 kg. The value 3.5 is:
A. Median average B. Mode average
C. Geometrical mean D. Arithmetic average

94. Relationship between two variables can be presented by:
A. Pie diagram B. Scatter diagram
C. Bar diagram D. Histogram

95. Calculate the median of these ten values.
1.9. 1.9, 1.9, 1.9, 2.2, 2.3, 2.4, 2.4, 2.4, 2.4
A. 1.9 B. 2.1 C. 2.25 D. 2.4

96. A number of cases of dengue are collected over 10 years with extreme variation in data. The best measure to calculate average is:
A. Arithmetic mean B. Mode
C. Geometric mean D. Median

97. Blood pressure samples from two communities are best compared by:
A. Paired t-test B. Student's t-test
C. Chi-square test D. Cohort study

98. In statistics, spread of dispersion is described by:
A. Median
B. Mode
C. Standard deviation
D. Mean

99. Among the measure of dispersion which is the most frequently used:
A. Range B. Mean
C. Median D. Standard deviation

100. The Chi-square test is used to measure the degree of:
A. Causal relationship between exposure and effect
B. Correlation between two variables
C. Association between two variables
D. Agreement between two observations

101. A researcher wants to determine some of the problems that are experienced by asthmatic clients when using a inhaler. The nurse researcher went into a clinic where he personally knows several asthmatic clients having problem with inhaler. The type of sampling done by the investigator is called:
A. Probability B. Purposive
C. Snowball D. Incidental

102. Which of the following test of significance can be used to compare unrelated variables when values are all binary?
A. t-test B. Chi-square test
C. Proportion test D. Correlation test

103. What is true about Chi-square test?
A. Expected and observed values are always equal
B. Mutually exclusive
C. Mutually non-exclusive
D. Indicates median

104. Regarding paired t-test true is:
A. Hypertension in a person before and after treatment can be studied
B. Continuous variables in a single sample
C. Different variables in a single sample
D. Unrelated samples can be compared

105. A useful measure of lethality of an acute infectious disease is:
A. Attack rate B. Incidence rate
C. Case fatality rate D. Mortality rate

106. Case fatality rate is:
A. Ratio
B. Proportion
C. Numerator is always constant
D. Numerator and denominator is are two separate quantities

107. Virulence of a disease is indicated by:
A. Proportional mortality rate
B. Specific mortality rate
C. Case fatality ratio
D. Morbidity rate

108. Descriptive epidemiology is study in relation to:
A. Time B. Place
C. Person D. All of the Above

109. Study of a person who has already contacted the disease is called:
A. Case control B. Cohort
C. Control cohort D. Longitudinal

110. Which of the following are true about case control studies?
A. Relative risk can be calculated
B. Backward study
C. Suitable for rare diseases
D. All of the Above

111. Prevalence is:
A. Rate B. Ratio
C. Proportion D. Mode

112. To compare two population, the best index is:
A. Standardized death rate
B. Infant mortality rate
C. Crude birth rate
D. Couple protection rate

113. Incidence is defined as:
A. Number of cases existing in a given population at a given moment
B. Number of cases existing in a given period
C. Number of new cases occurring during a specific period
D. Number of old cases present

114. Case control study is used for:
A. Finding rare cause
B. Finding multiple risk factors
C. Finding incidence rate
D. Finding morbidity rates

115. Best method to calculate the incidence rate is:
A. Case control study
B. Sentinel surveillance
C. Cohort study
D. Cross-sectional prevalence study

116. Percentages in the segments are indicated by:
A. Bar charts B. Histogram
C. Pictogram D. Pie charts

117. Which of the following test is done to find out the difference between the demographic variables of the groups:
A. T test B. Z test
C. ANOVA D. Chi square

118. Who was developed the grounded theory approach
A. Heidegger B. Glaser and Strauss
C. Husserl D. Denzin

119. Which of the research Deductive Reasoning is applied:
A. Qualitative research
B. Quantitative research
C. Action research
D. Applied research

120. Which is a qualitative research design where lived experiences of individuals are examined in their "life-world"?
A. Phenomenology B. Ethology
C. Ethnography D. Grounded theory

121. Which is a characteristic of qualitative research?
A. Deductive process
B. Control over the context
C. Fixed research design
D. Inductive process

122. Which design involves Qualitative research?
A. Emergent design
B. Correlative design
C. Experimental design
D. Cohort design

123. Nurse researcher disseminates the study findings to:
A. Improve career in profession
B. Publish study for achievement
C. Improve the nursing care and quality
D. Get recognition

124. Which is the qualitative methods focuses on description of cultural behaviour?
A. Phenomenology
B. Grounded theory
C. Ethnography
D. Symbolic interactionism

125. Which is the area of inquiry in grounded theory approach is
A. Holistic view of culture
B. Lived experiences
C. Behaviour observed over time in natural context
D. Social structural processes with in social setting

126. Which of the research design in the area inquiry is the manner by which people make sense of social interactions:
A. Grounded theory
B. Phenomenology
C. Symbolic interactionism
D. Ethnography

127. Which of the degree of consistency with an instrument measures the attribute it is supposed to be measuring is called:
A. Validity B. Reliability
C. Sensitivity D. Objectivity

128. Which has the reliability of a measuring tool aspects, except:
A. Stability B. Internal consistency
C. Efficiency D. Equivalence

129. Which of the extent same results are obtained on repeated administrations of the instrument is termed as?
A. Internal consistency
B. Validity
C. Stability
D. Sensitivity

130. Which stability index of a measuring tool derived through procedures that evaluate:
A. Inter-rater reliability
B. Internal consistency
C. Crombach's alpha
D. Test-retest reliability

131. The Spearman's-Brown formula is used to estimate:
A. Test-retest reliability
B. Internal consistency
C. Equivalence
D. Validity

132. The degree to which an instrument measures what it is supposed to be measuring is called as:
A. Validity B. Internal consistency
C. Sensitivity D. Equivalence

133. Which is NOT a type of validity index of a research instrument?
A. Predictive validity
B. Content validity
C. Concurrent validity
D. Homogenous validity

134. Which is the most common type of composite scale is:
A. Likert scale B. Visual analog scale
C. Checklists D. Thurstone scale

135. Which is sampling process where each element of the population get equal chance to participate in the study called as:-
A. Random Sampling
B. Non Random Sampling
C. Poisson sampling
D. Multistage Sampling

136. Data collection about everyone in population and has the advantage of accuracy and detail:
A. Census
B. Survey
C. Probability sampling
D. Cluster sampling

137. The FIRST stages of sampling process comprise:
A. Sampling and data collection
B. Specifying sampling frame
C. Specifying sampling method
D. Defining the population

138. A sampling method which proceeds with the selection of every k^th^ element from then onwards (where k= population size/sample size):
A. Simple random sampling
B. Stratified random sampling
C. Systematic sampling
D. Snowball sampling

139. Which are the considerations for choosing sample size include:
A. The degree of precision required
B. Method of sampling
C. Way in which results will be analyzed
D. All of the Above

140. Which are the Sampling bias or the error resulting from taking a non-random sample of a population include:
A. Pre-screening
B. Self-Selection Bias
C. Selection from a Specific Area
D. All of the Above

141. What is research hypothesis?
A. States there is no relationship between the variables.
B. Statement about the expected relationship of the variables.
C. States a negative relationship between the variables
D. All of the Above

142. What is Hypothesis testing called:
A. Exploratory data analysis
B. Power analysis
C. Deductive Reasoning
D. Confirmatory data analysis

143. Which of the following measure will provide information regarding how different the data are within the sets?
A. Analysis of variance
B. Measure of central tendency
C. Measure of dispersion
D. Measure of variability

144. What is the best statement of research?
A. Scientific and systematic search on a specific topic
B. Search new things
C. Examine carefully things
D. Search again

145. Why nursing research is essential in nursing?
A. For accountability
B. For autonomy
C. For new ways of practice
D. All of the Above

146. Which are the sources of Research knowledge?
A. Human experience
B. Trial and error
C. Authority
D. All of the Above

147. Which are the characteristics of research?
A. Non evidence B. Order and control
C. Un- Generalized D. Manipulation

148. Which data is Eyewitness actual observation or participant in an event? Records and reports, oral testimony.
A. Primary Sources
B. Null sources
C. Secondary sources
D. Ordinary sources

149. A small scale version, or trial rum of the major study is called as
A. Cohort Study B. Case control study
C. Pilot study D. Descriptive study

150. Which study result is formulation of hypothesis?
A. Cohort Study B. Case control study
C. Pilot study D. Descriptive study

151. A plan for gathering data for answering specific research questions.
A. Research type B. Research error
C. Research design D. Research data

152. A tentative statement ("educated guess") about the expected relationship between two or more variables.
A. Assumption B. Objectives
C. Statement D. Hypothesis

153. Which are the characteristics of hypothesis?
A. It should be reasonable
B. It should be stated in sum use possible terms
C. It is a educational guess or lunch
D. All of the Above

154. An attribute or characteristic of a person (or object) that can change from person to person called as:
A. Variable B. Objectives
C. Statement D. Hypothesis

155. Which are the types of variable?
A. Independent B. Dependent
C. Control D. All of the Above

156. Which is the aggregate of cases that confirm to the designated criteria and that are accessible to the researcher as a pool of subject s for a study of population called as?
A. Target population
B. Accessible Population
C. Sample population
D. All of the Above

157. Which is refers to the process of selecting a portion of the population to represent the entire population.
A. Target population
B. Accessible Population
C. Sample
D. All of the Above.

158. Allocation of the study that can affect results
A. Setting B. Sample
C. Data D. Error

159. Which is the last phase of the research?
A. Selecting a research design
B. Collecting data
C. Utilizing the Findings
D. Analyzing data

160. Which research are Pursuit of knowledge or finding truth, Generates, refines or tests theory and May be used later in development of treatment/drug/theory called as:
A. Basic Research B. Applied research
C. Practical research D. Evaluate research

161. Which research are Knowledge intended to directly influence clinical practice, Conducted in actual practice conditions and Solve problems, make decisions, predict/control outcomes
A. Basic Research B. Applied research
C. General research D. Evaluate research

162. Which are the Research manipulates, controls variable(s) and randomization observes effect in other variable(s)
A. Experimental B. Non- experimental
C. Cross sectional D. Longitudinal

163. Which is the research examines data already collected in the past
A. Experimental B. Non- experimental
C. Retrospective D. Prospective

164. Which are the research examines data already collected in the present
A. Experimental B. Non- experimental
C. Retrospective D. Prospective

165. Which are the research collects data at one point in time
A. Experimental B. Non- experimental
C. Cross sectional D. Longitudinal

166. Which are the research collects data at over a period of time
A. Experimental B. Non- experimental
C. Cross sectional D. Longitudinal

167. Theoretical sampling is considered as a critical feature of:
A. Grounded theory
B. Double-blind study
C. Experimental design
D. Action research

168. Which of the following refers to the independent variables in doing nursing research.?
A. Result B. Cause
C. Output D. Effect

169. The criteria for validity of a screening test is:
A. Accuracy
B. Predictability
C. Sensitivity and specificity
D. Cost effectiveness

170. A nurse researcher wants to do a study on this topic: "Effects of massage and meditation on stress and pain". Which of following type of research that best suits this topic is:
A. Applied research
B. Qualitative research
C. Basic research
D. Quantitative research

171. Which of the following Characteristics of content validity ?
A. Content of the measure is justified by other evidence.
B. Content validity entire range or universe of the construct.
C. Content validity is usually evaluated and scored by experts in the content area
D. All of the Above

172. A nonparametric test statistical significance used to assess wheather a relationship exists between two nominal variables is:
A. Crombach alpha test
B. ANOVA
C. t-test
D. Chi-square test

173. The term which refers to the extent to which the results of the study can be generalized to the larger population:
A. Internal validity B. Predictive validity
C. External validity D. Content validity

174. When subpopulations within an overall population vary, the best method of data collection is:
A. Simple random sampling
B. Stratified random sampling
C. Cluster sampling
D. Purposive sampling

175. An approach to construct validity that involves assessing the degree to which two methods of measuring a construct are similar:
A. Discriminant validity
B. Concurrent validity
C. Convergent validity
D. Divergent validity

176. The degree to which scores on an instrument are correlated with some external criterion measured at the same time:
A. Factor validity
B. Construct validity
C. Content validity
D. Concurrent validity

177. Data collection about everyone or everything in group or population and has the advantage of accuracy and detail:
A. Census
B. Survey
C. Probability sampling
D. Cluster sampling

178. The standard deviation of a sampling distribution is referred to as the:
A. Test statistic
B. Standard error
C. Confidence interval
D. Test of significance

179. What is TRUE about research hypothesis?
A. States there is no relationship between the variables.
B. Statement about the expected relationship of the variables =
C. States a negative relationship between the variables
D. Research hypothesis should always be directional.

180. Which of following is the most important characteristic of a sample?
A. Appropriate number
B. Location
C. Representativeness
D. Randomization

181. The research design that does not manipulate the independent variable is:
A. Experimental design
B. Quasi-experimental design
C. Non-experimental design
D. Descriptive design

182. The power of a statistical test is influenced by:
A. Size of the effect B. Sample size
C. Beta (β) D. All of the Above

183. A statistical expression of magnitude of relationship between two variables or magnitude of difference between two groups:
A. Effect size B. Eignvalue
C. p-value D. z-score

184. Which of the following classification of research designs is based on the dimension of control over independent variables?
A. Structured and flexible
B. Cross-sectional and longitudinal
C. Retrospective and prospective
D. Experimental/quasi experimental and non-experimental

185. The process in which each participant has an equal and known probability of being assigned to either the control or the experimental group is:
A. Randomization B. Manipulation
C. Research control D. None

186. The primary objective of experimental methodology is:
A. Ensure external validity
B. Improve internal validity
C. To eliminate type I error
D. To reduce ethical problems

187. Repeated-measures design is also known as:
A. Crossover design
B. Solomon four-group design
C. Time series design
D. With-in subjects design

188. A statistic calculated in ANOVA:
A. Chi-square
B. Correlation coefficient
C. Eta-squared
D. t-statistic

189. A correlation coefficient used to indicate the magnitude of a relationship between ordinal-level data:
A. Kendall's tau B. phi coefficient
C. Wilk's lambda D. *F*-ratio

190. A statistical procedure which typically used for testing causal models:
A. LISREL (Linear Structural Relations Analysis)
B. Survival analysis
C. Logistic regression
D. MANOVA

191. A multivariate statistical procedure which analyses relationship between multiple independent variables and categorical dependent variables:
A. ANCOVA
B. Logistic regression
C. Multiple regressions
D. MTMM

192. Which of following is the device or techniques an investigator employs to collect data?
A. Sample B. Instrument
C. Hypothesis D. Concept

193. A general method for fitting and testing path analysis models, based on covariances:
A. MTMM
B. Structural Equation Modelling
C. Multiple regressions
D. MANOVA

194. A nurse is conducting a research study on how mark, an AIDS client lives his life. A research design suited for this is:
A. Historical
B. Case Study
C. Phenomenological
D. Ethnographic

195. A design that unfolds in the course of a qualitative study as the researcher makes ongoing design:
A. Experimental design
B. Quasi-experimental design
C. Exploratory design
D. Emergent design

196. A branch of qualitative research associated with the field of anthropology:

A. Ethnography B. Anthropology
C. Etymology D. Epistemology

197. Which of the following is a qualitative method of research?

A. Ethnography B. Case Study
C. Survey/Sampling D. All of the Above

198. Which of the following is an assumption made by parametric tests?

A. Sample scores a have been drawn from a normally distributed population
B. The samples are assumed to have the same variance
C. DV is measured on an interval scale
D. All of the Above

199. Structural Equation Modelling (SEM) is also known as:

A. LISREL
B. Cluster analysis
C. Factor analysis
D. Correspondence Analysis

200. Intra-class correlation coefficient (ICC) is calculated:

A. Construct Validity
B. Test–Retest Reliability
C. Criterion Validity
D. Inter-ratter Reliability

201. The use of another person's ideas or wordings giving appropriate credit results from inaccurate attribution of materials to its sources. Which of following is referred to when another person's idea is inappropriate credited as one's own?

A. Plagiarism B. Quotation
C. Assumption D. Paraphrase

202. Upon gathering the data, which of the following can describe the most number of reasons of leave of absence?

A. Median B. Mode
C. Frequency D. Deviance

203. Which of the following are the reliable sources?

A. Interview B. Observation
C. Records D. All of the Above

204. In Quantitative data, which of the following is described as the distance in the scoring units of the variable from the highest to the lower?

A. Standard deviation
B. Mean
C. Median
D. Range

205. A hypothesis which a researcher tries to disprove is:

A. Positive hypothesis
B. Research hypothesis
C. Null hypothesis
D. Alternate hypothesis

206. The test for assessing patient's orientation and recall:

A. Beck depression inventory
B. Thematic appreciation test
C. Mini-mental status examination
D. Millon clinical multiaxial inventory

207. The major reason for conducting nursing research is to:

A. Promote the growth of nursing profession
B. Improve nursing care for clients
C. Ensure accountability for nursing practice
D. Document the cost effectiveness of nursing care

208. Facts generally accepted as true or correct are known as :

A. Assumptions B. Limitations
C. Delimitations D. Statistics

209. While counselling an individual an impotent principle to follow is:

A. Cooperation with patient
B. Continuity of interaction
C. Individual differences
D. Joint responsibility

210. Reliability of an instrument means that it:

A. Measure what it needs to measure
B. Measures consistently
C. Is feasible and applicable
D. Is standardized

211. Which method is the placement of a series of variables in ascending or descending order?

A. Ranking B. Rating
C. Q sort D. Likert scale

212. The first step in constructing a test is to:
A. Select a variety of items from which to choose
B. Define the objective of the course
C. Delimit the content to be covered by the test
D. Draw up a table of specifications-Blue print

213. Following are the properties of true scientific nursing research:
A. No Manipulation, control, nonrandomization
B. Manipulation, casecontrol, nonrandomization
C. Manipulation, control, randomization
D. Manipulation, control, nonrandomization

214. Random sampling ensures that each subject has:
A. Been selected systematically
B. An equal chance of selection
C. Been selected based on set criteria
D. Characteristics that match other samples

215. Which of the following property makes ex facto research different from experimental research:
A. Correlation is not found
B. Difficult to infer association
C. Difficult to infer causal relation
D. Manipulation is not possible

216. Nurse researcher carries out pilot study to:
A. Confirm the research design
B. Confirm the sample size
C. Help to modify tool
D. Confirm the feasibility of the study

217. Multistage sampling is also known as:
A. Systematic random sampling
B. Cluster sampling
C. Stratified sampling
D. Simple random sampling

218. Which of following communicate the results of the nursing research to the readers? They facilitate the description of the data.
A. Data collection B. Statistics
C. Research Problem D. Tables and Graphs

219. The collection and presentation of data used to explain characteristics of variables is known as:
A. Descriptive statistics
B. Inferential statistics
C. Demography statistics
D. Socioeconomic statistics

220. As a professional, a nurse you can do nursing research for varied reason Except:
A. Professional advancement through research participation
B. To validate results of new nursing modalities
C. For financial gains
D. To improve nursing care

221. Which of the following level data can be described by mean and median?
A. Nominal B. Ordinal
C. Continuous D. Ratio

222. This research topic has the potential to contribute to nursing because it seeks to
A. Include new modalities of care
B. Resolve a clinical problem
C. Clarify an ambiguous modality of care
D. Enhance client care

223. Which of the following is calculated in test retest reliability of an instrument which is administered to same subjects under same conditions at two different point of times:
A. Kuder Richardson
B. Standard deviation
C. Pearson
D. Correlation coefficient

224. This expresses the variability of the data in reference to the mean. It provides as with a numerical estimate of how far, on the average the separate observation are from the mean:
A. Mode B. Standard deviation
C. Median D. Variance

225. Scheffe's test is a:
A. A test for checking homogeneity
B. A test for checking normality of data
C. Post Hoc test of ANOVA
D. Non-parametric equivalent of ANOVA

226. Draw Lottery, Table of random numbers or a sampling that ensures that each element of the population has an equal and independent chance of being part of research is called:
A. Cluster B. Simple
C. Stratified D. Systematic

227. A Researcher want to know the average age of the nursing students who has the most number of leave of absence researcher will need:

A. Median B. Mode

C. Mean D. Deviance

228. Every year we discover new methods or gadgets to improve man's life. The research typed used of this nature is:

A. Applied research

B. Experimental research

C. Developmental research

D. Quantitative research

229. Kaplan–Meier estimator curves are related to:

A. Structural equation modelling

B. Cluster Analysis

C. Survival analysis

D. Canonical Discriminate Analysis

230. The recipients of experimental treatment are an experimental design or the individuals to be observed in a non-experimental design are called:

A. Setting B. Subjects

C. Treatment D. Sample

231. A method of analyzing qualitative data that involves an interactive approach to testing research hypothesis:

A. Analytic induction

B. Axial coding

C. 'Blind' review

D. Inquiry audit

232. A nurse researcher is to perform a study about how nurses perform surgical asepsis during World War II. A research design for this study is:

A. Historical

B. Case Study

C. Phenomenological

D. Ethnographic

233. Hypothesis testing is sometimes called:

A. Exploratory data analysis

B. Power analysis

C. Deductive Reasoning

D. Confirmatory data analysis

234. The plan for how a study will be conducted is called the:

A. Design

B. Hypothesis

C. Data – collection method

D. Research process

235. The principles of ethics in nursing research include:

A. Beneficence

B. Respect for human dignity

C. Justice

D. All of the Above

236. Which of the following is not true about a True Experimental Research?

A. There is a control group in true experiments

B. There is an experimental group

C. Selection of subjects in the control group is randomized

D. There is a careful selection of subjects in the experimental group

237. Cholesterol value are obtained in a group of people before and after giving drug A. the appropriate statistical test used to analyze the data is:

A. Paired t-test B. Unpaired t-test

C. Fischer's test D. Chi-square test

238. To obtain the desired data in a study, which of the following types of definitions is most essential?

A. Theoretical B. Dictionary

C. Conceptual D. Operational

239. Randomization is useful to eliminate:

A. Observer bias

B. Confounding factors

C. Patient bias

D. Sampling bias

240. Which of the following is not a measure of Central Tendency?

A. Mean

B. Variance

C. Standard Deviation

D. Range

241. Best method of variability is:

A. Mean B. Median

C. Range D. Standard Deviation

242. Nursing research has used which of the following reasoning processes?

A. Inductive

B. Deductive

C. Both inductive deductive

D. Neither inductive not deductive

243. The degree to which one can conclude that it was the interventional variable not the extraneous variable that produce the change in dependent variable is known as:

A. Content validity B. External validity

C. Construct validity D. Internal validity

244. Which of the following factors are important regarding the rights of the participants?

A. Confidentiality

B. Anonymity

C. Voluntary participation

D. All of the Above

245. The Client's rights should be protected when doing nursing research using human subjects. These rights below are correct EXCEPT:

A. Right of self-determination

B. Right to compensation

C. Right of privacy

D. Right not to be harmed

246. Anonymity is the name given to the procedure that ensures subjects that their responses:

A. Cannot be identified by anyone

B. Will not be shared with anyone

C. Will be destroyed at the end of the study

D. Will be kept under lock and key

247. The following statistics is used to measure the linear association between two characteristics in the same individuals:

A. Coefficient of variation

B. Coefficient of correlation

C. Chi-square

D. Standard error

248. Which of the following communication mediums could be used to present research findings?

A. Journals B. Research seminars

C. Poster sessions D. All of the Above

249. Blue print in research is known as:

A. Research decision

B. Methodology

C. Review of literature

D. Introduction

250. The final step of the research process, for the researchers, is to:

A. Collect the data

B. Analyze the data

C. Interpret the findings

D. Communicated the findings

251. The small group selected from a larger group to participate in a study is known as the:

A. Study population B. Sample population

C. Sample D. Element

252. Which of the following include in A research design?

A. A preliminary sketch

B. Blue print

C. Tentative plan and plan of action

D. All of the Above

❑❑❑

Answer Sheet

1.D.	2. A.	3. D.	4. B.	5B..	6. D.	7. D.	8. A.	9. C.	10. C.
11. D.	12. C.	13. A.	14. B.	15. A.	16. C.	17. D.	18. D.	19. A.	20. B.
21. C.	22. A.	23. D.	24. B.	25. B.	26. A.	27. C.	28. C.	29. B.	30. A.
31. C.	32. D.	33. C.	34. D.	35. D.	36. A.	37. D.	38. B.	39. C.	40. B.
41. D.	42. B.	43. B.	44. C.	45. D.	46. A.	47. D.	48. C.	49. D.	50. C.
51. A.	52. C.	53. D.	54. D.	55. B.	56. B.	57. D.	58. C.	59. D.	60. A.
61. D.	62. B.	63. D.	64. B.	65. C	66. A.	67. B.	68. B.	69. C.	70. C.
71. D.	72. B.	73. C.	74. D.	75. A.	76. D.	77. C.	78. D.	79. B	80. C.
81. D	82. B.	83. A.	84. D.	85. A.	86. A.	87. C.	88. B.	89. D.	90. A.
91. C.	92. B.	93. A.	94. B.	95. C.	96. B.	97. A.	98. C.	99. D.	100. B.
101. B.	102. A.	103. B.	104. A.	105. C.	106. A.	107. C.	108. D.	109. A.	110. D.
111. B.	112. A.	113. C.	114. B.	115. C.	116. D.	117. D.	118. B.	119. B.	120. A.
121. D.	122. A.	123. C.	124. C.	125. D.	126. C.	127. B.	128. C.	129. C.	130. D.
131. B.	132. A.	133. D.	134. A.	135. A.	136. A.	137. D.	138. C	139. D.	140. D.
141. B.	142. D.	143. D.	144. A.	145. D.	146. D.	147. B.	148. A.	149. C.	150. D.
151. C.	152. D.	153. D.	154. A.	155. D.	156. A.	157. C.	158. A.	159. C.	160. A.
161. B.	162. A.	163. C.	164. D.	165. C.	166. D.	167. A.	168. B.	169. C.	170. A.
171. D.	172. D.	173. C.	174. B.	175. C.	176. D.	177. A.	178. B.	179. B.	180. C.
181. C.	182. D.	183. A.	184. D.	185. A.	186. B.	187. A.	188. C.	189. A.	190. A
191. B.	192. B.	193. B.	194. C.	195. D.	196. B.	197. D.	198. D.	199. A.	200. D.
201. A.	202. B	203. D.	204. D.	205. C.	206. C	207. B.	208. A.	209. C.	210. B.
211. A.	212. B.	213. C.	214. D.	215. C.	216. D.	217. B.	218. D	219. A.	220. C.
221. C.	222. D.	223. C.	224. B.	225. C.	226. B.	227. C.	228. A.	229. C	230. B.
231. A.	232. A.	233. D.	234. A.	235. D.	236. D.	237. A.	238. D.	239. B.	240. B.
241. D.	242. C.	243. D.	244. D.	245. B.	246. A.	247. B.	248. D.	249. A.	250. D.
251. C.	252. D.								

10. Midwifery And Gynecological Nursing (MCQ)

1. The process by which ova are discharge from ovary is called:

A. Menstruation B. Mensuration
C. Ovulation D. Fertilization

2. Fusing of sperm and ovum is called:

A. Fertilization B. Transfusion
C. Combination D. None of the Above

3. The strongest ligament in the female pelvis is:

A. Reverse cervical
B. Oblique cervical
C. Transverse cervical
D. None

4. The alternate tern of normal labour is:

A. Procidentia B. Eutocia
C. Dystocia D. None of the Above

5. Grafian follicle of ovary secretes which hormones?

A. LH B. Progesterone
C. Oestrogen D. None of the Above

6. The screening cancer detection test for the most common cancer in women is:

A. Biopsy of cervical tissue
B. Dilation and curettage
C. Positive Kahn's test
D. Breast self examination

7. The causative organism of syphilis is ?

A. Ducrey's bacillus
B. Nisseria gonococcus
C. Treponema palladium
D. Welch's bacillus

8. The ultimate objective of M.C.H. Care is:

A. Lifelong health
B. Immunization
C. Promotion of breast feeding
D. Health communication and education

9. Drugs and X-rays should be avoided in the .... trimester of pregnancy:

A. Second B. First
C. Third D. None of the Above

10. Amniotic fluid otherwise known as:

A. Aqueous humor B. Liquor amni
C. Liquor chorion D. None of the Above

11. The first evidence of pubertal development in female is usually manifest as:

A. Onset of menarche
B. Appearance of axillary and pubic hair
C. Appearance of breast buds
D. Onset of growth spurt

12. .... Percent of water contains in amniotic fluid.

A. 80 B. 90 C. 70 D. 99

13. The killing of a new born child by its parents is called

A. Restitution B. Infenticide
C. Neocide D. Infantism

14. The function of amnion is:

A. Respiration
B. Shock protection
C. Endocrine function
D. Nutrition

15. MTP Act (1971) in india specifies all of the following except

A. Persons who should perform abortion
B. Conditions for abortion
C. Techniques of abortions
D. Place for conducting abortions

16. Which one of the following pairs regarding pelvis is not correct?

A. Gynecoid: Female type
B. Anthropoid: Ape type
C. Platypelloid: Flat type
D. Android: Male type

17. Compared to the use of the vacuum extractor, forceps delivery is associated with increased risk of:

A. Intracranial haemorrhage
B. Retinal haemorrhage
C. Minor facial injuries
D. Cephalohematoma

18. Which one of the following pairs regarding and presenting part in woman during labour is not correct?

A. Cephalic presentation: Chin
B. Face presentation: Face
C. Trails verse presentation: Shoulder
D. Breach presentation: Buttock

19. Which of the following response is expected in a mother suckling the baby?

A. Increase of adrenaline
B. Increase of prolactin-inhibiting factor
C. Increase of hypothalamic dopamine
D. Increase of oxytocin

20. A primigravida client who is little overweight asks how much weight she should gain over the 9 months. The most appropriate answer is :

A. For your size a little heavy about 15 pounds would be best

B. It really doesn't matter exactly how much weight you gain, as long as your diet is healthy

C. A gain of about 24-25 pounds is the best for the mother and baby

D. Because you are a little overweight, it would be best you not gain too much weight

21. During a prenatal check, a client asks nurse why menstruation ceases once pregnancy occurs. The nurse best response would be that this occurs because of the :

A. Reduction in secretion of hormones by the ovaries

B. Production of estrogen and progesterone by the ovaries

C. Secretion of luteinizing hormones produced by the pituitary

D. Secretion of estrogen hormones produced by the ovaries

22. The nurse teaches a multipara who has just delivered a large baby what to do to maintain a contracted uterus. The nurse recognize that teaching has been effective when the client states:

A. If I start to bleed, I will call for help

B. I will gently message my uterus to keep it firm

C. If I urinate frequently, my uterus will stay contracted

D. I will call you every15 minutes

23. A nurse is assessing a client with pregnancy induced hypertension. The nurse expects the client's blood pressure to be :

A. 150/100 mm Hg while standing and sitting

B. Elevated and accompanied by a headache

C. Above the baseline and fluctuating at each reading

D. 30/15 mm Hg over the baseline on two occasions 6 hours part

24. A client is gravida 4 para 3 and is in a labour room. After a vaginal examination it is determined that the presenting head is at station +C.The appropriate nursing action is :

A. Continue to observe client's contractions

B. Check the fetal heart rate for a prolapsed cord

C. Prepare to move the client quickly to the delivery room

D. Check with the physician to see if an Oxytocin drip is warranted

25. The nausea and vomiting commonly experienced by many women during the first trimester of pregnancy is an adaptation to the increased level of :

A. Estrogen

B. Progesterone

C. Luteinizing hormone

D. Chorionic gonadoptropin

26. Magnesium sulphate IM is administered every 4 hours to an eclamptic client which of the following symptoms is an indication for the next dose of Magnesium sulphate:

A. Absence of deep tendon reflexes

B. A respiratory rate of 16 per minute

C. Urine output of 50 ml over the last 4 hours

D. Complaint of being thirsty

27. The term dizygotic refers to twin who have ?

A. Developed from two separate ova and sperms

B. Been born several hours apart from each other

C. Developed physically a different rates from each other

D. Developed in one amnion and have one chorion

28. A nursing mother has cracked nipples. Which is appropriate nursing intervention in care of client:

A. Applying benzoin to tougher the nipples

B. Keeping the nipples covered with warm, packs

C. Offering to give baby a bottle

D. Exposing the nipples to air as much as possible

29. A client who is 32 weeks pregnant has just been admitted to the labour room in the first stage of labour. Which of the following clinical manifestations is considered abnormal and should be reported to the physician immediately?

A. Expulsion of a blood tinged mucous plug

B. Continuous contraction of 2 minutes duration

C. Feeling of pressure on perineum causing her to near down

D. Expulsion of clear fluid from the vagina

30. The nurse explains the treatment for fluid retention during pregnancy which is :

A. Adequate fluid and a flow salt diet

B. A low salt diet and elevation of the lower extremities
C. Adequate fluid and elevation of the lower extremities
D. Judicious use of diuretics and elevation of the lower extremities

31. In preparing a primigravida for breastfeeding, which of the following will you do?
A. Tell her that lactation begins within a day after delivery
B. Teach her nipple stretching exercises if her nipples are everted
C. Instruct her to wash her nipples before and after each breastfeeding
D. Explain to her that putting the baby to breast will lessen blood loss after delivery

32. You explain to a breastfeeding mother that breast milk is sufficient for all of the baby's nutrient needs only up to:
A. 3 months B. 6 months
C. 1 year D. 2 years

33. Women having normal limbs may sometimes give birth to babies with deformed limbs. This must be due to:
A. Spontaneous generation
B. Mutation
C. Inheritance of acquired character
D. Natural selection

34. Signs of true labour are the following except:
A. Painful rhythmic uterine contraction
B. Dilatation of the OS
C. Fetal movement
D. Show

35. Signs of separation of placenta are the following except:
A. Lengthening of the cord at vulva
B. Gush of blood is seen
C. Fundus raises upto umbilicus
D. Temperature rises

36. The permanent stopping of the menstrual cycle in women is called
A. Menopause B. Menarche
C. Dismenorrhea D. Amenorrhea

37. When are the chances of acute endometritis developing in a woman?
A. After menopause
B. After menarche
C. After abortion or childbirth
D. In childhood

38. The milk that is secreted at the starting of regular breast feeding that contains more proteins and sugar is known as
A. Mature milk B. Fore milk
C. Hind milk D. Transitional milk

39. Painful menstruation is termed as:
A. Menorrhage
B. Dysmenorrhea
C. Amenorrhea
D. Decreased production of prostaglandins

40. In following which is not a sexually transmitted disease?
A. Chancroid B. Syphilis
C. Fibroid uterus D. AIDS

41. When the umbilical cord lies in front of the presenting part and the membranes are intact it is known as:
A. Cord prolapse B. Cord presentation
C. Cord pulsation D. Cord delivery

42. Starting of menstrual cycle is called:
A. Ovulation B. Menstruation
C. Menarche D. Menopause

43. Secretion from mother's breast following delivery is called:
A. Seduestrum B. Colostrum
C. Lochia D. Leucorrhoea

44. During which stage of labour placenta is delivered?
A. Stage -1 B. Stage -2
C. Stage -3 D. Stage -4

45. 'Pap's smear" is used for screening of which of the following:
A. Ovarian cancer B. Endometrial cancer
C. Cervical cancer D. Breast Cancer

46. Which abdominal grip is used to assess the desecent of head in a pregnant woman?
A. Fundal B. Lateral
C. Pelvic 1 D. Pelvic 2

47. Movements of the baby felt by the mother are known as:
A. Lightening B. Engagement
C. Quickening D. Balottment

48. Bedrest is essential in pre-eclampsia since it:
A. Prevents eclampsia
B. Mobilizes tissue fluid thereby lowering blood pressure
C. Improves blood circulations and decreases oedema
D. Prevents premature labour

49. Bleeding after 24 hours of delivery is considered as past partum haemorrhage?
A. When blood loss is more than 500 ml.
B. When blood loss is more than 700 ml.
C. When blood loss is more than 100 ml.
D. When blood loss is more than 200 ml

50. In following which is the highest diameter of pelvis?
A. Anterio-posterior B. Lateral
C. Oblique D. All are equal

51. In following, which vaccine is given to a pregnant lady?
A. Measles B. B CG
C. Tetanus D. DPT

52. Primary feature of cervical cancer includes :
A. Polyurea
B. Irregular menstruation
C. Anorexia
D. Headache

53. Total number of antenatal visit by a pregnant lady should be at least:
A. 2 B. 3 C. 1 D. 5

54. Commonest complication of IUD insertion is:
A. Pain B. Bleeding
C. Perforation D. Ectopic pregnancy

55. In following which is the main cause of PID:
A. Abruptio placentae
B. Placenta previa
C. Ectopic pregnancy
D. PPH

56. During +2 station, position of foetal head is:
A. Below ischeal spine
B. Above ischeal spine
C. Behind ischeal spine
D. Just above of pelvic inlet

57. Corpus luteum of pregnancy is active till :
A. 6 to 10 weeks B. 12 to 14 weeks
C. 16 to 18 weeks D. 20 to 22 weeks

58. When the placental villi invade the myometrium, the placenta is termed :
A. Placenta Accreta
B. Placenta increta
C. Placenta percreta
D. Placenta extrachorialis

59. Which of the following is not a presumptive sign of pregnancy?
A. Vomiting
B. Increased frequency of micturition
C. Pain in breasts
D. Presence of foetal heart sound

60. By 28 weeks of pregnancy, the fundus of the uterus is :
A. Midway between the umbilicus and Xiphisternum
B. At 1/3rd (one-third).of distance between the umbilicus and xiphisternum
C. Just above the level of umbilicus
D. At 2/3rd (two-third).of the distance between the umbilicus and the xiphisternum

61. Spontaneous uterine contractions known as Braxton Hicks contractions begin by :
A. 10 weeks B. 14 weeks
C. 18 weeks D. 22 weeks

62. What is the best time to ask a woman to start taking folic acid supplements?
A. Second half of menstrual cycle
B. When she consult for a missed period
C. When pregnancy is confirmed
D. Once she plans a pregnancy

63. All of the following are characteristics of threatened abortion except :
A. Presence of vaginal bleeding
B. Pain in lower abdomen
C. Cervical os is open
D. Uterus corresponds to the period of gestation

64. For best result, medical method of termination of pregnancy is not recommended :
A. Beyond 5 weeks of pregnancy
B. Beyond 7 weeks of pregnancy
C. Beyond 9 weeks of pregnancy
D. Beyond 11 weeks of pregnancy

65. Human Chorionic Gonadotrophin levels are increased in all of the following, except:
A. Complete mole
B. Partial mole
C. Endo dermal sinus tumour
D. Embrional carcinoma

66. Functions of amniotic fluid include all of the following, except :
A. Cushioning effect to the foetus
B. Improves urine output
C. Maintains even temperature for the fetus
D. Promotes development of foetus

67. Which of the following movements occurs throughout labour in the mechanism of labour?
A. Restitution B. Internal rotation
C. External rotation D. Descent

68. If a newborn exhibits blue extremities and the body is pink the APGAR score should be?
A. 0 B. 1 C. 2 D. 3

69. When is fertilized ovum known as embryo?
A. 0-8 weeks B. 12-24 weeks
C. 0-12 weeks D. 8-32 weeks

70. Attitude of fetal head in occipito posterior position is:
A. Flexion B. Adduction
C. Deflexion D. Extension

71. Morbidly adherent placenta is called as:
A. Battledore placenta
B. Placenta accreta
C. Placenta succenturiata
D. Placenta circumvallata

72. Normal weight of placenta at term is:
A. l/4th of baby weight
B. l/6th of baby weight
C. 500 gms
D. 900 gms

73. Hormone responsible for hyperemesis gravidarum is:
A. Human chorionic genadotropin
B. Human placentral lactogen
C. Progesterone
D. Relaxin

74. Specific manifestation in menopause is:
A. Hot flashes B. Hypotension
C. Hypothermia D. Anorexia

75. Which of the following is correct with respect to the gamete intrafallopian transfer (GIFT) technique?
A. It is recommended for those females cervical canal restricts the passage of sperms
B. Whose ovary doesn't provide suitable environment for fertilisation
C. Who cannot produce an ovum
D. Whose uterus cannot retain the foetus inside it

76. Which one of the following statements is most appropriate to convince a mother for immunization of her child?
A. Immunization is okay for your baby
B. Government will take care of all post-immu-nization complications.
C. Vaccines are expensive and you are getting it free
D. Vaccines will prevent the occurance of the disease in future for which it is meant

77. After ovulation corpus luteum formed in the ovary releases:
A. Testosterone B. Aldosterone
C. Progesterone D. Estrogen

78. Which of the following is a risk factor for development of breast cancer?
A. Late menarche
B. Early menopause
C. No pregnancies
D. Early first pregnancy

79. The prenatal technique to determine the genetic disorder in a foetus is called :
A. Laparoscopy B. Amniocentesis
C. Abstinence D. Coitus interruptus

80. If a newborn exhibits a heart rate of 80 bpm the APGAR score should be?
A. 0 B. 1 C. 2 D. 3

81. Edward syndrome is characterized by :
A. Trisomy of 21st chromosome
B. Trisomy of 18th chromosome
C. Trisomy of 13th chromosome
D. Monosomy of 21st chromosome

82. The most common cause of urinary tract infection (UTI) in community is :
A. Salmonella B. Klebsiella
C. Corny bacterium D. E-coli

83. A possible complication of an infant delivered by cesarean section is:
A. Respiratory distress
B. Hypothermia
C. Hyperthermia
D. Anaemia

84. Which out of the following is not a feature of pre eclampsia?
A. Fits B. Oedema
C. Hypertension D. Proteinuria

85. Abnormal proliferation of uterine endometrial tissue outside the uterus is known as :
A. Metrorrhagia B. Cystic fibrosis
C. Endometriosis D. Menorrhagia

86. The primigravida reports thai her last menstrual period started on January 15 and ended on Janurary 20. Using nagele's rule, the EDD will be:
A. October 22 B. November 8
C. December 28 D. September 22

87. During which week of pregnancy lightening can be felt by the pregnant mother:-
A. 34 Weeks B. 36 Weeks
C. 38 Weeks D. 40 Weeks

88. Which of the following is most common cause of PPH :
A. Atonic uterus B. Clotting disorder
C. Traumatic uterus D. None of the above

89. During labour, the process of thinning and shortening of cervix is termed as :
A. Ballottement B. Dilatation
C. Effacement D. Insufficiency

90. Which of the following is main side effect of an intra uterine device:
A. Vaginal Bleeding
B. Pelvic Inflammatory disease
C. Uterine perforation
D. Ectopic pregnancy

91. A female who has given birth to the viable child first time, is termed as:
A. Primipara B. Multipara
C. Nulligravida D. Primigavida

92. "Crowning" is seen in which stage of labor :
A. First Stage B. Second Stage
C. Third Stage D. Fourth Stage

93. Which of the following hormones would be administered for the stimulation of uterine Contractions :
A. Prolactin B. Fetal cortisol
C. Oxytocin D. Progesterone

94. The best procedure to remove the embedded IUCD in the uterus with missing thread is :
A. Hysteroscopy B. Laparoscopy
C. Cystoscopy D. Laparotomy

95. Partograph is used for :
A. Admission of patient
B. Measuring progress of labour
C. Details of medicines of patient
D. Graphical presentation of outdoor patients number

96. Which of the following pregnant woman would be considered as being at high risk:
A. Height less than 4ft 10 inch
B. Systolic and diastolic BP 140/ 90
C. Edema
D. All of the Above

97. Which of the following cancer is found more in females:
A. Cervical Cancer B. Lung Cancer
C. Stomach Cancer D. Bone Cancer

98. A couple has a 2 years old child with cystic fibrosis. When planning their next pregnancy, the couple should undergo:
A. Genetic counseling
B. Psychological counseling
C. Counseling regarding transmission of sexually transmitted diseases
D. TORCH test

99. During which of the following stages of labor would the nurse assess "crowning"?
A. First stage B. Second stage
C. Third stage D. Fourth stage

100. Before birth, which of the following structures connect the right and left auricles of the heart?
A. Umbilical vein B. Foramen ovale
C. Ductus arteriosus D. Ductus venosus

101. Which of the following when present in urine may cause a reddish stain on the diaper of a newborn?
A. Mucus B. Uric acid crystals
C. Bilirubin D. Excess Iron

102. Early amniocentesis is done in which period of pregnancy?
A. 6-10 weeks B. 11-15 weeks
C. 16-18 weeks D. 9-11 weeks

103. Endometrium in pregnancy is known as:
A. Decidua
B. Decubitus
C. Trophoblast
D. Gravid endometrium

104. Hypertrophic sebaceous glands around nipples during pregnancy:
A. Montgomery's tubercle
B. Sebaceous cyst
C. Chloasma
D. Linea nigra

105. Average total gain during pregnancy is:
A. 8-10 kg B. 10-12 kg
C. 12-14 kg D. 16-18 kg

106. Fertilization takes place in fallopian tube in the:
A. Infundibulum B. Isthmus
C. Ampulla D. Fumbriae

107. Umbilical cord contains:
A. Two arteries and two veins
B. Two arteries and one vein
C. Two veins and one artery
D. One artery and one vein

108. Engaging diameter of vertex presentation is :
A. Suboccipito frontal
B. Suboccipito bregmatic
C. Submento bregmatic
D. Mento vertical

109. Which of the following matches the definition abnormal placenta development covering the cervix?
A. Placenta Previa
B. Abruptio Placentae
C. Multigravida
D. Proliferative phase

110. Physiologic anemia during pregnancy is a result of :
A. Increased blood volume of the mother
B. Decreased dietary intake of Iron
C. Decreased erythropoietin after first trimester
D. Increased detoxification of iron by the maternal lever

111. Sign and symptoms of placentaprevia include:
A. Sharp abdominal pain
B. Early rupture of membranes
C. Increased low back pain
D. Painless vaginal bleeding

112. During Induction of labor, a woman should be observed carefully for signs of:
A. Uterine tetany
B. Severe pain
C. Prolapse of the umbilical cord
D. Hypoglycemia

113. The most common cause of maternal mortality in India is:
A. Obstetric hemorrhage
B. Anemia
C. Abortion/ Septicemia
D. Obstructed labour

114. Which of the following are signs of true labour:
A. Painful uterine contractions, show, dilatation of cervix
B. Painful uterine contractions, show, taking up of cervix
C. Painful uterine contractions, show, lightening
D. Painful uterine contractions, show, rupture of membrane

115. Which of the following graph is used for recording of maternal and foetal condition during the labour:
A. Labour record B. Partograph
C. Vital sign graph D. Progress graph

116. During Laborassessment nurse observed signs of foetal distress, she immediately:
A. If on Oxytocin stop it, inform doctor, start I/V and oxygen
B. Inform doctor, start I/V and Oxytocin
C. Stop Oxytocin and inform doctor
D. Shift the patient to OT with I/V

117. In case lobe of placenta is left behind during post partum period it may lead to :
A. Infection B. Pain
C. PPH D. No problem

118. What is the shape of brim of the Gynaecoid or true pelvis:
A. Heart shape B. Oval shape
C. Round shape D. Bean shape

119. Which of the condition will result in case the amniotic fluid is more than 1500 ml in amniotic sac?
A. Polyhydramnios B. Oligohydramnios
C. Hydramnios D. Ahydramnios

120. What is the weight of the uterus at term of pregnancy?
A. 600 gms B. 700 gms
C. 800 gms D. 900 gms

121. Which of the following is not appropriately matched with the term: Braxton Hicks contractions?
A. Painless
B. Intermittent contractions
C. Edema
D. Irregular

122. Small nodules observed during 8 weeks of pregnancy on primary areola are known as:
A. Mask of pregnancy
B. Montgomery's tubercles
C. Areda tubercles
D. Linea nigra

123. Progesterone is secreted from a female's ____ to help the implanted embryo and continue the pregnancy.
A. Corpus luteum B. Mesoderm
C. Endoderm D. Thyroid

124. The average head circumference of newborn is:
A. 28 cms B. 30 cms
C. 32 cms D. 34 cms

125. In case newborn shows signs of asphyxia at birth, nurse should immediately:
A. Start oxygen B. Clear the airway
C. Stimulate crying D. Inform the doctor

126. A postnatal mother receiving treatment for deep vein thrombosis should be watched for:
A. Dysuria, ecchymosis and vertigo
B. Epistaxis, hematuria and dysuria
C. Hematuria, vertigo and hematuria
D. Hematuria, ecchymosis and epistaxis

127. At the time of delivery umbilical cord lengthening and spurt of blood form vagina is suggestive of :
A. Hematoma dislodgement
B. Uterine atony
C. Placental separation
D. Placenta previa

128. The most appropriate action by the nurse when the periodic acceleration in fetal heart rate is observed :
A. Notify doctor
B. Continue monitoring fetal heart rate
C. Reposition mother and monitor her vital signs
D. Document findings and inform mother about baby's well being

129. Antidote of opoid that mother has received during labour pains is :
A. Naloxane B. Mephentine
C. Clexane D. Bromexin

130. The mother is diagnosed with partial placenta previa. The nurse tells the client that the usual treatment for partial placenta previa is:
A. Bed rest

B. Administration of platelets
C. Immediate caesarean section delivery
D. Induction of labour with oxytocin

131. Which of the following hormones is not produced by placenta:
A. Testosterone
B. Estrogen
C. Progesterone
D. Human chronic gonadotropin

132. Genital tuberculosis occur mainly in women in the following organ:
A. Fallopian tube B. Uterus
C. Cervix D. Vagina

133. A nurse perform the assessment of patient posted for cesarean section delivery, which assessment would indicate the need to contact the doctor?
A. Hemoglobin of 11gm
B. Fetal heart rate 180 beats/min
C. Maternal pulse of 84 beats/min
D. White blood cells of 12,000/mm^3

134. Pfannenstiel incision is used for:
A. Caesarean section
B. Cholecystectomy
C. Inguinal Herniorraphy
D. Gastrectomy

135. Green Armytage forceps is used to arrest bleeding in:
A. Hysterectomy B. Ovariotomy
C. Cesarean section D. Myomectomy

136. Vaginal hysterectomy is done for:
A. Uterus prolapse
B. Fibroid uterus
C. Cervical erosion
D. Endometrial carcinoma

137. The most common side effect of IUCD insertion is:
A. Bleeding B. Pain
C. Pelvic Infection D. Ectopic Pregnancy

138. Which of the following danger signs should be informed immediately during the antepartum period:
A. Blurred vision B. Nasal stuffiness
C. Breast tenderness D. Constipation

139. If the LMP is January 31 the expected date of delivery (EDD.is :
A. Oct 7 B. Oct 24
C. Nov 7 D. Nov 8

140. Sperm count less than 20 million/Ml :
A. Aspermia B. Oligospermia
C. Azoospermia D. Asthenospermia

141. Lactational Amenorrhoea is due to:
A. Prolactin induced inhibition of GnRH
B. Prolactin induced inhibition of FSH
C. Oxytocin induced inhibition of GnRH
D. Oxytocin induced inhibition of FSH

142. Diagnostic criteria of pre eclampsia includes :
A. Presence of pitting edema over the ankles after 12 hours bed rest
B. Presence of pitting edema over the ankles after 2 hours bed rest
C. Presence of pitting edema over the ankles after 6 hours bed rest
D. Presence of pitting edema over the ankles after just after bed rest

143. In primigravida time period of latent phase in parto-graph is about:
A. 4 hours B. 8 hours
C. 12 hours D. 16 hours

144. A woman who has delivered a baby of above 4 kgs weight is normally screened for which of the following :
A. Malaria B. Typhoid
C. Jaundice D. Diabetes

145. Definitive treatment of placenta praevia includes:
A. Bed rest
B. Supplementary haematinics
C. Use of tocolytics
D. Caesarian section

146. In following which statement is false :
A. At birth the uterine body and the cervix ratio is about 1:2
B. When Menarche occurs the ratio between uterine body and the cervix become 1:1
C. After menarche the ratio becomes 2:1
D. After menopause the ratio remains 3:1

147. The peak point of a uterine contraction is called the:
A. Acceleration B. Acme
C. Deceleration D. Axiom

148. Which of the following danger signs should be informed promptly during the ante partum Period :
A. Constipation
B. Breast tenderness
C. Nasal stuffiness
D. Leaking amniotic fluid

149. Baby friendly hospital initiative are all except :
A. Breastfeeding on demand
B. Initiate breastfeeding with 4 hrs of normal delivery

C. Allow mothers and infants to remain together 24 hrs/day
D. Training of health care staff

150. The first thing that a nurse must ensure when the baby's head comes out is :
A. The cord is intact
B. No part of the cord is encircling the baby's neck
C. The cord is still attached to the placenta
D. The cord is still pulsating

151. The Symptom that divides eclampsia from pre-eclampsia is
A. Hypertension B. Edema
C. Convulsion D. Proteinuria

152. The main cause of breech presentation is :
A. Hydrocephalus
B. Prematurity
C. Multiparae with lax abdominal wall
D. Hydraminos

153. The brim of the anthropoid pelvis is.....shape.
A. Kidney B. Round
C. Heart D. Oval

154. Following fertilization the blastocyst secrets a hormone called?
A. Human Chorionic Gonadotropin
B. Oxytocin
C. FSH
D. LH

155. Which health related Act was made in India in 1971:
A. PCPNDT Act
B. RTI Act
C. Consumer Protection Act
D. Medical Termination of Pregnancy Act

156. The commonest lie of human fetus is :
A. Longitudinal B. Transverse
C. Oblique D. Unstable

157. Colour of Lochia Alba is :
A. Red B. Pink
C. Yellow D. Yellowish white

158. Which of the following is not a complication of eclampsia:
A. Renal failure
B. Cerebral haemorrhage
C. Thrombocytosis
D. Shock

159. Commonest type of ectopic pregnancy is :
A. Tubal Pregnancy
B. Ovarian Pregnancy
C. Abdominal Pregnancy
D. Cervical Pregnancy

160. If L.M.P. of a pregnant lady is 1 January then her EDD will be :
A. 01 October B. 08 October
C. 01 September D. 08 September

161. SBA services are given to:
A. Adolescents B. Pregnant woman
C. Lactating mother D. Elderly person

162. MUAC tape is used for :
A. Measuring height
B. Examining pregnant woman
C. Finding malnutrition in child
D. Applying on injury

163. MAPEDIR is related to which of the following :
A. Maternal and Infant Death Inquiry
B. Post partum maternal Death inquiry
C. Maternal and Perinatal Death Inquiry
D. Ante partum maternal Death inquiry

164. Small-for-date babies are prevented by:
A. Spacing of baby
B. Antenatal care
C. Nutritional supplement
D. Immunisation

165. The Nurse is caring a woman in 4th Stage of labour. The Nursing Care Plan should include:
A. Uterine constractions
B. Cervical dilation
C. Birth of baby and delivery of the placenta
D. Re-adjustment to the non-pregnant stage

166. Aspermia is the term used to describe:
A. Absence of semen
B. Absence of sperm
C. Presence of abnormal sperms
D. Absence of sperm motility

167. Assuming the menstrual cycle length as 32 days and LIMP as June 10th. Which of the following is most likely due date ?
A. March 12 B. March 17
C. March 21 D. March 27

168. Which one of the following is NOT a described type of female bony pelvis?
A. Android B. Gynecoid
C. Obstetroid D. Anthropoid

169. During pregnancy, placenta performs the following functions except:
A. Interchange of material present in the blood-streams
B. Acting as a selective barrier
C. Keeping the embryo moist and protecting it from desiccation
D. Acting as a selective barrier

170. **Excessive menstrual bleeding is :**
A. Epimenorrhoea B. Polymenorrhoea
C. Menorrhagia D. Oligo menorrhoea

171. **Massaging the uterus to make it hard is important in:**
A. Traumatic PPH B. Sub involution
C. Atonic PPH D. Inversion of uterus

172. **A newly married healthy couple is asking for the best method of contraception and which one of the following methods a nurse will advice?**
A. Barrier method
B. Rhythm method
C. Intrauterine devices
D. Combined oral pills

173. **All are high risk factors for endometrial carcinoma except:**
A. Obesity B. Multiparity
C. Diabetes D. Exogenous estrogen

174. **Which patient is having very high risk for developing ovarian cancer?**
A. 30 yrs old on oral contraceptives
B. 36 yrs old who had first child at 22 yrs
C. 45 yrs old who was never been pregnant
D. 40 yrs old who had 5 alive children, 1 abortion

175. **This is not included in the triple test :**
A. Maternal serum alpha fetoprotein
B. Progesterone
C. Unconjugated oestriol
D. HCG

176. **Increased prolactine level :**
A. Suppress lactation
B. Induce uterine relaxation
C. Suppress ovulation
D. Induce ovulation

177. **Third degree genital prolapsed is otherwise called:**
A. Procidentia B. Fibroid uterus
C. Retroversion D. Inversion

178. **The increased calorie need during puerparium is:**
A. 1000 kcals B. 800 kcals
C. 500 kcals D. 300 kcals

179. **Increased pulsation felt in lateral fornices of vagina in pregnancy is termed as :**
A. Chadwick' signs B. Oseander's sign
C. Goodel's sign D. Hegar sign

180. **HELLP syndrome is a complication of :**
A. Hepatitis B. AIDS
C. Leukaemia D. Pre-eclampsia

181. **A woman with 2 months of amenorrhoea and a positive pregnancy test is complaining of brown vaginal spotting, it may be suggestive of :**
A. Missed abortion B. Choriocarcinoma
C. Placenta previa D. Abruptioplacenta

182. **The weight of the placenta at term is about :**
A. 750 gm B. 100 gm
C. 1500 gm D. 500 gm

183. **......... Is a sexually transmitted disease :**
A. Molluscíim contagiosum
B. Hepatitis A
C. Gonorrhoea
D. Acne vulgaris

184. **First foetal movement perceived by mother :**
A. Quickening B. Engagement
C. Lightening D. Internal ballottement

185. **In vesicular mole, which hormone is found in excess:**
A. HCG B. FSH
C. Progesterone D. Oestrogen

186. **Which of the following is not a component of bishop's score?**
A. Cervical length B. Station of head
C. Cervical dialations D. Position of head

187. **After ovulation, the ovum is viable for :**
A. 24-36 hours B. 48-72 hours
C. 6-8 hours D. 8-12 hours

188. **Gravida denotes the:**
A. Previous pregnancy
B. Pregnant state
C. Pregnancy at the state of 30 and above
D. All of the Above

189. **Episiotomy is best done and commonly practiced in:**
A. J shaped B. Medially
C. Laterally D. Mediolaterally

190. **A multigravida 32 years old lady, admitted at 30 weeks with bleeding per vagina, which of the action the nurse should first do for her:**
A. Take consent for cesarean section
B. Perform a pervaginal examination
C. Provide perineal pads
D. Check the fetal heart rate and maternal blood pressure

191. **A patient progress from pre-eclampsia to eclampsia, the nurse's first action should be to:**
A. Administer oxygen by face mask
B. Assess the blood pressure and fetal heart rate
C. Clear and maintain an open airway
D. Administer magnesium sulphate intravenously

192. The foetus gets its food supply from:
A. Arteries of the mother
B. The placenta
C. The uterus
D. The amniotic sac

193. Disorders of uterine tube and ovaries are:
A. Tumours B. Ectopic pregnancy
C. Acute salpingitis D. All of the above

194. Which is the most appropriate time of IUD insertion?
A. Within 10 days of menstruation
B. About the midst of the cycle
C. Just before menstruation
D. At anytime of menstruation

195. Which is the most common and ideal pelvis?
A. Android B. Gynaecoid
C. Platypelloid D. Anthropoid

196. Bedrest is essential is preeclampsia, since it:
A. Prevents eclampsia
B. Mobilizes tissue fluid thereby lowering blood pressure
C. Improves blood circulation and decreases oe-dema
D. Prevents premature labour

197. Vaginal canal normally has:
A. An acid environment
B. An alkaline environment
C. A neutral environment
D. An environment difficult to determine

198. Ovulation is defined as:
A. Maturation of graffian follicle
B. Rupture of graffian follicle
C. Seepage of blood through vagina
D. Facilitate their maturation during embryonic development

199. The most difficult time to control diabetes during maternity cycles is:
A. First trimester
B. Last trimester
C. Labour and delivery
D. Puerperium

200. The process of giving birth is called:
A. Parturition B. Postpartum
C. Lightening D. Labor

201. What is the normal dilatation of cervix?
A. 20 cm B. 50 cm C. 7 cm D. 10 cm

202. The duration of puerperal period is:
A. From delivery to 1 week
B. Delivery to 4 weeks
C. Delivery to 6 weeks
D. Delivery to 10 weeks

203. The vaginal discharge during the first fortnight of puerperiuin is known as:
A. Show B. Lochia
C. Effacement D. Leukorrhea

204. What are the indications of cesarean section?
A. Fetal distress
B. Central placenta previa
C. Obstructed labor
D. All of the Above

205. The hormone responsible for lactation is:
A. Growth hormone B. FSH
C. Prolactin D. Corpus luteum

206. Fine downy hairs of the fetus is known as -
A. Vernix caseosa B. Amnion
C. Chorion D. Lanugo

207. Maternity nurse, must be aware that screening for Diabetes mellitus in pregnancy is done at:
A. 6 to 17 weeks B. 18 to 23 weeks
C. 24 to 28 weeks D. 29 to 32 weeks

208. Neonate of diabetic mother is at risk for all the following except :
A. Hypoglycaemia
B. Hypocalcaemia
C. Hyperglycemias
D. Hyperbilirubinemia

209. All of the following are complications of twin pregnancy except:
A. Abortion
B. Post maturity
C. Low birth weight
D. Congenital malformations

210. Severe vomiting in pregnancy is:
A. Nausea
B. Hyperemesis gravidraum
C. Morning sickness
D. None of the Above

211. The ideal pelvis for child bearing is.....pelvis :
A. Anthropoid B. Platypoid
C. Gynaecoid D. Android

212. Positive sign of pregnancy is:
A. Cullen's sign B. Hegar's sign
C. Foetal movement D. Morning sickness

213. Intrauterine contraceptive device are introduced postpartum at:
A. 6 months B. 12 months
C. 6 weeks D. 12 weeks

214. Physiologic anemia during pregnancy is a result of :
A. Decreased dietary intake of iron
B. Decreased erythropoiesis in the pregnancy
C. Increased plasma volume of the mother
D. Increased demands of the fetus

215. Which of the following is a barrier method of contraception?
A. Copper T B. Oral pills
C. Condom D. Tubectomy

216. Which of the following is a sign of toxemia in pregnancy?
A. Low blood sugar
B. High blood sugar
C. Low blood pressure
D. High blood pressure

217. The fundal height is at the level of xiphisternum at :
A. 28 weeks B. 36 weeks
C. 40 weeks D. 32 weeks

218. Immunity transferred to fetus from the mother through placenta is :
A. Passive natural immunity
B. Active natural immunity
C. Active artificial immunity
D. Passive artificial immunity

219. Anemia prophylaxis in pregnancy starts at the:
A. First month B. Second month
C. Fourth month D. Third month

220. Bleeding between menstrual period is called:
A. Amenorrhea B. Menorrhagia
C. Metrorrhagia D. Dysmenorrhea

221. A patient in active labor spontaneously ruptures membranes. The nurse should first:
A. Monitor the fetal heart rate
B. Call the doctor
C. Check vital signs
D. Monitor contractions

222. Acid medium of vagina is maintained by:
A. Doderleins bacilli
B. Staphylococci
C. Trichomonas vaginalis
D. E-Coli

223. Coomb's test is carried out to:
A. To asses for fetal chromosomal abnormalities
B. To detect neural canal defects
C. To detect the level of HCG
D. To detect antibodies against red cells of Rh negative babies of Rh positive mothers

224. A well fitting presenting part is essential while performing artificial rupture of membranes to:
A. Prevent cord prolapsed
B. Ensure progress of labor
C. To rule out cephalopelvic disproportion
D. Stimulate contractions

225. The risk of developing osteoporosis can be reduced by:
A. Eliminating caffeine from the diet
B. Increasing physical activity
C. Reducing exposure to sunlight
D. Adding iron rich food to diet

226. The narrowest part of the fallopian tube:
A. Ampulla B. Interstital part
C. Eustachian tube D. Isthmus

227. Women should increase daily intake of calcium to prevent:
A. Coronary artery disease
B. Atherosclerosis
C. Arteriosclerosis
D. Osteoporosis

228. Intrauterine fetal growth retardation results in:
A. For dates babies
B. Low birth weight babies
C. Post-term babies
D. Full term babies

229. The important landmark of the female pelvis is:
A. Iliac fossa
B. Hollow of the sacrum
C. Obturatory foramen
D. Sacral promontory

230. A gestational trophoblastic disease is known as:
A. Preeclampsia
B. Hydatidiform mole
C. Hyperemesis gravidarum
D. Eclampsia

231. Nurse taking care of a pregnant lady is being asked about when to start breast feeding. What should be her appropriate reply?
A. As soon as after delivery
B. 4 hrs after delivery
C. 6 hrs after delivery
D. 8 hrs after delivery

232. All the following are associated with increased chance of acquiring HIV infection in women except:
A. Chlamydia infection
B. Bacterial Vaginosis
C. Herpes simplex infection
D. Trichomonas vaginalis infection

233. Bleeding from the uterus due to premature separation of placenta during later weeks pregnancy is:
A. Vasaprevia B. Abortion
C. APH D. PPH

234. Weight of uterus is:
A. 30 gm B. 60 gm
C. 90 gm D. 120 gm

235. Majority of cases of mother-to-child (vertical) transmission of HIV-1 occur during:
A. Antepartum period
B. Intrapartum period

C. Postpartum period
D. Breastfeeding

236. Secretion from mother's delivery is called:
A. Sequestrum B. Colostrum
C. Lochia D. Leucorrhoea

237. During which stage of labour, placenta is delivered?
A. Stage 1 B. Stage 2
C. Stage 3 D. Stage 4

238. After delivery, which of the following medicines can be used to suppress lactation?
A. Estrogen-progesterone
B. Testosterone
C. Bromocriptine
D. All of the Above

239. Partograph was first deviced by:
A. Dr. R.H. Philpoter
B. Dr. A.L. Mudaliar
C. Dr. William Shaw
D. Dr. Shirodkar

240. Which abdominal grip is used to assess the descent of head in a pregnant woman?
A. Fundal B. Lateral
C. Pelvic 1 D. Pelvic 2

241. In 40 days of menstruation cycle the ovulation occurs at:
A. 14th day B. 20th day
C. 26th day D. 30th day

242. Regular rhythmic contraction can be felt during bimanual examination is called:
A. Palmer's sign B. Heger's sign
C. Uterine suffle D. Rovsign's sign

243. Morning sickness usually disappears by the end of:
A. 1 month B. 2 months
C. 3 months D. 4 months

244. Which formula is used for calculating EDD?
A. Naegele's rule B. Infant formula
C. Labor rule D. Rule of nine

245. Endometriosis is common in:
A. Nullipara
B. Multipara
C. Perimenopausal age
D. Virgins

246. During pregnancy increased need for:
A. Potassium B. Sodium
C. Iron D. Carbohydrate

247. Total calorie requirement for a pregnant women is:
A. 1000 to 1500 kcal
B. 2000 to 2500 kcal
C. 2500 to 2700 kcal
D. 2700 to 3000 kcal

248. Pearly white or silvery bright lines, headed after delivery Mark called:
A. Linea albicans B. Linea nigra
C. Striae gravidarum D. Striae nigra

249. Me conium mixed with liquor amnii indicates:
A. Congenital anomalies
B. Chromosomal
C. Fetal distress
D. Chorea

250. Presence of complete ring of bubbles at the meniscus in shake test indicates:
A. Maturity of fetal brain
B. Septal defect
C. Maturity of fetal lungs
D. Fetal cyancsis

251. Less than how many number of kicks in 12 hours indicates the failure of placental function?
A. 2 B. 5 C. 10 D. 20

252. Total weight gain of mother in pregnancy is:
A. 10 to 12 kg B. 18 to 20 kg
C. 12 to 14 kg D. 9 to 10 kg

253. Normal labor is called:
A. Spurious labor B. Dystocia
C. Eutocia D. False labor

254. 'Show' is the sign of:
A. True labor pain
B. False labor pain
C. Sign of abnormal labor
D. Sign of placenta previa

255. What is the total time period for the 3rd stage of labor primi and multi?
A. 15 minutes B. 30 minutes
C. 45 minutes D. 1 hour

256. After delivery the immediate care given to the baby is:
A. To clear the airway
B. To clamp the cord
C. Clean the cord
D. Initiate the feeding

257. Overlapping of the parietal bone during birth is called:
A. Caput B. Moulding
C. Hematoma D. Fixation

258. The procedure of removal and ligation of fallopian tube is referred as:
A. Mastectomy B. Vasectomy
C. Appendectomy D. Tubectomy

259. The best time for 1UD insertion is between which days of menstruation cycle?
A. Within 2 days B. 3 to 7 days
C. 8 to 10 days D. 11 to 14 days

260. The metal which is commonly used for family planning is:
A. Iron B. Aluminum
C. Copper D. Silver

261. Mala D is an example of:
A. Pill form
B. Injectable contraceptive
C. Vaginal diaphragm
D. Foam tablet

262. The immunoglobulin found in mother's breast milk is:
A. IgA B. IgM
C. IgD D. IgE

263. The realignment of fetal head with the body after the head comes out:
A. Expulsion B. Descent
C. Engagement D. Restitution

264. An incision made into perineum to enlarge the vagina during delivery is:
A. Amniotomy B. Episiotomy
C. Cesarean D. Forceps delivery

265. The most frequent causes of maternal death during child birth:
A. Injection B. Subinvolution
C. Haemorrhage D. None

266. Normal volume of amniotic fluid at term is. ... ml.
A. 500 ml B. 200 ml
C. 1000 ml D. 700 ml

267. The hereditary determinants of humans are received from:
A. Allele B. Genes
C. Nucleus D. Cytopalsm

268. The first sign seen in pregnancy is:
A. Quickening B. Amenonhea
C. Hegar's sign D. None of the Above

269. The failure of uterus to return to its normal size is:
A. Involution B. Subinvolution
C. Protrusion D. Retraction

270. Premature separation of the placenta from the uterine wall before delivery is:
A. Abruptio placenta B. Placenta previa
C. Fetal distress D. Cord prolapse

271.What is level of raise during ovulation?
A. 1°F B. 5°C C. 3°F D. 2°C

272. In managing a client with Pre-edampsia rest is important for the following reason EXCEPT:
A. Increases renal blood flow
B. Increases uterine blood flow
C. Decreases Blood pressure
D. Decreases placental blood flow

273. Which of the following instrument will be used in recording of uterine contractions from various parts of teh uterus?
A. Cardiotocography
B. Tocodynamometer
C. Tocometry
D. Topography

274. The progressive measurement of the pregnancy and calculation of errestional age by height of the fundus is done by
A. Naegle's rule B. Robert's rule
C. Mc Donald's rule D. Simson's rule

275. The instrument which is used to know the position and length of the uterine cavity is called
A. Uterine curette B. Uterine sound
C. Uterine forceps D. Uterine retractor

276. The binocular instrument providing a magnification to map the abnormal areas on the cervix is:
A. Colposcope B. Cystoscope
C. Colonoscope D. Proctoscope

277. When fetal kidney starts to produce urine?
A. 10 th week onwards
B. 12th week onwards
C. 13th week onwards
D. 14th week onwards

278. The time required for a spermatogonium to develop into a mature spermatozoon in about
A. 41 days B. 51 days
C. 61 days D. 71 days

279. The best contraceptive method to be adopted / within 72 hours by a women who have had unprotected intercourse is
A. IUCD
B. Morning -after pill
C. Norplant
D. Vaginal contraceptives

280. The best procedure to remove the embedded IUCD in the uterus with missing thread is
A. Hysteroscopy B. Laproscopy
C. Cystoscopy D. Laprotomy

281. The term "Phlegmasia alba dolens" refers to
A. Deep vein thrombosis
B. Varicose vein

C. Retrograde extension of pelvic thrombophlebitis
D. Venous thromboembolism

282. When applying forceps for a primigravida mother the traction (puil) required is estimated to be about
A. 13 kg B. 18 kg C. 14 kg D. 16 kg

283. Prolapse fo the cord during second stage of labour is treated by:
A. Caesarean section B. Forceps delivery
C. Episcotomy D. Cord resection

284. Placenta is directly anchored to the myometrium is:
A. Placenta acreata B. Bipartite placenta
C. Retained placenta D. Abruptio placenta

285. Health checkup done after the diagnosis of pregnancy which includes measurement of B.P., weight etc. is called:
A. Ante Natal Checkup
B. Post Natal Chekup
C. General Examination
D. None of the Above

286. What should be done to decontaminate the articles used in labour room to conduct delivery:
A. Wash with detergent & water
B. Place in 0.5 % chlorine solution for 10 minutes
C. Place in 5 % chlorine solution for 60 minutes
D. Wash with tap water

287. After Normal delivery, a woman should stay at hospital for how may hour:
A. 24 hour B. 36 hours
C. 48 hours D. 12 hours

288. Pink ribbon is associated with:
A. Lung Cancer B. Cervical Cancer
C. Breast Cancer D. Bone Cancer

289. Preterm baby is:
A. Born before 37 weeks
B. Born before 40 weeks
C. Born before 42 weeks
D. Born before 47 weeks

290. Simplified partograph should be used:
A. For every female in labour
B. For a female at risk to develop complication
C. On choice of nurse
D. Pregnant woman undergoing caesarian section

291. KMC should be continued for a neonate born preterm:
A. Up to 28 days after birth
B. Up to 4 month age
C. Up to 40th week of pregnancy
D. Till baby achieves 3500 gm weight

292. In which condition consent from guardian is needed for abortion:
A. Age less than 18 yrs
B. Mentally ill women
C. Both A and B
D. None of the Above

293. The factors which are mostly related to 2nd trimester abortions:
A. Endocrine factors
B. Cervico –Uterine factors
C. Metabolic Factors
D. Genetic Factors

294. All are the risk factors associated with big baby except:
A. Maternal obesity
B. Prolonged pregnancy
C. Previous large infant
D. Short stature of mother

295. Breast pain and tenderness 3 to 5 days after child birth is usually due to:
A. Breast Abscess
B. Mastitis
C. Breast engorgement
D. All of the Above

296. The serious complication of Intrauterine Fetal Death:
A. Choriocarcinoma
B. Disseminated Intravascular Coagulation (DIC)
C. Transfusion Syndrome
D. Retinopathy and Nephropathy

297. How many hormonal tablets are there in oral contraceptive pills strip?
A. 28 B. 30 C. 21 D. 7

298. Most common cause of Spontaneous Abortion is:
A. Cervical cause
B. Maternal illness
C. Germ plasma defect
D. Uterine cause

299. Placenta and Fetal membrane is formed by which:
A. Inner cell mass B. Trophoblast
C. Mesoderm D. Endoderm

300. MTP Act pertains to:
A. Termination of pregnancy
B. Medical Termination of pregnancy
C. JSY
D. None of the Above

301. Early skin to skin contact keeps the baby warm and is useful for low birth babies. This is known as :
A. Breastfeeding
B. Kangaroo Mother Care
C. Exclusive breast feeding
D. Rooming In

302. Human Papilloma Virus is linked to:
A. Cervical Cancer B. Lung Cancer
C. Brain Tumor D. Bone Cancer

303. Mission Indradhanush was started with the objective of:
A. Start pentavalent vaccination
B. Identifying color blind children
C. Immunizing drop-out and left out children
D. Campaigning polio vaccine

304. Janani Suraksha Yojana (JSY) aims at reducing maternal and neonatal mortality rate through:
A. Promoting institutional delivery
B. Health education
C. Distribution of iron and folic acid tablets to the mothers
D. None of the Above

305. Which of the following program is dedicated to reducing the MMR by targeting the High Risk Pregnancy:
A. Janani Suraksha Karyakram
B. Kushal Mangal Karyakram
C. Vande Matram Karyakram
D. Rashtriya Kishor Swasthya Karyakram

306. Which of the following is a definite indication of Caesarean Section:
A. Breech Presentation
B. Diabetes Mellitus
C. Moderate Preecclampsia
D. Cephalo Pelvic Disproportion

307. The ANC registration should be done at least by how many weeks of pregnancy:
A. 20 weeks B. 15 weeks
C. 12 weeks D. 4 weeks

308. When should the Breast feeding start after child birth:
A. After 1 hour
B. After half hour
C. After 2 hours
D. As soon as possible

309. The second stage of labor and delivery, how does a primigravida differ mainly from a multigravida:
A. Begins with full dilatation of cervix and end with delivery of placenta
B. Begins with true labor pains and ends with delivery of baby
C. Begins with complete dilatations and effacement of cervix and ends with delivery of baby
D. Begins with passage of show and ends with full dilatation and effacement of cervix

310. How many extra kilocalories are required by a pregnant women every day:
A. 300 kilocalories B. 500 kilocalories
C. 800 kilocalories D. 1000 kilocalories

311. At what reading of Dilatation of Cervix should the plotting of simplified partograph be started:
A. 2 cm B. 3 cm C. 4 cm D. 5 cm

312. What do you understand by Hyper emesis gravidarum:
A. Excessive vomiting during pregnancy which has a negative impact on the health of the woman
B. The growth of Placenta in the lower segment ofuterus
C. Early detachment of Placenta
D. Implantation of ovum at sites other than uterine cavity

313. PPH (Post Partum Haemorrhage) is:
A. 500 ml or more bleeding in 24 hours
B. 200 ml bleeding in a woman with 7 gm% of Hb
C. Changes Sanitary pad every five minutes
D. All of these

314. The type of abortion whose progress can be stopped by some interventions:
A. Complete Abortion
B. Inevitable Abortion
C. Threatened Abortion
D. Septic Abortion

315. How many doses of Inj.TT are given to a pregnant woman in an interval of one month:
A. Two B. Four C. Eight D. Ten

316. What is the surgery which involves the removal of uterus called?
A. Myomectomy B. Tubectomy
C. Hysterectomy D. Salpingectomy

317. Blood stained cervical mucus after starting of labor is called
A. Show B. Blood
C. Pus D. Cervical tear

318. What is an Ectopic Pregnancy:
A. Fertilization done by artificial method
B. Hemorrhage during pregnancy
C. Implantation of fertilized ovum outside the Uterus
D. None of the Above

319. If fever develops during pregnancy which test must be performed:
A. Test for malaria B. Urine test
C. Blood sugar level D. Hb level

320. Puerparium period begins just after:
A. Expulsion of Placenta
B. Expulsion of Foetus
C. Discharge from Hospital
D. Rupture of membrane

321. The length of the fallopian tube is
A. 10.5 cm B. 9 cm
C. 11 cm D. 10 cm

322. Fertilization almost always, occurs in the
A. Uterus
B. Uterine tube
C. Ampullary part of the uterine tube
D. Interstitial part of the uterne tube

323. The first course of oral pills should be started on the ..... day of menstrual cycle.
A. 2nd B. 7th C. 5th D. 10th

324. Consider the statements:
Regarding the cardinal movements during normal labour and find out which is in sequential order?
A. Engagement, descent, internal rotation, crowning, flexion extension
B. Engagement, descent, flexion, crowning, res-titution, lateral flexion
C. Engagement, descent, internal rotation, crowning, extension
D. Engagement, descent, flexion, internal rota-tion, crowning, extension, restitution, exter-nal rotation, lateral flexion of the statements

325. Women having their first pregnancy at or above the age of 30 years are called as
A. Grand multi para
B. Garand multi gravida
C. Elderly primi para
D. Elderly primi gravida

326. An immunoglobulin which crosses the placenta is:
I. IgG II. IgE
III. IgM IV. IgA
A. I and III B. I only
C. I and IV D. II and IV

327. Expected date of delivery for a lady whose LMP was Aug 15th is:
A. May 8th B. May 22nd
C. June 24th D. June 1st

328. The outermost membrane of the placenta is:
A. Chorion B. Amnion
C. Cotyledons D. Yolk sac

329. Physiological anaemia during pre-gnancy is a result of:
A. Increased blood volume
B. Increased detoxification demands on mother's liver
C. Decreased dietary intake
D. Decreased erythropoiesis after first trimester

330. The safest method of termination of pregnancy before 12 weeks is:
A. Lammaria tent
B. Prostaglandins
C. Suction evacuation
D. Dilation and curettage

331. Which of the following findings in a new born baby girl is normal?
A. Bleeding from umbilicus
B. Respiratory rate of 70/minute at rest
C. Yellow skin tone at 12 hours of age
D. Passage of meconium with in the first 24 hours

332. A woman delivered this morning, because this is her first child, which of the following goals is most appropriate?
A. Effective education of both parents
B. Minimal need for expression of negative feelings
C. Early discharge for mother and baby
D. Rapid adaption to role or parents

333. A woman had a midline episiotomy performed at delivery. The primary purpose of the episiotomy is to:
A. Enlarge the vaginal opening
B. Allow forceps to be applied
C. Eliminate the need for caesarean birth
D. Eliminate the possibility of lacerations

334. A vaginal fistula that opens into the rectum is called:
A. Rectovaginal fistula
B. Enterovaginal fistula
C. Vesicovaginal fistula
D. Colovaginal fistula

335. Obstetrical emergencies include all, except:
A. Ectopic pregnancy
B. Eclampsia
C. Placenta arterior
D. Placenta previa

336. The fertilization of ovum in female takes place in the
A. Vagina B. Cervix
C. Oviduct D. Uterus

337. The causes of physiological anemia in pregnancy is:
A. Haemodilution B. Haemolysis
C. Haemopoesis D. None of the Above

338. Injection TT is given to pregnant women to prevent:
A. Typhoid B. Meternal tetanus
C. Neonatal tetanus D. All of the Above

339. LMP was on 0.09.2009, then FDD is on:
A. 01/06/2010 B. 08/09/2010
C. 08/06/2010 D. 08/06/2009

340. Fertilized ovum up to 3-8 weeks is called:
A. Morula B. Embryo
C. Foetus D. Blastula

341. Humans placenta develops at...... months of pregnancy
A. 2 months B. 3 months
C. 1 month D. 4 months

342. Abortion is the termination of pregnancy before......weeks of pregnancy
A. 16th weeks B. 12th weeks
C. 10th weeks D. 24th weeks

343. Which assessment finding is most indicative of fetal distress?
A. Fetal heart rate of 140 beats/minute
B. Presence of fetal heart rate accelerations
C. Presence of green amniotic fluid
D. Increased amount of bloody show

344. Ovulation occurs during which of the following phases?
A. Menstrual B. Secretory
C. Proliferative D. Follicle

345. Weight of the placenta at term is:-
A. 250 gms B. 125 gms
C. 500 gms D. 600 gms

346. Increased pulsation is felt through the lateral fornix at 8th week is called
A. Osiander's sign B. Chadwick's sign
C. Goodell's sign D. Piskacek's sign

347. Indian MTP act allows abortion only to a period of?
A. 15 weeks B. 20 weeks
C. 28 weeks D. 12 weeks

348. The uterine fundal height of a pregnant patient is at the level of umbilicus. Her pregnancy is about :
A. 10-12 weeks B. 14-16 weeks
C. 22-24 weeks D. 30-32 weeks

349. Rho gram is most often used to treat____ mothers that have a ____ infant
A. RH positive, RH positive
B. RH positive, RH negative
C. RH negative, RH positive
D. RH negative, RH negative

350. The average blood loss during normal delivery is
A. Below 700 ml B. Below 500 ml
C. Below 250 ml D. Beloew100 ml

351. The nurse correctly explains that fertilization usually takes place in which structure?
A. Fallopian tube B. Ovary
C. Uterus D. Vagina

352. When the client asks the nurse about the viability of the sperm after ejaculation, during intercourse the nurse correctly explains that after ejaculation, the sperm remains alive for how many hours?
A. 2 hours B. 24 hours
C. 48 hours D. 72 hours

353. What is graphical record of cervical dilation?
A. Partograph B. Pictogram
C. Amino graph D. Hysterograph

354. The minimum birth weight for full term babies to be considered normal is:
A. 2,000gms B. 1,500gms
C. 2,500 gms D. 3,000gms

355. The following are ways of determining expected date of delivery (EDD).When the LMP is unknown EXCEPT:
A. Naegele's rule
B. Quickening
C. Mc Donald's rule
D. Batholomew's rule of 4

356. Which of the following is the most likely effect on the fetus if the woman is severely anemic during pregnancy?
A. Large for gestational age (LGA.fetus)
B. Hemorrhage
C Small for gestational age (SGA.baby)
D. Erythroblastosis fetalis

357. When the client asks why folic acid is important, which response by the nurse is most accurate?
A. "Folic acid helps prevent neural tube defects such as spina bifi da."
B. "Folic acid helps build strong bones for your baby."
C. "Folic acid helps your baby become resistant to infections."
D. "Folic acid prevents your baby from becoming anemic."

358. Which one of the following items should the nurse have available to meet the infant's priority need immediately after delivery?
A. Cord clamp B. Warm blanket
C. Bulb syringe D. Oxygen supply

359. The newborn is assigned an Apgar score of 7 at 5 minutes. The nurse understands that the newborn is in what condition based on the Apgar score?
A. Severely distressed
B. Moderately distressed
C. Stable but requiring close monitoring
D. Vigorous with no signs of distress

360. In a discussion about hormonal changes, the nurse informs the client that the placenta produces which hormone?
A. Estrogen
B. Testosterone
C. Oxytocin
D. Follicle-stimulating hormone

361. A 38-year-old participant, a gravid fifth, para I in the 10th week of pregnancy, tells the nurse of concerns that her age may affect the health of the baby. The participant asks the nurse if there is a test that can identify any genetic disorders that the baby may have at this point in the client's pregnancy, which test is typically used to detect genetic disorders?
A. Amniocentesis
B. Chorionic villi sampling
C. Rapid plasma regain
D. Ultrasound

362. Episiotomy best done in
A. Medially B. Laterally
C. Medio laterally D. J shaped

363. A nurse is monitoring the amount of lochia drainage in a client who is 2 hours postpartum and notes that the client has saturated a perineal pad in 1 hour.The nurse reports the amount of lochial flow as:
A. Scant B. Light
C. Heavy D. Excessive

364. The physician examines the client and determines that the cervix is dilated but the fetus and placenta are still in the uterus. Which nursing intervention is most appropriate when a spontaneous abortion is inevitable?
A. Prepare the client for dilation and curettage (D&C).
B. Place the client in Trendelenburg's position.
C. Prepare the client for placement of a purse-string stitch.
D. Place the client in the side-lying position.

365. Spinnbarkeit is an indicator of ovulation which is characterized as:
A. Thin watery mucus which can be stretched into a long strand about 10 cm
B. Thick mucus vaginal discharge influence by high level of estrogen
C. Thick mucus that is detached from the cervix during ovulation
D. Thin mucus that is yellowish in color with fishy odor

366. During an internal examination, the nurse palpated the posterior fontanel to be at the left side of the mother at the upper quadrant. The interpretation is that the position of the fetus is:
A. LOA B. LOP C. ROA D. ROP

367. A.You performed the leopold's maneuver and found the following: breech presentation, fetal back at the right side of the mother. Based on these findings, you can hear the fetal heart beat (PMI) BEST in which location?
A. Left lower quadrant
B. Left upper quadrant
C. Right lower quadrant
D. Right upper quadrant

368. The most common normal position of the fetus in utero is:
A. Vertical position B. Transverse position
C. Oblique position D. None of the Above

369. What event occurring in the second trimester helps the expectant mother to accept the pregnancy?
A. Lightening B. Ballotment
C. Pseudocyesis D. Quickening

370. When a pregnant woman experiences leg cramps, the correct nursing intervention to relieve the muscle cramps is:
A. Allow the woman to exercise
B. Let the woman walk for a while
C. Let the woman lie down and dorsiflex the foot towards the knees
D. Ask the woman to raise her legs

371. The following are ways of determining expected date of delivery (EDD).when the LMP is unknown EXCEPT:
A. Naegele's rule
B. Quickening
C. Mc Donald's rule
D. Batholomew's rule of 4

372. Which of the following is true regarding the fontanels of the newborn?
A. The anterior is triangular shaped; the posterior is diamond shaped
B. The posterior closes at 18 months; the anterior closes at 8 to 12 weeks
C. The anterior is large in size when compared to the posterior fontanel
D. The anterior is bulging; the posterior appears sunken

373. The umbilical vein carries _____ blood.
A. Deoxygenated B. Oxygenated
C. Both A & B D. None of the Above

374. A nurse massages the uterus of a postpartum client. Which assessment finding best indicates that the intended effect of this nursing action has been achieved?
A. Postpartal pain is relieved
B. The uterus becomes firm
C. The client passes clots from the vagina
D. Uterine contractions cease

375. What is the best evidence that a postpartum client's Kegel exercises are effective?
A. The client can perform deep-knee bends without back discomfort
B. The client can touch the toes without abdominal discomfort
C. The client can do several sit-ups without stopping
D. The client can stop and restart the flow of urine while voiding

376. The urine of a client who is 6 months' pregnant tests positive for albumin. The nurse correctly assumes that the client is probably developing which complication of pregnancy?
A. Preeclampsia
B. Liver impairment
C. Amniotic embolism
D. Gestational diabetes

377. The nurse informs a graduate nurse on a postpartum unit that the human chorionic gonadotropin (HCG) would no longer be detected in the client's blood at:
A. One week postpartum
B. Two days postpartum
C. Four weeks postpartum
D. One hour postpartum

378. .... is the permanent method of sterilization.
A. MTP B. D & C
C. Tubectomy D. Diaphragm

379. Which of the following urinary symptoms does the pregnant woman most frequently experience during the first trimester?
A. Incontinence B. Frequency
C. Dysuria D. Burning

380. Total weight gain during pregnancy is
A. 7-8 kg B. 13-14 kg
C. 10-11 kg D. 15-16 kg

381. Which of the following is not scored with the APGAR?
A. 0 B. Heart Rate
C. Color D. Tone

382. Which of the following urinary symptoms does the pregnant woman most frequently experience during the first trimester?
A. Incontinence B. Frequency
C. Dysuria D. Burning

383. Which of the following is not a germ layer during the 3rd week of development?
A. Mesoderm B. Ectoderm
C. Endoderm D. Exoderm

384. Which of the following develops into: bone, connective tissue, blood, and the spleen?
A. Notochord B. Endoderm
C. Mesoderm D. Ectoderm

385. What do you call the vague pain on either right or left lower quadrant that is sometimes felt by a woman during ovulation?
A. Dysmenorrhea B. Dyspareuni
C. Mettelschmerz D. Spinnbarkeit

386. Fever, foul lochial discharge and subinvolution of the uterus are signs of:
A. Puerperal sepsis
B. Puerperal psychosis
C. Hypertensive disorder
D. Postpartum hemorrhage

387. Rh factor contains
A. Antigen A B. Antigen C
C. Antigen D D. Antigen B

388 When is the most appropriate time for a women to perform breast self examination?
A. The first day of the menstrual period
B. One week after the start of the menstrual period
C. Just before the time of intercourse
D. Any convenient time of the month

389. Ovulation day is
A. 14 days of menses B. 10th day of menses
C. 9th day of menses D. 20th day of menses

390. Copper T is contra indicated during
A. Pregnancy B. Pelvic infections
C. Heart diseases D. All above

391. Sex hormones are
A. Thyroxine B. Insulin
C. Growth Hormone D. Testosterone

392. The tip of the sperm is called the ____.
A. Head B. Acrosome
C. Tail D. Nucleus

393. Difficult labour is called as
A. Dyspepsia B. Dysparenia
C. Dyspnoea D. Dystocia

394. Which of these is not considered a T.O.R.C.H. infection?
A. Rubella B. Herpes
C. Cytomegalovirus D. Croup

395. Which of the following develops into the ejaculatory duct and ductus deferens?
A. Paramesonephric duct

B. Mesonephric duct
C. Sympathetic duct
D. Parasympathetic duct

396. Which of the following is the result of poor fusion between the paramesonephric ducts in females?
A. Placenta Previa
B. Bicornuate uterus
C. Multigravida
D. Proliferative phase

397. Where does spermatogenesis occur?
A. Seminiferous tubules
B. Corpus spongiosoma
C. Prostate gland
D. Scrotum

398 Fertilization of ovam & sperm takes place
A. In uterus
B. Cervix
C. Vagina
D. Ampulla of fallopian tube

399. The vaginal vault is devided into
A. 6 fornices B. 3 fornices
C. 4 fornices D. 8 fornices

400. Pelvic bones are
A. Femur
B. Radius
C. Sacrum and coccyx
D. Humerus

401. Gynaecoid pelvis has
A. Oval shape brim B. Wedge shaped
C. Flat shape brim D. None of the above

402. As a client progresses through pregnancy, she develops constipation. What is the primary cause of this problem during pregnancy?
A. Prolonged gastric emptying
B. Decreased appetite
C. Inadequate fluid intake
D. Reduced intestinal motility

403. A client 37 years, visits the nurse practitioner for a regular prenatal check-up. She's 32 weeks pregnant. When assessing her, the nurse Reena should stay especially alert for signs and symptoms of:
A. Pregnancy-induced hypertension (PIH).
B. Sexually transmitted diseases (STDs).
C. Iron deficiency anemia.
D. Cephalopelvic disproportion.

404. The nurse is providing care for a pregnant client in her second trimester. Glucose tolerance test results show a blood glucose level of 160 mg/dl. The nurse should anticipate that the client will need to:
A. Monitor her urine for glucose.
B. Start using insulin.
C. Start taking an oral antidiabetic drug.
D. Be taught about diet.

405. The nurse is planning care for a 15-year-old client in the prenatal clinic. Adolescents are prone to which complication during pregnancy?
A. Iron deficiency anemia
B. Gestational diabetes
C. Varicosities
D. Nausea and vomiting

406. The nurse is caring for a client whose membranes ruptured prematurely 12 hours ago. When assessing this client, the nurse's highest priority is to evaluate:
A. Frequency and duration of contractions.
B. Maternal vital signs and FHR.
C. White blood cell (WBC) count.
D. Cervical effacement and dilation

407. Which of the following is the location where fertilization occurs?
A. Ovaries B. Vagina
C. Uterus D. Fallopian Tubes

408. Which of the following terms correspond with the phrase: a woman that is pregnant?
A. Gravida B. Parity
C. Spermatogonia D. Zona pellucida

409. Which of the following sign's may indicate pregnancy?
A. Chadwick's sign B. Turner's sign
C. Virchow's sign D. Kock's sign

❑❑❑

Answer Sheet

1. C.	2. A.	3. C.	4. B.	5. C.	6. D.	7. C.	8. A.	9. B.	10. B.
11. C.	12. D.	13. B.	14. B	15. D.	16. C.	17. A.	18. A.	19. D.	20. C.
21. A.	22. B.	23. D.	24. C.	25. D.	26. B.	27. A.	28. D.	29. B.	30. C.
31. D.	32. B.	33. B.	34. C.	35. D.	36. A.	37. C.	38. B.	39. B.	40. C.
41. B.	42. C.	43. B.	44. C.	45. C.	46. D.	47. C.	48. C.	49. A.	50. A.
51. C.	52. B.	53. B.	54. B.	55. D.	56. A.	57. B.	58. B.	59. D.	60. B.
61. A.	62. D.	63. C.	64. C.	65. C.	66. B.	67. D.	68. .B	69. A.	70. A.
71. B.	72. B.	73. A.	74. A.	75. C.	76. D.	77. C.	78. C.	79. B.	80. B.
81. B.	82. D.	83. A.	84. A.	85. C.	86. A.	87. B.	88. A.	89. C.	90. A.
91. A.	92. B.	93. C.	94. A.	95. B.	96. D.	97. A.	98. A.	99. B.	100. B.
101. B.	102. B.	103. A.	104. A.	105. B.	106. C.	107. B.	108. B.	109. A.	110. A.
111. D.	112. A.	113. A.	114. A.	115. B.	116. A.	117. C.	118. C.	119. A.	120. D.
121. .C	122. B.	123. A.	124. D.	125. B.	126. D.	127. C.	128. D.	129. A.	130. A.
131. A.	132. A.	133. B.	134. A.	135. C.	136. A.	137. A.	138. A.	139. C.	140. B.
141. A.	142. A.	143. B.	144. D.	145. D.	146. D.	147. B.	148. D.	149. B.	150. B.
151. C.	152. B.	153. D.	154.A.	155. D.	156. A.	157. D.	158. C.	159. A.	160. B.
161. B.	162. C.	163. C.	164. B.	165. D.	166. A.	167. C.	168. C.	169. C.	170. C.
171. C.	172. D.	173. B.	174. C.	175. B.	176. C.	177. A.	178. C.	179. B.	180. D.
181. A.	182. D.	183. C.	184. A.	185. A.	186. D.	187. A.	188. B.	189. D.	190. D.
191. C.	192. B.	193. D.	194. A.	195. B.	196. C.	197. A.	198. B.	199. C.	200. A.
201. D.	202. C.	203. B.	204. D.	205. C.	206. D.	207. C.	208. C.	209. B.	210. B.
211. C.	212. C.	213. C.	214. C.	215. C.	216. D.	217. B.	218. A.	219. C.	220. C.
221. A.	222. A.	223. D.	224. A.	225. B.	226. B.	227. D.	228. B.	229. D.	230. B.
231. A.	232. D.	233. C.	234. B.	235. B.	236. B.	237. C.	238. C.	239. A.	240. D.
241. C.	242. A.	243. C.	244. A.	245. D.	246. C.	247. C.	248. A.	249. C.	250. C.
251. C.	252. A.	253. C.	254. A.	255. B.	256. A.	257. B.	258. D.	259. B.	260. C.
261. A.	262. A.	263. D.	264. B.	265. C.	266. C.	267. B.	268. B.	269. B.	270. A.
271. A.	272. D.	273. B.	274. C.	275. B.	276. A.	277. A.	278. C.	279. B.	280. A.
281. C.	282. B.	283. A.	284. A.	285. A.	286. B.	287. C.	288. C.	289. A.	290. A.
291. D.	292. C.	293. B.	294. D.	295. C.	296. B.	297. C.	298. C.	299. B.	300. B.
301. B.	302. A.	303. C.	304. A.	305. B.	306. D.	307. C.	308. D.	309. C.	310. A.
311. C.	312. A.	313. D.	314. C	315. A.	316. C.	317. A.	318. C	319. A.	320. A.
321. D.	322. C.	323. C.	324. D.	325. D.	326. B.	327. B.	328. A.	329. A.	330. B.
331. D.	332. A.	333. A.	334. A.	335. C.	336. C.	337. A.	338. C	339. C.	340. B.
341. B.	342. D.	343. C.	344. C.	345. C.	346. A.	347. B.	348. C.	349. C.	350. B.
351. A.	352. D.	353. A.	354. C.	355. A.	356. C.	357. A.	358. C.	359. D.	360. A.
361. D.	362. C.	363. C.	364. A.	365. A.	366. B.	367. C.	368. A.	369. D.	370. C.
371. A.	372. C.	373. B.	374. B.	375. D.	376. A.	377. A.	378. C.	379. B.	380. B.
381. A.	382. B.	383.D .	384. C.	385. A.	386. A.	387. C.	388. B.	389. A.	390. D.
391. D.	392. B.	393. D.	394. D.	395. B.	396. B.	397.A .	398. D.	399. C.	400. C.
401. B.	402. D.	403. A.	404. D.	405. A.	406. B.	407. D.	408. A.	409. A.	

❑❑❑

11. Pediatric Nursing (MCQ)

1. **Which of the following is a clinical manifestation associated with imperforate anus?**
   A. Child Failure to pass me conium stool in the first 24 hours after birth.
   B. Child passage of currant jelly-like stools
   C. Sausage-shaped mass palpatec in the upper right abdominal quadrant
   D. Bile-stained faecal emesis

2. **What is the Normal birth weight of a new born?**
   A. 2.5-3 kg B. 3-3.5 kg
   C. 1.5-2.5 kg D. 3 kg.

3. **What is normal, length of a baby At the time of birth?**
   A. 35-40 cm B. 40-42 cm
   C. 50-60 cm D. 45-51 cm.

4. **A neonate touching by the nurse to the cheek near of the mouth causes turning of head towards the stimulation it is known as:**
   A. Moro reflex B. Sucking reflex.
   C. Doll's eye reflex D. Rooting reflex

5. **Rickets is caused by which Vitamin deficiency**
   A. Calciferol B. Ascorbic acid
   C. Folic acid D. Nicotinic acid

6. **When should be the introducing solid foods to her child?**
   A. 1 month B. 2 months
   C. 3 months D. 4 months

7. **A newborn diagnosis of esophageal atresia with tracheoesophageal fistula is suspected. The nurse expects to which of the most common sign of this condition documented in the record?**
   A. Severe projectile vomiting
   B. Choking with feedings
   C. Incessant crying
   D. Coughing at nighttimes

8. **What is a swelling on the neonate's scalp that crosses the suture line? This condition called as**
   A. Cephallic hematoma
   B. Caput succedaneum
   C. Hemorrhage edema
   D. Perinatal caput

9. **Which of the following developmental achievements would the nurse assess for one month old infant?**
   A. Smiling and laughing out loud.
   B. Rolling from back to side.
   C. Holding a rattle briefly.
   D. Turning the head from side to side.

10. **Which are the tasks is typical for an 18-month old baby?**
    A. Copying a circle
    B. Pulling toys
    C. Playing toy with other children
    D. Building a tower of eight blocks

11. **What is Marasmus ?**
    A. Nutritional deficiency disease
    B. Vitamin A deficiency disease
    C. Protein deficiency disease
    D. None of the Above

12. **What is a positive Babinski reflex indicates…**
    A. Immature muscle coordination.
    B. Immature central nervous system.
    C. Possible lower spinal cord defect.
    D. Possible injury to nerves that innervate the feet.

13. **If a baby's birth weight is 2.5 kg, then at 6 month weight of baby should be:**
    A. 7.5 kg B. 8 kg
    C. 5 kg D. 4 kg.

14. **What is Kwashiorkor?**
    A. Nutritional deficiency disease
    B. Vitamin A deficiency disease
    C. Protein deficiency disease
    D. None of the Above

15. **When will that the neonate's anterior fontanel will normally close by age…**
    A. 2 to 3 months B. 6 to 8 months
    C. 12 to 18 months D. 20 to 24 months

16. **A child hospitalalized with a diagnosis of pyloric stenosis. On admission assessment, which of the following data would the nurse expect to obtain with patient?**
    A. Vomiting large amounts of bile
    B. Watery diarrhoea
    C. Projectile vomiting
    D. Increased rate of respiration.

17. **The Physiological jundica appear in term babies at the age of-**
    A. Befor 24 hrs.
    B. Between 30-72 hrs
    C. 96 Hrs
    D. None of the Above

18. **What is the total body water in Infants-**
    A. 75-80% B. 60%
    C. 55% D. 90%

19. Koplik spot are found in-
A. Measies C. Polio
B. Rubella D. Mumps

20. What is causitive agent of dengue
A. Toga virus B. Rota virus
C. Arbo virus D. None of the Above

21. What is cushing traid of ICP-
A. Hypertersion, Tochycardir, Tachypnoea
B. Hypotension, Brady cardia, Bradypnoea
C. Hypertension, Bradycardia, Tachypnoea
D. None of the Above

22. Which of the following fluid would be infused in a patient with diabetic ketoacidosis?
A. Normal saline IV infusion
B. % dextrose IV infusion
C. NPK insulin IV infusion
D. Potassium IV infusion5

23. Suckling refliex disappears at the age of-
A. 6 months B. 8 months
C. 12 months D. 5 months

24. Active Immunizing agents are known as-
A. Sera B. Immunoglobulin
C. Vaccine D. None of the Above

25. The six-killer vaccine preventable disease in children are except-
A. Tuberculosis B. Poliomylitis
C. Pertusis D. Yellow fever

26. The examples of live attenuated vaccine are-
A. B.C.G B. OPV
C. MMR D. All of the Above

27. Which of the following age an infant can chew the food?
A. By 12 months B. By 7 months
C. By 3 months D. By 4 months

28. Which of the following primary nursing intervention in a child who diagnosed with Reye's syn-drome?
A. Changing position every 1 hours
B. Providing a quiet environment with dimmed lighting
C. Assessing hearing loss
D. Monitoring urine output and colour of sclera

29. A child has diagnosed with fluid volume deficit. Which of the following nursing assessment determines that the child condition is improving?
A. Capillary refill is more than 5 seconds
B. Capillary refill is less than 2 seconds
C. Urine specific gravity is 1.030
D. The child has no tears

30. What are the component of under five clinic-
A. Care in ellness & Immunization
B. Adequate Nutrition & Health education
C. Family planning
D. All of the Above

31. Which of the following item need to be placed at the child's bedside for a child who has risk for tonic-clonic seizures?
A. Padded tongue blade.
B. Tracheostomy set
C. Emergency crash cart
D. Suctioning equipment and oxygen

32. What is the normal, head circumference. At the time of birth?
A. 33 -35 cm B. 25-30 cm
C. 30-32 cm D. 35-40 cm

33. Which of the following primary nursing intervention in a child with tonic-clonic seizures?
A. Tracheostomy
B. Emergency epinephrine administer
C. Maintain airway and Suctioning
D. Prevent to child from injury

34. At which age a baby stand without support?
A. 10 months B. 22 months
C. 9 months D. 12 months

35. A child suspected for bacterial meningitis and cerebrospinal fluid (CSF) is obtained for analysis. A nurse reviews the results of the CSF analysis and determines that which of the following results would verify the diagnosis?
A. Cloudy CSF, elevated protein, and decreased glucose levels.
B. Clear CSF, increase lymphocytes, and elevated protein level
C. Cloudy CSF, decreased protein, and decreased glucose levels
D. Clear CSF, elevated protein, and decreased glucose levels

36. A therapy Commonly used for the treatment of thumb sucking :
A. Aversion therapy B. Desensitization
C. Psychoanalysis D. Implosive therapy

37. At which age child can sit with support?
A. 5 months B. 10 months
C. 8 months D. 3 months

38. Which of the following most appropriate method to assess the urine output in a infant with congestive heart failure who is receiving diuretic therapy?
A. Weighing the diapers
B. Inserting a Foleys catheter
C. Comparing intake with output.
D. Use condom catheter and water added to formula

39. Which of the following type toys should the nurse recommend for a 5-month-old child?
A. A big red balloon
B. A teddy bear with button eyes
C. A push-pull wooden truck
D. A colorful busy box

40. An infant has just returned after a surgical repair of a cleft lip on the Left side. The nurse places the infant in which best position at this time?
A. Left lateral position.
B. Right lateral position
C. Prone position
D. On the back side

41. Flag sign is found in-
A. Marasmus B. PEM
C. Kawashiorkar D. All of the Above

42. For assessment of Newborn for neurological examination what you will do-
A. CT Scan
B. X-Ray
C. Neonatal Reflax
D. Blood Investigation

43. In Infant which position is best for enema administration-
A. Sim's Position
B. Fowler's position
C. Kmee-chest position
D. None of the Above

44. What are the essential symptom for Kawashiorkar-
A. Retarted growth B. Edema
C. Mental change D. All of the Above

45. What is Lecithin-
A. Surfectant
B. Meconium
C. Sweat
D. Cynjucival seereaten

46. What is normal number of Temporary teeth.
A. 16 B. 28 C. 20 D. 24

47. Which of the following are the important characteristic of hypothyroidism except?
A. Increase Weight
B. Decreased BMR
C. Prone to hypothermia
D. Bulimia

48. Which of the following is most common chromosomal disorder in children?
A. Down syndrome
B. Edward syndrome
C. Hydrocephalus syndrome
D. Turner's syndrome

49. A nurse is preparing to care for a child with a diagnosis of intussusceptions .which symptom of this disorder documented by nurse?
A. Bright red blood and mucus in the stools or jelly like stool
B. Ribbon-like stcols
C. Tarry black colour stool
D. Watery diarrhoea

50. A nurse is preparing to care for a child with a diagnosis of Hirschsprung's disease. Which symptom of this disorder documented by nurse?
A. Projectile vomiting
B. Diarrhoea
C. Bright red blood and mucus in the stools or jelly like stool
D. Foul-smelling ribbon-like stools

51. Human foetus has coat of hair called as ..
A. Fur B. Scutes
C. Libids D. Lanugo

52. Which of the following are the Secondary prevention of Tuberculosis?
A. Rehabilitation
B. Early detection and treatment of MR
C. Immunization
D. Good antenatal care

53. Which of the following early sign of CHF assess by nurse in an infant with con-genital heart disease?
A. Tachycardia
B. Cough Pallor Cough
C. Slow and shallow breathing
D. Cough

54. Which of the following is the most common type of haemophilia?
A. Haemophilia C B. Haemophilia A
C. Haemophilia D D. Haemophilia B

55. Persistence of foramen ovale leads to
A. MOF B. ASD C. PDA D. TOF

56. A physician has prescribed oxygen as needed for an infant. In which of the following situation should the nurse administer the oxygen to the infant with congestive heart failure?
A. When drawing blood for electrolyte level testing
B. When collecting urine sample
C. When the mother is holding the infant
D. During feeding and sleeping time

57. Which of the following toys would best promote imaginative play in a 4-year-old providing therapeutic play?
A. Large blocks B. Dress-up clothes
C. Wooden puzzle D. Big wheels

58. When should measles, mumps, and rubella (MMR) vaccine at the recommended scheduled time.
A. In 6 months
B. In 1 year
C. At age 15-18 months
D. At age 2 years

59. What is meaning of Cryptorchidism?
A. Undescended testes
B. Enlargement of testes
C. Micro testes
D. Inflammation of testes

60. Which of the following confirming laboratory finding expected by nurse when a child suspected for rheumatic fever?
A. Antistreptolysin O titer
B. White blood cell count
C. Red blood cell count
D. Radiological examination

61. A nurse is caring for a child after a tonsillectomy. Which of the following observation indicates that the child is bleeding?
A. An elevation in blood pressure
B. A decreased pulse rate
C. Frequently child talking
D. Frequent swallowing

62. A mother concern about sudden infant death syndrome She asks the nurse how to position her baby for sleep. The nurse appropriately tells the mother that the infant should be placed on the:
A. Back and head below the level head
B. Side lying
C. Stomach with the face turned
D. Back rather than on the stomach

63. Which of the following is most common causative micro-organism is responsible for acute glomerulonephritis in children?
A. Streptococci B. Staphylococcus
C. Pseudomonas D. E.coli

64. The children hospital of eastern Ontario pain scale(Cheops) for rating post operative pain in children includes A/E?
A. Cry B. Touch
C. Torso D. Oxygen saturation

65. A clinic nurse reads the results of a Mantoux test on a 4 year old child. The results indicate an area of indurations measuring 10 mm. The nurse would interpret these results as:
A. Positive
B. Requiring a repeat test
C. Definitive Negative
D. None of them

66. The mother of an 6 year old child being treated for left lower lobe pneumonia at home calls the clinic nurse. The mother tells the nurse that the child com-plains of discomfort on the left side and that the ibuprofen is not effective.The nurse should tell the mother to:
A. Encourage the child to lie on the left side
B. Increase the dose of the ibuprofen
C. Encourage the child to lie on the right side
D.. Increase the frequency of the ibuprofen

67. Which of the following is the commonest cyanotic congenital heart disease?
A. Atrial septal defect
B. Patent ductus arterious
C. Tricuspid atresia
D. All of the Above

68. To help a young child retain tube feeding and avoid aspiration, the nurse should place the child in the-
A. Supine position
B. Left side lying position
C. Semi fowlers position
D. Prone position

69. Surgery of the clept lip is called-
A. Hernioplasty B. Pyeloplasty
C. Chieloplasty D. None of the Above

70. What is rate of O2 administration in children?
A. 7 liter/min B. 12 liter/min
C. 2 liter/min D. 10 liter/min

71. What is complication of O_2 therapy (Higher) in premature child-
A. Retrolental fibroplasia
B. Atelectasis
C. Induced apnoes
D. None of the Above

72. What is willms tumor-
A. Malignant tumor of Brain
B. Maluignant tumor of bone
C. Malignant tumor of ear
D. Malignant tumor of kidneys

73. What is exomphalos-
A. Umblical Hernia
B. Umblical infection
C. Diaphrgmatic hernia
D. None of the Above

74. Which is the posture shown by Infant at the time of birth-
A. Flexion & extension
B. Generalized flexion
C. Hyperflexed
D. Hyper extended

75. Which of The commonest complication of bronchial asthma in children?
A. Pleurisy B. Atelectasis
C. Emphysema D. Hyperpyrexia

76. Shortest incubation period is of
A. Influenza B. Hep B
C. Hep A D. Rubella

77. What are the Total number of temporary teeth in a children ?
A. 32 B. 30 C. 20 D. 24.

78. Which of the following illnesses would lead to pneumococcal meningitis in a 2 year old child?
A. Bladder infection.
B. Middle ear infection
C. Emphysema
D. Sepsis

79. Mid-day meal programme provides how many calories and proteins per day?
A. 300 calories and 6-12 gram of proteins
B. 200 calories and 6-12 grams of proteins
C. 300 calories and 8-12 grams of proteins
D. 200 calories and 8-12 grams of proteins

80. What is the age where normally eruption of teeth start in a child?
A. 6-8 months B. 4-5 months
C. 8-10 months D. 12-14 months

81. When will be the child's birth weight to triple?
A. 4 months B. 7 months
C. 9 months D. 12 months

82. Nurse caring a child with hydrocophalus. during examination nurse observe "Involuntry & free movement of eye ball". This task is sign of-
A. Atexia B. Frontal bossing
C. Nystagmus D. None of the Above

83. Which of the following should a frequent complication for a child with congenital heart disease?
A. Susceptibility to respiratory infection
B. Bleeding tendencies
C. Frequent vomiting and diarrhea
D. Seizure disorder

84. The Nurse in clinic must give a booster dose for polio to a child. The recommended vaccine is-
A. OPV B. DPT
C. IPV D. HIb

85. A child with type-1 diabetes has been addmitted in ketoacidosis. The nurse expects the child to exhibit-
A. Pyrexia B. Hyperpnea
C. Hypertension D. Brady cardia

86. The most area for bleeding to develop in a child with hemophiliia is the-
A. Joints B. Brain
C. Pericardium D. Intestine

87. The most common clinical type of ceribral palsy seen in childrens-
A. Spastic ceribral palsy
B. Athetoid
C. Ataxic
D. Mixed

88. Which of the following toys would the nurse suggest as most appropriate for an 8-month-old?
A. Push-pull toys B. Rattle
C. Large blocks D. Mobile

89. Which is characteristic of a preschooler with mid mental retardation?
A. Slow to feed self
B. Lack of speech
C. Marked motor delays
D. Gait disability

90. Which of the following findings would the nurse expected when a child diagnosis with the Wilms' tumour?
A. Stone in urine B. Hyperbilirubinemia
C. Petechiae D. Pallor

91. A six year old child is admitted to the hospital with pneumonia. An immediate priority in this child's nursing care would include all of the following except:
A. Give oxygen according to the programme
B. Assess respiratory status and signs of cyano-sis
C. Give fowler position/semi-fowler position
D. None of the Above

92. Which of the following finding would help to the nurse in assessment about celiac disease?
A. "Child is too long with blood in stool"
B. "Child stools are large,smelly and Protuberant abdomen"
C. "Child urine is dark in colour."
D. "Child belly is very small"

93. Which of the following would be the priority nursing assessment for an adolescent after an appendectomy?
A. The dressing on the surgical site.
B. Intravenous infusion site
C. Nasogastric tube function
D. Assessment about pain

94. Which of the following would be appropriate nursing role when A child diagnosis with severe gastroenteritis?
A. Use standard precautions.
B. Use regular eating plastic utensils
C. Place the child in a sterile deluxe room
D. Use sterile linens to cover child

95. The most common complication of mumps in children is:
A. Pancreatitis B. Orchitis
C. Aseptic meningites D. Peritoditis.

96. Incubation perod of hapatitis A:
A. 2 days - 2 weeks' B. 6 days - 6 weeks
C. 6 weeks-6 months D. 2 weeks - 2months

97. The causitive agent oral thrush is-
A. Candida albicance B. Toxoplasmosis
C. Asperglosis D. None of above

98. For trachoma treatment of choice for children is:
A. Oral tetracycline
B. Oral sulphacetamide
C. Tetracycline ointment
D. None of the Above

99. Bone dysphasia is due to:
A. Hormonal imbalance
B. Vitamin deficiency
C. Faulty development
D. Fault nutrition

100. Hormone responsible for skeletal maturation of fetus:
A. Progesterone B. Thyroxin
C. Estrogen D. Testosterone.

101. Maximum development of brain occur at:
A. School age
B. 1st trimester of pregnancy
C. Adolescence
D. Infancy

102. Three month old baby can do all, except:
A. Can turn supine from prone position
B. Lift head in prone position
C. Turn head to sound
D. Social smile

103. The reference protein is:
A. Lemon B. Rice
C. Egg D. Fish

104. Which of the following should the nurse do first after noting that a child with Hirschsprung disease has a fever and watery explosive diarrhea?
A. No need to do anything it is normal
B. Monitor child ever 30 minutes
C. Administer antidiarrheal medications
D. Notify the physician immediately.

105. When providing postoperative care for the child with a cleft palate, the nurse should position the child in which of the following positions?
A. Side lying B. In an infant seat
C. Prone D. Supine

106. Which of the following foods would the nurse encourage the mother to offer to her child with iron-deficiency anemia?
A. Pudding, green vegetables and rice
B. Macaroni, cheese and ham
C. Potato, peas, and chicken
D. Rice cereal, whole milk, and yellow vegetables

107. What is synonyms of Napkin rashes-
A. Amonia dermatitis B. Contact Dermatitis
C. Eczema D. None of the Above

108. When the evening colic is subside in Infant-
A. After 3 months of age of baby
B. After 6 months of age of baby
C. After 12 months of age of baby
D. After 18 months of age of baby

109. Which Refiex is disapear in 6 week to 3 months of neonate age-
A. Palmer grasp B. Gagging reflex
C. Rooting reflex D. Swallowing reflex

110. A child presents to the emergency room with the history of ingesting a large amount of acetaminophen. For which of the following would the nurse assess?
A. Headache
B. Right upper quadrant pain
C. Anuria
D. Hypertension

111. A 8 year old boy is returned to his room following a tonsillectomy. The nurse should place the child in which of the following positions?
A. Fowler B. Supine
C. Side-lying D. Sims'

112. A patient is admitted with meningitis and is receiving I.V.and oral fluids. The nurse should monitor this client's fluid intake because fluid overload may cause:
A. Hypovolemic shock
B. Heart failure
C. Dehydration
D. Increase ICP

113. Nurse is administering total parental nu-trition (TPN) through a peripheral I.V. line to a school-age child. What's the smallest amount of glucose

that's con-sidered safe and not caustic to small veins, while also providing adequate TPN?
A. 25% glucose B. 15% glucose
C. 10% glucose D. 5% glucose

114. When administering an IM injection to an infant, the nurse should use which site?
A. Vastus lateralis B. Ventrogluteal
C. Dorsogluteal D. Deltoid

115. During resuscitation in an infant, ratio of chest compression and ventilation breath should be:
A. 4:1 B. 5:1 C. 1:3 D. 1:1

116. Which of the following technique is most important in identified possible hydrocephalus in an infant with spina bifida:
A. Measuring head circumference.
B. CT scan and Obtaining skull X-ray
C. Performing a lumbar puncture
D. None of them

117. A child diagnosed with leukaemia who receiving chemotherapy. The nurse notes that the platelet count is below 20000 cells/ mm3. Based on this laboratory finding, which intervention would the nurse document in the plan of care?
A. Use a soft small toothbrush for mouth care
B. Initiate protective isolation precau-tions.
C. Monitor the temperature every 4 hours
D. Monitor closely for signs of infection

118. Which of the following would the nurse expect in a 2 year old child?
A. Child Tie his shoelaces
B. Child Ride a tricycle
C. Child Use blunt scissors
D. Child Kick a ball forward

119. Which of the following is priority nursing action when an infant with pyloric stenosis is admitted to the hospital?
A. Weight the infant
B. Provide prone position to child
C. Switch the infant to an electrolyte solution
D. Start intravenous infusion

120. What is the Toddler age?
A. 1-3 year B. 6-12 year
C. 0-1 year D. 3-6 year.

121. Which of the most common characteristic associated with nephrotic syndrome in a child?
A. Hypertension
B. Generalized edema
C. Increased urinary output
D. Hematuria

122. What is the most common cause of death due to diarrhoea?
A. Dehydration B. Vomiting
C. Abdominal cramp D. None of them

123. When neonate's head is turned slowly from right to left side, normally eye do not move is known as:
A. Blinking reflex B. Gagging reflex
C. Moro reflex. D. Doll's eye reflex

124. A child with haemophilia has slipped on the road and bumped his knee. The nurse should prepare to administer an:
A. Intravenous infusion of factor VIII.or cryoprecipitate plasma
B. Injection of factor X
C. Colloids
D. Administer injection of iron using the Z-track method

125. What id the Recommended daily intake of Vitamin D in a infant ?
A. 200 IU B. 400 IU
C. 300 IU D. 500 IU

126. What is the Treatment of pathological jaundice in a infant?
A. Administration of phenobarbitone
B. Exchange transfusion
C. Phototherapy
D. All of the the Above

127. Which of the position should the child get in postoperative care for the child with a cleft palate?
A. Supine B. Prone
C. In an infant seat D. On the side

128. Which of the following would be an important assessment finding for a 6 month old infant with severe diarrhoea?
A. Absent bowel sounds
B. Normal skin turgor
C. Dark yellow stool
D. Depressed anterior fontanel

129. Which of the following food should be avoided in celiac disease?
A. Rice B. Milk
C. Wheat D. Chicken

130. While caring for a newborn with an imperforate anus, the nurse assesses the neonate's urine output for which of the following?
A. Hematuria B. Meconium
C. Chyluria D. Bile

131. A promising treatment for some children suffering from Thalassemia is:
A. Steroidal therapy
B. Radiation therapy
C. Chemotherapeutic agents
D. Bone marrow transplantation

132. A child is diagnosed with bacterial conjuctivitis, a nurse educates the mother to do all, except:
A. Give eye drops as prescribed
B. Share towel and wash cloths
C. Clean eyes as prescribed
D. Wash hands frequently

133. The apgar scoring is done to appraise the infant for:
A. Emotional stability
B. RH-sensitization
C. Respiratory effort
D. Birth defects

134. Which of the vital sign is not included in Apgar score?
A. Temperature B. Heart rate
C. Respiration D. Colour

135. What is the most likely is the first two years of life, children with Broncho-pulmonary dysplasia requiring re-hospitalization?
A. Electrolyte disturbances
B. Immune deficiencies
C. Pulmonary hypertension
D. Respiratory tract infections

136. Which will be the deficiency of a four-year-old child, whose family follows a strict vegetarian diet, undergoes a prekindergarten physical examination?
A. Niacin B. Thiamine
C. Vitamin B_6 D. Vitamin B_{12}

137. Which laboratory value requires the nurse's intervention if a nurse is caring for a patient who received chemotherapy 10 days ago?
A. A blood urea nitrogen level of 10 mg/dL
B. A hemoglobin of 8.6 g/dL
C. A platelet count of $18 \times 10^3/\mu L$
D. A serum glucose of 110 mg/dL

138. When physiological jaundice appears in newborn baby?
A. First week after birth
B. On second day
C. On second week
D. At birth

139. Which of the following "fontanelle" in child is the first to close?
A. Mastoid B. Sphenoid
C. Occipital D. Frontal

140. Which of the following medications would the nurse anticipate to be prescribed in chelation therapy to remove iron overload?
A. Deferoxamine
B. Calcium gluconate
C. Atropine sulphate
D. Meropenem

141. To calculate the dose of a medicine for a child, which the following formula in used?
A. Young's rule B. Clark's rule
C. Fried's rule D. All of the Above

142. Which of the following game where a child could participate safely who has diagnosed with haemophilia
A. Field hockey B. Swimming
C. Basketball D. Soccer

143. In premature labour, which of the fol-lowing medicines is useful for the new-born?
A. Testosterone
B. Dexamethasone
C. Oxytocin
D. Magnesium sulphate.

144. Wilm's tumour is a tumour of:
A. Liver B. Testes
C. Brain D. Kidney

145. A nurse is planning care for a child with haemolytic uremic syndrome. The child has been anuric and will be receiving peritoneal dialysis treatment the nurse plans to:
A. Administer prescribed analgesics.
B. Encourage foods high in potassium
C. Care for the fistula
D. Restrict fluids as prescribed

146. Which of the following nursing finding help in assessment of the child about presence of scabies?
A. Fine greyish red lines on skin
B. Purple-coloured lesions on skin
C. Thick, honey-coloured crusts on skin
D. Clusters of fluid-filled vesicles on skin

147. Normal birth weight is:
A. 2.2-2.7 kg B. 3-3.5 kg
C. 2-2.5 kg D. 2.5-3 kg

148. A newborn is considered as LBW, is birth weight is:
A. Less than 3 kg B. Less than 2 kg
C. Less than 2.5 kg D. 2.5 kg

149. At which age a child can starts to brushhis teeth?
A. 20 months B. 4 years
C. 3 years D. 2 years

150. In following which vaccine is given at birth by intradermai route?
A. Measles B. DPT
C. BCG D. OPV

151. Causative organism of chickenpox is:
A. Bordetalla pertusis
B. Herpes simplex virus
C. Varicella zoster
D. Paramixo virus

152. While taking temperature from rectal route in children thermometer should be inserted about:
A. 1/2 inch B. 1 inch
C. 1/4 inch D. 2 inch

153. Anterior fontenella is ossified in:
A. At 5 years B. At 18 months
C. At 6 weeks D. Soon after birth

154. What is the criteria of LEW baby?
A. Birth weight <2.7 kg
B. Birth weight <3 kg
C. Birth weight <2.5 kg
D. Birth weight <2 kg.

155. In children which is the most appropri-ate route for measuring temperature?
A. Elbow B. Rectal
C. Axillary D. Oral

156. MMR vaccine is given by:
A. I.D. route B. I.V.route
C. S.C.route D. I.M.route.

157. Deficiency of Vitamin D in children may cause:
A. Beri-Beri B. Pellagra
C. Rickets D. Osteomalacia.

158. BCG vaccine is given to prevent:
A. Diphtheria B. Measles
C. Polio D. Tuberculosis.

159. Components of ORS include:
A. NaCl, KC1, $MgCl_2$, H_2O
B. NaCl, KC1, $NaHCO_3$, Sugar
C. NaCl, KC1, Sodium citrate, H_2O, Sugar
D. NaCl, KC1, H_2O, Sugar

160. In children which disease occurs due to protein deficiency?
A. Scurvy B. Beri-Beri
C. Kwashiorkor D. Marasmus

161. A child is suffering from dyspnea, first of all what nursing care will you provide to the child?
A. Start nebulization
B. Start O_2 therapy
C. Provide supine position
D. Start I.V.infusion

162. After birth of a baby, breast-feeding should be started:
A. After 1 week B. On second day
C. Within half hours D. Within 2 hours

163. Circumcision is used for the treatment of:
A. Epispadia B. Hypospadia
C. Cleft palate D. Phimosis

164. In an infant ideal ratio between cardiac compression and breathing during CPR should be:
A. 1:1 B. 5:1 C. 15:2 D. 3:1

165. In following which is not a preventive measure for tetanus neonatorum?
A. Penicillin antibiotic
B. T.T.immunization during reproduc-tive age
C. Follow five clinic rule
D. T.T.vaccination

166. A mother of a 3-year-old tells a clinic nurse that the child is rebelling constantly and having temper tantrums. The nurse most appropriately tells the mother to:
A. Punish the child every time the child says "no", to change the behavior
B. Allow the behavior because this is normal at this age period
C. Set limits on the child's behavior
D. Ignore the child when this behavior occurs

167. What is most essential assessment of neonate-
A. B.P. B. Pulse
C. Good/first cry D. Temprature

168. Which pgar (APGAR) Scare is showing mild depression-
A. 0-5 B. 3-5 C. 4-6 D. 0-3

169. A nurse is assigned to care for a 6 year old child with a diagnosis of a basilar skull fracture. The nurse reviews the physician's prescriptions and contacts the physician to question which prescriptions?
A. Suction as needed
B. Provide clear liquid intake
C. Maintain a patent intravenous line
D. None of them

170. What do you mean by child development-?
A. Net increase in weight
B. Net increase in Height
C. Maturataion of body argan
D. Functional & physiological Maturation

171. Which of the following nursing finding is associated with the diagnosis of glomerulonephritis?
A. Low blood urea nitrogen level
B. Hypotension and high urinary specific gravity
C. Low urinary specific gravity.
D. Brown coloured urine

172. What are most prevelent causes of I.M.R-
A. Diarrhoea
B. R.T.I.
C. Congenital abnormalities
D. Both A & B

173. Which assessment findings should the nurse expect to an adolescent client with diabetic ketoacidosis?

A. Sweating and tremors
B. Hunger and hypertension
C. Cold, clammy skin and irritability.
D. Fruity breath odour and decreasing level of consciousness

174. After a tonsillectomy, which of the following physician's prescriptions does the nurse question?

A. Give clear, cool liquids when awake and alert
B. Monitor for bleeding
C. Give no milk or milk products.
D. Suction every 2 hours

175. A child with type 1 diabetes mellitus has football practice.The school nurse provides instructions regarding how to prevent hypoglycaemia during practice.The school nurse tells the child to:

A. Eat normally food at lunch time
B. Take half the amount of prescribed insulin on practice days
C. Drink a cup of orange juice before practice
D. Take the prescribed insulin at practice time.

176. Which of the following observation expected by the nurse indicate strabismus in a 2 year old child?

A. The child consistently turns the head to see.
B. The child does not respond when spoken to
C. The child has difficulty to hold the head
D. The child consistently tilts the head to see

177. A nurse is preparing care plan for a child with acute bacterial meningitis. Based on the mode of transmission of this infection, which of the following precaution should be included in the plan of care?

A. Maintain enteric precautions
B. Maintain standard precautions
C. Maintain universal precautions
D. Maintain respiratory precautions for at least 24 hours after the initiation of antibiotics

178. Which of the following health education given by nurse to parents if a child diagnosed with bacterial conjunctivitis?

A. "They need to give the eye drops as pre-scribed"
B. "They need to wash my hands frequently" and not share towels and washcloths."
C. "They need to clean the eye as prescribed"
D. All of the above

179. Which of the following next nursing action after administer acetaminophen to a child with moderate fever?

A. Plan to administer salicylate (aspirin) in 4 hours.
B. Withhold oral fluids for 8 hours
C. Sponge the child with cold water
D. Remove excess clothing and blankets from the child

180. Which of the following would be the best nursing action in the care for an infant who has severe diarrhoea?

A. Monitoring sunken fontanels every shift
B. Monitoring abdominal skin turgor every shift
C. Monitoring the total 8 hour formula intake.
D. Weighing the infant each day

181. Which of the following positions is recommended for a child with a nasal bleeding?

A. Lying down with feet elevated
B. Sitting up with neck extended
C. Lying down with a small pillow under the head
D. Sitting up with head slightly leaning forward

182. A "Green stick fracture" is

A. A fracture at right angle to the bone
B. An incomplete fracture in which the bone is bent
C. A fracture in which a bone fragments in to several
D. Bone ends are no longer touching

183. Common fracture in child is:

A. Green stick fracture
B. Compleate fracture
C. Open fracture
D. Close fracture

184. Which international organization is concerned for the betterment of children?

A. UNESCO B. UNICEF
C. WHO D. FAO

185. Which of the following Health program provides Supplementary Nutrition and non formal education services as two major components?

A. Universal immunization program
B. ICDS
C. RCH program
D. NRHM

186. The normal respiratory rate of a new born is:

A. 20-30/minute B. 30-40/minute
C. 40-60/minute D. 60-70/minute

187. The infant's posterior fontanels usually closed by

A. 6-8 weeks B. 3 -6 months
C. 12-18 months D. 9-12 months

188. Human milk is preferable to cow's milk in child because:

A. Human milk has a non laxative effect

B. Human milk has more calories per ounce
C. Human milk has greater mineral content
D. Human milk offers greater immunologic effect

189. Erikson's theory provides a frame work for which of the following statement?
A. Clearly indicating the experience needed to resolve crisis
B. Emphasizing pathologic development
C. Coping with extraordinary events
D. Explaining children's behaviour in mastering developmental task

190. The best known theory of cognitive development in children was developed by
A. Sullivan B. Kohlberg
C. Erikson D. Piaget

191. The nurse is performing the 5 minute APGAR on a new born. Which one of the following observations is included in the APGAR score?
A. Blood Pressure B. Temperature
C. Muscle Tone D. Weight

192. All the following are sex chromosomal disorders except :
A. Turner syndrome
B. Klinfelter's syndrome
C. Hirsprungis disease
D. XXX syndrome

193. Which of the postoperative instruction following tonsillectomy is incorrect
A. Monitor for bleeding
B. Suction every 2 hourly
C. Give clear fluid when patient is awake
D. Give no milk products

194. Which of the following is not the risk factor for the development of duodenal ulcers?
A. Smoking B. Stress
C. Alcohol D. Antibiotics

195. The most commonly affected heart valve in RHD is
A Aortic B Mitral
C Pulmonary D Tricuspid

196. Chronic ulcerative colitis is characterized by muscular hypertrophy of bowel with its
A. Widening B. Shortening
C. Thinning D. Fibrosis

197. An acute condition characterized by diminished production and increased destruction of RBC, triggered by viral infection or folic acid deficiency is
A. Adrenal crisis
B. Aplastic crisis
C. Vasoocclusive crisis
D. Splenic crisis

198. A brain tumor located within the anterior two thirds of brain mainly cerebrum is called
A. Supratetntorial B. Inferior tentorial
C. Posterior tentorial D. Middle tentorial

199. Which of the following is NOT the sign of meningitis
A. Kernig's sign B. Bebinski's Sign
C. Brudzinski's sign D. Battle's sign

200. Features of brain stem being affected during the surgical removal of brain tumor is
A. Inability to swallow
B. Elevated temperature
C. Altered hearing ability
D. Orthostatic hypotension

201. A 7 weeks old child who has diarrhoea for 14 days but has no sign of dehydration, is classified as?
A. Persistent diarrhoea
B. Dysentery
C. Severe dysentery
D. Severe persistent diarrhoea

202. Maximum period of infectivity in Mumps is in:
A. Incubation period
B. Onset of swelling
C. After swelling appears
D. Prodromal period

203. All stages of rashes are seen in:
A. Measles B. Typhoid
C. Chickenpox D. Smallpox

204. Sub-acute sclerosing panencephaitis (SSPE) is seen in which of the following communicable diseases:
A. Measles B. Rubella
C. Mumps D. Chickenpox

205. An early sign or symptom of raised ICP in children is:
A. Increased vomiting
B. Bulging anterior fontanel
C. Increased head circumference
D. Complaints of frontal headache

206. A child with leukemia having nausea should be offered
A. Cold clear fluid B. Warm clear fluid
C. Low protein diet D. Low calorie diet

207. During the first year of life, the child is said to go through the which stage
A. Oral B. Anal
C. Genital D. Phallic

208. Which of the following is a hereditary hemolytic anemia?
A. Aplastic anemia
B. Pernicious anemia

C. Megaloblastic anemia
D. Thalassemia

209. Which of the following is not a precipitating factor related to pain crisis in the child with sickle cell anemia
A. Stress B. Trauma
C. Infection D. Fluid overload

210. Which of the following is a safe game for a child with hemophilia
A. Soccer B. Basket ball
C. Swimming D. Field hockey

211. At the age of 2 years child should be able to:
A. Use to eat fruits
B. Drink milk from cup
C. Pours own water in a glass
D. Cuts food using a knife

212. A child has third-degree burns of the face and chest. Which of the following nursing diagnosis takes priority?
A. Ineffective airway clearance related to edema
B. Disturbed body image related to physical appearance
C. Impaired urinary elimination related to fluid loss
D. Risk for infection related to epidermal disruption

213. What is the most com-mon assessment finding in a child with ulcerative colitis?
A. Profuse diarrhoea
B. Blood and mucus with stool
C. Severe vomiting
D. Abdominal cramps and distention

214. What is the Number of chromosomes in Turner Syndrome?
A. 45 B. 46 C. 40 D. 48

215. Knowledge of normal growth and development of the child is essential for the nurse because
A. It is basic to understand the sick child.
B. Most nurses have children
C. Most children do not get sick
D. It helps the nurse to be good father or mother

216. Hospital procedures for a child are
A. The same in each hospital
B. Different in basic principles from those for adults
C. Entirely different for each age group
D. The same in principle as the those for adults

217. The temperature of the child under 4 years of age should be taken by
A. Mouth B. Rectum
C. Mouth and rectum D. Axilla

218. To prevent accident when caring for children the nurse should remember to
A. Leave the crib sides up
B. Keep child in crib at all time
C. Have a gateway in door
D. Keep room tidy and environment safe

219. When playing with children, a toddler play can best be described as
A. Parallel B. Competitive
C. Cooperative D. Sharing

220. Early detection of possible erythrobastosis fetalis requires observation of
A. Jaundice soon after birth
B. Yellowtinged vervix caseosa
C. Susceptibility to eczema
D. Neurologic disturbances
E. Yellowtinged cord
F. PKU test
A. A B. A & B
C. A B & E D. C, D & F

221. The treatment of croup is
A. Highly humidified, cool oxygen and sedatives
B. Vaporized oxygen and sedatives
C. Highly humidified, warm air and syrup of ipecac
D. Rest, antibiotics and oxygen

222. A major priority of nursing care of child suspected of having meningitis is, to
A. Check the temperature and give the cold sponging
B. Isolate the child immediately
C. Administer the antibiotic as soon as it is ordered
D. Restrain the child to prevent accidents

223. The child's apical pulse is always checked before administering digoxin, the drug is not given if the pulse rate is :
A. Below 90 to 110 beats/minute
B. Above 90 to 110 beats/minute
C. Less than 60 beats/minute
D. More than 150 beats/minute

224. During the oedematous phase of nephrotic syndrome an important nursing, intervention is to:
A. Provide meticulous skin care
B. Encourage fluid intake
C. Encourage moderate activity
D. Weight the child every alternate day

225. Initial nursing assessment of an infant suffering with acute diarrhea and dehydration reveals:
A. Skin turgor B. Low hematocrit
C. Bulging fontanelle D. Weight gain

226. When the respiratory rate of a 12 months old child is 35 breaths/minute, the most appropriate nursing action is:
A. Notify the physician
B. Administer Oxygen
C. Reassess respiratory rate in 15 minutes
D. Document the findings

227. Which of the following "fontanelle" in child is the first to close?
A. Frontal B. Occipital
C. Sphenoid D. Mastoid

228. To calculate the dose of a medicine for a child, which of the following formula is used:
A. Young's rule B. Clark's rule
C. Fried's rule D. All of the above

229. In premature labour, which of the following medicines is useful for the newborn?
A. Magnesium sulphate
B. Oxytocin
C. Dexamethasone
D. Testosterone

230. A promising treatment for some children suffering from Thalassemia is:
A. Bone marrow transplantation
B. Chemotherapeutic agents
C. Radiation therapy
D. Steriodal therapy

231. A child is diagnosed with bacterial conjunctivitis, a nurse educate the mother to do all except:
A. Wash hands frequently
B. Clean eyes as prescribed
C. Share towel and wash cloths
D. Give eye drops as prescribed

232. The apgar scoring is done to appraise the infant for:
A. Birth defeats B. Respiratory effort
C. RH-Sensitization D. Emotional stability

233. Wilm's tumor is a tumor of:
A. Kidney B. Brain
C. Testes D. Liver

234. Normal birth weight is
A. 2.5 - 3 Kg. B. 2 - 2.5 Kg.
C. 3 - 3.5 Kg. D. 2.2 - 2.7 Kg.

235. What is the criteria of LBW baby?
A. Birth Weight < 2 Kg.
B. Birth Weight < 2.5 Kg.
C. Birth Weight < 3 Kg.
D. Birth Weight < 2.7 Kg.

236. At which age a child can starts to brush his teeth?
A. 2 years B. 3 years
C. 4 years D. 20 months

237. While taking temperature from rectal route in children thermometer should be inserted about:
A. 0.5 Inch B. 1 Inch
C. 1.5 Inch D. 2 Inch

238. MMR vaccine is given by:
A. I.M. route B. S.C. route
C. I.V. route D. I.D. route

239. Deficiency of Vitamin D in children may cause:
A. Osteomalacia B. Rickets
C. Pellagra D. Beri-Beri

240. In children which disease occur due to protein deficiency:
A. Marasmus B. Kwashiorkor
C. Beri-Beri D. Scurvy

241. After birth of a baby, breast-feeding should be started:
A. Within 2 hours B. Within 1/2 hour
C. On second day D. After 1 week

242. When physiological Jaundice appears in new born baby?
A. At birth B. On second week
C. On second day D. On First Week

243. In following which is not a preventive measure for tetanus neonatorum:
A. T.T. vaccination
B. Follow five clean rule
C. T.T. immunization during reproductive age.
D. Penicillin antibiotic

244. Causative organism of chickenpox is:
A. Paramixo virus
B. Varicella zoster
C. Herpes simplex virus
D. Bordetalla pertussis

245. Severe muscle wasting, growth failure and loss of subcutaneous fat are features of
A. Kwashiokor B. Beri-Beri
C. Scurvy D. Marasmus

246. The first indicator of protein Energy Malnutrition (PEM) in children is:
A. Over weight for age
B. Weak and lethargic child
C. Under weight for age
D. Child having less intake of food

247. Switching from mother's breast milk to normal feeding in infants is called:
A. Trail feeding
B. Weaning
C. Substitution
D. Replacement feeding

248. Phototherapy is effective when large surface area is exposed to the light therefore infant is unclothed but nurse be needs to take following precautions -

A. Cover Reproductive Parts
B. Cover Head, Eyes and Reproductive Parts
C. Cover eyes and heads
D. Cover head and face

249. Physiological jaundice in term babies subsides by
A. 5th day of birth B. 6th day of birth
C. 7th day of birth D. 8th day of birth

250. Bottle fed babies are more prone to
A. Cough and cold B. Diarrhea
C. Impetigo D. TB

251. In a child with the diagnosis of hyper pyloric stenosis, nurse should look for the possible sign of
A. Dehydration
B. Quality of cry
C. Coughing and feeding
D. Character of stool

252. Which precaution is used during phototherapy?
A. Leave the infant's clothes on
B. Check the infant's temperature once a day
C. Reposition the infant's infrequently
D. Cover the infant's eye

253. Head control is possible in an infant at:
A. 1 month B. 3 months
C. 5 months D. 6 months

254. Low birth weight baby is defined as:
A. Birth weight less than 1500 gms
B. Birth weight less than 2000 gms
C. Birth weight less than 2500 gms
D. Birth weight less than 1000 gms

255. Erikson theory of emotional development emphasized that 6-12 years of child wants adults to recognize him/her, have strong sense of duty and engage in many tasks; this is known as:
A. Sense of initiative B. Sense of identity
C. Sense of intimacy D. Sense of industry

256. What is the normal pulse rate of newborn:
A. 140 per minute B. 130 per minute
C. 120 per minute D. 110 per minute

257. Child with congenital heart disease suddenly had cyanosis and dyspnoea; nurse will immediately:
A. Change position to side with knee flexed and head elevated
B. Change position to upright position
C. Start oxygen and inform doctor
D. Provide comfort and rest

258. Child after hydrocephalus surgery is in post operative unit; nurse will assess the following on priority:
A. Routine vital signs and site of dressing
B. Vital signs every 15-20 minutes and papillary reaction
C. Routine vital signs and I/V fluid site
D. Blood pressure 1 hourly and papillary reaction

259. Which parts of the body are affected in case child had second degree burns?
A. All epidermis and dermis
B. All epidermis, dermis including muscles and bones
C. Epidermis 7/8 and dermis 1/2 appendages may be affected
D. Epidermis 1/2 and dermis 7/8 appendages are affected

260. Short and extended duration recommended for Kangaroo Mother Care as per Government of India guidelines is:
A. 2 hrs and 5-8 hrs B. 3 hrs and 10-12 hrs
C. 4 hrs and 5-8 hrs D. 5 hrs and 10-12 hrs

261. "Five clean Practices" under strategies for elimination of neonatal tetanus includes all except
A. Clean surface of delivery
B. Clean hands of the attendant
C. New blade for cord cutting
D. Clean airways

262. The important clinical parameter for assessing the degree of hypoxia at birth
A. Respiratory rate B. Colour of skin
C. Heart rate D. Muscle tone

263. Undescended testes is called
A. Cryptorchidism B. Inguinal Hernia
C. Unbilical Hernia D. Hydrocele

264. Old Man's appearance is seen in children in
A. Fever B. Marasmus
C. Jaundice D. Encephalopathy

265. What is meant by failure to thrive
A. Child is unable to drink
B. Child is unable to walk
C. Rate of weight gain is sluggish
D. Rate of length gain is sluggish

266 A midline cleft lip is due to failure of fusion of :
A. Maxillary Processes
B. Medial nasal processes
C. Medial & lateral nasal processes
D. Medial & maxillary process

267. APGAR score of a newborn baby born with severe respiratory depression
A. <3 B. 3-5 C. 5-7 D. >9

268. At what APGAR score at 5 minutes after birth should resuscitation be initiated
A. 1-3 B. 7-8 C. 9-10 D. 6-7

269. A reflex
- A. May involve very few neurons
- B. Is not under conscious control
- C. Is not learned
- D. All of the Above

270. Which program was launched on October 2, 2015 to address anemia in children
- A. National Iron Plus Initiative
- B. Weekly Iron Folic Supplementation
- C. National Anemia Eradication Program
- D. National Anemia Day

271. Which of the following are defects at birth
- A. Club Foot
- B. Cleft palate
- C. Vision Impairment
- D. Only A & B

272. MUAC tape can be used for children in the age group of
- A. 6 months – 59 months
- B. 0 months – 59 months
- C. 6 months – 72 months
- D. 0 months – 72 months

273. At the community level what are the symptoms to identify respiratory infection/pneumonia
- A. Difficulty in breathing
- B. High Respiratory rate
- C. High Temperature
- D. All of the Above

274. Vaccine D.T. is given to a child at
- A. 2 Years of age
- B. 6 Weeks of age
- C. 5 Years of age
- D. 10 Years of age

275. Drooling appears in which month of growth
- A. At Birth B. 4 Month
- C. 6 month D. 12 month

276. How many Sutures are present in Anterior fontanels
- A. 2 B. 3 C. 4 D. 5

277. After the delivery KMC is given to
- A. Neonate
- B. Lactating mother
- C. Child up to 1 year
- D. Malnourished childr

278. A 29 years old female expectant presents with active T.B. And delivers a child. All of the following are indicated except:
- A. Administer INH treatment to the baby
- B. Give anti-tetanus-Toroid (ATT) to the mother for the next 2 years
- C. Withold breastfeeding
- D. Ask the mother to ensure proper disposal of sputum

279. A 4-month-old child is brought to the sub-centre of a PHC with basic complaint of cough and fever. On the physical examination, there was chest-in-drawing and respiratory rate of 45 per minute. Which of the following is the best way to manage the child?
- A. Give an antibiotic and advice the mother to give proper home care
- B. The child should be classified as a severe care of pneumonia
- C. Reasses the child after 2 days or earlier if the condition worsens
- D. Refer urgently to the hospital after giving the first dose of an antibiotic

280. After surgical repair of a cleft lip for an infant, it is important for the nurse
- A. Keeping the baby NPO
- B. Give feeds by spoon
- C. Keeping the baby from crying
- D. Place in supine position

281. Congenital absence as closure of a normal body opening or tubular structure is called
- A. Atony B. Atresia
- C. Asthenia D. Ataxia

282. White monitoring an unconscious child admitted with a history of fall, nurse notices that the child suddenly has a fixed and dilated pupil. This indicates
- A. Neurosurgical emergency
- B. Eye trauma
- C. Indication of brain death
- D. Increased parasympathetic activity

283. WHO-ORS packet includes all except:
- A. Sodium chloride
- B. Potassium chloride
- C. Sodium bi-carbonate
- D. Calcium carbonate

284. Initial nursing assessment of an infant suffering with acute diarrhoea and dehydration revelas:
- A. Skin turgor B. Low hematocrit
- C. Bulging fontanelle D. Weight gain

285. The APGAR scoring is done to appraise the infant for:
- A. Birth defects B. Respiratory effort
- C. Rh-sensitization D. Emotional stability

286. What is the most common form of childhood cancer?
- A. Lymphoma B. Leukemia
- C. Brain tumour D. Osteosarcoma

287. Increased accumulation of cerebro spinal fluid in brain is:
A. NTD B. Spinal bifida
C. Hydrocephalus D. None of the Above

288. A new born baby has...... bones.
A. 213 B. 206 C. 256 D. 300

289. The average length of umbilical cord is....cm.
A. 25cm B. 30cm C. 10cm D. 45cm

290. A child's heredity is determined at the time of:
A. Viability B. Delivery
C. Conception D. Infancy

291. Growth retardation can be Identified by
A. Blood examination B. Feeding pattern
C. Apgar score D. Weight recording

292. Village health guide measures the state of malnutrition in an under 2 child by using
A. Mid arm circumference
B. Weight for age
C. Skin fold thickness
D. Height for age

293. Infant Mortality Rate belongs to the death of children in which age group
A. Up to 1 month B. Up to 1 year
C. Up to 6 months D. Up to 5 years

294. At which age an infant can transfer an object form one hand to another hand
A. 4 months B. 6 months
C. 9 months D. 12 months

295. 'Bregma' of infant should be closed at the age of
A. 6 weeks B. 18 weeks
C. 6 months D. 18 months

296. Normal length of umbilical cord is
A. 20 cm B. 30 cm C. 40 cm D. 50 cm

297. Extra Chromosome in 21 pair of chromosome (Trisomy-21) is related to
A. Down's syndrome B. Patau's syndrome
C. Turner's syndrome D. Edward's syndrome

298. Best characteristic to define diarrhea
A. Odour B. Amount
C. Frequency D. Consistency

299. To prevent the newborn from hypothermia, the newborn is placed in
A. Phototherapy unit B. Radiant Warmer
C. Open air D. None of the above

300. Deficiency of Vitamin D may lead to
A. Anemia B. Xerophthalmia
C. Marasmus D. Rickets

301. A child's weight falls in the Green colour of the growth chart, it indicates that the child is
A. Severely underweight
B Less weight
C. Normal weight for age
D. None of the above

302. Eyes need to be covered during phototherapy session because
A. To make sure that newborn has closed the eyes well
B. Reduce overstimulation from bright colors
C. Prevent injury to conjunctiva and retina
D. Limit excessive rapid eye movements and anxiety

303. Expressed breast milk can be stored in room temperature for how many hours
A. 4 B. 8 C. 16 D. 24

304. How many doses of Pentavalent vaccine given to the baby
A. One dose B. Four Dose
C. Three Dose D. Five Dose

305. Which disease can be fatal in malnutrition
A. Tetanus B. Anemia
C. Measles D. Polio

306. WHO recommend which of the following for management of diarrhea?
A. Electrolyte B. ORS +Zink
C. Rice water D. Sugar salted water

307. Cord clamping is delayed by 1-3 minute in neonates because
A. Prevents anemia in woman
B. Placenta separates easily
C. Prevents jaundice in neonate
D. Neonate gets cord blood

308. Therapy used for treatment of Jaundice in new born
A. Phototherapy
B. Adequate fluid therapy
C. Exchange transfusion
D. All of the Above

309. What is used to clear the airway in newborn
A. Mucus sucker
B. Penguin sucker
C. Manual suction machine
D. All of the Above

310. Right dose of inj. Vitamin K for babies born with weight less than 1 kg
A. 0.5 mg B. 1 mg
C. 0.1 mg D. 1 mcg

311. Brown Adipose Tissue is mainly found in
A. In adult B. In newborn
C. In old age D. Only in females

312. Amount of Potassium in ORS packet is
A. 2.6 gm/lit B. 2.5 gm/lit
C. 1.5 gm/lit D. 7.5 gm/lit

313. Newborn Stabilizing Unit has been established at

A. CHC B. PHC
C. District Hospital D. Medical College

314. Exclusive breastfeeding helps in
A. Controlling Diarrhoea
B. Preventing respiratory tract infections
C. Improving immunity system
D. All of the Above

315. Growth chart of a child indicates
A. Weight only
B. Height only
C. Height, Weight and nutrition level
D. Both A & B

316. Speech development may be delayed in a child if
A. Child suffering with Congenital Heart Disease
B. Child suffering with Cleft Palate
C. Child suffering with Mumps
D. Child suffering with Oral Thrush

317. Infection of the eye of Newborn due to Gonococci
A. Lymphogranulaoma venerum
B. Ophthalmia Neonatorum
C. Kernicterus
D. Moniliasis

318. At What age does an infant shows Social Smile
A. At One Month B. At Two Month
C. At Three Month D. At Four Month

319. Which category of children involved under national programme for control of blindness
A. Children under 5 years
B. Children under 8 years
C. Children under 6 years
D. Children under 10 years

320. Placenta should be disposed in which Color Bucket
A. Black B. Yellow
C. Green D. Red

321. Pitting edema in 2-3 years old child indicates
A. Liver disease
B. Kidney disease
C. SAM or Malnutrition
D. Injury

322. Reflex which never disappears in human life
A. Moro's reflex B. Rooting reflex
C. Swallowing reflex D. All above

323. What is incorrect about Thumb Sucking
A. Can lead to Malocclusion
B. Is a source of pleasure
C. Is a sign of insecurity
D. Must be treated properly in the1st year itself

324. The primary task to be accomplished between 12 to 15 months of age is to learn to:
A. Walk erect B. Say simple
C. Climb stairs D. Use a spoon

325. The basic emotional task for the toddler is:
A. Identification B. Trust
C. Industry D. Independence

326. An infection caused by canadia albicans often occurring in infants is:
A. Hepatitis B. Thrush
C. Dysentery D. Typhoid fever

327. Neonates are prone to:
A. Hypocalcemia B. Hypoglycemia
C. Hypergiycemia D. Hypercalcemia

328. Head circumference and chest circumference of child becomes equal at the age of:
A. 4 years B. 1 year
C. 2 years D. 3 years

329. A common finding in most children with cardiac anomalies is:
A. Mental retardation
B. Family history of cardiac anomalies
C. Cyanosis
D. Delayed physical growth

330. The most common cause of neonatal jaundice on the first day of birth is:
A. Physiological
B. Blood group incompatibility
C. Neonatal hepatitis
D. Biliary artesia

331. The risk of haemorrhage after Tonsillectomy and Adenoidectomy is:
A. 2-4 days after surgery
B. 12-13 days after surgery
C. 5-7 days after surgery
D. 8-10 days after surgery

332. The components of tetra logy of Fallot are the following except:
A. Over riding of the septal defect by the aorta
B. Right ventricular hypertrophy
C. Ventricular septal defect
D. Aortic stenosis

333. The APGAR score is based on the following evaluation except:
A. Heart rate B. Skin texture
C. Respiration D. Muscle tone

334. Iodine deficiency causes:
A. Beriberi B. Scurvy
C. Goiter D. Kwashiorkor

335. Causative organism of mumps is:
A. Paramyxovirus B. Variola
C. Retrovirus D. Rotaviras

336. While doing CPR in an infant what is the compression ventilation ratio with two rescuers:
A. 15:1 B. 5:1 C. 15:2 D. 30:2

337. The major cause of infant mortality rate in India is:
A. Acute respiratory infection
B. Diarrhoea
C. Congenital anomalies
D. Prematurity

338. Which of the following best describes typical annual growth during the school age years?
A. Few physical differences are noticeable between age mates throughout this period
B. Fat pads increase in number and add to the normal "chubby" appearance of the child
C. Child grows an average of 2 inches (5.2 cm) per year
D. Child gain an average of 3 pounds (1.4 kg) per year

339. Popcorn and nuts should not be given to a toddler primarily because they:
A. Will spoil the child's appetite
B. Can cause tooth decay
C. Are easily aspirated
D. Have very little food value

340. An acid-fast bacillus which is pathogenic:
A. Bacillus pertrussis
B. Salmonella typhi
C. Mycobacterium leprae
D. Coryne bacterium diphtheria

341. The neonate is vulnerable to hypothermia due to-
A. Physiological immaturity of the liver
B. Immaturity of hypothalamus
C. Low circulatory status
D. Immaturity of respiratory system

342. The baby friendly hospital initiative was formed for:
A. Promoting safe delivery at the hospital
B. Promoting the health of antenatal mothers
C. Promoting breastfeeding
D. Promoting growth monitoring at hospitals

343. A new born of one minute after vaginal delivery is pink with blue hands and feet. Has a lusty cry, having heart rate of 140 Prompt response to stimulation with crying and maintains minimal flexion with sluggish movement. The nurse should know that this newborn's Apgar score is:
A. 10 B. 8 C. 9 D. 7

344. Toddlers often participate in:
A. Opposite sex play B. Parallel play
C. Solitary play D. None of the above

345. The commonest type of jaundice in newborn:
A. Hemolytic B. Physiological
C. Obstructive D. Hepatogenic

346. The most common cause of heart disease in adolescence or young adult is:
A. Rheumatic fever
B. Congenital heartdisease
C. Anaemia
D. Melanization

347. Manifestation of anger in children:
A. Thumb sucking B. Temper tantrum
C. Nightmare D. Regression

348. Accidents are the largest single cause of mortality and disability between the age of:
A. 1-4 years B. 5-7 years
C. 9-10 years D. 10 years onwards

349. At what age does our brain stop further growth?
A. After 5 years B. After 10 years
C. After 15 years D. After 20 years

350. Which of the following is not present in bottle formula for newborn?
A. Amino acid
B. Complex carbohydrate
C. Electrolytes
D. Immunoglobulin

351. Klinfelter's syndrome is indicated by:
A. Chromosome 47XXY
B. Chromosome 23XY
C. Chromosome 47X
D. Chromosome 46XY

352. Birth trauma is a risk factor for:
A. Uterine prolapse B. Endometriosis
C. PID D. Abortions

353. Cyanosis in preterm baby is due to:
A. Jaundice
B. Cleft palate
C. Respiratory distress syndrome
D. Intracranial injury

354. In fully flexed cephalic presentation we feel:
A. Occiput of fetus
B. Sinciput of the fetus
C. Eyebrow of the fetus
D. Oral cavity of the fetus

355. In Babinski's reflex the movement of great toe undergoes:
A. Dorsi extension B. Dorsiflexion
C. Plantar flexion D. Plantar adduction

356. The urethra which opens on the dorsal surface of the penis is termed:
A. Epispadiasis B. Hypospadiasis
C. Cryptorchidism D. Anorchidism

357. Kernig's sign is a striking feature of:
A. Meningitis B. Nephritis
C. Neuritis D. Dendritis

358. Colle's fracture refers to the injury of:
A. Shoulder joint B. Knee joint
C. Wrist joint D. Elbow joint

359. If a newborn's head and trunk is allowed to fal? backward it elicits:
A. Step in reflex B. Plantar reflex
C. Startled reflex D. Moro reflex

360. A newborn who is above the 90th percentile on the Intrauterine Growth Curve is termed:
A. Post-term Baby
B. Large for Gestational Age
C. Small for Gestational Age
D. Preterm Baby

361. Crawling of an Infant occurs at:
A. 8 to 9 months B. 2 to 3 months
C. 4 to 5 months D. 6 to 8 months

362. Spot the correct statement in terms of "Epispadias". It is *an* abnormal urethral opening on the
A. Ventral aspect of the penis
B. Urethral serotal junction
C. Shaft of the penis
D. Dorsal aspect of the penis

363. Identify the wrong answer behavioral problems of childhood includes
A. Breath-holding spell
B. Temper Tantrums
C. Thumb sucking
D. Failure to thrive

364. Match the developmental stage with their psycho social development according to Erickson

	A	B
A.	Infancy	1. Sense of industry
B.	School age	2. Sense of intimacy
C.	Early adolescence	3. Sense of trust
D.	Late adolescence	4. Sense of identity

	A.	B.	C.	D.
A.	3	2	1	4
B.	3	2	4	1
C.	3	1	4	2
D.	3	4	2	1

365. A nurse suggests activities for a 7-yr old child with autistic disorder. Which activity is most likely to engage this child?
A. Playing checkers with another child
B. Building with blocks alone
C. Playing kickball with a small group of chil-dren
D. Having a birthday party with 6 to 8 other chil-dren

366. Find out the correct pair regarding nerve injuries that occur during birth
A. Facial Palsy - 7th cervical nerve root
B. Brachial Palsy - 6th and 7th cervical nerve root
C. Erb's Palsy - 5th and 6th cervical nerve root
D. Klumpke's Palsy - 5th cervical nerve root

367. Consider the following stages of personality by freud
1. Oral 2. Anal
3. Latency 4. Phallic
5. Genital

What is the correct order of stages by freud?
A. 1-2-3-4-5
B. 2-1-3-4-5
C. 1-2-4-3-5
D. 2-1-4-5-3

368. Mid arm circumference is measured in the age group of ___ children
A. 0-1 years B. 1-5 years
C. 5-10 years D. 10-15 years

369. Spot the incorrect statement regarding principles of learning according to JTFSL (Joint Task force on student learning)
A. Learning is an active process
B. Learning is an outcome of stimulation and motivation of the learner
C. Learning is an act of self-awareness
D. Learning is an act of self-identification

370. The clinical features of an infant with hydrocephalus are
1. Bulged tensed anterior fontanelle
2. Setting - sun sign
3. Macewer sign
4. Closed skull sutures

A. 1, 2 and 3 B. 2, 3 and 4
C. 1, 3 and 4 D. 2, 4 and 1

371. The process of functional and physiological maturation of the individual is known as
A. Growth B. Maturation
C. Intelligence D. Development

372. During the course of resuscitation, which of the following responses shows effectiveness of ventilation in the child
1. Adequacy of chest rise
2. Improved heart rate and pulse oximetry
3. Presence of increased abdominal rise
4. Improved color

A. Only 1 and 2 B. 1, 2 and 4
C. Only 3 and 4 D. 1, 2, 3 and 4

373. Funis is otherwise called as
A. Umbilical artery B. Umbilical vein
C. Umbilical cord D. Umbilicus

374. The formula used to calculate the estimated fetal weight is
A. Naegle's formula B. Johnson's formula
C. Nelson's formula D. Jacobson's formula

375. Infancy period is from
A. Birth to one month
B. One month to 1 year
C. 1 years to 3 years
D. 3 years to 5 years

376. The following are the signs of dehydration except:
A. Sunken tearless eyes
B. Loss of skin elasticity
C. Diuresis
D. Depressed fontanels

377. Repeated urination while sleeping, even after five years of age is called:
A. Eneuresis B. Tic
C. Stuttering D. Encopresis

378. Commonest cause of neonatal morbidity in India is:
A. Diarrhoeal diseases
B. Birth injuries
C. Congenital anomalies
D. Prematurity and low birth weight

379. A tracheoesophageal fistula should be suspected in a neonate immediately after birth if one of the following is present?
A. Jaundice
B. Absence of sucking
C. Excessive amount of frothy saliva in the mouth
D. Bile-stained vomitus

380. All of the following can be used to determine a chromosome analysis of the fetus except:
A. Chrionic vilus sampling
B. Percutaneous umbilical blood sampling (PUBS)
C. Aminocentesis
D. Fetal umbilical Doppler velocimetry

381. Grasping of object by closing fingers around it is by
A. Gagging reflex B. Palmer grasp
C. Rooting reflex D. Doll's eye

382. A child in postoperative ward under observation after tonsillectomy is suspected to have postoperative haemorrhage when the child:
A. Snores noisily
B. Complains of thirst
C. Become pale
D. Swallows frequently

383. Which of the following is an activity of underfive clinics?
A. Mid day meal programme
B. Child education
C. Growth monitoring
D. School health services

384. Which of the following is a cyanotic heart disease?
A. Carctation of aorta
B. Patent ductus arteriosus
C. Atrial septal defect
D. Tetralogy of fallot

385. "Flag sign" is a characteristic feature of which disease?
A. Poliomyelitis B. Kwashiorkor
C. Rickets D. Marasmus

386. Sequence of taking vital sign in a newborn infant is:
A. TPR B. PRT C. RPT D. RTP

387. Neonatal reflex elicited by touching the cheeks of the baby is:

A. Moro reflex B. Rooting reflex
C. Startle reflex D. Sucking reflex

388. VP shunt is the surgical management for:

A. Spina bifida
B. Brain tumor
C. Hydrocephalus
D. ASD

389. Macewen sign is an indication of:

A. Cerebral Palsy
B. Mental Retardation
C. Hydrocephalus
D. Meningitis

390. Inability of the liver to metabolize and remove bilirubin from the biliary system is:

A. Haemolytic jaundice
B. Obstructive jaundice
C. Hereditary hyperbilirubinemia
D. Hepatocellular jaundice

391. The freshly prepared ORS (Oral rehydration solution) should be used within:

A. 24 hours C. 36 hours
B. 12 hours D. 48 hours

392. Point out the incorrect statement

A. Growth and development is continuous and orderly
B. Growth and development is complex yet predictable
C. Growth and development is steady in rate at all stages
D Growth and development is unique and differs from individual to individual

❑❑❑

Answer Sheet

1. A.	2. A.	3. D.	4. D.	5. A.	6.D.	7.B.	8.B.	9.D.	10.B.
11. A.	12.B.	13. C.	14. C.	15.C.	16.C.	17.B.	18.A.	19.A.	20.C.
21. B.	22. A.	23. A.	24. C.	25. D.	26.D.	27.B.	28.B.	29.B.	30.D.
31. D.	32. A.	33. C.	34. D.	35. A.	36.A.	37.A.	38.A.	39.D.	40.B.
41. C.	42. C.	43. A.	44. D.	45. A.	46.C.	47.D.	48.A.	49.A.	50.D.
51. D.	52. B.	53. A.	54. B.	55. B.	56.A.	57.B.	58.C.	59.A.	60.A.
61. D.	62. D.	63. A.	64. D.	65.A.	66.A.	67.C.	68.C.	69.C.	70.C.
71. A.	72. D.	73. A.	74. B.	75.C.	76.A.	77.C.	78.B.	79. C.	80.A.
81. D.	82.C.	83. A.	84.C.	85.B.	86.A.	87.A.	88.C.	89.A.	90.D.
91. D.	92.B.	93. A.	94. A.	95.C.	96.B.	97.A.	98.A.	99.C.	100.B.
101. D.	102. A.	103. C.	104. D.	105. C.	106.C.	107.A.	108.A.	109.A.	110.B.
111. C.	112. D.	113. C.	114. A.	115.B.	116.A.	117.A.	118.D.	119.A.	120.A.
121. B.	122. A.	123. D.	124. A.	125.A.	126.D.	127.B.	128.D.	129.C.	130.B.
131. D.	132. B.	133. C.	134. A.	135.D.	136.D.	137.C	138.B	139.C.	140.A.
141. D.	142. B.	143. B.	144. D.	145.D.	146.A.	147.D.	148.C	149.C.	150.C.
151. C.	152. B.	153. B.	154. C.	155.C.	156.C.	157.C.	158.D.	159.C.	160.C.
161. B.	162. C.	163. D.	164. B.	165.A.	166.C.	167.C.	168.C.	169.A.	170.D.
171. D.	172. D.	173. D.	174. D.	175.C.	176.A.	177.D.	178.D.	179.D.	180.D.
181. D.	182. B.	183. A.	184. B.	185.B.	186.C.	187.A.	188.D.	189.A.	190.D.
191. C.	192. C.	193. B.	194. D.	195.B.	196.B.	197.B.	198.A.	199.D.	200.B.
201. D.	202. B.	203. C.	204. A.	205.A.	206.A.	207.A.	208.D.	209.D.	210.C.
211. B.	212. A.	213. A.	214. A.	215.A.	216.D.	217.B.	218.D.	219.A.	220.C.
221. C.	222. B.	223. A.	224. A.	225.A.	226.D.	227.B.	228.D.	229.C.	230.A.
231. C.	232. B.	233. A.	234. A.	235.B.	236.B.	237.B.	238.B.	239.B.	240.B.
241. B.	242. C.	243. D.	244. B.	245.D.	246.C.	247.B.	248.B.	249.C.	250.B.
251. A.	252. D.	253. B.	254. C.	255.D.	256.A.	257.A.	258.B.	259.D.	260.B.
261. D.	262. B.	263. A.	264. B.	265.C.	266.B.	267.B.	268.A.	269.D.	270.A.
271. D.	272. A.	273. D.	274. C.	275.B.	276.C.	277.A.	278.B.	279.B.	280.B.
281. B.	282. A.	283. D.	284. A.	285.B.	286.B.	287.C.	288.D.	289.D.	290.C.
291. D.	292.A.	293. B.	294. B.	295.D.	296.D.	297.A.	298.D.	299.B.	300.D.
301. C.	302.C.	303. B.	304. C.	305.C.	306.B.	307.D.	308.D.	309.D.	310.A.
311. B.	312. C.	313. A.	314. D.	315.D.	316.B.	317.B.	318.C.	319.B.	320.B.
321. C.	322. C.	323. D.	324. A.	325.D.	326.B.	327.B.	328.B.	329.D.	330.B.
331. D.	332. D.	333. B.	334. C.	335.A.	336.C.	337.A.	338.C.	339.C.	340.C.
341. B.	342. C.	343. D.	344. B.	345.B.	346.A.	347.B.	348.A.	349.C.	350.D.
351. A.	352. A.	353. C.	354. A.	355.B.	356.A.	357.A.	358.C.	359.D.	360.B.
361. A.	362. D.	363. D.	364. C.	365.B.	366.C.	367.C.	368.B.	369.D.	370.A.
371. D.	372. B.	373. C.	374. B	375.B.	376.C.	377.A.	378.D.	379.C.	380.D.
381. B.	382. D.	383. C.	384. D.	385.B.	386.A.	387.B.	388.C.	389.C.	390.B.
391. A.	392. C.								

12. Sociology (MCQ)

1. "Man is a social animal" said by-
   A. Aristole B. Cristo
   C. Plato D. Davis
2. Sociology is the scientific study of the:
   A. Study of Health System
   B. Study of Human behaviour
   C. Study of Society
   D. Study of Socio-economic institutions
3. Sociology is the study of-
   A. Human behaviour
   B. Society
   C. Political system
   D. Socio-political institutions
4. Which of following statement is true about society?
   A. An agglomeration of people
   B. A group of people bound by discipline
   C. A association which regulates membership
   D. An association patterned on the norm of interaction
5. The word "Sociology" is derived from:
   A. Society and study B. Societies and study
   C. Society and logus D. Society and student
6. Which following are the defects of sociology?
   A. Lack of objectivity
   B. Absence of purposes
   C. Lack of fixity
   D. All of the Above
7. Which of following statement in is true about society?
   A. Society means likeness
   B. Society implies differences
   C. Society mean mutual aid
   D. Society involves both likeness and difference
8. Which of the following sociologist sais "Society is a network of social relationships"?
   A. AugusteComte B. Aristotle
   C. C.H.Cooley D. MacIver
9. A group of people organized for a particular purpose is known as-
   A. Community B. Association
   C. Society D. Institution
10. Which of following two forces determined the "Man's behaviour in society"?
    A. Formal and informal
    B. Natural and unnatural
    C. Physical and social
    D. Psychological and philosophical
11. Which of the following is a common and important social problem in our country?
    A. Dowry system alcoholism
    B. Population explosion
    C. Unemployment
    D. All of the Above
12. Which of following is unit of social structures?
    A. Institutions B. Groups
    C. Associations D. All of the Above
13. In which of following condition a social process takes place?
    A. Integration B. Competition
    C. Assimilation D. All of the Above
14. What is the meaning of cultural change?
    A. Changes in field of technology
    B. Invention and discoveries
    C. Geographical environment
    D. All of the Above
15. Which following group is closest to tribe?
    A. Class B. An association
    C. Caste D. Community
16. Which of following is an example of organisation?
    A. Hospital B. Army
    C. Court D. All of the Above
17. What is the nature of a crowd?
    A. Permanent B. Transitory
    C. Continuous D. Learning
18. All are the elements of social system. Except
    A. Belief B. Sentiment
    C. Norms D. Salves
19. Which of the following year Hindu marriage act was passeded?
    A. 1953 B. 1971 C. 1945 D. 1955
20. Which of following is an example of institution?
    A. Family B. State
    C. Party system D. All of the Above
21. Which of following describes competetion ?
    A. Ways of emerging forth as superior
    B. Accomodation

C. Assismilation
D. Fixation of status in society

22. What is the meaning of Social changes?
A. Change in structure of society
B. Change in social development
C. Change in social relation ship
D. All of the Above

23. All of following are example of an organization. Except?
A. College
B. Factory
C. Many foreigners in Delhi
D. Prison

24. All are basic elements of a community? Except
A. Relationship with environment
B. Legal binding
C. Relationship with territory
D. Psychological feeling

25. Which of the following sociologist give the term Sociology?
A. MacIver and page in 1875
B. Auguste Comte in 1839
C. Simmer in 1865
D. Aristotle in 1730

26. Which of following makes a society ?
A. The people
B. The places of their residence
C. Reciprocity
D. Time boundness

27. A scientific study of relations between organism and environment is term known as:
A. Zoology B. Anatomy
C. Ecology D. Community

28. Which of following does not indicate status?
A. Bharat Ratna
B. Labouror
C. The title of knighthood
D. Use of Prefix Pandit

29. Which of the following is a basic characteristic of culture?
A. Every society has its own culture
B. Culture is man made
C. Culture is learned
D. All of the Above

30. Which of following is an example of the secondary group in sociology?
A. Church B. Labour union
C. Married people D. Family

31. Which of the following is a characteristic of a social group?
A. Common interest
B. Reciprocal relations
C. Sense of unity and relationship
D. All of the Above

32. Which of following is primary group in sociology?
A. Family
B. Students of sociology
C. Social workers
D. None of the Above

33. Which of the following is a unit of social structure?
A. Institution
B. Associations
C. primary and secondary Groups
D. All of the Above

34. Which of following describes marrige with in caste?
A. Endogamy B. Exogamy
C. Sagotra D. Hypergamy

35. Which of the following group is a example of primary group ?
A. Political group B. Family
C. Trade union D. School

36. Which of following is the most common marriage in the world?
A. Polyandry
B. Manogamy
C. Companionate marriage
D. Experimental marriage

37. Which of the following year The Dowry prohibition act was passed?
A. 1953 B. 1982 C. 1961 D. 1969

38. Exogamy is-
A. An experimental marriage
B. Marriage in same gotra
C. Marriage outside the group
D. Marriage with in prohibited degrees

39. What is the main reason behind urbanization?
A. Industrialization
B. Isolation from family
C. Growth of agriculture and horticulture
D. Movement of population

40. Social stratification implies

A. Social justice B. Social inequality
C. Social injustice D. Social equality

41. What is the Essential function of family?

A. Provision of home
B. Develop new generation
C. Sexual satisfaction
D. All of the Above

42. Social stratification means

A. Classification of society into two castes
B. Classification based on economic conditions
C. Classification based on power
D. Existence of group and inter-goup

43. What is Social stratification?

A. Classification of society into castes and class
B. Classification of society into group and intergroup
C. Classification of society into religious and economic group
D. None of them

44. All are correct about pertinent function of culture? Except

A. Regulation of social conduct of individuals
B. Teaching the individuals to live and behave in the society
C. Inculcating a sense of aggressive competition
D. Teaching the individuals manners good habits etc.

45. Which of the following types group is Family?

A. Kinship group B. Power full group
C. Religious group D. Public group

46. Norms in sociology indicate-

A. The normal standards of social behaviour
B. Tendency of human beings to more up
C. Ethical ideals of society
D. Standardised generalisation about normally expected modes of behaviour in people.

47. What is the meaning of Social stratification?

A. Social change B. Social development
C. Social equality
D. Social inequality

48. All of following are part of culture ? Except

A. Rail roads
B. Observance of sanskaras
C. Spirituality
D. Religious tolerance

49. Which of the following is a necessary and important criterion for the development of a family?

A. Mutual understanding
B. A form of marriage
C. Specific goal
D. Sense of unity

50. Which of following is the role a religion?

A. Harmonising
B. To bring the people closer
C. To provide faith to men in distress
D. All of the Above

51. Which of the following is an example of secondary group except?

A. Family B. Labour union
C. Political party D. None

52. Which following change refers of social change?

A. Value system B. Dress
C. Food habits D. Habitation pattern

53. Which of the following agency is responsible for socialization?

A. School B. Peer group
C. Family D. All of the Above

❑❑❑

Answer Sheet

1. A	2. C	3. A	4. A	5. A	6. A	7. D	8. D	9. B	10.C
11.D	12.D	13.C	14. D	15. A	16. D	17. B	18. D	19.D	20. D
21. A	22.D	23. C	24.C	25.B	26.C	27. C	28.B	29. D	30.B
31.D	32. A	33. D	34. A	35.B	36. B	37.C	38. C	39.D	40. B
41. D	42. A	43. A	44. C	45.A	46.D	47.D	48.A	49.B	50. D
51. A	52.A	53.D							

13. Nursing Administration with Professional Trends (MCQ)

1. **What is Laissez faire leadership?**
   A. Paternastic leadership
   B. Abdicratic leadership
   C. Directive leadership
   D. Creative leadership

2. **Which of the following is method of inventory control in which the items are classified on the basis of rate of consumption?**
   A. ABC analysis B. VED analysis
   C. HML analysis D. FSN analysis

3. **Which of following is first function of management?**
   A. Organizing B. Staffing
   C. Planning D. Directing

4. **Which of the following is the correct definition of administration?**
   A. It is the direction, coordination and control of many persons to achieve some objectives
   B. It is the activities of group co-operating to accomplish common goals
   C. It is organization and direction of human and material resources to achieve desired goals
   D. All of the following

5. **The power which is due to a higher position in a organization is known as:**
   A. Legitimate power B. Referent power
   C. Local power D. Coercive power

6. **In the critical path method of network analysis, the critical path is the**
   A. Shortest B. Longest
   C. Cheapest D. Costliest

7. **The material management started according to:**
   A. Demand estimation
   B. Maintenance & repair
   C. Procurement
   D. Storage

8. **The inventory control which is based upon necessity of items it is known as:**
   A. VED analysis B. ABC analysis
   C. Up to date analysis D. Priority analysis

9. **The basis of ABC analysis in inventory control is**
   A. Annual consumption value
   B. Criticality of items
   C. Unit cost of item
   D. Procurement difficulty, market availability

10. **Which of the following category are considered to The High cost items according to ABC analysis?**
    A. C category B. A category
    C. B category D. None of the Above

11. **In VED analysis of inventory control 'D' refers to:**
    A. Dryable B. Dispersible
    C. Demandable D. Desirable

12. **Hygiene factors and motivational factors are key concepts in**
    A. Maslow's hierarchy of needs
    B. Expectancy Theory
    C. Goal Setting Theory
    D. Herzberg's two factor theory

13. **What are the number of elements of communication process?**
    A. 3 B. 7 C. 5 D. 6

14. **Which of the following is not an element of communication?**
    A. Feedback B. Message
    C. Sender D. Noise pollution

15. **Which of the following concept is related to Frederick Taylor's theory of modern management?**
    A. Management is a true science.
    B. The selection of workers is a science.
    C. Workers are to be developed and trained.
    D. All of the Above

16. **Which of the following is a 5 'P' of effective communication except?**
    A. Purpose B. Price
    C. Participant D. Procurement

17. Which of the following are the stages of group dynamics?
A. Norming B. Storming
C. Forming D. All of the Above

18. Which type of leadership theories consider people inherit certain qualities that make them better suited to leadership?
A. Contingency Theories
B. Behavioural theories
C. Trait Theories
D. Situational theories

19. What is Assault?
A. Defamation of others
B. Intentional touching of body
C. Threat of others
D. All of the Above

20. Which kind of offence where a technician is doing a procedure of a young girl without taking consent?
A. Assault B. Battery
C. Tort D. All of the Above

21. Motivation-Hygiene theory (two-factor theory) of management was proposed by
A. Elton Mayo
B. W. Edwards Deming
C. Kurt Lewin
D. Frederick Herzberg

22. What is the meaning of the term Libel?
A. Malpractice
B. Defamation by speaking
C. Battery
D. None of the Above

23. A threat of unauthorized touching to a patient by health care provider is a term known as:
A. Battery B. Procedure
C. Assault D. Both A & C

24. Which of the following is an Indian Health Care Accrediting Agency?
A. Joint Commission International (JCI)
B. Joint Commission on Accreditation Of Healthcare (JCAHO)
C. National Accreditation Board for Hospitals & Healthcare Providers (NABH)
D. QHA Trent Accreditation

25. Unauthorized touching to a patient by health care provider is a term known as:
A. Battery B. Assault
C. Malpractice D. Negligence

26. Management by objectives (MBO) as an organization tool was first explained by
A. Robert Owen B. Hugo Munsterberg
C. Henry Towne D. Peter F. Ducker

27. Which of the following education provided to employees at the job setting to improve the work performance?
A. Induction training programme
B. Extra-mural education
C. In-service education
D. Continuing education

28. Who gives the Field and Hawthorne theory of human behaviour?
A. Frederick Taylor
B. Maslow
C. Elton
D. Douglas McGregor

29. Which of the following is an improvement technique of management?
A. Performance appraisal
B. PERT
C. MBO
D. Direction

30. "Management by objective works - if you know the objectives. Ninety percent of the time you don't" This was stated by
A. Peter Drucker B. Frederick Taylor
C. Henri Fayol D. Henry L. Gantt

31. Theory X and theory Y was proposed by
A. William Ouchi
B. Frederick Taylor
C. Mary Follett
D. Douglas McGregor

32. The famous 14 Principles of Management was first defined by
A. Elton Mayo B. Henri Fayol
C. Adam Smith D. James Watt

33. What is meaning of the androgogy?
A. Teaching children
B. Maturation of human being
C. Teaching girls
D. Teaching adults

34. Accreditation refers to one of the following:
A. Making assessment
B. Meeting predetermined standards
C. Making care cost effective
D. Ensuring Quality

35. Which of the following is the element of administration?
A. PUSCORB B. POSCORB
C. POSDCORB D. POSDRBO